The
WAR on
TRUTH

or

Everything you always wanted to know about the invasion of Iraq but your government wouldn't tell you

NEIL MACKAY

CASEMATE
Philadelphia

Published in the United States by
CASEMATE

© 2006 Neil Mackay

For further information please contact
Casemate Publishers, 1016 Warrior Road, Drexel Hill, PA 19026.

ISBN 10: 1-932033-62-9
ISBN 13: 978-1-932033-62-5

First published in the United Kingdom by Sunday Herald Books,
Glasgow, Scotland.
ISBN 13: 978-1-904684-15-2

Cataloging-in-publication data is available from the
British Library and the Library of Congress.

10 9 8 7 6 5 4 3 2 1

PRINTED IN THE UNITED STATES OF AMERICA

CONTENTS

To Susan Moody
who knew everything there was to know about truth.

INTRODUCTION
IN DEFENCE...

or

How Saddam actually did have weapons of destruction and how cats can pull stainless steel sinks from walls

Look, I know this appears to have nothing to do with Iraq, but can I ask if you've ever heard about a really strange ape called Koko the Gorilla?

Well, Koko is in her thirties and she's been raised by linguists at Stanford University in America who have taught her how to talk to humans using more than 1,000 expressions in sign language. Apparently, her keepers say, she knows many more words in spoken English.

One day, Koko got herself into a huge monkey* tantrum – as gorillas often do – and managed to rip a stainless steel sink from a wall. When the nearest human to hand confronted her with her wanton act of gorilla violence and asked her why she'd behaved so abominably, she pointed at a little kitten nearby, which weirdly was allowed to hang out with her for some reason, and signed: 'The cat did it.'

Koko did to that keeper exactly what Bush and Blair did to you and me. She told him a patently absurd and laughable lie. But instead of doing what the keeper did and say, 'Yeah, right, Koko, you're nuts, stop lying', we listened to the apes. We allowed Bush and Blair to take us to war; in fact, if the people of Britain and America had been that keeper, we'd have got Koko a gun and stood back and watched while that big bully of an ape shot the cat.

You know all those nasty jokes about Bush looking like a monkey? Well, he can certainly lie like one, that's for sure. His knee-jerk ability to tell a whopper at the drop of a Stetson really does appear to be shared by actual simians – as Koko proves.

*I know that a gorilla isn't a monkey. That's the only deliberately misrepresented fact that you'll find in this book – and at least I had the decency to tell you up front that it was a lie.

You have been lied to about Iraq on a daily basis by the British and American governments since before September 11, 2001. These weren't little accidental lies. Oh no, sir. These were big, fat, stonking, great lies of historic proportions – they were Koko-sized lies.

Today, we all know that Saddam had no weapons of mass destruction and that we invaded and beat up an entire country based on the lies of our leaders.

But our leaders didn't just lie to us. They terrified us with spectres of mushroom clouds; they attacked our patriotism if we questioned them; they insulted our intelligence if we said we doubted them; they mocked our reservations; they withheld information; suppressed facts; invented threats and deceived us into backing an illegal war which has left tens of thousands of Iraqis, Britons and Americans – who should still be alive and with their families – very, very dead indeed.

They only gave us half the facts and half the story. Sure, Saddam once had weapons of mass destruction – back before the First Gulf War – but his amazing weapons of doom were all long gone by the time the March 2003 invasion started.

And sure, Saddam was a moustachioed madman, a genocidal loon, a lover of rape rooms, torture chambers and mass graves, but what the hell has been going on in Abu Ghraib prison and that gulag over in Guantanamo Bay? I don't remember anything being agreed that said the democratic liberation of Iraq was dependent on some Iraqis being forced to masturbate with women's knickers on their heads, or beaten to death, or savaged with dogs, or covered in their own shit, or 'disappeared', or raped.

Again, we got half the story. Bush and Blair made out that Saddam was Darth Vader. They may as well have said that he had a Death Star and it was pointed right at us – that's how absurd their lies actually were. As a by-product of their lies they have crippled our intelligence services by forcing our spies to corrupt themselves and back up false government propaganda. In doing so, they have left our two countries more vulnerable than at any time since the Second World War. Just look to the Islamist atrocities in London in July of 2005 for proof of how this war has brought pointless religion-fuelled terror to our own doorsteps. If MI6 or the CIA found out that Krazy Kim over in North Korea had decided that he was a bit bored with life and so fancied topping himself and taking us all with him in a nuclear Armageddon, who would believe them? Would you? And Bush and Blair are the men who say that they want to make us safe and secure. The money-shot of this war was billed by our leaders as the denouement of a struggle which would end with 'the world as a safer place'. Tell that to London commuters.

We were mentally drugged with made-up phantoms, with half-truths, exaggerations, omissions and downright lies.

How dare these politicians who are servants of the people – who have their wages paid for by you and me and every other citizen – take our countries to war based on half the facts and half the truth.

This book attempts to fix that disparity. I'm going to give you the other half of the story. And I'm going to give it to you in the same unremitting fashion that Bush and Blair and their supporters and cheer-leaders in the right-wing establishment press on both sides of the Atlantic gave you their case for war. They weren't kind to those who opposed them; they insulted their 'enemies'; they mocked the opinions of anyone who differed with them; they humiliated and beat up on their opponents wilfully and cruelly; they lied openly about any person who had the temerity to challenge them or call them on their lies. So, it's pay-back time. On your behalf – you who were lied to, misled, told only half the tale, mocked and humiliated for your doubts – I am going to give them back exactly what they handed out to the 'doubters' in the first place. I'm a big believer in the principle of 'do as thy would be done to'. They did things to people that were wrong; they lied; so it's only fair that they are called on their lies and have done to them things which they don't like in return.

I spent the best part of four years researching this book as a newspa-per investigative journalist. This book is chock full of facts – one hun-dred per cent indisputable facts. Where claims are in doubt, I make clear they are in doubt or are speculative – but those moments are few and far between. There are hundreds of revelations in this book which prove completely just how duplicitous and corrupt this whole war was and is. I waste little time here rehearsing the arguments that Bush and Blair hollered again and again into our ears since 2002; they've had their say, and now it's time for someone to call them to a reckoning. We know their lying, treacherous claims, and we don't really need to hear them again. This entire book is meant to pull the rug brutally from beneath these liars, to trip them up, to expose them and to shame them for what they are and what they have done. But where they went on the attack with lies, here they are attacked only with the truth. That's the differ-ence, and that is also the moral measure of these people.

Their lies have corroded the democracies of Britain and America, reduced our two nations' moral standing in the eyes of the world, cost more than 100,000 lives, taken us into an illegal war, made the world a more dangerous place, given crazy killers inspired by the international al-Qaeda franchise an excuse to start lopping off the heads of innocent westerners, continued the repression of Palestine, eaten away at our civil liberties at home, fanned the flames of racism and religious hatred, brought the war on terror to Great Britain and turned Iraq into a vision of hell on earth.

An American friend asked me how I'd describe this book. I said that it was a yell back in the faces of Bush and Blair. It is meant to be a yell – a scream – at these liars. But it's a yell that has substance. When they yelled at us and told us we had to go to war, they provided us with absolutely no true facts as the basis of their claims or upon which we could judge their arguments. I provide you with a yell and with thousands of substantiated facts gathered over years spent investigating the roots of this war. My investigations have led to many shocking revelations which, I hope, make you question the nature of the democracy in which you live. I'm pretty sure that there is a lot more substance between the covers of this book than in all the memos, dossiers and documents that Bush and Blair put their names to over the last few years.

I make no apology for insulting these people. They have made me angry, and they should have made you angry too. Nothing has ever made me more angry than being lied to and being forced to watch my country, and the country of my good friends in America, taken into a criminal war which disgraces my nation and my species.

I sincerely hope that by the end of this book you will loathe their actions. I think you will. You've already heard all the garbage that they had to dole out over the years and it has been twisted, insubstantial fairy tales. Now – I hope – you can read this book and get the full picture. Then you can judge them, and if there is any sanity and decency left in a world that contains people like Bush and Blair you will find them wanting and hand out a guilty verdict. Perhaps we should ask ourselves if the judgement would be better handed down in a criminal court rather than in the court of public opinion.

Britain – in the shape of Tony Blair and his New Labour government – is a subservient lap-dog to a wilful, arrogant and dangerous American administration. Bush lied to our friends in America – the American people – and was aided and abetted in his lies by the corporate media. Once the media had terrified, cajoled and threatened the majority of Americans to back the war, it was a done deal that Britain would attack Iraq too. Why? Because Blair doesn't have the guts to stand up to America like a real friend should when his best mate is about to do something illegal, ugly and possibly suicidal.

We should have seen it coming. The people who stole the White House in the 2000 election are revolutionary ideologues who want to change the world radically. These neoconservatives – of whom you will read lots more about in Chapter 1 – have as their ideological guru one Mr Leo Strauss, an American philosopher. He just happens to believe that it is morally right for politicians to lie or conceal the truth in order to pursue goals in the greater good which simple folk, like voters, just wouldn't or couldn't understand. Of course, it is up to the politicians to decide what exactly is the 'greater good'. Is the greater good the interests of world peace? Keeping Iraqi children alive? Not squandering the lives of British and American soldiers? Or is the greater good helping your corporate buddies get rich in a war economy? Or using a brutal, bloody war to get the world whipped into shape behind American leadership – with its sidekick Britain ever to hand – for the rest of the course of the 21st century?

This book tells you how the Bush Team were planning to take out Iraq long before September 11; it tells you how oil was right up there on the Bush agenda as a reason for war; it tells you how Britain and America sold germs, nuclear gizmos and chemical weapons to Saddam; it proves, in the words of the world's leading weapons inspectors, that there were no WMD in Iraq at the time we invaded and that the west knew that; it proves how Britain and America collaborated with Saddam in his use of chemical weapons back in the 1980s when he did have WMD; it shows how British and American spies deliberately lied on behalf of the US and UK governments to take us to war; how our governments set out to literally destroy anyone who questioned their lies; how Blair could easily be impeached; how spies of all rank in both the UK and US feel they have been totally exploited by Bush and Blair; how British and American soldiers are dying because they haven't been given the right kit or training; how the US and UK spied on the United Nations; how Blair knew the war was illegal before it started; how the 'new' Iraq was carved up by US big business after the invasion; how responsibility for the war crimes at Abu Ghraib goes right to the top of the US administration; how Tony Blair was told that British soldiers were carrying out war crimes in Iraq but did nothing; how British spies knew the war in Iraq would bring the war on terror to London; how British spies underestimated the 'Iraq effect' on the al-Qaeda franchise in the UK; and how the corporate media caved in and became frighteningly effective propaganda agents for Bush and Blair ... and finally, it also, sadly and shamefully, tells you how the only nations to ever use weapons of mass destruction since September 11 have been Britain and America ... and we just happened to use those WMD – uranium-tipped bombs – against Iraqi civilians of all people.

So, there are quite a few revelations along the way that should get your blood boiling at the very thought of the Tony-and-George show. This book is a full-frontal assault on their hypocrisy. As I said, there are quite a few nasty asides against that pair throughout the book, but I hope you understand that although I'm a journalist, I am a human being, too, and like you I get angry when I see a bastard acting like a bastard. There is a time and a place for dispassionate 'objective' journalism – whatever that is – but it's not now and not here. No journalist should be expected to hold their tongue and quell their principles when crimes are being committed in their name. In times like these, when innocent people are dying because dangerous people have told lies, the wrong-doers amongst us – to use the language of Washington and Whitehall – must be called to account for their sins.

When people are dying for nothing every day because of Blair and Bush, I think it's incumbent on every one of us to stand up and say, 'This is wrong; this disgusts me.' That's what I've tried to do here. I hope you enjoy getting disgusted; I hope it informs you, and I hope it also entertains you a little. I hope it puts a little balance back into the world after Bush and Blair's efforts to turn night into day, paint black as white and make 2+2=5. I urge you, if you come across information in here that you think people need to know about then lend them the book or stick bits of it up on the internet or just talk to them about it to get them thinking for themselves again after the west's long vacation from the truth. We have lived with lies and the suppression of the truth for too long, let's allow the facts to speak for themselves now. And let's stop allowing visionless, narrow-minded, corrupt, amoral politicians – on the make – to keep us dumb, to silence us and to do our thinking for us. Remember, information is a hand grenade. So, if you see Bush and Blair chuck this book at them for me.

Neil Mackay
February 2007

THE TRUTH WAS ACTUALLY OUT THERE

or

The secret revolutionary plans of the Bush White House as discovered by me

We invaded Iraq because we thought that Saddam had big scary weapons of mass destruction. Right? Wrong.

Weapons of mass destruction had nothing to do with why we invaded Iraq, and you know it. Right now, though, I'm going to tell you one of the main reasons why we did invade. It's quite simple really ... it was all down to oil.

Now, don't moan and groan and roll your eyes muttering 'conspiracy theory' at me. In fact, don't even take my word for it. Take it from one who knows – a certain US Secretary of Defense Donald Rumsfeld.

I've got a copy of a letter that Rumsfeld wrote to President Bill Clinton back in January 1998. In it, Rummy says that Clinton should 'aim, above all, at the removal of Saddam Hussein's regime from power'. So, as far back as 1998, Rumsfeld was targeting Saddam for regime change. That's long before September 11, long before any of those bogus intelligence claims linking Saddam to the 9-11 hijackers and long before any made-up mullarky about weapons of mass destruction. So why would Rummy want to turn his fire on Saddam?

Well, Rummy tells us in his letter: if Saddam is allowed to continue in power, then, 'a significant portion of the world's supply of oil will all be put at hazard'. It's right there in black and white.

Saddam wasn't targeted by a White House full of jitters about rogue states linked to terror groups and building deadly piles of doomsday machines. He was targeted by a White House full of jitters that Saddam, a lunatic who hated the United States and its allies with the passion of Beelezebub, was sitting on top of the world's second biggest oil reserve.

'Removing Saddam Hussein and his regime from power ... now needs

7

to become the aim of American foreign policy,' the letter says. 'We urge
you [Clinton] ... to turn your administration's attention to implement-
ing a strategy for removing Saddam's regime from power.' According to
Rummy, 'this means a willingness to undertake military action as
diplomacy is clearly failing'.

Rummy goes on to suggest that Clinton should basically tell the
United Nations to go screw itself. 'We believe the US has the authority
under existing UN resolutions to take the necessary steps, including military steps, to protect our vital interests in the Gulf. In any case,
American policy cannot continue to be crippled by a misguided insistence on unanimity in the UN Security Council.'

When I stumbled on this letter, it left me gobsmacked. Here was one
of the men who led the US government, at the time of the invasion and
occupation of Iraq, suggesting long before he came to power that not
only should Saddam be 'regime changed' but that he should be regime
changed in order to protect US oil interests. And it showed that Rummy
of the neocons had about as much respect for the UN as Osama bin
Laden has for the Vatican. That letter was strangely prescient. But the
gist of it sure didn't sound like the WMD spiel the world was given by
the US in the run-up to the invasion of Iraq.

There was something weird about that letter, too. It was signed by
Rumsfeld, but there were a whole load of other signatures on it as well.
And these other signatures seemed spookily familiar.

There was Paul Wolfowitz. His name certainly rang a bell. He was
Rumsfeld's deputy over at the Pentagon at the time of the invasion. He's
been called 'Wolfowitz of Arabia', described as the 'architect' of the
invasion of Iraq and has now taken over the World Bank for George W
Bush.

Now, who else signed that letter? Hmm ... James Woolsey. He's the
former director of the CIA, and a man with business interests in the
Titan Corporation. The Titan Corporation is one of the US military
firms which provided military interpreters for interrogation sessions in
Abu Ghraib prison where all those Iraqis were raped, tortured, humiliated and killed.

Another person who signed the letter was Elliott Abrams. He was
indicted by the Iran-Contra special investigator for giving false testimony before Congress in 1987 over his role in illegally raising money for
the Nicaraguan Contras. In the end, Abrams ended up pleading guilty
to a couple of lesser offences (only withholding information from

Congress) in order to avoid a spell in jail. He was eventually pardoned by President George Bush Senior.

Abrams was later appointed Special Assistant to the President (that's George Dubya) and Senior Director of Near East Affairs. According to a December 3, 2002 press release from the State Department his job would involve Arab/Israeli relations and US efforts to promote peace in the Middle East. For 'efforts to promote peace' one should read, 'invading creaking, weak regimes run by madmen and stocked full of oil'.

Now, who else signed that letter? Oh yes, Paula Dobriansky. She became Dubya's Under-Secretary of State for Global Affairs.

Zalmay Khalilzad was also a signatory on the letter. He was appointed Bush's ambassador to Afghanistan in 2003, and then ambassador to Iraq in 2005.

Oh, and Richard Perle. I almost forgot him. He's got a really cool nickname – the 'Pentagon's Prince of Darkness'. He used to be chair of the Pentagon's influential Defense Policy Board (DPB) until he resigned over a conflict of interest due to his businesses connections. Well, when I say, he resigned, I mean he resigned as chair but still sits on the Board. The DPB, by the way, essentially hands out military contracts to big business.

There was also Peter W Rodman, Assistant Secretary of Defense for International Security Affairs. He's a *protégé* of Henry Kissinger.

John Bolton was another signatory. He was a prime architect of Baby Bush's Iraq policy and he served both Bush Senior and Reagan in the State Department, Justice Department and US Aid (the government department which hands out those lucrative Iraqi reconstruction contracts to primarily pro-Republican firms).

Bolton became Under-Secretary for Arms Control and International Security in Bush Junior's State Department. His appointment was intended to destabilise then Secretary of State Colin Powell, the token little dove in Bush's parliament of hawks. Bolton was also one of Bush's ballot counters during the 'stolen' 2000 election. For those of you who don't remember, that's the election where Bush's baby brother, Jeb, the Governor of Florida, purged mostly black voters (i.e. Democrats) off the election roll and swung the presidency for Dubya.

Bolton is a great guy. He opposes the Comprehensive Test Ban Treaty on nuclear arms and has even hinted at targeting Cuba as part of the war on terror. He's also got plenty of financial interests in oil and arms firms. The latest feather in Bolton's hideous cap came when Bush promoted him to represent the US as its ambassador to the United Nations – if you can believe it.

Those were just a few of the guys and gals signing that smoking gun of a letter back in 1998. But then I noticed another thing. It wasn't just signed by the top guns of the Bush administration – it was on the headed notepaper of some outfit called 'The Project for the New American Century'.

Now that sounds about as wacko and scary as it is possible to be. The New American Century? It gave me little shivers down my spine. But I thought I'd better check it out given that half of Bush's cabinet seemed to be members.

Well, you'll never guess what. The PNAC, as the Project for the New American Century likes to call itself, was set up by the Bush cabinet and the Bush family. The signatories of the PNAC's founding statement of principles include Dick Cheney (the Vice-president), Jeb Bush (that's Dubya's helpful vote-counting baby brother again) and Lewis Libby (who is known as Scooter, was Cheney's Chief of Staff and is now awaiting trial for perjury, as it just so happens).

Other founders include some of the charmers mentioned above – Wolfie, Abrams, Dobriansky, Khalilzad, Rodman and, of course, good old Donald Rumsfeld. Oh, and another of the founders was Dan Quayle: he who couldn't spell 'potato' while Vice-president of the United States of America.

That was an interesting little cabal, I thought. And here they were calling for Saddam's head on a platter, with a side order of oil, back in 1998. I wondered what else they'd been up to during those inconvenient Clinton years while they were waiting to win – ahem – the US election.

So, I had a poke around in the PNAC's vaults. Oooh ... you oughta see what I found, baby. A hefty tome called *Rebuilding America's Defenses: Strategy, Forces and Resources for a New Century*. Not to put too fine a point on it, this has been called the *Mein Kampf* of the neo-conservatives now running the White House. It's known as *Mein Kampf* because I give it to friends and colleagues, ask them to read it and they then return it to me saying, 'My God, that's like *Mein Kampf*.'

Now, where do I start with describing *Rebuilding America's Defenses*? Well, it was written in September 2000 – that's before Bush 'won' the election, before 9-11, and before all that 'Saddam has WMD' stuff. It clearly shows that Dubya and his cabinet were planning a premeditated attack on Iraq to secure regime change.

Here's a taster: 'The United States has for decades sought to play a more permanent role in Gulf regional security. While the unresolved conflict with Iraq provides the immediate justification, the need for a substantial American force presence in the Gulf transcends the issue of the regime of Saddam Husscin.'

Transcends the issue of the regime of Saddam Hussein. I see. That means they intended to take control of the Gulf region whether or not Saddam was around. That's not frightening or militaristic or illegal. Is it?

The document calls for a worldwide Roman Empire-style 'Pax Americana'. It also supports 'a blueprint for maintaining global US pre-eminence, precluding the rise of a great-power rival, and shaping the international security order in line with American principles and interests'. You might see why some of the folk I showed this document to started to go for the *Mein Kampf* schtick around this point.

The PNAC also points out that preserving a 'Pax Americana' could well lead to, 'theatre wars spread across the globe'. While I wish that meant actors hitting each other with handbags; it doesn't. It's just a polite way of referring to a perpetual world war. The neocons, as you will know by the end of this book, are big on World War III.

But, oh my, oh my, the PNAC chums are only getting started. This American grand strategy must be advanced 'as far into the future as possible' and the US must 'fight and decisively win multiple, simultaneous major theatre wars' as a 'core mission'. This is sounding disturbingly familiar. Aren't we fighting two wars now? There's the War on Terror and the War on Something in Iraq.

The maintenance of 'America's global leadership' relies on 'the preservation of a favourable balance of power … in the Middle East and surrounding energy-producing region'. Sounds like that old 'oil' word creeping back in there again, I fear. The bottom line is that the White House has to 'translate US military supremacy into American geopolitical pre-eminence'. 'Global reach, global power' is the hip, new buzz-phrase.

As the PNAC puts it: 'American military pre-eminence will continue to rest, in significant part, on the ability to maintain sufficient land forces to achieve political goals such as removing a dangerous and hostile regime when necessary.' Translated, that means: as long as we can kick the ass of tin-pot tyrant losers like Saddam we can be the biggest bully in the playground and tell the rest of you suckers what to do.

It just goes full-scale Orwellian from this point onwards. The PNAC starts to get off over weapons, describing the US armed forces as 'the cavalry on the new American frontier' – the 'frontier' by the way is global. The PNAC document gives Wolfie and Libby a little nod, too. It adds its support to a document they wrote which said that the US must 'discourage advanced industrialised nations from challenging our leadership or even aspiring to a larger regional or global role'.

I can't believe you are normal if you get to this part of *Rebuilding America's Defenses* and don't think the world is screwed. But there is more to come. More screwing, more humiliation and more sand kicking. Allies like the UK are seen as, 'the most effective and efficient means of exercising American global leadership'. Mr Blair must have really polished up on *Rebuilding America's Defenses* when Dubya rode into Washington.

The PNAC shows exactly what the Bush regime thinks of the rest of the world. Peacekeeping missions, according to the creepy document, 'demand American political leadership rather than that of the United Nations' – so bugger the UN. We're told that the US has to take on long-term 'independent' constabulary missions. That means United Nations resolutions for military action are just a stupid inconvenience. From this political position, it's just a philosophical hop, skip and a jump to spying on Kofi Annan and shoving Freedom Fries up the noses of hand-wringing Frenchies on the Security Council. Suffice to say that the PNAC isn't too fussed on the European Union either as it might rival the US. Time to go 'pro' on the single currency, I think, voters.

In line behind the UN for a good kicking come 'non-proliferation treaties', 'diplomacy' and 'the 1972 Anti-Ballistic Missile Treaty'. That darn old ABM Treaty just got in the way of building more weapons apparently. Curses.

Oh, what else can I tell you about *Rebuilding America's Defenses*? It's such a rich bag of goodies. A little Santa sack bursting with neocon horrors. How about this one: the creation of 'US Space Forces'. Now this really is big, rich boys getting all turned on by their big, rich toys.

The PNAC – effectively the brain of the Bush administration – wants 'a global network of space-based interceptors or space-based lasers'. That's the Star Wars project to you and I – but the neocons just make it sound too Dr Evil for words. They go on to say that if the US military is to continue to enjoy its 'unequivocal supremacy in space' then 'Space Command' must be able to 'deny others the use of space'. Remember all that kerfuffle over Bush announcing his new space programme with Mars and Moon shots? Well, call me a cynic, but after reading *Rebuilding America's Defenses*, I tend to think that he might have had an ulterior motive other than pioneering exploration of the the solar system and pure scientific endeavour.

It's kind of, like, given away, you know, on page 56 of the policy paper: 'Maintaining control of space will inevitably require the application of force both in space and from space,' it says. So get those lasers on the moon quick.

Cyberspace also gets turned into a battleground under the neocons. 'Any nation wishing to assert itself globally must take account of this other new "global commons",' we're told by the PNAC.

The neocons make it clear that they want a 'revolution' in military affairs. With some sort of horrible spooky foresight, the PNAC cabal says that the process of this 'revolutionary change, is likely to be a long one, absent some catastrophic and catalyzing event – like a new Pearl Harbour'. Is it wrong to say '9-11'?

Here's their glimpse of the future, courtesy of *Rebuilding America's Defenses*: 'Although it may take several decades for the process of transformation to unfold, in time, the art of warfare on air, land and sea will be vastly different than it is today, and "combat" likely will take place in new dimensions: in space, cyberspace and perhaps the world of microbes.'

Can you hear the tune to the *Twilight Zone* playing in your head as you read this?

'Air warfare may no longer be fought by pilots manning tactical fighter aircraft sweeping the skies of opposing fighters, but a regime dominated by long-range, stealthy, unmanned aircraft. On land the clash of massive, combined-arms armoured forces may be replaced by the dashes of much lighter, stealthier and information-intensive forces, augmented by fleets of robots, some small enough to fit in soldiers' pockets.'

I swear this is all true and I am making none of it up. 'Control of the sea could be largely determined not by fleets of surface combatants (that's ships to mere mortals like you and I) and aircraft carriers, but from land and space-based systems, forcing navies to manoeuvre and fight underwater. Space itself will become a theatre of war, as nations gain access to space capabilities and come to rely on them; further, the distinction between military and commercial space systems – combatants and non-combatants – will become blurred. Information systems will become an important focus of attack, particularly for US enemies seeking to short-circuit sophisticated American forces. And advanced forms of biological warfare that can "target" specific genotypes may transform biological warfare from the realm of terror to a politically useful tool.'

Did you get the last bit? The bit about targeting 'genotypes' and using biological weapons as a 'politically useful tool'? Am I just a chicken-shit 'old' European for finding that statement totally terrifying?

The neocons are modern-day revolutionaries. They are changing the way armies fight; they are changing the rules that armies fight by and they are changing the causes that armies fight for. Dubya's doctrine of pre-emptive attack against countries which America thinks might be a risk to US security stands a century of consensus on warfare, diplomacy and international law on its head.

Here's some more sci-fi horror from the White House neocons: 'Future soldiers may operate in encapsulated climate controlled, powered fighting suits, laced with sensors, and boasting chameleon-like "active" camouflage. "Skin patch" pharmaceuticals help regulate fears, focus concentration and enhance endurance and strength. A display mounted on a soldier's helmet permits a comprehensive view of the battlefield – in effect to look around corners and over hills – and allows the soldier to access the entire combat information and intelligence system while filtering incoming data to prevent overload. Individual weapons are more lethal, and a soldier's ability to call for highly precise and reliable indirect fires – not only from Army systems but those of other services – allows each individual to have great influence over huge spaces. Under the 'Land Warrior' program, some Army experts envision a "squad" of seven soldiers able to dominate an area the size of the Gettysburg battlefield – where, in 1863, some 165,000 men fought.'

All I can say is that it's lucky the Republicans got Arnie Schwarzenegger in as the Governor of California so they can use his expertise when it comes to fighting aliens, robots and other assorted monsters. Meanwhile, they'll just have to carry on killing Arabs armed with sticks and rocks. *Hasta la vista* democracy!

Are you ready for the neocon future? I sure am. I can't wait for cyborg policemen shooting at the earth from outer space. Many, not me, I assure you, would call this kind of talk the fantasies of complete raving Armageddonists and maniacs. Sorry, that's not quite accurate. When I first wrote about the PNAC in the *Sunday Herald*, I called *Rebuilding America's Defenses* 'a secret blueprint for US global domination'. So, that kind of implies that I thought it sounded like the work of dangerous nutters.

In 2002, Tam Dalyell, the then British Labour MP, father of the House of Commons and one of the leading rebel voices against the invasion of Iraq, was among the first people I told about the PNAC's plans. By then, of course, most of the PNAC were running the world from the White House. Here's what Mr Dayell, a military veteran, had to say: 'This is garbage from right-wing chicken-hawks – men who have never seen the horror of war but are in love with the idea of war. Men like Cheney, who were draft-dodgers during the Vietnam War (he could also have included President Bush).

'This is a blueprint for US world domination – a new world order in their making. These are the thought processes of fantasist Americans who want to control the world. I am appalled that a British Labour prime minister should have got into bed with a crew which has this moral standing.'

Tam was speaking to me back in September 2002 before the war started, and I'm sure I'm not putting words in his mouth when I say that it's pretty unlikely he'd be surprised by anything Tony Blair would do or say today as part of his unbreakable pact, forged in blood, with a revolutionary US government. Getting into bed with Bush was just the start. God knows what the pair of them plan during their little telephone chats these days.

What other treats do the Masters of the Universe have in store for us as revealed in *Rebuilding America's Defenses*? Well, let's get back to that tricky old subject of Saddam. The PNAC tells us, 'even should Saddam pass from the scene', bases in Saudi Arabia and Kuwait will remain permanently – despite domestic opposition in the Gulf regimes to the stationing of US troops within their borders and the fact that having GIs in the Arab peninsula is one of the best recruiting sergeants for the al-Qaeda franchise. Having US bases in the Gulf is also the cause of most of those nasty outbreaks of fundamentalist violence which end with the dead bodies of western oil workers being dragged through the streets of Saudi cities.

In fact, spreading the US armed forces around the globe like a military margarine is high on the agenda. 'American forces must remain deployed abroad, in large numbers,' the PNAC says. In a post-Saddam world, we are told, 'even should US-Iranian relations improve, retaining forward-based forces in the region would still be an essential element in US security strategy given the long-standing American interests in the region'. Put simply: 'Units operating abroad are an indication of American geopolitical interests and leadership.'

North Korea, Libya and Iran are all pinpointed as dangerous regimes whose existence justifies the creation of a 'worldwide command and control system'. No surprises there, given the 'Axis of Evil' rhetoric that's roasted the ears of the free world for the last couple of years. What is interesting about North Korea is that, unlike Iraq, the crazy hermit nation is acknowledged by the PNAC back in 2000 as actually possessing 'a small nuclear arsenal'. North Korea is even said to be, 'on the verge of deploying missiles that can hit the American homeland'.

Wouldn't it have been wiser, then, to deal with nuked-up Kim Jong-il, the freaky NK dictator, rather than the poverty-stricken cowardly lion that was Saddam? Or maybe tackling a nation which really has got big scary bombs – instead of taking out a country which has, as its best weapon, a war-time propaganda minister who threatens to beat coalition forces with his shoe – isn't a good idea. But then perhaps I'm being too naive and should just leave it to the neocons to do my thinking for me.

And damn if the neocons didn't do exactly as they said they were going to when they finally got into the White House. They invaded Iraq, screwed the UN, buggered diplomacy and swaggered with six-shooters around the globe like a frat boy auditioning for *Dirty Harry*.

In the introduction to *Rebuilding America's Defenses*, the neocon cabal demanded an increase in defence spending to 3.5 per cent of the US's gross domestic product. Guess what? In October 2002, the US Senate approved the biggest increase in military spending in two decades by agreeing to a defence budget of $355 billion for 2003. In 2004, the annual defence budget was $369 billion, or 3.5 per cent of GDP – bang on the PNAC recommendation – and a grand total of 17.5 per cent of all US spending. Year on year, the bomb budget just keeps growing and growing and growing. The White House spends big on defence, just as the neocons promised in *Rebuilding America's Defenses*. And, of course, this all has nothing to do with the financial links between the Bush administration and the arms industry. Heaven forbid that I'd make such a suggestion.

How do they pay for this military spending anyway? Don't worry, citizens, the neocons had it all thought out before they got into office ... as we now know courtesy of *Rebuilding America's Defenses*. It's simple really – they screw the poor – or as they put it: 'In the coming decades, the network of social entitlement programs, particularly social security, will generate a further squeeze on other federal spending programs.' Hence, jobs drop, unemployment rises, kids get less education, parents work longer hours, families become unhealthy, prison numbers rise, but the bombs still get built and the bullets still whizz at those damn camel-jockeys in the Gulf. Welcome to the wonderful revolutionary world of Dubya's neocons!

There's a few promises that the PNAC didn't quite live up to, however, like vowing to improve the quality of life for the military which they said had been 'degraded' by Clinton. Senator Blanche Lincoln, in April 2004, criticised the way Team Bush has treated servicemen, pointing out that disability pay is deducted from a disabled veteran's military pension. The Federal Government won't even pay the travel expenses for soldiers' trips home on leave from Afghanistan and Iraq. What a way to make sure you have a global military elite ready to kick *cojones* all around the world – don't even pay their travel expenses.

I think the ending – the climax – of *Rebuilding America's Defenses* should speak for itself. Here we go – to the tune of 'Land of the Free': 'We cannot allow North Korea, Iran, Iraq or other similar states to undermine American leadership, intimidate American allies or threaten the American homeland itself. The blessings of the American peace, purchased at fearful cost and a century of effort, should not be so trivially squandered.

'Keeping the American peace requires the US military to undertake a broad array of missions today and rise to very different challenges tomorrow, but there can be no retreat from these missions without compromising American leadership and the benevolent order it secures.

'This is the choice we face. It is not a choice between pre-eminence today and pre-eminence tomorrow. Global leadership is not something exercised at our leisure, when the mood strikes us or when our core national security interests are directly threatened; then it is already too late. Rather it is a choice whether or not to maintain American military pre-eminence, to secure American geo-political leadership and to preserve the American peace.'

And then I wept.

GETTING AWAY WITH MURDER

or

How Rummy kissed Saddam's ass and gave the Butcher of Baghdad the green light to 'chemicalize' the Iranians

It's time to bring out the Great Hypocrite again. This ought to make you sick.

OK. So, we've established that way back in the late 1990s, Rumsfeld, on behalf of the whole neocon cabal of Cheney and Wolfowitz *et al*, was tugging at Clinton's sleeve and yapping at his heels to give Saddam a good hiding – to whack Iraq and take over all that lovely oil. Well, if Rumsfeld and all the boys just hated Saddam, then they had the right to think like that. Right?

If that's the case, how do you explain the photograph that's lying on my desk? Because if Rumsfeld hated Saddam so much then why have I got this photo of them shaking hands in Baghdad in December 1983?

OK, OK. Maybe Saddam was a good guy back then?

Nope, he wasn't. I've just checked.

He was gassing Iranian soldiers in the early 1980s and the US knew all about it. And it wasn't as if Donald Rumsfeld was blissfully, unimpeachably ignorant about Saddam's war crimes either, because in 1983 he was President Ronnie Reagan's Special Envoy to Iraq. So Rummy was pretty much in the loop when it came to all things Iraqi. And it's definitely Rummy in that picture. I'd know that vain, arrogant face anywhere. And it's definitely Saddam, too. There he is with his moustache, his military uniform and his bunch of 'Saddamalikes' standing around. Saddam and Rummy are shaking hands, all smiles. It's a beautiful scene – two men of such towering abilities – *mano-e-mano* and clearly in love.

Jeez. It kinda takes some explaining, though, don't you think? Saddam and Rummy getting it on like boyfriend and girlfriend. But let's give it a go, anyway.

Thanks to the formidable academics and researchers over at George Washington University's National Security Archive we've got the full skinny on what Rummy was up to in Iraq – and it's pretty disgusting.

Just a quick history lesson though before we get down to shaming Rumsfeld: the Iran–Iraq war kicked off in 1980 and ran for eight years. The US was 'officially neutral' over this little desert dust-up. That must make me 'officially neutral' over whether or not Tony Blair gets sent to the Tower for crimes against his country. It was with such even-handed 'official neutrality' that America supported Iraq against Iran with money, intelligence and weapons. Such acts of neutrality paid off wonderfully by prolonging one of the most brutal wars of the 20th century and ramping up the body count.

America was freaked out by the idea of a bunch of stars-and-stripes-burning ayatollahs running a big country like Iran. So, Iraq (which had cut off diplomatic relations with the US after the 1967 Arab–Israeli war) was quietly removed in 1982 from the State Department's list of states that supported terrorism. That eased things nicely for money to start flowing from America into Saddam's coffers. Both the White House and the State Department bullied the export–import bank to cough up more dollars for Iraq. That made Iraq's balance sheet look so healthy that it could then go off and get more money from other international banks.

What do you think Saddam spent all that lovely money on? Dolls for Baghdad schoolgirls? Maybe free counselling for all the people who managed to live through one of his torture sessions or a spell in Uday's rape rooms? A cheese and wine party for the Kurds? Nope. I think he spent it on guns and chemicals and anthrax and stuff like that. Oh, and he bought swathes of this top quality killing kit from Britain. Yes, the Yanks and Brits just lined up to flog barbaric equipment and technology to a man who admitted to being inspired by Hitler and Stalin. Good call.

Joyce Battle of the National Security Archive at George Washington University says: 'Although official US policy still barred the export of US military equipment to Iraq, some was evidently provided on a "don't ask, don't tell" basis.' Battle points out that in March 1983 a congressional aide asked whether heavy trucks, recently sold to Iraq, were intended for military purposes. A State Department official replied: 'We presumed that this was Iraq's intention and had not asked.'

It wasn't until November 1984 that the US restored full formal relations with Saddam's Ba'athist Iraq, although for years Ronnie Reagan had been ordering that Iraq receive intelligence and military support in secret. It's strange, though. Why would America restore relations in November 1984, when in the summer of 1983 Iran started moaning on about those pesky Iraqis dropping chemical weapons on their soldiers. You'd think Reagan would have had no dealings with some low-life dictator with an arsenal full of mustard gas. Wouldn't that mean that America was a pal and a sponsor of a country which murdered its own people and used weapons of mass destruction against its enemies? Surely, that can't be? It doesn't add up.

All those Iranian claims were probably lies, though. I mean who's going to trust some fundamentalist with a beard and a robe when you have a secular tyrant with a moustache and a uniform to believe.

But how about this: those Iranian claims weren't lies after all, apparently. The US knew all along that Saddam was gas-happy. It had intelligence confirming that Iraq used chemical weapons on an 'almost daily' basis. A November 1983 memorandum from the bureau of politico-military affairs to the then Secretary of State George Shultz headed *Iraqi Use of Chemical Weapons* confirmed that.

There was another State Department memo, also written in November 1983; and this time from the office of the Assistant Secretary for Near Eastern and South Asian affairs. It says that maybe the US should mention to Saddam that they knew his boys had been dropping poison gas all over Iranians because – wait 'til you hear this – that would 'avoid unpleasantly surprising Iraq through public positions we may have to take on this issue'. 'Unpleasantly surprising' Iraq? I think it was the Iranians who were getting unpleasantly surprised in this instance – primarily by huge clouds of noxious lethal fumes wafting over their tanks and turning the faces of their soldiers green.

And, I should point out that some other intriguing State Department cables were sent around this time, including one which said that Iraq used chemical weapons in October 1982 and in July and August 1983, 'against Kurdish insurgents'.

Let me just remind you that the US had this information a full year before normal relations with Iraq were formally re-established and before Rummy went on his grotesque Baghdad junket to suck up to Saddam.

While all this was happening, Iran was adrift in a sea of mustard gas and the world didn't give a goddamn. The Geneva Convention says that the entire world – every nation on earth – must take action against any country that uses chemical weapons. However, the great countries of the globe shuffled their feet, looked at the ground and left those nasty little fundamentalists in Tehran to their isolated and apparently much deserved fate.

Not only did Britain and America know that all this horror was going on, and not only did they look the other way (because they'd rather a monster like Saddam came out on top in a fight with Iranian fundamentalists) but they also helped the Butcher of Baghdad to commit his crimes. Among State Department papers, there's a document which says that the American government had decided to limit its 'efforts against the Iraqi CW (chemical weapons) program to close monitoring because of our strict neutrality in the Gulf War'. Here was the world's policeman saying it was happy to stand by and watch while mass murder and war crimes were committed in front of America's eyes and with its silent acquiescence.

The State Department knew by the end of 1983, just as Rummy was about to brown-nose Saddam, that 'with the essential assistance of foreign firms, Iraq has become able to deploy and use CW and probably has built up large reserves of CW for further use'.

One of the documents that Joyce Battle and her team at GWU got declassified under the Freedom of Information Act was Ronnie Reagan's National Security Decision Directive NSDD 114. The directive was entitled *US Policy toward the Iran–Iraq War* and dated November 26, 1983. This was just a few weeks before Rummy whored himself, his president and his country to Saddam. Sorry if I keep going on about Rummy debasing himself, it's just such a sweet fact that it bears repeating ... and repeating ... and repeating.

NSDD 114 says that Iraq is under the control of a genocidal madman; that the war should stop; that America and the west have disgraced themselves through their collective failure to denounce Saddam; that assistance to Iraq in any form is illegal and that chemical weapons are the work of Satan.

Sorry, that was a joke. I was being daft, imagining that someone with a spark of human decency in their soul had written the National Security Decision Directive.

What Ronnie Reagan actually said was: 'Because of the real and psychological impact of a curtailment in the flow of oil from the Persian Gulf on the international economic system, we must assure our readiness to deal promptly with actions aimed at disrupting that traffic.' So, no mention of chemical weapons or the fact that an entire generation of Iraqi and Iranian youth was being bled white and gassed green on the plains of Mesopotamia. Nope. None of that. Just oil, oil, oil.

So, Ronnie looked around him. He needed someone to haul ass over to Iraq, kiss Saddam's butt and keep them *I-rak-ees* sweet on sending lots of oil stateside. Hmm. Bonzo the chimp was otherwise engaged, so Rummy, President Gerald Ford's former Defense Secretary, stepped in to fill the breach. He looked like the kind of guy who'd get down on his knees before an evil lunatic and do whatever it took to keep the oil flowing. On December 20, Rummy met the big man himself – Prez Saddam. Those guys loved each other. They got on like a house on fire.

I've got the secret State Department document that tells all about the Rummy – Saddam love-in. Do you want to hear a bit of it? 'Saddam Hussein showed obvious pleasure with President's letter and Rumsfeld's visit ... Rumsfeld told Saddam US and Iraq had shared interests in preventing Iranian and Syrian expansion. He said US was urging other states to curtail arms sales to Iran and believed it had successfully closed off US-controlled exports by third countries to Iran.' Don't blame the bad grammar and staccato telegram-style on me, it's those Ivy League diplomats' fault.

It's so cute. They chatted about oil for a while, with Rummy telling Saddam that it'd be just great if Iraq 'increased oil exports'. The State Department says: 'Our initial assessment is that meeting marked a positive milestone in development of US–Iraqi relations and will prove to be of wider benefit to US posture in the region.'

Then we get a little colour about how the meeting went. I hope Rummy's reading this right now. If he is, then I bet he's going to be wishing he were dead in about 20 seconds. Describing Rummy's introduction to Saddam and Tariq Aziz, the State Department secret memo says: 'Both Iraqi leaders were in military dress with pistols on hips ... Rumsfeld opened by conveying President's greetings and expressing his pleasure at being in Baghdad.' Saddam and Rumsfeld both agreed that 'having a whole generation of Iraqis and Americans grow up without understanding each other had negative implications and could lead to mix-ups'. Is that simply plain old black humour or are they both being clairvoyant and using comical understatement?

We're also told that 'France in particular understood the Iraqi view', which is probably why all those French firms sold weapons to Saddam – along with the Brits, the Americans, the Russians and the Germans –

but we'll come to that later. Rumsfeld then tells Saddam: 'Our understanding of the importance of balance in the world and the region is
similar to Iraq's.' Rumsfeld goes on to say that he's worried about 'the
circumstances of the Palestinian people'. Poor man, the last 20 years
spent fretting about those folk in Gaza must be the reason his hair's so
silvery-white.

Rumsfeld agreed with Saddam 'about the effects of generations of
Iraqis and Americans not having kinds of interaction that were natural
at all levels. If this situation persisted, it would contribute to areas of
ignorance and warped, unclear views that were in no-one's interest'.

The briefing goes on: 'Regarding war with Iran, Rumsfeld said, "US
agreed it was not in interests of region or the west for conflict to create
greater instability or for outcome to be one which weakened Iraq's role
or enhanced interests and ambitions of Iran. We thought conflict should
be settled in a peaceful manner which did not expand Iran's interests
and preserved sovereignty of Iraq."' So, Rumsfeld knows Iraq has been
using internationally outlawed weapons of mass destruction against the
Iranians. Saddam knows he knows and here's Rummy saying to
Saddam, 'We're on your side.' He might as well have filled the artillery
shells with mustard gas himself and given them to the Republican
Guard's War Crimes Battery. Rumsfeld's meeting with Saddam was
nothing more than a free hand to one of the world's most dangerous and
cruel leaders to carry on breaking international law wantonly and committing as many atrocities as he pleased. And all this while the Iranians
were pleading for the UN to listen to their complaint that they were
being slaughtered with chemical weapons. He's a good guy our Rummy,
don't you think?

Rummy quickly tires of weighty affairs like war and soon moves back
to oil. He starts talking about a new pipeline, but that doesn't seem to
satiate his junkie cravings for gushing, black crude. The greedy boy just
can't help himself and suggests that perhaps, actually, two new pipelines
might be a better idea.

Saddam's more interested, however, in closing down nations who are
selling arms to Iran, and starts whingeing about Libya and Syria flogging the Ayatollah weapons. Rumsfeld's answer has to be listened to
with the thought in your mind that America and its sidekick Britain
were selling nuclear, biological and chemical capabilities to Saddam
throughout the 1980s. With a straight face, Rumsfeld says: 'Countries
which acted in such a manner were short-sighted, looking at a single

commercial transaction while their more fundamental interests were being harmed ... People should know that terrorism has a home in Iran, Syria and Libya.' It's that old 'Axis of Evil' mob again, but, hey, one's missing. Iraq's not on that little list – even back then when it was using weapons of mass destruction. Work that one out ... because I can't.

Rumsfeld then starts denouncing Syria, telling Saddam that Damascus should withdraw from Lebanon. He describes the behaviour of the Syrian Government as 'unacceptable'. Not a word, however, not a single solitary word from Rumsfeld throughout the entire meeting about Saddam's use of chemical weapons on the battlefield.

His behaviour is entirely consistent with the policy of the US. A State Department memo from November 1, 1983 notes that Saddam got 'CW production capability' possibly from a US company's foreign subsidiary. Two sentences later the memo reads: 'As you are aware, presently Iraq is at a disadvantage in its war of attrition against Iran. After a recent meeting on the war, a discussion paper was sent to the White House for a National Security Council meeting, a section of which outlines a number of measures we might take to assist Iraq.' At the time the memo was written, the State Department said that Iraq's use of chemical weapons wasn't even on the NSC meeting's agenda.

So, that was Rummy's meeting with Saddam. One more thing though. Just as an aside, I thought you might like to hear the following words that fell from Rumsfeld's quivering lips during his dewy-eyed encounter with 'the world's most evil man'. The secret US report on the meeting reads: 'US, said Rumsfeld, sought to promote a fair peace between Arabs and Israelis, one that recognised the circumstances of the Palestinian people.' I don't think I need to comment on that, do I? Suffice to say, Saddam has a soft spot for the Palestinians – probably because he has the same view of Jews as Hitler did – and such comments were a great way for Rummy to kiss the dictator's hairy Babylonian ass. As we know, since Baby Bush took power the people of Palestine have suffered horrendously under Israel, so one has to doubt Rumsfeld's commitment in the early 1980s to equanimity for both Palestine and Israel.

The following spring – May 9, 1984 to be exact – another State Department memo said that the US was reviewing its policy on 'the sale of certain dual-use items to Iraq nuclear entities' and that 'preliminary results favour expanding such trade to include Iraqi nuclear entities'. In case you are wondering, a 'dual-use' item could be something like a chemical used to make fertiliser which also just happens to be the key component of a nerve gas. Or it could be a bit of machinery used in a heart machine which also just happens to be essential if you want to build a nuclear bomb. So this is what is done in Britain and America: these 'dual-use' thingummyjigs are sold to dictators just as long as the dictator promises that he won't make weapons of mass destruction out of them. Once Britain and America hear that someone like Saddam plans to use these 'dual-use' items to make some nice fertiliser to grow corn along the banks of the Euphrates or to build lots of heart machines for the old folk in the Basra Twilight Home for Retired Members of the Fedayeen Militia, then everything is A-OK.

It's not surprising then, given the level of oversight by western powers on what happened to the 'dual-use' kit sold to dictators like Saddam, that in September 1984 the US's Defense Intelligence Agency found that Iraq was continuing to develop its 'formidable' chemical weapons arsenal and would 'probably pursue nuclear weapons'. Can you believe it? Britain and America gave them fertiliser stuff and what-you-may-call-its for heart machines and those guys went and made sarin and started their own Manhattan Project. Disgraceful.

After Rummy gave Saddam the old nod and the wink to go on gassing the Iranians, the Iraqis really got going in the war crimes stakes. In February 1984 Iraq publicly told Iran: 'The invaders should know that for every harmful insect there is an insecticide capable of annihilating it whatever the number and Iraq possesses the annihilation insecticide.' These guys weren't messing about – they had the annihilation insecticide and they wanted to use it.

Only now – only when Iraq, so cocky because of Rumsfeld's Baghdad bum-licking, went public with threats to use weapons of mass destruction (aka the 'annihilation insecticide' in Ba'ath-speak) – did Washington decide to raise the issue of chemical weapons. Well, America didn't quite raise the issue. It waited until March before publicly condemning a man who was obviously a genocidal lunatic. When I say 'publicly condemn' I mean America put its hand over its mouth so that the rest of the world couldn't quite hear and whispered very quietly that Saddam was a bit naughty. This is the way the US put that madman Saddam in his place: 'While condemning Iraq's chemical weapons use ... The United States finds the present Iranian Government regime's intransigent refusal to deviate from its avowed objective of eliminating the legitimate government of neighbouring Iraq to be inconsistent with the accepted norms of behaviour among nations and the moral and religious basis which it claims.' So it was the Ayatollah who got the bollocking for having the temerity to allow Saddam to drop poison gas all over his troops. And, just for the record, it was Iraq which attacked Iran first in September 1980.

In *Shaking Hands with Saddam Hussein: The US tilts towards Iraq 1980–84*, Joyce Battle says that following this 'denunciation' the State Department was asked if Iraq's use of chemical weapons would have 'any effect on US recent initiatives to expand commercial relationships with Iraq across a broad range'. A State Department official said: 'No. I'm not aware of any change in our position. We're interested in being involved in a closer relationship with Iraq.'

Iran was obviously not very impressed with the tough hand that America was taking with Iraq and the fulsome concern that the White House had shown for all those gassed Iranian soldiers; so the mullahs in Tehran started to threaten that they too would develop weapons of mass destruction. Iran then lodged a draft resolution with the United Nations asking the world to condemn Saddam's use of chemical weapons. That prompted American diplomats to go scuttling around the UN headquarters telling friendly pushover nations to go for a 'no decision' ruling on the resolution. The US was also ready to abstain in the vote, rendering the entire process a redundant farce.

Iraqi diplomat Nizar Hamdoon, who later became Iraq's ambassador to the UN, met the US Deputy Assistant Secretary of State, James Plack, and made it clear that Iraq didn't want the resolution passed – no surprise there – but could live with a Security Council presidential statement which did not name any country for using chemical weapons. That is exactly what happened on March 30, 1984. During Plack's meeting with Hamdoon, the American said that he didn't want chemical weapons 'to dominate our bilateral relationship nor to detract from our common interests'.

On the same day that the UN effectively did nothing about the Iraqi atrocities against Iranians, the State Department's bureau of Near Eastern and South Asian affairs sent a memo to Plack letting him know that the UN statement contained everything that 'Hamdoon wanted'.

Then, a few months later in November, as I mentioned earlier, the US and Iraq restored diplomatic relations. Here's what Joyce Battle had to say, not long before the invasion of Iraq in 2003, about the lessons we could all have learned from the shared past of Iraq and America: 'The current Bush administration discusses Iraq in starkly moralistic terms to further its goal of persuading a sceptical world that a pre-emptive and pre-meditated attack on Iraq could and should be supported as a "just war".'

She goes on to say that during the years when Iraq really was using weapons of mass destruction 'actual rather than rhetorical opposition to such use was evidently not perceived to serve US interests; instead the Reagan administration did not deviate from its determination that Iraq was to serve as the instrument to prevent Iranian victory ... Chemical warfare was viewed as a potentially embarrassing public relations problem that complicated efforts to provide assistance. The Iraqi Government's repressive internal policies, though well known to the US government at the time, did not figure at all in the presidential directives that established US policy toward the Iran–Iraq War. The US was concerned with its ability to project military force in the Middle East, and to keep the oil flowing.'

ARMING SADDAM

or

How America gave bugs, bombs and poison gas to our friendly dictator in the Gulf

It pretty much sucks, really, doesn't it? All that turning a blind eye and allowing war crimes and atrocities to go ahead without lifting a finger is about as low as it can get, isn't it? Isn't it?

Wrong. It's just about to get worse. But what can be worse than allowing Saddam to chemicalise Iranians? Well, how about selling him weapons of mass destruction that even Dr No wouldn't dream of using? That oughta do it.

You probably don't believe me, do you? There's no way America would have sold Saddam bio-weapons, you're thinking. Well, once again, don't believe me. Next time you're in Washington take a wander over to the Senate and see if you can dig out a much forgotten document called *The Riegle Report*. It took nearly a year to research and was finally concluded in May 1994. It was carried out by the Senate's Committee on Banking, Housing and Urban Affairs under the chairmanship of Senator Donald W Riegle Junior.

One day back in October 1992, this rather prosaically named committee, which is responsible for overseeing US exports, was told by UN inspectors during a hearing that they had 'identified many US-manufactured items exported pursuant of licences issued by the US Department of Commerce that were used to further Iraq's chemical and nuclear weapons development and missile delivery system development programmes'.

Now, around this time – after the First Gulf War – lots of GIs who fought against Iraq in 1991, and their wives and kids, were coming down with a whole host of really nasty illnesses and diseases – symptoms which would later come to be known as Gulf War Syndrome. The

29

Senate Committee thought there might be a connection between sales of WMD capabilities to Iraq from America and this spate of horrible illnesses that was affecting soldiers who fought in the Gulf. If this scary WMD stuff from America was turning up in Iraq, then maybe that's what was making those soldiers sick. But, hang on, that would mean that America was effectively killing its own soldiers because the government was selling all these banned weapons to Baghdad. Now, that is sick.

In August 1993, Riegle says he 'began to research the possibility that there may be a connection between Iraqi chemical, biological and radiological warfare research and development programs and a mysterious illness which was then being reported by thousands of returning Gulf War veterans'. Government officials, scientists and veterans were interviewed and consulted.

The Committee also contacted the US Department of Commerce and requested that information on the sale of biological materials to Iraq before the war be handed over. The records only go back to 1985, but what they reveal is astonishing. Included in the sales from America to Iraq, up until 1989, were the following germs – all of which can be 'weaponised':

> *Bacillus Anthracis* – aka anthrax. It was the major component of Iraq's bio-warfare programme prior to 1991, according to the Department of Defense. Anthrax is usually fatal. Death follows fever, difficulty breathing, chest pain and blood poisoning. Once the illness is advanced, drugs are useless and death is inevitable.

> *Clostridium Botulinum* – aka botulism. It causes vomiting, constipation, thirst, weakness, headache, fever, dizziness, double-vision and paralysis of the muscles used to swallow. It is often fatal.

> *Histoplasma Capsulatum*. This little beauty is sort of like TB and it can kill. It can cause pneumonia, enlargement of the liver and spleen, anaemia, flu-like symptoms, acute inflammatory skin diseases. It also attacks the lungs, brain, spinal membranes, heart, peritoneum and the adrenal glands.

> *Brucella Melitensis*. It's a bacteria that causes chronic fatigue, loss of appetite, profuse sweating even when at rest, pain in the joints

and muscles, insomnia, nausea and damage to the major organs. You'd be lucky to survive.

Clostridium Perfringens. This highly toxic bacteria causes gas gangrene. The toxins move along the body's muscles killing cells and producing necrotic – dead – tissue that the bacteria can then use to grow in before moving off and eating other parts of your body. Eventually, the toxins move into the bloodstream and you're finished.

As well as those five bacterial brutes, the US also sent Saddam's scientists E. coli and genetic material including human and bacterial DNA. America wasn't under any illusions where this stuff was going – they were posting it directly, in most cases, to the Iraqi Atomic Energy Commission and the University of Baghdad's Department of Microbiology. Collectively, they're the guys who usually make atomic bombs and build bio-weapons for war.

In other words, Saddam was being given nerve gas, bio-weapons and nuclear gizmos almost right up until the outbreak of the First Gulf War. Everything he needed – the technology and the materials – to develop nuclear, chemical and biological weapons of mass destruction was being sold to Saddam by America and Britain.

Let's go through that list of exports that Senator Riegle and his staff were able to extract from the Department of Commerce.

Here we are on May 2, 1986. There's a big shipment from the US heading straight for Iraq's Ministry of Higher Education. What do you think's in it? Well, there are three batches of anthrax, five batches of botulism, three batches of clostridium perfringens and two batches of tetanus. In total, 23 batches of deadly germs winged their way to Baghdad on that day alone.

On August 31, 1987, the Iraqi State Drug Company got eight batches of germs including salmonella and E. coli. On July 11, 1988, the Iraqi Atomic Energy Commission got three batches of germs, one of which is E. coli.

America was still delivering biological material to the Iraqi Atomic Energy Commission on April 26, 1988. By the way, that's just a few weeks after Saddam's chemical-weapons shock troops killed some 5,000 Kurds in just one hour in the town of Halabja on March 17, 1988.

On September 29, 1988, the Iraqi Ministry of Trade got a big bundle of fun from stateside in the shape of 11 batches of germs including anthrax, clostridium perfringens and botulism. That delivery came just over a month after Saddam attacked another Kurdish village. This time mustard gas, nerve gas and sarin were all dropped by Iraqi aircraft over the town of Birjinni on August 25, 1988. Four people died and survivors said victims were writhing in agony and coughing up blood. Scientists at Britain's Porton Down military research establishment confirmed CW had been used against the people of Birjinni.

Iraq is also suspected of using biological agents during an attack in 1984. This was not long after Rummy left Baghdad after glad-handing with Saddam. The attack was on Majnoon Island during the Iran–Iraq War and involved the use of cholera and typhus.

The deliveries just go on and on. There's botulism being shipped to Officers' City in Baghdad; bugs, including West Nile fever, going to the University of Basrah's Department of Biology; typhus being sent to the Ministry of Health. In total, Saddam was trying to weaponise at least ten germs that America was sending him in the post. There were at least 17 individual shipments, during which a total of 80 batches of bio-material were sent to Iraq.

'The US government actually licensed the export of deadly micro-organisms to Iraq,' said Riegle. 'It was later learned that these micro-organisms exported by the United States were identical to those the United Nations inspectors found and recovered [in the 1990s, after the First Gulf War] from the Iraqi biological warfare programme.' These were, Riegle says, 'full pathogens capable of being reproduced' that America was sending to Iraq.

You all know what blow-back is, right? It's when you've done something stupid and wicked years ago and then it comes back to haunt you – to bite you in the ass. Gulf War Syndrome was the first blow-back from the British and American policy of arming Saddam. James J Tuite III was the principal investigator for Riegle's committee. He found that America had 'exported chemical, biological, nuclear, and missile-system equipment to Iraq that was converted to military use in Iraq's chemical, biological, and nuclear weapons program. Many of these weapons – weapons that the US and other countries provided critical materials for – were used against us during the war'.

So, guess who sat on Senator Riegle's committee? You're probably thinking they were a bunch of nobodies or that all the members have died or resigned or lost their seats, yeah? Because surely no-one who sat on that committee and heard how the US was selling anthrax to Iraq could still be holding office today and not be howling from the top of the Capitol building about the hypocrisy of the invasion of Iraq. Riegle's team included a chap called Senator John F Kerry of Massachusetts. That would be John 'The Chin' Kerry – that boring guy we saw on TV now and again during the 2004 presidential election. He's the guy who voted for the war, even though he didn't really like the idea of the war. Yeah, that's right, he's the fella who stood as the Democratic Presidential nominee against Bush. Yep, he was on the Riegle committee. And he still voted for the war, even though he knew fine well how Saddam had been armed to the teeth by the US.

How could Kerry vote for the war after hearing Don Riegle say these words on October 27, 1992 as the committee investigations got all accusatory? 'We now know that between January 1985 and August 1990, when the invasion of Kuwait took place, the executive branch of our government approved 771 different export licences for sale of dual-use sensitive equipment to Iraq.' That's a lot of stuff. Saddam could have either made one helluva a lot of heart machines and fertiliser with that amount of kit or he could have really got started on cranking up the old sarin gas production lines prior to the First Gulf War. Riegle said he thought the statistics were 'a devastating record'.

The Senate report also notes that: 'The United States provided the Government of Iraq with "dual-use" licensed materials which assisted in the development of Iraqi chemical, biological and missile-system programs.' This 'assistance', we discover, included 'chemical warfare-agent precursors, chemical warfare-agent production facility plans and technical drawings, chemical warfare filling equipment, biological warfare-related materials, missile fabrication equipment and missile system guidance equipment'. Damn, that's almost enough to start World War Three.

Riegle said that 'at least 17 licences were issued for the export of bacteria or fungus cultures to either the Iraqi Atomic Energy Commission or the University of Baghdad. Licences to export computers [for] missile activity, and computers and electronic instruments to the Iraqi Atomic Energy Commission, were issued to a known procurement agent for Iraqi missile programmes. A licence was issued to export equipment for general military applications such as jet engine repair, rocket cases etcetera.'

Riegle then told the world that: 'The records also indicate that the US government understood exports that it was licensing could enhance

Iraq's conventional military capability.' Trouble was, however, that the world didn't listen to Riegle, or, perhaps, remember what he said, come 2003 and invasion time. Or else maybe the leaders of Britain and America just didn't give a damn about their past crimes, or simply didn't have a conscience.

One other fella who testified in front of Riegle's committee was some guy called David Kay. Now, that wouldn't be the same David Kay who was appointed by the CIA to head the Iraq Survey Group (ISG) after the fall of Saddam, would it? The man tasked by America to uncover the location of all those WMD that Saddam was supposed to have stashed away? The man who then resigned from the ISG saying 'we were all wrong' to believe the damned things were in Iraq? The man who called Tony Blair 'delusional' for saying the ISG would find the mythical unicorn-like weapons of mass destruction? Yep, it was him alright.

Back in the early 1990s, Kay was the head of the UN's nuclear weapons inspections in Iraq. Here's what the man had to say to Riegel: 'The simple answer to the question of whether US-produced equipment and technology has been found to be part of the Iraqi nuclear weapons programme is "yes". It was there. It was an essential part.' Well, you can't get clearer than that, can you?

The committee even heard that documents found in Iraq were an effective blueprint for Saddam's first nuke. Of course, Saddam's scientists wouldn't have had a clue how to put the thing together unless there'd been plenty of help stateside from big business and government. Gary Milhollin, director of the Wisconsin Project on Nuclear Arms Control, testified in front of the committee that some '40 American companies got more than 100 licences to supply sensitive dual-use equipment to Iraqi nuclear and ballistic missile sites'.

'American equipment,' he said, 'contributed vitally to the Iraq nuclear programme, the missile programme and the chemical programme, and I am afraid I also believe that we knew that the risk was very high, if not certain, that it would contribute when we licensed.'

The US government, said Milhollin, 'knew about which Iraqi end-users were making nuclear and chemical weapons and ballistic missiles, and knew that there had been many exports to those entities'. To translate Milhollin's very diplomatic language: America knew it was selling 'heart machine' parts and 'fertiliser' chemicals to people who wanted to turn them into 'nuclear bombs' and 'annihilation insecticide' (aka poison gas).

This revolting game of passing weapons of mass destruction under the table to Saddam wasn't just down to old cowboy Ronnie Reagan. George Bush Senior was up to his turkey-neck in this nasty charade as well. The House Committee on Banking, Finance and Urban Affairs heard on May 29, 1992 that Pappy Bush's government used 'the intelligence agencies, not just the State and Commerce Departments, but the Agriculture Department, and the Justice Department to facilitate a program of aiding and abetting Saddam Hussein'. As Irene Gendzier, Professor of Political Science at Boston University, says: 'As the same hearings confirmed, major US corporations were encouraged by the administration to do business with Iraq. National Security Directive 26, issued by the first Bush administration on October 2, 1989, after the end of the Iran–Iraq war, endorsed the US "tilt" towards Baghdad, no longer justifying it in terms of Iran's feared victory.' So, America under Bush Senior got all cosy with Saddam, even when there was no risk of the evil Ayatollah getting his wicked way.

In 1990, after the invasion of Kuwait, the same Pappy Bush administration then passed the Iraq Sanctions Act. So, let me get this right, American foreign policy works this way: they arm this nutter Saddam to the teeth with WMD and tell him they are on his side. The policymakers turn a blind eye to his live experiments in chemical warfare on Iranian soldiers and Kurds, and then only get pissed off when he does what any insane tyrant propped up by a selfish, thoughtless superpower is meant to do and goes and invades another country – namely Kuwait. This sort of rank hypocrisy reminds me of the kind of parent who swears in front of their kid and then beats the same kid senseless if the youngster is unlucky enough to repeat the curse word. 'Do as I say, not do as I do' seems to be the watchword of US foreign policy.

Not only that, but Pappy Bush and Co. then started to go around blaming the weasels over in Europe for arming Saddam. Well, Pappy Bush was right in that respect – the weasels over in Europe were arming Saddam – but so was America under his presidency and the presidency before him. Nevertheless, the passage of the Sanctions Act gave the administration the chance to make such a big noise about other nations arming Saddam, that nobody thought of looking in the direction of Pappy Bush and asking what he and Ronnie Reagan had been doing during the 1980s. Perfect cover.

Pappy Bush didn't stop there, though. It wasn't just a case of his government lying by omission by blaming Europe and not having the *cojones* to accept their own misdeeds. Oh no, half-measures wouldn't do for Pappy. He needed a full-fat lie – nothing less would suffice. So, noticing that his government was obliged under the 1990 Iraq Sanctions Act to – in Don Riegel's words – 'prepare a report on the transfer or sale to Iraq of nuclear, biological, chemical or ballistic missile technology', Pappy went ahead and did just that, putting out a government report which had dead simple findings. This is what it said: 'Reflecting both US government policy and responsible sales practices of American firms, United States suppliers did not contribute directly to Iraq's convention-al or non-conventional weapons capability.' Nuff said.

So, the Riegle report was discovering that America had been tripping over itself to stuff Saddam's pockets with germs and gas and nuclear gee-gaws, but Bush Senior was saying, 'Nope, we never sold the guy nuthin'!' You've really got to hand it to Pappy – he was the master behind some audacious lies. Obviously, he does nothing by halves. Imagine a drug dealer caught shooting PCP into the veins of a 15-year-old schoolboy by a cop. The cop says: 'Hey, drug dealer, what are you doing? You can't give powerful, illegal and dangerous drugs to 15-year-olds.' And the drug dealer says: 'Reflecting both US government policy and responsible sales practices of drug dealers, I did not contribute directly to the angel dust flowing through this 15-year-old's veins that has turned him into a rampaging, murderous monster.' That's Pappy – an in-your-face liar. So daring in his lies that most people can't even believe he's lying. The cop should grab the drug dealer by the balls and cart him off to jail – and the world should have done the same to Pappy, but instead we just shrugged our shoulders and let him slip away to raise his brood. It's not that facing down 'Saddam, the Invader of Kuwait' was bad – far from it – it's just that facing down a man you've armed leaves *nobody* on the side of right. It just means everyone involved is corrupt.

And it wasn't just Pappy Bush lining up to swear that black was white. In June 1990, the Senate Foreign Relations Committee began investigating US–Iraqi relations. US Assistant Secretary of State for Near Eastern and South Asian Affairs, John Kelly, told the committee: 'We do not sell items on the munitions list to Iraq. We do not co-operate with Iraq's nuclear programme.'

The problem is that these guys just don't give a tinker's fart about the truth. As Senator Riegle said as recently as May 2003: 'It is exceeding-ly difficult to force the military bureaucracy to come clean – and now we have essentially the same cast of characters back in power in Bush II. The truth, as always, is a powerful disinfectant – if it can be brought to light.'

The current British government is doing all it can to make sure that the truth gets treated like disinfectant – flushed down the toilet. Following my investigations, scores of British MPs of all parties signed an Early Day Motion in the House of Commons (October 20, 2005) entitled *Biological and Toxin Weapons Convention and Iraq*. In effect, this motion says that as Senator Riegle has proved that the US sold bio-weapons to Iraq, then the UK is bound – as a signatory to the Biological and Toxin Weapons Convention (BTWC) – to squeal on America by informing to the United Nations Security Council. The MPs also reminded Blair of his 'recent commitment in the April 2002 Green Paper, *Strengthening Biological and Toxin Weapons Convention*, that those at every level of responsibility for any breach of international law relating to the use of such weapons will be held personally accountable because compliance with BTWC is an issue the international community cannot avoid'. In other words, if Blair was as good as his word then he would go to the UN and say that the American government stood in total breach of international law for selling bio-weapons to Iraq.

Blair certainly couldn't have forgotten about bio-weapons in the run-up to war because that's when poor Brits were being frightened out of their wits daily with the spectre of Saddam nuking/chemicalising/anthraxing them. So, I take it that you – just like me – believe Blair must by now have seen the error of his ways and be currently heading straight to Kofi Annan's office to tell him all about America's nasty little secrets and how the US armed Saddam?

Umm ... not quite.

On March 14, 2004 the Bishop of Oxford asked this question of Her Majesty's Government while sitting in the House of Lords: 'Whether, in accordance with the Biological and Toxin Weapons Convention, they will report to the Security Council of the United Nations the reported sale of biological weapons to Iraq by the United States?'

Here's what Labour's Baroness Symons said in response: 'My Lord, no. The materials were exported by the United States in accordance with export controls in place at the time. The United States did not believe that they would be used for anything other than legitimate research purposes and therefore did not knowingly export the materials to assist a biological weapons programme. There are therefore no grounds for reporting a breach of the Biological and Toxin Weapons Convention.'

Yeah, right. America thought that Saddam would get out his home chemistry set and microscope and start brushing up on his O-level science when he got all those lovely bugs and germs. There's no way he'd use his new bio-arsenal for anything evil – especially after chemicalising the Kurds and the Iranians.

America armed the Fifth Horseman of the Apocalypse and Britain is too yellow-bellied to say a damn thing about it. Instead of standing up for the truth, the UK fights wars for the US. That's how Britain does its bit for democracy and decency. But then of course, as I'll show you in the next chapter, Britain armed Saddam, as well – as did most other western powers. So, it might be a bit hypocritical of the Baroness to go grassing up the White House without dobbing in Number 10 to the UN, and most other heads of state in the free world, too.

But, hang on a minute. Perhaps we are just being naive here. I mean, the Ayatollah was a loon as well, wasn't he? That is just as indisputable as Pappy Bush's administration lying like a puppet-show full of Pinocchios, and Saddam being a blood-thirsty despot. Maybe the Americans just had to do a deal with the devil and jump into bed with Saddam to make sure the lesser of two evils won the day. And hell, if that means chucking Saddam a few million litres of nerve agent along the way, well so be it. And you know what? If you're doing the right thing, then maybe you have to tell a few lies, too. After all, the public aren't that sophisticated; it's not like they've all got degrees in international relations or anything. *Realpolitik* just isn't something the punter in the street is generally all that savvy about.

At least rationalising the facts that way – thinking that it's all down to some hard truths that are beyond the workaday understanding of most drones in the US and UK – isn't quite as bad as admitting to yourself that the people who run our countries are all amoral, dangerous, self-serving liars who don't give a damn about wallowing up to their armpits in the blood of innocent people.

Just so we don't get confused here, let's spell out just how horribly real the politics of the west were and just how far up the chain of command this complicity with Saddam really went within the US government. We know that the CIA aided Iraq for a period of at least two years during the war with Iran by secretly supplying Saddam with detailed intelligence, including data from sensitive US satellite reconnaissance photography. This helped the Iraqis bomb Iran's oil terminals and power plants.

And we should not forget a guy called Howard Teicher. He was a former US National Security Council advisor between 1982 and 1987 who just happened to accompany Rumsfeld on his infamous little jaunt to Baghdad in 1983. You remember: the one where Rummy kissed Saddam's ass. In 1995, Teicher lodged a sworn declaration in the US District Court in the Southern District of Florida. This is what it said: 'While a staff member to the National Security Council, I was responsible for the Middle East and for Political-Military Affairs. During my five-year tenure on the National Security Council, I had regular contact with both CIA Director William Casey and Deputy Director Robert Gates ... CIA Director Casey personally spearheaded the effort to ensure that Iraq had sufficient military weapons, ammunition and vehicles to avoid losing the Iran–Iraq War ... in 1986, President Reagan sent a secret message to Saddam Hussein telling him that Iraq should step up its air war and bombing of Iran. This message was delivered by Vice-president Bush who communicated it to Egyptian President Mubarak, who in turn passed the message to Saddam Hussein. Similar strategic operational advice was passed to Saddam Hussein through various meetings with European and Middle Eastern heads of state.'

I'd like to give Don Riegle the last word on this steaming pile of lies and hypocrisy – he is, after all, the one man who's done the most to bring out the whole disgusting truth of how the west armed, encouraged and then beat up and destroyed Iraq. 'It is obvious from the record,' he says, 'that our own government fostered the development of the military strength of Saddam Hussein, which we then had to turn around and go and confront directly with American military forces. And lives were lost in the process. And an enormous amount of money was spent as well.'

On second thoughts, let's give the floor finally to the American Gulf War Veterans Association (AGWVA). With all due respect to Don Riegle, they are the ones who lived through the hellish results of American foreign policy towards Iraq, so it's really no surprise to find out that they have a clincher of a comment to make.

'If our Secretary of Defense,' the AGWVA wrote in October 2002, referring to Rumsfeld as the momentum for war became unstoppable, 'is unaware of the sales of biological materials to a country with which we are about to go to war, or if he is in denial over the fact that these sales occurred, the AGWVA believes that he represents a clear and present danger to the lives of our military, our country and the American people, and should be considered a very serious threat to the national security. It is for this reason that the AGWVA calls for his resignation and removal from office.'

Now who would disagree with those guys?

WHY BRITAIN WAS SADDAM'S DIRTY LITTLE WHORE

or

How the UK sold WMD to the man with the most evil moustache in the world

Attention all Brit readers. Please do not sit there reading this book and thinking smugly to yourself: 'Why those bloody awful Americans. They're despicable, they are. They'd do anything, they would. Not like good old Blighty.'

Remember: Britain armed Saddam, too. Britain is every bit as culpable and despicable as those awful, awful Americans. In fact, Britain is probably a bit more despicable than America. While the US was selling deadly weapons to Saddam so they could ensure the 'chemicalisation' of Iranians, Britain was selling weapons of mass destruction to Saddam simply for the green folding stuff. Filthy lucre was all that mattered to the Brits – they didn't have the cover of complicated geo-political ends to protect their asses. The American motive might have been morally warped and criminal, but at least there was some sort of ideology behind the US's nasty actions. All Britain cared about was making money. It couldn't have given a damn who Saddam killed or what side he was on, it just wanted the contents of his wallet.

Now, I know that you know all of this. Don't you remember a little incident, almost a decade ago, called the Scott Inquiry? That's it – it's all coming back to you now. You can remember just how loathsome we can be as a nation, can't you? Well, if you can't, I'm going to remind you … in detail.

I also know that some of you are reading this and thinking 'the Scott Inquiry'? Wasn't that some really boring, endless Whitehall hearing about export licences? Uh-uh. It was nothing of the sort. The Scott Inquiry was one of the first times in their national history that the British people were able to see their leaders for what they really are – a bunch of cowardly, amoral, dirty liars.

The Scott Inquiry – and its subsequent report – pulled back the skin on the body politic of the UK and showed the maggoty, rotten heart of what passes for the British government. What it revealed was a fundamental enmity between government and honesty. Both the Tories and today's Labour Party seem incapable of being honest with the people who elect them. I don't know if politicians imbibe a lie serum as soon as they're elected, but it seems that the minute they get a whiff of power they vanish to the dark side and into a world of lies where black's white, good's bad and nuclear bombs are heart machines. It's like Ian McDonald, the head of the Ministry of Defence's Defence Sales Secretariat, said when he was quizzed during the Scott Inquiry: 'The truth is a difficult concept.' Well, as far as I can work out, it is if you are Tony Blair, or any other British leader for that matter, going all the way back to the Battle of Hastings in 1066.

The truth is not just 'a difficult concept' for the British government. The truth is constipated in Westminster. It's backed up by years of lies that have clogged up democracy and calcified honesty and withered away the spirit of the United Kingdom. It's time, then, that Britain took an enema and purged itself of the wasteful sludge that's holding it back – namely, the political classes.

Don't let the lies of the Labour administration, however, blind you to the lies and failures of the government that came before it. Labour's bad, sure, but the Tories are bad, too. Worse, actually. You might think that Tony Blair deserves to be strung up for taking Britain into the Iraq War – at least I hope you'll think that by the time you've finished reading this book – but if you ever think, even in your darkest moments, that Blair's betrayed you so much that you just might go and vote for the Tories, then I have one piece of advice for you: bookmark this chapter for just such an occasion. Then you can quietly sit down and rediscover just what a lying, duplicitous, amoral whore of a government the Tories put in place the last time the UK was stupid enough to let them into power. Did we look the other way? Were we sleeping? Were we drunk? How did these people rule this country for nearly 20 years?

Remember, Blair is bad for cosying up to Bush and taking us into an illegal war on the basis of lies. But that doesn't make the Tories any better. They sold Saddam weapons of mass destruction. They went to war against him for invading Kuwait because he thought he could get away with it on the strength of his friendship with the UK and the US. They backed sanctions because Saddam had WMD, without admitting that they had sold the weapons to Iraq in the first place, and then proceeded to lie their arses off to the public, claiming that the arms sales had never taken place. To some extent Blair, like America under Bush, is driven by ideology and belief. The Tories, however – cheap little tarts that they are – only get turned on by pound signs.

OK, so just what did the Scott Report show us about the slut-politics of the Tories? Well, do you remember the name 'Matrix Churchill'? It was an English firm which sold 'machine tools' to Iraq. These machine tools just happened to be perfect for building missiles. Matrix Churchill also provided know-how to help Saddam's nuclear programme. There was one little problem, though. The Tories were telling the British people and the world that Britain wasn't selling weapons to Saddam. And, as the UK had agreed to a UN arms embargo during the Iran–Iraq war, selling A-bomb technology to Saddam was a little out of order, to say the least. I should also point out that Matrix Churchill was selling all this wonderful kit to Saddam with the full knowledge, blessing and support of both the Tory Government and MI6.

Britain saw the Iran–Iraq war as a lucrative little blood-bath on which the UK's biggest corporations could get fat. So, throughout the 1980s, the Tory Government allowed mass arms sales. Bugger the UN arms embargo, they thought. What they don't know won't hurt 'em – that was the policy of the Tories when it came to the British electorate and the international community.

Typical of this sneaky, duplicitous way of conducting government was Trade Minister Alan Clark – a barking mad testosterone-fuelled toff who actually found Margaret Thatcher sexually attractive. This was the man who once held a meeting in 1988 with British arms manufacturers and told them to make it seem on export licences as if the equipment they were transporting to Iraq was for civilian, rather than military, use. No point in alerting HM Customs to the fact that we were arming Hitler Mark II to the eyeballs with WMD – so went the Clark/Tory school of thought. So, Matrix Churchill, and many other firms, felt it was completely hunky-dory to sell Saddam all the expensive little gizmos he needed to build things like atomic bombs.

And, some other UK companies also started to sell stuff to Saddam. Stuff like sodium cyanide for chemical weapons and plutonium and gas spectrometres – which any self-respecting Iraqi 'father of the bomb' would need to build a nuke. Two British companies, Walter Somers and

Forgemasters, even began making parts for Saddam's notorious 'Super Gun' which could fire shells filled with anthrax some 700 kilometres. The British government knew about the existence of the 'Super Gun' a full year before parts of it were seized by British customs.

Anyway, the government put out some fantastic lies long before the Scott Inquiry started, claiming that it wasn't flogging doomsday machines to Iraq. But those jobsworths down at Customs & Excise just ruined it all. Customs officers had a look at all this WMD technology that Matrix Churchill was wrapping up in frilly paper and sending to Saddam and thought to themselves, 'Hang on, this is incredibly danger-ous, illegal and possibly suicidal. We'd better arrest this lot.'

In November 1990, Customs & Excise began its legal action against the directors of Matrix Churchill. The only problem for the government was that the directors of Matrix Churchill couldn't quite get their heads around why they were being dragged up before the beak. Why are we in court, they thought, when the government – and MI6 – told us it was OK to sell these hugely expensive parts for weapons that could help annihilate us and the rest of the world?

So, the defence team for the Matrix Churchill folk asked the govern-ment if they could have a look at some government documents which they thought might prove what the Matrix Churchill bosses were say-ing. But that didn't happen. Oh, no. The Tories' Attorney-General, Sir Nicholas Lyell – a lovely chap – then told a bunch of government min-isters to sign 'public interest immunity certificates' – gagging orders – which said the government didn't have to hand over anything – not a sausage – to the courts.

If you have children, you will be able to understand exactly what the Tories were up to. Let's say your youngest child comes towards you screaming, crying and blubbing that her big sister just burned her with matches. You find big sis and ask her what's going on. Then you notice that she's holding something behind her back that's shaped suspiciously like a box of Swan Vestas matches. You ask to see what she's got. She refuses to show you. 'There's nothing there,' she says. 'Oh, yes, there is,' you say, 'show it to me.' She screams 'No!' and runs in the opposite direction from you hollering 'I didn't do it! I didn't do it!' The result is that you have to wrestle the child to the ground and pull the matchbox from her hand only to hear her yell 'These matches aren't mine! I never had them!' Well, that kid's behaviour is more or less the way the Tories conducted themselves. They were so smugly dim that they couldn't see how obvious it was to the rest of us that they were lying. So the Scott Inquiry had to rugby-tackle this big wanton dumb party to the ground and kick it in the nuts to get it to confess to its multifarious sins.

Just in case you've missed the significance of the Matrix Churchill case, let me spell it out. The Tories were willing to allow innocent men to go to jail in order to cover up the fact that the government had been allowing arms sales to Saddam. Well, when I say innocent men, I mean innocent insofar as they were sanctioned by the government to sell WMD capability to a foaming-at-the-mouth genocidal madman. I'd find it a bit odd if anyone saw these men as morally righteous. After all, the type of machines their 'tools' were building were lethal ones.

Just to add to the disgusting yellow streak running down the back of the John Major and Margaret Thatcher governments, it turned out that MI6 didn't just know that the Matrix Churchill people were flogging Saddam weapons – that would be much too above-board. MI6, it just so happened, was also receiving lots of lovely top-grade intelligence on Iraq's WMD programme from one of Matrix Churchill's head honchos.

The blackest mark against the government during the Matrix Churchill case was down to the issuing of those public interest immunity certificates which stopped the court accessing documents proving the firm had the backing of the British state. Alan Moses, the senior prosecutor in the Matrix Churchill case, said that if he had seen the documents which the government concealed before the trial he would have stopped the case in its tracks. Moses was completely unaware of a key 1989 intelligence report which showed Whitehall knew the company's 'machine tools' were being used to make weapons in Iraq. Isn't it weird then that after the Scott Report was published, Sir Nicholas Lyell, the UK's Attorney-General, told Parliament that 'all the relevant documents were before the court before the trial began'. Someone was lying – either Moses or Lyell. But nevertheless when Lyell put out his flim-flam, the Tories in the House of Commons honked like a bunch of geese with sinusitis and waved their dispatch papers in the air. Did they forget that Scott had said that the 'major responsibility for the inadequacy of the instructions to Mr Moses must, in my opinion, be borne by the Attorney-General'? Did they also forget Scott saying that Lyell was 'personally at fault' for the handling of the Matrix Churchill case?

It was the collapse of the Matrix Churchill case in the autumn of 1992 that led to the setting up of the Scott Inquiry – a wide-ranging investigation into what the Thatcher and Major governments had been up to during the 1980s and early 1990s when it came to arms sales to Saddam. The proceedings kicked off soon afterwards under the eye of Sir Richard Scott, a rather maverick judge who'd spent his formative years in India and South Africa, and who irritated the hell out of the Tories on every count, including the fact that he cycled to work. That was way too anti-Establishment for the Conservative Party back then.

Scott was never going to kick the government square in the balls, but he did give the 'powers that be' a rather nasty slap in the testicles. The slap rather than the kick was delivered in perfect Whitehall jargon, but regardless of the prissy language it sure did make the Tories' nuts hurt bad. When Scott published his 1,800-page report in February 1996, he left no-one in any doubt over the duplicity of the Conservative Government. 'In circumstances where disclosure might be politically or administratively inconvenient,' he wrote, 'the balance struck by the government comes down, time and again, against full disclosure.' Just replace the words 'full disclosure' with 'telling the truth' and you get the measure of the fork-tongued fat cats prowling around Westminster back in the late '80s and early '90s.

Obviously, Scott ruled that the Matrix Churchill case should never have been taken. As a judge, he was a little more keenly aware than the average cabinet minister that it isn't a good legal precedent for the government of the day to try to jail people who have simply been doing its bidding as well as passing sensitive intelligence in the interests of national security to MI6.

Picture if you can, for a moment, the abiding image of the Scott Report. Remember Alan Clark? The posh bloke we spoke about earlier who was the Tory Trade Minister? The guy who told companies that were selling WMD kit to Iraq to make it look like they were selling civilian gear? He became the living, breathing symbol of what a bunch of tossers the Tories really were. Here is a man who colluded in selling weapons of mass destruction to a mass murderer, yet, when confronted with the truth of his actions under cross-examination during the Scott Inquiry, insouciantly said, without a flicker of shame or remorse, that he had been 'economical with the *actualité*' and that he had indeed known full well that the 'machine tools' could be used to make weapons.

In Britain, 'economical with the *actualité*' has become something of a cliché. It's the sort of line political journalists throw out over a drink when some politician has been caught lying. But it's not funny and it shouldn't be a cliché. Clark, an old-school aristocrat, had such scorn for the public, or maybe just thought about the public so little, that making a smart-ass comment about the lies he told over arming Iraq came as natural to him as gassing a Kurd came to Saddam.

Clark was a liar, and a smarmy, spoiled, little rich boy as well, but he at least held up his hands and admitted he'd acted like a shit. Clark confessed that discussions he'd had with the 'Machine Tool Technologies Association could be regarded as advising companies to stress the civil applications of their equipment even though they knew that it could be used for military purposes'.

Scott found that the Tories had 'failed to inform Parliament of the current state of government policy'. What's more 'this failure was deliberate' and the rationale behind the silence was 'that no publicity would be given to the decision to adopt a more liberal, or relaxed, policy'.

'Answers to the parliamentary questions about the government policy on defence exports to Iraq,' said Scott, 'were inadequate and misleading.'

Like Reagan, the British government decided to go on secretly arming Saddam even after the chemical bombing of the Kurdish town of Halabja. In fact, David Mellor – a buck-toothed geek of a minister who anyone would have picked on at school – was even in Baghdad around the time Saddam ordered that 5,000 men, women and children from Halabja should make their slow, painful, choking, gas-filled exit from the world. Those weapons, by the way, which killed the people of Halabja were made with German chemicals. The Germans haven't really learned the risks of poison gas, have they?

Hearing about old Mellor cosying up to Saddam kind of makes you reconsider the way you look at the world, doesn't it? America doesn't seem like a lone villain anymore. In fact, all these nasty facts about Britain's murky past with Saddam make you think twice about Blair. It's not like the sins of the Tories are any greater than his – it's just that all Tony is doing is continuing a policy of deception that's been in place since before I was born. If Blair ends up in the Seventh Circle of Dante's hell then you can be sure that the old Tory cabinet will be roasting right there beside him. In fact, Satan may chuck a little extra petrol on the fires of torment for the Tories if he remembers that there were actually noises made by the Conservative Government which questioned whether or not chemical weapons had been used against the Kurds. Obviously, securing all those juicy arms contracts with Saddam was far more important than the mass murder of a few thousand Kurds.

The anti-war journalist, John Pilger, tells a good story about Mellor and his greasy little trip to Iraq. Pilger was there in 1999 and met a hotel manager who said to him: 'Ah, a journalist from Britain! Would you like to see where Mr Douglas Hurd stayed and Mr David Melon [it's not clear whether the Iraqi hotelier was referring to the shape of Mellor's head or whether he just had a little difficulty with the pronunciation of the name, but he was definitely talking about David Mellor] and Mr Tony Newton and all the other members of Mrs Thatcher's government? These gentlemen were our friends, our benefactors.'

Pilger says the hotelier then showed him some newspaper clippings from way back when Britain loved the proliferation of weapons of mass destruction and when WMD were one of our favourite exports rather than a reason for invading another country. Pilger says there was always a photograph of Saddam on the front page, and each edition was different only because of the changing face of the British government minister sitting alongside him. There's Douglas Hurd – twice – and once he's even bowing to Saddam. Oooh, that must really hurt Hurdy today. And Mellor's there, too, pictured in 1988, not long before the gas attack on Halabja. He's on the sofa and he's snuggling up beside big old beautiful Saddam Hussein. It'd bring a tear to a glass eye.

A month after Halabja, Tony Newton, the Trade Minister, returned from a trip to Baghdad leading to Tory celebrations over Saddam's status as Britain's biggest customer of dual-use machine tools. Don't you wish these guys were back in power? Aren't they just the bee's knees?

After the Iran–Iraq war, Foreign Secretary Sir Geoffrey Howe – of whom a lot more later – wrote a brutal, cold and calculating government paper called *The Economic Consequences of the Peace*. This was the sort of thing the Tories really excelled at – making dirty money. Howe said that the arms market in Iraq presented British industry with 'major opportunities'. Howe, however, cowardly venal toad that he is, was scared that if his amoral little plan leaked out he'd incur the wrath of the British public. For all our faults we've never been ones to sit back and say that arming a Hitler-wannabe with WMD is fine by us. In a brilliant 'no shit, Sherlock!' moment, one of Howe's officials told the Scott Inquiry that it would have looked 'very cynical if so soon after expressing outrage about the treatment of the Kurds, we [adopted] a more flexible approach to the arms sales'.

Scott rightly pointed out that changing the policy on arms sales to Iraq and then lying to the public and to Parliament was probably just a wee bit more cynical. But Howe's cynicism was only just getting going. Ian Blackley, a senior Foreign Office official, said that Howe's office ordered *The Economic Consequences of the Peace* to be hushed up until – in what seemed like a tasteless reference to the gassing of Halabja – 'the cloud had passed'.

Feel free to say whatever you want about the Tories right now. Let 'em have it. They made sick jokes about the ethnic cleansing and mass murder that they aided and abetted.

The Tories couldn't have given a damn about morality, decency, honesty, accountability or democracy. Instead, they wanted to line the pockets of big business and arm Saddam with technology that ministers and officials knew could be used for military purposes. 'Public opposition in this country might have been embarrassingly vociferous,' said Scott, 'particularly in view of the use by Iraq of chemical weapons.'

Howe claimed that he wanted to protect British business from 'malicious commentators' and 'emotional misunderstandings'. This fine specimen of democracy-in-action also said that not telling the truth to Parliament about the shift in policy regarding the sale of arms to Iraq was 'perfectly legitimate management of news'.

Howe was about as cynical as the Tories came, back in those days. This man had the audacity to tell Scott that: 'There is nothing necessarily open to criticism in incompatibility between policy and presentation of policy ... [The Government] is not necessarily to be criticised for difference between policy and public presentation of policy.' In other words – it's OK to lie. It's OK to do one thing and tell the public – who elect you and pay your wages – something completely contradictory. Can you believe that none of these people went to prison? The sad fact is that not one of them even resigned.

Howe is part of the same party, incidentally, that carp on endlessly about the Blair government's dependence on spin. God forgive me for getting into Blair's corner, but he's only doing what the Tories taught him to do over a decade ago: lie your arse off and do anything to save your unworthy hide just so long as the pay-back for that soul you sold to Satan is the chance to cling on to another desperate day in power.

Perhaps the best summation of the way the government behaved comes from Mark Higson, who was the former head of the Iraq desk in the Foreign Office. He said simply that there was a 'culture of lying' within government; a culture that continues to allow all those elected MPs who call themselves ministers of state, all those diplomats and mandarins who forget that they are civil servants – servants of the people – to lie to the British public and to the British Parliament over and over and over again.

Higson also said that Foreign Office ministers like William Waldegrave were also well aware that British arms were being sold to countries like Jordan and then sneakily shipped straight on to Baghdad so it looked like Britain had nothing to do with arming Saddam. 'Iraq was regarded as the big prize,' he said. The public, he added, got just as much truth as the government 'could squeeze out'. Higson, to his undying credit, said squarely: 'We told downright lies.'

Just so that nobody could miss that the Tories of the Thatcher and Major governments actually were a bunch of pant-pissing weasels, Downing Street insisted on having eight days to prepare for its response to the publication of the Scott Report in 1996. Robin Cook, then the Shadow Foreign Secretary, was granted a staggering two full hours to prepare – on the condition that he accepted being locked in a room in the Department of Trade after he handed over his mobile phone. *Two hours*. To read 1,800 pages. The rest of the nation's Opposition MPs were allowed ten minutes.

Scott even tried to do the Tories a favour when he warned them that not giving the Opposition a fair crack of the whip and a chance to read the report would make them look like total losers. Well, he didn't quite use those words. What he said to the government, through his secretary, was this: 'You seem to be apprehensive about most MPs, members of the House of Lords and the media having access to the report at the same time access is given to those who are criticised in it.'

But to no avail. In fact, Scott even had to slap down Ian Lang, the Trade Secretary, for having the cheek to suggest that the former Foreign Secretary Geoffrey Howe – a lovely man, we all agree – be given an easy ride.

If that wasn't pathetic enough, Scott also uncovered evidence that showed just how much John Major was quaking in his Y-fronts over the publication of the report. In November 1992, Stephen Wall, John Major's then Private Secretary, told his boss: 'The most that can be said against you ... is that as Chancellor of the Exchequer [a post Major held from 1989 to 90] you knew that the government had decided to change the (export) guidelines.' Major had also been told when he was Foreign Secretary that there were plans to sell Hawk jets to Iraq. He, too, was fully aware of all this chicanery.

When the Scott Report came out and bitch-slapped two successive Tory administrations, people like Geoffrey Howe – if you can believe it – stumbled out of the shadows to say it was all totally 'unfair'. What was unfair – to the public and democracy – was that Tory spin-doctors prepared a doctored 'press pack' for journalists who hadn't been given any time to read the report. This 'press pack' highlighted a couple of pathetic phrases from Scott which weren't all that damning of the government. The condemnatory quotes were left out and the piddling little 'get-out clauses' were kept in. The result: the Conservative press machine used this abortion of the truth to try and save their masters' miserable asses.

Another Tory who shuffled out of his coffin to have a pop at the Scott Report was Douglas Hurd. Hurd, who had hair like a Mr Whippy ice-cream cone, was the same Foreign Secretary who chaired a meeting in July 1990 which agreed to scrap all restrictions on arming Saddam. Hurdy was ready for a real end-of-season WMD sale. It was obviously going to end with vats of sarin gas, whole flocks of anthrax-infected sheep and ready-to-use A-bombs heading straight to Saddam's presidential palaces. Except Saddam went and ruined it all for Hurdy by invading Kuwait a little while later. Stupid Saddam! Imagine stopping the British arms industry earning all that lovely lolly so the weapons manufacturers could then give donations to the Tory party.

One of the biggest conman of the lot was William Waldegrave. It was Waldegrave, Scott said, who wrote letters to MPs regarding armament sales to Iraq 'that were apt to mislead the readers as to the nature of the policy on export sales to Iraq'. Robin Cook, despite being given those measly two hours to prepare his ammunition, was able to accuse Waldegrave of misleading Parliament some 30 times – that's 30 reasons for resignation. Waldegrave, Chief Secretary to the Treasury, approved the sale of equipment which he knew could be used for military purposes. Even when officials from the Ministry of Defence warned Waldegrave that Britain was equipping Saddam with nuclear technology, the Tory heavyweight shooed them away. He said that if the licence to export the equipment was turned down it would look like Britain was 'looking for excuses to irritate Iraq for no reason'.

Waldegrave even had the brass neck to tell the Scott Inquiry that 'damaging British firms for no perceptible gain in diplomatic or other policy objectives seemed to me to be stupid then and still does now'. A man like Waldegrave needs to be careful when he is bandying big words like 'stupid' around. He could easily hurt himself.

How Waldegrave had the nerve to brazen out this kind of bare-faced effrontery is staggering. During the Scott Inquiry he was accused of approving the sale of chemical, biological and nuclear exports to Iraq. The report itself accused him of a 'deliberate' failure to inform Parliament of a change to the arms sales policy to Iraq. Scott also referred to the 'duplicitous nature' of Waldegrave's claims; said he was engaged in 'sophistry' and that he knowingly misled MPs. Yet Waldegrave had the audacity to go live on ITN within two hours of the report being published to claim he was vindicated.

Waldegrave signed 38 letters to MPs in 1989 in which he insisted that the government had not relaxed its export policy to Iraq. Scott's take on this was that Waldegrave 'knew, first hand, the facts that, in my opinion, rendered the "no change in policy" statement untrue'. Scott went on to say that: 'It is clear in my opinion that policy on defence sales to Iraq did not remain unchanged.' If the judge was you or me, he would have called Waldegrave a big, fat, chinless liar.

Scott saw a very grave danger in the way that the Tories, by then a fag-end of a political party, misused democracy by misleading Parliament about the arms sales to Iraq. 'A failure by ministers to meet the obligations of ministerial accountability by providing information about the activities of their department undermines, in my opinion, the democratic process,' he said.

Interestingly, one of the other characters who came in for criticism from Scott was a certain Sir Robin Butler. At the time he was Cabinet Secretary and Head of the Civil Service. Today he is better known for chairing the Butler Inquiry into the way intelligence was used by Blair's government to claim that Saddam had WMD. Yeah, that's right, that's the same intelligence that took us to war against the tin-can tanks of the Iraqi Republican Guard when we were expecting a barrage of sarin-filled missiles to rain down on our expeditionary forces. Scott slapped Butler down for having the cheek to claim that 'half the picture can be true'. That's a very telling and worrying phrase to be used by a man who was later tasked to investigate the deliberately manipulated and massaged data which built the case for war. As you'll recall, Blair survived the gruelling inquisition of the Butler Report – which incidentally was held behind closed doors – effectively unscathed. Maybe Butler thought that Mr Blair's decision to give the British public only half the picture about Saddam's weapons of mass destruction in 2002–2003 amounted to a version of the truth as well.

The half-truth that Blair gave then was that Saddam owned weapons of mass destruction. The other half of the truth, that he suppressed, was that Saddam didn't have these weapons of mass destruction by the time we invaded the country.

By the way, Blair seems to have learned from the mistakes of his Tory predecessors. Sir Richard Scott was picked by Major to investigate his government and the Thatcher government. Although Scott could have ruined the Tories, he didn't. But he still gave them a fairly ruthless roasting. Blair certainly didn't want to be ruined. In fact, he didn't even want a roasting. He wanted a get-out-of-jail-free card. So, Blair picked Butler. You've just read about what sort of an Establishment bum-licker Butler is, but Scott was much more independently minded. He'd already given the Thatcher government a bloody nose by the time he came to oversee the inquiry into the sale of arms to Iraq. Major should have known what lay in store for him after Scott's dismissal in 1987 of the government's attempt to prevent the press from publishing the contents of *Spycatcher*. *Spycatcher* was the memoir of the former MI5 agent Peter Wright, and told how the British intelligence services tried to undermine a Labour government. When the judge told the government to sling its hook and gave the green light to go right ahead and publish, Scott said: 'The ability of the press freely to report allegations of scandal in government is one of the bulwarks of our democratic society. The importance to the public of this country of the allegation that members of MI5 endeavoured to undermine and destroy public confidence in an elected government makes the public the proper recipient of the information.' Again, Scott loves his jargon, but what the judge was doing was warning the government of this country that it should curb its tendency to behave undemocratically and to hide the truth from the people it is meant to serve.

The Tories, however, were never too keen on the public getting fully abreast of the facts. Take this toad – Tristan Garel-Jones. He was one of that group of Tory ministers who signed those public interest immunity (PII) certificates in the Matrix Churchill case. This was a man arrogant enough to say that the publication of Scott's report was 'inimical to the interests of the state'. When a creature like this refers to 'the state', he does not, like you or me, mean our nation and the people who live in it; what he means by 'the state' is the interests of the power-hungry clique that he happens to be a part of. Garel-Jones continued his denunciation

of the Scott Report, adding: 'Damage will have been done to the standing of the public service with little or no contribution to the better gov-
ernance of the Kingdom.' Aside from how awful his syntax is, you have
to ask yourself what did Garel-Jones mean by these comments? What
did he expect Britain to do? Listen to him and tell Scott to rip up four
years of work because Tristan said so? The answer, I'm afraid, is that he
probably did. Arrogance above all else, was the watchword in the dying
days of Tory rule.

Others who signed those PII certificates, by the way, included another nonentity of Garel-Jones' calibre called Lord Trefgarne. William
Waldegrave and Alan Clarke also signed away their decency. Michael
Heseltine signed as well, but only after a minor tussle with his conscience when he raised concerns about the gagging orders. Scott criticised Sir Nicholas Lyell, the Attorney-General, for failing to pass on
Heseltine's concerns to the prosecution.

Like the Labour government today, the Tories back then treated the
trust of the British people like a casual lay – a cheap pick-up to be
played with and used and abused whenever they felt so inclined. Tony
Blair would have been well advised, then, to listen to what that old stal-
wart of British politics, Menzies Campbell, had to say back in 1996
regarding the blow to public trust that an episode like the Scott Report
can have on democracy. The elder statesman of the Lib-Dems said that
Tory 'arrogance' and 'unwillingness to be held accountable' had led to
a 'deep cynicism among the electorate about the whole process of gov-
ernance in Britain'.

The Tories – like Labour– used our trust like toilet paper. They sickened the people with a diet of disinformation, propaganda and self-serving lies told only to further their own loosening grip on power.

But what did our Tony say at the time of the Scott Report's publication? You'll just love this one. He attacked the government for – wait
for it (prepare yourself Mr Blair if you are reading) – 'gloss and spin'.
He said the question of whether the government had misled the public
stood out like a 'beacon demanding to be answered'. What a rhetorical
flourish. What a democrat. What a bullshit artist.

But even the odd Tory felt a bit perturbed by all those lies. One,
Richard Shepherd, said the Attorney-General and Waldegrave should
resign, telling a TV interviewer: 'It is absolutely unacceptable to mislead
Parliament and the public – within our democratic system that is an
absolute trust.'

But would the Tories take their punishment? Would they buggery. They began to invent whole new theories of government to get their sorry asses out of a sling. Just a wee reminder about the nature of government. The prime minister is responsible for the actions of his or her cabinet and each minister is responsible for the actions of his or her department – the buck stops with them. I don't need to tell you that not one amongst this useless bunch of tax-spongers resigned over the Scott Report. However, it was almost worth having them stay in office to see them wriggle like little worms when Labour MPs – in Opposition preaching about high standards and morality – started to stick their boots so far up the Tories' arses, in the wake of the publication of the Scott Report, that their heels almost vanished.

Take Roger Freeman's contortions of reality and linguistics. While trying to fend off calls for mass resignations, the Public Service Minister said: 'The minister in charge of a department is the only person who can be said to be ultimately accountable for the work of his department … it is manifestly impossible for him to take all the decisions or be personally involved in every action of his department.' So, the minister is accountable, but he can't be held to account – that seems to be the answer from Freeman. In other words, a Tory government minister was there to pick up a big fat salary, screw with people's lives, rubber-stamp some papers and then get off Scott-free – no pun intended – when the shit hits the fan.

The Tories were so devoted to the cause of open and honest government that they even tried to lean on Scott while he was preparing his report. Pressure was put on him by none other than Cabinet Secretary, Sir Robin Butler. That's right – the guy who conducted the inquiry into British intelligence. Scott made it clear to government that his team would 'not be intimidated'. However, there is some evidence to suggest that his criticisms were toned down between the draft stage and the final version of the report.

Even if Scott couldn't be intimidated, he still had his work cut out for him, what with officials shredding documents after smuggling Chieftain tank hulls to Iraq via Jordan. It's hard to keep tabs on a rogue government when it's got its minions standing by the old shredder. So who knows what Scott missed in the final analysis. It was this type of abusive, corrosive secrecy that Scott tried to take on in his report – but, sadly, as we can see from the way our government works today, the man failed. 'Is it any longer satisfactory,' Scott asked, 'that the Parliament and the British public are not entitled to be told to which countries and in what quantities goods such as artillery shells, land mines and cluster bombs have been licensed for export?'

Apparently, such withholding of information is satisfactory if you happen to be a Tory government minister. It also seems that if you are a Labour government minister then it is equally satisfactory that the British public – and its representatives in Parliament – is not entitled to be told the truth about the reasons for its army being sent into war.

WE MUST INVADE IRAQ...WE HAVE THE RECEIPTS

or

How Saddam told the world which Western powers gave him huge illegal bombs, but we still kicked his ass—and some information on how Britain continues to sell WMD to the world's worst monsters

You can probably guess that after the Scott report, the British government wasn't too keen on talking about arms sales to Iraq anymore. But the problem was, that when Tony Blair decided to get jiggy with George Bush and back up the young Caesar over the invasion of Iraq, Saddam thought that he'd remind the world why the US and the UK seemed to be so dang adamant that he had huge stockpiles of WMD. Saddam decided to tell the nations of the world that the reason America and Britain knew about the weapons of mass destruction was because they had the receipts. All they had to do was go and rummage about in the attic, find a big box marked WEAPONS OF MASS DESTRUCTION WHICH WE SOLD TO SADDAM WHEN WE LIKED HIM IN THE 1980s and check which chemical, biological and nuclear equipment went from London and Washington to Baghdad.

Late in 2002, while Blair and Bush were talking all sorts of crap about Saddam's WMD arsenal and how Saddam and bin Laden were the best of buddies, Iraq compiled a hefty big dossier and sent it to the United Nations. It contained information on every single company and country on earth which had helped Iraq build its WMD programme in the 1980s, and into the 1990s.

Of course Saddam only told the truth 'cos his back was against the wall and he knew he was in for a touch of the old shock-and-awe, as it was now inevitable that Britain and America were going to invade his country.

In his December 2002 dossier, Saddam named around 80 companies across the world which had supplied him with nuclear, biological, chemical, rocket and conventional weapons technology.

The names were buried in a 12,000-page report submitted to the UN. Strangely, the Security Council agreed to a US request to censor thousands of pages – including those sections naming western businesses which aided Iraq's WMD programme. Funnily enough, each of the five permanent members of the Security Council – France, Britain, the US, China and Russia – are all named as allowing companies inside their borders to sell weapons technology to Saddam.

In February 2003, I got my hands on the full list of companies named by Iraq as having supplied Saddam with weapons. The identities of 17 British firms were published in the *Sunday Herald* newspaper. Only one of those companies – which Iraq said supplied rocket technology – denied any connection with Saddam, on pain of legal action.

Here's Saddam's list of the other 16 UK companies he said supplied Iraq with weaponry:

> Euromac Ltd, UK: for supplying nuclear know-how
> C Plath-Nuclear: also for supplying nuclear know-how
> Endshire Export Marketing: again for supplying nuclear know-how
> International Computer Systems: for supplying nuclear, rocket and conventional capabilities
> MEED International: for supplying nuclear and chemical capabilities
> Walter Somers Ltd: for supplying rocket technology
> International Computers Limited: for supplying nuclear and conventional technology
> Matrix Churchill Corp.: nuclear
> Ali Ashour Daghir: nuclear
> International Military Services: rocket
> Sheffield Forgemasters: rocket
> International Signal and Control: rocket
> Inwako: nuclear
> TMG Engineering: conventional
> XYY Options Inc.: nuclear

International Military Services, incidentally, is part of the Ministry of Defence. This demonstrates that a department of state, which is meant to protect British citizens from tyrants tooled up with banned weapons, was actually selling WMD to a man who was to become our deadly enemy. The dossier also shows that some 24 US firms sold weapons to

Iraq. These included Hewlett-Packard, which Saddam says was selling nuclear, rocket and conventional technology; Dupont, which sold nuclear technology; Eastman Kodak which sold rocket technology; and that old friend of the Bush administration, Bechtel. Bechtel sold conventional technology and is now cleaning up in the money-go-round of post-war Iraqi 'reconstruction' contracts which the White House is throwing around like a drunken sailor on shore leave in Rotterdam.

According to Iraq, China allowed three companies, including the China State Missile Company, to sell them nuclear, chemical, conventional and rocket know-how. Eight French companies were flogging WMD to Saddam, along with six companies from the former Soviet Union. From Japan there were five companies selling to Saddam; three from Holland; seven from Belgium; three from Spain; and two from Sweden including Saab-Scania. The dossier also says that some '50 subsidiaries of foreign enterprises conducted their arms business with Iraq from the US'.

Now, we could well dismiss this as a dodgy dossier – just as dodgy a dossier as the one that Tony Blair presented to the British people and Parliament to convince us to back his neocon war. And just as dodgy as the garbage-can information that Colin Powell served up to the UN Security Council in the run-up to the invasion when he waved his little vials of anthrax around and warned us of the risk of global Armageddon stemming from the WMD stockpiles of Saddam.

But to dismiss what Saddam was saying as complete propaganda would be to forget the Riegle Report and the Scott Inquiry. There must have been some truth in what Saddam was saying – because the UK and the US had already been caught out selling him WMD capability. And then there's the fact that in some cases the countries which armed Saddam were implicating each other – and proving Saddam's claims. Classified US Defense Department documents show that Britain sold Iraq the drug pralidoxine, an antidote to nerve gas, in March 1992 . And that was after the First Gulf War. Pralidoxine, by the way, can be reverse-engineered to create nerve gas.

The censored parts of Saddam's dossier made horrific reading for the western powers. It claimed that the US ministries of defence, energy, trade and agriculture, as well as America's Lawrence Livermore, Los Alamos and Sandia National Laboratories all supplied Saddam with WMD.

It didn't look very good for old Europe either. It seemed that maybe

France and Germany weren't really the peace-loving nations they were pretending to be. Perhaps the reason they didn't want to attack Iraq was that they knew they'd been propping up a murderous dictator with shipments of arms for years. Germany, after all, was shown by Iraq to be its biggest arms-trading partner, with some 80 companies sending WMD technology to Saddam – including the firm Siemens. It sold medical machines with dual-purpose parts that could be used in nuclear bombs. The German government also reportedly 'actively encouraged' weapons cooperation, and assistance was allegedly given to Iraq in developing poison gas which Saddam used against the Kurds.

The German Ministry of Economics tolerated and actively supported the illegal arms deals with Iraq up until the outbreak of the First Gulf War, even though Germany's own domestic laws forbade it from arming Iraq because the Iran–Iraq war made it a 'region of tension' which could not even be sold conventional weapons. But German firms were assisting Saddam way past the outbreak of hostilities in 1991, following Iraq's lunatic invasion of Kuwait. The German government was warned by its own arms control experts about a micro-electronics firm's relationship with Iraq in 1999. Officials told the government that supposed civilian equipment going to Iraq could be used for military purposes. Didn't the Germans hear about the Riegle Report or the Scott Inquiry? Couldn't they learn from other countries' mistakes?

Not surprisingly, the United Nations quickly caved in to the US demand to censor the Iraq dossier. The global public was then forced to listen to a load of nonsensical claims which were spun to have us believe that publicly naming the companies would be counter-productive. Rather, what the supine UN should have said was that publicly naming these companies would have shown that the world was quite happy to arm Saddam until he started to piss off America and Britain. And, furthermore, naming these companies would totally derail the case for war, as it would show the brutal, cold and sinister hypocrisy of Washington and London.

In reality, the US had simply taken the Iraq dossier before any nation had a chance to look at it, cut huge chunks out of it and then handed a censored version to the UN. A whole 24 hours passed before the permanent members of the Security Council had a chance to see the document. But it took two weeks, from the day of the delivery of the dossier by Iraq, for the US to hand over the doctored version to the non-permanent members of the Security Council – all the other nations apart from the UK, US, Russia, China and France. In total, some 3,000 pages had been cut out with the agreement of the permanent member states – all of whom had flogged weapons to Saddam.

Foreign companies supplied Iraq's nuclear weapons programme with detonators, fissionable material and parts for a uranium enrichment plant. Foreign companies also provided Iraq's chemical and biological programmes with basic materials; helped build labs; assisted with the extension of missile ranges; provided technology to fit missiles with nuclear, biological and chemical warheads and supplied Scud missile launch pads. None of which, I'm sure you will agree, is remotely dangerous.

Although most of this arms trade with Saddam ended in 1991 on the outbreak of the First Gulf War, at least two of the five permanent Security Council members – Russia and China – traded arms with Iraq in breach of UN resolutions after 1991. Incidentally, all trade in WMD technology has been outlawed internationally for decades.

UNSCOM – the UN weapons inspectors – found documents showing preparations by the Russian firms, Livinvest, Mars Rotor and Niikhism, to supply parts for military helicopters in 1995. In April 1995, Mars Rotor and Niikhism sold parts used in long-range missiles to a Palestinian who transported them to Baghdad. In 2001 and 2002, the Chinese firm Huawei Technologies sent supplies to Iraqi air defence.

However, long before the 2003 invasion of Iraq nearly all the weapons that were supplied had been destroyed, accounted for or immobilised, as I'll show you in the next chapter, using the words of the UN's own weapons inspectors.

When I got hold of Saddam's list of firms which he claimed supplied him with top WMD kit, I rang the Foreign Office and asked them what they were going to do about it. Here's what one of the automatons who man the press telephone lines told me: 'The UK will investigate and, if appropriate, prosecute any UK company found to have been in breach of export control legislation.'

I can't remember if I wet my pants laughing or if I broke my hand by punching a wall. What the Foreign Office was telling me was that they were going to prosecute – among others – an arm of the Ministry of Defence and ... wait for it ... Matrix Churchill, which as we all know had already been wrongly prosecuted for arming Saddam – a prosecution which exposed the whole sorry, dirty business of the way the British government colluded in arming Saddam in the first place. It really was

Alice in Wonderland, through the looking-glass stuff.

The Department of Trade and Industry simply refused to cooperate, saying that details on export licences, including information on weapons sold to Iraq was 'unavailable'. Forgive the cynicism, but if Saddam had the info, you'd think Tony Blair might have the same facts to hand as well.

I then started ringing around the companies that Saddam had named. Some didn't exist anymore – no surprise really; bad karma hopefully caught up with the bosses and threw them into bankruptcy for giving weapons to a mad tyrant. But a few were still on the go. Endshire Export Marketing was alive and well, and one of their staff told me that the firm had sold a consignment of magnets to a German middleman who then sold them on to Iraq. I pointed out that certain types of magnets were pretty essential for building nuclear bombs. He said: 'I've no idea if that is the case. I couldn't tell one end of a nuclear bomb from the other.'

I asked him why the company was included on a US boycott list in 1991. He told me that the company considered the deal 'genuine business' at the time, but with the 'benefit of hindsight' the firm would never have taken part in the transaction.

A spokesman for the Ministry of Defence's International Military Services said he couldn't tell me a damn thing as there were no staff from before 1991 – the time of the First Gulf War – on the payroll anymore and not a single document from that time still existed.

Given that nobody was going to tell me a thing, I decided to talk to a few folks who I thought would slag off the government and these firms for their past behaviour. At least it would make me feel better to talk to someone who found this whole twisted mess as twisted and as messy as I did.

So, I had a chat with a guy called Mick Napier from the Stop the War Coalition. I kinda knew already what he was going to say, but what I really wanted to hear was him spluttering with rage as I recounted the facts of what was in Saddam's dossier. 'How can we support a government,' he said, 'which says it's against mass murder when its record is one of supporting and supplying Iraq? This government depends on public mass amnesia.'

I was glad that I'd spoken to Mick as 'public mass amnesia' is a brilliant expression. I looked around for someone equally gobby. This wasn't really an issue on which people were going to be a little miffed – this was an issue which was obviously, as Mick showed, going to drive folk up the wall with rage.

So, I called the Scottish Socialist Party. Now, the response from this hard-line left-wing group was going to be fairly predictable too, but we were just weeks away from war at this point and I felt that every dissenting voice that could be heard should be heard. The government was spinning a line of crap to me about its own record of selling weapons to Saddam, so I thought I'd let a team of top-class tub-thumpers get their tuppence worth in. 'The evidence,' the SSP spokesperson said, 'of British armament companies, with central government support, arming the Butcher of Baghdad lays to rest the moral garbage spewed from the British government. It exposes the fact that Britain, along with America, France and Russia, armed Saddam to the teeth while he was butchering his own people.'

Good for you, SSP spokesperson, I thought. I'd never get that kind of stuff from the Foreign Office or the Ministry of Defence. To complete my triumvirate of peaceniks, I called my old pal Tam Dalyell – he who referred to the PNAC back in Chapter 1 as power-crazed chicken hawks intent on taking over the world.

Well, he was on form again. Chicken hawks were back on the menu. He started off being very flattering – Tam is a gentleman, after all – saying that the info I'd got hold of was 'of huge significance'. I have to say I knew that, but it was very complimentary of him to say so. The list of firms, said Tam, 'exposes the hypocrisy of Blair and Bush. The chicken hawks who want war were up to their necks in arms deals. This drives a coach and horses through the moral case for war.'

Wow, I thought, Tam really hates these guys. I'm not alone. At least three other people thought like me. I can't take all the credit for this story, though, by any means. Andreas Zumach over in Germany, on the paper *Die Tageszeitung*, beat the *Sunday Herald* to the scoop – but then the truth isn't a competition. So applause for Herr Zumach. What the *Sunday Herald* did do, though, was bring this rank hypocrisy to the breakfast tables of the British and American people.

The bitter stinky pill that the British people have to swallow, however, is that these nasty arms exports are often paid for by ... the British people. That's all thanks to something called the Export Credit Guarantee Department (ECGD). When countries which are greedy for guns but short on funds fail to pay up for the weapons they bought from Britain plc, it isn't the armament companies which lose out – no, no, no,

no, that's too obvious and equitable an arrangement for the British government. No, thanks to the ECGD, it's you and me and all the other tax-
payers that cough up money to compensate the weapons companies if
some shady, murderous regime welches on its payments.

This sick piece of make-believe government nonsense amounts to an
insurance policy through which the British government will pay
weapons companies huge sums of money if foreign governments fail to
pay their bills. Immediately after Tony Blair rose to power in 1997, the
ECGD guaranteed a total of £3.4 billion across the entire spectrum of
British industry – and the arms trade alone that year accounted for nearly a quarter of ECGD cover. Some 75 per cent of that ECGD cover for
military purposes went to countries in the Middle East.

The Thatcher and Major governments poured somewhere between
£650 million and £1 billion down the toilet in ECGD loans for Iraq.
Saddam never paid his bills. We – you and I – paid for Saddam to get
nuclear, biological and chemical weapons from British companies at the
behest of the British government. And then a decade later another
British government invaded Iraq, killing British soldiers and thousands
of Iraqi men, women and children on the false pretext that Saddam still
had these British-made weapons of mass destruction.

Dr Mark Phythian, an expert on the arms trade and a respected political scientist, says: 'Simply, the government pays the British company
selling the arms up-front for the weapons, and the ECGD is then supposed to reclaim the loan from the country that's buying the arms. If
that doesn't happen, the taxpayer coughs up. We extend such an appeal-
ing credit line to get other countries to buy our weapons. Superficially,
it keeps jobs and boosts British prestige overseas, but it's also fair to ask
why we should pay for arms companies like BAE to sell arms.

'There is no doubt that exporting arms in this way is not beneficial to
this country, either economically, politically or in security terms. One
also has to question the morality of some of the sales.'

When Thatcher was guaranteeing ECGD loans for Iraq, the credit
was extended under a special provision for deals supposed to be in
Britain's 'national interest'. In the middle of the Iran–Iraq war Thatcher's
ECGD was guaranteeing £25 million worth of military sales to Iraq a
year. Suffice to say, Iran didn't get such kind treatment. At the end of the
Iran–Iraq war, the ECGD was guaranteeing sales worth £100 million a
year. In some years, net annual subsidies meant to boost the arms trade
ran to £763 million. That's about 10 new hospitals or 100 new schools.

Under Thatcher and Major, the 'export guarantees' for Iraq were only supposed to cover civilian goods, but you know the Tories – civilian schmavilian, that's their view. Racal, which donated £75,000 a year to the Tories, was provided with a secret 'defence allocation' of £42 million in ECGD insurance after getting a contract with Iraq in 1985. Saddam was then able to import military radios from Racal which enabled the Republican Guard to stop any enemy jamming their communications. When the First Gulf War broke out, the government had to write Racal a cheque for £15.7 million.

In 1987, Marconi Command & Control had a taxpayer-guaranteed loan of £10 million for the sale of AMETS (Artillery Meteorological System) to Iraq. Because the ECGD's secret 'defence allocation' had been used up on Racal by this time, the Ministry of Defence reclassified the Marconi contract as civilian. Marconi wound up with a cheque – courtesy of you and me – for £8.2 million.

The Tory cabinet even refused to cease signing away loans for exports to Saddam's regime after Farzad Bazoft, a journalist for a British newspaper, *The Observer*, was executed in Iraq. The reason, they said, was that they didn't want to damage British industry.

The British arms trade and the British government are two tarts from the same brothel. In the late 1980s, the British firm Tripod Engineering cut an £18 million deal with the Iraqi air force for a fighter pilot training centre. Would you be surprised to learn that Tripod was able to get the deal classified as civil despite its obvious military function? A RAF air vice-marshal even helped Tripod close the deal. No conflict of interest there, I'm sure you'll agree. Incidentally, Tripod was later paid nearly £3 million by the government thanks to ECGD compensation.

In 1988, David Hastie, one of British Aerospace's high-flying execs, was seconded to the MoD's arms sales department. In 1989, he reverted to being a British Aerospace exec for a few days so he could attend a Baghdad arms fair which MoD staff had been banned from attending. This jiggery-pokery allowed Alan Clark to later tell the Commons that no MoD staff had been at the arms junket.

So, not only did we sell arms to Iraq which we then used as an excuse to beat the shit out of the Iraqi people, but us suckers, the taxpayers, had to cough up for the arms sales. It's pretty disgusting, right? You know when I ask you that, that I'm going to tell you something even worse, don't you? I am.

We are still selling weapons of mass destruction. Right now, today, chemical weapons components are being sold to North Korea, Libya and Iran – all so-called 'Axis of Evil' countries' – by the United Kingdom, the country that went to war behind America to wipe out weapons of mass destruction.

Back in the summer of 2002, I got a call suggesting I check out the apparent sale by the UK to a couple of dozen countries of stuff called 'toxic chemical precursors' (TCPs). TCPs are those wonderful things known as dual-use chemicals. You know what they are, we've talked about them before. You can either use them to make fertiliser or you can turn them into sarin nerve agent. Back then, in 2002, we were selling TCPs to 26 countries. As of 2004, when I last checked, we were selling TCPs to 40 countries. So, in the space of time that it took to fight a war over the proliferation of weapons of mass destruction, we managed to arm 40 nations with chemical weapons.

The UK, then, is one of the world's leading exporters of weapons of mass destruction. We have armed both North Korea and South Korea with TCPs – can you believe that? Other regional conflicts that we thought we'd exploit by selling chemical weapons to both sides included India and Pakistan. It's not as if those guys didn't have enough to worry about – what with their nuclear arsenals and sectarian madness. We also sold Iran some TCPs, which is maybe just pay-back for flogging Saddam all that WMD kit back in the 1980s when he was chemicalising the Ayatollah's armies.

We also like to sell TCPs to really impoverished nations like Sudan. You just know it makes much more sense to encourage brutal governments to buy our WMD technology than to get them to put food in the empty bellies of their people or quit genociding the populace. Other states which have positively glowing human rights records – such as Saudi Arabia (where for saying 'Allah sucks' or being gay or shagging behind your husband's back you have a good chance of getting executed) – are keen to buy lots of lovely chemical weapons from good old Britain, too.

It's pretty ironic really that we are selling weapons to Sudan given that in August 1998 President Clinton blew the shit out of the El Shifa pharmaceutical plant on the outskirts of Khartoum claiming it was a chemical weapons factory making VX nerve agent. It wasn't a chemical weapons plant at all, by the way. But if America was to apply these standards to the UK, then a stealth bomber should drop a daisy-cutter on Number 10 tomorrow.

It is totally against international law and the Chemical Weapons Convention to sell chemicals to any state which might use them to make weapons. The gas which killed 12 people when the Japanese doomsday cult Aum Shinrikyo blitzed the Tokyo subway system came from TCPs. One lovely TCP is thiodiglycol. It can be turned into mustard gas simply by adding hydrochloric acid or household drain cleaner. So if you're North Korea's Kim Jong-il, you just buy some TCPs from the UK and then give it to your scientists along with a big bottle of Drano and let them get on with your plans for world domination/Armageddon.

The Department of Trade and Industry which is responsible for the export of TCPs admitted to me that there is no way that the British government can know whether these chemicals are being used to fertilise fields or turned into poison gas once they leave the UK. Holland considers the sale of TCPs to countries like Sudan so dangerous that it has banned the trade in dual-use chemicals for both civilian and military purposes.

Sudan tried to buy TCPs from the Dutch, saying they wanted to make fertiliser but the Ministry of Economic Affairs outlawed the transaction, saying it had 'indications that [the chemicals] might be used for other ends', including the manufacture of nerve gas.

Alastair Hay, Professor of Environmental Toxicology at Leeds University's School of Medicine and the biochemist who carried out forensic tests that proved Saddam used poison gas against the Kurds, says the sale of TCPs is a 'matter of real concern'. He adds: 'Many TCPs have no other purpose other than the making of chemical weapons. It has to be considered as a real possibility that a country is buying chemicals for allegedly innocuous reasons but planning to use them for lethal purposes.'

When I spoke to him, Richard Bingley, of Campaign Against the Arms Trade, added: 'We don't even know that if we sell these chemicals to a seemingly decent regime that they won't sell them on to a repressive and dangerous nation. Yet we've taken that a step further by actually selling these chemicals to repressive systems and nations which one day could use the chemical capabilities we gave them against us or our allies.'

The DTI told me that TCPs were sold overseas 'under the belief' that they would be used 'benignly' for agricultural purposes or turned into detergent. The DTI also admitted that the main assurance it relied on to trust foreign powers that they wouldn't turn TCPs into chemical weapons was 'an end user undertaking'. That basically amounts to a promise from a country like North Korea – a mad hermit nation with a nuclear arsenal and a famine-depleted population – that it wouldn't use the TCPs for military means.

'We aim to minimise risk,' I was told, 'but obviously it is very diffi-cult to say what happens to these things once they get to their final des-tination. It is impossible to clamp down 100 per cent. It is impossible to know what happens to them in the stages that come after they leave Britain.'

You'd think that we could just do what the Dutch do and tell nasty little countries with the track records of serial killers to sling their hook when they try and buy chemical weapons from us, but, no, that is just not the done thing in Blighty.

Professor Julian Perry is a chemist at the Science and Technology Policy Research Unit at Sussex University. He's also the man who helped draft the Chemical Weapons Convention (CWC) and a member of the CWC's UK National Authority Advisory Committee. You can't get more clued-up about chemical weapons than Perry. He says TCPs are the main constituent in chemical weapons and adds that the nation should be worried about the sale of these items 'especially given the rather weak assurances from the DTI'.

He said that one TCP, dimethyl methylphophonate, was the 'perfect dual-use chemical'. On its own it's a top quality flame retardant, but mix it with other chemicals and – *wowee zowee* – you've got sarin. 'Once you have your hands on dimethyl methylphophonate,' says Perry, 'you are well on the way to making sarin. Every single chemical warfare agent can be made from toxic chemical precursors.'

Dr Mark Phythian, the political academic and the author of *The Poli-tics of British Arms Sales*, says: 'Such chemicals are sold with political approval. Any government would be hard pushed to say it didn't know the consequences of such sales, although it is hard to make sense of that policy in the present climate of concerns about terrorism and war.

'It appears this is an extension of our policy on the sales of conven-tional weapons. That is, a policy of sustaining the UK's industrial base, protecting jobs in the weapons industry and maintaining our image as a global player in arms. The government's desire to maximise trade seems to be at odds with its rhetoric about security. History would suggest that to err on the side of trade over security is a very short-sighted policy.'

HOW THE UN DEFANGED SADDAM AND KILLED HALF A MILLION IRAQI KIDS

or
Finding excuses to beat up dodgy Arab dictators
who are armed with sticks and rocks

So, Saddam was sold huge stockpiles of weapons of mass destruction by the US, the UK and most of the world's other 'big power' industrialised nations throughout the 1980s and into the 1990s.

Let's forget the black morality and the dumb hypocrisy of that situation for a moment and accept that because we sold Saddam WMD we had to go to war to take them off him again. It's a totally sick and criminal scenario, but at least that would allow Bush and Blair to say that they took us to war against a lethal madman who really was sitting on top of a big pile of very real nukes and VX and anthrax.

That argument, though, doesn't stand up, because if Saddam did have WMD then where did they all go to? They sure weren't lying around waiting to be found by David Kay, the CIA-appointed head of the Iraq Survey Group, whose job it was to find weapons of mass destruction in post-invasion Iraq. At the time of going to print not one weapon of mass destruction has been found – not even a BB-gun filled with stink bombs.

Kay resigned, and later, as you may remember, said in the middle of 2004 that Tony Blair was 'really delusional' for still claiming that Saddam had weapons of mass destruction.

The comments by Blair, that Kay was responding to, were very subtly phrased. What Blair said was: 'We know Saddam had weapons of mass destruction. He used them. What we know also is that we haven't yet found them.'

Now Blair was being awfully clever here. It's true that Saddam had WMD, after all we sold them to him. Again, it's true that Saddam used them. We all remember the gassing of the Kurds in Halabja and how the

US was quietly backing Saddam's Iranian 'chemicalisation' programme. After stating the bloody obvious, puzzled Tony then scratched his head and said: 'What we know also is that we haven't yet found them.' Blair knew exactly where those weapons were – master sophist that he is, Blair was lying by omission in the most flagrant way. The weapons had all been destroyed by sanctions and by UN weapons inspections – a fact that Blair knew only too well.

If Blair didn't know of the destruction of Saddam's banned arsenal then he must pay scant regard to the United Nations and its weapons inspectors. Since the end of the 1990s, and right through to the 2003 invasion, some of the UN's most senior voices and some of the world's most respected weapons inspectors – people who spent huge chunks of their lives in Iraq hunting for WMD – told successive British and American governments that Saddam didn't have outlawed weapons anymore.

After Saddam invaded Kuwait and was then defeated by allied forces in 1991, the ensuing economic sanctions and long-running weapons inspections by the United Nations completely destroyed Saddam's WMD arsenal and his ability to reconstitute WMD programmes. Incidentally, the UN sanctions also reduced the country to a pre-industrial wasteland and killed about 1.5 million Iraqis – at least a third of them children.

The bottom line is that when we invaded in 2003, Iraq had no WMD. Sure, we'd sold Saddam lots of nasty weapons years before – and allowed him to use them – but when he pissed us off in 1991 by invading Kuwait we ground his country and his people into the dirt and left him completely de-fanged.

Back in September 2002 when I wrote in the *Sunday Herald* about how the US had sold biological weapons to Saddam – weapons like anthrax – I thought I should find a former UN weapons inspector who could explain to me where this stuff might have gone. Was it still there, I wanted to know? So I contacted a guy called Scott Ritter. He was the UN's former Chief Weapons Inspector in Iraq, a former US marine intelligence officer, a card-carrying Republican who voted for George W Bush in 2000 and a veteran of the First Gulf War.

He sounded like the kinda guy who'd say Saddam still had all those lovely, evil weapons. But did he? Hell, no. This guy was angry. This guy was sitting in his home in America and throwing his toys out of his pram. Something wrong – very wrong – was happening, he felt, and he needed to speak out about it. The truth was being buried; lies were being told. The British and American people were sleepwalking into an illegal war and the end result would be massive loss of life for Americans, Britons and Iraqis.

Ritter told me that he knew categorically that the UN destroyed most of Iraq's weapons of mass destruction. Some 90–95 per cent of Iraq's WMD were decommissioned, Ritter said. Also, the remaining stockpiles would have been unusable by 2003 and Saddam didn't have the where-withal anymore to restart his WMD programmes. We were going into a war, then, Ritter was saying, that was based on total and utter lies. Downing Street and the White House were telling us that Saddam had to be pre-emptively attacked because he had WMD, but in reality Saddam didn't have WMD. Once again, Bush and Blair were leading their public through the looking-glass and into a back-to-front make-believe world – a world in which lots and lots of people were going to needlessly die in the most dreadful and bloody ways imaginable.

Ritter came straight to the point and called Bush and Blair 'liars' when we spoke. All this talk about Saddam having a nuclear capacity or being on the verge of attaining one was total bullshit. Ritter said that gamma-ray atomic radiation from the radioactive materials in warheads would have been detected by our surveillance satellites. It would have been the same deal if Saddam had been manufacturing chemical or bio-logical weapons – western satellites would have spotted them.

'We saw none of this,' Ritter said. 'If Iraq had been producing weapons, we'd have had definitive proof.' Not long after I spoke to Ritter, I also had a chat with a guy called Hans von Sponek – a truly charming gentleman who was also the UN's former Coordinator in Iraq and the UN's Under-Secretary General. He too was adamant that the west was lying about Iraq having WMD.

Von Sponeck had visited the al-Dora and Fallujah factories near Baghdad in 1999 after they were 'comprehensively trashed' on the orders of UN inspectors because the sites were suspected of being chem-ical weapons plants. He'd just come back from revisiting the site when we spoke in late August/early September of 2002.

He'd returned with a German TV crew and found that both plants were still wrecked. 'We filmed the evidence of the dishonesty of the claims that [these plants] were producing chemical and biological weapons,' he said. 'They are indeed in the same destroyed state which we witnessed in 1999. There was no resumed activity at all.'

Around the time that I was talking to former UN big hitters like Ritter and von Sponeck, an American activist called William Rivers Pitt was doing the same. He talked on the telephone to Scott Ritter off and on for a few days in August 2002. In the telephone conversations, Ritter told Pitt exactly the same as he had told me. Pitt went into meticulous detail with Ritter about the destruction of Iraq's WMD programme, and published the interview in full in a tiny book called *War in Iraq*, in which his discussions with Scott Ritter form the centre-piece. It's a fascinating read – it's just a shame nobody listened to what the book had to say. Published in the run-up to the invasion it was one of the first attempts by a journalist and a highly placed whistle-blower to get the truth out. Sadly, they failed to change a damn thing in London or Washington.

Ritter told Pitt: 'Since 1998, Iraq has fundamentally disarmed: 90–95 per cent of Iraq's weapons of mass destruction capability has been verifiably eliminated. This includes all of the factories used to produce chemical, biological and nuclear weapons, and long-range ballistic missiles; the associated equipment of these factories; and the vast majority of the products coming out of these factories ... We have no evidence Iraq retains either the capability or material. In fact, a considerable amount of evidence suggests Iraq doesn't retain the necessary material.'

OK, let's give Bush and Blair the benefit of the doubt and imagine that Saddam still had 5–10 per cent of his old WMD arsenal. Isn't that still enough to cause global Armageddon? Not so, according to Ritter. 'We have to remember that this missing 5–10 per cent doesn't necessarily constitute a threat. It doesn't even constitute a weapons programme. It constitutes bits and pieces of a weapons programme which in its totality doesn't amount to much ... Likewise, just because we can't account for it doesn't mean Iraq retains it. There's no evidence Iraq retains this material.'

Iraq, Ritter said, continually demonstrated 'over and over a willingness to cooperate with weapons inspectors'. It was the US which ruined the inspections by sparking a crisis which led to the removal of weapons inspectors. America, he said, violated the terms of UN resolutions on weapons inspections 'by using their unique access to operate inside Iraq in a manner incompatible with Security Council resolutions, for example, by spying on Iraq'.

For seven years, until inspections ended in 1998, UN teams razed Saddam's WMD arsenal to the ground. Ritter says that when he left in

1998 Iraq's nuclear programme 'had been 100 per cent eliminated'.

'There's no debate about that,' he said. 'All of their instruments and facilities had been destroyed.' Ritter's team were monitoring Iraq for gamma-rays – which would have proven Saddam was enriching plutonium or uranium. 'We never found anything,' he added. 'We can say unequivocally that the industrial infrastructure needed by Iraq to produce nuclear weapons had been eliminated.'

Iraq could, however, have rebuilt its nuclear programme between 1998 and 2003, couldn't it? The answer appears to be a categorical 'no'.

'For Iraq to re-acquire nuclear weapons capability, they'd have to basically build from the ground up enrichment and weaponisation capabilities that would cost tens of billions of dollars.' Iraq simply couldn't have done it as the UN sanctions regime was so severe that basic necessities like some medicines were banned from being sold to the country. How on earth, then, could Saddam have got the hi-tech gizmos and geegaws needed to enrich uranium and plutonium into the country under the sanctions? Even if he could have bust the sanctions and smuggled in bits of kit like centrifuges, western satellites would have detected his scientists happily going about their business of building nuclear bombs. No evidence of this was ever found.

'Centrifuge facilities emit gamma-radiation, as well as many other frequencies,' said Ritter. 'It's detectable. Iraq could not get around this.' Claims, then, made by US Vice-president Dick Cheney that Saddam was two years away from acquiring a nuke were 'nonsense' in Ritter's eyes.

So, that's nukes taken care of. If Ritter's to be believed – and there is no reason why a man who was assigned to the staff of General Norman Schwarzkopf as an intelligence officer charged with tracking Scud missiles in the First Gulf War should lie to save the hide of a tyrant whom he despised – then Iraq was nuke-free. So, what about the chemical weapons? Did Saddam really lose all those, too?

Again, if you believe Ritter, the answer is 'yes'. Saddam produced his chemical weapons at the Muthanna State Establishment – a huge chemical weapons factory. It was blown to bits during the First Gulf War. After that 'weapons inspectors came and completed the task of eliminating the facility', he says. Iraq only manufactured three kinds of nerve agent – sarin, tabun and VX. With Muthanna gone, Iraq lost its manufacturing base for chemical weapons.

'We destroyed thousands of tons of chemical agent,' says Ritter. 'We had an incineration plant operating full-time for years, burning tons of the stuff every day. We went out and blew up bombs, missiles and war-heads filled with agent. We emptied Scud missile warheads filled with agent. We hunted down this stuff and destroyed it.'

Even if Iraq had managed to hide some of these deadly poisons, sarin and tabun only have a shelf life of five years. Ritter says that if there were secret caches of chemical weapons hidden in Iraq it would have been 'nothing more than useless, harmless goo' by the time of the invasion.

As for VX it also ceased to be a concern after the bombing of Muthanna. 'Even if Iraq had held on to stabilised VX agent,' said Ritter, 'it's likely it would have degraded [by the time of the invasion]. Real questions exist as to whether Iraq perfected the stabilisation process [for VX]. Even a minor deviation in the formula creates proteins that destroy the VX within months.' So was there a VX nerve agent factory in Iraq by the time we invaded? 'Not on your life,' says Ritter.

'The manufacture of chemical weapons emits vented gases that would have been detected if they existed.' Like a nuclear programme, western satellites would have picked up on chemical weapon production. Ritter is certain that if Iraq had been making sarin or tabun or VX then we would have had 'definite proof, plain and simple'.

'From 1994 to 1998, we had monitoring inspectors blanketing the totality of Iraq's chemical industrial facilities, installing sensitive sniffers and cameras, and performing no-notice inspections. We detected no evidence of retained or reconstituted prohibited capability.'

Right, that's chemical weapons dealt with – what about bio-weapons? Iraq – thanks to the efforts of Ronnie Reagan's administration – actually did make anthrax in 'liquid bulk agent form' and 'produced a significant quantity of liquid botulinum toxin'. Both were 'weaponised' and put into bombs.

According to Ritter, the Iraqis lied until 1995, saying they didn't have bio-weapons, but 'when they finally admitted it in 1995 we got to work on destroying the factories and equipment that produced it'.

Ritter and his boys blew up the Al Hakum factory – the main bio-weapons plant in Iraq. Under 'ideal storage conditions' liquid anthrax germinates in about three years and becomes totally useless, Ritter explained. 'So, even if Iraq lied to us and held on to anthrax – and there's no evidence to substantiate this – Iraq [had] no biological weapons [at the time of the invasion], because both the anthrax and botulinum toxin [were] useless. For Iraq to have biological weapons [at the time of the invasion], they'd [have had] to reconstitute a biological manufacturing base.

'We blanketed Iraq – every research and development facility, every university, every school, every hospital, every beer factory: anything with a potential fermentation capability was inspected – and we never found any evidence of ongoing research and development or retention.'

To summarise, Ritter says: 'I never found any evidence of conceal-ment of biological weapons ... we know enough to say that as of December 1998 we had no evidence Iraq retained biological weapons nor that they were working on any. In fact, we had a lot of evidence to suggest Iraq was in compliance.'

So, nuclear, chemical and biological weapons were all destroyed by UN weapons inspections. Let's forget about WMD then and see if Iraq was even able to deploy long-range bombs against its enemies.

The Iraqi rocket programme was run by 'intelligent energetic ama-teurs who were just not getting it right' said Ritter. 'They manufactured rockets that would spin and cartwheel, that would go north instead of south, that would blow up.'

As of the eve of the invasion, Iraq didn't have 'the capability to do long-range ballistic missiles', said Ritter. 'They didn't even have the capability to do short-range ballistic missiles,' he added.

'The idea that Iraq can suddenly pop up with a long-range missile is ludicrous,' Ritter went on. 'There's a lot of testing that has to take place, and this testing is all carried out outdoors. They can't avoid detection.'

Iraq also continued to declare its missile tests – usually carried out about eight times a year. 'Our radar detects tests,' said Ritter, 'we know what the characteristics are, and we know there's nothing to be worried about.'

The CIA had claimed that L-29s – Czech single-engine jets – were being modified by the Iraqis and turned into drones which could deliv-er WMD. Ritter talked to the 'best experts in the Israeli air force' – Saddam's sworn enemies – about the L-29s, and here's what happened: 'They were dismissive,' said Ritter. 'They said it just doesn't make sense – to deliver agent, you'd have to make modifications to the aircraft that are very specific and detectable. These modifications would also have an impact on range and fuel.'

Ritter finally sent inspectors to investigate the L-29s. They 'found no evidence of the Iraqis modifying L-29s along the lines the CIA sug-gested'. Yet, the CIA continued to say that the L-29s were a potential delivery system up until the 2003 invasion.

Nor was Saddam able to circumvent UN sanctions and buy parts for banned weapons on the global black market. Iraq found it almost impossible to buy spare parts for its tanks, helicopters and planes on the black market, let alone source and buy the equipment needed to build WMD.

Ritter tailed hundreds of Iraqi intelligence 'front companies' which Saddam set up around the world in the hope of using them to sanctions-bust. 'We travelled everywhere investigating them,' he says. 'We never found concrete evidence of any involvement in acquiring proscribed items.'

Weapons inspectors would undoubtedly have stayed in Iraq and maintained scrutiny of Saddam's military capabilities if Britain and America hadn't colluded in subverting inspections and turned a UN-authorised international inspection team into a spying outfit. 'The second you start allowing inspections to be used to gather intelligence information unrelated to the mandate [weapons of mass destruction], you've discredited the entire inspection regime,' said Ritter.

'Several programmes – most importantly a signals intelligence pro-gramme I designed and ran from 1996 to 1998 – were allowed to be taken over by the CIA for the sole purpose of spying on Saddam. This was wrong, and I said so on numerous occasions.' Ritter says that this was one of the reasons he resigned from his post in 1998.

It's not hard, then – after listening to Ritter deconstruct the London–Washington case for war, and trample on claims that Saddam posed a threat to the west and its allies because of weapons of mass destruction – to agree with his bald summation of the invasion: 'This war with Iraq is the dumbest thing I've ever heard of.'

Ritter was warning before the invasion that the US was going to find itself in another Vietnam-style situation. He compared what would hap-pen to the American and British army in Iraq to the hideous running sore of the Russian military action in Chechnya. 'This is a war that has everything bad about it. There is no good end for this war,' he said.

It's people like Scott Ritter that – thankfully – take the anti-American poison out of the anti-war movement. If you oppose the war, then you need to listen to people like Ritter. He confounds the stupid stereotypes in Europe that Americans are dumb, trigger-happy cowboys. Here's a proud patriot – a one-time cheerleader for George W Bush – saying his country got it wrong. He's not a traitor or a weasel or a coward or an appeaser – he's a man who had the facts at his fingertips and realised he was being lied to, and that the case for the war that he was being sold was a bunch of bullshit. He was a man who wouldn't lie to himself just because he was told it was the loyal, flag-waving thing to do. He represents the best of the American spirit – independence of thought and action, a refusal to do as he's told just because he's told to do it and an unwavering belief that at the heart of government there must be an unbreakable bond of honesty and respect between the nation's leaders and the people. He also has the balls to say 'fuck you' to anyone he thinks is a liar, a cheat or a fraud.

Here's Ritter's definition of what it means to be an American: 'Our primary responsibility is not to sit and nod dumbly while elected representatives say whatever they want in Washington DC. Our duties and responsibilities are to make American democracy function, and American democracy can only function when citizens are involved, when citizens are empowered with facts. My speaking out has everything to do with empowering democracy, and absolutely nothing to do with treason or betraying my country.

'I wore the uniform of a Marine for 12 years. I went to war for my country. I serve my community today. I'm doing all of this not out of sympathy for the people of Iraq but because I love my own country.'

Let's hear from some other senior UN figures. This time from Dennis Halliday, a delightful Irishman and the former UN Assistant General-Secretary and UN Humanitarian Coordinator in Iraq. A man, then, who's pretty much up to speed on all things Iraqi.

I'd found out from Ritter that Iraq had effectively complied with UN weapons inspections. Now I wanted to know what life in Iraq had been like under sanctions. Could Ritter have been wrong? Could Iraq have been financially able to reconstitute its WMD programme?

Halliday told me that under UN-imposed sanctions at least one million people died in Iraq. He was being conservative in his estimate – other UN aid agencies have said that about 1.5 million Iraqis, including some 565,000 children – were dead by the mid-1990s thanks to sanctions. Do you fancy an example of the kind of horrific, sadistic and murderous mind-set that typified the US and UK government since their application of sanctions? Try this one. In 2002, the US blocked contracts for water tankers on the grounds that they might be used to haul chemical weapons, even though UNMOVIC – the UN's new weapons inspectors – had no objection. This was at a time when the country was in the grip of a severe drought and lack of water was a major cause of child deaths.

A declassified document for the US Defense Intelligence Agency in 1991 entitled *Iraq's Water Treatment Vulnerability* noted what would happen to Iraqis under economic sanctions: 'Iraq depends on importing specialised equipment and some chemicals to purify its water supply,' the document said. 'Failing to secure supplies will result in a shortage of pure drinking water for much of the population. This could lead to increased incidences, if not epidemics, of disease. Although Iraq is already experiencing a loss of water treatment capability, it probably will take at least six months before the system is fully degraded.' Some would say that statement amounts to proof of a premeditated war crime as evidence that the US knew full well it would be killing Iraqi civilians wholesale through its use of targeted sanctions.

Up to July 2002, some $5.4 billion in humanitarian aid was being obstructed by the US with the support of Britain. In March 1996, the World Health Organisation said sanctions had caused a six-fold increase in the mortality rate of Iraqi children aged under-five. In October of the same year, UNICEF said some 4,500 Iraqi children were dying every month as a result of sanctions-induced starvation and disease. To get the measure of the kind of soulless creatures who run Britain and America, take a look at one Madeline Albright. This woman was Bill Clinton's US Secretary of State. An interviewer once asked her on the US TV show *60 Minutes*: 'We have heard that a half-million children have died ... I mean that's more children than died in Hiroshima. And, you know, is the price worth it?'

Here's Albright's chirpy reply: 'I think this is a very hard choice, but the price – we think the price is worth it.'

Halliday doesn't think so: 'Children were dying of malnutrition and water-borne diseases. The US and UK bombed the infrastructure in 1991, destroying power, water and sewage systems against the Geneva Convention. It was a great crime against Iraq.'

Once we'd bombed the hell out of Iraq in 1991, we then slapped on brutal sanctions. 'Thirteen years of sanctions made it impossible for Iraq to repair the damage,' Halliday told me. I was speaking to him shortly after the bombing of the UN station in Baghdad by the post-invasion Iraqi resistance in August 2003. He said the reason the UN headquarters in Baghdad had been attacked – leaving 23 dead including many of Halliday's own friends – was because the United Nations had been taken over by the US and turned into a 'dark joke'; a 'malignant force'; an aggressive arm of US foreign policy. The murderous attack was payback for sanctions.

Let's play a maths game. If sanctions killed more than 1.5 million Iraqis over 13 years, that means that each year US and UK-backed UN sanctions were killing 115,384 Iraqis. That's 9,615 Iraqis a month or 2,403 a week or just a mere 343 a day. That means six Iraqis died every hour. Every ten minutes for 13 years, then, UN sanctions claimed one Iraqi life. In terms of death toll, who's worse? Us or Saddam?

'The west sees the UN as a benign organisation, but the sad reality in much of the world is that the UN is not seen as benign,' said Halliday – who was nominated for a Nobel Peace Prize in 2001, following his resignation from the UN in 1998 in protest over the continued use of sanctions. 'The UN Security Council has been taken over and corrupted by the US and UK, particularly with regard to Iraq, Palestine and Israel.'

'That is why we have such tremendous resentment and anger against the UN in Iraq. There is a sense that the UN humiliated the Iraqi people and society. I would use the term genocide to define the use of sanctions against Iraq.'

It all makes sense now, doesn't it? The UN inspections took Saddam's arms off him and the UN sanctions took Iraq back 100 years. That's why it was so easy for our troops to waltz into Baghdad, knocking the Republican Guard over like skittles.

Halliday says that 'further collaboration' between the UN and America and Britain 'would be disaster for the United Nations as it would be sucked into supporting the illegal occupation of Iraq'.

'The UN has been drawn into being an arm of the US – a division of the State Department. Kofi Annan was appointed and supported by the US and that has corrupted the independence of the UN. The UN must move quickly to reform itself and improve the Security Council – it must make clear that the UN and the US are not one and the same.'

As the war got going, Halliday remained resolutely defiant of London and Washington, saying that 'Bush and Blair misled their countries into war. By invading Iraq and placing the US inside the Islamic world, America invited terrorists to come on the attack.' The war, as we all know today, made the world a much more dangerous place for Brits and Americans. Halliday believed back in 2003, when the invasion had just happened, however, that 'once the US goes from Iraq, the terrorist will go as well'. Now that the country has tipped into civil war that hope seems tragically futile.

Halliday's analysis, which he says he shares with many leading figures still working in the UN today, is that the invasion of Iraq made the world a place of fear and terror for people from Glasgow, Chicago, Cardiff, New York, London, San Francisco, Belfast and Seattle. It wasn't just a war based on lies, then, it was a war based on lies which didn't even do us any good. It was a war based on lies which made life worse for us. As nations, we've debased ourselves morally by lying and we've made hatred the common currency between the peoples of the Middle East and the peoples of Europe and North America. We've gone a long way toward screwing up the entire world.

Mr Blair and Mr Bush, on behalf of the free peoples of the US and the UK, I would like to thank you for disgracing our countries. You have taken two nations which could still cling to the idea that we were both good guys because we were the ones who'd beaten Hitler in the Second World War and you've pissed that heritage and self-belief up against the wall. And all for the sake of invading a tin-pot country like Iraq which posed us no threat. Why?

A NASTY, BLACK
THREE-LETTER WORD
or
How Enron, energy blackouts and jamming megawatts up Grandma Millie's ass made Iraqi oil too rich a prize for the White House to ignore

You know the kind of people who I think are stupid? The folk who believe that it's only some sort of conspiracy-theory wacko who would even dare to mention that oil might be a possible explanation – or even just one of the reasons – for the US and the UK's decision to invade Iraq.

Why shouldn't a government worry about energy? Why shouldn't a government worry about money? In fact, why wouldn't a capitalist government want to make sure it had access to a plentiful supply of cheap energy in order to keep its economy chugging along? Don't you worry about money? If you couldn't keep the lights on in your house or make sure you had enough fuel to heat your home wouldn't you try to do something about it?

Why should we think of governments as being any different to people? People do terrible, stupid, greedy things for money, so why do we presume that countries and governments can't be just as base as individuals when it comes to filthy lucre? A government is just a collection of people, after all, so why can't the institution be just as dumb and cruel as the people who comprise its membership? Why must we suppose that a government always acts from lofty principles? Can't a government be as corrupt and venal as you or me?

I have to confess that the old 'they did it for the oil' theory always left me a little cold. Nevertheless, if you are a journalist and you are watching the world prepare for war while the White House is full of oil men and oil women, and the country they are planning to invade sits on top of the planet's second largest oil reserves, it's kinda incumbent on you to at least ask a few questions about oil as a possible war motive.

Especially, if everywhere you turn people are carrying placards in the street saying NO WAR FOR OIL and the talk among every anti-war protester you speak to is of 'oil, oil, oil'. The peaceniks were good at saying oil was the driving force behind the war, but when you asked them 'why?' or asked them to prove what they were saying, they couldn't do it. They'd just say: 'Well, it is.' That's not good enough, really. That is a conspiracy theory – it's a blind belief, an act of faith almost. So, I decided to start hunting around to see if I could either prove or disprove this belief that somehow oil was motivating Bush, Cheney *et al* in their little Iraqi escapade.

After a lot of talking to oil men, financiers, academics and business types in the autumn of 2002, I was pointed towards a policy paper prepared for Dick Cheney, the Vice-president, by none other than James Baker, the former US Secretary of State under George Bush Senior. Cheney and Baker were old pals. Dick Cheney, you will remember, was Secretary of State for Defense under Daddy Bush, leading the charge against Saddam in the First Gulf War. After Daddy Bush screwed his chances of getting a second term in the White House and had his ass whipped by Clinton, Cheney made out with the oil industry for most of the 1990s and ran Halliburton, the oil mega-corp, before he returned to office under Baby Bush in 2000 as VP. As we all know, Halliburton won many of the US contracts to 'reconstruct' Iraq post-invasion. James Baker is one of the Bush family's closest advisors and was instrumental in helping Dubya pull off the 2000 election.

This paper that Baker prepared for Cheney was called *Strategic Energy Policy Challenges for the 21st Century*. It sounds as dull as ditchwater, but believe me, it is dynamite. It proved what all those tree-hugging leftie hippy types had been saying about oil all along. Using this document as a policy blueprint, the Bush cabinet agreed in April 2001 that Iraq was a risk to world oil markets and therefore America as well. As a consequence, military intervention was deemed necessary. That's the long and the short of it.

It was all there. When the *Sunday Herald* reported what Cheney was up to, in a front-page investigation based on the Baker document, it created quite a storm. Cheney, who chairs the White House Energy Policy Development Group and heads the administration's Energy Task Force, received the report from Baker's Institute for Public Policy in April 2001. The conclusion to the report prepared for Cheney was this: 'The United States remains a prisoner of its energy dilemma. Iraq remains a destabilising influence to the flow of oil to international markets from the Middle East. Saddam Hussein has also demonstrated a willingness to threaten to use the oil weapon and to use his own export programme to manipulate oil markets. This would display his personal power, enhance his image as a pan-Arab leader and pressure others for a lifting of economic sanctions against his regime. Therefore the US should conduct an immediate policy review toward Iraq, including military, energy, economic and political/diplomatic assessments.'

UN sanctions allowed Iraq to export some oil. In fact, the US was importing almost a million barrels of Iraqi oil a day back then, even though American firms were forbidden from direct involvement with the regime's oil industry. In 1999, Iraq was exporting about 2.5 million barrels a day across the world.

Remember that this Cheney/Baker document was finalised in April 2001 – some five months before September 11. So, understandable paranoia in the wake of the terror attacks on the US had nothing to do with the Bush administration targeting Saddam at this stage. The use of possible military intervention against Iraq was not to do with weapons of mass destruction, links to al-Qaeda or Saddam as a threat to regional or global peace. The use of possible military intervention against Iraq had everything to do, however, with oil – as the document Cheney got from Baker proves.

The White House was fixated on kicking Saddam's ass and getting all that lovely Iraqi oil. As Cheney's document showed: 'The United States should develop an integrated strategy with key allies in Europe and Asia, and with key countries in the Middle East, to restate goals with respect to Iraqi policy and to restore a cohesive coalition of key allies.'

This oil obsession should come as no surprise. George Bush Junior, after all, has strong personal connections to the US oil industry and once owned the oil company, Spectrum 7. This Cheney document, then, fundamentally questioned the motives behind the Bush administration's desire to take out Saddam. It pulled the rug from under all that fake talk about WMD and al-Qaeda, and brought oil – that nasty, black three-letter word – front and centre.

What's interesting is the way Cheney's document mulls over the use of military force. A variety of scenarios are thrown up. On the one hand it recommends using renewed UN weapons inspectors as a means of controlling oil by cowing Saddam and then moving in to take control of Iraqi oil. But it also supports straightforward military intervention.

'Once an arms-control program is in place,' it says in typical turgid bureaucratese, 'the US could consider reducing restrictions [sanctions] on oil investment inside Iraq.' The reason for this is that 'Iraqi [oil] reserves represent a major asset that can quickly add capacity to world oil markets and inject a more competitive tenor to oil trade'.

This course of action, however, may not be as effective as simply taking out Saddam, we're told. The report admits that an arms-control policy will be 'quite costly' as it will 'encourage Saddam Hussein to boast of his "victory" against the United States, fuel his ambition and potentially strengthen his regime'. It adds: 'Once so encouraged, and if his access to oil revenues was to be increased by adjustments in oil sanctions, Saddam Hussein could be a greater security threat to US allies in the region.'

One of the 'consequences' of the US remaining 'a prisoner of its energy dilemma', the report wearily concludes, may be a 'need for military intervention' in Iraq.

But what lay at the heart of this re-think in energy policy under the watchful eye of Uncle Dick? Well, it was down to the woeful mismanagement of US energy policy – surprise, surprise. Because the government screwed up, Iraq and its oil reserves became a nice juicy prize on the horizon.

The report was written against the backdrop of huge power cuts which plunged the west coast of America into darkness. These power cuts were not good for the White House, given the fact that the government had recently deregulated the energy markets in California and consumers were blaming this policy for the outages and shortages. The Cheney/Baker report warned of 'more Californias' ahead, and said the 'central dilemma' for the US administration was that 'the American people continue to demand plentiful and cheap energy without sacrifice or inconvenience'. With the 'energy sector in a critical condition, a crisis could erupt at any time [which] could have potentially enormous impact on the US and would affect US national security and foreign policy in dramatic ways'.

The main cause of any future crisis, we're told, is 'Middle East tension' and that means the 'chances are greater than at any point in the last two decades of an oil supply disruption'. The report says the US is not 'energy independent' and is becoming too reliant on foreign powers supplying it with gas and oil. The response, the Cheney document says, is to put oil at the heart of the administration – a 'reassessment of the role of energy in American foreign policy'. Just as Blair told the UK people that he'd put 'edakayshun, edakayshun, edakayshun' at the heart of all government policy, so Cheney wanted oil central to everything the Bush administration would do.

The US energy crisis, Cheney's report says, is exacerbated by growing anti-American feeling in the oil-rich Gulf States. 'Gulf allies are finding their domestic and foreign policy interests increasingly at odds with US strategic considerations,' it says, 'especially as Arab–Israeli tensions flare. They have become less inclined to lower oil prices. A trend towards anti-Americanism could affect regional leaders' ability to cooperate with the US in the energy area. The resulting tight markets have increased US vulnerability to disruption and provided adversaries undue political influence over the price of oil.'

The attention then turns back to Iraq. The nation is described as the world's 'key swing producer turning its taps on and off when it has felt such action was in its strategic interests' and so forcing variations in oil prices – an act frowned on fiercely by free market America. Cheney's report even speculates that 'Saddam may remove Iraqi oil from the market for an extended period of time' creating a volatile market.

What are the consequences of these shortages in oil supplies and jumpy energy prices? Well, first of all there are those blackouts in California. The report says that 'unprecedented energy price volatility' led to the recurring blackouts. And those blackouts, the report goes on, are having a bad effect on voters; in fact they are a possible election loser. For that reason, Cheney has to create 'a new and viable US energy policy central to America's domestic economy and to [the] nation's security and foreign policy'. The report says that energy and security policies should be integrated to stop 'manipulations of markets by any state'. In fact, energy policy-makers should include 'representation from the Department of Defense'.

'Unless the United States assumes a leadership role in the formation of new rules of the game,' the report tells us, 'US firms, US consumers and the US government [will be left] in a weaker position.'

When you pore over the text and decipher the policy-wonk talk this is what the Bush administration was thinking in terms of its energy policy: We hate Saddam. He's got lots of oil and we don't. He can screw about with us by making oil prices fluctuate. Oil prices are causing all that shit over on the west coast with those blackouts and stuff. Voters don't like those blackouts. They blame us. We could lose the next election. Maybe we need to think about whacking that Saddam bastard so our oil supplies are nice and safe. We certainly need to do something because sure as shit our energy supply is just as important as our national security. OK. Maybe we will kick that camel-jockey's ass one day.

Ain't it funny though, the type of people who can influence the thoughts and ideas of a government? Baker didn't knock up his oil report for Cheney all by himself. Oh, no. He had lots of little helpers. And I'm sure Cheney knew most of them. After all, as the former Chief Executive of Halliburton based out of Texas, he's bound to have known Texan Ken Lay. Do you know Ken Lay? You're bound to. Not only was he one of Baker's key advisors drafting the oil report for Cheney, he was also the disgraced former Chief Executive of Enron, the US energy giant which went bankrupt (not long after the Cheney/Baker report was written, in fact) because of massive accountancy fraud. Ken Lay was found guilty in May 2006 of fraud in the wake of Enron's collapse. Enron, by the way, has been the single biggest financial supporter of George W Bush's entire political career. Lay died on holiday in Aspen, Colorado, of heart disease on July 5, 2006 before he could be sentenced.

Other advisors to Baker included the likes of Luis Giusti, a Shell non-executive director; John Manzoni, Regional President of BP; David O'Reilly, Chief Executive of ChevronTexaco; Sheikh Saud al Nasser al Sabah, former Kuwaiti Oil Minister; and Steven L Miller, Chairman of the Board of Directors, President and CEO of Shell Oil Company.

Of course, Cheney's connections to Halliburton obviously had no influence on his thinking regarding Iraq. Heaven forbid.

Halliburton is a bit like a 21st-century East India Company – the corporation the British Empire used to spread its power across the world. Whither America goes, Halliburton goes these days.

'I have no financial interest in Halliburton of any kind and haven't had now for over three years,' Cheney said. Well, I hope Dick forgives me being so coarse, but that's total bollocks. He's got a deferred annual salary and nearly 450,000 shares of unexercised Halliburton stock options. His shares are worth millions. Every time Halliburton makes a buck then Cheney's future bank balance gets fatter and fatter. Cheney left Halliburton with a $34 million payout and the company has now got some of the biggest government contracts in US history.

In fact, Halliburton was given a secret $7 billion contract by the Pentagon before the invasion of Iraq even took place to rebuild and run the country's oil industry. When questioned about that contract, Cheney got more than a little uppity and said he wasn't involved in any way in the deal being awarded to his old corporate *alma mater*. 'As Vice-president, I have absolutely no influence of, involvement of, knowledge of – in any way, shape or form – of contracts led by ... the federal government.'

Hmm, that doesn't really tally with an email which the redoubtable government watchdog organisation Judicial Watch prised from the cold, grasping fingertips of Pentagon spin-doctors. It's dated March 2003 and it says that the Halliburton contract 'has been coordinated with VP's [Vice-president's] office'. On March 8, the Army Corps of Engineers gave the no-bid contract to Halliburton.

Cheney says he has 'no idea' why there was no bidding for the contract. But if that's true then what about a 10-page Pentagon document which Judicial Watch also got its hands on. This showed that Halliburton landed the contract because it was the only corporation which the Pentagon deemed capable enough of handling the task. I should point out that Halliburton was the only corporation deemed fit for the job because the Pentagon had given the firm an unfair advantage over other companies. This was done by not only giving Halliburton access to secret contingency plans in November 2002 but also allowing Halliburton to 'pre-position equipment and personnel' for the Iraqi oil operation a full month before the contract was agreed.

Incidentally, in 1998 Halliburton – then controlled by Cheney – did $15 million worth of business with Saddam, selling him parts he needed to repair his oil infrastructure. How weird is that? Just a few years later Cheney was calling Saddam a 'murderous dictator'? Jeez, times sure do change fast in US politics and big business.

It shouldn't come as much of a surprise then that a man like Cheney was prepared to listen to the musings of a creature like Enron boss Ken Lay when it came to mulling over what to do about oil, Iraq and war. After all, Ken Lay was running a gigantic US energy company that was operating in California – the state where all those voter-unfriendly blackouts were happening. Lay certainly had a reason to be listened to, then, don't you think? I'm sure you will agree, particularly when you find out that it was Enron which was helping to illegally cause those blackouts and then cashing in on the catastrophe.

Enron traders were caught on tape gloating and praising each other for helping to create the power crisis in California and then reaping the massive financial dividends caused by the mayhem brought about by their criminal conspiracy. The tapes, from Enron's California trading desk, show how traders deliberately drove up prices by screwing with power production. Vince Gonzales of *CBS News* in America led the way in exposing the role Enron had in the California blackouts with a series of scoops based on the tape recordings of Enron's sinister, soulless staff.

Here's the taped proof that Enron staff started exporting energy out of California so the company could drive up prices regardless of the effects:

> *Enron worker 1*: What we need to do is to help in the cause of, ah, the downfall of California. You guys need to pull your megawatts out of California on a daily basis.
> *Enron worker 2*: They're on the ropes today. I exported like fucking 400 megs [megawatts].
> *Enron worker 3*: Wow, fuck 'em, right!

These sickos came up with geeky nerdy terms for their money-grubbing little plots – codenames like Death Star, Ricochet and Fat Boy were given to the ruses used to manipulate the market.

'You wanna do some Fat Boys or, or whatever, man, you know, take advantage of it,' says one trader. A Fat Boy sees traders using fake power sales to hide megawatts. This shrinks the energy supply and drives up the price.

A 'Ricochet' involved Enron sending power out of California and then reselling it to the hapless state. This avoided price caps for deals which took place solely within the state of California.

The company also created 'phantom' congestion on electricity transmission lines. A memo written by Enron lawyers in December 2000 explains that the 'net effect' of a Death Star 'is that Enron gets paid for moving energy to relieve congestion without actually moving any energy or relieving any congestion'.

As an investigative report for *CBS News* put it: 'They also used the oldest trick in the book: lies.'

One tape goes like this:

> *Enron worker 1*: It's called lies. It's all how well you can weave these lies together, [colleague's name], alright, so.
> *Enron worker 2*: I feel like I'm being corrupted now.
> *Enron worker 1*: No, this is marketing.
> *Enron worker 2*: OK.

Another tape shows Enron weasels getting power supplies shut down so they can hike up prices. It goes like this:

Enron worker 1: If you took down the steamer [part of the power plant], how long would it take to get back up?

Enron worker 2: Oh, it's not something you want to just be turning on and off every hour. Let's put it that way.

Enron worker 1: Well, why don't you just go ahead and shut her down.

On another tape a trader's heard trilling 'burn, baby, burn. That's a beautiful thing' when a forest fire shuts down a major transmission line into California, cutting power supplies and raising prices.

Another tape has this conversation:

Enron worker 1: He just fucks California. He steals money from California to the tune of about a million.

Enron worker 2: Will you rephrase that?

Enron worker 1: OK, he, um, arbitrages the California market to the tune of a million bucks or two a day.

Or how about this tape:

Enron worker 1: They're fucking taking all the money back from you guys? All the money you guys stole from those poor grandmothers in California?

Enron worker 2: Yeah, Grandma Millie, man!

Enron worker 1: Yeah, now she wants her fucking money back for all the power you've charged right up, jammed right up her asshole for fucking $250 a megawatt hour.

One tape even contains this immortal line from an Enron worker: 'It'd be great. I'd love to see Ken Lay Secretary of Energy.' Another has a member of Enron staff saying that he knows Bush will allow no limits to energy prices: 'When this election comes Bush will fucking whack this shit, man. He won't play this price-cap bullshit.'

That turned out to be pretty bang on the money. In May 2001, Bush said: 'We will not take any action that makes California's [energy] problems worse and that's why I oppose price caps.'

Both Enron and the Justice Department tried to prevent the release of the tapes, but their contents were finally secured by the Snohomish Public Utility District near Seattle in 2004. Even the Federal Energy Regulatory Commission (FERC), the agency meant to control energy corporations, tried to stop the tapes being released despite the fact that FERC investigators knew about their existence as far back as 2002. Eric Christensen, a Snohomish spokesman, said: 'This is the evidence we've all been waiting for. This proves they manipulated the market.'

Snohomish and other utility companies are trying to get Enron to cough up for the money the firm's actions cost them. California senators are seeking a refund worth almost $9 billion.

The sheer cruelty, exploitation and greed of Enron is shocking – particularly for a company with a boss who is supposed to be helping the Bush government get to grips with these rolling blackouts in California. And those blackouts – which Enron helped create – caused many in the administration to start thinking that maybe they had to go do something about those energy problems. Maybe oil was the answer. Maybe it was time to target Iraq in order to secure oil and stop this damn unsettling energy crisis at home which could lose Georgy-boy the next election.

Relentlessly, the Enron cruelty continued – even though some parts of the state of California were literally lit by car headlights and people were even trapped in lifts – and still the Enron traders laughed and counted their wodge.

One trader says on tape: 'Just cut 'em off. They're so fucked. They should just bring back fucking horses and carriages, fucking lamps, fucking kerosene lamps.'

When a businessman complained to an Enron trader about the sky-rocketing prices, the trader said: 'I just looked at him. I said "Move." (*Laughter*) The guy was like horrified. I go, "Look, don't take it the wrong way. Move. It isn't getting fixed anytime soon."'

The intention was to ruin California in order to make a quick, illegal buck. One worker is recorded saying: 'You gotta think the economy is going to fucking get crushed, man. This is like a recession waiting to fucking happen.' Another says: 'This is where California breaks.' His pal responds: 'Yeah, it sure is, man.'

And it's not as if the staff didn't know that their conspiracy to shut down plants and drive up prices was a disgrace. They weren't that stupid. Here's a testament to the fact that these guys were bad and loving it:

> *Enron worker 1*: This guy from the *Wall Street Journal* calls me up a little bit ago ...
> *Enron worker 2*: I wouldn't do it, because first of all you'd have to tell 'em a lot of lies because if you told the truth ...
> *Enron worker 1*: I'd get in trouble.
> *Enron worker 2*: You'd get in trouble.

When the lies and the conspiracy were finally uncovered, one trader is heard on tape trying to protect his sorry behind and saying: 'I'm just ass-fucked, I'm just trying to be an honest camper so I only go to jail once.'

Don't be mistaken – companies like Enron played a role in this war happening. The horrible irony is that states on the west coast of America which were hit by the energy crisis ended up owing millions of dollars to Enron even though the company fixed the markets and caused the blackouts. Enron and other energy companies hope to rescue themselves from bankruptcy by collecting on contracts and are even suing their own victims.

Russ Campbell, a lawyer acting for the Nevada Power Company, said: 'We had to go out and buy energy to keep our system in the red, to keep our lights on, to keep the strip up and running and we had to do so at exorbitant prices.'

In America, they call this 'gouging the consumer' – we call it fraud. Enron actually forced utility companies in Nevada to sign expensive long-term contracts at the very height of the power crisis.

Nevada was as much a target of Enron exploitation as California, as this tape shows:

> *Enron worker 1*: I wanna see what pain and heartache this is going to cause Nevada Power Company. I want to fuck with Nevada for a while.
> *Enron worker 2*: What do you mean?
> *Enron worker 1*: I just, I'm still in the mood to screw with people, OK?

Russ Campbell says: 'This is not a smoking gun, this was an audiotape of the bullet coming out of the chamber, hitting the victim and the killer standing over the body and laughing about it.'

Enron still denies any role in an energy crisis which saw wholesale power rates increase by tenfold, left three investor-owned power utilities facing financial ruin and caused misery for millions of Californians caught in rolling blackouts.

In a way, then, Enron, can really be said to have helped cause the war. The White House was freaking out about the blackouts on the west coast – imagining the dire electoral consequences if similar power-cuts spread around the 50 states. And all along it was Enron which was helping to cause the blackouts, even though the company's jailbird boss, Ken, was giving the government advice which boiled down to 'invade Iraq for oil so we don't have to worry about energy shortages and power-cuts anymore'.

It's not just ironic; it's not just hypocritical or grim or repellent; it's a world where black's white and night's day, a world built on lies and gross deception and a complete disregard for the lives of ordinary people. Of course, Enron and its shenanigans and the energy crisis and power-cuts weren't the only reason that Bush and Co. targeted Iraq. Far from it; in fact, that would just be hyping the significance of these events way too much. But this gross little vignette shows that oil did, as we can now see, play a significant role in making solid the decision to hit Saddam; it focused the minds of the administration's prime movers and made energy, or rather the lack of it, a central policy issue – a matter that had to be looked at in terms of foreign policy and military intervention.

Black gold, then, did have a part to play in the war. In the run-up to the invasion, the Pentagon's pet Iraqi, Ahmed Chalabi, a convicted fraudster and the head of the exile group the Iraqi National Congress (and a man who would later turn out to be accused of working for Iranian intelligence), was running around telling representatives of foreign oil firms that 'American companies will have a big shot at Iraqi oil'. It didn't take a genius to work out that with a deposed Saddam and a pro-American Iraqi in power the US would reap billions in post-war Iraq and solve its energy worries.

Maybe that's why Dick Cheney and his buddies over at the Energy Taskforce spent much of 2001 poring over charts detailing Iraqi oil and gas projects and also drew up a March 2001 list entitled *Foreign Suitors for Iraqi Oilfield Contracts*. This list also includes information on how well the 'foreign suitors' are getting on with the job of wooing America for the chance to get their mitts on Iraqi oil. All this was happening nearly two years before the invasion and half a year before the September 11 attacks. Now, if that ain't a hint that America planned to whack Iraq and take its oil, then I surely don't know what is.

By the way, just so as you know, Dick Cheney refused to make public a whole series of documents from his Energy Taskforce. In June 2004, the US Supreme Court declined to compel Cheney to release secret papers detailing meetings of the Energy Taskforce. Judicial Watch has been trying to get its hands on the documents since 2002. The Sierra Club, the US lobby group which campaigns on environmental issues, also filed a suit for access to the papers. The two organisations believe the Bush administration was way too close to Enron.

Well, surely the Supreme Court can't be in on this, too, can it? Umm

... well, Justice Antonin Scalia did refuse to step down from hearing the case against Cheney even though he'd taken a hunting holiday with the Vice-president at the very time when the court was actually considering the verdict. Judge Scalia, by the way, played an integral role in securing the 2000 presidency for Bush even though Dubya lost the popular vote. Eugene Scalia, Antonin Scalia's son, was a lawyer with Gibson, Dunn & Crutcher, the law firm that represented Bush before the Supreme Court over the election debacle in November 2000. The Supreme Court gave the election to Bush by ruling that the ballot counting had to stop.

It was Scalia who gave the explanation – even though his own kid was acting for Bush. Here's what he said: 'The counting of votes that are of questionable legality does, in my view, threaten irreparable harm to petitioner [Bush], and to the country, by casting a cloud on what he [Bush] claims to be the legitimacy of his election.' What that means is 'we have to make Dubya the president as all this ballot-counting and stuff is making him sad'.

Let freedom reign and oil flow!

HOW THE LIES WERE TOLD: PART I

or

Inside the wicked, wicked world of the UK's secret spying spin machine

OK. So we know that weapons of mass destruction had very little to do, really, with the decision to whack Iraq. We know that concerns over oil and empire were a lot more significant than the old vials of anthrax or canisters of VX that we'd sold Saddam and then couldn't find.

But how were we – that's Britain and America – going to get our mitts on Saddam; how were our governments going to finagle the unleashing of our two countries' armed forces in order to kick his ass? How were we going to get around the tricky fact that Saddam really didn't have much in the way of weapons anymore? Sure, he had some sticks and rocks and could throw sand in our eyes, but all the really nasty kit had been eliminated after the First Gulf War. The facts – those bastards – showed that Saddam was pretty much compliant with UN disarmament requirements. So how were we going to twist the truth – some would call that lie – and make it look as if Saddam was up to his sweaty little armpits in illegal weapons?

Our governments did what governments have been doing down the ages to their peoples. They lied: big-time. They lied like a person who's just been diagnosed a compulsive liar. They lied like someone bred from the pure DNA of George Bush and Tony Blair. They lied like politicians.

A more polite way to put it would be to say that the Labour government 'politicised intelligence'. Politicising intelligence works this way: imagine that I'm the Prime Minister, or the President, or the Vice-president or maybe even the Defence Secretary or the Foreign Secretary. I say to one of my spy chiefs: 'Oh, Spy Chief, come here, please. Take a seat. I would like you to go away and find out lots of bad stuff about Iraq for me. I'm not really interested in any of the good stuff. Just find me stuff that makes Saddam look evil and scary. Thank you, Spy Chief, your knighthood is in the post.'

The Spy Chief goes away and tells his spies: 'Spies, oh my spies, go forth and find me bad things about Saddam. None of that stuff about him getting rid of his weapons, OK? Just find me nasty stuff. Stuff that makes him look dangerous. Thank you, your promotions are in the post.'

The spies then go for cream teas and spy-cakes in the spy canteen and look at each other over the rims of their china cups and think 'we're screwed'. The big problem for Britain's spies was that the best available intelligence showed that although Saddam was obviously very mad indeed, he was also very un-armed. The other big problem for Britain and America is that really good spying depends on what the spooks call 'humint' – human intelligence. You and I would call this 'other spies'. If MI6 had a spy in one of Saddam's presidential palaces – that's humint. If the CIA had a spy at the top of the Iraqi army – that's humint. It's men and women on the ground in Iraq in important positions who will tell our spies something that's secret.

Countries like France and Russia had lots of 'humint' on Iraq. We didn't. How do I know this? Well, I spoke to our spies for a start. The *Sunday Herald* had, in the run-up to war, briefings with plenty of disgruntled spies and military brass in both the UK and America. It wasn't just me listening to spooks giving their tuppence worth on the folly of the planned invasion, there were at least three other senior members of staff getting regular briefings from within the 'intelligence community' about the misuse and abuse of intelligence as well.

Most of the chat came in the form of whining from low-level staff in the intelligence community. They'd talk about low morale, about how staff were pissed off at the path the government was taking. They'd continually say we didn't have the humint in Iraq to be able to say what we were saying – namely that Saddam was armed to the teeth and a danger to Britain. Some talked about the cherry-picking of intelligence – about staff being asked to select certain types of information which suited the government's agenda. In other words, spooks were being told to go off and find info that showed Saddam was dangerous, and to overlook info that showed him UN-compliant. Once again, I would call that a lie.

This was good stuff. But it was just a selection of moans, groans, complaints and accusations from fairly ordinary and anonymous folk not very high up the chain of command in the British and American intelligence services.

Then, one day, I decided to give Scott Ritter another call. I couldn't work out how the British government had the audacity to make crazy claims – like the one which said that Saddam could hit UK targets with weapons of mass destruction within 45 minutes – if the intelligence to back up such an allegation didn't exist. I wanted to know how the government could think it could get away with such totally behemoth-sized lies.

If I was cynical about the government before I placed this call to Mr Ritter, I was capable of believing anything after I hung up. He revealed everything he knew about a British intelligence operation called Operation Rockingham. Put bluntly, Operation Rockingham was used as much against the British people as it was against the Iraqi people. While it may have justified the wholesale killing of thousands of Iraqis, it made the British people complicit in this slaughter by turning known lies into truth. It was the most grotesque little experiment in deception and myth-making that I'd ever heard of in my life. It poisoned the minds of the British population, making it seem for the citizens of the UK that truth was lies and lies were the truth.

When I found out about Operation Rockingham, the *Sunday Herald* ran the story on its front page under this headline: REVEALED: THE SECRET CABAL WHICH SPUN FOR BLAIR. That was a little unfair to Blair because Rockingham had been running long before he ever got a whiff of the toilet that is Number 10, but it was Blair who used Rockingham in the vilest way.

In effect, Rockingham was a covert dirty tricks operation designed solely, it would seem, to produce misleading intelligence that pointed towards Saddam having weapons of mass destruction. It'd been doing this for years, but the nonsense it was churning out didn't see the light of day, or have much relevance for ordinary British people, until, of course, Blair started to up the tempo of the drums of war. It was then that some 'facts' were required to provide him with a justifiable excuse to wage war against Iraq alongside the US.

Operation Rockingham was established by the Defence Intelligence Staff (DIS) within the British Ministry of Defence in 1991 after the end of the First Gulf War. Its creation had one purpose: to cherry-pick intelligence proving an active WMD programme in Iraq and to ignore and quash intelligence which indicated that Saddam's stockpiles had been destroyed or wound down. Rockingham, then, treated the truth in the same way my children treat their Christmas dinner. They like the gravy, turkey and the stuffing, so they'll have some of that, but they hate the sprouts, the spuds and the buttered carrots, so they won't be having any of that, thank you very much. I really can't be bothered with the term cherry-picking – it's 'spookese' for a lie and I think in these days of double-talk that we need to call it what it is, and to me a lie is a lie. If a person knows that 95 per cent of all the information at their disposal points towards something not being true – such as Saddam having a WMD arsenal – but uses the remaining 5 per cent of the facts they have to prove that this lie is in fact true – then, to me anyway, they're just liars. And that's precisely, according to Ritter, what the boys and girls over at Operation Rockingham were doing.

Ritter, who you will remember is the former UN Chief Weapons Inspector and a US Military Intelligence Officer, said he knew members of the Rockingham team. He'd worked with them and they'd told him exactly what they were up to. Today, he describes the unit as 'dangerous'. He says – and this is important – that there is no way you could describe the Rockingham team as 'rogue agents' acting without government backing. 'The policy was coming from the very highest levels,' he says. The Rockingham team was simply doing what they were paid for – following the orders of their political masters. Just like the soldiers in Iraq who know that sticking a hood over a teenager's head is wrong or the pilots who know that dropping explosives on residential areas is wrong, these men did what they did because to do otherwise would end their careers. And, you know, sometimes it's hard for good people to question those who stand in authority over them, especially when you believe that the cost of your mortgage or the kids' school fees outweigh the price to be paid for the sin of helping to lie your country into a pointless and illegal war.

'Rockingham was spinning reports, and emphasising reports that showed non-compliance [by Iraq with UN inspections] and quashing those reports which showed compliance,' Ritter told me. 'It was cherry-picking intelligence.'

All this came amid that small kerfuffle, you may remember, to do with the BBC claiming that the government had 'sexed up' the intelligence about Saddam's weapons. Sexed up? If Operation Rockingham was anything to go by, Blair and his boys had pumped the intelligence full of Viagra, fed it a diet of Amsterdam hardcore porn and paid for it to go on a have-it-away-day in Madame Cyn's House of Pain. Sexed up? This intelligence was so hot and horny that it didn't know whether it was coming or going.

Ritter was not the only current or former member of the intelligence services on both sides of the Atlantic who I spoke to about Rockingham – but he was the only one to go on the record. Ritter and these other sources said without hesitation that the staff of Operation Rockingham and MI6 were supplying skewed information to the Joint Intelligence Committee – you remember the old JIC, don't you? That's the little British committee which signed off on Blair's so-called dodgy dossier about Iraq's non-existent weapons of mass destruction; the dossier that ludicrously said Saddam could hit UK assets with WMD within 45 minutes. That, as we all know, turned out to be unadulterated bullshit. Saddam didn't have the wherewithal in 2003 to hit himself in his own arse with a missile in under 45 minutes, let alone bomb a UK 'asset' with chemicals. But once you realise that the JIC was getting handed these heavily skewed reports from the Rockingham crew, you can quickly see how it could publish such nonsense.

Yet, didn't the man who was the chairman of the JIC, John Scarlett, get promoted after the war to become the head of MI6? Call me a cynic, but I tend to think that anyone that high-up in the intelligence community must have known of the existence of Operation Rockingham and therefore must have known that the information that the JIC was using to say Saddam was armed and dangerous was rubbish in the first place. Scarlett was also the first chairman of the JIC to come from within the intelligence community. Up until his appointment, the head of the JIC was usually some career civil servant/policy-wonk type. Scarlett's very appointment to the chairmanship of the JIC pointed towards the increased politicisation of intelligence under Blair.

What we are left with then is an un-virtuous circle of lying. It really does make your head spin. The politicians tell the spies to go and find them some skewed facts. The spies pass this fake information to the JIC, which is run by spies, and the JIC then turns this skewed info into a dossier which is then given to the politicians. The politicians then use the dossier based on lies to terrify the British public and Parliament and convince us all that war's a must. Is it possible to think of a more debased system of governing? Using lies of your own making to back up lies which you are yet to tell. Blair duped us all. He duped Parliament, he duped the public, he even duped his own intelligence services as they are the ones who come out of all this looking like liars and idiots, while

Blair and his cronies can blame it all on inept spooks. There are more than a few in Britain's spying community who believe Blair has done more damage to the reputation of British intelligence than Philby, Burgess, MacLean and every other Soviet era double-agent in British spying history put together ever did.

Intelligence sources have made clear to me on a number of occasions that the JIC was following political instructions. When I contacted the MoD and Number 10 and asked them what they had to say about Ritter's revelations regarding Operation Rockingham, they sighed like I was an idiot and reminded me that 'the government never comments on security matters'. I found this an hilarious answer. For months we'd been listening to the government tell us Saddam was a threat to security, but here they were refusing to utter a word about security. When they say, 'We don't comment on security matters', what they actually mean is, 'Piss off, your story will embarrass my master, you irritating prick.'

The staff of Operation Rockingham deliberately overlooked 'mountains' of mainstream reports and intelligence documents, said Ritter, which proved that Saddam was destroying his arsenal. Instead they depended on a handful of 'selective intelligence' from just a tiny pool of data and used this to create a false and misleading picture that Saddam was a threat to the west.

'As inspections developed throughout the 1990s,' Ritter said, 'it became clear that Unscom was accomplishing a great deal. This became a liability for the UK and the US. Because of the level of Iraqi disarmament, France, China and Russia began talking about lifting sanctions. This wasn't what Britain and America wanted to hear – they wanted sanctions and regime change.

'Operation Rockingham became part of an effort to maintain a public mindset that Iraq was not in compliance with the inspections. They had to sustain the allegation that Iraq had weapons of mass destruction, even though Unscom was showing the opposite.'

Operation Rockingham staff, said Ritter, began to liaise with Unscom – ostensibly the liaison was meant to share intelligence with the UN weapons inspectors from within the UK's spying community, but it soon became clear that this covert operation had a hidden agenda: deliberately turning Saddam into a clear and present danger who was armed to the teeth in the eyes of the British people.

'Operation Rockingham,' says Ritter, 'received hard data but had a pre-ordained outcome in mind. It only put forward a small percentage of the facts when most were ambiguous or noted no WMD.' Some staff connected to Rockingham were believed to be linked to the Iraqi Survey Group (ISG) which hunted fruitlessly in post-invasion Iraq for those damned elusive weapons of mass destruction.

Interestingly, John Scarlett – he of the chairmanship of the JIC and now head of MI6 – sent an email to the head of the ISG, Charles Duelfer, way back in March 2004. In the email Scarlett asked Duelfer to include 10 'golden nuggets' in the ISG's report on WMD in Iraq, including claims that Iraq had smallpox weapons, possessed mobile bio-weapons labs and that Saddam was developing a 'rail gun' which could propel an object at enormous speed along a track. Given that none of these things is true (do you remember getting infected with smallpox?) Scarlett's suggestion to Duelfer sounds a little like good old Rockingham-style cherry-picking to me.

The man who made the claim about the email was Tom Mangold, a respected journalist and a close friend of the family of Dr David Kelly. Dr David Kelly was the British weapons expert who killed himself after being exposed as the source behind the BBC claim that the government 'sexed up' its dossier on Iraqi weapons. David Kelly, who was also a UN weapons inspector, testified before Parliament's Intelligence and Security Committee, the day before he died, that he had worked with Operation Rockingham. Kelly said simply: 'I liaise with the Rockingham cell.' This being Britain, no-one took a blind bit of notice of what he was saying as no-one knew then what Operation Rockingham was, and being Britain no-one really could be bothered to find out. The Butler Inquiry into intelligence failures in Iraq also proved the existence of Operation Rockingham – more than a year after I revealed its existence and duplicitous shenanigans in the *Sunday Herald* – by including a few pedestrian paragraphs on its connection to Unscom in its report.

Kelly, said Ritter, was Rockingham's 'go-to person for translating the often confusing data that came out of Unscom into concise reporting that could be forwarded to analysts in the British intelligence community as well as political decision-makers'. Kelly, then, was intimate with Rockingham and appears to have been one of the operation's key technical assets. If there was ever a guy who knew about 'sexing-up', then, it must have been Dr David Kelly.

Ritter also contends that Kelly – at least for a while – supported the government's position on Iraq, and hinted that he helped shape public opinion with his frequent discussions with journalists.

'Given Rockingham's penetration of Unscom at virtually every level,' said Ritter, 'there existed a seamless flow of data from Iraq, through New York to London, carefully shaped from beginning to end by people working not for the UN Security Council, but for the British government. Iraq's guilt, pre-ordained by the government, became a self-fulfilling prophesy that only collapsed when occupied Iraq failed to disgorge that which Rockingham and the rest of the UK intelligence community had said must exist.'

'Rockingham,' he added later, 'institutionalised a process of cherry-picking intelligence produced by the UN inspections in Iraq that skewed UK intelligence about Iraqi WMD towards a pre-ordained outcome that was more in line with British government policy than it was reflective of ground truth.

'Operation Rockingham was, in fact, more reflective of an institutionalised predisposition towards the politicised massaging of intelligence data that resulted in the massive failure of intelligence that we all have tragically witnessed regarding Iraq and WMD.

'The role played by Operation Rockingham in this failure should be fully investigated by an independent committee of Parliament.'

To back up his claims that Operation Rockingham was deliberately 'cherry-picking' intelligence and producing misleading reports, Ritter described the inner workings of the operation and revealed how its staff blatantly ignored proof of Saddam's compliance. 'Britain and America were involved in a programme of joint exploitation of intelligence from Iraqi defectors,' he said. 'There were mountains of information coming from these defectors, and Rockingham staff were receiving it and then selectively culling reports that sustained the claims that weapons of mass destruction were in existence. They ignored the vast majority of the data which mitigated against such claims.'

Think back to that 45-minute warning. Remember that it came from a single source. This is exactly the type of fake and exaggerated rubbish that Rockingham excelled in making fact. Its staff would wade through the de-briefings of countless Iraqi defectors all telling the same bland un-usable truth about what they knew: that Saddam was effectively compliant. Then a lone report from a single Iraqi source would pass their desk claiming to have proof of Saddam's WMD programmes and they'd be jumping for joy. Of course, these single Iraqi sources were inevitably linked to someone like Iyad Allawi, of the anti-Saddam exile group the Iraqi National Accord (INA), who later became the leader of the 'new' post-invasion Iraqi interim government. Without wishing to state the obvious, the interim government was seen by many of Allawi's fellow countrymen and women as a puppet regime of the British and Americans.

If these single Iraqi sources weren't connected to the INA, then they were usually linked to another dodgy outfit like the Iraqi National Congress (the discredited exile organisation headed by the discredited Ahmed Chalabi).

One such lone report – coming from a single source and connected to Iyad Allawi – was indeed the 45-minute claim; a claim which the people of Britain subsequently learned was absurd. It later turned out that the Iraqi military source, one Lieutenant-Colonel al-Dabbagh, behind this particular piece of 'intelligence' had in fact never seen inside the purported chemical weapons crates upon which his 45-minute claim was based. The information was passed from al-Dabbagh to his brother-in-law General A J M Muhie who helped get the claim to the London HQ of the Iraqi National Accord.

People like Allawi and Chalabi would literally have done anything to get rid of Saddam (post-invasion they both vied to run the country, after all) and some of their followers and fellow-travellers were more than happy to just make stuff up about Saddam. Quite why anyone needed to make things up about a genocidal, invasion-happy psychopath is beyond me, but maybe Britain and America felt they needed that extra make-believe cherry on top of the Saddam cake of horrors. It wasn't really all that bad, surely, to add a few extra crimes to the already long and ugly charge sheet of a total bastard? Why not throw in the odd claim that there was a bio-weapons site up and running or that Saddam could chemicalise British bases in Cyprus in the time it takes to watch an episode of *ER*? The motive for these unnecessary lies was that a few leading Iraqi defectors of the INC/Allawi-stripe realised that Saddam needed to be constantly represented to the west as a fresh, current threat, not some old bogeyman from history. They wanted him gone now, they couldn't hang around for natural wastage to do away with Saddam, so a few lies fed to Britain and America – with Britain and America happy in the knowledge that they were being handed the very lies they wanted to hear – helped oil the war machine and get the public in the mood for shock and awe.

'In theory, Rockingham wasn't dangerous,' says Ritter, 'In theory, it was a clearing house for intelligence. But what is dangerous is the policy behind Rockingham. When I was an intelligence officer, I didn't tell my commander what he wanted to hear, I told him what the facts were. In combat, we have an old saying – if you lie, you die.

'Operations like Rockingham become a danger to democracy if they lose their integrity. They are behind the scenes, in the shadows and away from public scrutiny. When a government is corrupt by way of such a policy, the public has a hard time holding the government accountable. We were all subject to a programme of mass deception, but now the lie has been exposed. In practice, Rockingham was dangerous.'

Ritter insists that the intelligence officers involved in cherry-picking selective intelligence were acting directly on political orders. 'In terms of using selective intelligence,' he says, 'this policy was coming from the very highest levels.' Until Ritter spoke out, the only written reference to Operation Rockingham was to be found in a 1998 parliamentary report. In it, Brigadier Richard Holmes, who was giving evidence to the defence committee, refers, in what appears to be an off-the-cuff aside, to Operation Rockingham and linked it to Unscom inspections in Iraq.

Ritter was loath to expose too much information about the men and women who worked inside Rockingham – and it is to his credit – because of the risk to their personal security. What he would say, however, was that the staff included some military officers, others came from the ranks of the intelligence services such as MI6 and others were civilian MoD personnel. From 1991 to 1998, it had three chiefs – one man and two women – and anyone who headed up Operation Rockingham was guaranteed a very senior intelligence job after their stint running the unit.

Its tactics, Ritter says, included leaking false information to the weapons inspectors, and then using the resulting inspectors' search of an Iraqi site as 'proof' of the existence of WMD. You have to marvel at such a strategy for its low-down dirtiness. 'Rockingham was the source, in 1993, of some very controversial information which led to inspections of a suspected ballistic missile site,' said Ritter. 'We went to search for the missiles but found nothing. However, our act of searching allowed the US and UK to say that the missiles existed.'

The Unscom inspectors, says Ritter, were 'played like fiddles' by the Rockingham team. Ritter repeatedly offered to give evidence – to both the Hutton Inquiry into the death of Dr David Kelly and the Butler Inquiry into the use of British intelligence on Iraqi WMD – about the nature of Operation Rockingham. His offer was never accepted.

Surprise, surprise, Ritter's revelations caused a few spies I know, who were full supporters of the war, to ask questions about the behaviour of the government and the role their agencies had in ramping up the case for war. One, who had strong personal links to the military, told me: 'I'd like to know if troops were sacrificed because we kept hyping up weapons of mass destruction.'

MI6, according to Ritter and other intelligence sources I interviewed after speaking to him, was also involved in this 'selective intelligence gathering' using handpicked intelligence sources 'to sustain the concept of WMD. Other sources who contradicted evidence about WMD were ignored. Only data which sustained the myth was used'.

Ritter is clear that this skewed info gathered by the Rockingham team and MI6 would have ended up in the hands of the JIC. One source in British intelligence said the JIC, or at least some members of it, knew that the information it was handling was unreliable, distorted and cherry-picked, but nevertheless used these twisted facts to help the government build a fabricated case for war.

This contra-flowing web of deceit created by the politicians and acquiesced to by the spooks played into Blair's hands wonderfully. When Blair came under attack in the Commons for sexing-up information – particularly the 45-minute claim – he could say that there was 'no attempt by any official or minister … to override the intelligence judgements of the JIC, including the so-called 45-minutes, a judgement made by the JIC and by them alone'. Of course, he is technically right. No minister did override the JIC on the 45-minute claim because everyone knew what the rules of the game were – and the spies had climbed into bed with the government, ripped off their knickers and got down to some serious whoring for their political paymasters. The spies knew just what the politicians wanted so they didn't have to be told what to say – that was the sublime nature of the operation.

I can equate this, a little, to some of the worst follies of journalism. All journalists know editors who ask reporters to go out and find them a story on topic X. It may well be that topic X is rubbish, or that topic X doesn't exist, but if you don't come back with a story on topic X then you are in trouble. In some newspapers it is implicit in the reporter–editor relationship that you do what you are told – even if it means telling lies; lies that could seriously hurt other people. Similarly, the government, by asking for info on Saddam's WMD programme and making it clear that it wanted to receive this data come what may, were implicitly telling British spies to 'go out and find us some bullshit lies we can tell the people'; the spies duly complied and handed it to a JIC controlled by a government placeman spy. The JIC then wrote a dossier giving the government exactly what it wanted in the first place. The whole process is, as one ex-military intelligence officer told me, a 'mind fuck'. That's precisely what the government did to us – used skewed information which was gathered and processed in such a convoluted manner that we couldn't do anything else but believe that the WMD claims were all true at the time that the information was being given to us. It was disgusting but masterly.

At the time, though, when these lies were being spun, there were a few good guys ready to stand up and tell the truth. Not all of them, like Ritter, were prepared to go on the record, as they had families and mortgages like the rest of us; and not only did they fear for their livelihoods, they also risked a few years in jail under the Official Secrets Act if they were caught blabbing to bothersome reporters. One guy springs to mind. I contacted him regarding the 45-minute claim and asked him what he thought of it. His answer was: 'Bollocks'. It didn't really give me a lot to go on in terms of quotes for a story, but at least he was being straight with me. The 45-minute claim he said was from an unreliable Iraqi source and the vast majority of information stemming from this source was 'fabricated'.

This has all been a disaster for British intelligence. 'Old school' spies I spoke to – guys who fought the Cold War in places like West Berlin during the 1960s and 1970s – say Blair has ruined their profession. Spying was never a gentleman's game, they admit, but ultimately it lives or dies on intelligence officers being able to tell politicians the absolute truth so that decisions can be taken in the best interests of the UK and its people. Blair closed that gap, that buffer zone, between the intelligence community and the government. The intelligence community became a politicised arm of the Labour Party, not an independent part of government. By allowing this to happen, the spies committed professional suicide because they found themselves in the firing line over the lies and spin that went into Blair's case for war. The Prime Minister was able to continually pass responsibility for the nature of the intelligence on to the spies rather than on to people like him – the politicians – by saying things like: 'The intelligence that formed the basis of what we put out [in September 2002 in the 'dodgy dossier'], that intelligence came from JIC assessments.' What he doesn't say is that it was British government policies which corrupted the JIC in the first place making it a tool of British government deception. Now the JIC is disgraced, MI6 is saddled with a wounded leader in the shape of John Scarlett, a man who everyone takes as a government lap-dog who sold his soul, and British intelligence is humiliated once again around the world. Many people joke that British intelligence is the ultimate oxymoron – they are wrong. I've met many men and women who serve or have served in British intelligence and they have mostly been honourable, brave and decent – it's their political leaders who are the disgrace.

Imagine if Britain really were in peril from a foreign power tomorrow – maybe an Iran armed with nuclear weapons – who would believe our leaders then? That is the real danger to national security and that's thanks to Tony Blair. As many in the spying community today believe, Britain is more at risk now than ever before. The war made the world a more dangerous place to be British, not a safer one.

One politician who stands out as decent among all the other horrors that crowd the benches of the House of Commons is Michael Meacher, Blair's former Environment Minister. Here was a senior politician who attacked the government over Operation Rockingham and he did so after voting for the war – a decision, he says, which he took because, like so many other decent Brits, he believed what the Prime Minister was telling him at the time. 'Within the UK intelligence establishment – MI6, MI5, GCHQ and defence intelligence,' Meacher said, 'Rockingham had a central, though covert, role in seeking to prove an active Iraqi WMD programme.'

Referring to what he calls the 'shoe-horning of intelligence data to fit pre-fixed political goals,' Meacher says that 'Rockingham was an important tributary flowing into the government's rationale for the war'. Disinformation, according to Meacher, 'served the Rockingham purpose only too well'.

He's right. Not long before his death, Dr David Kelly told Parliament's Intelligence and Security Committee that there was only a '30 per cent probability' that Saddam had WMD. Instead, all the public got fed was a diet of headlines like *The Sun*'s BRITS 45 MINS FROM DOOM. 'Rarely,' says Meacher, 'can the selective use of information have had such drastic consequences.

Lies, then, became the currency of this war. As Scott Ritter said: 'Not one single piece of information was proved. We went to war based on garbage.'

Miscellaneous Porky Pies – Operation Mass Appeal

Here's another little jewel in the crown of British intelligence which Scott Ritter blew the whistle on: Operation Mass Appeal. Imagine that you're a British spy and you want to get some bullshit facts out there in the public domain and the mass media, but you don't want it traced back to you. Nor do you want to annoy British newspaper editors if they rumble that the facts you are trying to peddle are as false as a Labour Party manifesto pledge. What do you do? It's such a dilemma. I'll give you a little clue. It beings with 'l' and ends in 'ie'.

Why not invent a ridiculous sounding intelligence operation and then instruct all your spooks who have contact with journalists (half of them probably are journalists) to plant fake facts in the foreign press about how scary Iraq really is? Hey presto! You've got Operation Mass Appeal on your hands, created solely to gently coax the British public around to believing that Saddam was armed to the gunnels and that his country should be invaded.

Initially, Operation Mass Appeal was there to prop up the sanctions regime, but it soon became a conduit for planting stories in papers which showed that there was no other way to deal with Saddam but military intervention.

It was launched in the late 1990s on Tony Blair's watch and saw claims crop up – or 'surface' as the spooks like to say – about Saddam developing nerve agents and other evil super weapons of doom. These appeared in newspapers in countries like Poland or India or South Africa. Nations which were all non-aligned at the time.

Once the stories appeared in a foreign paper, dumb-ass British reporters would leap on them joyfully as free copy and reprint them back home. It was a job well done as far as the government was concerned, and it just goes to show you how useless so much of the British press really is. Too many journalists are lazy, conservative by nature, cheerleaders for the Establishment and the ruling class and unquestioning supporters of the status quo. Another swathe is so cynical that the bulk of them have had a humanity-bypass and barely blink when confronted with something truly immoral. Operation Mass Appeal was the perfect confection to feed lazy, drugged and jaded little sheep. You know when you hear about a journalist taking a politician to lunch? Well, think Operation Mass Appeal on a tiny scale. That journalist is there so he or she can repeat to you in print the lies that the politician is telling him or her face-to-face. The hack is your bullshit intermediary; your crap channel. That's freedom of information for you in Britain today.

The government has admitted that Operation Mass Appeal did exist, but swears that no misinformation was planted. Yeah, right. One government spokesman even had the audacity to say: 'There were things about Saddam's regime and his weapons that the public needed to know.' What he meant to say was: 'There were made-up things about Saddam's regime and his non-existent weapons that we wanted the public to know.' I often wonder how these 'government spokesmen' – who are, after all, supposed to be unpartisan civil servants – sleep at night.

Ritter says he sat in on meetings where MI6 officers discussed the best way to manipulate public opinion. 'The aim was to convince the public that Iraq was a far greater threat than it actually was,' he added. 'Stories ran in the media about secret underground facilities in Iraq and on-going programmes [to produce WMD]. They were sourced to western intelligence and all of them were garbage.'

One of the key figures involved in Operation Mass Appeal was Sir Derek Plumbly, former director of the Middle East department at the Foreign Office and now the UK's Ambassador to Egypt. Plumbly worked hand-in-glove with MI6 to promote the UK's Middle East policy.

Ritter met two men and a woman from MI6 at a lunch in London in June 1998 to discuss Operation Mass Appeal. They discussed what information could be planted in foreign papers which would inevitably 'feed back' to Britain and America. 'What MI6 was determined to do by the selective use of intelligence was to give the impression that Saddam still had WMD or was making them, and thereby legitimise sanctions and military action against Iraq.'

Ritter again pointed to Dr David Kelly's possible involvement in underhand intelligence activities, either wittingly or unwittingly, when he noted that Kelly may have been used by MI6 to pass on fake facts to journalists. 'Kelly was a known and government-approved conduit with the media,' he said. What an irony that Kelly's own flirtation with the BBC contributed to his suicide and caused the playing-card walls of the government's case for war to come tumbling down.

This use of MI6 as a so-called 'back channel' for government lies was judged a success by all those involved. The cack that was being printed in the papers about Saddam hiding his weapons and building assorted doom-machines ramped up public support for sanctions and laid the foundation stones for the British people and Parliament listlessly backing the inevitable use of military force. It's a wonder that MI6 didn't get totally carried away and plant a story saying that Saddam had developed a laser on the moon or a Death Star with which he planned to destroy the entire planet. If they had, then the press mob in the UK would have sucked it up like leeches and run a graphic showing Saddam kitted out in a full Darth Vadar Nazi space-costume under the headline EARTH: 45 MINUTES FROM SPACE-STATION DESTRUCTION.

HOW THE LIES WERE TOLD:
PART II
or
Inside the wicked, wicked world of the USA's
secret spying spin machine

Not to be outdone by the Brits and Operation Rockingham, the Americans created their own little *ad hoc* lie factory. It was given the wonderfully Orwellian name of 'The Office of Special Plans'.

The Office of Special Plans had one purpose – to twist any fact that its staff could get their hands on and make it look as if Saddam was a threat to the west, linked to Osama bin Laden and engaged in developing weapons of mass destruction.

What the OSP did was make sure that the politicians got precisely the kind of information they wanted to get when it came to Saddam and Iraq. Right back at the very start of the Bush II presidency, the administration began overtly seeking out the sort of intelligence that the hawks wanted to see on Saddam – you know, stuff on nukes, sarin, anthrax and so on. Once the OSP gathered the faked-up info that the administration was looking for it was 'stovepiped' – as intelligence insiders put it – to the Prez and the VP. Bush and Cheney were handed the OSP's garbage without real intelligence experts, like analysts in the CIA, getting a look at it first. Kenneth Pollack, a former National Security Council expert on Iraq, says the Bush administration, in its haste to invade Iraq, managed to dismantle an intelligence filtering system that had been in place since the end of the Second World War.

The story of the OSP begins just as Bush comes to power in late 2000. The very first meeting of Bush's National Security Council, in January 2001, pinpointed Iraq for regime change. But the problem for Bush and Cheney and Rumsfeld was that the CIA and the conventional intelligence agencies just weren't coming up with the goods on Saddam. According to those stupid spooks, Saddam was pretty much disarmed,

111

not really trying to build up a WMD arsenal and on similar terms with Osama bin Laden as the Rev. Dr Ian Paisley is with Gerry Adams.

In January 2001, Ahmed Chalabi's Iraqi National Congress – within the ranks of which there were Iraqis who felt they had to make things up about Saddam to get him removed by the US – started getting big wodges of cash from the American government. This was under what was called the 'Information Collection Programme' which existed to help them buy up defectors who could then start spilling the beans on Saddam's links to terror and his WMD arsenal to American spies.

Just to remind you about the INC – Vince Cannistraro, the former head of CIA counter-terrorism, says this about the Iraqi group's so-called intelligence: 'Much of it is propaganda. Much of it is telling the Defense Department what they want to hear, using alleged informants and defectors who say what Chalabi wants them to say, [creating] cooked information that goes right into presidential and vice-presidential speeches.' Cannistraro says that although Bush and his crew wanted Saddam's nuts in a vice, 'the administration had to find the rationale to do it. So they set up a secretive group which started producing information on Iraq that was more compatible than the CIA.' That group was the OSP – an organisation which Cannistraro refers to as 'the bat cave'. It eventually grew out of the Information Collection Programme.

The Information Collection Programme, says Colonel Patrick Lang, a former intelligence officer specialising in the Middle East with the Defense Intelligence Agency (DIA), provided 'a steady stream of raw information useful in challenging the collective wisdom of the intelligence community where the "War with Iraq" enthusiasts disagreed with the intelligence agencies'. In other words, the American taxpayer forked out billions a year to pay for US intelligence agencies, but because Bush and his cronies didn't like what spies in the CIA were telling them, they invented a new and very costly way to get the information they wanted – namely getting exiled Iraqis to make up the claims that they needed to justify the toppling of Saddam. You know what the bottom line was? The CIA's analysts were telling the truth, or at least a version of the truth which dovetailed with the available facts the agency had to hand, and Bush and his hangers-on didn't like that. They wanted some good old juicy lies – ahem, 'strategic intelligence' – that they could use to terrify and confuse the US public. After the invasion, someone inside the Defense Intelligence Agency leaked a report which found that the INC had not provided any real intelligence to America at all. You can't really blame the disgruntled DIA staffer who leaked the document. The OSP, which peddled the myths and fairytales of Iraqi exiles, had, after all, been set up within the Pentagon to directly push the DIA into the cold and give Rumsfeld an alternative source of intelligence which he could use to target Saddam.

In order to sell the war, says Lang, 'information had to be available with which to argue against what was seen as the lack of imagination and timidity of regular intelligence analysts. To facilitate the flow of such "information" to the president, a dedicated apparatus centred in the Office of the Vice-president created its own intelligence office, buried in the recesses of the Pentagon, to "stovepipe" raw data to the White House, to make the case for war on the basis of the testimony of self-interested émigrés and exiles.'

These people – the Bush administration – always wanted to hit Iraq, they just couldn't figure out a way to get the American public to go along with their scheme. On September 15, 2001, at a war-cabinet meeting at Camp David following the hits on the World Trade Center and the Pentagon, Paul Wolfowitz urged an immediate invasion of Iraq – not Afghanistan, where the Taliban was playing host to al-Qaeda. Why? Because, in Wolfie's words, Iraq was 'do-able' and because America one day 'would have to go after Saddam at some time if the war on terrorism was to be taken seriously'. On September 17, Bush signed a top secret directive detailing the invasion of both Afghanistan and Iraq.

With the decision now inked onto paper that America would take out Saddam, it was time for the Information Collection Programme to morph into something a lot more sinister – something that would quickly provide the lies to justify a pointless war to the American people. Come October 2001, the Pentagon's Under-Secretary of Defence for Policy, Douglas Feith, had created a tiny intelligence cell which he ordered to trawl through all existing government databanks for anything that might link Saddam to the 9-11 attacks. The cell was known as the Policy Counter-Terrorism Evaluation Group. This organisation was under the command of Rumsfeld, but was the brainchild of Paul Wolfowitz. Both men allowed Feith to turn it into his private fiefdom. The Policy Counter-Terrorism Evaluation Group, and the INC informants who were linked to the Information Collection Programme, were the forerunners of the OSP. Staff inside the OSP, incidentally, would later go on to proudly describe themselves as 'the cabal'.

Claims that Saddam was linked to 9-11 were treated as gibberish by respected, professional members of the intelligence community. Here's Colonel Lang on that subject: 'The permanent, statutory agencies of the national intelligence community could not support such beliefs on the basis of what they saw in their own files. Therefore, some other means was sought to obtain the conclusion that the Iraqi Government had been involved in 9-11.

'The team's mission was to cull the massive holdings of the intelligence database and to uncover intelligence reports accumulated on the subject of Iraq/al-Qaeda links. The issue of whether or not the intelligence agencies considered these reports to be true was thought immaterial. Not surprisingly, some of the sweetest cherries picked in the data searches came from informants provided by the INC's Information Collection Programme.'

This gross manipulation of wholly untrustworthy information under the direction of Douglas Feith gave rise to what US intelligence insiders sarcastically labelled 'Feith-based intelligence' – faith-based, feith-based – geddit? Feith was a great guy for getting his buddies and fellow travellers good jobs. Back in 1996, Feith had authored a study for Israel's right-wing Likud Party which advocated toppling Saddam because he posed the greatest threat to the state of Israel. Another member of the team which authored that report was David Wurmser, a fellow of the pro-Israeli American Enterprise Institute – an organisation which seems to be something of a frat house for the Bush neocons.

Guess who Feith chose to start his cherry-picking operation at the Policy Counter-Terrorism Evaluation Group? Why, it was David Wurmser. He began sucking in every piece of nonsense that the INC's handpicked informants from the Information Collection Programme could pass his way.

It was only a matter of time until the cherry-picking exercise was given a more permanent form. This is where retired Navy captain and arch neocon William Luti comes into play. After his appointment by Cheney to take over the Pentagon's Near East and South Asian Affairs (NESA) office – the team which deals with the Middle East – Luti began to systematically 'de-professionalise' NESA of its intelligence officers. The Iraq desk of NESA was soon to morph into the Office of Special Plans, and the last thing that those with a political agenda wanted around them in the Pentagon were objective analysts who might have told them something they didn't want to hear: namely, the truth.

To get a handle on some of the other characters running the Pentagon, let's take a look at Harold Rhode. Feith got Rhode to help organise the plans for the invasion of Iraq. And it was Rhode who, like Luti, also started purging the professionals from the Pentagon, and undermining all those long-standing defence officials who refused to buy the neocon argument about Iraq and couldn't bring themselves to support the war. One analyst said: 'They wanted nothing to do with the professional staff. And they wanted us the fuck out of there.' Rhode also infamously humiliated one visiting Arab diplomat, telling him that there would be no 'bartering in the bazaar anymore. You're going to have to sit up and pay attention when we say so.'

Until the neocons decided that they needed a war with Iraq, staff at the NESA office worked daily with a defence intelligence officer – a DIO – from the Defense Intelligence Agency. That system was scrapped as the purge of expert analysts began. Colonel Patrick Lang believes this 'night of the long knives' targeting intelligence professionals was down to the actions of one honest soul – Bruce Hardcastle, the DIO attached to NESA in the run-up to the war. Hardcastle refused to tell Luti what he wanted to hear about Saddam. On Luti's orders, Hardcastle was excluded from meetings on Iraq.

'Hardcastle brought with him the combined wisdom of the professional military intelligence community,' says Lang. 'The community had serious doubts about the lethality of the threat from Saddam Hussein, the terrorism links and the status of the Iraqi WMD programmes. Luti could not accept this. He knew what he wanted: to bring down Saddam Hussein. Hardcastle could not accept the very idea of allowing a desired outcome to shape the results of analysis.'

By August 2002, the Iraq desk of NESA was transformed into the Office of Special Plans, and it soon began to burn white hot as OSP staff dug up every bit of speculative trash they could get their sweaty little paws on in order to help Bush convince the American people and Congress that the US should invade Iraq. Luti appointed Abram Shulsky to head up the OSP. Surprise, surprise, Shulsky was a time-served neocon. He'd even written a paper which declared that – wait for this – intelligence was all about deception! Well, knock me down with a feather, he certainly proved his point, didn't he? Lang says of Shulsky: 'For Shulsky, the goal of intelligence is to serve the needs of policy-makers in making possible the attainment of policy goals ... Shulsky seems to have set out to use the OSP as the means for providing the Bush administration policy-makers all the ammunition they needed to get their desired results.

'Interestingly, neither Shulsky nor the great majority of the people employed at one time or another by all these *ad hoc* intelligence groups were people with any previous experience of intelligence work. They were former congressional staffers, scholars and activists of one kind or another. They were people embarked on a great adventure in pursuit of a goal, not craftsmen devoted to their trade.'

I can't overstate the importance of Lang's last point. These people were not spies or intelligence analysts, they were ideologically motivated amateurs – policy-wonks, politicised mandarins and Washington insiders – put in place to destabilise, undercut and sideline the real guys in the know: the professional spies. Can you imagine if, in the UK, a political apparatchik of the Labour Party – let's say someone like Tony Blair's former Director of Communications, Alistair Campbell, for argument's sake – was suddenly able to manipulate intelligence reports and bypass the analysis of the real professional spies? And all so that his boss, the PM, could freak out the British people and get us to back his plan to invade Iraq?

Sorry, that's a bad example, it's already happened.

Greg Thielmann, who ran military assessments at the State Department's Bureau of Intelligence and Research Unit until he retired shortly before the war, says of the OSP: 'Do they have any expertise in Iraqi culture? Are they missile experts? There's no logical explanation for the office's creation except that they wanted people to find evidence to support [the policy of invading Iraq].' Thielmann went on: 'There's a formal, well established intelligence process in Washington, which Rumsfeld apparently wanted to circumvent.'

Here's one of the more pathetic examples of how these people pursued the lies they needed in order to pursue the war: the Arab media was scoured for anything that would incriminate Saddam, without checking whether it was true and without running it past the CIA. The claims in the Arab press and on Arab TV were fed straight to the American public. Can you imagine China deciding to invade the UK because of something some commissar read in *The Sun* or launching a pre-emptive strike at America based on a claim in the *National Enquirer*?

The OSP also had extremely close ties to an intelligence unit within the office of the then Israeli Prime Minister, Ariel Sharon. This Israeli unit had a similar purpose to the OSP. Where the OSP cut the CIA out of the equation, Sharon's unit cut out Mossad. The Israeli cherry-pickers fed the OSP with such outlandish threat assessments about Iraq that Mossad officers refused to put their names to the reports.

The crazy actions of these congressional staffers and activists inside the OSP eventually led to their total exposure. The real professionals – people like Lt Colonel Karen Kwiatkowski – could not take what was happening to their much loved craft anymore and eventually went public about the lie machine. Kwiatkowski worked inside NESA for a year, leaving in March 2003 just as the war began. When I spoke to her, she was still reeling from her time inside this madhouse. One of the things that riled her most was the obvious politicisation of the whole intelligence process – typified by Luti answering directly to Lewis Libby, VP Dick Cheney's Chief of Staff who is now awaiting trial for perjury – and the incestuous links between the OSP and the media. OSP staff were pumping their garbage directly into the willing ears of right-wing, bean-brained, docile hacks who then used lunatic scare stories about the might of Saddam to slowly ramp up the national passion for war.

Of course, none of the information coming from discredited Iraqi defectors was checked or verified by the OSP. All it took was one happy, smiling Iraqi to come forward to the OSP – courtesy of the Iraqi National Congress, of course – and claim that Saddam was up to something horrible, and lo and behold! it was in the papers the next day or in a speech by Bush. I even remember one story doing the rounds in the run-up to war – which came from unnamed 'Iraqi sources' – purporting that Saddam had a team of beautiful, seductive, female assassins in deep cover in the UK as sleeper agents and posing as belly-dancers. I mean, Ian Fleming wouldn't have written that kind of crap in one of his James Bond books, but the war party were happy to allow this sort of rubbish to leak out from their cherry-picking operations into the media and from there into the homes and minds of the British and American people. The belly-dancing assassins claim, incidentally, came from the Iraqi National Accord which was run by Iyad Allawi, who went on to become leader of the Iraqi interim government after the invasion.

As Kwiatkowski says: 'This information would make it straight out into the knowledge base without waiting for intelligence analysts to come by with their qualifications and reservations.'

'At the OSP, what they were doing was looking at all the intelligence they could find on WMD. That was the focal point, picking bits and pieces that were the most inflammatory, removing any context that might have been provided in the original intelligence report, that would have caused you to have some pause in believing it or reflected doubts that the intelligence community had, so if the intelligence community had doubts, these would be left out.'

Kwiatkowski is a lovely woman – genteel, intelligent and charming. After speaking to her, I liked her, so I'm loath to put words in her mouth. But what I think she is trying to say is that the information from the OSP – the information which basically made up the Bush case for war – was utter bollocks.

'They would take items that had occurred many years ago, and put them in the present tense, make it seem like they occurred not many years ago,' she says, adding: 'They would not talk about dates … they would say things like "he could do it tomorrow", which, of course, wasn't true. The other thing they would do would be to take unrelated events that were reported in totally unrelated ways and make connections that the intelligence community had not made. This was primarily in discussing Iraq's activities and how they might be related to al-Qaeda or other terrorist groups that might be against us, or against Israel.'

These links and connections were 'made in a calculated way to form an image that is definitely not the image that anyone reading the original reports would have. The summaries that we would see from intelligence did not match the kinds of things that OSP was putting out. So that is what I call propaganda development. It goes beyond the manipulation of intelligence to propaganda development.'

She means the OSP was telling lies. Not only were they getting dodgy Iraqis to make up fairy stories for them, they were also culling snippets of outdated claims from years ago, splicing them together with other suspect facts and creating the 'storyline' they wanted in the first place. How ironic that an outfit with such an Orwellian-sounding name should have perfected the art of making 2+2=5. In fact, in a wonderful exercise in mind-control, Luti was behind the production of what he called 'talking points' on Iraq – you know, stuff like Saddam had lots of deadly weapons and was behind 9-11. These were written by the director of the OSP, Abram Shulsky. On Luti's orders these 'talking points' were to be the official line on Iraq – no variation from the theme was to be tolerated. If the war party said it was so, then it was so. These 'talking points' were in effect anything the INC could think up, passed through the 'scamulator' of the OSP, pumped out of all proportion and then handed to Bush, Cheney or some stooge in the media from whence it went right into your brain. What a wonderful Soviet way of disseminating propaganda and disinformation.

Kwiatkowski left her job in the Pentagon because she felt she was being 'propagandised'. The creation of the OSP, she said, had led to the 'functional isolation of the professional corps' who were then replaced with right-wing political appointees. Kwiatkowski now calls herself a 'soldier for truth' and gladly speaks out to any reporter who will listen to her about the actions of the OSP. Does it surprise you that the mainstream media still barely recognises that she exists? She calls the OSP Bush's 'spin enforcers'. Kwiatkowski compares the insular, mindless cruelty of the Bush ideologues to the bitchy spite of high school 'mean girls', prom queens and cheerleaders. 'This cliquishness is cause for amusement in movies such as *Never Been Kissed* or *Hot Chick*,' she says. 'In the development and implementation of war planning, it is neither amusing nor beneficial for American security because opposing points of view, and information that doesn't fit, aren't considered.'

The OSP prom queens barely even spoke to the CIA, treating former director George Tenet's boys like a bunch of sexless nerds, swots and geeks. And even General Tony Zinni – Bush's former Middle East envoy – was treated like some spotty loser with no pals by the in-crowd at the Pentagon. After he attacked the administration for its Iraq policy saying he didn't know 'what planet they lived on' – and then lost his job – Kwiatkowski says she heard him called a 'traitor' by OSP staff. They even delighted in slagging off Secretary of State Colin Powell, just because he was a little more pro- UN than they were. What a bunch of hissy-fit little girls, they sound.

Kwiatkowski recalls being told to rewrite background papers regarding Libya numerous times because she was including verified intelligence that the country was trying to 'regain the respect of the international community'. But real intelligence – ie the truth – wasn't good enough for Luti. 'They made me go back and change it and change it,' says Kwiatkowski. 'They'd make me delete the quotes from intelligence so they could present their case on Libya in a way that said it was still a threat to its neighbours and that Libya was still a belligerent, antagonistic force. They edited my reports in that way. In fact, the last report I made, they said "just send me the file".'

This editing of the truth plumbed truly desperate depths. 'We were instructed by Bill Luti, on behalf of the Office of Special Plans, on behalf of Abe Shulsky, that we would not write anything about Iraq, WMD or terrorism in any papers that we prepared for our superiors except as instructed by the Office of Special Plans,' says Kwiatkowski. 'And it would provide us with an electronic document of talking points on these issues. So I got to see how they evolved.'

So, the OSP – a bunch of political hacks and think-tank members – was telling a seasoned analyst like Kwiatkowski – a woman with 20 years' service to her country under her belt – exactly what to say and not to say, and think and not to think, regarding Iraq.

'It was very clear to me that they [the talking points] did not evolve as a result of new intelligence, of improved intelligence, or any type of seeking the truth. The way they evolved is that certain bullets [a single talking point] were dropped or altered, based on what was being reported on the front pages of the *Washington Post* or the *New York Times*.

'One item that was dropped was in November 2002. It was the issue of the meeting in Prague prior to 9-11 between Mohammed Atta [leader of the September 11 hijackers] and a member of Saddam Hussein's intelligence force. We had this in our talking points from September through mid-November. And then it was dropped totally. No explanation. Just gone. That was because the media reported that the FBI had stepped away from that that the CIA said it didn't happen.'

The only time that Kwiatkowski got angry when I spoke to her was when she recounted the story of this non-existent meeting between Atta and Iraqi intelligence. 'They presented it as fact, and that's pretty close to lying,' she told me. 'They didn't come in to look at intelligence and make decisions, they came in and looked at the intelligence and made it fit the decisions. It's a classic case of the perversion and distortion of the truth.'

While the OSP inflated the threat from Saddam, Kwiatkowski says 'intelligence was showing he was not stronger, but getting weaker and weaker'. Nevertheless, the message from Luti and Shulsky was clear: 'Saddam needed to go.' Kwiatkowski told me that Iraq wasn't even identified by intelligence assessments as a country which posed a direct threat to America, although it was listed as a country which concerned the US. 'I would say Cuba was more of a realistic threat,' she said.

As far as Kwiatkowski is concerned, 'the talking points were political, politically manipulated. They did have obvious bits of intelligence in them, but they were created to propagandise ... Things were not debated. To them, Saddam Hussein needed to go ... They spent their energy gathering pieces of information and creating a propaganda storyline, which is the same storyline we heard the President and Vice-president tell the American people in the fall of 2002 ... These people have total disrespect for the Constitution. We swear an oath, military officers and NCOs alike swear an oath, to uphold the Constitution. These people have no respect for the Constitution. The Congress was misled, it was lied to. At a very minimum, that is subversion of the Constitution. A pre-emptive war based on what we knew was not a pressing need is not what this country stands for.'

The INC-sourced drivel that the OSP was producing allowed Dick Cheney to kick some serious ass over at the CIA. The Vice-president paid three trips to the CIA headquarters at Langley in Virginia in the run-up to war demanding more 'forward leaning' intelligence on Iraq's status as a threat to the US. Such visits were unheard of in intelligence history and point to the blatant decision by the Bush administration to politicise intelligence – aka tell lies. Vince Cannistraro said of the VP's visit to the CIA: 'The Vice-president going to the CIA? Cutting ribbons and giving speeches, yes. But sitting down with analysts and going over intelligence. I've never heard of that.'

Cheney was able to rattle the spooks and intimidate them, demanding to know why they weren't coming up with the sort of hard-hitting stuff the OSP was uncovering. I'm sure many spies wanted to yell 'because we don't bloody make stuff up' at Fat Dick, but when a lowly spy has the Vice-president of America roasting them on a spit, they might be forgiven for losing their bottle and caving in to his bully-boy tactics. It's the same old story. Anything for a quiet life – even if that means being complicit in an illegal war. That's precisely what happened. Cheney was able to use the OSP to terrorise the CIA into complicity with the Bush war plan. One example of the way this terrorisation of professional spies worked was exhibited by the pressure that was piled onto report officers in the CIA's Directorate of Operations. These men and women sift through reports from agents and informants around the world. They are meant to bin anything which is patently absurd or not backed up by hard facts. Thanks to Cheney and his *Blitzkrieg*, the CIA didn't dump anything. So the OSP was then able to read all the crazy claims in these reports that should never have seen the light of day. And then turn them into concrete 'facts' which were then told to the world by people like Dubya and Cheney. It's so horrible, it's perfect.

Colonel Lang – who we mentioned earlier – has a neat phrase to sum up what happened inside the professional intelligence community thanks to the Machiavellianism of the Bush administration: 'the spies drank the poisoned Kool-Aid'. Once upon a time, spies like Lang would tell their bosses that they'd rather 'fall on their sword' – commit professional suicide – before doing something that would dishonour themselves, their trade and their country. However, under the terror regime of the Bush administration spies began to 'drink the Kool-Aid' – that's the soft-drink that was famously laced with cynanide during the Jonestown Massacre when the cult followers of Rev. Jim Jones topped themselves *en masse*. In other words, the spies were coerced into destroying themselves and disgracing their profession and their country.

'The subversion of the intelligence process,' Lang says, 'was death by a thousand cuts, a cumulative process of badgering in which the pipeline of disinformation from the INC, through OSP, to the desk of the Vice-president played a decisive role.'

Mel Goodman, a former CIA official and intelligence expert with the National War College, described the OSP as 'true believers' in the plot to whack Iraq. Members of the outfit were also, he told me, experts in bullying. Professional intelligence staff, such as analysts with the Defense Intelligence Agency, were harassed 'to produce the kind of intelligence that the OSP and the Defense Secretary [Donald Rumsfeld] wanted'. So, OSP chiefs were basically telling the professional spies to go away and not come back until they'd written reports that suited the OSP's political line.

Goodman added: 'The OSP was established by Rumsfeld for one reason and one reason only. He was dissatisfied with the intelligence provided by the CIA.' Rumsfeld wanted to make sure that he could get the White House the kind of 'alarmist messages' that the President required to target Iraq.

'OSP managers would task the Pentagon's Defense Intelligence Agency, with assignments on Iraqi WMD or Iraqi links to al-Qaeda, and analysts were told ... exactly what they should say on their intelligence assessments,' Goodman explained. 'Some DIA analysts refused to play this game, but most did. In this way, the OSP got alarmist and discredited views to the White House with the imprimatur of the Pentagon. The OSP also "leaked" information to ... the *Weekly Standard* [a neo-con newspaper closely linked to the White House] so that ... the journal could publish intelligence information on a regular basis. This was the worst type of politicisation that was practised by the Pentagon.

Meanwhile, Secretary of Defense Rumsfeld regularly tried to bully CIA director [George] Tenet to produce more alarmist views for the White House.'

Goodman also says that there is 'no question' that Tony Blair was briefed with OSP 'intelligence'. He was 'brought along at the highest level' by Bush and Rumsfeld, says Goodman, adding that the Prime Minister was 'vulnerable because of his own evangelical bent' over bringing democracy to the Middle East.

Greg Thielmann, the State Department intelligence official, says he was pressurised to massage intelligence to fit policy. 'The al-Qaeda connection and nuclear weapons issue were the only two ways that you could link Iraq to an imminent security threat to the US,' Thielmann said. 'And the administration was grossly distorting the intelligence on both things.' Thielmann says the OSP 'surveyed data and picked out what they liked. The whole thing was bizarre. The Secretary of Defense had this huge defence intelligence agency, and he went around it.'

This blatant bullying is why men like George Tenet, the director of the CIA, signed-off on Bush's claim in his January 2003 State of the Union speech that Saddam was trying to get uranium from Niger. Lt Col Karen Kwiatkowski says the claim about Saddam trying to get nuclear material in Africa 'was something he'd [Saddam] done in the 1980s, but they made it seem as if it was yesterday'.

Khadir Hamza represents the kind of 'source' that the OSP was using for the wild allegations it was peddling, courtesy of Chalabi's INC mob, of course. Hamza was an Iraqi nuclear scientist who defected in 1994. He came to the US with help from the INC. In 1998, he tried to write a book saying that Saddam's attempts to turn Iraq into a nuclear bomb-owning nation had effectively 'fizzled' out. Unsurprisingly, no-one really wanted to publish such a boring book. In 2000, however, he wrote a book hyping the hell out of the threat from Saddam's nuclear programme.

Other bullshit claims that came from the INC and were trundled out as indisputable fact by the OSP included allegations that Saddam was importing aluminium tubes for development of a nuke (the tubes were totally unsuitable for building nuclear weapons), reports that Iraq had mobile bio-weapons labs, and stories that Saddam had got his hands on unmanned airborne vehicles (UAVs) that could be used as a delivery system for chemical and biological weapons.

The source of the mobile bio-weapons labs report was an Iraqi military defector who the INC had latched onto thanks to the Information Collection Programme. The CIA and the Defense Intelligence Agency both thought the guy was a bullshit artist – but no-one heeded a word they said. The labs, as I hope you remember, turned out to be used for filling weather balloons. Lies that turn weather balloons into weapons of mass destruction – could the OSP have been more stupid, more duplicitous, more manipulative and more sinister? Top brass at the US Air Force believed – correctly – that the UAVs were solely for reconnaissance.

Perhaps the most disgusting lie perpetrated by the OSP was the claim that Saddam was linked to 9-11. Without that claim seeping into the consciousness of middle America the war would never have taken place. At the time of the invasion some 60 per cent of Americans believed Saddam was behind 9-11. Even exploiting the dead of September 11, then, isn't beneath Bush and his ideologues.

The OSP's raping of intelligence protocol cost American soldiers – as well as British troops and more than 100,000 Iraqis – their lives. As Greg Thielmann says: 'The rosy assumption about troops being greeted with flowers and hugs – that came from [the OSP] stream of intelligence.' If the lies hadn't been told, then, the boys wouldn't be coming home in body bags today.

Only a few US politicians have raised an eyebrow over the role of the OSP. Democratic Representative Ellen Tauscher, a member of the House Armed Services Committee, said: 'The concern is they were in the cherry-picking business – cherry-picking half-truths and rumours and only highlighting pieces of information that bolstered the administration's case for war.'

Another Democrat, this time Congressman David Obey, says: 'That office was charged with collecting, vetting and disseminating intelligence completely outside of the normal intelligence apparatus. In fact, it appears that information collected by this office was in some instances not even shared with established intelligence agencies and in numerous instances was passed on to the National Security Council and the President without having been vetted with anyone other than political appointees.'

Colonel Patrick Lang admits, sadly, that the OSP pulled off everything it set out to do. It dominated foreign policy, got Chalabi's trash-intelligence into the minds of the American people, left the Defense Intelligence Agency cowed and beaten, and faced down the CIA. Thanks to the OSP, American intelligence became nothing other than a White House propaganda tool, and America disgraced itself on the world's stage, offended its allies, belittled the United Nations and launched a criminal war which has left thousands of innocent people dead. Will the OSP – its staff and its leaders like Luti, Shulsky, Feith, Wolfowitz and Rumsfeld – ever pay the price for this disgusting betrayal of the American people? All I can tell you is that in July 2003, Donald Rumsfeld's Pentagon quietly changed the name of the Office of Special Plans to the Northern Gulf Affairs Office. It's as if it never happened. With an Orwellian flourish, the OSP has disappeared down the memory hole – where the neocons hope and pray it and its legacy will remain forgotten forever.

DON'T £*©$ WITH US!
or
How to get ruined by the Bush White House for proving the Prez lied over Iraqi nukes

How did a man like Ambassador Joseph C Wilson IV – a man who George Bush Senior called an all-American hero – end up Public Enemy Number One in the eyes of George W Bush's administration? And why did Wilson's wife, an undercover CIA agent, end up having her life put at risk by someone very, very close to Dubya inside the White House? You must be able to guess what the answer is by now, surely? It's quite simple really: the Wilsons proved that Bush and his mob were a bunch of liars, and in return got one almighty kicking from the White House.

The story of how the Bush administration tried to destroy two of the most patriotic servants of America in the country today goes back, as everything does in this tale, to the wild and ridiculous claims about Saddam's WMD capabilities that were pouring out of Whitehall and the White House in the run-up to war. In this case, the claim centred on Iraq trying to buy 500 tonnes of uranium from the African state of Niger – that's enough to make 50 nukes.

It all begins in February 1999. It was then that Wissam al-Zahwaie, the Iraqi ambassador to the Holy See in Rome, set off on a series of rather unglamorous diplomatic jaunts to a number of African countries including Niger – a nation known for its prodigious exports of goats, onions and ... uranium.

Sometime after the Iraqi ambassador's trip to Niger, Italy's Military Intelligence and Security Service, SISMI, came into possession of some highly suspect documents purporting to show that Saddam was after Niger uranium. Details of Iraq's attempt to buy yellowcake (uranium ore) and copies of the documents were handed by SISMI to Britain's MI6 which in turn passed them to America's CIA, some time after

September 11, 2001 but before the end of October of the same year. The information was pure gold and soon caught the eye of arch chicken hawk Dick Cheney. These totally unsubstantiated claims 'proved' in Cheney's eyes that Saddam was trying to reconstitute his nuclear weapons programme. Or, at least, in the VP's opinion, the dubious allegations might convince the average blue-collar American that that was what Saddam was up to. And if that's what Saddam really was up to, well then who could possibly disagree with the Brits and Yanks blowing the daylights out of his country? There was just one hitch, though. The entire claim that Saddam was trying to buy uranium was balderdash of the highest order and the documents were childish forgeries. Concerns were raised about the intelligence almost immediately, with the CIA thinking it was totally without credibility, and analysts over at the State Department's Bureau of Intelligence and Research equally sceptical.

Do you think that worried Bush and Blair, though? Not a chance. Here's what Blair's infamous dossier called *Iraq's Weapons of Mass Destruction: The Assessment of the British government*, said on September 24, 2002: 'There is intelligence that Iraq has sought the supply of significant quantities of uranium from Africa. Iraq has no active civil nuclear power programme of nuclear plants and, therefore, has no legitimate reason to acquire uranium.' The only reason that Blair did not directly name Niger as the source country for the uranium was that the CIA told him that its spooks were uneasy with the value of the Italian intelligence. Jack Straw, the British Foreign Secretary until mid-2006, has confirmed that the CIA 'expressed reservations to us about the [Niger] element in the September dossier'. Hard as it may be to believe this, Blair – the last man standing as ever – still claims that Iraq sought uranium from Niger. It's not yet clear if the Prime Minister still believes in Father Christmas or babies being delivered by storks but it's quite likely given his track record. Britain has said that it has separate intelligence to back up the Niger–Iraq claim. So far, it hasn't been produced.

A highly placed source in the International Atomic Energy Agency – the IAEA, which is the UN's nuclear inspection team – told me: 'As far as I know, the only other evidence Britain has about the Niger connection is based on intelligence coming from other western countries which saw the same forgeries. Blair's claim that he has other evidence is nonsense. These foreign intelligence agencies are basing their claims on the same forgeries as the Brits.' The Foreign Office has admitted that the other evidence to support the Niger connection does not include 'any UK-originated material'. In other words, the Brits are claiming that reports compiled by foreign intelligence services – probably Italy's SISMI – on the fake Niger documents, are fresh evidence to support the Niger connection. It's pitiful and mad ... and dangerous. And it should be criminal.

A few months after the British dossier slithered into public view, the US government reiterated the claim in a fact sheet dated December 19, 2002. It was headed *Illustrative Examples of Omissions from the Iraqi Declaration to the United Nations Security Council*, and in it, under the heading 'Nuclear Weapons', it reads: 'The declaration ignores efforts to procure uranium from Niger. Why is the Iraqi regime hiding their uranium procurement?' Yet, just a few months earlier, in October 2002, a classified national intelligence estimate from the State Department's Bureau of Intelligence and Research said: 'Finally, the claims of Iraqi pursuit of natural uranium in Africa are, in (our) assessment, highly dubious.'

Nevertheless, George W Bush took the lunatic allegations into the stratosphere when he uttered these now infamous 16 words during his State of the Union address, on January 28, 2003: 'The British government has learned that Saddam Hussein recently sought significant quantities of uranium from Africa.' Bush didn't stop there, though. Oh no. He went on to say that there would be 'mushroom clouds' unless Saddam was stopped. Senior CIA officers tried to prevent Bush making these ridiculous comments, in what one British intelligence source described to me as 'a wise attempt at an ass-saving manoeuvre'. In fact, on October 6, 2002, the CIA faxed the White House stating: 'The Africa story is overblown.' George Tenet, the CIA director, stopped Bush mentioning Niger during a speech in Ohio, and even told the Deputy National Security Advisor that the President 'should not be a fact witness on this issue ... (as) the reporting was weak'. But in the end, under pressure from the politicians, the spineless and whipped CIA decided to sign-off on the text. The best the CIA chiefs could do was tell themselves that if they got rumbled then what Bush had said could be blamed on the stupid Brits. After the inevitable rumbling, that's precisely what happened. The CIA, said George Tenet, 'concurred that the text in the speech was factually correct, ie that the British government report said that Iraq sought uranium from Africa'. Tenet added: 'This did not rise to the level of certainty which should be required for presidential speeches, and the CIA should have ensured that it was removed.' The poor bastards in the CIA were going to get a whuppin' whatever they did. If they tried to get the claim taken out, then they were lily-livered cowards and failures as spies; but if they left it in then it was Tenet and his boys and girls over at Langley who'd carry the can for the catastrophic cock-up.

The CIA had a little more success warning Secretary of State, Colin Powell, not to include claims about Iraq getting uranium from Niger in his spectacularly stupid address to the UN in February 2003 on the threat posed by Saddam. You must remember that address – Powell sure didn't make any comments about Niger but you might recall him waving pretend vials of anthrax about and showing us satellite images of Saddam's non-existent WMD on the move.

Bush's 16 slippery words were a beautiful exercise – nay, a master class – in double-speak. 'The British government has learned that Saddam Hussein recently sought significant quantities of uranium from Africa.' The phraseology kept US intelligence out of the picture, the sentence didn't refer to those dodgy documents or any evidence at all – just British speculation – and yet the comment still got the threat out there big-style. The phrasing of the sentence meant that the lie could be told that Saddam was after African uranium with the President avoiding any blame for the lie. In fact, to make it even more perfect, all the blame would go to his little sidekick over in Downing Street, London.

Now these wild Niger claims by Bush and Blair gave a few people some pause for thought – not least the International Atomic Energy Agency. The IAEA had said that Saddam was nuke-free – basing its claim on the fact that Britain and America bombed Iraq's nuclear facilities into dust during the First Gulf War. In October 1997, the IAEA issued a report stating: 'There are no indications that there remains in Iraq any physical capability for the production of amounts of weapon-grade usable nuclear material of any practical significance.'

Someone else who was a little taken aback by the State of the Union address was Ambassador Joseph C Wilson IV. You see, he'd taken a trip to Niger on behalf of the CIA to investigate the uranium claim and discovered that it was total nonsense.

Between 1976 and 1998, Wilson was a career diplomat. In 1990, he was the last US diplomat to confront Saddam before the start of the First Gulf War. He was an ambassador in West Africa under Bush Senior and helped direct policy on Africa for Clinton in the National Security

Council. So he wasn't exactly some partisan leftie with a grudge against his country and a penchant for despotic regimes and mad moustachioed tyrants.

'In February 2002, I was informed by officials at the Central Intelligence Agency that Vice-president Dick Cheney's office had questions about a particular intelligence report,' he recounted. 'While I never saw the report, I was told that it referred to a memorandum of agreement that documented the sale of uranium yellowcake by Niger to Iraq in the late 1990s. The agency official asked if I would travel to Niger to check out the story so they could provide a response to the Vice-president's office.'

Remember all those trips Cheney was taking to the CIA in the run-up to the war? And how he was harassing the spooks to give him the facts he wanted to hear? Well, the uranium claim was just music to Dick's ears and he wanted to push the allegations as far as possible. Enter Wilson, who undertakes to go to Africa in an attempt to make the Niger claim stand up for the Vice-president. Incidentally, Wilson took on the job free of charge as a public service to his country; all the US government had to do was pick up his expenses: costs like his flights, food and hotels.

When he arrived in the Niger capital, Niamey, in late February 2002, Wilson's first port of call was the office of the US Ambassador, Barbro Owens-Kirkpatrick. 'The ambassador told me that she knew about the allegations of uranium sales to Iraq and that she felt she had already debunked them in her reports to Washington.' The claims had also been kicked into the gutter by high-ranking members of the US military.

Wilson then 'spent the next eight days drinking sweet mint tea and meeting with dozens of people: current government officials, former government officials, people associated with the country's uranium business. It did not take long to conclude that it was highly doubtful that any such transaction had ever taken place.

'Given the structure of the consortiums that operated the mines, it would be exceedingly difficult for Niger to transfer uranium to Iraq. Niger's uranium business consists of two mines, Somair and Cominak, which are run by French, Spanish, Japanese, German and Nigerian interests. If the government wanted to remove uranium from a mine, it would have to notify the consortium, which in turn is strictly monitored by the International Atomic Energy Agency. Moreover, because the two mines are closely regulated, quasi-governmental entities, selling urani-

um would require the approval of the Minister of Mines, the Prime
Minister and probably the President. In short, there's simply too much
oversight over too small an industry for a sale to have transpired.'

I should point out that at the time Wilson set out on his trip in
February 2002, he had no idea that the documents – as I'll show you
later – were pathetic forgeries. He was working on the assumption that
they were genuine.

In early March, Wilson was back stateside. He told the CIA, which
had been asked to get to the bottom of the whole Niger-uranium allegations, that the claims were rubbish – that Iraq just couldn't have got
uranium from Niger. Wilson gave the same report to the State
Department. You can understand, then, why Wilson was more than a
little confused when Blair in September 2002 and Bush in January 2003
went out of their way to say that Saddam was buying uranium from
Africa. The allegation was repeated in March 2003 by Dick Cheney.
Wilson said: 'If ... the information [which he provided on there being
no bid by Iraq to buy uranium from Niger] was ignored because it did
not fit certain preconceptions about Iraq, then a legitimate argument
can be made that we went to war under false pretences.' Just to make
the import of what the ambassador is saying perfectly clear, remember
that Bush had said that Iraq was trying to get uranium from Africa
almost a year after Wilson came back from Africa saying the claim was
nonsense. The Prez was telling a big, fat, hairy spider of a lie.

Wilson says that, based on his 'experience with the administration in
the months leading up to the war, I have little choice but to conclude
that some of the intelligence related to Iraq's nuclear weapons programme was twisted to exaggerate the Iraqi threat'. Understandably,
Wilson added: 'It begs the question 'what else are they lying about?'

Within days of Wilson going public on July 6, 2003 about what had
really gone on during his trip to Niger, the neocons in the White House
decided to ruin him and his family. After Wilson spoke out on the pages
of the *New York Times*, the White House, through gritted teeth, conceded that the Niger claim should never have been included in the State
of the Union address. The Director of the CIA, George Tenet, had to
stagger blinking into the media glare to take the whipping for his boss
Mr Bush. By the time Tenet resigned to tend his garden in 2004, the ex-
CIA Director must have had calluses on his ass the size of walnuts after
all the beatings he took to save Bush's own sorry behind. Tenet, in full
mea culpa mode, said the CIA was to blame for the inclusion of the 16-

word whopper and hadn't properly warned the White House that the Niger allegation was 'highly dubious' in the eyes of agency analysts. No-one seemed to have the sense to point out that Tenet was far less culpable than Bush and was obviously taking the fall for his boss. The White House – remember – was fully conversant with the fact that the uranium claim was rubbish because Wilson had scotched the allegation after being dispatched by the CIA on behalf of Dick Cheney to Niger. Tenet – as you can see – drank the poisoned Kool-Aid a long time ago. He was Bush's prize bitch.

Wilson was now a marked man. He'd dared to question the neocons. His pay-back came just a week after an extensive article by him appeared in the *New York Times*' op-ed section saying his travels in Niger on behalf of the Bush administration had uncovered proof that Iraq couldn't have acquired uranium from the little African nation. Pay-back came in the form of a syndicated column on July 14, 2003 – just over a week after Wilson publicly refuted the Niger-uranium claims – by the right-wing pundit Robert Novak. It came out, quoting anonymous government sources, saying that Wilson's wife, Valerie Plame, was a CIA officer and she'd got her husband the Niger gig. The implication was that Wilson had only got the job because his wife was in the CIA and that he wouldn't have had the credentials to get picked for the task without her. The sub-text was that he was incompetent for the assignment and his findings and theories therefore couldn't be trusted. The column was an ugly attempt to smear Wilson with the dirt of nepotism. It was, however, a pretty pathetic effort to undermine his credibility given that Wilson's CV reads like the track record of a high-achieving polymath and über-patriot.

The attack on Wilson should, by rights, have died away. This was a man, after all, who had had praise heaped on him by two former presidents. But the sneaky little neocons had been a little too overweening this time. This slur wasn't going to go away, because by impugning Wilson's name they'd also, as a by-product of their scheming, exposed the identity of his wife – and it is a criminal offence in the US to 'out' a serving undercover CIA officer. Whoever it was in the White House who exposed Plame's name and revealed her job, they'd broken the 1982 Intelligence Identities Protection Act and that carries with it a fine of up to $50,000 and ten years in jail. Ten years! What a wonderful prospect! At least two senior White House officials, it is now known, spoke to six Washington journalists – including slimy Novak – to dribble poison in

their ears about Wilson and Plame. Wilson was nothing short of a traitor, ran the spin from the White House. He was a liar, the real liars lied.

Someone was going to get their balls fried for this one. Wanna hear
the clincher to this shoddy affair? Valerie Plame was a spy whose job it
was to monitor the proliferation of weapons of mass destruction. In
fact, Valerie Plame was a so-called NOC – a spy who works in 'non-offi-
cial cover'. That means she doesn't work out of an embassy pretending
to be diplomatic staff in order to conceal her true identity as a spy.
Rather what NOCs do is build a cover by pretending to be a student, a
journalist, a visiting professor, a business executive – that kind of thing.
It costs the CIA up to $1 million to build a NOC's cover. A NOC is also
at real risk of being killed or arrested since unlike the spies based in
embassies they have no diplomatic immunity. You can see why Valerie
was known to be something of a crack shot with an AK-47.

So, let's get this straight. To discredit Wilson, a man whose only
crime, so far as I can see, was to do something for free for his country
and then tell the truth about it, the White House ruined his wife's career.
Cool. Not only that, but Team Bush risked the national security of
America by endangering any sources or informants Plame might have
had overseas. To top it all, they put her life at risk too. Great guys. The
White House stooge who squealed on Plame 'compromised an entire
career of networks, relationships and operations', Wilson said, referring
to his wife's history as a high-flying CIA officer. Plenty of al-Qaeda
inspired terrorists would love to whack a CIA spy – even if she did happen to be married to a man who wanted to stop the invasion of Iraq.
Don't forget that CIA station chiefs in Beirut and Greece have been
assassinated. Mentioning her name in public was enough to put this
woman's life in grave danger.

'I have been subjected – along with my wife, Valerie Plame – to a partisan Republican smear campaign,' said Wilson. 'I've been accused of
being a liar and, worse, a traitor … Administration sources leaked to the
media that my wife was an undercover CIA operative – an unprecedented betrayal of national security and a possible felony … It was a
malicious act meant to keep others from crossing a vindictive administration.'

Wilson named a number of men he believed were behind the leaks,
including Karl Rove, Bush's Brain, aka the President's Political Advisor.
He claimed that a meeting was called in the White House in March
2003 – around the time that Wilson was beginning to make it discreet-

ly known to the administration that he felt Bush should 'fess up to putting that 16 word lie about African uranium in his January 2003 State of the Union address. The meeting centred on Wilson and how to damage him. Wilson says: 'Either the Vice-president himself or, more likely, his Chief of Staff, Lewis Libby, chaired a meeting at which a decision was made to do a work-up on me.'

A work-up, according to Wilson, meant that the White House 'basically mounted an intelligence operation to find out everything they could on me and my habits and everything else. Which in and of itself I find rather appalling ... Somebody decided that his or her political agenda was more important than the national security of my country and that this person was prepared to betray a national security asset [his wife, Plame] to defend that agenda.' In Wilson's words, those people at that meeting decided to 'drag my wife into the public square and administer a beating on her'. It was a shot across his bows, and the bows of other whistle-blowers, Wilson believed. It was a clear message, he added: 'If you talk, we'll take your family and drag them through the mud.'

Wilson was called partisan and labelled a Democrat, even though he'd given money to Bush's 2000 presidential campaign and his mission to Niger had been undertaken for Bush's own administration. 'I brought back a report which, if it had been accepted by my government, would have kept the President of the United States from actually lying to the American people,' he said.

It's frightening to think that some of the most powerful men in the world would sit around a table and devise ways to make another man's life a misery. There is no higher good in these corridors of power– just good old-fashioned revenge and dirty tricks. 'Destroy the messenger' – that was the battle-cry of these guys – at whatever cost. Team Bush was out to out-Nixon Nixon. Don't forget, Watergate was just about a petty break-in and nasty Nixon trying to get himself re-elected; Yellowcakegate, Niger-Gate, Plame-Gate, whatever you want to call it, was a crime of massive deception played out against the American people which also ruined the career of a top US spy.

According to Wilson, the policy decided at the meeting was to deflect attention away from the lie in the State of the Union address by launching a personal campaign against Wilson designed to humiliate him and destroy his credibility. His wife, it seemed, was a legitimate target in this plan. Karl Rove, according to Wilson, then circulated information from the work-up on him within the administration after making it clear that Valerie Plame was 'fair game'. Hardly surprising then that Wilson said: 'At the end of the day, it's of keen interest to me to see whether or not we can get Karl Rove frog-marched out of the White House in hand-cuffs. And trust me, when I use that name, I measure my words.' I just love that quote. The mental image conjured up is nothing short of beautiful.

Of course, the White House came out and defended Rove, with Press Secretary Scott McClellan saying: 'He wasn't involved ... The President knows he wasn't involved ... It's simply not true.' If I was to use the same kind of reductive, biased reasoning that Team Bush and the Blairites used to justify this war, then from that above sentence, I could conclude, without question, that Bush was part of the criminal conspiracy to out Plame. If Bush 'knows' that Rove *isn't* involved, then logically he must know who *is*. Ergo Bush is concealing the identity of whoever leaked Plame's name to the press in the plot to ruin Wilson and his wife. It's the same clumsy logical tripe as saying 'we know Saddam has weapons of mass destruction, but Saddam will not hand over those weapons. Therefore Saddam is hiding the weapons and we must as a consequence invade Iraq to take the weapons from him'.

Those neocons were about as low as a flea on a rat's belly thanks to their scam to destroy Wilson and Plame. But their ugly machinations left Wilson free to moonwalk on the moral high ground. 'Valerie and I realised that for all the hardship it may have imposed on us, the real crime was the crime against the national security of this country,' Wilson said. 'We have tried to avoid giving the impression that we thought of ourselves as victims. We thought that the country was the victim.'

Ouch! Killer comments like that must be some kick in the gonads for Bush and Co. Wilson piled on the pressure saying that after Valerie was 'outed', her colleagues 'made it very clear that there had been a breach of trust between the clandestine service of the CIA and the White House'. The Wilson-Plame-Niger-Yellowcake affair made Bush look like the real enemy of the state. To Wilson, the US government came after him 'either because they wanted to discourage other people from stepping forward and telling the truth, or out of simple revenge ... It was truly un-American. It was a betrayal of the country ... It was treasonous.' Ouch again, Ambassador Wilson! With all those put-downs, you are spoiling us.

'This is my country,' said Wilson, skewering the Bush administration with its own patriotism, 'and it is a great country, and the American people have every right to know what their government is doing and what their government has done with the false pretences under which this government launched this war on Iraq.'

While this disgusting display of bullying, character assassination and treachery to America was unfolding within Team Bush, the truth was also emerging about what was really in those Niger-uranium documents which started the whole wild goose chase in the first place. The IAEA had been begging to see proof that Iraq was seeking to get uranium from Niger since the British government dossier was published in September 2002. When the papers were finally handed over on February 4, 2003, a senior IAEA official told me that it took them just a few hours to figure out that the documents were 'total bullshit'. They were childish forgeries – so childish that one telltale mistake was flagged up by a simple Google search. 'There were more than 20 anomalies in the Niger documents,' the IAEA official told me. 'It's staggering any intelligence service could have believed they were genuine for a moment.'

So, just how easy is it to tell a fake contract for nuclear material from an impoverished African country to a tin-pot dictatorship? Actually, it seems pretty easy indeed. In one of the documents – there were 17 pages in all, written in French – which was a letter from the President of Niger, a reference is made to the constitution of May 12, 1965, which is a pity, given that the constitution is dated August 9, 1999.

A three-page accord agreeing the uranium sale was accompanied by another letter, dated October 10, 2000 and signed by the Foreign Minister Allele Elhadj Habibou. However, Habibou stopped being Foreign Minister in 1989. The heading of this letter also referred to the Conseil Militaire Supreme, a body which was abolished in May 1989. In another, an obsolete government letterhead is used, including the wrong symbol for the office of the president. References to state bodies like the Council for National Reconciliation don't match with the dates on the letters. One letter bearing the obviously faked signature of Niger's president Tandja Mamadou was so woefully executed it looked like it'd been done on an Etch-a-Sketch.

The day after the IAEA discovered the documents were completely cooked up, Colin Powell, then US Secretary of State, made his case before the UN Security Council for war against Iraq. Significantly, Powell didn't mention Niger. IAEA director, Mohamed El Baradei, tried

again to bring reason to the table on March 7 when he told the UN
Security Council – just before Iraq was invaded – that his team and 'outside experts' had worked out that 'these documents ... are in fact not
authentic'. But it was to no avail. The lie had been told, vast swathes of
the American population believed that Saddam was a nuclear threat and
that was all that was needed to green-light the invasion of Iraq in the
eyes of the Bush administration.

A senior IAEA official told me: 'I know that we told Britain and
America, two weeks before El Baradei made his statement to the UN in
March, that the documents were forgeries. At that point, the IAEA gave
them a chance – they asked the US and UK if they had any other evidence to back up the claim apart from the Niger forgeries.

'Britain and America should have reacted with shock and horror
when they found that the documents were fake – but they did nothing.
The IAEA had said that it would follow up any other evidence pointing
towards a Niger connection. If the UK and US had such evidence they
could have forwarded it and shut the IAEA up – El Baradei would never
have gone public if that had happened. My analysis is that Britain has
no other credible evidence.

'If I was prosecuting someone in a court of law and I brought in what
I knew to be forgeries in an attempt to get a conviction, the case would
be thrown out immediately and it'd be me in the dock. The case wasn't
thrown out against Iraq, however, and what we are left with is an ominous sense of the way intelligence was treated to promote war. There are
only two conclusions: one, is that Britain has intelligence but kept it
from the weapons inspectors, which they should not have done under
international law, or that they don't have a thing. If they did have intelligence, then why not show it to the world now that [the invasion] is
over?'

The IAEA and El Baradei, he said, were bitter and humbled – just as
were Hans Blix and his UN weapons inspectors in UNMOVIC – after
their experiences at the hands of the Bush administration, 'but perhaps
now we may have some solace as the truth seems to be coming out. It's
obvious that we could have done this without war – but the evidence
shows war would have happened regardless of what the inspectors
could have done as that was the wish of Bush and Blair. Everyone, it
seems, was working for peace – except them.'

The British government's claim that it had additional intelligence
which proved that Saddam was seeking uranium from Niger was a bla-

tant lie. Just have a look at this April 2003 letter from the State Department to the Democrat House of Representatives member Henry Waxman, who'd been demanding answers about what the hell all this Iraq-Niger stuff was about. The letter says that the US received intelligence from the UK and another 'western European ally' – which many believe to be Italy – that Iraq was trying to buy yellowcake from Niger. But it adds: 'Not until March 4 did we learn that, in fact, the second western European government had based its assessment on the evidence available to the US that was subsequently discredited.'

In other words, as one intelligence source told me: 'Italian intelligence had based its reports on the same crap the British used.' That's no surprise since it was the Italians who gave the British the faked-up documents in the first place. The junk intelligence that the Brits and the Italians had was then happily sucked up as Holy Scripture by Team Bush. Everyone was using everyone else's intelligence – but it was all based on the same forged documents. It was a merry-go-round of lies and disinformation between the Brits, the Yanks and Berlusconi's boys in SISMI. Given that this letter to Democratic representative Henry Waxman was dated April 29, 2003, it kind of makes you wonder why the White House didn't admit that the Niger claim was rubbish until early July 2003 – after Wilson went public and revealed that allegations of Saddam trying to buy uranium in Africa were completely bogus. Of course, by the time the Bush administration finally admitted the allegations were false, the March 2003 invasion of Iraq was completed.

When El Baradei came out and rained on the war party's parade by telling the world that the documents supporting Bush and Blair's pet theory on uranium supplies to Iraq from Niger were a bunch of crap, he was given the usual treatment that the neocons mete out to anyone with a Middle Eastern-sounding name who contradicts or stands up to them. Cheney gave it to that awkward Arab, shock-and-awe style. 'I think Mr El Baradei frankly is wrong,' Cheney said, as his nose grew all the way down to his ankles. '[The IAEA] has consistently underestimated or missed what it was Saddam Hussein was doing. I don't have reason to believe they're any more valid this time than they've been in the past.' Even the word of the UN's chief expert on nuclear weapons wouldn't suffice for Cheney. If he said it was so, then it was so, despite what the CIA, the IAEA or anyone else said or did. That's not a man of self-confidence and assured leadership, that's a plain old-fashioned autocrat.

Quite how Dick squared these comments about El Baradei with the fact that an internal CIA memo from June 17, 2003 said 'we no longer believe there is sufficient other reporting to conclude that Iraq pursued uranium from abroad', is beyond me, but then being weird, contradictory and confusing seems to be something of a badge of honour in the Bush White House.

Here's another weird, contradictory and confusing aside in the Niger-Iraq uranium story. From December 2001, the State Department's Bureau for Intelligence and Research had been saying that Iraq didn't have a nuclear programme. So why would Colin Powell, the man in charge of the State Department, tell the House International Relations Committee in February 2002 that 'with respect to the nuclear programme, there is no doubt that the Iraqis are pursuing it'?

It's also interesting to note that prior to Bush uttering the infamous 16-word lie in his January 2003 State of the Union address, the State Department's Bureau for Intelligence and Research had concluded that the documents were 'clearly a forgery'. So, that means Bush knew before making his bogus claim that Saddam was after African uranium, that the papers backing this allegation had been labelled as fake – yet he still went ahead and spouted that Iraq had sought uranium from Africa. If that's not telling a downright lie, then you can smear my ears with honey and tie me to an anthill. On April 5, 2003, not long before the March invasion, the National Intelligence Council issued a memo that stated: 'We judge it highly unlikely that Niamey sold uranium yellowcake to Baghdad in recent years.'

I should also point out that getting 500 tonnes of yellowcake from Niger to Iraq is a little more difficult than getting your weekly supermarket shopping home after late night opening on Thursday. There's the small matter of taking 500 tonnes – which is a lot of tonnes by the way – across the Sahara Desert and then getting it shipped from West Africa to Iraq. After that it's just a small matter of transporting it from one of Iraq's southern ports to Baghdad. That should be pretty easy given that before the invasion Iraq was the most surveyed nation on earth – so it's not as if the UK or US would have spotted this illicit trade in yellowcake from the satellites we had zooming in on every camel that took a dump in the Iraqi desert.

Where in fact did these forged documents come from which started the whole made-up Niger claim in the first place? One theory is that either Italian intelligence, or Italian intelligence working with MI6, cooked up the whole thing themselves with the full backing and support of American intelligence. There's also a suspicion that the spooks were assisted by a disgruntled or easily bribed diplomat or office worker from Niger at the country's embassy on Via Antonio Baiamonti in Rome who passed over documents like forgeable letterheads and official stamps. The documents could also have been doctored versions of papers relating to a real attempt by Iraq to buy uranium from Niger in the late 1980s – when the US and UK were arming him, as you'll remember. Perhaps, the dates of papers were altered by western spooks to make it look as if the attempted trade took place much later.

The visit by Wissam al-Zahwaie, the Iraqi ambassador to the Holy See in Rome, to Niger was just a serendipitous trip which made the entire scam look more plausible. Incidentally, today al-Zahwaie says that his mission to Africa was to invite statesmen to Baghdad so that they could be persuaded to speak out against UN sanctions. 'I had no other instructions,' he says, 'and certainly none concerning the purchase of uranium.'

Whatever happened, there was certainly a break-in at the Niger embassy in Rome in December 2000 – and all that was stolen was a cheap watch and a few bottles of perfume. Rocco Martino, a shady operator who once worked for SISMI, the Italian intelligence agency, says SISMI forged the papers in late 2000 and early 2001. If this is true, then God help Italy. If this nation relies on an intelligence agency which can't even get the right name for Niger's Foreign Minister on a forged document that they are trying to pass off as proof that Saddam bought yellowcake from Niger, then the country is even more screwed than we thought. But then I suppose a country's intelligence services come to resemble a country's leader just the way a dog comes to look like its master. Under Blair's watch, Operation Rockingham turned UK spying into a slithery, slimy craft built on carefully constructed lies; Bush turned the OSP into a swaggering, macho operation that lied blatantly and for the hell of it; and under Silvio Berlusconi, it appears, the Italian spooks became even dumber and more bumpkin-like than they'd ever been before – and that's saying something.

The forged documents then surfaced publicly in Italy in October 2002, when Elisabetta Burba – a reporter for *Panorama*, an Italian news magazine owned by – *ba-da-bing*! – none other than former Italian premier Silvo Berlusconi – got a call from Martino in which he said he had information about Saddam trying to buy uranium in Africa. When they met, he offered to sell her the Niger documents for about $10,000. The paper's editor-in-chief, Carlo Rossella, who had close ties to Berlusconi's administration, ordered Burba to hand the documents over to the US Embassy. She did just that. Burba herself later checked the documents out and quickly concluded that they were a faked-up pile of steaming dung. They really are hiring the wrong people in the intelligence services these days, aren't they? I mean if one solitary reporter could work out that the Niger papers were fake, it just makes you wonder, doesn't it, why all those British, Italian and American spies couldn't for the life of them see the same thing? You'd almost imagine that they were deliberately not looking.

The Niger-uranium saga unveils one of the key strategies of the Bush and Blair governments: allowing information which the administrations knew to be fake and phoney to be aired in order to convince the US Congress, the British Parliament and the people of the UK and America, that they should support war.

The truth about this massive con job finally began to sink in, even to Washington insiders on bodies like the Senate Intelligence Committee. One of its members, Senator Jay Rockefeller, who voted for the war after having the daylights scared out of him by the President, just like most other American citizens, says now: 'There is a possibility that the fabrication of these documents may be part of a larger deception campaign aimed at manipulating public opinion and foreign policy regarding Iraq.'

With the image of British and American spooks and their political masters looking utterly ridiculous and sinister around the world after these events, George Tenet at least tried to salvage a little credibility and decency for himself by calling on the Justice Department to investigate the leaking of Plame's name and her covert role in the CIA to the press – well, what else could he do? She was a CIA officer and he was her boss, so he did have a duty of care to help her.

Lousiana's Democrat Senator, Mary Landrieu, said: 'This betrayal by someone or some people in the administration has reached a new low. There's an unwritten rule in politics that no matter how rough the politics gets, families are off-limits, particularly spouses and children.'

It took more than two months – until the end of September 2003 – for the Bush administration to order an inquiry. In the meantime, people like Scott McClellan, the White House spokesman, kept saying things like: 'I'm telling you, that is not the way the White House operates ... No-one was certainly given any authority to do anything of that nature.' Dick Cheney even said: 'I don't know Joe Wilson.' Cheney, if you need to be reminded, was Defense Secretary under George Bush the Elder during the First Gulf War. As the acting US Ambassador in Baghdad in the weeks before the war, it was Wilson who helped evacuate thousands of foreigners from Kuwait and negotiated the release of more than 100 US hostages whom Saddam had taken prisoner. Wilson also sheltered some 800 US citizens in the American Embassy. For his trouble, Dubya's father wrote to Wilson saying: 'Your courageous leadership during this period of great danger for American interests and American citizens has my admiration and respect. I salute, too, your skilful conduct of our tense dealings with the government of Iraq. The courage and tenacity you have exhibited throughout this ordeal prove that you are the right person for the job.' In a cable to Baghdad, Bush Senior told Wilson: 'What you are doing day in and day out under the most trying of conditions is truly inspiring. Keep fighting the good fight.' So, sure, Dick Cheney, had never heard of Wilson. Wilson likes to pick up that last quote from Daddy Bush – the one about fighting the good fight – and turn it on Baby Bush. 'I guess,' says Wilson, referring to Bush the Elder, 'he didn't realise that one of these days I would carry that fight against his son's administration.'

The investigation into the leaking against Plame was eventually opened – but not before Dick Cheney told America on the news show *Meet the Press* that the claim in the British dossier of September 2002 stating Saddam had been seeking uranium in Africa was 'revalidated'. The man is unbelievable in his ability to tell stonking big lies and think he can get away with it. Cheney was saying this in September 2003 – while weapons inspectors across newly occupied Iraq were wandering around, scratching their heads and wondering where all those lovely big WMD had gone to that they thought they would find just lying around in palaces or propped up against a palm tree at a desert oasis.

Anyway, back to that investigation into the outing of Plame. It was opened by the Justice Department, then under the command of John Ashcroft, Bush's Attorney-General. This is a man who believes he sits at God's right hand; he's a Christ-bothering warrior for the Lord and the kind of guy who you could well imagine thinks quite fondly of Margaret Atwood's vision of an America run by crazed theocratic patriarchs in *A Handmaid's Tale*.

But hang on a minute, here, isn't getting Ashcroft to investigate an alleged White House leak simply a case of one nasty little apparatchik investigating another? Having Bush's top lawman in charge of an inquiry into shenanigans by those in the President's inner circle is a bit like getting me to investigate my best mate. The Justice Department gave whoever leaked Plame's name a head-start to cover their tracks. Ashcroft's minions informed the White House on the evening of Monday September 29, 2003 that the investigation was about to begin – effectively the Justice Department might as well have said, 'OK guys, we'll be round tomorrow first thing to get going on this investigation.' Of course, what that meant was that the White House leaker or leakers had an entire night to clean out the closet.

The White House totally opposed the appointment of a special independent prosecutor. Scott McClellan – the Voice of Bush – told reporters that an independent investigation just wasn't appropriate, and besides, he said, 'the President believes leaking classified information is a very serious matter'. Well, that's alright then – if the President says that he's really upset about Plame's life being put at risk then everything must be fine. Nothing to worry about, citizens. Go back to sleep.

Wasn't Clinton impeached for simply dissembling about a bit of harmless hanky-panky behind the back of his missus? For saying 'I never had sex with that woman' when he kinda had? Wasn't the investigation into whatever Clinton did – if my memory serves, it was getting a little oral love from some chick at the office and then lying about it – undertaken by a special independent prosecutor rather than a partisan pro-administration Justice Department? Ashcroft took more than a passing interest in the Plame investigation. His aides regularly briefed him on the progress of the inquiry, passing him the identities of those who'd been interviewed. I'm sure Mr Ashcroft kept all these details totally to himself and would never have thought of relaying information to Bush or Cheney or any of his other friends, mentors and bosses.

Eventually, even the Bush team had to relent, and in December the Justice Department handed the investigation over to Special Prosecutor Patrick Fitzgerald.

US grand jury investigators have interviewed Bush, Cheney and Powell, as well as the White House Weasel-in-Chief, Scott McClellan, the press spokesman. Although all grand juries are secret, it's leaked out that witnesses allegedly told the grand jury that Bush knew about, but took no action to stop, the release of Plame's identity. Bush has already got himself an outside lawyer to deal with the coming fall-out from any investigation.

Finally, the truth began to stagger into sight in the summer of 2005. That's two years after the whole scandal broke – enough time to make sure that America had forgotten about the affair, got bored and moved on to discussing which actress had the nicest hooters in *Desperate Housewives*.

After threats, harassment, bullying, general ass-kicking and nipple-tweaking, information about *Time* magazine reporter Matt Cooper's off-the-record briefings regarding Wilson's wife with none other than a certain Mr Karl 'Brain of Baby Bush' Rove made its way to the grand jury. Cooper, as any decent journalist would, had fought tooth-and-nail to protect his source. To a journalist, even Karl Rove has to be protected – no matter what – and Cooper had faced the threat of jail over his attempts to respect the pact between reporter and source. He was saved from jail when his bosses at *Time* went over his head and handed his emails, relating to secret discussions with Rove, to the grand jury. Cooper also agreed to testify. Another reporter, Judith Miller from the *New York Times*, was jailed for not talking. Ironically, Miller had been a complete ra-ra girl for the war from the get-go, pedalling all sorts of bogus Chalabi-inspired rubbish about Saddam's mighty arsenal of WMD on the front pages of her newspaper in the lead up to war.

As an aside, you might like to know that when Cooper first met Bush – at a time when the reporter was staring into the maw of a possible spell in the can for protecting one of the lizards on Bush's West Wing – the President gallantly said: 'Cooper! I thought you'd be in jail by now.'

One of the emails which Cooper was forced to give up is just great. Not only does it appear to indicate that Rove was part of a criminal and treacherous conspiracy to out Plame, but it also contains a pretty cool reference to the John Belushi movie *Animal House*. See if you can spot it. It's just perfect when you think about the frat boys currently running America.

Here it is, in all its ungrammatical, badly punctuated and misspelled glory:

> Spoke to Rove on double super secret background for about two mins before he went on vacation ... it was, KR said, wilson's wife, who apparently works at the agency on wmd issues, who authorized the trip. not only the genesis of the trip is flawed ans suspect but so is the report. he implied strongly there's still plenty to implicate iraqi interest in acquiring uranium fron Niger ... some of this

is going to be dclassified in the coming days, KR said. don't get too
far out in front he warned. then he bolted.

(In case you are wondering, 'double super secret background' is the line
taken from *Animal House*.)

Let's be clear about this – that email proves Rove told Cooper that
Wilson's wife worked for the CIA. At the time of the discussion, July 11,
2003, less than a week after Wilson revealed publicly that the Niger-uranium claims were nonsense, and just a few days before Plame was first
'outed' as a spy in the press – all any reporter had to do to find out the
identity of Joe Wilson's wife was Google 'ambassador joseph c wilson
iv + wife' and the result would be – bingo! – Valerie Plame. Little Karl
was playing a deeply nasty game called jigsaw identification, and by
doing so he leaked the identity of a national security asset.

Dubya's daddy once called people who unmasked spies 'the most
insidious of traitors'. Baby Bush promised to sack the leakers. Karl Rove
sure looks like he is one of the leakers. Does that not mean that Karl
Rove is a traitor and should be sacked? Yet still he remains … It is also
a criminal offence to identify a spy. But Karl Rove seems to have identified a spy. Shouldn't he be in jail? Yet still he remains …

Just for the record, Rove's claim to Cooper that it was Plame who
authorised the trip to Niger is another lie. A declassified Senate
Intelligence Committee report, dated July 7, 2004, reveals that it was
the Deputy Chief of the CIA's counter-proliferation division who gave
the Niger expedition the green light. It also appears that once Plame's
ID was out in the public domain this presented foreign intelligence services with something of a heyday. Spooks from around the world started to piece together the life of Valerie Plame in order to work out just
how the CIA might be operating in their countries. Well, there's a real
boon to US national security courtesy of White House apparatchiks.

Satan loves his own. So far, Rove has been lucky and it looks like he
is sure to avoid having his collar felt by the long arm of the law,
although he and other White House officials are still facing a lawsuit
filed by Wilson and Plame. Dame Fortune however, has not smiled quite
so kindly on Rove's crony, Lewis 'Scooter' Libby, Vice-president Dick
Cheney's Chief of Staff.

On October 28, 2005, Patrick Fitzgerald, the US attorney in Chicago
who was appointed Special Counsel in the CIA leak investigation,
revealed that a federal grand jury had returned a five-count indictment

against Libby. He was charged with one count of obstruction of justice, two counts of perjury and two counts of making false statements.

Note that no-one has as yet been charged with leaking Plame's name – Libby has just been charged with lying his ass off – allegedly – to the investigating grand jury. There may well yet come a time when other senior figures in the Bush administration face the music over outing Plame. Libby is just the first casualty in what will turn out to be a very lengthy and bloody war of attrition for the Bush regime.

Here is how Libby shafted himself, according to Fitzgerald. In October 2003, the FBI interviewed Libby, and what he essentially told the Feds was this: he was at the end of a long chain of phone calls with the press. He spoke to one journalist, Tim Russert, who Libby claimed told him: 'Hey, do you know that all the reporters know that Mr Wilson's wife works at the CIA?'

Fitzgerald goes on: 'He [Libby] told the FBI that he learned that information as if were new, and it struck him. So, he took this information from Mr Russert and later on he passed it on to other reporters ... He told the FBI that when he passed the information on [to other reporters] ... that he passed it on the understanding that this was information he had gotten from a reporter; that he didn't even know if it was true.'

Libby went to the grand jury twice in March 2004 and said the same thing under oath. But that, in the eyes of the grand jury, was just a pack of lies. 'It would be a compelling story,' Fitzgerald said, 'if only it were true. It is not true.' In fact, as Patrick Fitzgerald explained, Libby had first learned from Dick Cheney – in June 2003 and prior to his conversation with Russert – who Joe Wilson's wife was. Libby later claimed to have forgotten this chat with his boss, the Vice-president.

In all, Libby had 'discussed the information about Valerie Wilson at least half a dozen times before the conversation with Mr Russert ever took place, not to mention that when he spoke to Mr Russert, Mr Russert and he never discussed Valerie Wilson or Wilson's wife,' Fitzgerald revealed. The indictment alleges that Libby 'learned the information about Valerie Wilson at least three times in June 2003 from government officials'.

Libby, Fitzgerald discovered, had actually had at least seven discussions with a number of government officials about Valerie Plame all *before* the date when he said he'd learned about her and her CIA role from the reporter Tim Russert. Libby had also, apparently, spoken to Karl Rove and to White House Press Secretary, Ari Fleischer, and even went so far as to testify that he had told reporters he 'did not even know if Mr Wilson had a wife'.

Here's Fitzgerald's take on Libby: 'He was at the beginning of the chain of phone calls, the first official to disclose this information outside the government to a reporter, and then he lied about it afterwards, under oath and repeatedly.'

The damage of revealing Plame's identity, said Fitzgerald, 'wasn't to one person. It wasn't just Valerie Wilson. It was done to all of us ... anyone who would go into a grand jury and lie, obstruct and impede the investigation has committed a serious crime.' He added: 'For people who work at the CIA ... they have to expect that when they do their jobs, that information about whether or not they are affiliated with the CIA will be protected ... they have to make sure that they don't run the risk that something bad is going to happen to them from something done by their own fellow government employees.'

Fitzgerald has sworn not to 'end the investigation until I can look anyone in the eye and tell them that we have carried out our responsibility sufficiently to be sure we've done what we could'.

Bush is on shaky ground, too. Libby said in court papers that he had been told by Dick Cheney in July 2003 – after Wilson publicly announced that the Niger-uranium claim was rubbish – that he had President Bush's authority to discuss classified material with journalists. Team Bush says that even if this is true no harm's been done as Bush has the power to declassify information and order its release. Which is about as logical as saying 'Bush can do what the hell he wants as he's the president'.

Court papers have also revealed hand-written notes – written prior to Plame's identity being leaked – by Cheney in the margin of Wilson's newspaper column which dismissed claims that Saddam was seeking uranium from Niger. Cheney's note reads: 'Have they [the CIA] done this sort of thing before? Send an Amb. [ambassador] to assess a question? Do we ordinarily send people out pro bono to work for us? Or did his wife send him on a junket?'

Incidentally, Libby could face up to 50 years in prison if found guilty. We can only dream that justice comes for him and all the other toads who are up to their warty necks in this deceitful game. But experience tells us that is doubtful.

There are few men who know what real political bastards are like, but John Dean, the former Nixon White House Counsel, is one of them. He has written: 'To put it bluntly, if Bush has taken Congress and the nation into war based on bogus information, he is cooked. Manipulation or deliberate misuse of national security intelligence data, if proven, could be a "high crime" under the Constitution's impeachment clause. It would also be a violation of federal criminal law, including the broad federal anti-conspiracy statute, which renders it a felony "to defraud the United States, or any agency thereof in any manner or for any purpose".'

And then, after pausing to think about the 'work-up' exacted on Wilson and Plame, Dean added: 'If I thought I had seen dirty political tricks as nasty and vile as they could get at the Nixon White House, I was wrong ... Nixon never set up a hit on one of his enemies' wives.'

WHITEWASH IN WHITEHALL
or
How the UK government sexed-up the case for war, f**ked the press, and Blair damned himself forever in the eyes of history

I remember thinking the day before the Hutton Inquiry Report was published that Tony Blair was finished. I remember nearly every other journalist I knew thinking the same thing – and nearly every intelligence source I had in my contacts' book was of the same opinion. After listening to the mountain of evidence that Lord Hutton, one of Britain's most senior judges, sucked into his brain during his public inquiry into the death of Dr David Kelly we were all sure that Blair was well and truly screwed. How wrong we were.

Kelly, you'll remember, was the Ministry of Defence scientist and acclaimed UN weapons inspector who was the source for the claim by the BBC reporter Andrew Gilligan that the Labour government 'sexed up' the dossier on Saddam's weapons of mass destruction that it presented to the British public to justify war against Iraq. The Beeb had said that Alastair Campbell, Blair's odious spin-doctor, was responsible for the exaggeration. And the biggest fib told in the entire document, the Beeb added, was the allegation by the government that Saddam could use weapons of mass destruction within 45 minutes of the order being given. That little gem led to headlines in British papers such as *The Sun* which read BRITS 45 MINUTES FROM DOOM. Kelly was finally outed by the Ministry of Defence as the Beeb's source, under Blair's orders. The BBC mole subsequently killed himself, triggering the entire Hutton affair.

The reason all us hacks and all those spies and I'm sure nearly everyone else from Aberdeen to Plymouth felt that Blair was going down was because we'd all heard the same evidence that Hutton had. And being rational human beings we thought the old goat of a judge would think the same way we did. Hutton, of course, isn't a rational human being.

He's a fully paid-up member of the Establishment. As a judge in Northern Ireland during the Troubles, you can't really get much more pro-government than a man like Lord Hutton. The fact that he has the word 'Lord' before his name shows you just how much he's on the side of people like you and me.

Hutton absolved the government and blamed the BBC. As a result, Alastair Campbell and Blair survived, and were never called to account for their actions. Meanwhile, over at the BBC heads rolled and people lost their jobs. These included: Andrew Gilligan, the reporter who made a claim which, as you will see, was correct; Greg Dyke, the Beeb's Director-General; and Gavyn Davies, the Chairman of the Beeb's Board of Governors and one of Tony's cronies – a pal of the PM and a bankroller of the Labour Party who moved in lofty, powerful circles. Davies's wife is the Private Secretary to Gordon Brown – the Chancellor of the Exchequer, and the second most powerful man in British politics. Davies, then, was hardly a man with an anti-government agenda.

The BBC journalists and managers who had the temerity to point out to the public that the British government was comprised of a bunch of liars who'd taken us into an illegal war, had their careers ruined and were personally trampled on while the government went on its merry, duplicitous way.

Well, let's do Lord Hutton's job for him. Or rather, let's complete it. Where his summing up was only based on half the evidence, and his ruling gave just half the story – the government's side of the story – let's explore the other half of the story and the evidence. Let's use the very evidence that was laid before this wilfully blind and deaf system – evidence which was patently ignored – to show how the Hutton inquiry really did come to learn that the government sexed up the case for war, but chose to ignore the truth in order to save Blair's miserable ass.

OK. Let's start with the most important allegation first. Could a paragon of virtue such as Alastair Campbell have possibly had a hand in exaggerating allegations – made in the British government's September 2002 dossier on Iraqi WMD which was cooked up for the consumption of the British public – that Saddam was a clear and present danger to the west, and Britain in particular, as he had stockpiles of WMD? Prior to becoming Blair's henchman-in-chief, Campbell's CV read something like this: reformed booze-hound, ex-porn mag writer and tabloid hack.

Campbell admits that he was involved from a 'presentational point of view' with the dossier and made 'some recommendations' on how the dossier should be written. First question: why does a chap like Ali 'Soupy' Campbell, a media-tart who had become a hired-gun, bully-boy and spin-doctor for Blair, need to look at a dossier which was meant to belong solely to the intelligence services? It was the Joint Intelligence Committee, the body which liaises between the UK's spying services and the British government, which was meant to be in full control of this dossier – nobody else. Sir John Scarlett, the MI6 officer who chaired the JIC, was meant to 'take ownership' of the dossier so that the document would be a pure distillation of intelligence service thinking rather than politicised propaganda. I'd like to point out that Campbell considered Scarlett to be his 'mate'. Blair, I'd also like to point out, would later go on to make Scarlett the head of MI6. Obviously, then, there was no cronyism to worry about at all.

We know from evidence submitted to Hutton that Blair was desperate for the dossier to be packed full of details like how many chemical and biological warheads Saddam had. Of course, the spies didn't have any material like this at all because Saddam didn't have any chemical or biological warheads left, so the JIC sent out a plea to the intelligence services saying: 'No 10, through the chairman, wants the document to be as strong as possible within the bounds of available intelligence. This is therefore a last (!) call for any items of intelligence that agencies think can and should be included.'

It really was desperate. As we now all know, thanks to reading the earlier chapter on Operation Rockingham, the entire dossier was made up of selectively culled claims which were years old, totally discredited and based on the allegations of a few highly suspect Iraqi informers; and key claims, like the 45-minutes allegation, were based entirely on the reports of a single, solitary, untrustworthy Iraqi intelligence source. So desperate, in fact, was this government to get its wicked way and launch a war – whilst keeping its double-dealing out of sight and out of mind – that some members of the JIC weren't even given the fine detail of the intelligence reports before they signed-off on the dossier – they just had to take the government's word that the claims were all *bona fide*.

However, the desperation paid off as the day after the JIC made its pathetic plea for more intelligence on Iraqi naughtiness, Sir Richard Dearlove, then head of MI6, visited Blair and told him that his spies had some new, super-duper intelligence on Iraq. The public, however, has still not been told what the new super-duper intelligence was that

Dearlove brought to the PM.

Campbell had also received an email from his senior special advisor saying: 'Re draft dossier. Very long way to go, I think. Think we're in a lot of trouble with this as it stands now.' It was intelligence-lite, to say the least, and there was no way that the British public was going to be suckered into believing that Saddam was a danger to us based on the scrappy facts presented in the draft dossier. Something had to be done.

Here's the kind of massaging it took to turn the draft dossier from the laughable shambles that it was at this stage into the kind of document that could get a front page in *The Sun* and scare the bejesus out of the British people. Initially, the most contentious claim was handled like this in draft form: 'Chemical and biological munitions could be ... ready for firing within 45 minutes.' When the dossier was published for public consumption the passage read that the warheads 'are deployable within 45 minutes'. So, the threat of Saddam moved from being a possibility to a certainty. That sounds like sexing-up, in my opinion.

As a little aside, readers should know that words like 'could' and 'are' are very important in the world of journalism – a world that a man like Alastair Campbell, a one-time tabloid reporter, knows all about. If a reporter has a story that says, 'Tony Blair *could* be a liar', it is far less likely to get a spot on the front page than the story which says, 'Tony Blair *is* a liar', Newspaper folk don't like doubt to enter into their relationship with the reader – they want certainty, shock and sensation.

Campbell told his 'mate' John Scarlett that there were nine passages in the draft that he thought could be strengthened or were weak. Scarlett wrote back: 'We have been able to amend the text in most cases as you proposed.' So, let me ask you, do you now think Campbell – that one-time soft porn writer and master of the tabloid sensation – sexed up that dossier?

In the week prior to the dossier's publication, Dr David Kelly visited the Defence Intelligence Staff twice to run over the contents of the draft. While there, a scientist complained to him about 'the spin merchants of this administration'. The consensus was that the dossier would hopefully turn into 'tomorrow's chip wrappers'.

Spin merchants? Who could that scientist have meant? These spin merchants, whoever they were (did someone say the name 'Campbell'?), aided and abetted their master, Tony Blair, by helping him write in the foreword to the dossier: 'What I believe the assessed intelligence has established beyond doubt is that Saddam Hussein has continued to produce chemical and biological weapons.' As we now know, that statement is complete and utter bollocks. In any other job, Blair would be seen as either a scheming liar, an incompetent moron or both – either way he'd have been sacked. But no such fate lies in wait for those who lead us, or rather lead us on.

One man who went on the record about the kind of chilling deception that was underway was Dr Brian Jones, the Defence Intelligence Staff's most senior analyst on weapons of mass destruction. He wasn't buying these claims about Saddam's arsenal for a second. At the Hutton Inquiry, he said of the dossier: 'There was an impression that there was an influence from outside the intelligence community.' He was asked if the intelligence community was happy with this interference and he replied: 'No.'

Jones told his own bosses – the Director and Deputy Director of Defence Intelligence, who both happened to serve on the JIC – that 'the intelligence available to me ... has not established beyond doubt that Saddam has continued to produce chemical [and biological] weapons'. He also told the Hutton Inquiry: 'Some of my staff said they were unhappy ... my expert analyst on chemical weapons expressed particular concern ... they were really about a tendency in certain areas, from his point of view, to, shall we say, over-egg certain assessments in relation particularly to the production of CW [chemical weapon] agents and weapons since 1998.' Jones also went on to say that 'our concern was that what we were hearing was second-hand information' and that 'the whole dossier was unusual'. During parliamentary investigations into the use of intelligence in the run-up to war, Jones's concerns and the fears of his experts were never mentioned by government ministers.

Jones talked of 'over-egging'. Gilligan spoke of 'sexing-up'. Is there really any difference? Let's not quibble about metaphors. Both mean the same thing to me: spin, hype, distortion ... perhaps even lying. How on earth, you find yourself asking, after listening to and reading the evidence laid before that dusty old Ulster judge, did Hutton ever come to the conclusions he reached? He deserves the Orwell Prize for Doublethink.

Here's another little taster of some – ahem – obviously minor alterations to the dossier just prior to publication. Jonathan Powell, Blair's Chief of Staff, stumbled upon a paragraph which he thought was 'a bit of a problem'. It read: 'Saddam is prepared to use chemical and biological weapons if he believes his regime is under threat.' As Powell rightly interpreted, this passage stated that Saddam would only unleash his mighty weapons of doom if the Brits and the Yanks rolled over his borders – otherwise he'd leave us and the rest of the world alone. As it stood, then, Saddam was only a threat to the west or his neighbours in the region if we attacked him. That kind of claim just wouldn't do. Powell told the JIC to rewrite that section. When the dossier was published the offending passage read: 'Saddam is willing to use chemical and biological weapons.' It's got the fingerprints of politicians and their spin-doctors all over it. Such a distortion isn't quite a lie, but it is a pubic hair's breadth away from being one. It is a disgusting use of semantics and chicanery at the expense of the British people – utterly misleading and completely undemocratic.

Some of the vast team of press officers working for Campbell even had security clearance to sit alongside intelligence officers while drafts of the dossier were discussed. One press officer, Danny Pruce, emailed Campbell saying: 'Much of the evidence is largely circumstantial so we need to convince our readers that the accumulation of these facts demonstrate an intent on Saddam's part.' Phil Bassett, a senior special advisor to Blair, sent out an email after reading a draft of the dossier describing it as 'intelligence-lite', claiming there was a 'very long way to go' and adding: 'We've got to find a way to get over this by having better intelligence material.'

Blair himself said of the 'sexing-up' accusation: 'Had the allegation been true, it would have merited my resignation.' Can I just ask you a question, Tony? If that's the case then why did you remain in power one more day?

One of John Scarlett's predecessors as head of the JIC is Sir Rodric Braithwaite. He told the BBC's acclaimed *Panorama* programme that Scarlett became far too close to the government and that Campbell should never have been allowed to hold any sway over the dossier.

'The JIC is there to try and produce a dispassionate assessment on some problem usually involving a threat to this country,' he said. 'It's not there to be helpful, it's there to try and make an honest judgment which is very difficult ... It's not [the JIC's job] to fiddle with documents in order to make them more presentable to the public. If they start doing that, they get involved instead of in analysis, which is their job, in presentation, and presentation means not falsifying the facts but presenting them in an order which is designed to produce a particular impression on the audience. It's ceasing to be objective, it's becoming an advocate.'

You could also call it cherry-picking, sexing-up, over-egging or propa-gandising – you choose.

Referring to Jones telling his bosses that he was unhappy with the dossier, Braithwaite said that 'means that something abnormal is going on and you can't just dismiss it ... I can think of a few examples from the past. Of course, it's something that superiors and politicians don't like, but you don't do it lightly if you're an official.'

Braithwaite said that the behaviour of the JIC – the way it rolled over and allowed bits of the dossier to be rewritten at the behest of Blair's bagmen – was not the committee's 'finest moment', adding: 'If your job is simply to analyse things, boring job basically, not very sexy, you have to avoid getting into the magic circle which always surrounds any prime minister, not only this one. A prime minister has to be surrounded by people who support him personally because it's a very tough and wear-ing job, who believe in what he's tried to do, who advocate what he's tried to do and very often will stick at nothing to ensure that what he's trying to do actually happens. That's all legitimate. But if you are part of an analytical process you have to keep outside that. It's very difficult to do that and from time to time it fails. You get people who should be dispassionate being passionately involved in things.' Braithwaite told the BBC that he felt the JIC 'unwittingly became a tool of Downing Street in presenting or trying to rally a sceptical British public to the case for war'.

Three weeks after Bush and Blair declared war on Saddam, David Kelly met the BBC reporter Andrew Gilligan. Gilligan said that Kelly told him the dossier was 'sexed-up'. He pointed out the 45-minute claim as one of the most egregious passages and blamed the spin and hype on Campbell. Gilligan reported on air that the 'government had ordered intelligence to be put into the dossier – even though it probably knew the intelligence to be wrong'.

I ask you, given all that you have just read, could anyone object to that claim made by Gilligan. The report was the truth, but to the gov-ernment it was a lie. Blair and Campbell went ape shit. Excerpts from the diary of Le Campbell read like an overheated melodrama, with Ali sounding like a po-faced Bridget Jones. For example: 'It's grim. It's grim for me and it was grim for TB [Tony Blair] and there is this huge stuff about trust.'

Campbell and Blair had been gunning for journalists for months. With the Tories still a spent pathetic force at this stage, the Liberals a joke and the Labour Party reduced to a bunch of whipped cowering curs, the only real opposition to the all-powerful Blair was the press. Campbell had complained to the BBC 13 times about its journalism.

Kevin Marsh, the editor of the *Today* radio programme which aired Gilligan's report, read the text of the complaint about Gilligan's report from Campbell and flipped. 'It's all drivel,' he said, 'and frankly it'd be easy to get as confused as Campbell is. The man's flapping in the wind.' Like many journalists, Marsh seems to have felt that Campbell was a little freaky – he had control issues and problems with power. It gives me the willies, sometimes, even just to think about him.

Campbell made it clear in his diary that he wanted to hammer the BBC into submission. He got his chance when David Kelly lost his bottle, came forward to his bosses at the MoD and said that he thought he might be Gilligan's source. Kelly insisted, however, that he hadn't attacked the government, criticised the dossier or said the intelligence had been sexed-up.

Campbell could smell blood. Salivating at the thought of being able to beat up on journalism in general, he wrote in his diary: 'Geoff Hoon [the defence secretary] and I agreed it would fuck Gilligan if that [Kelly] was his source.' Isn't it inspirational to know that a man almost as powerful as the prime minister would write such a thing? That he'd say he wanted to 'fuck Gilligan'. He sounds like some jail-house bull-queen – the hetero hard-man who likes raping new boys on the wing just to show them who's the daddy.

The use of language is a telling psychological give-away about the minds behind the men. 'Sexing-up' documents and 'fucking' reporters – you get the feeling that the fellas in power in the UK absolutely get off on being in control. Power really must be the great aphrodisiac. Shame they're all so bloody ugly, though.

So, in order to 'fuck' Gilligan, the Prime Minister started to chair a series of meetings – four in all – in Number 10 on how Kelly would be dealt with. The decision was taken to say that a source had come forward. To undermine the BBC, Campbell wrote in his diary: 'It was agreed ... we should get it out that the source was not in the intelligence community, not involved in drawing up the dossier.'

The next day, *The Times* carried the words: '[The source] is not a member of the Intelligence Services and was not involved in drafting the report.' Hmm ... quite similar to the words in the diary of journalist-fucker-in-chief Alastair Campbell. *The Times* – owned by Blair's media master Rupert Murdoch – was the favoured mouthpiece of Campbell. He later admitted to briefing senior journalists and editors about 'the source', and telling the press that the BBC informant was not a senior intelligence official or centrally involved in the drawing up of the dossier.

Campbell wanted Kelly's name out in the open as he believed that would discredit the BBC's story. The thinking was that if Kelly kept to his story that he hadn't attacked the dossier and hadn't accused Mr lily-white Campbell of sexing-up the dossier then the BBC and Gilligan would indeed be well and truly fucked.

Blair chaired three meetings in one day on Kelly, with the Foreign Secretary, three Permanent Secretaries, his Chief of Staff, the Chair of the Joint Intelligence Committee, a number of Special Advisors and the wearyingly ubiquitous Campbell. A press release was put out describing the source as an advisor to the MoD and an expert in weapons of mass destruction. That narrowed down the field of possible candidates. Journalists were soon sifting through reference books trying to find WMD experts who worked in the MoD so they could get the scoop and name the BBC informant.

Soon someone high up in the government was pouring even more details about Kelly into the ears of journalists – particularly those over at *The Times*. It was related that the BBC source was a former UN weapons inspector – well, there aren't many of those in the world who also worked for the MoD. The list of suspects was getting shorter and shorter. *The Times* was also told that the source was an advisor to the Proliferation and Arms Control Secretariat at the Ministry of Defence. It was now just a matter of time before Kelly's identity was guessed. Some sinister, cynical, spiteful character at the very highest echelons of the government had dripped out enough information on Kelly to ensure that he was outed. This was an act which the government knew would discredit the BBC's story as Kelly had panicked and denied he'd poured scorn on the dossier and Campbell.

Who could have been behind this disgusting manoeuvring which would eventually lead to David Kelly – a loyal servant of the British government – killing himself? I have no idea. Alastair Campbell did write in his diary, by the way, that 'the biggest thing needed was the source out'.

Geoff Hoon now creeps out of the woodwork like a dirty little louse to ease the passage of ruin for Kelly. Hoon – for the benefit of readers who don't know this nonentity – was the Defence Secretary; he was in charge of running the UK's wars. If it didn't sound like a compliment, I'd say he was no Donald Rumsfeld – but I won't. He looks like a maths teacher or a lecturer in town planning. He has the charisma of an ailing carp. He smacks of typical self-serving New Labour nothingism – a cypher ready to say whatever it takes to ensure his slow climb up the greasy pole of power and politics.

Hoon told his press officers that they could confirm Kelly's name to journalists if the journalists got it right. Now, I'm a journalist and I can't imagine any game quite so sick. As lawyers for the Kelly family later said, the government was playing Russian roulette with a man's life. All employers have a duty to care for their staff. The MoD by law should have done all it could to save Kelly from the press – instead they threw him into the arena.

One journalist literally played 20 Questions with the MoD press team – listing name after name of possible suspects. On his 21st guess, he asked if David Kelly was the source. A MoD press officer confirmed that Kelly was the source. Kelly was called at home and told he had been outed. His world collapsed. The man must have been wondering if he was going to be arrested under the Official Secrets Act, if his career was over, if the press would paint him as a traitor. Kelly was a man who'd served his country well and personally taken on Saddam after the First Gulf War over Iraq's – at that time for real – stockpiles of WMD. Now, his reputation was in the gutter.

If creatures like Hoon and Campbell were central to the ruination of Kelly, then what of the Prime Minister's role? Was he, like some Whitehall Zeus, above such lowly mortal machinations? Or was he as up to his armpits in the dirt and the muck and the blood as the rest of them?

Sir Kevin Tebbit, the Permanent Under-Secretary at the Ministry of Defence – in other words the MoD's top civil servant – told the Hutton Inquiry that he'd been present at a committee meeting, along with Blair, when the decision was made to out Kelly – not by releasing his name – but by confirming it if a reporter asked the right questions. He added that the government believed that if Kelly's name was out in the public domain then Gilligan's 'sexing-up' story for the BBC would be totally rebutted.

What a government. What leaders. What courage. What character. They have the nobility of syphilis.

To think of one of the most powerful men in the world – the Prime Minister of this once great country of ours – sitting in a back room racking his brains in order to work out some way of ruining a loyal servant of the British Isles, so he could save his own skin and put the boot into his critics in the press, is profoundly depressing. Blair, ever the slippery lawyer, told the Hutton Inquiry: 'I think the view was: we could not give people wrong information or mislead them, on the other hand we had not volunteered the name.' Once again, Blair's mastery of semantics and double-dealing served him well. He walked a tightrope over a pool filled with the effluent of his own lies, and somehow managed not to fall in and drown. The smell, however, has never left him, and never will.

The nation saw through Blair and his slithery silver-tongued manoeuvrings in an instant. The people watched the Inquiry unfold, certain that there'd be a hanging party at the close of the hearing and that Blair, Hoon and Campbell would all be dangling from the end of ropes. But, as we've seen so often, Satan really does love his own.

The Kelly family weren't buying the bullshit from Blair and Co. either. Mrs Kelly told the Inquiry that her husband had been 'totally let down and betrayed' by the MoD when his name was released. All the while the MoD insisted that it had treated Kelly in an 'outstanding' fashion. This is just another example of the kind of idiotic and schizophrenic way that the MoD treats the English language. Liberating people means killing them; stockpiles of WMD mean a few tanks and some machine-guns, and 'outstanding' care means putting your boot into someone's head when they are already down.

With Kelly now publicly outed, the government decided to use him – their new human toy – to best advantage. Campbell wrote that 'this is now a game of chicken with the Beeb – the only way they will shift is if they see the screw tightening'. Kelly was the ace in the hole in this game of chicken, so the government ordered him to go before two parliamentary committees knowing that he'd say the BBC exaggerated its reporting. Kelly – while a decent man for anonymously bringing the truth about the government's distortions to the public via Gilligan – was just like most of the rest of us when it came to the crunch: he wanted to protect himself and his family, and no-one can blame him for that.

Blair had been told that Kelly had 'uncomfortable views' about the Prime Minister's claim in the dossier that intelligence had 'established beyond doubt' that Saddam had WMD.

But that wasn't Blair's only worry. Kelly had been telling other journalists that it was only 30 per cent likely that Saddam had chemical weapons. In fact, he'd gone further and told at least one journalist that the 45-minutes claim was indeed hyped up. If that came out, then any statement by Kelly claiming that he hadn't told Gilligan that he thought the 45-minutes claim was sexed-up would look somewhat dubious. Why would he say one thing to one reporter and then deny saying something similar to another reporter? Such a position by Kelly just wouldn't have made any sense and the lies behind the government dossier would have been effectively exposed. Kelly's denials would also have made him look like a man who was dissembling in order to protect himself and his career.

BBC journalist Susan Watts had recorded Kelly's comments to her about the 45-minutes claim. This time he'd said: 'I knew the concern about the statement. It was a statement that was made and just got out of all proportion. They were desperate for information. They were pushing hard for information that could be released.' To me, that expression – 'just got out of all proportion' – sounds more than a little like Kelly saying that he felt the dossier had been sexed-up.

Unsurprisingly, an email from the Prime Minister's Chief of Staff said that Blair wanted Kelly well schooled before he gave evidence to the parliamentary committees. He was, the email read, 'to be properly prepared'. These instructions came all the way from Tony Blair. The MoD was told to 'strongly recommend that Kelly is not drawn on his assessment of the dossier but to stick to what he told Gilligan'. MoD meeting notes show officials were panicking about Kelly being questioned on 'tricky areas'.

The two committees Kelly had to go before were the Intelligence and Security Committee – which sits in private – and the Foreign Affairs Select Committee (FAC) which sits in public before TV cameras. The chairman of the FAC, Donald Anderson, a Labour loyalist, agreed to demands by Geoff Hoon about what Kelly could and could not be asked. Kelly was not to be asked about weapons of mass destruction.

One of the most ugly moments during Kelly's interrogation before the FAC was his grilling by MP Andrew Mackinlay, who harangued Kelly saying: 'I reckon you are chaff; you have been thrown up to divert our probing. Have you ever felt like a fall guy? You have been set up, have you not?' Mackinlay's behaviour was all wrong – he was publicly humiliating Kelly – but his point was bang on the money: Kelly was a fall guy; he had been set up to take the BBC down.

Kelly – like Kafka's *homo domesticus* – could only reply: 'I accept the process that is happening.' He was trapped in the arms of a dehumanising bureaucracy and he was as helpless as a child. In a bid to protect himself and protect the government, however, Kelly stupidly lied to Parliament. He told the Committee that he did not recall telling the BBC's Susan Watts that the 45-minutes claim 'got out of all proportion'. Kelly, it would turn out, had also told the government that he had not discussed the dossier with Watts. He'd lied twice so far, therefore, and for a man whose career and reputation rested on his trustworthiness, Kelly must have realised that he was all but finished as a scientist.

Mrs Kelly would later say that her husband now 'looked so desperate … distracted and dejected'. She said he seemed to have 'a broken heart … he had shrunk into himself. I couldn't comfort him.' Kelly found himself in the middle of a system of government that does not like the truth. His attempt at telling journalists the truth had sucked him into a process that demanded he now lie to save himself. It was obviously a bargain of conscience that he couldn't stomach. If Kelly's character is to be measured, then it should be by the great public good he did by alerting a few journalists to the fact that something was wrong with the intelligence that the government was using to justify this war against Iraq. Kelly should not be judged by the couple of lies he told to save his own skin. Who wouldn't lie to protect their jobs and their family and their reputation? His failings were simply very human and not something a man should be condemned for when he has tried to do the decent thing most of his life.

Kelly, however, was his own worst judge – he condemned himself to death. On June 30, 2003, Kelly had come forward to say that he was the source. One July 9, 2003, he'd been named in the press as the source and on July 17, 2003, Kelly took his own life when he walked out of his country house, slit his left wrist and took a mouthful of painkillers. He died slumped under a tree.

On the same day that Kelly was bleeding to death in a field in middle England, Blair was prancing across the world like a prima donna. July 17 was to see Blair go down in the history books as the first British prime minister since Churchill to get the Congressional Gold Medal of Honour in the USA. Churchill got his for standing up to the Nazis when the whole world – including America – looked the other way as Britain got blitzed to bits by German bombers. Blair got his for bootlicking George W Bush and lying his arse off. Blair has an almost fetishistic obsession with his place in history. A long time ago, he might have gone down in the history books as a fairly populist PM who made Britain feel good about itself after the wasted, sleazy, greedy, spiteful, pitiless years of Toryism. Blair gave us Cool Britannia; he brought rock stars to Number 10 for drinks and canapés; he didn't wear a tie all the time; he was a bit like a dull version of Bill Clinton. But then the pull of his place in history dragged him into this war – this illegal, monstrous invasion of Iraq. If anything, historians will see him as the man who bankrupted the trust of the British people and betrayed what lingering spirit of Churchill still resided in Number 10. Under Blair, the highest office in the land had been turned into that of American's number one lackey-in-chief; it was no longer a place of leadership and vision.

So, while Kelly bled to death, Blair waited for his pat on the head. When he received his choc-drop medal from the Americans and got his tummy tickled by Congress, he couldn't help himself but bring up his place in history one more time – this time for the benefit of the US lawmakers. 'If we are wrong,' he said of the invasion, 'we will have destroyed a threat that at its least is responsible for inhuman carnage and suffering. That is something I am confident that history will forgive.'

As Blair arrived in Tokyo from America he found that the fixed present was far less forgiving than any imagined future that he'd been dreaming about in Washington. 'Have you got blood on your hands, Prime Minister?' shouted the journalists as he got off the plane to face the truth of Kelly's suicide. Blair's face was so deathly white that it looked as if he didn't have any blood in his head, let alone on his hands. He looked shaken to his soul; he looked like a man who'd suddenly been confronted with the enormity of his misdeeds. His actions had led to the death of a loyal British citizen and Blair – just momentarily – looked disgusted with himself. His shit-eating smarmy grin was replaced by a grey pallor of panic. He looked scared. If he wasn't such a liar, you could – almost – have felt sorry for him.

To add to the catalogue of his wrongs, Blair spun a web of semantics before the journalists who asked if he'd authorised the release of Kelly's name. While Sir Kevin Tebbit, the MoD's number one mandarin, would later say that Blair presided over the meetings which ruled that certain bits of information about Kelly could be dribbled out to the press and then Kelly's name confirmed if journalists inevitably guessed his identity, Blair, however, indignantly put on an act declaring that he had nothing to do with the naming of Dr David Kelly. 'Emphatically not,' he said when asked if he'd given the go-ahead for Kelly to be named. 'I did not authorise the leaking of the name of David Kelly ... I believe we have acted properly throughout.'

That, ladies and gentleman of the jury, is the alternative take on the evidence given to the Hutton Inquiry. Does it, do you think, add up to a watertight case against the BBC? Does it prove that the government didn't lie about weapons of mass destruction; that the government really did look after David Kelly when he most needed its support; and that David Kelly didn't tell the BBC that the dossier for war was a less than satisfactory document?

I look at the evidence that Hutton heard and I conclude: Kelly knew the dossier was hyped out of all proportion; the government forced the intelligence services to exaggerate what little intelligence the spies had; under the direction of Blair, Hoon and Campbell, Kelly was used, abused, outed and humiliated until the poor man could take it no more and killed himself. Hutton was one almighty whitewash – the biggest cover-up job in British history – and what makes it all the more galling is that it was done right in front of our faces. It was shameless. Hutton pointlessly undermined British democracy. What electorate can really believe that it has the power to hold its leaders accountable when they are protected by handpicked members of the Establishment? But the beauty of Hutton is that his whitewash was just too white. If he had maybe attributed a little blame, just a *soupçon* perhaps, to Blair or Campbell then the public might have had some sugar to coat a bitter pill, but that wasn't to be the case. The damning of the BBC was to be as complete as was the exculpation of the government.

We Brits may be a lot of things, but we aren't stupid. We could see that no-one deserved to get away Scott-free from the inquiry. Hutton's biggest mistake was to offend the British sense of fair play. And Blair would have to pay a deliciously ironic price for being saved by Hutton. From the moment Hutton gave his verdict, Blair's place in history was assured: he would go down in the minds of future generations as the most distrusted leader this country has ever had; as the prime minister who sold out British democracy; as a liar and as a coward. Hutton saved the prime minister for the time being, but he damned him in the eyes of history forever.

SPIES AND LIES

or

**What the UK's top spooks really knew about
the invasion of Iraq—in their own words**

The *Sunday Herald* newspaper received a series of detailed briefings from members of the British intelligence and security services both directly before Lord Hutton published his findings and shortly after the report went public. If I was being diplomatic about how the spies felt, I think I'd have to say that they saw Tony Blair as a less than effective prime minister. If I wasn't being diplomatic, I'd probably say that they considered him an oily little tosser with a forked-tongue.

One week after the January 2004 resignation of David Kay (the CIA-appointed Head of the Iraq Survey Group tasked to find Saddam's WMD, who quit his post saying there weren't any stockpiles of illegal weapons), I took a number of phone calls which outlined the feelings within the UK's key intelligence services over Blair's war in Iraq. Significantly, the briefings were given to me just a few days before Hutton's report was due to be published. Back in late January 2004, everyone thought that Hutton was going to give Blair a bit of a kicking and one of the purposes of this briefing was the spies taking the opportunity to send a message to the prime minister. That message was: if Hutton comes after you, don't go blaming us or we will seriously screw with you in return.

Even after Kay's outright statement that no WMD had been manufactured in Iraq since 1991, Hutton still didn't go after Blair, as we all know, so the spies' pre-emptive shot across the PM's bows was ultimately unnecessary. But thank God they fired that panicked salvo in the first place, as their warning to Blair gives a fascinating insight into just how manipulative the New Labour government has been.

Blair never looked weaker than in the days before the publication of

Hutton's findings. Kay's comments were the equivalent of slashing a boxer's Achilles tendons just minutes before he gets into the ring for the title fight of his life. What Kay said seemed to tally spookily with the general thrust of Andrew Gilligan's controversial broadcast on BBC Radio 4's *Today* programme. You may remember that Kay's successor Charles Duelfer also said that he did not believe banned weapons would ever be found. One day after the *Sunday Herald* received its briefing from British intelligence, Colin Powell, the US Secretary of State, conceded that Iraq may not have possessed any WMD. That was rather nice of him, given that it was Powell who went to the United Nations and started a war by saying Saddam was up to his moustache in WMD in the first place.

When a survivalist politician like Blair is on the ropes, he becomes a dangerous beast. Staying alive is all that counts; if he could find someone to blame for the intelligence failures, then he'd do it just to save his political skin – at least that's what the spooks thought.

The pre-Hutton intelligence briefing I received included the views of some of the most senior representatives inside Britain's main intelligence organisations including: the Defence Intelligence Staff, who helped supply intelligence for Blair's dodgy dossier of September 2002; the Joint Intelligence Organisation (which then included John Scarlett, current head of MI6 and then chair of the Joint Intelligence Committee, the body which liaises between the intelligence services and the government, and which was supposed to have overall control of the drafting of the dossier); the JIC's support staff; and MI6, the country's prime intelligence agency. MI6, or the Secret Intelligence Service, was the main agency responsible for gathering the intelligence which went into the dossier.

It is impossible to be more specific about how exactly representatives of these organisations spoke to the *Sunday Herald* and the ways in which the briefings were given, as many of those who let their views be known to the newspaper are still senior members of the intelligence community. Those who passed on their feelings to the newspaper represented a significant number of intelligence professionals at some of the highest levels of their field.

They were speaking out as they were sure Blair was going to blame them for failing to gather accurate intelligence. They didn't want to be the fall guys for the PM's lies. The briefings they gave were far from a *mea culpa*; what came through in the briefings was a warning to Blair that they were not prepared to be the whipping boys for the failure to prove the case for war, the death of David Kelly, the quagmire that the government found itself in on the eve of the Hutton Report's publication and the lack of WMD in Iraq.

This is what they had to say.

Firstly, there was a problem with Iraq, particularly over the interpretation of the WMD issue. Many said they had been openly sceptical about the presence of WMD in Iraq for years. There was a systematic failure, they believed, in the way intelligence was interpreted. This was because they were under pressure to provide the government with what it wanted to hear – namely that Iraq was indeed in possession of WMD and that it posed a clear and present danger to British interests.

Secondly, they said that intelligence was 'cherry-picked' – their word, not mine – over Iraq and that damning intelligence against the country was selectively chosen, whilst intelligence assessments which might have worked against the build-up to war were sidelined. The government was looking for anything that would cast Iraq in a negative light.

Thirdly, this group of spies, analysts and intelligence professionals claimed that a political agenda had crept into the work of the intelligence community and they found themselves in the invidious position of taking orders from politicians. In other words, the vitally objective work of intelligence officers was subordinated to the subjective needs of politicians. When asked if direct lies were told to the British public, the answer was that the intelligence they supplied was one-sided and produced on demand to politicians.

Fourthly, the intelligence community got into the habit of making worst-case scenarios and these were then used to make factual claims by politicians. The spies accepted that intelligence was used for political ends, but they also said that their understanding of their job was that it was not meant to help politicians justify their actions as that distorts the nature of what their profession is all about. The way the spies see it, the intelligence game is all about protecting British interests no matter what – and the war on Iraq didn't do that.

The spies also said they realised it was high time that changes were made to the way British intelligence operates – if only for the purpose of saving the almost ruined reputation and integrity of UK spooks. Blair had taken the existing intelligence system and destroyed it; after him, a new start was needed for the profession to recover.

Hours after this briefing from the intelligence community, Donald

Anderson – the Labour loyalist who chaired that devastating session of the Foreign Affairs Select Committee hearings during which David Kelly was humiliated and degraded – came out and said that he felt the failings over WMD were more the fault of the intelligence services than the politicians. His comments just reinforced the belief within the intelligence services that slippery New Labour was going to shaft the spooks – who they'd already used and abused to get their way and start a war with Iraq – now that the shit was about to hit the fan.

This pre-emptive strike by some of the most senior members of British intelligence was quickly forgotten amid the stunned bewilderment that greeted Hutton's whitewashing of Blair and his cabal in Westminster. But the spies were not going to forgive and forget. Not long after Hutton's absurd findings were delivered, the *Sunday Herald* received another briefing – this time from one of the very highest ranking officials in the Ministry of Defence. The source is among the most senior players in the Ministry, has the highest of security clearances and is a central figure in the intelligence loop. The source knows exactly what went down inside the corridors of power as the case for war was rushed through by Blair, Hoon and Campbell.

Regrettably, in order to protect the source, that person will have to remain a sexless 'they' – even referring to their gender might narrow the field on the list of possible candidates, and I wouldn't want to help the government in yet another dirty little game of 'let's jigsaw identify confidential anonymous whistle-blowers'.

Our war planners, the high-placed MoD source said, really wanted to move against *bona fide* rogue states such as North Korea – which does have nuclear weapons – but it was because of the very fact that Kim Jong-il's Korea had nukes that we didn't pursue wars against such nations. In other words, Britain and America are prepared to kick the weedy little psychopaths around – nasty runts like Saddam – but big bad Kim and his hydrogen bomb are just way too heavy to take on. That is nothing but a recipe for imperial swaggering by the US and the UK which leaves the real villains still posing terrible risks to the British and American people.

With 9-11 as a backdrop, Iraq became an immediate target, the source explained. The MoD started 'doing scenario planning' for invading Iraq. 'We thought we might get three for one,' the source said. 'If we hit Iraq then we thought that Iran and Libya might topple, too. We'd always wanted to remove [Libyan leader] Colonel Gaddafi from power in Tripoli as Libya is strategically important to us. We thought that if we were getting into this war then we should use it to sort out as many rogue states as possible.'

Libya, incidentally, sits on vast oil wealth. When it comes to Iran, however, the MoD couldn't have got it more wrong. Instead of the war against Iraq destabilising the mullahs in Iran, the MoD now believes that it was the Iranians who were pulling strings behind the scenes to get the west to hit Iraq and take out Saddam – the bitterest enemy of the ayatollahs in Iran.

It gets complicated here. Bear with me. Everyone remembers Ahmed Chalabi, the leader of the exiled Iraqi National Congress, which was desperate to have Saddam deposed? Chalabi was also a convicted embezzler and was one of the men funnelling wonky intelligence into Whitehall and the White House – intelligence which made all manner of outlandish claims about Saddam's WMD capabilities.

Well, the Bush administration and its spying services now believe that Chalabi was an Iranian spy who was supplying the mullahs with info on US plans for Iraq – a claim that Chalabi vehemently denies. US officials said that electronic intercepts showed that Chalabi and some of his top aides were discussing Iraq with Iran. Chalabi, obviously denying everything, was cut adrift from the US administration. Financial aid was cut off to his Iraqi National Congress and the US raided his HQ in Baghdad.

Chalabi, the Americans allege, was telling the Baghdad station chief of Iranian intelligence that the US was reading Iran's secret communications. Chalabi was rumbled, apparently, when the Iranian spymaster in Baghdad sent a cable to Tehran recounting what Chalabi had told him. Obviously, as the US was reading Iran's encrypted messages, they found out that Chalabi had informed on them to the Iranians.

So what else did Chalabi or another spy within the INC tell the Iranians? Well, if British intelligence is to believed the INC double-agents told everything they could – but more importantly they were also feeding Iranian-inspired disinformation right back to the intelligence services in London and Washington. Here's how that very, very senior source in the British Ministry of Defence put it: 'We have come to see that Iran carried out one of the biggest intelligence coups of the century. It got the US and UK to go to war against Iraq – its biggest enemy – by infiltrating our intelligence services in the most subtle of ways. The operation was quite brilliant.'

Do you see how it works? The Iranians tell the INC some made-up nonsense about Saddam; the INC then tells British and American spooks the same nonsense; the spooks tell the politicians, and the politicians use the information to prove to the public that the US and UK must go to war with Iraq. And it was all based on lies and rubbish in the first place. It is, indeed, quite brilliant.

The MoD chief both slaps Blair around and praises him. First of all, the source says, that if it hadn't been for British pressure coming straight from Number 10 then Bush would have gone to war probably as much as a year earlier. 'We had to fight hard to stop that happening,' the source said. The MoD and Number 10 were 'desperate' to get a second resolution on Iraq from the United Nations which would have justified war. 'This was a prime concern for us both in terms of the legality of the war and also to give the operation legitimacy in the eyes of the soldiers and officers,' the MoD chief said. Many senior British army officers still believe they may be committing war crimes simply by being in Iraq because of the almost non-existent legal basis for the invasion. That has tied British hands in Iraq and limited their desire to take on Iraqi insurgents – a fact that is contributing to the casualty figures for UK forces.

So, in the eyes of this top-drawer MoD figure, Blair tried to go down the UN route and tried to rein in Bush. But – and it's a big but – once the UN route was closed down and Bush was off the leash, Blair went right along behind the neocons believing that fighting a war based on lies was in the best interests of the UK as it would keep in place the inviolable ties of the special transatlantic relationship between Britain and America. To Blair, lying to the British people so he could fight a war in order to keep on the right side of the US was a better option than acting as a true friend of America, and a British patriot, by telling the US that it was wrong and bang out of order to whack Iraq. That is what senior intelligence and military figures find so intolerable. 'Hutton was completely wrong not to criticise Blair,' the source said. 'He should have given it to Number 10.'

Of course, the MoD chief is worried that the Prime Minister manipulated intelligence and peddled half-truths and myths to get the UK into a shooting match, but after a career spent trying to defend Great Britain what worries this source most is the detrimental effect Blair's machinations have had on British national security. The source is quite clear that there can be no more wars fought by Britain for quite some considerable time – not only because our troops are overstretched, but also because Parliament and the people would not support a war. That is a recipe for disaster to a career soldier or spy. What if, one day soon, we *really* need to go to war? What if real intelligence comes in to MI6 that an enemy state is planning to hit us? How does the prime minister convince the people and Parliament that this time he's telling the truth? Blair's self-serving dissembling has seriously hobbled the UK's ability to defend itself. If wars are out of the question for a while, then military brass – like this source – believe that diplomacy must be used to improve global stability.

That is why, this source says, that 'from the point of view of the Foreign Office and the MoD, Israel and Palestine must be dealt with as this situation is still the biggest threat to world peace'. If the Iraq war has made the world a more dangerous place, then the only way to make the planet – and by extension the UK – safer is for the poison of the Palestine–Israel question to be drawn. It is this conflict which, the MoD chief believes, is fuelling world terror. However, Blair is insignificant in the Israeli scheme of things – all Tel Aviv cares about is American opinion, not the views of the British people, the source added. Blair also failed to get Bush to properly tackle a political solution to the Palestine–Israel conflict; a fact, the MoD chief says, which shows 'that he hasn't as much influence with Bush as he likes to think he has'. Britain was equally weak when it came to standing up for Hans Blix, the former UN chief weapons inspector, who was continually undermined by the Bush administration. The UK wanted to keep Blix and his weapons inspectors in place in Iraq 'as he was doing a good job', the MoD source added, but Washington would have none of it and London gave up the fight like a meek little lamb.

One of the most fascinating comments made by the MoD chief was that 'Israel is not actually that strategically important to the US'. According to the source's analysis, Israel fixated on Iraq – seeing it as the biggest threat to security and peace in the Middle East. There are two reasons why America wants to keep Israel safe at all costs – even if that means spinning the case for an illegal war against Iraq. Firstly, and unsurprisingly, there is the electoral clout of the powerful Jewish lobby in the US. A president who turns his back on Israel – or a presidential candidate who did the same – is a contradiction in terms: in America such a thing just can't and won't happen. That's why Democrats and Republicans have less than a hair's breadth between them over their respective policies on the Middle East. But another – and certainly far greater – reason to protect Israel is that Tel Aviv is nuked-up. The MoD source said that if any nation in the Middle East really threatened Israel, and Tel Aviv felt itself abandoned by the US, it would launch nuclear strikes against its enemies without hesitation. America, therefore – at least according to the MoD chief – is locked into protecting Israel; the US is trapped by its own policy. To prevent nuclear war, it has to be Israel's ever vigilant guard-dog.

Any time I talk to someone senior in the intelligence world, the discussion raises more questions than it can ever possibly answer – it's the nature of this 'through the looking-glass world' that spies live in. If there were no WMD in Iraq, the source was asked, then why did we have a war in the first place? The MoD chief gave a pretty unsatisfactory answer, but here it is anyway: 'To avenge Saddam's attempted assassination of George Bush Senior.'

Bush Senior had been targeted for assassination by Saddam during a 1993 visit to Kuwait. Baby Bush is on record as saying Saddam was the 'guy that tried to kill my dad'. Clearly, there was personal business to be attended to in this war.

The MoD source did not go easy on their erstwhile colleague, Dr David Kelly, either. Kelly, the source said, killed himself because he lied to Parliament about speaking to Susan Watts, the other BBC journalist whom he briefed about WMD. Kelly, the source added, was getting most of his information about the dissatisfaction of the intelligence community with Blair's dossier from senior figures in the Defence Intelligence Staff. The source added: 'When he talked of unhappiness within the intelligence community he didn't mean MI6.' There was no elaboration on this remark, but one can take it to mean that those at the top of MI6 were playing along with the government's manipulation of the facts, while elements within the DIS – the Ministry of Defence's intelligence wing – were bitterly opposed to such duplicity. Given that Blair's lying machine – Operation Rockingham – was located within the DIS, it's not surprising to learn that it was from inside the DIS that most of the intelligence communities' concerns emanated.

Nor was Kelly all that popular with the staff and bosses at the MoD. The bosses felt he rated himself too highly. 'He was always asking for a pay rise,' the source said. And he was a bit of a loner. 'He was always off on his own professionally,' the source added, pointing out that the Ministry of Defence had learned lessons from the Kelly affair – such as not to let any member of staff become a one-man band – which they hope will avoid future disastrous leaks.

A big worry in the minds of MoD chiefs is that the invasion of Iraq has totally taken the UK's eye off the ball in Afghanistan. 'That country is a total mess,' the source said. But neither the UK nor the US has the manpower to deal with the deteriorating situation. Some of the MoD's biggest hitters clearly believe that the War on Terror – or at least the elimination of the Taliban and its safe haven for al-Qaeda – was a war worth fighting, while the invasion of Iraq was pointless. Their thinking is nothing more than self-evident 'War Planning 101'. The Taliban in Afghanistan were harbouring al-Qaeda. Al-Qaeda kills westerners. Therefore, the Taliban must go in order to take out al-Qaeda and protect the UK.

That logic works – that's all fairly simple.

However, the logic on invading Iraq is as fuzzy as static on a TV with a bad reception during a Force 10 gale in the Outer Hebrides. The logic on not invading Iraq is a lot clearer. It goes like this: Iraq is controlled by Saddam. We aren't sure if Saddam has WMD. Saddam doesn't appear to be a threat to the west. Therefore, there is no point in taking out Saddam as it won't protect Britain's interests – in fact, hitting Saddam might spread anti-western feeling and make the UK more vulnerable. That's the way our best military minds were working – but that is not the way the minds of people like Blair, Hoon and Campbell were operating.

The MoD source says the Defence Ministry is proud of the number of active al-Qaeda operatives who have been taken out of circulation both here and abroad who were planning to hit British interests. 'We've lifted so many al-Qaeda guys that you wouldn't believe it,' the source said, adding that successes such as this and the 'stifling of al-Qaeda funds' have been overshadowed by the Iraqi quagmire. As an aside, the source castigated Bush for continually and 'deliberately' equating al-Qaeda and 9-11 with Iraq and WMD. They are two separate issues, but an easily confused public was lured into supporting a hit on Saddam because his spectre was continually raised in the same breath as comments made about al-Qaeda.

And for the future? What happens now to British spying? Well, for a start, the MoD chief thinks it's a disgrace that John Scarlett, the JIC chairman, was made the head of MI6 in the wake of the Hutton Report. It damaged irreparably British intelligence forever in the eyes of the public and made spying seem like just another arm of Number 10. 'Scarlett was not the man for the job. He should go,' the source said. The MoD chief said that a complete rethink had to be undertaken to preserve the future of British intelligence. Everything from a merger of the major agencies to the appointment of an intelligence czar needs to be put on the table for discussion if British intelligence is to save its image overseas and keep the trust of the UK public at home.

Finally, and most tellingly of all, the MoD chief said: 'We've got to stop cosying up to Bush. The 21st century is the century when India and China will come to dominate the globe – it's these guys we need to get close to now. That's the new reality.'

Proof of the shoddy use of intelligence that my sources spoke about could even be gleaned from public statements made by leading spies before and after the war. When 'C' – Sir Richard Dearlove, the head of MI6 at the time of the Iraq war and the Hutton Inquiry – gave evidence by audio link to Hutton (famously never showing his face in order to keep a semblance of secrecy around a service that leaks as much as a Victorian lavatory), he admitted that the claim that Saddam could use WMD in 45 minutes was based on the flimsiest of proof: the word of a single Iraqi army officer.

Dearlove also admitted that he didn't even know what type of munitions the Iraqi officer was specifically talking about. Nor did he know where the alleged munitions were. He even said that the dossier should never have appeared to suggest that Saddam could launch chemical and biological weapons against British bases in Cyprus within 45 minutes. In other words, the whole claim was crap.

Dearlove tried to explain this all away by saying that the press gave 'undue prominence' to the 45-minutes claim. The press? I don't remember any working journalists writing the dodgy dossier? Wasn't it the MI6 spies and the politicians who were in cahoots? Wasn't it the Westminster spin-doctors who drip-fed lies to the press – lies like the 45-minutes claim, which workaday journalists then in turn stupidly and unwittingly peddled to the public?

Dearlove then went on to say that 'the original report [on the 45 minutes-claim] referred to chemical and biological munitions and that was taken to refer to battlefield weapons. I think what subsequently happened … was that it was taken that the 45 minutes applied, let us say, to weapons of a longer range.'

That means the MI6 spies and the PM knew that if Saddam was able to ready WMD in 45 minutes that those weapons would only have been able to hit British troops on the battlefield – inside Iraq. There was never any risk of Saddam targeting UK interests overseas. Blair was never questioned about this by Hutton. No-one asked him why short-range weapons like mortar shells were suddenly upgraded in the eyes of the British Establishment to long-range weapons like Scuds.

Geoff Hoon admits that he deliberately left this lie festering in the minds of the British people to breed fear. He was asked why no 'corrective statement' was put out after scaremongering headlines in newspapers like *The Sun* warned that Britain could be hit in 45 minutes by Saddam's banned arsenal. With an inconceivable degree of arrogance, he told the inquiry: 'I have spent many years trying to persuade newspapers and journalists to correct their stories. I have to say it is an extraordinary time-consuming and generally frustrating process.'

When Hoon was asked if he accepted that he had 'an absolute duty' to correct misconceptions in the public mind, he replied: 'No, I do not.' Hoon also refused to accept that the reason he issued no apology was that 'it would have been highly embarrassing because it would have revealed the dossier as published was at least highly capable of being misleading'.

Other Labour ministers weren't quite so brutally on message as Hoon, Blair's favourite pre-programmed android. The usually fearsome Blair enforcer John Reid was the Labour Party Chairman in the days after the invasion. He went on to fill Hoon's shoes – not a hard job, I'm sure – as Defence Secretary, before becoming Home Secretary. A member of the Labour Party called Alun Harford came forward to tell me that he had taken part in a telephone conference with Reid in which the Labour hard man said it would have taken 'more than 48 hours' for Saddam to get his WMD operative. Harford, who has now quit the party, said: 'I can tell you, I am absolutely confident that that is what Dr Reid said.'

To me, it is nothing short of a Christian miracle that Blair managed to get away with taking this country to war. Anyone who had a brain in their head was against it from the start; it's hard now to find anyone, apart from the hollowed-out ghosts that Blair fills his cabinet with, who actually supports the invasion.

A long-standing British military intelligence source of mine told me: 'There was absolute scepticism among the British intelligence agencies over the case for the invasion of Iraq. [Alastair] Campbell's claims that the dossier wasn't sexed-up are utter rubbish.' People like Clare Short, the former cabinet minister, backed this spook up: 'The suggestion that there was the risk of chemical and biological weapons being weaponised and threatening us was spin. That didn't come from the security services,' she said in the months following the war. 'It was a political decision that came straight from the Prime Minister.'

Short said she'd seen intelligence from all the security services and it did not mention anything to do with the 45-minutes claim in the briefings. Menzies Campbell, then the esteemed Lib-Dem Foreign Affairs Spokesman and now the party's leader, said: 'It was one of Whitehall's least well kept secrets that, throughout the Iraq crisis, the intelligence services have been uneasy about the use being made of the product of their labours.'

The same military intelligence source who poured scorn on Campbell told me that France and Russia had the best intelligence on what was going on inside Saddam's regime and they were telling the US and the UK that 'there was effectively no real evidence of a WMD programme' in Iraq.

Don't think that the Washington neocons and their Westminster bootlickers didn't know – unlike France, Russia and my friendly spy – that there were no WMD in Iraq. In May 2003, US Defense Secretary Donald Rumsfeld blew the whistle on himself when he said that Iraqi leaders possibly destroyed their WMD before the invasion. If that was true then Iraq had fulfilled the criteria of UN Resolution 1441 – which required them to disarm. That meant that there was no legal basis for the war to proceed – at all. Rumsfeld made a total fool of himself with his comments, and gave us a quick glimpse of the blood all over his podgy little hands. The US had mocked Hans Blix, the UN chief weapons inspector, saying he wasn't up to the job of finding Saddam's arms caches – but if the weapons were destroyed, as Rumsfeld suggested, then there was nothing for Blix to find.

The chilling, oleaginous Paul Wolfowitz went even further. He said the US only focused on WMD because it was a politically convenient way of justifying war against Iraq. 'For bureaucratic reasons we settled on one issue, weapons of mass destruction because it was the one reason everyone could agree on,' he said. It was also the one claim that scared the living daylights out of westerners in the wake of 9-11.

Rumsfeld added later: 'The coalition did not act in Iraq because we had discovered dramatic new evidence of Iraq's pursuit of WMD. We acted because we saw the evidence in a dramatic new light – through the prism of our experience on 9-11.'

The UK's mainstream spies were telling their political masters that the intelligence on WMD was pathetic and not anywhere near strong enough to build a case for war. 'The intelligence we were working on was basically of a technical nature coming from satellite surveillance and eavesdropping. The only real humint [human intelligence] that we had was from Iraqi exiles and we were sceptical of their motives,' one military intelligence source said.

It was this 'tainted' intelligence which was used to compile the crucial dossier on Iraq which Blair presented to MPs in September 2002. On the 45-minutes claim, the military intelligence officer said: 'The information had been lying around for ages. The problem was we didn't really trust the defectors as they were working in their own self-interest and really doing their master's bidding – by that I mean us, the UK. They also had one eye to the future and their role in any new Iraqi Government.'

The intelligence used to make the 45-minutes claim was based on information at least 10 years old stemming from the time of the First Gulf War, the military intelligence source said: 'We are talking about information relating to 1991 and afterwards.' This military intelligence officer had served in the First Gulf War.

'We told the government that this information was old but they ignored the fact.' Claims that Iraq could hit British interests in 45 minutes related to information about Iraqi missile systems in 1991 such as the Scud.

'These were mobile missiles. A good Iraqi team would take 20 minutes to get them active, an average team would take 45 minutes – that is where the government claim comes from.

'The government elected to use this to say Saddam Hussein could deploy chemical weapons in 45 minutes. But it's rubbish. Saddam's capabilities were destroyed. Iraq simply wouldn't have had this ability when we invaded. There was only the very remotest possibility that he had long-range missiles or chemical weapons left.

'It can't be denied that Saddam once did have this capability, but when intelligence handed this information to the government, the 45-minutes claim was extracted in isolation and misrepresented. You can't use 10-year-old intelligence as the basis for anything. People like Alastair Campbell are able to fall back on the fact that Saddam once had the ability to deploy in 45 minutes, but there is a fear within intelligence that people like him can turn around and blame us for passing old intelligence.'

Sir Richard Dearlove, the former head of MI6, in his evidence to the Hutton Inquiry, admitted that 'there was no new intelligence at all after 9 September [2002] which related to the 45-minutes claim'.

Keep that date in mind when you recall that it was on September 11 2002 that John Scarlett's team at the JIC sent out their infamous note on behalf of Blair making a 'last (!) call for any items of intelligence that agencies think can and should be included' in the dossier.

In response to the September 11, 2002 email, Dearlove arrived at Downing Street the next day – September 12, 2002 – and told Blair that he had new and highly sensitive intelligence on Iraq. Whatever it was (as I've said before the public still hasn't been told what this information concerned) it had nothing to do with Iraq being able to ready weapons in 45 minutes. So, that means that at a time when Number 10 and the spin-doctors and spooks who were in Blair's cabal were panicking and trying to get extra intelligence to pad out the dossier, the details of the 45-minutes claim were already well known in intelligence circles. The 45-minutes claim was not some final-hour fact uncovered by British spies that they failed to check thoroughly as the clock was ticking; it was a tatty old bit of nonsense that had been lying around gathering dust on a shelf at Spook HQ for years, and everyone knew it to be well dodgy. It was taken down from that shelf, dusted off and given a nice new glossy lick of spin-doctor paint to make it all the more attractive to a British public gullible enough to believe that the UK's leaders wouldn't deceive them when it came to putting their sons and daughters in the military in harm's way in Iraq.

Dearlove also briefed senior BBC executives, telling them that Syria and Iran posed a greater threat than Iraq, and claimed that Iraq was not viewed by the intelligence services as a primary threat. Dearlove even added that in terms of WMD and terrorism Iraq was not a priority. The briefing took place before the BBC's infamous report on radio which said that the 'dodgy dossier' had been 'sexed-up' by the government.

Our servicemen and women were sent out to die in the desert even though our allies like France were saying, 'don't do it, don't go, this war is pointless, there are no WMD'. The military intelligence officer told me: 'French intelligence was telling us that there was effectively no real evidence of a WMD programme. That's why France wanted a longer extension on the weapons inspections. The French, the Germans and the

Russians all knew there were no weapons there – and so did Blair and Bush as that's what the French told them directly. Blair ignored what the French told us and instead listened to the Americans.'

Other intelligence sources have speculated that Blair went along with America because of Israel. One source said that 'the real over-arching strategic reason' for the war was the road map for peace in the Middle East designed to settle the running sore of the Israeli–Palestinian conflict. 'I believe that Britain and America saw the road map as fundamental. They were being told by Ariel Sharon [Israel's former premier] that Israel would not play ball until Saddam was out of the way. That was the condition. So he had to go.'

A few spooks and spies who I spoke to said they believed that Saddam had a tiny WMD arsenal which he shifted over the border and into Syria prior to the invasion – however, sources who made this claim tempered their comments by adding that they believed such allegations were stemming from hardliners in America who could, perhaps, have been angling to take the war to Syria next.

Others said they were 'very unhappy' with the dossier; some were 'pissed off' and one said the claim about WMD being battle-ready in 45 minutes was 'complete and utter bollocks'.

One well-placed intelligence source told me: 'The spooks were being asked to write this stuff. The dossier had been lying around for months. When it came time for publication, Downing Street said it wasn't exciting or convincing enough. The message was that it didn't cut the mustard in terms of PR as there wasn't much more in it than a discerning newspaper reader would know. The intelligence services were asked if there was anything else that could be added to it. Intelligence told Downing Street that the 45-minutes claim hadn't been added in as it only came from one source who was thought to be wrong. The intelligence services were asked to go back and do a rewrite even though Downing Street was told the 45-minutes claim was unconvincing.'

Those who have lined up to attack Bush and Blair for this politicisation of intelligence make for a long and impressive list. Just a few include folk like former Labour Minister, Glenda Jackson, who thinks Blair should resign; the formidable, courageous and now sadly dead Robin Cook, who said the PM should admit he was 'wildly wrong' when he presented his intelligence dossier to Parliament (Cook also said: 'Now that even the White House has admitted they may have got it wrong, it's embarrassing to watch our government still trying to deny reality. The game is up.'); Air Marshall Sir John Walker, the former Chief of Defence Intelligence, who said it was clear that claims about Saddam's WMD capabilities were 'wrong' and who scorned the idea that British intelligence chiefs weren't influenced by Number 10; and former Labour Defence Minister Peter Kilfoyle, who said 'evidence was used selectively from intelligence reports to fit the case' and added that the failure to prove the case for war to the British people had 'shattered trust' in the government. Peter Kilfoyle then went on to ask the House of Commons library if impeachment was still a part of the UK constitution – he was told that it was. Around the same time, prosecutors at the International Criminal Court at The Hague were asked to consider a request by an international body of lawyers to investigate Mr Blair for alleged war crimes.

Oh dear, Mr Blair does seem to have run out of friends. It may, therefore, come as no surprise to you that the people Blair hangs out with now when he has a holiday aren't the celebrity high-roller types like Bill and Hillary Clinton, but people like Cliff Richard and Silvio Berlusconi. For readers unfamiliar with Cliff Richard, he is an ageing English Christian 'pop' star who likes tennis. For anyone unfamiliar with Mr Berlusconi, I can tell you that I have heard him described as Italy's answer to Tony Blair. Enough said.

TONY IN THE TOWER

or

How Mrs Cherie Blair could impeach her lying, conniving husband and have his head set on Traitor's Gate for crimes against Britain

Can you imagine how wonderful it would be to see Tony Blair one day led away in handcuffs for what he has done to Britain and the world? It would be a true bonfire of the vanities; a moment when someone who considers themselves to be one of the masters of the universe is brought back to earth with a bone-shattering bump and then taken for a ride in a Black Mariah for an appearance before the beak (for non-UK readers, that means he's taken in a police truck to the local courthouse).

I know, I know. You think this can't happen. Leaders never get punished, right? No matter what they do, they retire with bank accounts stuffed with cash and life peerages and a battalion of armed Special Branch officers to keep them safe. Just look at the cosy, twilight years of that lovely old grandpa of global statesmen, General Pinochet of Chile.

But what if it could happen to Blair – regardless of whether or not the British electorate or the Labour Party has booted him out of office for single-handedly turning Britain into a corrupt cesspit? Subjecting Blair to a trial might be the only way to really save democracy in the UK. If a leader can take it upon himself to lie to the people of this country and the Parliament to get us into an illegal war in order to keep on the right side of the US, then what right do we have to keep the 'Great' in Great Britain anymore? If such a thing can happen, we are a democracy in name only. Culturally and historically, Blair has disgraced this nation. Once, the UK, for all its faults, both ancient and modern, could at least hold its head up as the one nation that stood alone against Hitler for two years. Then, we were the resistance; now, we are the occupier.

Blair was given custody of the highest office in this land and he corrupted it; in turn he has corrupted the country and its people. He has failed in his duty. But he should be held to account not because he is incompetent, but because he lied and he cheated. Remember, Blair is our servant. We voted him into office and we pay his wages. If you part-owned a company and a member of staff was just rubbish at their job, you wouldn't call the police, you'd just sack them quickly and get on with hiring someone else to do the job better the next time. But if you find that an employee has lied to you, assumed powers they didn't have, wrecked your reputation and put you in peril, then you'd probably have the right to consider calling the cops.

Well, that is what is happening right now. The machinery for impeaching Blair has already clanked into life. It's been many, many years since Britain used the power of impeachment against one of its leaders, but the old law has been taken down from the shelves and dusted off, and, unluckily for Blair, it looks as if his behaviour is the very definition of impeachable conduct.

The case for impeachment was drawn up for the Welsh Nationalist Plaid Cmryu MP Adam Price. The document, called *A Case to Answer* was put together by two of the UK's best academic brains – the redoubtable Messrs Glen Rangwala and Dan Plesch. Much of what appears in *A Case to Answer* is already known – such as Blair's lies over WMD – but the masterstroke of the exercise is that the authors have put this document together forensically, setting out the case for impeaching Blair with the surety of a legal standard of proof. And it is brilliantly convincing.

In fact, if a really shit-hot ambitious lawyer got their hands on this document, they could use it as the basis for putting together the prosecution of the British Prime Minister. Imagine the fame and celebrity that would come to any lawyer who was able to successfully prosecute Blair. I'm not saying that they'd succeed in putting him behind bars – that's not going to happen. Just having him impeached would be a gold standard legal and political coup. If he's still in public office, then strip him of his premiership. If he's either resigned, been booted out by Labour MPs increasingly fearful that he will take the party down with him, or been dumped by a nihilistic British electorate, then ban him for life from holding public office ever again. It would forever signal to future leaders that we – the people – will exact a punishment on them if they lie to us or mislead us. The successful prosecution of Blair would be a turning point in western history and a testament to the British people's belief in national and global democracy. It would show the true power of the people ... and it would also make whichever lawyer decided to take the case on, a very rich person and a hero of democracy.

So, I got to thinking: 'Which lawyer could do this?' We'd need someone who really understands the inner workings of government; someone with a sharp legal mind who isn't afraid to take on the Establishment or fight for the underdog; someone independent-minded; wilful; ruthlessly ambitious; a performer. Then it hit me – Cherie Blair! Cherie is the only lawyer capable enough to take on her own husband and bring him down. So, I'd pick Cherie to prosecute Tony. Wouldn't it be a beautiful thing to behold? Finally, the Blairs – both lawyers – would be able to settle which one of them really was the king or queen of the courtroom. And, damn, if I wouldn't be praying for Cherie's coronation.

Let's set out the case for impeaching her husband for Cherie, courtesy, of course, of the sterling research of Rangwala and Plesch. The biggest 'charge' against Blair is, of course, that his claims about Iraq's WMD were made up, or, if you wish to be more diplomatic about it, 'unsupported by the intelligence assessments available to him'.

Now, if Cherie were prosecuting Blair, she'd quote from *A Case to Answer* and say: 'A considerable number of the claims made by the Prime Minister about Iraq's NBC [nuclear, biological and chemical] weapons from early 2002 onwards drew upon the authority of the intelligence services for their validation.'

An example would be when Blair told the Commons on September 24, 2002: 'I am aware, of course, that people are going to have to take elements of this [the case for war against Iraq] on the good faith of our intelligence services. But this is what they are telling me.'

A few months earlier on April 3, 2002, Blair said: 'We know that [Saddam Hussein] has stockpiles of major amounts of chemical and biological weapons, we know that he is trying to acquire nuclear capability, we know that he is trying to develop ballistic missile capability of a greater range.'

A week later, Blair told the House of Commons: 'Saddam Hussein ... is developing weapons of mass destruction, and we cannot leave him doing so unchecked. He is a threat to his own people and to the region and, if allowed to develop these weapons, a threat to us also.'

OK. So, let's have a look at some of the intelligence reports that were available to Blair around the same time and see what they say about Iraq. Don't forget, Blair said that he was basing his argument on what the intelligence services were telling him.

But now things get really strange. The Joint Intelligence Committee assessments of March and April 2002 were nowhere near as certain as Blair was about the threat posed by Saddam or about Iraq's WMD stockpiles. Was Blair, Cherie would have to ask herself, ignoring the mainstream intelligence and seeking his facts from elsewhere? Was he cherry-picking intelligence? Was he taking worst-case scenario information and ignoring the vast swathe of intelligence which didn't back up his lust for taking part in America's war? Was he using the type of twisted intelligence that came from Operation Rockingham or the Office of Special Plans and quashing the considered analysis of long-standing intelligence specialists?

It seems so. If Cherie did take on this case, she'd be rubbing her hands in glee to read the JIC assessment of March 15, 2002. It says: 'Intelligence on Iraq's weapons of mass destruction and ballistic missile programmes is sporadic and patchy ... We believe Iraq retains some production equipment and some small stocks of CW [chemical weapons] agent precursors ... there is no intelligence on any BW [biological weapons] agent production facilities.'

So at the same time that Blair was saying that Saddam had 'stockpiles of major amounts of chemical and biological weapons', the intelligence services were reporting that there were few real facts about Iraqi WMD and at best Saddam had small stocks of chemicals – although nothing was known about bio-weapons. The two perspectives seem very, very far apart – especially on a subject which is going to be used as the basis for a war.

The JIC said that Saddam 'may have hidden small quantities of [chemical] agents and weapons'. May have hidden? May? That's substantially different from Blair's emphatic 'we know that he has stockpiles'. You wonder if, by the time Cherie gets this far in her preparation for the case, her eyes don't stray from the pages of her briefing papers to her hubby sitting at the other end of the couch, strumming his guitar. Might the thought of having to raise her kids as a single mum, while Tony does porridge down at the Scrubs, run through her mind?

Blair also told the Commons on April 10, 2002: 'There is no doubt at all that the development of weapons of mass destruction by Saddam Hussein poses a severe threat not just to the region, but to the wider world.' This is the next plank of Blair's argument – not just that Saddam had WMD but that he was also a risk to British national security and global wellbeing. Blair even told the TUC (Trades Union Conference) in September 2002 that Saddam had 'enough chemical and biological weapons remaining to devastate the entire Gulf region.' Saddam, according to Blair, was the Fifth Horseman of the Apocalypse and he had to go. Death, War, Pestilence and Famine would have to get on without Saddam.

In the dodgy dossier of September 24, 2002, Blair wrote in his foreword that Saddam was 'a current and serious threat to the UK national interest … I am in no doubt that the threat is serious and current'. In other words: we gotta hit Saddam before he hits us. It was only a matter of time before the despot in the desert chemicalised us like he chemicalised the Iranians, Blair was telling us.

'The intelligence is clear,' Blair told the House of Commons on February 25, 2003, 'he continues to believe his WMD programme is essential for internal repression and for external aggression.'

I hate to state the obvious, but Blair is a past-master at talking bollocks. Parliament's own Intelligence and Security Committee decided in September 2003, after reading all the Joint Intelligence Committee assessments that Blair had read, that 'Saddam was not considered a current or imminent threat to mainland UK'.

Inter-departmental advice based on JIC assessments and given to ministers in March 2002 said that Saddam 'has not succeeded in seriously threatening his neighbours'. It also said that the only time Saddam would use WMD would be 'if his regime were threatened'. JIC assessments also had it that only battlefield weapons – not long-range strategic weapons – would be used if Saddam were attacked. That hardly makes Saddam a clear and present danger to the UK and the world. In addition, it completely undermines all that rubbish about Saddam hitting UK interests and assets with WMD within 45 minutes of giving the order to bomb. I'm also guessing that Israel, Britain, France, China, America, Russia, Pakistan and India – in fact just about any country with stockpiles of WMD and nuclear bombs – would, like Saddam, consider using any weapons they had if their sovereign territory was attacked by another nation which was nuked-up itself.

Interestingly, Blair cut a reference in the draft September dossier which referred to the impossibility of Saddam launching a nuclear attack on London. Perhaps, our leader didn't want to prevent the suggestion of a mushroom cloud hanging over Westminster lingering in the minds of readers.

Blair was ramping up the case for war like a carnival barker trying to sell you tickets to see the bearded lady. 'Roll up, roll up and see the incredible WMD of evil Saddam!' he huckstered. But when we finally got inside the tent, all we saw was a lady with a hairy mole on her top lip rather than a full-on man-beard. You'd be forgiven for asking for your money back, or calling the local cops because you felt you'd been fleeced by a sharp-suited conman with the gift of the gab. You'd want a phoney, snake-oil charlatan like that run out of town, wouldn't you?

Or as Rangwala and Plesch rather more sedately put it: 'There were repeated statements by the Prime Minister in 2002 and 2003 that Iraq constituted a threat to the world and to the UK. The Prime Minister sourced his claim that Iraq sought nuclear, biological and chemical weapons for the purpose of external aggression to the intelligence services. These statements were in direct contrast to the JIC assessments at the time, which were available to the Prime Minister, and which did not assert that Iraq had the intention to use NBC weapons outside its borders except in the case of a US-led attack on Iraq. If Iraq was not thought to have had such an intention, it would not constitute the threat as claimed by the Prime Minister.' That sounds like a big, old bruiser of a lie to me. And that's just for starters.

But, Blair, as we know to our cost, is a master of semantics. Like the carnival barker, he knows how to be slippery with words. One of his endless tricks was to consistently claim that armaments, which hadn't been found by the time the last round of UN weapons inspections ended in 1998, still existed.

During the debate leading up to the vote by Parliament on whether or not to go to war, Tone told the Commons: 'When the inspectors left in 1998, they left unaccounted for 10,000 litres of anthrax; a far-reaching VX nerve agent programme; at least 80 tonnes of mustard gas, possibly more than ten times that amount; unquantifiable amounts of sarin, botulinum toxin and a host of other biological poisons; an entire Scud missile programme. We are now seriously asked to accept that in the last few years, contrary to all history, contrary to all intelligence, he decided unilaterally to destroy the weapons. Such a claim is palpably absurd.'

UNSCOM and UNMOVIC – the UN weapons inspection teams successively tasked to hunt for WMD in Iraq – continually said that the US and the UK couldn't just assume that because something couldn't be found that it therefore necessarily existed. The kind of logic that the US and UK were engaged in can be used to prove the existence of fairies and

Santa Claus. It runs along these lines: 'I've been told that X exists. [For X replace: nerve gas, nuclear weapons, Oberon, King of the Fairies, or werewolves, or whatever else takes your fancy.] I can't see X. Therefore X must be hiding somewhere. Therefore X exists.' Lo and behold!, we've proved the existence of fairies, werewolves and WMD in Iraq.

As the world lurched towards war, Hans Blix tried to get America and its happy lackey, the UK, to stop pretending that fairies exist for just a few minutes before it was too late. He told the UN Security Council in February 2003: 'Many proscribed weapons and items are not account-ed for. To take an example, a document, which Iraq provided, suggest-ed to us that some 1,000 tonnes of chemical agent were 'unaccounted for'. One must not jump to the conclusion that they exist.'

And, as we've already noted, JIC assessments also said that at worst Iraq 'may have hidden small quantities of agents and weapons'.

Blair, however, was now in full-blown 'let's-just-make-stuff-up' mode. On September 24, 2002, he told the Commons: 'His WMD programme is active, detailed and growing. The policy of containment is not work-ing. The WMD programme is not shut down. It is up and running.' Blair's dossier published on the same day said: 'The picture presented to me by the JIC in recent months has become more not less worrying.'

Oh, really? That's intriguing, because the inter-departmental advice given to ministers in March 2002, based on JIC assessments, said that sanctions had halted Iraq's nuclear programme. The advice also claimed that Iraq hadn't been able to rebuild its chemical weapons stockpiles to pre-First Gulf War levels, that its development programme for bio-weapons and chemical weapons had been hindered and that its ballistic missile programme was restricted. 'Active, detailed and growing'? I don't think so, Mr Blair.

Even the Butler Report – based on Lord Butler's inquiry into the use of pre-war intelligence – found that Blair's drive for war 'was not based on any new development in the current intelligence picture ... what had changed was not the pace of Iraq's prohibited weapons programmes, which had not been dramatically stepped up, but tolerance of them fol-lowing the attacks of 11 September, 2001'. Remember that the US neo-cons said themselves that they saw Saddam anew through the 'prism' of 9-11 and decided that they simply had to remove him from power no matter what. Blair, drugged by the transatlantic special relationship and hypnotised by his proximity to total power in the shape of George W Bush, bought the neocon ideology hook, line and sinker. He was a 'true believer' in neocon speak; a convert; and converts, as we know, are always the most zealous of the faithful. Many joked in the run-up to the invasion that Blair seemed like Bush's Foreign Secretary as he travelled the world beating the drums of war. As Butler's comments show, he more or less was. Here was a British prime minister, according to Butler, interpreting the UK's interests through the filter of American fears.

Butler added for good measure: 'There was no recent intelligence that would itself have given rise to a conclusion that Iraq was of more immediate concern than the activities of some other countries.'

In order to trigger the war, Blair needed a legal excuse. When weapons inspectors returned to Iraq in November 2002 they were authorised to do so by UN Resolution 1441. For Iraq to be legally invaded, Saddam had to make a 'material breach' of Resolution 1441. For an old Machiavellian like Blair this must have been a fascinating challenge.

Britain's Attorney-General told Blair that if war against Iraq was going to be legal then the UK had to show 'that Iraq had failed to take the final opportunity to comply with its disarmament obligations under relevant resolutions of the Security Council and that it was possible to demonstrate hard evidence of non-compliance and non-cooperation with the requirements of Security Council Resolution 1441'. By the way, that explanation of the Attorney-General's opinion on the legal basis for war comes not from the British government but courtesy of Lord Butler. The actual opinion was kept secret from the British people. The above explanation was Butler's summation of the Attorney-General's thinking.

To prove non-compliance, Blair told the world on February 25, 2003 that UN inspectors were not getting unrestricted access to Iraqi scientists. He said the inspectors were not being allowed to conduct interviews away from government minders and outside Iraq.

How weird, then, is it, that just a few days earlier on February 14, 2003, Dr Mohammed El Baradei, the Director General of the International Atomic Energy Agency [the UN's nuclear weapons monitoring organisation], told the UN Security Council: 'The IAEA has continued to interview key Iraqi personnel. We have recently been able to conduct four interviews in private – that is without the presence of an Iraqi observer.'

El Baradei went on: 'I should note that during our recent meetings in Baghdad, Iraq reconfirmed its commitment to encourage its citizens to accept interviews in private, both inside and outside of Iraq.'

Blair was saying that war was necessary as the Iraqis were getting in the way of weapons inspectors and therefore in breach of Resolution 1441. The weapons inspectors, however, were saying the complete opposite. How often does Blair think that he can just say the opposite of what everyone else knows to be the truth and the British people will believe him? Does he really despise us so much that he considers us that dumb, that lacking in depth and understanding that we will pad along behind him like little puppies, the way he pads along behind the bullshit rhetoricians running the United States?

In March 2003, Hans Blix said in a report to the Security Council that 'the Iraqi side seems to have encouraged interviewees not to request the presence of Iraqi officials (so-called minders)' and that 38 people had asked for private interviews. It seemed as if Saddam, as wily a genocidalist as there ever was, had figured out the tactics of Blair, and was trying to abide by the letter of Resolution 1441.

So, Blair started to claim that Saddam wasn't providing 'evidence of destruction of the biological and chemical agents and weapons' that he was suspected of owning after the First Gulf War. They're the ones we sold him as I'm sure you'll remember from previous chapters. Well, if Saddam wasn't providing evidence of destroying his WMD, then how does Blair explain Iraq inviting the weapons inspectors to excavate the al-Aziziya range near Baghdad where bombs filled with biomaterial had been destroyed. Hans Blix said: 'The investigation of the destruction site could, in the best case, allow the determination of the number of bombs destroyed at that site.'

Iraq also gave a six-page air force report to weapons inspectors in November 2002 that was meant to explain the use of the chemical weapons which crop-sprayed the Ayatollah's armies during the Iran–Iraq war. In December of the same year, Blix told the Security Council: 'Iraq has further explained its account of the material balance of precursors for chemical warfare agents.'

Blix also told the Security Council in March 2003 that 'more papers on anthrax' had been handed over and that 'Iraq proposed an investigation using advanced technology to quantify the amount of unilaterally destroyed anthrax dumped'. One earlier chemical analysis of an Iraqi site had indeed established that anthrax had been dumped. Yet Blair maintained right up to the outbreak of war that there was 'no proper production or evidence of the destruction of … the ten thousand litres of anthrax'.

In the Commons on March 18, as he pushed Parliament to back his war, Blair told a stonking big fat lie. He said that the weapons inspectors, UNMOVIC, had recently published a report – a 'remarkable document', he called it – which 'lists 29 different areas in which the inspectors have been unable to obtain information' on issues like the use of a nasty form of gunk called mycotoxins, such as aflatoxin and trichothecenes, as weapons.

What he was referring to was UNMOVIC's *Clusters Document*, which was released on March 7, 2003. UNMOVIC didn't say that it had been unable to obtain information, but rather that it sought further information. There's a big difference. Blair's position makes it seem as if Saddam was refusing to cooperate, whereas the inspectors are simply saying they need more detail.

In fact, the inspectors had said in the *Clusters Document* that the development of trichothecene hadn't gone beyond the research stage and that any stocks of aflatoxin would have become degraded with age and not be usable. Blair ignored these facts completely and once again made something that happened a long time ago look like a threat in the present tense. UNMOVIC's comments that it needed more information from Iraq were taken by Blair and spun until it became a matter of fact that Saddam had refused to give information to the inspectors. Massaging the truth? Manipulation? Propaganda? Sexing-up? Lying? Which word would you choose to describe the Prime Minister's conduct?

Blair claimed that the UNMOVIC *Clusters Document* said: 'Documentation available to UNMOVIC suggests that Iraq at least had had far-reaching plans to weaponise VX.' That particular quotation is taken from the background part of the document which recounts the history of Iraq's weapons programmes. Prepare yourself for this ... the actual quote related to Iraqi plans in 1988. That's three years before the First Gulf War – at the very time when we in the west were arming Saddam to the teeth. In fact, UNMOVIC said that Saddam effectively had no VX capability.

Saddam, Blix told the Security Council in March 2003, had undertaken 'numerous initiatives which ... can be seen as active, or even proactive' in the way the Iraqis cooperated with weapons inspectors.

According to Rangwala and Plesch: 'It is clear from the accounts of the UN inspectors, before the Prime Minister's statement, that Iraq was providing evidence of the destruction of chemical and biological warfare agents that were unaccounted for in 1999. The statement from the

Prime Minister is in direct contradiction to the account of the weapons inspectors.'

They added: 'Allegations made by the Prime Minister in the House of Commons on March 18, 2003 resort to direct misrepresentation of the reports of UN inspectors in order to make the case that Iraq was in material breach of Security Council Resolution 1441. The Prime Minister thus did not fulfil the requirement laid down by the Attorney-General that he make sure there were strong factual grounds for concluding that Iraq was not complying or cooperating with its obligations. In presenting what he had been told by the Attorney-General was crucial evidence for the invasion to be lawful, the Prime Minister resorted to exaggeration, misquotation and fabrication.'

Inter-departmental ministerial advice circulated in March 2002 said that to trigger war, the UN Security Council would have to believe that Iraq had breached UN resolutions on disarmament. 'They would need to be convinced that Iraq was in breach of its obligations regarding WMD and ballistic missiles,' the UK government wrote. 'Such proof would need to be incontrovertible and of large-scale activity. Current intelligence is insufficiently robust to meet this criterion.'

The other ways to trigger the war, the government had worked out by now, would be an Iraqi refusal to re-admit inspectors or the expulsion of weapons inspectors engaged in the hunt for WMD. The UN weapons inspectors were always going to be used as the cover for war. So, prior to the invasion Blair played as fast and as loose with the truth about inspections as he possibly could.

Then, after the invasion was over, Blair really got going with the made-up stuff. First of all, he pretended that proof of WMD had been found. He claimed in May and June 2003 that two mobile bio-weapon labs had been found in Iraq. You might recall that these were trailers used to fill balloons with hot air – perfectly symbolic of Blair's claims about Iraq's WMD. This kind of desperate behaviour would end, embarrassingly, with the coalition claiming that Iraq had been engaged in 'weapons of mass destruction-related programme activity'. I could say that a 15-year-old schoolboy was engaged in 'weapons of mass destruction-related programme activity' if I caught him reading his chemistry O-level textbook.

First, Saddam had weapons of mass destruction. Then, he had WMD programmes and, finally, the charge sheet was reduced to 'weapons of mass destruction-related programme activity'. It was truly pitiful. But the deterioration of the allegations shows just how flimsy the lies were that Bush and Blair told.

As an aside, guess who established that those trailers were not mobile bio-weapons labs? None other than Dr David Kelly.

Plesch and Rangwala divide the evidence for Blair's impeachment into two categories: the stuff that Blair made up, exaggerated and lied about; and the facts that he suppressed, ignored and lied about.

Had the British people been in full possession of these suppressed and distorted facts at the time of the build-up to war, we could have used them to negate Blair's case. Blair's greatest crime is his attempt to keep us ignorant. His style of government reduces the electorate to a mob which he wishes to cynically sway in one way or the other by use of a carefully designed argument which paints a biased picture of the world. To keep us stupid, he deprives us of information, leaving us with nowhere to turn for facts but to himself.

As Plesch and Rangwala say: 'The government, including the Prime Minister, has been in possession of a substantial amount of information that undermined the case that it was presenting to the public about Iraq's weapons, but which it chose not to disclose.

'In consequence, members of Parliament and the public were unable to make a properly informed judgement of the scale of the threat posed by Iraq at the time they were asked by the government to support the invasion. The retention of information has also prevented the government and the Prime Minister from being adequately exposed to properly informed criticism after the invasion.'

The suppressed facts, they say, 'strongly indicate that the Prime Minister and his officials held back material that would have substantiated the viewpoint that Iraq was not a serious threat, particularly in comparison with other potential threats to the UK, and did not have a substantial programme to develop or stockpile NBC weapons.'

Cherie would be delighted and horrified by the evidence she's now about to read in preparation for the impeachment of her husband. Delighted because the facts make the prosecution a walk in the park and a conviction a certainty; but horrified as the poor woman knows that she will soon have to be standing in line with all those junkie mums and their snotty-nosed malnourished kids to get in to visit Tony once a week at one of Her Majesty's guest-houses for the criminally naughty.

This next example of Prime Ministerial duplicity should have you reaching for the phone to dial 999 on our rogue leader. Read the facts, and weep.

Saddam's son-in-law and the director of Iraq's Military Industrialisation Corporation, Hussein Kamel, became one of the west's most prized defectors when he escaped to Jordan in 1995. Damn, how Britain and America must have been salivating at the mouth at the prospect of Kamel spouting all of Saddam's delicious WMD secrets into a CIA tape-recorder. But they were to be sadly disappointed. Here's what Kamel told the UN's weapons inspectors: 'I ordered the destruction of all chemical weapons. All weapons – biological, chemical, missile, nuclear – were destroyed.'

Oh, dear. That must have put a spanner in the works. It fairly screws up a war plan built on the premise of taking out Saddam because he has WMD if the chap in charge of Iraq's banned weapons says they've all been scrapped.

The British government was aware of this fact as far back as August 24, 1995, just two weeks after Kamel's defection. On that day, the JIC said: 'Hussein Kamel claims there are no remaining stockpiles of agents.' So why then did Blair tell the House of Commons on February 25, 2003 – nearly eight years later – that 'it was only after ... the defection of Saddam's son-in-law to Jordan that the offensive biological weapons and the full extent of the nuclear programme were discovered'.

The answer is: because he could. Kamel's account wasn't public. Blair could say what he wanted as the people had no way of contradicting him. Blair even claimed that Kamel 'defected to Jordan and admitted that they had an offensive biological weapons programme'. A person could only interpret Kamel's comments that 'all weapons had been destroyed' as proof of an active bio-warfare programme if their brain had been removed from their head and replaced the wrong way around.

Tony was in Wonderland. He proceeded to completely vanish through the looking-glass when he said that Saddam's 'lies were revealed by his son-in-law. Only then did the inspectors find over 8,000 litres of concentrated anthrax'. Rangwala and Plesch say: 'One can only assume that this information was made up by the Prime Minister as inspectors never found live anthrax in Iraq and the factory at which anthrax had been produced before 1991 was under UN monitoring from at least October 1991.'

Rangwala and Plesch also raise an interesting aside which points to a concerted effort to suppress truths that the UK government didn't want out in the public domain: namely, why were the British intelligence services not dispatched to interview former Iraqi ambassador, Wissam al-Zahwaie, after his retirement to Amman in Jordan in 2001? This was the man, after all, at the centre of allegations that Iraq had tried to secure uranium from Niger. Rangwala and Plesch suggest that the failure by MI6 to speak to al-Zahwaie 'raises the issue of whether questions were not asked because no-one was interested in answers that would not support the presumption of Iraq's active nuclear ambitions'.

While the intelligence held by Britain on Iraq was pitifully meagre and totally shonky from the start – and about as reliable as a roof estimate from an Essex builder – Blair was telling the world that the UK had 'vast' amounts of intelligence on Saddam's WMD.

When he released the dodgy September 2002 dossier, he told the Commons: 'The intelligence picture [that the intelligence services] paint is one accumulated over the past four years. It is extensive, detailed and authoritative.' That statement was rubbish. As we know, the UK had basically no human intelligence – humint – on Iraq at all.

Only a handful of unreliable Iraqi sources were used by Blair to build the case for war. For example, British intelligence knew that the 'sub-source' who provided the intelligence that Iraq could use WMD in 45 minutes had 'links to opposition groups' and that there was 'the possibility that his reports would be affected by that'. As we know, the sub-source was connected to the Iraqi National Accord – the political group of the Iraqi Interim Prime Minister Iyad Allawi. The Butler Report said that 'post-war validation by SIS has raised serious doubts about the reliability of reporting from this new sub-source'.

Incidentally, Blair says he had no idea that the 45-minutes claim related to short-range battlefield weapons, not long-range missiles which could target UK assets, such as bases in Cyprus. This admission in itself should be enough to get Blair impeached for criminal negligence. How can the leader of this country not know what weapons may or may not be threatening the UK? Do you really think that during the Cold War, Harold Wilson or Margaret Thatcher were clueless about the Soviet arsenal? Or that during the Second World War, Churchill never really bothered to find out what doodlebugs could do to London? Blair's defence against lying makes him look like an incompetent fool who couldn't be left in charge of a corner shop, let alone allowed to lead one of the world's most powerful nations.

The Butler Report also uncovered that more than four-fifths of all the intelligence on alleged Iraqi weapons concealment came from just two sources; and two-thirds of this intelligence came from just one person. The reliability of both sources is now highly questionable.

Similarly, Butler also discovered that two-thirds of intelligence on Iraq's WMD circulated in 2002 came from only two sources. One of these sources reported directly to UK intelligence and there is now 'serious doubt' over the reliability of the other source. 'The vast majority' of intelligence on mobile bio-weapons came from one source – an Iraqi defector codenamed 'Curveball' who was in Germany and had never been interrogated by British intelligence.

In total, then, nearly all the significant intelligence on Iraq's WMD came from just a handful of people, with suspect motives, who were being used unquestioningly as the basis upon which to take the UK into a ghastly war. If you had known this – if MPs had known this – do you think we would ever have invaded? Answer: NO.

These sources, quite frankly, were used to provide Blair with the allegations he needed to justify war. Iraqi defectors were also, obviously, using Blair. And he was just delighted to play along. By passing exaggerated or fake intelligence to the UK, they knew they could hasten the demise of the dictator Saddam, and, perhaps, they also thought that they might be able to feather their post-invasion nests.

One source who later proved to be unreliable provided information to the government which, Butler said, 'had a major effect on the certainty of statements in the government's dossier of September 2002 that Iraq possessed and was producing chemical and biological weapons'.

In September 2002, a report from a 'new source on trial ... did provide significant assurance to those drafting the government's dossier that active, current production of chemical and biological agent was taking place'. Guess what? In July 2003 – after the invasion was all over – that particular report from that particular source was withdrawn. Butler also made it clear that Blair was briefed by the head of MI6 and told that this new source 'remained unproven'.

Using the royal 'we', Butler said: 'We were struck by the relative thinness of the intelligence base supporting the great firmness of the JIC's judgements on Iraqi production and possession of chemical and biological weapons.'

Butler's inquiry revealed that four sets of intelligence reports – three on weapons and one on concealment – which made up the vast bulk of the government's case against Iraq were later withdrawn or discredited.

The first report from the 'new source on trial' was withdrawn in July

2003 by MI6 as 'the sourcing chain had by then been discredited'. The second report from the source connected to the Iraqi National Accord also included the infamous 45-minutes claim. After the invasion, MI6 found 'serious doubts about the reliability of reporting' from this source.

The third report – from the source who gave info about weapons concealment – was also a pile of rubbish. MI6 said after the invasion that it had 'doubts about the reliability of the reports provided by the source'. Finally, the fourth report from the source who gave 'the vast majority of the intelligence' on mobile bio-weapons labs was assessed by MI6 and found badly wanting. Butler said: 'We conclude that there must be some doubts about the reliability of all the reports received from this source.'

On July 8, 2003, at the same time that MI6 was saying post-war that their sources were full of crap, Blair was still keeping the myth alive. He told Parliament: 'I also stand entirely by the intelligence we put into the September dossier ... I have absolutely no doubt whatever that he was trying to reconstitute WMD programmes and that the intelligence that we were getting out of Iraq about those programmes and about the attempt to conceal them was correct.'

Blair says he had no idea that reports from Iraqi sources were being withdrawn because they were unreliable. Even if you are inclined to believe that a PM, who made this war his own personal crusade, is unlikely to have been briefed about the collapse in MI6 confidence in the defectors and informers who provided him with his case for war, then you still have to deal with this claim as an admission of total incompetence. How could the Prime Minister not have known that the sources' reports were being withdrawn? Blair's excuse for not being a liar is that he was asleep at the wheel.

Here's some more concealed info that Blair hid away from us: in September 2002, the JIC was clear that Saddam wouldn't use any WMD outside his own country. 'There is no intelligence to indicate that Iraq has considered using chemical and biological agents in terrorist attacks,' the JIC said. It also found that Saddam would only use WMD 'if he believes his regime is under attack'.

Why didn't Blair tell us these things? Rangwala and Plesch say the reason Blair kept us in the dark was because he 'was ready to allow a highly alarmist view of Iraq's weapons to spread. This view was in direct contrast with the perspective of the intelligence services, but enabled a political climate of fear to be generated in which an invasion of Iraq could be justified to a substantial proportion of the population.'

Blair wilfully set out to make sure that the world would not be treated to a fair and balanced debate on Iraq. It was all good guys and bogeymen from the get-go. On December 8, Iraq submitted a declaration to the UN saying it had no WMD. You might remember that in an earlier chapter I told you how I'd got hold of some of the censored information from this Iraqi document which named the western companies which had sold WMD capability to Saddam.

Speaking at the time, Blair said that 'not a single member of the international community seriously believes' the declaration. Just before the war started he claimed: 'The December 8 declaration is false.' Hmm ... I wonder what President Vladimir Putin of Russia would say about that? He told his good buddy Blair in October 2002: 'Russia does not have in its possession any trustworthy data which would support the existence of nuclear weapons or any weapons of mass destruction in Iraq, and we have not received from our partners such information.' Russia, unlike the UK and USA, had good human intelligence assets inside Iraq.

The Iraqi declaration was some 12,000 pages long. British intelligence spent just a few days analysing it. Butler 'noted the limited time given to evaluation' of the document.

Blair also ignored chief weapons inspector Hans Blix's comments to the UN Security Council about the declaration when Blix said it gave further explanation about chemical weapons and provided a 'good deal of information' about missiles. Similarly, it also presented 'new material and information' about bio-technology. 'This is welcome,' Blix said.

However, Blair's most dreadful offence against the British people is that he deliberately hid from us the fears from within UK intelligence that an invasion of Iraq would turn the country into a terrorist hotbed and a zone of almost total anarchy – a place which would spawn killers like Abu Musab al-Zarqawi, the most celebrated and brutal of the many al-Qaeda affiliated terrorists who washed up in Iraq post-invasion, hoping to turn the nation into a crucible of terror aimed at destroying the west; and a place that would create victims like the British civilian Ken Bigley, horribly murdered by al-Zarqawi's organisation.

Parliament's Intelligence and Security Committee revealed in September 2003 – long after the occupation – that prior to the war 'the JIC assessed that al-Qaeda and associated groups continued to represent by far the greatest terrorist threat to western interests and that threat would be heightened by military action against Iraq'.

The JIC also assessed 'that any collapse of the Iraqi regime would increase the risk of chemical and biological warfare technology or agents finding their way into the hands of terrorists, not necessarily al-Qaeda'. The JIC also believed before the war that Iraq's NBC capability was smaller and less of a threat to the UK than other so-called rogue nations like Iran or North Korea.

The Intelligence and Security Committee noted 'that the Prime Minister was aware of this'. What on earth was this man playing at? He knew that the invasion would increase terrorism, but he didn't tell us. He was told that the invasion could lead to terrorists getting their hands on WMD, but he didn't tell us. He knew that other nations were a greater risk to our security, but he didn't tell us. Does he really give a damn about Great Britain? He increased terror and failed to tackle the real threats to the UK which needed to be dealt with immediately. The family of Ken Bigley, and the families of the victims who died on July 7, 2005 in London, have Blair to thank for their loved ones' fates; and if a dirty bomb goes off in London, then we'll all know who to thank as well. Stand up, Mr Prime Minister, and take a bow as the real enemy of the British people.

Blair struck out on claim after claim in the September dossier. His dossier said that the al-Sharqat factory was producing nitric acid for use in the building of nuclear weapons. The IAEA visited the site just before the war and found 'no indication of resumed nuclear activities'. The Fallujah II plant was supposed to be making chlorine for chemical weapons. UNMOVIC went there five times before the war started and discovered 'the chlorine plant is currently inoperative'. Nothing was found at two other sites which were linked to chemical weapons production in the September dossier.

Did Blair order a massive shake-up of intelligence in the wake of these intelligence disasters? Not on your Nelly, my friend. Butler noted, using the royal 'we' once again: 'We are surprised that neither policy-makers nor the intelligence community, as the general negative results of UNMOVIC inspections became increasingly apparent, conducted a formal re-evaluation of the quality of the intelligence and hence of the assessments made on it.'

Blair stubbornly stuck to his lies as the weapons inspectors found nothing time and time again during their pre-invasion searches for

WMD, which started in November 2002 under the auspices of the recently passed UN Resolution 1441.

Before the invasion, more than 400 weapons inspections were carried out at over 300 sites. All were performed without prior notice and the Iraqis always allowed the inspectors free access. Even presidential sites and private homes were inspected without any moaning or jiggery-pokery from the Iraqi side. I guess, the Iraqis would, by this point, have cooperated with pretty much any request as they knew that one almighty ass-kicking was coming their way and there wasn't much they could do about it. Yet Blair didn't give a damn. The war was going ahead no matter what. Even when his absurd claims in the September dossier were shown post-war to be nonsense, Blair stood by them. Blair is either a liar *par excellence* or a delusional self-convincer in need of psychiatric help.

Yet another part of the impeachment case put together by Plesch and Rangwala for Adam Price MP centres on a bizarre email that briefly made it onto the front pages of British papers back in March 2004. The email was from none other than John Scarlett, then head of the JIC and soon to be Chief of MI6, to Charles Duelfer, the head of the Iraq Survey Group which had been dispatched by the CIA to locate those missing WMD in occupied Iraq. As we now know, the ISG eventually ruled that there were no weapons of mass destruction in Iraq at the time of the invasion.

Scarlett, *The Times* said, suggested to Duelfer that an 'ISG report should be cut from 200 pages of detailed analysis to 20, and left sufficiently vague to protect Blair's stand on Iraq's weapons menace'. Scarlett wanted the report to keep alive the prospect that weapons would still be found, according to *The Times*.

Scarlett even asked the ISG to add 'ten golden nuggets' to the report to boost the belief that Saddam was armed, such as making mention of mobile bio-weapons labs and equipment used in nuclear research. Duelfer has confirmed he received this email.

Rangwala and Plesch say: 'If the allegations are true, it provides further decisive indications that the attempt by the British government to mislead the public and members of Parliament on the subject of Iraq's weapons did not end with the invasion, but has continued to the present day.'

The last raft of evidence against Blair that Rangwala and Plesch turn their attention to deals with the allegations that Blair entered into a secret agreement with Bush to go to war against Iraq. Unlike the lies and the suppression it is hard to back up this allegation with a welter of documents from within the British government itself. There are plenty of smoking guns lying around to show that Blair misled the country and hid the truth from us, but the allegation that Blair had a secret pact with Bush is much more difficult to sustain because only those two men really know the truth. But we don't need to prove that Blair huddled around a private cauldron of spin with Bush to weave a spell of war over the world in order to have him impeached; he is already damned by his lies – lies which can be proved time and time again.

Nevertheless, Rangwala and Plesch have made a pretty damned good case for claiming that there was certainly something fishy going on between the Prez and the PM.

Here's what they say: 'The evidence available to the public strongly indicates that the Prime Minister understood that the United States was planning to invade Iraq from late 2001, unless Saddam Hussein was deposed through other means; that he made a decision to support the United States in this action during the course of mid-2002; and that he used the claims about Iraq's weapons inspectors throughout this period as a way to win support from the public and other countries. In effect, the Prime Minister had committed the UK to assist the US with the invasion of Iraq, but had not disclosed this commitment to Parliament, to his own cabinet or to the British public.'

Well, let's hear how Rangwala and Plesch prove this incendiary claim. Sir Christopher Meyer, the former British Ambassador to Washington, says that Blair knew the US was going to take out Saddam from September 20, 2001 onwards. In just over a week from the attack on the World Trade Center and the Pentagon, Blair was in the loop and knew that Saddam now had top ranking on America's 'big board of bad people that we must beat up'. Meyer was quoted in *Vanity Fair* saying that on September 20, Blair arrived in Washington for talks in the White House. Iraq was discussed, the magazine quoted Meyer as saying, adding: 'At dinner in the White House, attended also by Colin Powell, Condi Rice, and the British Ambassador to the United States, Sir Christopher Meyer, Bush made clear that he was determined to topple Saddam.' Meyer told *Vanity Fair*: 'Rumours were already flying that Bush would use 9-11 as a pretext to attack Iraq. On the one hand, Blair came with a very strong message – don't get distracted; the priorities were al-Qaeda, Afghanistan, the Taliban. Bush said, "I agree with you,

Tony. We must deal with this first. But when we have dealt with Afghanistan, we must come back to Iraq.'"

By January 2002, Bush had promoted Iraq to membership of the Axis of Evil in his State of the Union address. Soon Blair would pledge himself to back America come what may – long before he asked Parliament in March 2003 for its approval to support the US in a war against Iraq. In April 2002, Blair said that when America fights, the UK 'fights with her ... side by side ... Britain will be at America's side'.

At the same time, all the inter-departmental advice for British government ministers was stating that the 'current objectives towards Iraq' were 'the reintegration of a law-abiding Iraq, which does not possess WMD or threaten its neighbours, into the international community. Implicitly, this cannot occur with Saddam in power.' So, implicitly, Blair had committed his government to removing Saddam with no mandate from the people or Parliament. His mandate came from a higher power: the President of the United States of America.

The same inter-departmental advice said that 'the use of overriding force in a ground campaign is the only option that we can be confident will remove Saddam'. Blair was now secretly committing us to war. British military planners began preparing for the invasion of Iraq with their US counterparts from early June 2002, according to Air Marshall Brian Burridge, the national contingent commander for Operation Telic, the MoD's codename for the invasion of Iraq.

In July 2002, Blair held a 15-minute telephone conversation with President Bush. In the same *Vanity Fair* article, called 'The Path to War', author Bryan Burrough quotes a US official from the office of Vice-president Dick Cheney. This source had read the conversation transcript, and he told Burrough: 'The way it read was, come what may, Saddam was going to go; they said they were going forward, they were going to take out the regime, and they were doing the right thing.

'Blair did not need any convincing. There was no, "Come on, Tony, we've got to get you on board." I remember reading it and then thinking, OK, now I know what we're going to be doing for the next year.' The source added: 'It was a done deal.'

Tony Blair was like the desperate little kid in the playground who wants to be the tough guy's best pal. He'll do anything to please his idol. He'll tell his new pal, 'Sure you can come round to my house to play with my new XBox,' even though he hasn't got an XBox. So, what does he do? Wheedle and beg his mum to buy him an XBox so he can bring his cool American friend over for dinner and his cool American friend won't be disappointed in him. By the way, for 'XBox' read 'mandate from the British people and Parliament to invade Iraq'. It's desperate. It's a sell-out. It's treachery to the spirit of what Britain stands for. It's cheapening. It's degrading.

So, the deal was done. By 2002, Blair had made a pact with the devil to go behind his country's back and secretly sign up to Bush's war against Saddam without the authority of Parliament. The Butler Report points out that in April 2002, Bush and Blair were at a meeting at the President's ranch in Crawford, Texas, where they discussed 'the need for effective presentational activity'. In other words, they were working out how to sell their little plot to the British and American people.

Not only were the British people kept in the dark – the very people who pay Blair his wages – but Parliament was cut out and lied to, as was Blair's own cabinet. This really was Blair's war. On July 26, 2002, Clare Short, the International Development Secretary, wrote in her diary that she raised her 'simmering worry about Iraq' with Blair saying she wanted the issue debated in cabinet. Blair told her a debate was a bad idea as 'it would get hyped'. He then told her that 'nothing [was] decided and wouldn't be over summer'. What a bare-faced lie. In the same month, he and Bush had agreed on the phone to topple Saddam, but Blair determinedly lied to his own cabinet ministers about his schemes.

On September 9, 2002, Short notes again in her diary that 'TB [Tony Blair] gave me assurances when I asked for Iraq to be discussed at cabinet that no decision made and not imminent [sic]'.

Rangwala and Plesch say that all this makes it 'reasonable to conclude that the Prime Minister had made a secret alliance to go to war by September 9, 2002, and that his subsequent presentation of material on Iraq's NBC weapons was an attempt to win public and international support for a predetermined policy outcome'.

It's hard to think of a politician in a western democracy who deserves impeachment more than Blair – or who provided the planks for the prosecution so eloquently with his own words. So what does this impeachment process involve? Well, all it takes to get the wheels of justice to turn is for just one MP to accuse Blair of the marvellously named offence of 'high crimes and misdemeanours'.

The only problem is that the House of Commons forbids MPs from slagging off and generally insulting the Prime Minister – and that includes accusing the PM of lying. When the MP John Baron told the

Commons, 'We as a country were misled by the Prime Minister' he ended up on the receiving end of a rather severe bollocking from the Deputy Speaker of the House (for non-UK readers the speaker is sort of like the guy who referees the bun fight that passes for democracy over in these parts). The Deputy Speaker ruled Baron out of order, telling him that he 'should be very careful with the words he uses'. If an MP continues to call the PM a big, fat, smelly liar then he can get physically hauled out of the chamber by one of the many men in stockings who are supposed to defend the Houses of Parliament from al-Qaeda, rogue assassins, people who like fox-hunting, militant lesbians and dads fed up with the family court system.

Any attempt to call Blair and his cronies to account for lying to the British people is therefore scuppered by the stupid, creaking and antediluvian protocol of Parliament. Quite a democracy, eh? It's hard to get your head around the madness of this convention. MPs cannot accuse Blair of lying – even though my pet spaniel knows Blair couldn't be trusted to open his can of doggie chunks at teatime – because MPs can't call the Prime Minister a liar.

Nevertheless, thanks to Adam Price, the Welsh Nationalist MP, commissioning the sharp minds of Rangwala and Plesch to construct a legal case for impeachment, Blair now stands accused of 'high crimes and misdemeanours' by a fellow MP: Mr Price. Unable to challenge Blair adequately – so far – in Parliament, Price had to think outside the box to get his voice heard. I'm no supporter of nationalism wherever it rears its head, but British democracy needs more MPs like Price. He's a rising star in his own party and had no compunction in accusing Blair of 'contempt for the rule of international law and scant regard for the lives of our soldiers'. Blair was 'unfit for any office, let alone the highest in the land', he said. Ouch – that's gotta sting. Well done, Mr Price.

Just to rub salt into the wounds of our Billy Liar premier, Price said impeachment was 'a weapon of mass democracy on behalf of the millions of people that the Prime Minister had deceived'. I would have added 'and the thousands he's helped kill', but nevertheless Price's contribution to the debate around Iraq is so valuable that I think England should cede Wales to the Welsh immediately and recommend Price be made King of Cardiff by way of a small 'thank you'.

The 'high crimes and misdemeanours' that Price, Rangwala and Plesch accuse Blair of are 'subversion of the constitution, the abuse of power and the betrayal of trust'.

Impeachment is totally feasible. A 1967 Parliamentary Select Committee said that it was a legitimate legal process. Impeachment means to accuse a public official of conduct unbecoming of their high office. Once a person is impeached they are tried by the two Houses of Parliament – the lower house, the House of Commons, where MPs elected by the British people sit; and the House of Lords, where a bunch of un-elected bishops, barons and bum lickers – who get their peerage and their right to sit in the Lords by kissing the asses of past and present PMs – dribble senility down their old school ties, waste taxpayers' money and come for a snooze when the heating systems in their stately homes break down.

The House of Lords carries out the trial and the House of Commons decides on the sentence. If Blair was convicted, I don't think we should be too harsh on him. I think we should just strip him naked, wrap him in a big American flag and leave him in downtown Baghdad to find his way back to London. If he makes it back, then we can lock him up in the Tower until the Tories get back into office so, hopefully, he should be free sometime around 2050.

Britain has impeached loads of people over the centuries, but the practice hasn't really been used at all over the last 100 years or so. That is a shame. The thought of getting prosecuted for being a useless, dishonest leader would certainly have added a bit of truth and dignity to the careers of people like Margaret 'Monster' Thatcher and her sleazebag successor John Major. Or as William Holdsworth says in *A History of English Law*: 'If ministers were made criminally responsible for gross negligence or rashness, ill considered activities might be discouraged, real statesmanship might be encouraged and party violence might be moderated.' Others have described impeachment as 'a safeguard of public liberty well worthy of a free country'. Impeachment is the last tool in a democracy's arsenal to uphold the supremacy of the people over the Prime Minister, his cabinet and the Parliament. In fact, to not impeach Blair would be undemocratic.

In the 1600s, the House of Commons used to refer to impeachment as 'the chief institution for the preservation of the government'. However, the impeachment process was overtaken historically by the convention in British politics that if an MP misleads the House of Commons – and is caught out – they have to resign. That convention remained unbroken down the decades – but what's a little democratic convention to Mr Blair?

Did you know that Blair has actually admitted that he misled the House of Commons? I watched him do it. It was at the Labour Party Conference at the end of September 2004 down in Brighton. He had the whole herd there – all the Labour party apparatchiks, nodding like members of the Politburo circa 1975 at a Leonid Brezhnev speech – when suddenly Blair (for once) told the truth. He admitted that he talked utter crap.

Here's what he told the party faithful: 'The evidence about Saddam having actual biological and chemical weapons, as opposed to the capability to develop them, has turned out to be wrong. I acknowledge that and accept it ... I can apologise for the information that turned out to be wrong, but I can't, sincerely at least, apologise for removing Saddam.'

So, there we are ... Blair finally, half-heartedly, admitting his claims about WMD were total nonsense and that the country went to war on a completely false premise. There is no way of looking at this state of affairs but to see Blair guilty of misleading the House of Commons – an offence which requires compulsory resignation. Two of Blair's cabinet colleagues – Beverly Hughes and Peter Mandleson – resigned for misleading the House. Although I have no wish to be kind to any of Tony's cronies, I have to say that Hughes resigned over a fairly trivial matter and her deception of the House was seen by many as unintentional. Yet still she resigned ...

Mandelson, you may recall, is one of the architects of the New Labour project, as well as being Blair's bestest buddy and the holder of 'the most sinister man in Britain' title. Half the reincarnation of Niccolò Machiavelli and half a living shop dummy, Mandelson told a few half-truths and summarily lost his job. Good. No-one should fib in public office and get away with it. But Mandy's sins were as nothing compared to Blair's. However, here's what Blair told his pal when Mandy offered his resignation post-fibbing: 'I accept [that comments made by Mandelson were] misleading and resulted in the House of Commons and the Lobby being misled – and I accept his resignation on that basis.'

Commenting on Mandelson's resignation, Blair once told the former leader of the opposition, William Hague – a useless, bald bloke from northern England who is famous for being useless, bald and a bloke from northern England – that 'if people did something wrong, they would pay the penalty'. Tough talk. So why doesn't he sack himself? Blair makes an abject mockery of the promise he gave the British people when he came to power that he would 'uphold the highest standards in public life'.

Blair would obviously rather suck Saddam's sandals live on *The National Lottery Show* on Saturday night TV than resign, so impeachment is the only method of going after him, given that MPs are forbidden by the speaker from casting aspersions on our leader's glorious reputation.

*

Not long after Rangwala and Plesch produced *A Case to Answer* for Adam Price, the heat intensified on Blair. His secrets were leaked and the public learned exactly what he had known before the war. These secrets were namely: Blair knew that the war was illegal; that the invasion would turn into a quagmire that could last for generations, and that it was more than likely that, once Saddam was overthrown, a new Iraqi government, even a democratic one, would start developing weapons of mass destruction.

These warnings were contained in a series of top-secret documents that Blair read and digested long before the invasion. These papers were leaked to Britain's *Daily Telegraph* newspaper in September 2004. It was a mighty scoop – for it effectively proved the case that Price, Rangwala and Plesch were pushing: that Blair should be impeached for lies and suppression. After digesting the contents of these secret documents it's little wonder that Menzies Campbell, then Liberal Democrat Foreign Affairs spokesman, described the revelations as 'the crown jewels'. The documents show that, despite the reservations of his own Foreign Secretary and the Cabinet Office Overseas and Defence Secretariat, Blair was swept along by George W Bush into a war that the British people did not want.

On the week that the leaked documents went public, Blair was trying to draw a line under Iraq and move on to more elector-friendly domestic issues. At the TUC Conference in Brighton, he attempted to put Iraq on the back burner by talking up his domestic agenda. His choice of words couldn't have been more ironic: 'Even if I've never been away, it's time to show I'm back.' He could have been talking about the spectre of Iraq hanging over his career and British politics: Iraq has never gone away, and it keeps coming back with a vengeance. Iraq is Banquo's ghost at the feast for Tony 'Macbeth' Blair. It's proof of the truth in that old adage: 'Be sure your sins will find you out.'

The contents of the documents couldn't have been revealed at a worse time for Blair. The week before, Kofi Annan had said the invasion of Iraq was 'illegal'; and it was also a foregone conclusion that the Iraq Survey Group would say that Saddam had no stockpiles of banned weapons.

The day before the documents were published President Bush brought more gloom to his forlorn Gauleiter in London by warning that guerrilla attacks in Iraq would get worse. On the same day a highly classified US National Intelligence Estimate, put together during the summer of 2004 by the American government's most senior analysts, was revealed as saying that Iraq could spiral into full-blown civil war.

The Foreign Relations Committee in the US came out furiously at a request from the State Department to divert some £2.82 billion out of Iraqi reconstruction funds, worth a total of £15 billion, to security and economic development, such as the improvement of the oil industry.

The claims in the secret documents came, then, as yet another nail was hammered into the coffin of a prime minister fixated on his place in the history books. They show that he was not motivated by passion or commitment but by a carefully calculated mix of self-interest and loyalty to America.

The secret documents disclose that, a full year before the invasion, Blair was told that any hope of getting a stable government for post-invasion Iraq would take 'many years' and would be impossible without putting thousands of British troops into the country. Foreign Secretary Jack Straw also expressed grave reservations about the war, the nation learned, with his officials telling Blair that Iraq could 'revert to type' post-war and start to build up stockpiles of anthrax, sarin and nuclear weapons.

Blair was also warned that Bush considered taking out Saddam Hussein to be 'unfinished business' – a 'grudge match' – and that if Britain wanted to go to war legally against Iraq, Blair would have to 'wrong-foot' Saddam and get him to slip up over weapons inspections in order to give the UK an excuse for invasion.

Straw told Blair in March 2002, in a letter stamped SECRET AND PERSONAL that there was no proper understanding of what would happen in Iraq post-invasion. 'There seems to be a larger hole in this than anything,' he wrote. Referring to the American thirst for regime change, Straw added: 'No-one has satisfactorily answered how there can be any certainty that the replacement regime will be any better. Iraq has no history of democracy so no-one has this habit or experience.'

Straw was deeply worried about the legality of any invasion. He said British action had to be 'narrated with reference to the international rule of law'. Straw added that his legal advisors had told him it would take a new UN resolution to make the war legal, despite the US having no interest in these kinds of niceties.

In an options paper dated March 8, 2002, prepared by senior ministerial advisors and marked SECRET UK EYES ONLY, the Cabinet Office Overseas and Defence Secretariat spelled out just how depressing the interlocked futures of Iraq and Britain would become in the event of war. It said: 'The greater investment of western forces, the greater our control over Iraq's future, but the greater the cost and the longer we would need to stay.'

It added: 'The only certain means to remove Saddam and his elite is to invade and impose a new government, but this would involve nation-building over many years.' Putting a 'Sunni strongman' in place in order to get British troops out of Iraq quickly would be completely counter-productive. 'There would be a strong risk of the Iraqi system reverting to type. Military coup could succeed coup until an autocratic Sunni dictator emerged who protected Sunni interests. With time he could acquire WMD,' the paper added.

Even a democratic government would be likely to try to acquire WMD for two reasons: firstly, because of the nuclear capabilities of its two enemy states – Israel and Iran – and secondly, because the Palestine question was the unresolved source of conflict in the Middle East. If a democratic government was to survive in Iraq, 'it would require the US and others to commit to nation building for many years. This would entail a substantial international security force.'

Lord Butler referred in passing to the Cabinet Office options paper in his report saying it indicated that regime change was illegal and had 'no basis in international law'. The government paper also said there were serious difficulties in finding a legal justification for war, adding: 'Subject to law officers' advice, none currently exists.'

Not only that, but the paper also said Saddam was not an increased risk and that there was no evidence Saddam was backing international terror. 'This makes moving to invade legally very difficult,' the options paper concluded.

The US believed a legal basis for war already existed, and that Saddam's alleged flouting of UN resolutions on disarmament was a legitimate trigger for any invasion. With that mindset, the US was dead set against continuing a policy of containment. The British government document said that 'the swift success of the war in Afghanistan, distrust of UN sanctions and inspections regimes, and unfinished business from 1991 are all factors' which contributed to the quickening of the US's appetite for destruction.

Washington, the paper warned, would not be 'governed by wider political factors. The US may be willing to work with a much smaller coalition than we think desirable.' Peter Ricketts, Foreign Office Policy Director, said there were 'real problems' with the US policy line. 'Even the best survey of Iraq's WMD programmes will not show much advance in recent years,' Ricketts wrote. 'Military operations need clear and compelling military objectives. For Iraq, "regime change" does not stack up. It sounds like a grudge match between Bush and Saddam.'

Ricketts, however, advised that Blair should stick close to Bush: 'By sharing Bush's broad objective, the Prime Minister can help shape how it is defined, and the approach to achieving it. In the process, he can bring home to Bush some of the realities which will be less evident from Washington. He can help Bush by telling him things his own machine probably isn't.'

Ricketts also explained why the war was an inevitability: 'The truth is that what has changed is not the pace of Saddam Hussein's WMD programmes, but our tolerance of them post-September 11.'

At the same time, MI6 was arguing against Blair's decision to publish a dossier of declassified information designed to convince the British public that Saddam was dangerous. MI6 was saying that the intelligence didn't support the claims that Blair wanted to make. Jack Straw felt the dossier would be meaningless.

As we've seen, JIC assessments dated March 2002 said intelligence on Saddam's WMD was 'patchy', and the toughest the language could get was: 'We believe Iraq retains some production equipment and some small stocks of chemical precursors, and may have hidden small quantities of agents and weapons. There is no intelligence on any biological agent production facilities.'

Blair was advised in the spring of 2002 in the Cabinet Office options paper to work slowly towards a legal justification for war, by building international support and ramping up the pressure on Saddam by pushing for weapons inspectors to return to Iraq.

The chance to wrong-foot Saddam could come from him refusing to re-admit the inspectors or blocking their inspections. 'He has miscalcu-

lated before,' the paper says. The intention was war come what may –
by hook or by crook. Of course, Saddam accepted the return of weapons inspectors in the autumn of 2002, and, as we've seen, effectively
cooperated with their demands, scuppering Blair's little plot, and leaving the US and UK no alternative but to pursue a blatantly illegal war.

Other documents show that the Foreign Office and the Bush administration were poles apart in terms of how they saw the conflict unfolding. The Foreign Office was alarmed at just how eager the US was to hit
Iraq, whether or not it had the support of its allies.

In a letter to the Prime Minister marked SECRET – STRICTLY PERSONAL,
Sir David Manning, Blair's Foreign Policy Advisor, summed up the talks
he had in Washington in March 2002, saying: 'I think there is a real risk
that the administration underestimates the difficulties. They may agree
that failure isn't an option, but this does not mean they will necessarily
avoid it.'

Bush 'still has to find answers to the big questions', Manning wrote,
including a solution to the most vital problem: 'What happens on the
morning after?'

The Americans were fully aware of the invidious position in which
Blair found himself. He was being dragged two ways at the same time:
the US expected the UK, its closest ally, to get onboard for a war in Iraq,
but more than half the British people were polled as opposed to the war.

Manning had briefed Sir Christopher Meyer, the then British
Ambassador to the US, and had spoken to US National Security Advisor
Condoleezza Rice – now US Secretary of State. Manning told her that
Blair wanted Bush not to rush into war until the invasion was deemed
legal – something that would need the full support of the UN Security
Council. A springtime memo from Meyer was circulated which warned
UK policy-makers not to underestimate Bush's passion for ousting
Saddam. With Washington pushing for an invasion of Iraq to go ahead
in the autumn of 2002, Blair's advisors told him that 'if any invasion is
contemplated [for] this autumn, then a decision will need to be taken in
principle six months in advance'. In other words, the decision had to be
taken almost immediately. It's stating the obvious to point out that this
left Blair little or no time to make the case for war legally watertight.

Manning was dispatched to Washington to explain to the administration just how difficult life was for Blair. Manning's memo on the trip
read: 'Prime Minister, I had dinner with Condi [Condoleezza Rice] on
Tuesday ... these were good exchanges, and particularly frank when we

were one-on-one at dinner. We spent a long time at dinner on Iraq. It is clear that Bush is grateful for your support and has registered that you are getting flak.

'I said that you would not budge in your support for regime change but you had to manage a press, a Parliament and a public opinion that was very different than anything in the States. And you would not budge on your insistence that, if we pursued regime change, it must be very carefully done and produce the right result. Failure was not an option. Condi's enthusiasm for regime change is undimmed. But there were some signs, since we last spoke, of greater awareness of the practical difficulties and political risks.

'From what she said, Bush has yet to find the answers to the big questions: how to persuade international opinion that military action against Iraq is necessary and justified; what value to put on the exiled Iraqi opposition; how to coordinate a US/allied military campaign with internal opposition (assuming there is any); what happens on the morning after? Bush will want to pick your brains. He will also want to hear whether he can expect coalition support. I told Condi that we realised that the administration could go it alone if it chose. But if it wanted company, it would have to take account of the concerns of its potential coalition partners.'

Manning told Rice that pushing for weapons inspections could help bring Europe along, adding: 'Renewed refusal by Saddam to accept unfettered inspections would be a powerful argument.' Manning also told Rice that it was 'paramount' that Israel and Palestine be dealt with. Failure to do so could lead to the allies 'bombing Iraq and losing the Gulf'.

Manning told Blair: 'Bush wants to hear your views on Iraq before taking a decision. He also wants your support. He is still smarting from the comments by other European leaders on his Iraq policy. This gives you real influence: on the public relations strategy; on the UN and weapons inspections; and on US planning for a military campaign. This could be critically important.' Manning added that the 'US scrambling to establish a link between Iraq and al-Qaeda is so far unconvincing. To get public and parliamentary support for military options we have to be convincing that the threat is so serious/imminent that it is worth sending our troops to die for.'

Blair then travelled to Bush's ranch in Crawford, Texas, in the spring of 2002 to talk war with the President. Here was how Jack Straw interpreted the meeting: 'The rewards from your visit to Crawford will be few. The risks are high both for you and the government.' Straw said there was a long way to go before Parliament could be convinced about 'the scale of the threat from Iraq and why this has got worse recently; what distinguishes the Iraqi threat from that of, for example, Iran and North Korea so as to justify military action; military action in terms of international law; and whether the consequences of military action really would be a compliant, law-abiding replacement government.'

Straw added: 'I know there are those who say that an attack on Iraq would be justified whether or not weapons inspectors were re-admitted, but I believe that a demand for the unfettered re-admission of weapons inspectors is essential, in terms of public explanation, and in terms of legal sanction for military action.'

Straw said there were 'two potential elephant traps': firstly, wanting regime change did not justify military action; and secondly, US opposition to a 'fresh mandate' (another resolution supporting war) from the United Nations. Straw added that: 'The weight of legal advice here is that a fresh mandate may well be required.' It's good of Jack to make the point – not that his private reservations stopped him from being a public rah-rah boy for the war – but it really is a no-brainer: for the US and UK to invade Iraq, the UN had to rubber-stamp the war for it to have any legality. Working that out isn't exactly rocket-science. The UN didn't rubber-stamp the war – so Tony and George are war criminals.

Blair lied to us all; he took the people of Great Britain into a war of his making, not for the sake of our friends in America – the American people – but on the whim of one of the most warmongering, right-wing US presidents the world has ever seen. Thousands have died. Britain is disgraced on the world's stage and at a greater risk than at any other time since the Second World War. For Britain to successfully come back from the place of shame the nation is now in, Blair must go, and he must be seen to go in shame. His shaming will remove our shame – the collective shame of the British people. For that reason, there is quite simply nothing else that the British people can do than to demand from their representatives in Parliament that Blair be impeached – and sent to the Tower where all our worst traitors once went.

WAR ON THE UNITED NATIONS

or

How a really nice English girl rumbled Britain and America's spy ring inside the UN, got arrested and then proved that the invasion of Iraq was illegal

I wonder what you make of this email. It's from a guy called Frank Koza. He's one of the big boys over at the NSA, the National Security Agency – that's America's ultra-secretive spying arm; an outfit so shady that it used to be referred to as 'No Such Agency'.

The email, marked TOP SECRET, was sent on January 31, 2003 just after midnight and the subject box read prosaically 'reflections of Iraq debate' – referring to the pre-war diplomatic wrangling surrounding the US–UK push to take out Saddam. It was sent to a series of British and American spy chiefs including senior staff at Britain's listening post, GCHQ (General Communications Headquarters) in Cheltenham.

It said: 'As you've likely heard by now, the Agency is mounting a surge particularly directed at the UN Security Council (UNSC) members (minus US and GBR of course) for insights as to how membership is reacting to the on-going debate re Iraq, plans to vote on any related resolutions, what related policies/negotiating positions they may be considering, alliances/dependencies, etc – the whole gamut of information that could give US policy-makers an edge in obtaining results favourable to US goals or to head off surprises.'

The email goes on to talk of a 'surge effort to revive/create efforts against UNSC members Angola, Cameroon, Chile, Bulgaria and Guinea, as well as extra focus on Pakistan UN matters'.

In case you were wondering, those states – Angola, Cameroon, Chile, Bulgaria, Guinea and Pakistan – all sat as non-permanent members of the UN Security Council in the run-up to the invasion of Iraq and the support of these 'six swing states' was key to getting UN backing for the war. The email also said that Britain and America must 'pay attention to existing non-UNSC member UN-related and domestic comms for anything useful related to UNSC deliberations/votes'.

Now, that is quite a lot of spook-speak to deal with, but if you haven't worked it out already let me explain: this email exposes how Britain and America spied on members of the UN Security Council in the run-up to war in the hope that they could learn something which would help them secure UN support for the invasion.

Let's run over that wording again. The email talks of:

- Mounting a surge – that is, spying effort – at the permanent members of the UN Security Council. That means Russia, France and China were to be spied on;
- A surge effort against the other non-permanent members – Angola, Cameroon, Chile, Bulgaria, Guinea and Pakistan;
- 'Paying attention' to non-UN Security Council members and their UN-related or domestic communications. In other words, any country on earth with a UN mission in New York was liable to have its diplomatic communications at the UN bugged by the UK and US.

A week after the email was sent US Secretary of State Colin Powell went to the United Nations in an attempt to convince the world that Saddam was a clear and present danger. He wiggled fake vials of anthrax at delegates, showed us a host of pointless satellite photos and delivered his hymn in praise of war with scaremongering cant. The email noted that the spying effort 'will probably peak (at least for this specific focus) in the middle of next week following the Sec State's presentation to the UNSC'. So while Colin Powell was trying to convince the world that Saddam was going to Armageddonise us all, British and American spies were bugging members of the Security Council and trying to undermine the United Nations – the one body on the planet which is meant to symbolise cooperation between the nations of the earth and a desire for universal peace between their peoples. Hardly a rush to the moral high ground.

The war against Iraq was by extension a war against the United Nations. The PNAC and the neocons who stole power in the 2000 US election had been saying for years that the UN was an impediment to US global power. If America was going to run the world, then it had to do something about the United Nations. To successfully launch the war in Iraq, America would have to take on and undermine the UN. That's because there was no way the United Nations would support the war as the UN was the body which put the weapons inspectors into Iraq and was therefore the body which knew pretty damned well that Saddam wasn't armed to the teeth. It was also the body which shamefully allowed sanctions to degrade the Iraqi people, so the UN therefore also knew that Iraq couldn't put up much of a fight and hadn't had the wherewithal to reconstitute its weapons programme after the First Gulf War.

But Iraq, for the leaders of America, was one stop on a long journey – a journey which the neocons believe will end with the US in an unassailable position militarily, economically and diplomatically. To create an American empire and hegemony, the UN had to be cowed by Team Bush. The ground had been laid for this long before the spying operation got going. We'd become used to hearing the Bush administration disparage both the UN itself and its leading members of staff – men like weapons inspectors Hans Blix and Mohammed El Baradei – simply because they dared to disagree with America's twisted take on the state of Iraqi weapons.

Any spying undertaken against friendly nations such as France by GCHQ would have been sanctioned all the way up to Jack Straw, who as then Foreign Secretary had overall control of GCHQ, and the Prime Minister. Such spying on the UN is expressly forbidden by the Vienna Conventions which outlaw espionage at UN missions. This spying venture wasn't just a suggestion – it happened. The UK and the US did spy on the UN. The email directing the spying operation against the UN came to light because an ordinary linguist at GCHQ had access to it and leaked its contents. Such a low-ranking official would not have been able to read shocking and revealing information about illegal and top secret spying missions unless they were required to use their language skills to help with the operation. Put bluntly, someone so far down the chain of command would never have had access to this email unless the operation it spoke of was already underway.

While the espionage effort against the UN was typical of America's contempt for the United Nations, the spying had much more to do with British self-interest than anything else. Remember that America was quite happy to go to war against Saddam in the face of world opinion. Bush had much of the American public behind him, having scared them silly with all his crap about mushroom clouds, but Blair wasn't in quite so untroubled a position. He desperately needed a resolution from the

UN Security Council that expressly gave the green light for military action against Iraq in order to give the war any legal and moral authority in the eyes of the British people and Parliament. America wanted to do its best by its faithful UK sidekick and was prepared to throw Blair a bone in the shape of a big push to get the requisite UN resolution. And if a little cloak-and-dagger mullarky at the UN helped, well, so be it.

In November 2002, the UN Security Council passed Resolution 1441 saying in effect that Saddam had to prove to the world that he'd disarmed or face war. As we all know, Saddam had no weapons, so he couldn't disarm; he also told the world that he had no weapons; Iraq cooperated with the arrival of weapons inspectors in Baghdad in late 2002 and the inspections teams found no WMD throughout early 2003 in the run-up to the invasion.

The sane countries of the world wanted to give the weapons inspections much longer so that teams could search through Iraq to prove definitely that there were or were not WMD lurking in the sand dunes. But America was locked and loaded and wanted a fight.

The logic of this war is truly terrifying: America said Saddam had banned weapons so the world agreed this was a risk and sent in inspectors to find the weapons; when the weapons weren't found that meant that in American eyes Saddam was hiding them and the war was on. Obviously, if the inspectors had found any weapons the war would have started anyway as Saddam would have been in breach of Resolution 1441. It's a bit like the way we tested for witches in medieval Britain. If an old hag was suspected of being a witch we'd chuck her in a pond. If she floated, she was guilty so we burned her; if she sank she was innocent and not a witch – but of course she was by now dead.

Most of the world, however, wasn't buying this kind of sicko psychopathic logic, and Britain knew it. That's why Blair in the dying days of 2002 and the new year of 2003 was desperate to get a second resolution from the UN which would justify the war. Perhaps Blair's mind was a little more focused than Dubya's as Britain had signed up to membership of the International Criminal Court which prosecutes war crimes; the US, however, had not. Many senior British army officers are terrified at the prospect of war crimes trials for taking civilian lives in an illegal war in Iraq. And I'm sure the thought of standing in the dock at The Hague must have crossed Blair's mind at least once. Understandably, then, Blair wanted the reassurance of a second resolution that would have made the war legal in the eyes of the world, the British people,

Parliament and the UK armed forces.

Thus, the spying surge against the UN as revealed in the email from the NSA.

The only problem with wicked plans – and spying on the UN is a wicked act – is that good people sometimes find out about them. You should, of course, not be shocked at Britain and America spying on the UN. Nor should you be shocked that countries like Russia and France or China would spy on the United Nations either. Shock has faded in this new world of ours. We are no longer shocked to hear that Catholic priests have abused children or that bosses put their workers' lives at risk to cut corners and up profits. It disgusts us, but shock? No. However, the absence of shock does not make something morally acceptable.

This is now where Katherine Gun enters stage left. Katherine was an expert in Mandarin Chinese working at GCHQ in January 2003. She was a gifted linguist who'd excelled at Durham University after a childhood in the Far East. With little interest for the *Boys' Own* world of espionage she joined GCHQ – signing the Official Secrets Act of course – because it gave her an opportunity to use her language skills in her professional life.

The NSA email came to Katherine's attention presumably because America and Britain were engaged in spying on the Chinese UN delegates and Katherine was a Chinese linguist. She says that when she read the email, she thought it 'pretty outrageous' so she printed a copy off and popped it in her bag. The contents of the email drove her nuts, niggling away at her for an entire weekend. Messrs Bush and Blair should take note of Ms Gun's behaviour here. You see, good people sometimes have sleepless nights and gnawed-at consciences when they think that bad things are going to happen, and sometimes they even feel compelled to 'do the right thing'.

So, Katherine passed this email to a friend of hers who in turn passed it to a journalist. 'I felt that the British intelligence services were being asked to do something which would undermine the whole United Nations democratic process,' she said. This story should have hit the news' stands like one of Saddam's mythical A-bombs – but it didn't. It caused a mild public reaction and then drifted away … until, that is, Katherine was arrested and charged with what amounted to treason.

But, of course, even though the news of the spying email died out in the public mind relatively quickly, it penetrated the brains of UN diplo-

mats like Bunker Busters dropped on Tora Bora. The world was right
on the brink of war, painful diplomatic negotiations were underway and
Bush and Blair were being outed as a pair of sneaky spies.
Diplomatically, the spying revelations spelt the end of Britain and
America's attempts to get the world to follow their lead over Saddam
and secure a second resolution from the Security Council giving the
thumbs-up to an invasion of Iraq. Who would want to tag along behind
a little rat and a big bully anyway? The email galvanised thinking within nations like France and Russia that it was time to start considering
how to shift away from the uni-polar world in which we live – a world
dominated by the US – to a multi-polar world where other countries are
not all submissive to the will of America.

The email revealed the sinister thinking, the self-serving scheming and
the black motives of Bush and Blair. Why would the UK and the US
have to spy on the United Nations in the midst of trying to get a second
resolution to justify war against Iraq on the grounds that Saddam was
armed to the teeth if their reasons were legitimate? Surely, if Saddam
was tooled up with nukes and sarin and anthrax then the world would
find out through the weapons inspectors in good time and we could
then all happily and legally march off to war to disarm him. Why the
need to rush it when containment, sanctions and bombing raids in the
north and south no-fly zones had worked since 1991? Why the need to
use spying? Why the need to try to wrong-foot other nations like France
and Russia? Because, Bush and Blair were totally at it. They knew their
argument that Saddam had dangerous stockpiles of WMD was crap,
they knew it wouldn't stand up to scrutiny and they needed to coerce
the world into war – they needed to confuse people, scare people and
panic them into making decisions that they didn't have the time or information to hand to make properly.

That's why the decision was made to bug the offices and homes of
senior UN officials and diplomats. Bush and Blair knew they couldn't
win by fair means, so they were quite content to succeed by foul ones.

People like Katherine Gun, however, are different creatures altogeth-
er. Bush and Blair kiss their wives goodnight each evening after their
decisions have cost thousands of innocent lives and drift off into a
dreamland of global domination, deception and stealth taxes. Good
people, however – people like Katherine Gun – sometimes find it hard
to live with the consequences of their actions even if they have acted for
the greater good. Even though she'd exposed a terrible wrong, Gun still

felt horrified about having betrayed her employer. Don't you wish that women like Gun would enter politics? But then why would a decent, honest person want to whore their principles for a few years of transient power?

Shortly after the publication of the spying email, in a crisis of conscience, Gun told her bosses what she'd done. GCHQ certainly treats whistle-blowing staff a lot better than the MoD. While Dr David Kelly was hounded to his death, Katherine Gun was allowed to cry on her boss's shoulders – literally. However, she was then taken directly to Cheltenham Police Station and charged under the Official Secrets Act.

The Official Secrets Act is one of the most insidious pieces of legislation in the canon of great big shitty British laws. It gags anyone who wants to speak out against government misdeeds at the highest or lowest level. All that is needed to jail someone under the Act is for the prosecution to prove that a person is covered by the Act. This is easy to do, given that most government employees sign the damn thing in order to get a job. The next step is to prove that the accused revealed information covered by the Act. Given that Gun had admitted leaking an email headed TOP SECRET, she looked well and truly shafted.

But there's one thing governments tend to overlook – the British people. The British people sit on juries, and juries can be troublesome things, just like electorates, facts and the truth.

When another British civil servant, Clive Ponting, was prosecuted in the 1980s for passing evidence to an MP that Margaret Thatcher's government had misled Parliament about when and where the Argentine battleship, *General Belgrano*, was sunk during the Falklands War, it too looked like an open-and-shut case. Ponting confessed, just like Gun, and the judge virtually ordered the jury to convict. The jury was having none of that, however – no uppity Establishment judge was going to lecture them on matters of a man's personal conscience – so they acquitted Ponting.

However, memories of Ponting didn't help much when the government banned Gun from saying anything to her lawyers about her work at GCHQ, crippling her defence. Gun was scared. She realised the 'whole government machine' was pitted against her, but she took solace from her husband who told her the matter was very simple. It all boiled down to a case of 'do nothing and die, or fight and die'.

'I didn't feel at all guilty about what I did,' she said, 'so I couldn't plead guilty, even though I would get a more lenient sentence.' Despite the prospect of jail, Gun was sure that if she had to re-live the event, she'd still have leaked the email – it was that important.

She decided to fight her corner on the defence of 'necessity' – in other words, her legal team would argue that she needed to leak the document in order to save lives which would be lost in an illegal war. That circumvented the sneaky government trick of banning her talking about her work at the listening post to her lawyers.

The world is filled with lesser people than Gun. How many other people in other spying agencies read that email, thought it disgusting, yet still did nothing? A young woman like Katherine Gun, aged just 29, showed that she understood better and cared more for the spirit of British democracy than Tony Blair and all his sidekicks put together. They talk about the principles of democracy – she acts on them. They took lives, she tried to save them. 'I have only ever followed my conscience,' she said.

Her bravery earned her many admirers and supporters in her hour of need; among them were the Hollywood actor Sean Penn, the Rev. Jesse Jackson and Daniel Ellsberg.

Ellsberg was a US State Department official who was almost destroyed by the Nixon administration in the early 1970s when he leaked the so-called Pentagon Papers which showed how consecutive presidents from Kennedy onwards had repeatedly lied to the American people about the Vietnam war. Ellsberg's biggest regret is that he leaked the information too late. If he'd acted sooner, he believes, many American and Vietnamese lives might have been saved.

'I can only admire the more timely, courageous action of Katherine Gun, the GCHQ translator who risked her career and freedom to expose an illegal plan to win official and public support for an illegal war, before the war had started,' he wrote. 'Her revelation of a classified document urging British intelligence to help the US bug the phones of all the members of the UN Security Council to manipulate their votes on the war may have been critical in denying the invasion a false cloak of legitimacy. That did not prevent the aggression, but it was reasonable for her to hope that her country would not choose to act as an outlaw, thereby saving lives. She did what she could in time for it to make a difference, as indeed others should have done, and still can.'

Ellsberg added: 'Exposing governmental lies carries a heavy personal risk, even in our democracies. But that can be worthwhile when a war's worth of lives is at stake.'

As well as a handful of celebrities and a fellow whistle-blower, Gun also had the British civil rights organisation, Liberty, weigh in on her side against the massed ranks of New Labour. With their help, her lawyers began planning her defence. It was a defence that would rise and fall on one simple question: was the war in Iraq legal?

This was exactly what Blair did not want. He hadn't won that second UN resolution which would have given him legal cover for invading Iraq, and the last thing he wanted was the legality of the war questioned in a British court of law – especially by the woman who leaked the spook email which doomed to failure Britain and America's attempts to win support for their ass-covering resolution among the other members of the UN Security Council.

In February 2003, as the year crept inexorably towards war, more than a million people marched in Britain protesting against the planned invasion of Iraq. Russia, France and Germany were also pressing for greater diplomacy not militarism. Meanwhile, the UK and the US began increasing their strikes against Iraqi air defences in the northern and southern no-fly zones which were established at the end of the First Gulf War. On the day that details of Gun's leaked email hit the news stands, Iraq claimed that UK and US bombers had killed six civilians during no-fly zone raids on Basra – and the war hadn't even started yet.

It was January 31, 2003, when Gun first read the spying email. Its contents were made public on March 2, 2003. China, France and Russia soon released a joint declaration stating that a UN resolution authorising war would not be allowed to pass. On March 17, 2003, the three countries made clear that there was no support for war inside the Security Council. The resolution was abandoned by the US and the UK.

America and the UK had been pushing for a second resolution triggering war in the face of mounting evidence from the weapons inspectors that Saddam didn't have any WMD. Many countries wanted more time to continue the hunt, not a pointless war of aggression.

Hot on the heels of China, France and Russia slapping down Britain and America's much sought after resolution, there came yet another report from Hans Blix, the chief weapons inspector, which again didn't provide the necessary excuse for war: the discovery of hidden weapons. For his crime of not finding things that didn't exist, the grand inquisitors of the US administration painted Blix as the village idiot of global diplomacy.

Jack Straw, the UK Foreign Secretary, had called on the UN to set an ultimatum that Iraq would be invaded by March 17. France responded by saying it would veto any such resolution. While Iraq experienced its first casualties of the Second Gulf War in Basra in pre-war 'softening-up' raids, the Prime Minister was just about to take his first bloody hit as well. Andy Reed, a parliamentary aide to Blair loyalist Margaret Beckett, resigned over the looming war, and Clare Short, the at times flaky International Development Secretary, threatened to resign if the UN failed to pass a second resolution.

Donald Rumsfeld then waded in, flippantly saying that the US would go it alone if Blair couldn't rally his political troops due to the failure to get a second resolution. Rummy's little psyop paid off, with Blair responding that Britain would fight alongside the US in any attack. Jacques Chirac, the French President, then called Blair, reiterating that France would veto military intervention.

Bush and Blair rushed to the Azores for an island summit with the leader of the Spanish government and Iberian slimeball-in-chief, Jose Maria Aznar. He is the right-wing liar who got kicked out of office for telling the grieving Spanish people that the Madrid train bombings were the work of Eta – the domestic separatist terror group – rather than the handiwork of al-Qaeda affiliates. In the Azores, this triumvirate of liars and fantasists said war would be declared within days if Saddam didn't disarm. With hindsight, this summit takes on a terrible nightmarish quality. The world was being dragged into a ghastly war whether it liked it or not.

China, France and Russia responded to the Azores summit by yet again restating their opposition to any attack proving once more – as if it needed to be proved – that the US and the UK were beat, at least in the diplomatic war. They withdrew attempts to get a second resolution passed and blamed the goddamn French. French fries were replaced with 'Freedom Fries' in diners across the mid-West and Fox News all but called for Paris to be bombed.

Robin Cook, the Leader of the House of Commons and former Foreign Secretary, then resigned saying he couldn't support a war without 'international authority nor domestic support', while Bush gave Saddam and his sons 48 hours to get outta town. With diplomacy up the creek, Bush reverted to gunslinger mode, telling the Hussein gang that they were wanted dead or alive.

British politics sustained even more casualties. Government ministers John Denham and Lord Hunt resigned, along with four other government aides. On March 18, 2003, a parliamentary debate ended in both success and failure for Blair. The government motion endorsing the war was passed by 412 votes to 149, but some 139 Labour MPs rebelled. Another government aide, David Kinley, resigned, bringing the total government casualties over Iraq to nine before the first shot of the war proper was even fired.

More than 170,000 US and UK forces massed by the Kuwaiti border to invade as more 'softening-up' air strikes against Iraq took place. Germany, France and Russia all condemned what was happening, saying that war was illegal and not sanctioned by the United Nations. But Bush and Blair blanked them and the war began on March 20 with a failed assassination strike against Saddam Hussein. Operation Shock-and-Awe was underway.

While all these historic events were unfolding, Katherine Gun was plotting her defence – and the belligerent disregard of America and Britain to the wishes of the rest of the world would prove very handy for Ms Gun and her legal team, keeping, as they did, the diplomatic controversy and questionable legality surrounding the war alive in the minds of the British people.

By February 2004, Gun's trial was getting closer and closer. Katherine was preparing herself for a spell behind bars and being branded a traitor in what appeared to be an open-and-shut case for the government. Then suddenly on February 25, the charge against her was dropped. The prosecution offered no evidence against her, saying that there wasn't a 'realistic prospect of conviction', and she walked away from court a free woman.

Of course, the reason the government didn't hound Gun to her grave like David Kelly had nothing to do with Blair's humanity or a change of heart – rather the slimy bastards didn't want to be caught out in their lies. Gun's lawyers were going to say that she broke the law out of necessity as the war was illegal. To disprove her defence of necessity the government would have been forced to bring into public the legal advice it took in the run-up to war. 'Was the war legal?' was not a question Blair wanted examined in a British court.

As the Butler Report subsequently told us, the British Attorney-General, Lord Goldsmith, informed Blair that if the war was to be legal then the UK had to show 'that Iraq had failed to take the final opportunity to comply with its disarmament obligations under relevant resolutions of the Security Council and that it was possible to demonstrate

hard evidence of non-compliance and non-cooperation with the requirements of Security Council Resolution 1441'. As we know, there had
been no material breach of Resolution 1441, so the war was illegal. It
wasn't as if the government and Blair didn't know all this. After all,
Elizabeth Wilmshurst, the Foreign Office's Deputy Legal Advisor, told
Lord Goldsmith, the Attorney-General and Britain's highest-ranking
law officer, that the legal basis for war didn't stand up and then resigned
– as did two other Foreign Office legal advisors. Nearly all Foreign
Office lawyers believed a second UN resolution was required to make
the war legal. While the principled Wilmshurst resigned, her boss,
Michael Wood, did not. He received a knighthood in 2004.

It was Goldsmith's job to rule whether invading Iraq was lawful or
not, so before he gave the war a big legal thumbs-up he asked the PM
for assurances that there were 'strong factual grounds' and 'hard evidence' that Saddam was failing to comply with Resolution 1441. Of
course, Blair, the ultimate self-convincer, patted Goldsmith on the head
and told him Saddam was definitely in non-compliance as the weapons
existed.

Understandably, poor old Blair didn't want any of the mad contents
of his head – or the ropey legal justification for the war which had been
cobbled together after he'd boxed the Attorney-General into saying that
attacking Saddam was above board – revealed in open court during
Katherine's trial. Let's not forget that Blair is a lawyer, so he's as slippery as a trout down a poacher's trouser leg when it comes to anyone
trying to catch him out.

It is the Attorney-General, Lord Goldsmith, who must approve any
prosecution under the Official Secrets Act. It is also Lord Goldsmith
who decides whether prosecutions under the OSA should be scrapped.
So, the man who knew how dodgy the legal case for war was, had
decided to bin a trial under the Official Secrets Act in which he knew
that the question of the legality of the war was central.

When Shami Chakrabarti of Liberty, which supported Gun, suggested that the reason for the prosecution being dropped just might have
something to do with a criminal trial being a 'little too embarrassing',
the government muttered that 'it would not be appropriate to go into
the reasons for this decision'. You bet.

The day before the government suddenly and unexpectedly chickened
out of prosecuting Gun, her lawyers had served papers on the administration demanding to see all legal advice surrounding the war. Facing

the prospect of a fair fight in a British court of law, and the bogus legal foundations of the war being exposed, the government ran for the hills and dropped the prosecution. From beginning to end, Katherine Gun displayed an integrity, humanity and intelligence that's all too easy to think long gone in Britain. Smiling from ear to ear as she walked from court a free woman, she said: 'Obviously, I'm not prone to leak secrets, left, right and centre but this needed to get out. The public deserved to know what was going on at the time.' Simple, just and true.

Goldsmith may appear to be something of a conniving villain in this tale, but he is, in fact, a man more sinned against than sinning; albeit a weak and manipulated one. Blair, it seems, broke his Attorney-General, forcing Goldsmith to corrupt his integrity and compelling him to do his bidding. In the end, by the time war came, Goldsmith had been squeezed by both Blair and Bush to such an extent that he had swung from believing that any invasion would be illegal to giving Blair the strained, convoluted legal go-ahead that was required from him to trigger the war that the PM wanted so desperately.

Goldsmith was no expert in international law. He was a commercial barrister, and, most crucially, a friend of the Blairs. The Prime Minister told his sceptical 'friend' to say nothing about the war until any comments he had would advance the case for invading Iraq. Goldsmith must have taken being ordered to shut his mouth by the Prime Minister very much to heart as he later told the Butler Inquiry team that he could not show them his legal opinion for the government on whether or not the war was justified. He only produced his legal findings for the Butler team when they said they'd abandon the Inquiry if he didn't cooperate. As you know, the legal advice may have been seen by the Butler Inquiry, but it was never made public by the government.

Between September 2002 and February 2003, Goldsmith was saying behind closed doors that he couldn't back the war legally without the explicit say-so of the United Nations. Resolution 1441, in Goldsmith's opinion, was not enough to justify the invasion.

The US, meanwhile, was in a legal Cloud Cuckoo Land. The leading members of the Bush administration believed – or rather had convinced themselves – that UN Resolution 1441 and also UN Resolution 687, which was passed in 1991 after the First Gulf War, was enough to trigger war if Iraq was deemed by America to be in breach of its disarmament obligations.

Come January 2003, Goldsmith wrote a memo to Blair outlining his legal concerns about the war. He was then dispatched in February to Washington DC to meet with the US Attorney-General, John Ashcroft, and John Bellinger, the Senior Associate Counsel to the President and the Legal Advisor to the National Security Council. Meeting that pair would be a horrible prospect for anyone to face – even a lawyer who works for the Blair government.

Maybe they threatened Goldsmith with a spell in Guantanamo Bay, because when he returned to good old Blighty, the Attorney-General produced the legal advice Blair had been looking for ... sort of. The problem was that the advice was filled with too many 'ifs' and 'buts', too many caveats and qualifications, and it also described what legal challenges could be mounted against the case for war. Furthermore, the advice, against all protocol, didn't get circulated to the cabinet. Blair later told Lord Butler that he held back the legal findings as he couldn't trust some members of his own top team. Such dictatorial rule prompted Butler to remark: 'We are concerned that the informality and circumscribed character of the government's procedures which we saw in the context of policy-making towards Iraq risks reducing the scope for informed collective political judgement.'

As the war approached, Goldsmith's advice was sent to Admiral Sir Michael Boyce, Chief of the Defence Staff, who said he found it too equivocal. Boyce wanted something tougher and more definitive; something that would set the minds of military top brass at ease and reassure them that they were not engaging in an illegal war which could end up with them languishing in some international nick awaiting war crimes trials.

Goldsmith wrote to Blair asking for confirmation that 'it is unequivocally [in] the Prime Minister's view that Iraq has committed further material breaches as specified in ... Resolution 1441'. The next day, the PM's office told Goldsmith 'it is indeed the Prime Minister's unequivocal view that Iraq is in further material breach of its obligations'.

Goldsmith was being forced to provide the legal mechanism to take the UK to war solely on the say-so of Tony Blair. His legal opinion following his return from America had been full of notes of caution, which would have undoubtedly made the British people and Parliament question the legality of any invasion, but when Goldsmith appeared before the cabinet on March 17 – just a few days before the war started – he read out a short statement stripped of all qualifications which, in effect, said simply that the invasion of Iraq was legally justified. Influenced by

Blair, Goldsmith had made the legal findings stronger and more assured; complexity, nuance and ambiguity had been replaced by the kind of strident self-assurance that Blair craved. The cabinet – abject in its collective spinelessness – was not allowed to ask any questions. On March 18, the House of Commons voted for war and two days later the invasion began.

All that can really be said in Goldsmith's defence is that friends claim he felt his position was intolerable throughout early 2003 and that he seriously contemplated resigning his post.

Why didn't Goldsmith follow his heart? Why can someone like Katherine Gun take the hard road to truth, integrity and honour, while others, like Goldsmith, succumb to power and betray themselves and the spirit of their country? Nothing can ever explain that.

CARVING UP THE NEW IRAQ
or
How the American military-industrial complex got fat on Iraqi blood

What is at the heart of all the lies that were spun by Bush and Blair to get this war started? When searching for answers there's no better advice in any hunt for the truth than to 'follow the money'.

This conflict was started by war profiteers who had a revolutionary political ideology that they wanted to further. Getting the bombing underway suited both their philosophy and their bank balances.

I want to take you on a journey to two very specific points in the war. The first is the halfway point of the 'war proper' itself – mid-April 2003. The war began on March 20, 2003 and was declared over by Bush on May 1, 2003 when the Prez flew onto the deck of an aircraft carrier, no doubt with a pair of socks tucked down the crotch of his flight suit, to tell the world that it was 'Mission Accomplished' in Iraq.

By mid-April, Saddam's armies were well and truly defeated, and Iraq was drifting into chaos. It was at this precise time that American companies, heavily linked to both the US military and political establishments, began to pull down massive US government contracts for the reconstruction of Iraq. Of course, to the sane mind, the concept of reconstruction in a country where a hundred deaths a day in suicide bombings is not uncommon makes about as much sense as offering botox injections to the Elephant Man.

After we examine the first, early orgy and rush by the war profiteers to pull down the big contracts, I will take you forward just over a year to the late summer of 2004. By then, the Iraqi interim government had been installed by the US under the leadership of Iyad Allawi. The passage of a year had allowed US firms to really get their fangs into Iraq. By now, the reconstruction contracts that they were securing were bringing them fortunes beyond the wildest of imaginations. The irony was that nothing was being reconstructed; Iraq itself was like one burning cauldron of chaos, anarchy, terror and repression. Simply staying alive was more important for Iraqis, US soldiers and American contractors than completing all those reconstruction jobs that they'd been paid for. Yet, still the contracts kept flowing.

These two points in time – the spring of 2003 and the summer of 2004 – are meant to be illustrative of how American business, with the full backing of the American government and military, raped and exploited what was left of Iraq. The period between spring 2003 and summer 2004 charts the passage of a policy of war profiteering from its inception to a point where it became a grotesque perversion of reconstruction and nation-building. By midway through 2004, US companies were getting rich off the back of a country that was one endless tableau of rape, kidnap and murder. These corporate raiders were capitalist Neros, fiddling while Baghdad burned.

Surprise, surprise, from the early stages of the reconstruction process in the spring of 2003, right through to today, the big winners – in fact nearly all the winners – were American companies closely tied to the Bush administration. Britain and Australia and all the other countries who sent their boys to die for Bush were lucky if they picked up a few sub-contracts for reconstruction work from the big US firms. They were like dogs begging for bones from the king's table.

OK. So let's return to our starting point – mid-April 2003 – in an attempt to find out just how the ugly world of war profiteering works. This was when Bush's favoured US firms began to jockey for position, hoping to get a slice of Iraq. Iraq was teetering on the brink of collapse and the capitalists in stovepipe hats back in the US started to drool in anticipation at the prospect of the big wodges of cash that they knew the Bush administration would send flowing their way.

As they rubbed their hands, Iraq, by mid-April, lay in ruins. Its cities were bombed; its buildings had been torched by teenage arsonists; its shops, hospitals, factories, museums, art galleries and homes were looted. Iraq stood facing its very own Year Zero. The old regime was all but gone. It was now the duty of the United States to rebuild this country literally from the ground up.

By that spring, America had its reconstruction plan in place. Answering directly to Centcom commander General Tommy Franks, was retired Lt Gen Jay Garner, the man initially put in charge of the reconstruction effort. This soldier – who during his time in Iraq came to be known as the Sheriff of Baghdad – was aided by a series of military hard men, diplomats and Republican Party placemen. He planned to help the United States create 'Free Iraq' – a pipe dream that he believed he could will into existence with the aid of Iraqi exiles returning to get their share of the spoils.

Garner's job later passed to career diplomat, Ambassador Paul Bremer, who headed the Coalition Provisional Authority until the so-called hand-over of power to the un-elected Interim Iraqi Government in June 2004. From 1989 to 2000, Mr Bremer, an old Yale man *á la* President Bush, was Managing Director of Kissinger Associates, a strategic consulting firm headed by former Secretary of State, Henry Kissinger. Lawrence S Eagleburger, who served Bush Senior as Secretary of State, is the President of Kissinger Associates. Eagleburger is also a Director of Halliburton, the oil company once run by Vice-president Dick Cheney and now scooping up the biggest of big bucks in Iraqi reconstruction contracts. Bremer, then, as we can see, is symbolic of the crony culture that fed off the reconstruction project; he was as besmirched as the rest of the reconstruction team by the multi-layered conflict of interests that underpinned everything to do with the big business carve-up of the 'new' Iraq.

This 'reconstruction' project was no selfless exercise by any of the participants; rather, it was a self-interested network of fellow travellers umbilically tied to each other by financial kick-backs, political pay-backs, the buddy-system and ferocious ideology; this is what propped up the entire reconstruction scheme, not love for the Iraqi people or a single-minded celebration of the joy of 'democracy'.

At the time, the US denied that men like Jay Garner were the first wave of a military occupation. The Bush administration insisted that it wanted these men to work their way out of a job as quickly as possible. Laughably, some mentioned three months as the possible length of their tenure in Iraq – others, realistically, claimed five years was a more likely term, taking the length of the US occupation of post-war Japan as the best comparison.

Today, we know that the west will be entrenched in this nation for decades to come. The irony is that now – with the bombs flying, bullets raining and heads of all shapes, sizes and colours rolling – the west would much rather get the hell out of Iraq than hang around.

But things were different back in April 2003 when the colonisation process really began. It was a seminal moment in Iraqi history – the moment that American capitalists, lured by wealth and heedless of the coming horror, carved up the New Iraq with their military and political pals; the moment when all talk of freedom and nation-building was subordinated to greed.

The roots of the reconstruction process are, like everything about this war, easily traced back to the ideologues – the neoconservatives running the US government – who devised the invasion and the occupation; the people who thought that we'd be greeted as liberators by flower-throwing Iraqi children, rather than as invaders by the masked killers who stalk every Briton or American who now dares to set foot in Iraq today.

As we know, these ideologues are the men who see the US military as the 'cavalry on the new American frontier'; men who wanted Saddam 'regime-changed' long before Bush took power and who have long dreamt of a permanent US satellite in the Gulf. They are the men who wanted Iraq's oil fields.

Documents from Vice-president Dick Cheney's Energy Task Force – obtained by the pressure group Judicial Watch under America's Freedom of Information Act in 2003 – showed how these vultures were salivating for their booty.

The documents, dated March 2001 – long before September 11 and the sabre-rattling over Saddam and his non-existent WMD began – included a map of Iraqi oil fields, pipelines, refineries and terminals, as well as two charts detailing Iraqi oil and gas projects and a list entitled *Foreign Suitors for Iraqi Oilfield Contracts*. Spookily, the documents also contained maps of Saudi Arabian and United Arab Emirates oilfields and pipelines. The Bush administration tried long and hard to keep the workings of Cheney's Energy Taskforce secret.

For the Bushites, ideology is ideology, sure, but philosophy has to take second place to hard capitalist truths; in the good ol' US of A, government political theory goes hand-in-hand with big business. The inevitable end result of the esoteric musings of Republican hawks fashioning the concepts behind the new world order is money-grubbing for the Yankee dollar. When the Americans took us to war in Iraq, the world didn't just watch some clumsy, ugly attempt to bring freedom and liberty to the people of Iraq, it became a dumb spectator in a conquest by and for American big business as well.

The term 'military-industrial' complex brings to mind all sorts of crazy conspiracy theories, but let's consider the expression again. Back in 1961, the Republican President Dwight D Eisenhower warned in a speech delivered as he left the White House that 'we must guard against the acquisition of unwarranted influence, whether sought or unsought, by the military-industrial complex. The potential for the disastrous rise of misplaced power exists and will persist.'

The companies in the running for, or in possession of, contracts to reconstruct Iraq are either major Republican donors or have government staff working for them. Their donations to the Republican Party – and also to George W Bush himself – run into millions. They are arms companies and oil companies who are cleaved to Washington's political cadre. It's a ready-made oligarchy.

The war became pay-back time for the men who bankrolled the American political establishment – and that was just fine by the guys in government. To them, greasing palms and whoring for cash is just business as usual. In the UK, connections like this between big business and politicians would be front page news for months and would certainly result in sackings and resignations. Yet, there is more to this than just kick-backs. The Americans call it 'the favour bank', we call it cronyism. The myriad connections between those reconstructors is frankly staggering. They are the networked new elite; the new masters of the universe ... and they are all the best of mates.

If these people aren't in the same think-tank together, then they work for the same companies, have the same friends and interests or went to college together; they are all interconnected like some sprawling dysfunctional, incestuous family. Just look at one example. Over the next few pages, I have divided the people who moved into Iraq as reconstructors in the final days of the fighting in mid-April 2003 into a variety of categories: the ideologues, the power-brokers, the generals, the neocons and so on. Under the power-brokers section you will find Andrew Natsios. He's the head of USAid, the United States Agency for International Development – the government department which hands out those juicy Iraqi reconstruction contracts. Would it surprise you to find out that Natsios has a connection to a company called Bechtel which is – of course – war profiteering like there is no tomorrow? Oh, and by the way, all of the contracts that are handed out by the US government to its pals in big business are negotiated in secret.

According to the Federal Election Commission, Bechtel handed over almost $770,000 to the Republican Party between 1999 and March 2003 when the war broke out. Donald Rumsfeld once acted as a liaison between Bechtel and the Iraqi regime in a bid to smooth the building of an oil pipeline. Other successful contractors for Iraqi reconstruction include the Washington Group International which has given $438,700 to the Republicans over the same period – on top of a donation to Bush – and the Louis Berger Group which gave $26,300 to the party.

Then there's the International Resources Group (IRG). As of April 2003, there were just eight government contracts up for grabs, but IRG was 'lucky' enough to secure one of those lucrative contracts. Are you shocked to learn that IRG has four vice-presidents and 24 other senior members of staff who at one time worked for USAid which doles out the Iraqi contracts? IRG also made significant donations to the Republican Party and won a $38 million contract.

Or what about John Hemingway, President of Stevedoring Services of America which won the Iraqi reconstruction contract to manage the port of Umm Qasr? He has made personal donations to the Republican Party. SSA was one of the first companies to win a contract. It was worth $4.8 million.

There's also Halliburton, the oil giant once run by Dick Cheney, and its subsidiary Kellogg, Brown & Root, both of which are making billions of dollars out of reconstruction. Since 1999, Halliburton has given 95 per cent, or some $700,000, of its political donations to the Republicans. Kellogg, Brown & Root won the first Iraqi reconstruction contract – a single deal valued at $500 million. The Flour Group has also made a killing. It gave the Republicans $275,000 and has ties to a number of intelligence and defence procurement officials.

As a word, 'corruption' cannot do justice to what American businessmen and their political pals are engaged in inside occupied Iraq. With only a few exceptions, there is a smoking gun for all those behind the reconstruction work. Whether it's a seat on a board, shares in a firm, a favour owed here or there, there are serious questions to be asked about the impartiality of some mega-powerful people and the levels of self-interest that lie behind the invasion and the rebuilding of Iraq.

In the early days of the invasion, with Iraq free of Saddam, it looked to the neocon hawks and their business cronies that the Iraqi nation was going to be one of the most lucrative countries on earth for America for the foreseeable future ... of course, that was before Iraq turned into a vision of hell on earth which sucked up lives and money like a vacuum cleaner on speed.

When hostages start having their heads sawn off live on TV, money really ceases to have any meaning. That's when reality kicks in; and when reality kicked in for the Iraq project, the neocons were exposed for what they really were deep down inside: petty emperors in new clothes – stupid, arrogant men who have riches but nothing else.

Here, listed over the next few pages, are the people who carved up the New Iraq at the very start – at that seminal moment in mid-April 2003 when the old regime was just disappearing and the new one was just moving in, sniffing for the money and the pay-off. But what is most chilling about the creatures you read about in the coming pages is the way in which they meld the corporate world with the world of the military and channel it into the heart of the government of the US. As an aside, and as nothing more than an aside, I'd like to remind you that it was the Italian dictator Benito Mussolini who said: 'Fascism should more accurately be named corporatism, since it is the merger of state and corporate power.'

Anyway, here they are; the people, the companies and the think-tanks that began the 'reconstruction' (some would call it corporate looting) in April 2003 and were jockeying for riches and power during that Baghdad spring. As ever, the first place on any list to do with the Iraq War, must go to:

THE NEOCONSERVATIVES

Paul Wolfowitz

At the time of the invasion, Wolfie was the Deputy Defense Secretary, the arch-ideologue of the Bush administration and the key architect in the Pentagon of the post-war reconstruction of Iraq. Like many of the reconstructors, Wolfowitz of Arabia, as he is known, is a high ranking member of the leading neoconservative think-tank, the Project for the New American Century (PNAC), which advocated regime change in Iraq even before George W Bush took office. He is, also, like many of the reconstruction team, a key member of the ultra-right-wing Jewish Institute for National Security Affairs (JINSA) – a think-tank that puts Israel and its security at the heart of US foreign policy. Many of the reconstructors – known as Wolfie's People or the True Believers – were hand-picked placemen chosen by the neocon grandee. Wolfowitz is the ideological link in Team Bush's grand scheme. His thinking was and is central to the war and its aftermath.

Lewis Libby

Known as Scooter, he was, prior to his earlier mentioned arrest, Vice-president Dick Cheney's Chief of Staff and a long-standing face at the Pentagon, having served in the defence department during George Bush Senior's presidency. He is also friend, confidant and a neocon fellow-traveller with Wolfowitz, and a founding member of the PNAC. He sits on the board of the Rand Corporation, a research and development company which has a huge number of contracts with the Pentagon. Zalmay Khalilzad, Bush's special envoy to Iraq, was also an employee of Rand Corporation. Libby owns shares in armament companies and has various oil interests. He is a consultant to Northrop Grumman, the defence contractor, which has an influential voice on the Defense Policy Board (DPB), the so-called brains of the Pentagon, and an organisation which advises the defence department on all things military and influences defence contracts. Rand Corp., which won $83m in Pentagon contracts, is also linked to the DPB.

Donald Rumsfeld

A founding member of the PNAC, the Pentagon supremo is probably one of the best connected men in American politics. It was Rumsfeld who personally designed the Iraqi invasion plan. Every detail of the post-war reconstruction has to be cleared by the Defense Secretary. Each and every neocon in the Pentagon owes their position to him. One fact he doesn't want to be reminded about is his former glad-handing with Saddam as Reagan's special envoy to Iraq in the early 1980s. While Saddam was blitzing the Ayatollah's armies with chemical weapons in the Iran–Iraq war, Rumsfeld spent most of his time talking to the Ba'ath Party about the building of an oil pipeline on behalf of the construction company Bechtel. Bechtel's former Vice-Chairman is George Shultz, Reagan's Secretary of State. Bechtel is one of the front-runners when it comes to the reconstruction contracts.

Douglas J Feith

Under-Secretary for Policy at the Pentagon, Feith picks and selects members of the powerful Defense Policy Board and is on the board of advisors of JINSA. As a lawyer, Feith represented Northrop Grumman, the defence contractor. He was a Pentagon placeman when Richard Perle was Assistant Defense Secretary in the 1980s and hired Michael Mobbs (see *Power-brokers*) to work at his law firm Feith & Zell. Zealously pro-Israeli, Feith is a keen fan of the disgraced Ahmed Chalabi (see *Arabs*), as are Perle and Rumsfeld.

Richard Perle

The Pentagon's Prince of Darkness is a key member of JINSA and a prominent member of the American Enterprise Institute (described by Ronnie Reagan as one of the most influential right-wing US think-tanks) along with Dick Cheney's wife, Lynne. He also sits on the Foundation for the Defense of Democracies, another right-wing think-tank, along with former CIA Chief James Woolsey, who was at one point tipped to become the Information Minister in post-war Iraq. Perle acted as an advisor to the lobbying firm run by Douglas J Feith – the Pentagon's Under-Secretary of Defense. Perle was also chair of the DPB until he resigned following a scandal over a conflict of interests relating to his business connections. However, he remained on the board of the DPB. Perle has sought permission from the Committee on Foreign Investment, on which the Defense Secretary Donald Rumsfeld sits, to run telecommunications businesses in Asia. He is also a member of neo-con think-tanks such as the American Enterprise Institute, and worked as an aide to ultra-right-wing former Israeli premier, Benyamin Netanyahu. Perle advised clients of Goldman Sachs, the investment house, on post-war investment opportunities in Iraq. Perle is also a director of the software company Autonomy Corp., which has clients including the Pentagon. Autonomy said it expects its profits to increase dramatically as a result of the war in Iraq.

Dick Cheney

Capitol Hill's resident hawk-in-chief, is a PNAC founding member and was on JINSA's board of advisors. The Vice-president was Defense Secretary under Bush Senior and has been fantasising about getting Saddam's head on a plate for over a decade. He was Chairman and CEO of oil company Halliburton, the corporate behemoth. Halliburton's subsidiary Kellogg Brown & Root secured contracts worth up to $7 billion from the US Army's Corp of Engineers to put out oil well fires in Iraq. He is a Trustee of the American Enterprise Institute and has had numerous oil interests. He has links to Chevron, for whom he negotiated the building of an oil pipeline from the Caspian Sea. Condoleeza Rice, the National Security Advisor at the time of the invasion, was the Director of Chevron until 2001 – and even had an oil tanker named after her. During Condi's tenure, Chevron's CEO Kenneth Derr once said: 'Iraq possesses huge reserves of oil and gas reserves I'd love Chevron to have access to.' Dick Cheney's wife Lynne sat on the board of Lockheed Martin, which manufactures Cruise missiles and now has an $800 million military satellite designed to assist troops in Iraq.

Michael Joyce

The former President of the Bradley Foundation, one of the largest and most influential right-wing organisations in America. It set up the PNAC led by William Kristol. Kristol's *Weekly Standard* is viewed in Washington as the in-house paper for Team Bush. The *Standard* is bankrolled by Rupert Murdoch. Joyce once said that Bush's key people such as Cheney, Rumsfeld and Wolfowitz 'were clearly influenced by Bradley Foundation thinking'. Joyce's 'best buddy' is William Bennett, Reagan's Education Secretary and Bush Senior's drug czar, who sniffed around some involvement in Iraq's post-war education system. Neil Bush, Dubya's brother, has also been spoken of in connection with rebuilding the education system in Iraqi. Joyce has phoned Bennett with the words: 'This is coach Joyce and this is what I want you to do.' Joyce is a self-styled moral guardian of American family values who, along with James Woolsey, is an advisor to Americans for Victory over Terrorism, a group that wants to stifle criticism of American military muscle.

James Woolsey

A long-time supporter of war on Iraq, and PNAC and JINSA member. The former Director of the CIA was named early on as a possible Minister of Information in the new Iraq. His business interests have included: the arms company British Aerospace; the Titan Corporation, which provided military interpreters to Abu Ghraib Prison, and DynCorp, which provides bodyguards for Hamid Karzai, the Afghani president, and has installed a police force monitoring service in Bosnia. DynCorp was sued for human rights violations in Bosnia, environmental health disasters in Ecuador and fraud in America. He was a partner in the law firm, Shea & Gardner, which acted as foreign agents for the Iraqi National Congress, led by Ahmed Chalabi. He is Vice-president of Booz Allen Hamilton, a corporate consultancy firm, which won a contract to develop a computer model of post-war Iraqi society. Booz Allen is also closely linked to the Defense Policy Board. Woolsey said that 'only fear will re-establish [Arab] respect for us ... we need a little bit of Machiavelli'. He has also said: 'We really don't need the Europeans. Anyways, they will be the first in line patting us on the back following our success and saying they were with us all along.'

THE POWER-BROKERS

Robert Reilly

Former Director of Voice of America, the pro-US radio service, Reilly was to be entrusted with overhauling Iraqi radio, television and newspapers. The Bush administration gave Reilly the green light to operate Radio Free Iraq. This involved using transmitters that had been sent to the Middle East for the military's psychological operations. Reilly is closely involved with an American administration plan to establish a media network in the Middle East beginning with a satellite TV station worth tens of millions of dollars. He is a very close friend and business partner of Ahmed Chalabi.

Michael Mobbs

A Pentagon lawyer and the overall civilian coordinator who had a powerful say in many of the Iraqi ministries. Mobbs wants US citizens imprisoned indefinitely without charge for terrorist offences. A notorious hawk and close friend of Richard Perle, Mobbs also worked for Douglas Feith's law firm. As a Pentagon consultant, he created the legal framework for the indefinite detention of al-Qaeda suspects at Camp X-Ray in Guantanamo Bay, which was built by Bechtel for $16m. He's also a former member of the US arms control agency under former President Ronald Reagan.

George Shultz

A Republican heavyweight and former Secretary of State under Nixon, Shultz was Bush Junior's presidential campaign advisor. He became one of the administration's key thinkers on running post-war Iraq. He was also on the board of directors at Bechtel, which chased Iraqi contracts after regime change. Like Perle, he has lucrative financial relationships, which bring his impartiality into question. Shultz is Chairman of the International Council of JP Morgan Chase, the banking syndicate in which Lewis Libby has heavy investments. Morgan Chase lent Saddam's regime $500m in 1983. Shultz is a member of the Committee for the Liberation of Iraq and a patron of the American Enterprise Institute.

William Eagleton

Like George Shultz, a contemporary of George Bush Senior and revered by the right as one of the grand old men of Republican foreign policy. The pair went to Yale together and both served in the Far East during the Second World War. A career diplomat, Eagleton was based in Iraq between 1980 and 1984 as Chief of US Interests Section in Baghdad. His tenure there came at a time when Iraqi use of chemical weapons against Iran was being studiously ignored by Washington. In April 2003, he was tipped to be the 'Mayor of Kirkuk', the oil-rich city in northern Iraq, or Kurdistan.

Andrew Natsios

The head of USAid, the United States Agency for International Development, Natsios is the man who hands out the post-war reconstruction contracts. Only US companies can bid for these lucrative deals. One of the most controversial episodes of his career saw him, as CEO of the Massachusetts Turnpike Authority, oversee the 'Big Dig' construction project of a three-mile underground highway in Boston, undertaken by Bechtel. The budget spiralled out of control costing up to $10bn more than it should have, with the largest budget rises under Natsios's tenure. The 'Big Dig' was meant to provide a series of tunnels to alleviate traffic congestion in and around Boston. Today, the tunnels are like Swiss cheese with water flooding them constantly. A former Massachusetts House of Representatives congressman, he is the author of a book called *US Foreign Policy and the Four Horsemen of the Apocalypse* and a retired Lieutenant Colonel from the First Gulf War. He was also the Chairman of the Massachusetts Republican Party for most of the 1980s. Natsios was assisted in the reconstruction project by Michael Marx, the head of USAid Disaster Assistance Response Team (DART) and a former US Army officer. Marx previously headed the DART team after the conflict in Afghanistan. Lewis Lucke, another USAid senior staffer, was to oversee the Iraqi reconstruction process. He headed the USAid mission team in Haiti alongside Timothy Carney (see *The Grey Suits*), one of the former US ambassadors who became involved in administering 'Free' Iraq. Their attempts at establishing democracy in Haiti failed, with elections collapsing amid allegations of electoral manipulation and fraud. Haiti soon descended into bloodshed and chaos.

Clint Williamson

In April 2003, Clint Williamson was getting ready to head the Iraqi Ministry of Justice. A former prosecutor at The Hague's International War Crimes Tribunal, he helped compile evidence against Slobodan Miloseviç. Williamson worked at Condoleezza Rice's National Security Agency. His skill in preparing indictments against war criminals should – one would hope – make him a valuable asset in dealing with abuses of Iraqi detainees by US soldiers in Abu Ghraib prison.

John Bolton

A prime architect of Bush's Iraq policy, Bolton served Bush Senior and Reagan in the State Department, Justice Department and USAid and became Under-Secretary for Arms Control and International Security in Bush Junior's State Department. His appointment was intended to counter the perceived 'dove-ishness' of Colin Powell. Bolton led Rumsfeld's charge to destabilise Powell's multilateralism. Bolton is part of the Jewish Institute for National Security Affairs, the Project for the New American Century and is a Vice-president at the American Enterprise Institute. He was also one of Bush's chad-counters during the Florida count in the 2000 race for the presidency. Bolton has long advocated Taiwan getting a UN seat – he's been on the payroll of the Taiwanese Government. The US unilateralist is a regular contributor to William Kristol's right-wing *Weekly Standard* and has vilified UN Secretary General Kofi Annan. This made Bush's elevation of Bolton to his current position as US ambassador to the UN all the more remarkable. Bolton was an opponent of the Comprehensive Test Ban Treaty and a cheerleader for the Star Wars Defense System. He has hinted at targeting Cuba in the war on terror. His financial interests include oil and arms firms and JP Morgan Chase, like Shultz. There is scary gossip about Bolton that – like many in the Bush administration – he believes in the inevitability of Armageddon. Like Woolsey, Bolton is said to believe we are in the midst of World War Four (the Cold War was World War Three, in case you were wondering) which he estimates could take 40 years to finish. Despite evidence to the contrary he apparently believes Iraq was involved in September 11. With Rumsfeld, Wolfowitz,

Khalilzad, Bennet, Woolsey, Perle and Kristol, Bolton co-signed a letter in 1998 urging President Bill Clinton to take military action in Iraq to protect oil interests.

THE THNK-TANKS

These are the right-wing foundations and intellectual powerhouses stuffed with Republican Party hacks, which have successfully influenced Bush's Iraq policy since he took power.

The Jewish Institute for National Security Affairs (JINSA)

With its aims of informing Americans of the continued importance of Israeli security, and of the need for an Israeli 'victory' in the Middle East, JINSA places itself firmly on the extreme right wing. It has repeatedly praised Israel for what it views as 'remarkable restraint' in the face of a centrally orchestrated campaign of terror from the Palestinian Authority, and its ranks include most of Bush's neocons. In April 2003 it supported both Garner and Chalabi.

The Project for a New American Century

Founded by the likes of Rumsfeld and Cheney in 1997 to counter what it viewed as Clinton's drifting foreign and defence policies, this think-tank would come to form the nucleus of Team Bush. It has always lobbied for regime change in Iraq and for America to play a more permanent role in the Middle East. It also believes American foreign policy to be by definition, inherently 'right'. Many see it as attempting to mastermind a US-controlled 'new world order'.

The American Enterprise Institute

One of America's biggest and most established think-tanks, the AEI has been pushing its conservative agenda for over 50 years in both foreign and domestic policy. With 14 of its members in Bush's administration, it claims to be better represented than any other think-tank in the current US government.

The Bradley Foundation

During the 15-year tenure of Michael Joyce heading up this organisation, which has charitable status, the century-old foundation increased its profile dramatically and can now claim to be cash-rich and very powerful. It even provided the seed money needed to set up the Project for a New American Century. The Republicans love it and some even call it the patron saint of hawkish causes, thanks to the considerable amounts of money it splashes out for the benefit of neocons.

THE CORPORATE PLAYERS

Stevedoring Services of America

This world-leading Seattle port company won one of the first USAid contracts for Iraqi reconstruction – a $4.8m deal to manage Iraq's strategic port, Umm Qasr. Known for its union-busting activities, it turns over around $1bn a year and its President, John Hemingway, has made personal donations to Republican Party candidates. SSA's contract angered the British government and army, and Trade Secretary Patricia Hewitt unsuccessfully called on Washington to intervene. The British shipping giant P&O is also angered about missing out and about not being told why they lost. EU commissioner Chris Patten called the US-exclusive bidding 'exceptionally *maladroit*'.

Bechtel

As of April 2003, Bechtel was scooping up contracts worth $900m. The total amount of business for Bechtel from Iraqi reconstruction could total $3bn. Bechtel has donated $1.3m to political campaign funds since 1999, with the majority going to the Republican Party. George Shultz is Bechtel's former CEO and is still on the board of directors. Other Republicans linked to the company include former Reagan Defense Secretary Caspar Weinberger. General Jack Sheehan, retired Marine Corp General, is its Senior Vice-president; he also sits on the Pentagon's influential Defense Policy Board. Just to remind you: in the 1980s Bechtel proposed building an oil pipeline through Iraq with Rumsfeld as an intermediary for the company to Saddam.

International Resources Group

The Washington-based company won contracts worth $38m to establish the humanitarian aid programme in Iraq. Obviously this involves an exceptionally close working relationship with USAid, which awards the contracts. Four of IRG's vice-presidents have all held senior posts with USAid, and 24 of the firm's 48 technical staff have worked for USAid.

Halliburton

This was Dick Cheney's old oil company until he joined Team Bush, walking out the door with a pay-off worth around $30m. There have also been deferred payments of $180,000 a year. Since 1999, Halliburton has given 95 per cent, or just under $700,000 of its political donations to the Republican Party. It also gave George Bush nearly $18,000. Halliburton's subsidiary, Kellogg Brown & Root (KBR), was the first company to be awarded an Iraqi reconstruction contract by the Pentagon to cap burning oil wells; the deal was reportedly worth $500m. The contract was awarded by the Army Corps of Engineers without any open competitive bidding process thanks to federal laws allowing the negotiations to take place in secret in the interests of national security. KBR has won a string of lucrative contracts despite failing to control the cost of work in the Balkans and being fined $2m following claims of fraud at a military base. KBR was also one of two contractors chosen by the Defense Threat Reduction Agency to undertake the disposal of weapons of mass destruction. That hasn't been a very taxing job so far. KBR subcontracted some of its work to two Houston firms – Wild Wells, and Boots & Coots, which was close to bankruptcy at the time. Boots & Coots had a capital deficit of $17m. They were given a $1m loan from a Panama-registered investment company, Checkpoint, run by Texas oilmen. It claimed Boots & Coots defaulted and demanded it file for bankruptcy.

Best of the rest

In April 2003, the other companies in the running to pull down big bucks included *Fluor Corp.*, which donated $275,000 to the Republicans and $3,500 personally to George Bush, and had ties to a number of intelligence and defence procurement officials. These included Kenneth J Oscar, former Acting Assistant Secretary of the army, and Bobby R Inman, a retired admiral, former NSA Director and CIA Deputy Director. Also in the running was *Parsons Corp.*, which donated $152,000 to the Republican Party and $2,000 to Bush. It has helped reconstruct Kosovo and Bosnia and built the Saudi 'military city' of Yanbu. Bush's Labour Secretary Elaine Chao served on its board before joining the cabinet. In April 2003, it had the chance of $900m in reconstruction contracts and worked closely with Halliburton. Chao's husband, assistant majority leader and majority whip Mitch McConnell, has links to defence contractor Northrop Grumman. He has also received donations from, among others, Halliburton and arms firm Lockheed Martin. In mid-April 2003, California congressman, Darrell Issa, was lobbying for firms such as *Lucent Technologies* to rebuild Iraq's decrepit telecoms system – a deal worth around $1bn. Pentagon Under-Secretary, Douglas Feith, has up to $500,000 invested in Lucent. *Raytheon Corp.*, alongside KBR, was another company apparently chosen by the Defense Threat Reduction Agency to deal with WMD. Cheney's sidekick, Lewis Libby, has shares in this company. The *Louis Berger Group*, which gave $26,300 to the Republicans and also implemented the USAid Croatia development programme, was also in prime position in April 2003 to make plenty of cash from the Iraqi chaos.

THE DEFENCE PLAYERS

The arms companies and military bodies inextricably tied to the reconstructors:

SY Coleman

It is a key company connected to the US Patriot missile system. The fact that the company is headed by Lt Gen Jay Garner, the one-time Sheriff of Baghdad, caused consternation amongst both aid agencies and the UN. Garner seems to have had a career policy based on blowing things up and then rebuilding them.

Northrop Grumman

One of the biggest winners under Bush's increases in defence spending, the firm won $8.5bn in defence contracts in 2002, in the run-up to the invasion. It has links with JINSA and the AEI and key Bush administration hawks. The company planned a merger with Lockheed Martin, another defence giant, which had Dick Cheney's wife Lynne on the board.

DynCorp

Linked to former CIA Director James Woolsey, it provides security in world trouble spots where America has felt compelled to act as the policeman. Woolsey's DynCorp links tally with his intellectual inclinations – both he and Richard Perle sit on the Foundation for the Defense of Democracy, a pro-military think-tank.

The Defense Policy Board

This is the massively influential Pentagon advisory group, headed by Richard Perle until he was forced to resign over a conflict of interest. Currying favour with the DPB is the key to getting a Pentagon contract. At least eight DPB members have links to firms that have won defence contracts including Northrop Grumman, Bechtel and Rand Corp., which is linked to Lewis Libby and Zalmay Khalilzad. DPB members included General Jack Sheehan, who is connected to Bechtel, the CIA's James Woolsey and former Republican Secretary of Defense James Schlesinger.

THE ARABS

Ahmed Chalabi

Prior to the invasion, he was leader of the London-based Iraqi National Congress (INC). Chalabi's supporters include Paul Wolfowitz and Donald Rumsfeld, who pushed for him to be the interim leader of post-war Iraq. He later fell out of favour with the US administration over allegations that he'd been spying for the Iranians. Before his fall, he was backed by the think-tank JINSA and linked to the American Enterprise Institute. Convicted in absentia in Jordan for his part in a massive embezzlement scandal, Chalabi and his organisation received up to $12m from Washington after the First Gulf War. He planned to work with Robert Reilly on broadcasting and communications in the New Iraq. Often referred to as 'Cheney's *protégé*', he is deeply unpopular in Iraq and was loathed by Colin Powell's State Department. Before the war, he fell out of favour with the CIA, which in the early 1990s funded the INC to the tune of $325,000 a month. Other Iraqis in 2003 who were yapping to get involved in a future government – at the behest of Wolfowitz – included INC members Salem Chalabi (Chalabi's nephew) and Aras Habib, director of intelligence for the Iraqi National Congress and Ahmed Chalabi. Wolfowitz also wanted jobs to go to Chalabi's friends, Tamara Daghestani and Goran Talebani.

Zalmay Khalilzad

Afghanistan-born Khalilzad has been Bush's special envoy to both Afghanistan and Iraq and has a wide variety of oil interests. He co-wrote an article on Saddam, entitled 'Overthrow Him', with Wolfowitz, his former boss. A consultant with the oil company Unocal, he was pushing for a natural gas pipeline in Afghanistan during the Taliban regime, and worked under Condoleezza Rice when she served as Director of Chevron. He is also a close associate of George Shultz, and encouraged using Iran to help topple Saddam. He is a former Rand Corp. employee and a charter member of the PNAC.

THE MILITARY

Maj Gen Bruce Moore and Gen Buck Walters

Moore and Walters, who are both retired US Army officers, were hand-picked by the Pentagon to run the north and south of Iraq respectively. Walters, a recently retired businessman, originates from President George W Bush's home state of Texas.

Lt Gen John Abizaid

Tommy Franks' Number 2 at Central Command in Qatar, Abizaid is the most senior military officer of Arab descent in the US Army and at the time of the invasion was the Director of the Joint Staff. He served in the First Gulf War as well as in Bosnia and was given a significant voice in post-war Iraq.

Lt Gen Ron Adams

Former Commander of the Bosnia Stabilisation Force, in the First Gulf War he was Assistant Divisional Commander of the 101st Airborne. He has held the office of Deputy Chief of Staff for Operations and Plans and was hand-picked by Lt Gen Jay Garner to be his deputy on the civil reconstruction committee.

Lt Gen Jay Garner

Nicknamed variously the Sheriff of Baghdad, Iraq's king, pro-consul, or just plain old president, Garner fought in the First Gulf War and was coaxed out of retirement to be the Director of the Office of Reconstruction and Humanitarian Assistance for Iraq. A fan of JINSA, he has praised the Israeli defence force for its 'remarkable restraint in the face of lethal violence orchestrated by the leadership of the Palestinian Authority'.

After one JINSA junket he also said: 'A strong Israel is an asset that

American military planners and political leaders can rely on.' He is
President of SY Coleman, the defence firm that specialises in Patriot
missiles and which was awarded a billion-dollar-plus contract to provide logistic support to US special forces. SY Coleman is a subsidiary of
L-3 Communications, the ninth-largest contributor to US political parties from the defence electronics sector. He is a Pentagon placeman who
is directly answerable to General Tommy Franks, head of US CentCom.
This was jumped on by many in April and May of 2003 as proof that
the reconstruction work was at best a Pentagon operation and at worst
a military occupation. A Vietnam veteran and former Assistant Chief of
Staff, Garner was no stranger to Iraq, having headed the Kurdish relief
programme after the First Gulf War. He is a close friend of Cheney and
Rumsfeld, who co-opted him to work on the extension of missile
defence in space.

Gen Jerry Bates

General Bates was to lead the logistical and administrative support
operations for General Garner. He took part in military intervention in
Haiti and is Senior Vice-president of the National Group, an arm of the
MPRI (Military Professionals Resources Inc.), which has been condemned for being a Pentagon-funded mercenary outfit.

Col George Oliver

A former head of the Army War College's Peacekeeping Institute and a
Pentagon insider, Oliver has trained Israeli military staff and was a delegate to the United Nations' Military Staff Committee. He also served
as a military advisor to the US Permanent Representative to the UN.

Col Richard Naab

Naab was the Commander of allied forces during Operation Provide
Comfort in the Kurdish areas in northern Iraq following the First Gulf
War and, like Garner, is seen as a friend by the Kurds. He is also an
advisor to the Iraqi Institute for Democracy.

Cap Frederick 'Skip' Burkle

Burkle is a medical doctor and the Iraqi team's only *bona fide* polymath.
He has worked for the World Health Organisation and USAid. This
highly decorated Vietnam and Gulf War veteran was to play a key role
in the Iraqi health ministry.

THE GREY SUITS

The diplomats and mandarins involved in the reconstruction process.

Barbara Bodine

Nicknamed the 'Mayor of Baghdad', she was to coordinate Iraqi central affairs. Deputy Principal Officer to the US Embassy in Baghdad and Deputy Chief of Mission in Kuwait during the First Gulf War, Bodine was US Ambassador to Yemen when al-Qaeda bombers killed 17 American sailors on the *USS Cole* in 2000. The FBI accused her of frustrating investigations.

Timothy Carney

The former US Ambassador to Haiti and Sudan, he was hand-picked by Wolfowitz to head the industry ministry. While Osama bin Laden was in Sudan, the Sudanese government offered to arrest him, to help improve their relations with the US. America repeatedly refused the offer and bin Laden eventually fled to Afghanistan to plot September 11.

Robin Raphel

She began her career as a CIA economic analyst, specialising in oil. She has also worked for the State Department and USAid and, as Under-Secretary of State, was responsible for America's Afghan policy in the early 1990s during the rise of the Taliban. She was US Ambassador to Tunisia and was tipped to head up the Iraqi Trade Ministry.

John Limbert and David Dunford

Limbert was US Ambassador to Mauritania, a country now hiving with al-Qaeda affiliates. A Middle East expert, he was to play a key role in the Ministry of Culture. He taught in Iran, where he was held hostage for 14 months. Deputy Ambassador to Saudi Arabia, Dunford has worked extensively as a consultant for oil and defence companies and was tipped for a ministerial position under the American occupation.

George Ward and Robert Gifford

Former US marine, Vietnam veteran and ambassador to Namibia, Ward was expected to have a government role in the Coalition Provisional Authority involving humanitarian assistance. Gifford was the USA's pre-eminent security expert and Director for Police Peacekeeping with the

Bureau for Narcotics and Law Enforcement Affairs. He was to set up Iraq's new police force.

*

So that is how the first phase of the reconstruction process looked in April 2003. That's the list of the people who had already got their slice of the Iraqi cake – either in the shape of money or power – and the list of those who were jostling to get their noses in the trough for a share of the spoils. Now you understand the nexus of corruption and cronyism that existed between the people and organisations with the power to hand out the contracts, and those who were getting the contracts.

So, how did it all shape up more than a year later – by the time, significantly, that the US had 'symbolically' handed over power to the Iraqi interim government under Iyad Allawi? Do you think the Americans got it together and put a stop to their greed? Did the rising flood of Iraqi blood, British blood, the blood of fellow Americans and the innocent blood of hostages stop their profiteering? Not a chance. The money just kept flowing and the doors of the favour bank just kept revolving. While Iraq burned and Iraqis died, the American corporate raiders just kept getting richer and richer. Of course, some things had changed. By the summer of 2004 Ahmed Chalabi was sidelined as a possible Iranian spy; Jay Garner had come and gone and been replaced by Paul Bremer, who administered the country like Pontius Pilate for Imperial Rome pending the fake and pointless handover of nominal power to the Iraqis.

John Negroponte took over from Bremer when he became US Ambassador to Iraq (making him in effect the American tasked to run the country in the post-handover period) even though he was implicated in the covert funding of the Nicaraguan Contras and the covering up of human rights abuses carried out by CIA-trained death squads in Honduras in the 1980s. After his tour of duty in Iraq, Negroponte was made the USA's National Intelligence Director in 2005. When Negroponte left Iraq, he was replaced as Ambassador by Zalmay Khalilzad.

Despite the fact that by spring 2003 we could all see that the reconstruction of a humiliated, ruined and raped nation was going to take place using the Enron business model, nothing could stop the money torrent. Acquisitions and mergers went hand-in-hand with executions and murders.

Here's how the situation shaped up as of summer 2004. Let's look at some of the businesses which have been the biggest contributors to Republican Party coffers between 1990 and 2002.

According to the Federal Election Commission, in terms of the donations they made to all party political campaigns, those among the biggest corporate contributors included:

Vinnell Corporation (Northrop Grumman) – $8.5 million
BearingPoint Inc. – $5 million
Science Applications International Corp. – $4.7 million
Flour Corp. – $3.6 million
Bechtel – $3.3 million
Kellogg, Brown & Root (Halliburton) – $2.4 million
American President Lines Ltd – $2.2 million
Parsons – $1.4 million
DynCorp – $1.2 million
TECO Ocean Shipping – $1.2 million
United Defense Industries – $1 million
Readiness Management Support – $464, 995
Tetra Tech Inc. – $223, 770
Louis Berger Group – $212, 456
Management Systems International – $121, 656

Now let's see how these big bankrollers did when it came to pulling down those Iraqi reconstruction contracts as of the time of the handover and mid-summer 2004. Here are the same companies, but this time with the value of their reconstruction contracts, rather than the payments they made to politicos:

Vinnell Corporation (Northrop Grumman) – $48 million
Bearing Point Inc. – $240 million
Science Applications International Corp. – $159 million
Flour Corp. – $3.8 billion
Bechtel – $2.8 billion
Kellogg, Brown & Root (Halliburton) – $11 billion
American President Lines Ltd – $5 million
Parsons – $5 billion
DynCorp – $50 million
TECO Ocean Shipping – $7.2 million
United Defense Industries – $4.5 million
Readiness Management Support – $173 million
Tetra Tech Inc. – $1.5 billion
Louis Berger Group – $28 million
Management Systems International – $15 million

You don't have to be Russell Crowe playing the 'hard sums' genius John Nash in *A Beautiful Mind* to work out the maths and see that in the US it pays to pay it forward. If you put out, then someone else will put out for you ... it's yet another unvirtuous circle of kick-backs and favours; a gravy train *par excellence*.

Here's an example of cronyism in practice: as you know, Bechtel's bosses have included former Secretary of State George Shultz. Other company helmsmen have been the State Department's Charles Redman and the former Marine Four Star General Jack Sheehan, who also just happens to sit on the Defense Policy Board.

Other companies that we've previously mentioned as being close to the Republican Party included Raytheon, which gave contributions of nearly $90,000 to all party political campaigns and got contracts worth more than $12 million; similarly, Stevedoring Services of America, which paid out almost $19,000 and got back more than $14 million, and International Resources Group paid contributions worth $3,830 and secured contracts with a value of $38 million.

You get the point by now. In Britain, this really wouldn't be tolerated. It is corruption of the highest order and it is also an affront to democracy with un-elected corporate raiders pulling the strings of the men and women who hold the very highest offices in the land.

According to the excellent Centre for Public Integrity – without whom whole swathes of this chapter would have been impossible to research – Halliburton received more money from government contracts in 2003 than it did in the five years between 1998 and 2002. In 2003, it got contracts alone worth $4.3 billion; in the years preceding 2003, Halliburton was getting around $500 million per annum in contracts.

Not only that, but those models of corporate rectitude over at Halliburton had the audacity to screw the US taxpayer over prices. Remember, Cheney ran this company before taking office as VP. The Defense Contract Audit Agency (DCAA) found a number of cock-ups in the way Kellogg, Brown & Root – the Halliburton subsidiary – was billing Uncle Sam for food for soldiers. The DCAA is withholding some $186 million in payments for food services from Kellogg, Brown & Root until the company shows it actually provided the meals it said it did. There we have it – old Dick Cheney's firm apparently screwing soldiers out of a warm meal for the sake of a few cents.

A criminal investigation, initiated in February 2004 by the Pentagon Inspector General, was tasked to probe whether Kellogg, Brown &

Root overcharged the government for fuel, and the Securities and Exchange Commission fined Halliburton some $7.5 million in August 2004 because of dodgy and misleading accounting practices. The scam meant that pre-tax income was higher than declared. For example, in the second quarter of 1998 pre-tax income was reported at $228.7 million when it should have been $183.3 million. Four former accountants of the company have stated as part of a shareholder class action that the company systematically committed accounting fraud to give a false impression of profits.

Kellogg, Brown & Root have five main contracts in the Hades that is Iraq. The juiciest is probably the $5.6 billion contract with the army's Logistics and Civil Augmentation Programme. KBR managed to secure the contract despite going over budget by some 32 per cent while working for the US government in the Balkans. Contracts have been awarded to KBR without open bidding. The government said this was because of the classified nature of the work the company would be doing.

Of course, the privatisation of war has other costs than the damage to public trust that the whiff of corruption and kick-backs it inevitably brings in its wake. Privatising war means that crazies from the world of capitalism end up with people's lives in their hands. Take Abu Ghraib prison. It wasn't just ugly, hillbilly trailer-park nutters like Lynndie England – the pervert GI seen sexually torturing Iraqi detainees in the infamous pictures of abuse which leaked out of Abu Ghraib – who were roaming around that prison, the place was awash with contractors from the private sector, too.

One of the firms to send members of staff to Abu Ghraib was CACI International Ltd. Thanks to a lack of properly trained army interrogators some 11 contracts with a value of more than $66 million were given to CACI to provide 'interrogation support and analysis work for the US army in Iraq'. These freelance interrogators were allowed to interrogate prisoners, debrief army personnel and write up intelligence reports. To you and me the idea of a private company being paid to do work that under the British system would be carried out by representatives of military intelligence or MI6 is stupid and gross, but not to the zealous free marketeers running the US.

An army investigation by Major General Antonio Taguba into the horrors in Abu Ghraib – which we will deal with in a later chapter – accused CACI staff of complicity in the serious physical abuse of prisoners. In total, CACI is thought to have had 31 interrogators in Iraq.

Unbelievably, a third of these people had no 'formal training in military interrogation policies and techniques'. Can you imagine if someone like you or me – someone who had no idea how to interrogate a prisoner – was given the job of trying to get information out of a man you thought might be a Jihadist? What would you do? Beat him? Rape him? Kill him? All of that – beating, raping and killing – was going on inside Abu Ghraib. The army itself hadn't even bothered to check if the civilians working in Abu Ghraib as interrogators had any training and were up to the job – they just took CACI's word for it. It was money, money, money, on all sides. Firms like CACI wanted to make cash; the army was trying to save cash; and somewhere in the middle this quest for more and more filthy money started costing us our humanity.

It gets better though. The out-sourcing of jobs that should be undertaken by government staff just keeps on mounting. Military Professional Resources Inc., the private military company which was hired to write the Pentagon's own rule book on the use of private companies – *Contractors on the Battlefield* – has proved very useful to the Pentagon. The manual that MPRI produced in January 2003 studiously avoided making any mention of whether it's a good thing or a bad thing to use private contractors in the fields of intelligence-gathering and interrogations, even though in December 2000, Assistant Secretary of the Army Patrick Henry said contracting out intelligence should not be allowed as it posed a risk to national security.

I should also point out that MPRI has won contracts itself in Iraq from the Department of Defense worth $2.6 million.

US government investigations into the contracting process have found that the official agencies handing out the contracts are short-staffed and overworked, and employees are badly trained and have little knowledge of the actual contracting process. That means they end up stretching the rules beyond the acceptable limit. There has also been poor overseeing of contractors once they've secured the deal, says the General Accounting Office and the Inspector General at the Pentagon. Of 24 contracts handed out by the Defense Contracting Command-Washington, that were examined by the Pentagon's Inspector General, 22 did not adhere to Federal Acquisition Regulations. Officials handing out the contracts even allowed contractors to start work before the price had been agreed.

This is typical of the Republican *laissez faire* attitude. They just don't give a damn about the rules basically. Regulation and control are too costly and difficult, so it's better to just waltz around handing out bundles of tax dollars to your friends and not bothering to act when they rip off the taxpayer, damage the country, hurt others or just plain screw up – as long as the money-go-round keeps turning, then all is right in the world of the blinkered, zealous capitalist.

The sleaze went right to the top in every direction. The Office of Reconstruction and Humanitarian Assistance (ORHA) – in effect, the one-time American administration in occupied Iraq – made sure its friends got well looked after, thanks to a little jiggery-pokery, of course, which saw people who were friends and private-sector colleagues of top ORHA execs getting well-paid contracts to work in Iraq as protocol officers.

The 'Iraqi Free Media' contract awarded to Science Application International Corporation (SAIC) initially cost $15 million. Now, as a journalist I think it's pretty good value for money to get a *bona fide* functioning fourth estate and integral part of democracy for less than the cost of the average British movie. However, the cost of the SAIC contract soon shot up to $82 million. Why the hike? Well, could it be anything to do with having people on the staff like one senior manager who bought a Hummer and a Ford pick-up truck, and then chartered a jet to fly the vehicles to Iraq so he could use them?

The amount of money that the US taxpayer has to cough up for these privateers is also left effectively uncapped. DynCorp has a contract in Iraq worth some $50 million, but it could grow in value to $800 million. It's an unforgivable 'who cares' attitude from Bush and his hangers-on in industry. But who cops the pain? Everyone else – that's who.

But, you know, we all allow our pals to get away with things we wouldn't tolerate in others. I've got a mate who's a taxi driver, and he often waives part of the fare – the extras – for me as a favour if I've had to make a few stops on the way home and kept him waiting for me. That's what pals do, but if the government is pals with big business and Team Bush goes and does its corporate mates some favours then they are doing those favours with the American tax-payers' money, not their own – that's the crucial difference. Take Science Application International Corp. – the ones who spent all that money flying Hummers to Baghdad and then boosted the cost of their contract with the US government by five times the original price. SAIC is a good pal of the government as it has shown by forking out many millions for national political campaigns over the years. In return, some 69 per cent of its business comes from the government. The Centre for Public Integrity has said 'its company roster is a revolving door of government-corporate interests'.

Among the past luminaries who worked for SAIC there was David Kay – the man hired by the CIA to find weapons of mass destruction in Iraq. Then there's Christopher Henry, who left SAIC as Vice-president of Strategic Assessment and Development in February 2003 and became Bush's Principal Deputy Under-Secretary of Defense for Policy. That means Henry now effectively oversees the relationship between his old company and the government.

Other government connections include Duane Andrews who was Assistant Defense Secretary under George Bush Senior until he joined SAIC in 1993. Board member W A Downing was a general and the Deputy Assistant Director for International Counter-Terrorism on the National Security Council until he joined SAIC in 1996. Bobby Ray Inman was a Director of the National Security Agency and a Deputy Director of the CIA. He was a SAIC board member until late 2003 and is also a member of the board of directors at Fluor.

It's easy to see how contracts can boom in price if the government is hiring the mates of leading members of the administration as the chief contractors. But they aren't just hiring mates, they are hiring companies that no-one else on earth would touch as well – companies like WorldCom. It went bankrupt, had to pay the Securities and Exchange Commission a fine of £500 million for overstating its cash flow by almost $4 billion and was banned for a time from receiving federal contracts. Yet, the Pentagon hired a company called MCI, which grew out of WorldCom, as part of a $45 million project to build communications systems in Baghdad. Critics said that MCI had little experience of the work it needed to undertake in Iraq and were angry that the contract wasn't even put up for competitive bidding.

If company bosses have got a man on the inside of the political administration, then it's a helluva lot easier to make sure that when governments come to think of where to allocate the tax-payer dollars that they think of their firm. Take Creative Associates International Inc. It has contracts worth $273 million in Iraq. Over the years it has stumped up some $10,000 in campaign contributions. One of its contracts was given out by USAid for educational development work in Iraq worth $157 million. Creative, by the way, describes itself as a private for-profit aid company – whatever the hell that contradiction in terms means.

Four months before the contract was awarded, USAid hosted a small conference on Iraqi education. Frank Dall attended on behalf of Creative. He is also a former USAid employee. Dall got briefed by USAid four months before the contract was handed out; the other companies who were asked to bid had only two weeks' notice. USAid eventually had to admit 'that only one of the five contractors that were subsequently invited by USAid to bid on the contract participated in an initial round table discussion ... We conclude that USAid bureau officials did not adhere to the guidance on practical steps to avoid organisational conflicts of interest.'

Creative went on to subcontract to three of the four companies which had bid unsuccessfully for the contract, including the firm Research Triangle Institute. That's a very cosy little relationship, particularly as Creative is in turn subcontracted by Research Triangle Institute on its own Iraqi contract which is worth some $466 million. The Research Triangle Institute is also a political donor.

My own favourite story of government-business back-scratching, however, has to be the Sullivan Haave Associates affair. Here's how it goes: Sullivan Haave was subcontracted by SAIC to spend four months in Iraq as a consultant to a number of Iraqi ministries. Terry Sullivan – the Sullivan in the name Sullivan Haave Associates – happens to be married to none other than a certain Carol Haave, who is the Deputy Assistant Secretary of Defense for Security and Information Operations. Carol swears she has nothing to do with the company even though her name is in the company title. Well, that's alright then. We believe her, don't we?

To add to this madness, the US government has resorted to contracting other firms to oversee the work being done by contractors because federal staff just aren't up to the job. Like all conservative ventures, attempts at saving cash just end up costing the taxpayer more.

However, the silly situation of having to hire someone else to make sure that the people you hired in the first place are doing their job properly is also open to massive conflicts of interest. A report by the House Committee on Government Reform and the Senate Democratic Policy Committee found that Parsons and CH2M – two firms hired to oversee other companies – were partners in projects with the very corporations they were meant to be supervising. It's like me being asked to police my own brother. One of the companies that Parsons was supposed to be cracking the whip over was Fluor. But Fluor and Parsons work together on a $2.6 billion joint venture in Kazakhstan.

USAid has said: 'To ensure that US tax dollars are utilised efficiently and effectively, USAid is providing a transparent monitoring and evaluation system to ensure that contractors are meeting their goals and staying on schedule.' If you believe that, you'll believe that Saddam's WMD will be found by next Ramadan.

The contrary opinion to that kind of government bullshit can be gleaned from the thankfully outspoken US politician Henry Waxman, a Californian Democrat in the House of Representatives. He says there is 'evidence that favoured contractors like Halliburton and Bechtel are getting sweetheart deals that are costing the taxpayer a bundle but delivering scant results'. That's the understatement of the war so far, I think.

Now, it's only thanks to hard work by organisations like the Centre for Public Integrity that I'm able to pass on to you this sort of information. Government and big business guard facts such as these like dragons guard gold. If it wasn't for America's wonderful Freedom of Information laws, we'd be blind and deaf to the corruption and abuse of power that continues. But even Freedom of Information requests come up against stiff opposition thanks to Republicans and their fawning love for their corporate backers.

In 1987, Ronnie Reagan signed off on Executive Order 12600. This ruled that companies have the right to forbid the release of facts, figures and documentation under the Freedom of Information Act if it relates to contracts with the US government which are commercially sensitive. Hey! Talk about the Republicans wanting to let freedom prosper. Seven contracts awarded to SAIC were released to the Centre for Public Integrity under Freedom of Information laws but the values of the contracts were blacked out. The army said the documents had been censored 'due to the sensitive nature of the Iraqi contracts' and the mere act of releasing the figures would lead to 'substantial competitive harm to the contractor'.

That's not a bad protection from public scrutiny, but Bush Junior – ever desperate to be the heir to Reaganomics – went further and protected his corporate buddies in the oil business from criminal prosecution while in Iraq. On May 22 2003, Bush signed Executive Order 13303 which forbids 'any judicial process' against anyone with interests in Iraqi oil as legal action would constitute an 'extraordinary threat to the national security' of the US. Tom Devine, the Legal Director of the Government Accountability Project, says the law amounts to 'a licence to loot Iraq and its citizens', is a 'blank sheet for corporate anarchy' and 'cancels the rule of law for the oil industry'.

The reconstruction effort has been such an unmitigated balls-up – for everyone, that is, apart from the corporate cronies of the Bush administration – that the US is now having to go around the commonwealth of nations of the earth with its begging bowl asking for a hand-out to help stabilise and rebuild the country it unnecessarily invaded in the face of contrary world opinion.

Because of the nightmarish state of security in Iraq, America has had to shift billions in reconstruction funds into beefing up security. Money that was meant to be spent building schools and hospitals that the coalition blew up is now being spent on fighting an insurgency that never existed until Britain and America gatecrashed Baghdad. As a result the US expects other nations – like France, Germany and Russia – to pitch in and fix its mistakes with money from the pockets of their own tax-payers; tax-payers who more than likely opposed the war in the first place. Of course, good lackeys like Britain and Japan have already dug deep to help out big brother in Washington.

Remember: Bush promised to completely reconstruct Iraq, to give it the best infrastructure in the Middle East and to leave it stable and rich enough to embrace democracy. But with the economy in the USA totally up the left and the price of merely keeping US troops and war profiteers alive in Iraq escalating by the nano-second, Bush and his tin-pot posse have effectively called it quits. They are planning to leave the Iraqis high and dry; they're gonna welch on the deal and leave the dirt poor folk in Baghdad, Mosul and Basra to clear up the mess the USA made.

The Bush administration is not going to seek any new funds for reconstruction – that's official. Now that the big business buddies of Baby Bush have milked all they can out of the country, and now that the security situation is so bloody and dangerous that even the most fanatical capitalist can't make any more money without fear of losing their head – it seems the logic of reconstruction has run out for Republicans and their corporate henchmen. If Bush's cronies can't make any more cash from the damn reconstruction project, then why bother with the project in the first place; that's the thinking in Washington.

As of June 2007, the current $18.4 billion dollars earmarked for reconstruction will run out. No more money is being sought by the Bush administration from Congress after that date. Just flick on your TV set and look at the streets of any Iraqi town or city and tell me if you think all the reconstruction work has been done. I don't know about you, but living in a ruined shell, with shit in the street, sewage up to my ankles, no electricity or water and madmen wandering about wanting to gouge out my daughter's eyes because she can read does not equate with 'the best infrastructure in the Middle East'. Needless to say, none of the utilities like oil, electricity, water and gas is even anywhere near their degraded pre-invasion capabilities. The average Iraqi is lucky to have electricity from breakfast time to supper time. Iraqis will have to spend billions of pounds of their own money fixing the things that the Americans blew up and then swore on their mothers' lives that they would fix. Quite how they are going to do that is another question. Iraq's oil wealth was meant to help fund the reconstruction but with refineries producing just 1.8 million barrels a day compared to 2.6 million barrels before the invasion – thanks to sabotage by anti-coalition forces – there really isn't much in the bank for the Iraqi government to play with. Just keeping an Iraqi official alive is an expensive game.

Half the US money intended for reconstruction had to be spent on security. Billions meant for schools and hospitals have been sucked up fighting the insurgency and preparing for Saddam's trial. Money intended to rebuild the country went on training specialist bomb squads, hostage rescue teams and putting up prisons and safe houses. Of course, the end to US reconstruction money is proof that both the Brits and the Yanks want the hell out of Iraq as quickly as possible – now that they have come to secretly realise the murderous folly of their grand game. But while it might be a piece of cake just to be mean and stop signing cheques, it is a different, and much less easy, matter when it comes to extricating Britain and America from Iraq. Unless the US wants to treat the world to some Siagon-style images of GIs and diplomats leaping on to Black Hawk helicopters from the roof of the Green Zone as they flee Baghdad, the pull-out process will take years. Britain and America will be lucky to be out of Iraq by the time Blair qualifies for his pensioners' bus pass.

Of course, now the US tells us that the reconstruction process was never meant to fully rebuild Iraq. It was 'just supposed to be a jump-start' says Brigadier General William McCoy, the Army Corps of Engineers commander who has overseen what passes for the reconstruction process. Needless to say, McCoy is telling someone else's lies for them.

So, America has cut off the money – despite all its empty promises – and left the Iraqis to do the rebuilding themselves. Another little problem facing any future attempts by the Iraqi government to fix America's cock-ups and rebuild the busted nation is the fact that Iraqis are more than likely to see some $200 billion – that's about £120 billion – of their national wealth go zooming out of the country, primarily into the pockets of western oilmen. Why? Well, because the US wants to hand over the development of Iraqi oil reserves to mainly American and British companies.

Needless to say this colonialist asset stripping seems to indicate that oil did have quite a role in the ousting of Mad Saddam. A report by War on Want and the New Economics Foundation called *Crude Designs* said the policy was thought up prior to the invasion. Foreign investors will seek rates of return between 42 and 162 per cent. A gangland money-lender would be proud to get away with such a mark-up. Louise Richards, Chief Executive of War on Want, said: 'People have increasingly come to realise the Iraq war was about oil, profits and plunder.' Remember, US and UK government officials were holding the pens of the Iraqis who wrote the country's new post-Saddam constitution – a constitution which gave foreign firms a big say in the future of the nation.

So, the US bombs a country into the Stone Age based on a bunch of lies, uses the bombing as an excuse to make the pals of the government rich, reneges and welches on its promises, screws up any attempt at reconstruction and then wants the world to come and fix the disaster it created. If America shat in its own pants it would probably expect the world to come running to pay good money to help it clean its ass. Maybe the world should just leave America to wallow in its own dirty mess for a little while – that way it might figure out the true, filthy cost of this war.

GOD, GUNS AND GOVERNMENT

or

On the campaign trail with Dubya's
dookie disciples `

In late August 2004, I decided it was time to find out, first hand, a little more about the people backing Bush – not the millionaire corporate sponsors or the military men but the ordinary folk who were fuelling this War on Truth by giving their unwavering support to the President. Now, the British Labour Party is a party riven with dissent over the invasion of Iraq. Many of Blair's once most loyal supporters are disgusted at the duplicitous manoeuvring by Blair to take the UK to war. They are angry that Blair slavishly followed George W Bush and America's Republican Party to war. There's even an attempt underway to impeach the great British leader for the lies he told to sell the British people this American war.

On the eve of his second presidential election victory, however, the Republican Party of George 'Dubya' Bush was as united as the Labour Party was divided.

So, if I wanted to find out what made the flag-wavers for this war tick it wasn't the likes of the good burghers of Swansea, London, Edinburgh or Belfast that I had to understand, it was the folk in Kansas, Austin and Cincinnati that I needed to get a handle on.

So, I took myself off to America. If I wanted to come face to face with the ideologies, the thought processes and the hearts and minds of the people who voted Bush into power and wanted him to continue with this seemingly endless war on all fronts, then there was nowhere better to be than at the Republican Party's National Convention in New York City between late August and early September 2004, where the entire party, from the groundlings to the elite, spent a week cheerleading for a second Bush term with the presidential election just two months away.

265

Of course, today, as we know, both Republican swagger and the almost robotic worship by the party faithful of their President have waned considerably as the steady flow of blood from Iraq has eroded the spell and the promise of George Bush, leaving him with support in the opinion polls at an all-time low. But in the days leading up to his successful 2004 election, he was a man with his party and his nation in the palm of his hand. And that meant that overseas he could do damn well what he pleased.

Here are some recollections written at the time to give you a flavour of the Bush cult in 2004.

The last day of the convention started with a circus sideshow that left me wondering whether President George W Bush was a demagogue or a demigod.

At midday on Thursday, September 2, 2004, on the third floor of the skyscraper New Yorker Hotel, across the street from Madison Square Garden where the convention had run for most of the week, Colorado evangelist Ted Beckett was greeting the Republican Party faithful and treating them to a little bit of cinema history: the screening of the film *George W Bush – Faith in the White House*.

His film, like the President's God-laced performance which would come some ten hours later at the finale of the convention, sent Republicans into raptures. 'This nation, under George W Bush,' said Beckett, 'has a mandate from the Lord to be the world's policeman.

'The President is a born-again Christian. I support him as a by-product of his faith. He stands for a strong morality and family values which are under attack in America from the likes of the homosexual community. President Bush is a man's man. He runs three times a day. He's put respect back into the Oval Office. He doesn't go to his work without a shirt and tie, he makes sure people are on time for meetings – there's no Dress Down Friday in his White House.

'The love that we can all see between himself and his family shows that he does what he espouses – he talks the talk, and he walks the walk. Under President Bush, this nation is protecting the free world just like we did back in the 1940s. Remember if it wasn't for us, you Brits would be talking "Sprechen Sie Deutsch".'

This myth that America was Britain's knight in shining armour, or perhaps a better metaphor would be that America came charging over the hill like the Seventh Cavalry to save the doomed British in the Second World War, was a recurring theme of conversations with

Republicans. It was hard to tell whether it was constantly raised in the hope of creating some common bond or in an attempt to evoke a sense of obligation or even humiliation – but crop up it did, constantly. Beckett and the other 1941ers don't like it pointed out to them that it's plain wrong for America to pretend that it bailed out Great Britain during the Second World War or came to our rescue. From 1939 until 1941, the British people waited in vain for their friends in America to help them in their lone fight against Nazism – the country's and democracy's greatest hour of need – as German bombs rained down on British cities day and night. No help came. After Japan bombed Pearl Harbour in December 1941, America declared war on Japan, and Nazi Germany, which was allied to Japan, declared war on America in return. As history shows, America didn't bravely come to Britain's aid, instead America defended itself against Japan and in turn was sucked into the war in Europe.

But the simplified, Americanised parody of history still resonates in the brain of people like Beckett. When it comes to Iraq, Beckett fancifully believes that Bush's actions are a continuation of what he sees as America's heroic and selfless role in the Second World War. 'We have liberated, but we never occupy,' he says. 'Just look at Germany and Japan. The best thing that can happen to a nation is for it to be overthrown by America. History will see the President as a great liberator.

'I believe that he is God's man for this hour. Four years of John Kerry [the Democratic presidential candidate] would be inconceivable. Who knows what might happen to the world? The times need a man who can stand up and lead the free world. He identifies with God's mandate and God has blessed him for that.'

What Beckett says isn't out of step with what many of the Republican Party's most senior speakers said throughout the week of the Republican Convention – a veritable marathon of neoconnery. Time and again, Bush was portrayed as a straight-talking, down-to-earth guy with guts; an old-fashioned type of fella who did the right thing, told it how it is, and was there looking out for America and for freedom and liberty. And, above all, everyone could see that he was a good God-fearing Christian. Beckett was merely a little more colourful and direct in his language than the party elite.

Chrissie Nicolle had dropped by to watch the movie. 'President Bush has dignity,' she told me. 'He is honest and he has brought class back to American politics after the disgrace of the Clintons. He's a spiritual person and it's important to Americans for their politics to be combined with a belief in God. We can't separate God from such a noble endeavour as leading the United States.

'The President is a likeable guy; he's like a cowboy – a true American hero. He reminds me of President Reagan in the way that he embodies that whole spirit of what America is all about.' To Nicolle that means preserving the faith of the founding fathers, being humble, kind, open, generous and magnanimous. And Laura Bush, she says, is a 'true First Lady. She's so refreshing after the horror of Hillary Clinton. She was so unfeminine and such an opportunist. You just knew the Clintons' relationship was all about power. George and Laura love each other – that's wonderful and it's a true inspiration.'

Laura and the image of family is a real vote winner for Bush. At the end of the convention, with the entire audience at Madison Square Garden on its feet and cheering, as the red, white and blue confetti, ribbons, balloons and streamers fell to the floor, Laura walked onto the circular stage with the Bushes' twin daughters. Then came Barbara Bush, the President's mum; his dad, former President George Bush Senior – the entire first family was at George's side and the message was clear: this is a man of family values; just like all you voters in the American heartlands. They were followed by the entire second family – Vice-president Dick Cheney, his wife Lynne and their children and grandchildren. It was a tactic which had been used all that week – bringing out Laura to soften the President's image and to portray him as a kind and loving husband, father and President.

This was a convention which often disparaged Hollywood – demonising the land of the right-wing's favoured hate-figures, Barbra Streisand and Martin Sheen, as a symbol of the liberal elite and Democratic decadence; but the Republican Party's stage-managers were happy to steal plenty of the tricks of Tinseltown. Apart from Arnold Schwarzenegger – or Conan the American as the *New York Post* took to calling him – the Convention Jockeys were perhaps the epitome of the vacuous happy-clappy showbiz veneer that the Republicans took on. The ConJocks were pretty, perky, white-toothed girls who bounced around the floor of the convention while MOR funk music and soul blasted in the background as they interviewed delegates MTV-style and sang the praises of the party and the President. Their forays into party propaganda were projected onto giant TV screens dotted around the auditorium.

Carole McLean, one of the publicists at the screening of *George W Bush – Faith in the White House*, knows that in politics, the message – and its presentation – is everything. 'The President is an exemplar to America,' she said. 'He is asking us to believe in ourselves and the original intent of our founding fathers – which was the love of liberty and freedom for all. The founding fathers made hard choices for the sake of freedom and so has our President. His is a poetic and inspiring vision for America.'

The Republicans seem to see the US Constitution and the Ten Commandments in the same light: both are inviolable and written in stone. The bible says homosexuality is bad – so homosexuality must remain an evil, *ad infinitum*. The Constitution says citizens have the right to bear arms in case another King George tries to yoke the American people into serfdom, so, to Republicans, guns must remain at the root of liberty forever. The passage of time, the coming of modernity and the rise of new values and beliefs are not allowed to alter the sacrosanct principles of the founding fathers or the teachings of God. It's no wonder, then, that even right-wingers in Europe are confused and bewildered by the crusading zeal of Republicans, whether it comes in the shape of promoting family values, allowing assault weapons to be sold or invading other countries under the banner of freedom and democracy. Europe does not understand the myth of America that has captured the hearts and minds of Republican believers: it is the promise of a land free from repression where family, faith and flag are at the centre of life. It is a simple myth of good versus evil – with America eternally cast in the role of the hero. Of course, the myth glosses over the genocide of the Native Americans, the horrors of slavery and the barbarism of the Vietnam war, but these chapters of American history may as well never have happened for the myth-makers of the modern Republican Party – the men who are busy building the storyline and narrative for a new and revolutionary American ideology: men like Karl Rove, who masterminded Bush's election victory in 2004 against an insipid John Kerry from the Democratic Party.

Even Bush's pro-business, anti-taxation platform is seen by his followers as a romantic throwback to the days of the Revolutionary War. 'Individual enterprise and ownership is the best way forward,' said Carole McLean, after the showing of the film. 'The founding fathers felt that if a person owned their own land then they would prosper,' she added.

McLean has also been wooed by the Middle American ideal of womanhood that Laura Bush seems to radiate. 'I try to emulate her as a wife,' she said. 'She's talented, she's a good mother and a good wife. I can't find a fault with her.' Referring to Bush's past problems with alcohol, McLean, in Tammy Wynette mode, added: 'She even stood by her man when what was going on must have been really hurting her. He was wild – a party-animal.'

But the President appears to have a charisma all his own which attracts women like McLean. 'He seems powerful, strong and masculine,' she said. 'And he's also pretty cute. I've often thought to myself "damn what a catch". We're about the same age and I wondered to myself "where was I when he was single". His character resonates with me as he's so down-to-earth. His Texas way of calling a spade a spade and shooting from the hip is really admirable.

'I can't relate to John Kerry at all. He doesn't seem real. He tells you what he thinks you want to hear. He looks at what way the wind is blowing before he says anything. Kerry gives me the willies. He and his brother even speak French together when they don't want people to know what they are talking about.'

For these people, the Bush message has worked. The convention was one of the slickest propaganda machines ever trundled out in American history and it dealt John Kerry some terrible body blows. Where the Democrats at their convention avoided attacking Bush, the Republicans beat the daylights out of Kerry for four full days with spin and disinformation the key weapons in their arsenal. The joke doing the rounds amongst US political hacks was that Kerry's famously big chin – a chin so big in fact that it earned him the nickname 'Lurch' after the lantern-jawed monster butler in the TV show *The Addams Family* – came in handy during the Republican convention as it could soak up all the left hooks and right jabs that Team Bush was landing on it on an almost minute by minute basis.

Kerry's apparent failure to support additional funding for US troops was brought up continually, but what the Republicans didn't mention was that he had in fact supported the increase in troop expenditure as long as it didn't add to America's already crippling deficit. Cherry-picking the truth was the order of the day as ever with the Republicans. Each time Kerry's so-called betrayal of the troops was raised, the Republican delegates booed fit to shake the rafters of Madison Square Garden and swung their arms from side to side like windscreen wipers chanting 'flip-flop, flip-flop', mocking his inability to make a decision and stick to it – a character trait which was grossly exaggerated and spun wickedly out of proportion by the Republican Party. Kerry's condemnation of American atrocities in Vietnam when he returned from active service there was taken, turned against him and used to belittle his patriotism – and patriotism, above everything else, was the theme of this convention. But only patriotism of a certain stripe was acceptable to the Republican Party. Kerry's war record – one of heroism which led to him being decorated many times for bravery in combat in Vietnam – was sickeningly twisted by Republican activists and used perversely to portray him as a coward and a liar.

People like the renegade Democratic senator for Georgia, Zell Miller – or Zell from Hell as the Democrats now call him – were put on stage to make a monster out of Kerry. 'Senator Kerry has made it clear that he would use military force only if approved by the United Nations,' Miller said. 'Kerry would let Paris decide when America needs defending. I want Bush to decide.' The crowd booed Kerry, cheered Bush and then Miller added with contempt and to wild applause: 'And this politician wants to be leader of the free world?' At this rally, you could always rely on a comparison between the Democrats and the French to bring down the house.

Touching on themes that could be heard from the rank and file on the floor and from the plinth on the stage time and again, Miller added: 'I admire President Bush. I am moved by the respect he shows the First Lady, his unabashed love for his parents and his daughters, and the fact that he is unashamed in his belief that God is not indifferent to America … I have knocked on the door of this man's soul and found someone home, a God-fearing man with a good heart and a spine of tempered steel. The man I trust to protect my most precious possession: my family … In this hour of danger, our President has had the courage to stand up.'

The Republican Convention was awash with militarism. Images of soldiers, helicopters and jets were flashed constantly before the crowds' eyes on huge plasma screens mounted around the auditorium. Amidst the patrician militarism, there was plenty of blue-collar 'fun' to be had – to the left of the main speakers' stage there was a smaller stage, which ascended from the bowels of Madison Square Garden; each time it rose there'd be some country kid singing C&W or a never-been-heard-of-before-and-never-would-be-heard-of-again singer wailing a song destined to go straight into the elevator at the local shopping mall.

Crippled cops were trundled out to deliver patriotic messages, along with sports figures, a Miss America, the C-list Hollywood actor Ron Silver, fire-fighters, police chiefs, old soldiers and every person with a different shade of skin colour to President Bush that Republican Party organisers could lay hands on.

Mingling amidst all the militarism, patriotism, faith and family values, there was the unmistakable whiff of dynasty. Dozens of Bushes seemed to be at the convention. There was even a sort of royal box where the Republican Party's leading lights were allowed to sit beside the likes of Pappy and Mommy Bush. It reminded me of those pictures of Soviet Politburo meetings in the 1980s when the grey wrinkly faces of communist leaders from decades before – from the 1950s and 1940s – still loomed over Russian politics long after their youth had faded with their abilities and relevance.

Barely a speaker made it to the stage without mentioning September 11 and the continuing terrorist threat to the United States. New York's suffering was whored for political gain. Rudy Giuliani, Mayor of New York when the twin towers were toppled, set the mood from the first night when he wrung every last drop of pain from the memory of the attacks and claimed Bush had made the planet a safer place while Kerry would jeopardise America and the world. Recalling the words he said to his police chief on September 11, Giuliani told the crowd: 'I say it again tonight, "Thank God George Bush is our President".'

A simple, clear, easily digestible Middle American message was banged home over and over and over and over again from the podium, and it was mirrored by the logos on the walls – A NATION OF COURAGE, A PEOPLE OF COMPASSION, A LAND OF OPPORTUNITY, FULFILLING AMERICA'S PROMISE: A SAFER WORLD, A MORE HOPEFUL AMERICA. From the mantra of 'Compassionate Conservatism' – which rests on the intervention of the churches in the lives of the poor, the homeless, the disabled and the vulnerable – to California Governor Schwarzenegger's exhortation to those who shy away from unbridled capitalism – 'Don't be economic girlie men!' – this was a party saying 'We are right, we are best for America, you are un-American if you are not with us.' Like the war on terror and the war in Iraq, when it comes to domestic politics you are either with the Republicans or you are against them.

These incessant messages – the militarism, the tax cuts, stopping patients suing negligent doctors, the faith-based initiatives as a salve for social horrors, America's manifest destiny to lead and protect the world – were finally funnelled on a sultry Thursday night at 10 o'clock into the mouth of George W Bush for his closing speech to the delegates – a speech that blurred the line between politics and faith.

'To everything,' the President told an audience that was at times awed, at times hysterical with support, and at times visibly moved by what he was saying, 'we know there is a season; a time for sadness, a time for struggle, a time for rebuilding. And we know we have reached a time for hope. This young century will be liberty's century. By promoting liberty abroad, we will build a safer world. By encouraging liberty at home, we will build a more hopeful America. Like generations before us, we have a calling from beyond the stars to stand for freedom. This is the everlasting dream of America, and tonight, in this place, that dream is renewed. Now we go forward, grateful for our freedom, faithful to our cause, and confident in the future of the greatest nation on earth. God bless you, and may God continue to bless America.'

His speech began and ended on the theme of 9-11: 'In the heart of this great city, we saw tragedy arrive on a quiet morning. We saw the bravery of rescuers grow with danger.' From 9-11, the President moved straight to America's war against Iraq, praising it as an extension of the War on Terror that began in September 2001 – conflating the two separate conflicts in the minds of his followers. 'We have seen Americans in uniform storming mountain strongholds, and charging through sandstorms and liberating millions with acts of valour that would make the men of Normandy proud ... We have made the hard journey, we can see the valley below ... I believe the most solemn duty of the American President is to protect the American people. If America shows uncertainty and weakness in this decade, the world will drift toward tragedy. This will not happen on my watch.'

Bush spoke of Laura saying, 'Americans have come to see the goodness and kindness and strength I first saw 26 years ago, and we love our First Lady.' He spoke of his father, his mother, his children and told the crowd that the spirit of Ronald Reagan – 'his optimism and goodwill and decency' – was in the hall with them that night.

He praised the American worker, entrepreneur, farmer and rancher, and said that's why he'd 'unleashed the largest tax relief in a generation'. That the rich benefit most from his tax breaks made no difference to his supporters, whether they were wealthy, aspiring or poor – the tax breaks themselves represented Bush's commitment to rugged individualism and that's what mattered. Taxation means big government and big government means socialism – and socialism is evil to the Republican world-view. From tax cuts Bush naturally segued into a pledge to reduce the size of the government, stating that 'the government should help people improve their lives, not try to run their lives'. He then invoked the spirit of George Washington, saying: 'Our nation's founding commitment is still our deepest commitment: in our world, and here at home, we will extend the frontiers of freedom.'

Like nearly all the speakers before him had, the President took a swipe at the telegenic running mate of John Kerry, the Vice-presidential hopeful John Edwards. Edwards' soft spot was his profession – he's a lawyer who's taken on doctors over medical malpractice. The policy of limiting such lawsuits was a big theme of the Republican Convention. Bush reminded the audience that he was 'on the side of working families' – not slick lawyers. Once again, a storyline was being created: the Democrats are liberal elitists, they have jobs like lawyers and diplomats, they are not like us Republicans: ordinary people who are honest, god-fearing and true.

Edwards got off mildly compared to Kerry. Kerry was characterised as a politician of higher taxes, as a leftist radical, while Bush was a man of caring, compassionate conservatism. 'In this world of change, some things do not change: the values we try to live by, the institutions that give our lives meaning and purpose. Our society rests on a foundation of responsibility and character and family commitment,' Bush told the faithful.

The biggest cheers of the evening – the whistles, the *yee-has* and the standing ovations – came as Bush hit the theme of morality. 'Because a caring society will value its weakest members, we must make a place for the unborn child. Because religious charities provide a safety net of mercy and compassion, our government must never discriminate against them. Because the union of a man and a woman deserves an honoured place in our society, I support the protection of marriage against activist judges.' For days, the talk among the conventioneers had been as much about gay marriage, abortion and stem cell research as it was about Iraq, terrorism and tax cuts. Bush's followers opposed gay marriage, abortion and stem cell research – clear signs of the liberal godlessness that was eating away at America. The same godlessness and sloppy morality was seen as a reason why Democrats and liberals opposed the invasion of Iraq.

While Bush was a champion of God's laws, Kerry, on the other hand, believed that 'the heart and soul of America is found in Hollywood'. The crowd booed. Kerry saw Reagan's presidency as eight years of 'moral darkness'. The crowd booed. Kerry was the flip-flopper – Bush the steadfast, loving leader. 'Since [September 11], I wake up every morning thinking about how to better protect our country,' the President said. 'I will never relent in defending America whatever it takes.'

His presidency was 'staying on the offensive, striking terrorists abroad so we do not have to face them here at home'. And his presidency 'would prevail'. Afghanistan, Iraq, the disarmament of Libya, the fight against terrorism by Pakistan and Saudi Arabia were all hailed as great victories for and by America. 'We have led, many have joined, and America and the world are safer.' Bush was telling his audience and America that these are times of terror and fear, but I will make you safe; I will protect you. He evoked nightmares and then promised to lay them to rest.

Iraq, Bush said, was his 'toughest' decision. 'We knew Saddam Hussein's record of aggression and support for terror. We knew his long history of pursuing, even using, weapons of mass destruction. And we know that September 11 requires our country to think differently: we must, and we will, confront threats to America before it is too late.' His comments recalled earlier speakers and the sabre-rattling threats they delivered to nations like Iran and Syria.

'Do I forget the lessons of September 11,' the President said, 'and take the word of a madman, or do I take action to defend our country? Faced with that choice, I will defend America every time.' The question of the lies told about WMD or of the failure to capture Osama bin Laden were not even put on the table for discussion; instead Bush said his actions had liberated more than 50 million people and established democracies in Afghanistan and Iraq – and when the job was done, he promised, 'then our troops will return home with the honour they have earned.' Not a word was said about the horrors of Abu Ghraib and the torture, sexual abuse and murder of Iraqi men, women and children by coalition soldiers.

Throughout the convention the theme of respect for what Republicans call 'citizen soldiers' was writ large to offset the memories of the military failure to contain the resistance in Iraq and the spectre of the war crimes committed by US forces. Bush told the troops that they were 'involved in a struggle of historic proportions ... because of you, women in Afghanistan are no longer shot in sports stadiums. Because of you, the people of Iraq no longer fear being executed and left in mass graves.' From here he could shift into yet another swipe at Kerry saying: 'There is nothing complicated about supporting our troops in combat.' Complexity, ambiguity and doubt were there to be mocked as weakness.

The war on terror was not a war for oil, power or empire, according to the Bush message, but instead a war in pursuit of global liberty. 'The terrorists know that a vibrant, successful democracy at the heart of the Middle East will discredit their radical ideology of hate.' It was at this point that one unquestionable truth was uttered – and it came from Bush. He said: '[The terrorists] know that men and women with hope and purpose and dignity do not strap bombs on their bodies and kill the innocent.' Of course, he is right. If Iraqis or Palestinians or Chechens had any hope left that they would one day be free, or if their dignity hadn't been crushed out of them by the killings of their loved ones, then they would be doing what you are doing – reading a book, watching TV, playing with their children – instead of setting off with a bomb around their belly to get revenge for a life ruined by state-sponsored violence and terror. But, of course, that's not what Dubya meant, for he added: 'Freedom is their greatest fear and they should be afraid, because freedom is on the march.' To the Republicans, it is not freedom which these people are fighting for, rather they are fighting against freedom. In this strange topsy-turvy world, the occupation of Palestine by Israel is somehow an act of liberation, and resistance of occupation in Iraq an act of repression.

'I believe in the transformational power of liberty,' Bush continued. 'The wisest use of American strength is to advance freedom ... Americans of all people should never be surprised by the power of liberty to transform lives and nations. That power brought settlers on perilous journeys, inspired colonies to rebellion, ended the sin of slavery and set our nation against the tyrannies of the 20th century.' Summoning up the spirit of yet another dead Republican president – Abraham Lincoln – Bush said: 'I believe that America is called to lead the cause of freedom in a new century ... freedom is not America's gift to the world, it is the Almighty God's gift to every man and woman in this world.'

When the fiery rhetoric was done, Bush turned on his down-home folksy charm and easy sentimentality. He made jokes at his own expense

– 'I have a few flaws,' he said, 'some folks look at me and see a certain swagger, which in Texas is called "walking".' People in the audience cried when he spoke of 'returning the salute of the wounded soldiers', 'holding the children of the fallen', 'meeting with parents and wives and husbands who have received a folded flag'. 'In those military families,' he said, 'I have seen the character of a great nation: decent and idealistic and strong.' He was describing what the delegates on the floor saw in him.

He ended as he began on September 11 – a tragedy which has defined his presidency and given him, his party believes, the right to have his face carved into the rock of Mount Rushmore. 'For as long as our country stands,' Bush told the crowd, 'people will look to the resurrection of New York City and they will say: here buildings fell, and here a nation arose'.

As the crowd cheered him to the echo, the Republican Party convention planners did what they'd done best throughout the week – they put on the schmaltzy razzmatazz. The song 'Put a little love in your heart' blared over the PA and then Cardinal Egan came on to give the closing benediction – a prayer for America and Dubya. He gave thanks to God for the wonder of America, for the fact that Americans 'are the creatures of your Hand, fashioned in your image'. He offered up prayers for the unborn child, for the President, for the Vice-president, for the policeman, the fire-fighter and the soldier 'in lands across the sea'.

'Lord of all,' said the Cardinal, 'we are Your children, "one nation under God", a people called to be a light of righteousness in a troubled world, a city set on a mountain-top from which all mankind might draw strength, inspiration and hope. Help us to measure up to this wondrous calling, this unique vocation, as You send us forth from this place in peace, justice, compassion, virtue and holiness, now and forever. Amen.'

Unlike the Democrats – as exhibited by what US liberals have deemed the treachery of Zell Miller – there was no wobble amongst the Republicans, no schisms; they were all singing from the same hymn sheet. From the Yukon to the Panhandle, these delegates were behind Bush 100 per cent – they had bought the vision, they wanted to see it continue and they were going to vote in their millions to make sure it did continue for 'four more years'. Minutes before Bush came on stage, Alaska delegates June and Roy Burkhart were almost devotional in their praise for him. Roy is a wheelchair-bound Korean war veteran. 'Kerry isn't for family values,' he said. 'He won't support a constitutional amendment to stop gay marriage or make it a crime to desecrate the flag of the United States of America. He says burning the flag is free speech. If that's the case then why is it a crime for me to make a racist comment? President Bush answered the attacks of 9-11 by going on the attack. He's the man we need to lead us.'

June said: 'President Bush exemplifies everything that every American family raising young children thinks is necessary for the safety and well-being of their children. He cares about children. He's a man of God – I'd hate to think of an atheist in the White House. He has such great charisma. He can sit down with anyone and in minutes he will connect with them. President Bush is a real man of the people.

'He showed leadership and tenacity when he made those terribly hard decisions to go to war in Afghanistan and Iraq. We had to do it to break down that wall of terrorism that started here in New York City. I'll never forget him saying that we would attack back and that he'd pro-tect us. He'll be my president forever.'

Jenny Haning is a fashion student from Texas. When I met her she looked like a stunning cartoon, dressed in red, white and blue knee boots, her hair red, her blouse white and her denim skirt blue, she'd topped it off with a Stetson and a star-spangled neckerchief. Here's why she adores her Commander-in-Chief: 'He'll protect us, he'll cut taxes and benefit businesses, he dealt with Iraq and he is taking a stand against abortion, stem cell research and gay marriage. Gay marriage, you know, has been the cause of the fall of several civilisations over the course of history. And he stood up to France – that country had deals with Saddam Hussein.'

Rabbi David Stone, another delegate, backed Bush because 'the secu-rity of the borders of Israel is the most important issue to me'. Many in the Jewish lobby buy the idea that if Bush had been around in 1938 then the Holocaust wouldn't have happened, such is his unshakeable soli-darity with the nation of Israel. Stone opposed the creation of a Palestinian state that touches any of the 'biblical borders of Israel'. 'Forcing Israel to give up land for peace is a Democratic issue,' Stone said. 'The Democrats reward terrorism and create more terrorism. Those Palestinians danced and sang when 9-11 happened – they hate America. I'm a Republican and a Bush supporter because the Repub-licans and President Bush support Israel.'

Linda White, an Arizona delegate with the words BLONDES FOR BUSH emblazoned across her T-shirt, said simply: 'I love my President.' So did the rest of the crowd. Each time a speaker endorsed Bush or called for his re-election the crowd went wild chanting 'USA! USA!', or else they held four fingers in the air, and waved their hand backwards and forwards like a military salute, yelling 'Four more years! Four more years!' It was a suspiciously scary-looking way of adoring one's leader. Try it in the mirror, and see what you think.

What got the delegates most, though, was the repeated image of Bush three days after the attacks on the World Trade Center, standing at Ground Zero with his arm around a fire-fighter and a bullhorn in his hand shouting: 'I can hear you, the whole world can hear you and pretty soon the people who knocked those buildings down will hear you.' The Republicans say it is his Churchill moment – his 'we will fight them on the beaches' speech. It is the moment when, to the Republicans at least, Bush became a man – as Senator John McCain said – who was the leader of a country which had a 'rendezvous with destiny'.

To the Republicans, Bush is power. Take Mike Brown. Clad in a Stars and Stripes sweatshirt, this bodybuilding attorney from Long Island, was sweaty and ecstatic as he left Madison Square Garden minutes after Bush had ended his rabble-rousing speech. 'He was purposeful, strong and vibrant,' said Brown. 'He's a real man – a real leader. He gave us the message we wanted to hear, and that message is that he has made America strong and four more years will make America even stronger still. He's a great guy. I'm a real fan of President George W Bush.'

*

A day before Bush was hailed as an almost mythological being by his party, I watched Ann Bunting freak out as she sat at an end table in the Tick-Tock Diner on the corner of West 34th Street and Eighth Avenue, directly across the road from Madison Square Garden. Ann showed me that beneath the swaggering strength of America lies real fear – a fear that triggers the need to be strong.

Ann suddenly started babbling that she thought that Michael Moore was lurking three tables away, listening to her hold forth on God, guns and the government. Sure, the guy was fat, wore a baseball cap and had a straggly beard on his chin, but anyone could see that he wasn't Michael Moore – the liberal filmmaker-cum-devil-incarnate for the American right wing. Being stalked by the likes of Michael Moore wasn't the only thing that Ann was a bit paranoid about – Canada, socialism, the Democrats, France, the liberals she has to deal with in everyday life, gun control, abortion, stem cell research, gay marriage, terrorism

... Ann's list of phobias, hates and fears seemed to stretch on like a New York street. Guess who is the panacea to all her woes? You better believe it – it's George W Bush.

In the UK, this subservience to leadership would be seen as dangerous, frightening and more than a little pathetic. A party which evoked God and the gun as solutions to the biggest problems of the world and all domestic questions would be hammered in the polls and more than likely wiped off the political map in the UK or France or Germany or probably any other European or western nation – but not so in America. In America, the cult of personality surrounding the President is fiercely encouraged and it's the politicians who don't get jiggy with God and the gun who are in electoral trouble.

Ann, a former lawyer turned college English teacher, was with her husband Bill, a gun instructor who owns a personal arsenal of some 75 weapons including German Lugers from the Second World War. They were up in New York from Florida where Bill is a Republican county chairman – that makes him a pretty big wheel in the party and he's proud to be a delegate to the 2004 Convention. With them were two young Republicans from Nebraska – Nate Pattee and Paul Cordes. They were dressed in neat blazers, ties and slacks despite the broiling New York weather. They were also sporting very proper haircuts for 17-year-olds. Bill was schooling them in the ways of the party and the press. 'Just tell it like it is when you're doing an interview,' he said to the boys.

For the record, the Buntings said, they should be considered fairly mainstream in Republican terms. In fact, they used to be Democrats – until the likes of Hillary Clinton came along. 'That woman wants to chip away at our second amendment rights,' said Bill. The second amendment to the US Constitution guarantees citizens the right to keep and bear arms.

Bill said that Americans need guns because 'an armed populace doesn't have to worry about a government getting too big and over-running us'. Ann chipped in: 'The second amendment ensures our personal freedom. In order to be free you have to be armed. It's a question of independence, self-protection, self-assertion, self-confidence. It's basic to being an American.' These are themes she'd return to many times over.

To Bill, liberal politicians like Hillary Clinton are betraying the spirit of America. Man, do the Republicans hate Hillary. The only women I've ever heard pull down more vitriol on their heads were Myra Hindley and Margaret Thatcher. 'When politicians like Hillary Clinton put their hand on the bible and swear to uphold the Constitution of the United States of America, they can't pick and choose which amendments they like and which they don't,' he said.

Welcome to the Two Americas – a land now as polarised (if not more) by politics as it was in the 1960s when the nation was riven over the rise of the Permissive Society, racial equality and the Vietnam War. On one side stand the liberals, the Democrats and the independents; on the other, the Republicans, the religious right and the conservatives. Each loathes the vision for America that the other espouses – whether it's on foreign policy like Iraq and the United Nations, domestic policy like taxation or social issues like abortion and gay rights, both camps have never been further apart. The result is a nation locked in a cultural war – a cultural war that is fuelling global war. It was family, faith and flag that most Republican supporters voted for, securing the President another four years in office. The global consequences of Bush's US mandate is a more aggressive America and a more violent world. America's domestic decisions have become the planet's difficulties.

For Ann, the gun is the quintessential symbol of American grit; the object which makes this country of hers great. One of the logos plastered over Madison Square Garden during the Republican Convention was A NATION OF COURAGE. It chimes with Ann. To her, the gun answers questions and gets things done. 'I am 100 per cent behind the President on the War on Terror,' she said. 'You have to stand up to a bully. If you back down and show any fear then they will be all over you. Going into Iraq was the right thing to do and we had to do it.' Like nearly everyone in her party, Ann conflated September 11 with the invasion of Iraq. It doesn't matter to them that Osama bin Laden hates secular Saddam or that Iraq had nothing to do with the attacks on America. In fact, a lot of Republicans think that Saddam was the mastermind behind the toppling of the twin towers. Paul Cordes, the 17-year-old from Nebraska being mentored by Bill and Ann during the convention, said categorically that Saddam and al-Qaeda were linked: 'It's a fact. The War on Terror is our World War Three and September 11 was our Pearl Harbour.'

The concept of freedom is dear to these people, so it's remarkable how easily they accept the controversial Patriot Act, which has massively eroded civil rights in the US and given the government sweeping powers including the right to search a person's home without notice. 'Extraordinary times call for extraordinary measures,' explained Ann.

Nate Pattee, wearing a Stetson with a star-spangled hatband and decked out in pro-Bush badges, warmed to the theme, his anger peaking at the tens of thousands in the anti-war lobby who took to the streets of Manhattan that week condemning Bush and his war. 'What gets me going is the way these protestors feel they have to come out and demonstrate about these things,' the teenager said. 'I support the war in Iraq because I support President Bush. We have to deal with countries that take in terrorists and foster them – Saddam did that, and I hope more European nations will stop doing that as well.' Europe isn't too popular with the Republican Party at the moment.

The surety of many Republicans comes straight from the pages of the bible. Over and over again during the convention, God was evoked. His blessings were called down on delegates, on President Bush, on America. The thousands of Republicans who flocked to Madison Square Garden were told by Ronald Reagan's son, Michael, that God had a special plan for this nation. Images of the US as a New Jerusalem were constantly summoned up – one favourite and over-used metaphor being America as a 'shining city on a hill'. It is from this part of the Republican psyche that the culture wars and the unwavering support for Israel have come. Where once the US was indeed 'one nation under God', it is now two nations – a conservative one under God and a progressive one which wants nothing to do with God.

'Our founding fathers,' said Bill, 'based the constitution on Judeo–Christian values. If you look at our coins they say 'In God We Trust'. God is mentioned everywhere. What we now have is a country divided. The atheists have their beliefs and that's fine with me, but don't try and force that agenda on these young people sitting here,' he said, gesturing to Paul and Nate. 'That is exactly what is going on and we are not going to accept that change.

'If Senator Kerry and Ted Kennedy [another liberal politician who's a Republican *bête noire*] want to get married in Massachusetts [a state seen by conservatives as a sort of Land of Sodom] then that's fine. They can live there together, but they aren't going to do it in the state of Florida because we have laws that say we won't recognise gay marriage. Gay couples are going up to Massachusetts and getting married and then coming back to states like mine and expecting us to recognise the marriage. We aren't going to accept that.'

There are now moves underway within the Republican Party to get a constitutional amendment that would specifically forbid same-sex unions. If Bush came out in favour of such a policy then Ann said she'd support him. 'I believe in traditional family values,' she said. 'Marriage is the best way to raise children.'

When Bush retook the White House until 2008, many liberals feared that his second term would be 'revolutionary' – that he would amend the constitution to prohibit gay marriage, that he'd support a ban on abortion, that medical research would stall, and that he'd appoint hard-line Republicans to the Supreme Court so that his own Christian conservative footprint would be left on American society for generations. There were even some liberals who believed that Bush would attempt to change the Constitution to allow him to stand for a third term, citing national security and continuity of leadership in a time of war.

As in every home across America, the culture clash is on the table at the Tick-Tock Diner just as much as the ubiquitous ketchup and Frenchie's squeezy mustard. Paul sallied forth with his take on the culture wars. 'The political issue that I'm most passionate about is abortion,' he said. 'I was raised with strict moral values handed down to me by my family which is almost completely Catholic. When I think of abortion, I think that anyone else would go to prison for killing, but not in this case. I believe life starts at conception.'

Paul had no truck with the term 'pro-choice' – a baby doesn't choose to die, he said. Paul, however, was pro-death penalty. He saw no disparity. A baby is innocent, a murderer is guilty. There was no moral equivalency for him. Stem cell research is given just as sound a moral thrashing – it's playing God. It's as simple as that.

When it comes to matters fiscal, the Buntings wanted to see taxes slashed to the bone. 'The government will always spend the money it gets, the individual is the best person to hold the purse strings,' said Bill. 'The more tax is reduced the more jobs and security there will be and that means people will spend more money. It's trickle-down economics.' For a system that doesn't work, Bill added, 'just look at socialist countries like Canada'. In Republican eyes, their northern neighbour is just one step up from Castro's Cuba.

So, if there's little taxation, how do you look after the poor? Around the corner from the Tick-Tock Diner on Eighth Avenue, there was a guy who says he is called Barney. He told me he slept in the street every night. He was black. He was a Vietnam vet and mentally ill. He was so disturbed that apart from his name and the fact that he served his country fighting communism, Barney wasn't really coherent about anything else. I asked him if he knew that the Republican Party Convention was taking place just a few yards away from where he bedded down on the sidewalk each night. He didn't have a clue what I was talking about, but he did say that he thought there'd been a lot more police about than usual. I never heard the Republicans talk about old, broken-down soldiers like Barney when they spoke of the respect, love and honour that the Bush presidency is supposed to have for American fighters overseas and military veterans.

How would the Buntings help a lost patriot like Barney?

'First of all,' said Ann, 'I don't think we should start with the assumption that it is the government's responsibility to take care of people in the community. It is for the individual, and of course other human beings should help their neighbours. If you start with the concept that the government is the solution to all social problems then nothing will be solved. Socialism is a dead-end economic system. The government has to help people to help themselves. It has to help them get educated, get a job and become independent so they can fend for themselves. The idea of Big Brother helping you is destructive to the human spirit.

'It's not an accident that in the short history of the USA this country has been the most productive and creative society on earth. Look at our technology, music, motion pictures, telecommunications, computers, manned flight, mass production, pharmaceuticals. Why? Because we have a free market system that rewards entrepreneurs and creativity. In socialist countries you don't have that vibrant dynamic going on.'

Ann and Bill were pretty well off. They didn't live in the America of crowded jails, poverty, drug addiction, falling educational standards, no health insurance, ramshackle housing, minimum wage, job losses and union busting. The middle-class Americans that Ann and Bill spoke for either couldn't or wouldn't see the lives that the Barneys of America live day in and day out.

Bill said he had the answer to helping poor, homeless, mad Barney off the streets – faith-based organisations. That's charity from churches. 'Faith-based organisations can screen out those who are really in need of care from those who don't care about themselves,' he said. 'When they ask for money at my church and there is a reason, then I put money forward. People with money will give money.'

These socialist countries – like France and Germany and Canada – have got it all wrong when it comes to tax, the welfare state, social issues and, most importantly, their relations with the US, the group believed. 'The countries that are drifting away from America are doing so because of their leadership,' said Paul. 'Jacques Chirac needs to go. Somebody needs to step up in France and move it back to having better relations with America. They need to stand up for what is right in the world. Chirac is nothing short of a coward. France's position on issues both social and foreign is just pathetic.'

Tony Blair, on the other hand, gets a mini thumbs-up from Nate. 'His support of President Bush is excellent, but to be honest I haven't paid much attention to him.' Bill Bunting, however, wasn't quite so sure. 'Blair is no Thatcher or Johnny Major, is he?' he said. 'They made better and more clear decisions. Blair seems to waffle in your houses of Parliament. One country that has turned around into a good democracy though is Italy. They used to have a new government every nine months, now they're stable and they've taken control of the Mafia. Berlusconi is doing a great job.'

France and the Democratic Party are one and the same to Ann. The diplomatic conflict between the US and France is 'a fight between socialism and free enterprise' as is the bitter battle between the two parties. 'I think a lot of Democrats are real socialists – if not communists,' she said. Bill added that the French just don't have the 'work ethic' the way Americans do.

The Democrats don't even want to instill a culture of hard work in the American people, Ann added. To solve social problems they want a bigger government – funded through higher taxes – that will provide education, minimal care and social services. That, said Ann, breeds a 'culture of dependency'. That's what's ruining America, she added. 'Republicans want to foster independence and self-assurance,' Ann said. 'The Democrats want to keep us dependent to shut us up.'

Just look at education, said Ann. One of her teacher colleagues said recently to her that education should be free. 'Why should it be free?' Ann said angrily. 'When any socialist country has a system where they take taxpayers' dollars to pay for the education of all people, children don't reach their full potential.' Although America has one of the poorest educated populaces in the western world, Ann was convinced that paying for education was what 'made this country so great'.

Most Republicans feel victimised by what they see as the left. 'A lot of these Democrats and protestors need to recognise that we have a voice too,' said Ann. 'Their notion of tolerance is hypocritical. My liberal so-called colleagues at school don't want to tolerate my conservative tradition. They get all upset that I think I should have the right to carry a gun onto campus.'

Nate – the kid with the cowboy hat covered in Bush-Cheney badges – was told to 'go fuck himself' in the street on the way to the diner and someone 'flipped him the bird' right in his face. Paul got a tough time from teachers and pupils at his school when he set up a Young Republicans club because the sex education classes were getting 'way too left'. It's for parents to teach their kids about sex, he said.

'The liberals can't step on our rights or take them away,' said Bill. 'I don't want them living off our backs because we make more money. We worked for our money. They can have their liberal agenda but they better goddamn well get out there and work for themselves.'

Paul and Nate were disgusted with the way the Democrats behaved. They are disrespectful, said Paul, to Bush. 'He holds the highest office in the land and he deserves the respect of all the people, yet they call him a liar and a murderer.'

Nate added: 'Nobody thinks it's cool to be a Republican. But it's cool these days to be a Democrat. I get a hard time for my politics, but in a way I enjoy it. I want to stand up for what I believe in, and the way people react to me just shows you the true face of the Democrats.'

*

People like Bill and Ann and Nate and Paul weren't welcome in New York – one of the most liberal and democratic cities in the US – in the late summer and early autumn of 2004. Their arrival hurt many New Yorkers. Dan Jones, one of the founders of the September 11 Families for Peaceful Tomorrows organisation, felt their presence keenly.

It was a sweltering Thursday evening in Union Square and Jones was trying to explain to me how his children felt when they lost their favourite uncle – his brother-in-law – on September 11, 2001. Suddenly, his face crumpled and he started to cry. He quickly composed himself. It had been a rough week for him.

His brother-in-law, he felt, had been wrapped in the Stars and Stripes and his death expropriated by the Republican Party, which came to town just days before the third anniversary of the attacks on America for its pre-election convention. The decision to hold the convention just a few blocks from the site where nearly 3,000 people died in the World Trade Center was condemned by many opponents of the Republican Party as a gross exploitation of America's suffering. Each day of the convention saw the continual evocation of the memory of 9-11 as a reason to 'never forget and never forgive'; each day delegates called on 9-11 as a reason to justify war.

If the convention and the memory of his family's loss had made this a harrowing week emotionally for Jones, it had also been a hard few days for him physically as well. He'd just completed the mammoth task of dragging a 5,000-lb tombstone – inscribed with the words 'To the unknown civilians killed in war' – from Boston to New York in time for the convention. The 'Stonewalk' saw some 500 people, led by Jones, pulling this hulk of granite along the same route that the planes which crashed into the Twin Towers took when they were taken over by the 9-11 hijackers.

The Tombstone now takes centre stage in Union Square. This usually bohemian, bustling little patch of ground was turned into a shrine for all those who had died since 9-11. Surrounding the tombstone were 978 pairs of boots – a set for every soldier who had lost their life in Iraq as of that Thursday evening in early September 2004. Hundreds of kids' shoes and women's shoes and the shoes of men were there as well – each pair representing a dead Iraqi. The names of all those who had died during the invasion and occupation of Iraq were being read out as Jones tried to describe the pain and anger his family has felt – pain at losing his children's uncle, Bill Kelly, and anger at the Bush administration for using their suffering, as they see it, as an excuse for war across the globe.

Bill Kelly was at a breakfast meeting in the Windows on the World restaurant at the World Trade Center when the first plane struck. His body was never found. 'My children lost their favourite uncle,' said Kelly, a 39-year-old social worker in the New York school system. 'We didn't want to see any other family going through what we did. My children are still very afraid. The shock and horror hasn't left them. No other children anywhere in the world should go through what they went through. The city in which they live saw planes crashing into buildings and the buildings falling down.

'We knew that if our country waged war that other families would be put in the same position that our family was put in – children would lose uncles and parents, people would lose their brothers and sisters, parents would lose their children.

'We wanted justice not war. War is no way to get justice. It took a long time for the man who blew up the plane over Lockerbie to come to justice but it happened in the end. We wanted this pursued as a crime, not to be considered as an act of war. The war in Afghanistan has not brought those who plotted my brother-in-law's murder to justice. And the war in Iraq has certainly not served that purpose either.'

The tombstone that he and the other members of September 11 Families for Peaceful Tomorrows dragged to New York was meant to quietly and symbolically show their President what they thought of his foreign policy as he staged his party's national convention.

Not every anti-Bush protestor in New York that week was as eloquent as Jones and the 200 or so other families in his organisation, but nearly all shared his sentiments. From the day before the convention started Manhattan became a sea of protest. Sunday alone, the eve of the convention, saw at least 200,000 people take to the streets in a demonstration aimed solely at one man – George W Bush. The poor, the homeless, military veterans, former police officers and fire-fighters who responded to 9-11, the gay community, the unemployed, anarchists, hippies, Muslims, Christians, soccer moms – someone from every segment of the myriad ways of life in America – took to the streets of New York to tell their President to stop what he was doing and to let him know that they wanted him out of the White House. Most were dignified and some were silly – such as the panty protest down at Battery Park where women flashed their knickers bearing slogans like FUCK BUSH. Only a very few were violent and a handful were pointless – there were more than a couple of wasted stoners desperately wandering New York looking for something to protest about but unable to locate the nearest demonstration.

The police arrested more than 2,000 people, many for the slightest infractions. The NYPD operated a policy of pre-emptive arrest, cracking down hard on anyone who so much as looked like they were about to step out of line. But although draconian, the police were generally not too heavy-handed with the protestors. That's not surprising. Few would have had the guts to test the patience of the police in a city that looked as if martial law had been declared. A giant NYPD spy blimp, replete with camera company adverts written on the side in towering letters, floated over the city as helicopters patrolled the skies. On every street corner in Manhattan there were dozens of police. Streets were blocked off in all directions by anti-car bomb barriers. Flotillas of motorcycle cops sped around as officers on horseback and with batons drawn idled in the streets. Madison Square Garden itself looked as if it was under siege, ringed by secret service agents, the National Guard and thousands of police armed to the teeth. This was not a city taking any chances.

This was a city that had been sent into turmoil because of the politics of George Bush. The crazy levels of security seeped paranoia into the minds of New Yorkers, many of whom were sure that there was going to be a terrorist attack on their city. One off-duty cop in a bar told me straight-faced that he'd heard that the Brooklyn Bridge was going to be blown up.

The Republicans delighted in disparaging the demonstrators as a bunch of leftie hippies who cost the city a fortune in security. The response from the demonstrators was that the Republicans should have taken their convention elsewhere and not cost the city a fortune in trying to provide security in the first place.

But Dan Jones is not the type of protestor that the Republicans are ever likely to pick on. He's their worst nightmare – a victim of terrorism who is also a pacifist and an opponent of America's wars.

As bells rang in Union Square for everyone who had died in the Iraq war, Jones said: 'The philosophy of our organisation is to highlight civilian deaths. Our family members went to work, got on aeroplanes, went to breakfast, responded to an emergency and were killed because they were in the wrong place at the wrong time. We don't want our loved ones used as an excuse to start war.

'Yet the death toll of the innocent people in Iraq and Afghanistan just keeps going up. Like our families, these people were in the wrong place at the wrong time. We just want peace and justice. Our organisation takes its name from something that Martin Luther King said – 'Wars are poor chisels for carving out peaceful tomorrows.' That's all we want – a peaceful tomorrow – and these wars we are involved in are no way to bring that about. The stone that we've brought to New York is a compliment to the tomb of the unknown soldier. It is a mark of respect to the suffering and anguish of the families of soldiers who have lost loved ones overseas. It's a reminder about the human toll of war.'

As Jones spoke, the names of dead Iraqi children were being read out. 'Some of them were just two years old,' Jones said. 'I have children and it is horrible to think of the one day of terror that we lived through in New York. But the nightly bombings in Iraq is terror raining down every day, and the soldiers over there wondering each time a car passes whether or not it is going to blow them up are living with a constant threat of death.'

American politics, Jones said, has now become a 'fiery cocktail'. 'These wars haven't made my country safer,' he added, 'and even if they

had, the means aren't justified. The entire world is a far more dangerous place, due in large part to the actions of my government.'

Jones believes that what is happening overseas is an act of revenge by
America. He quoted an old college buddy of his – a navy veteran – who
told him that it was military doctrine that no army should take part in
a war for the sake of vengeance because vengeance is dishonourable and
the military lives or dies by its honour.

'If the horror of those pictures from Abu Ghraib prison hasn't
shocked us into admitting that we have no moral authority anymore,
then I don't know what can stop this,' he said. 'The genie is out of the
bottle and I don't know how to get it back in. I wish I did.'

Jones hasn't lost hope though. He says he and all the other millions
of protestors around America have to keep on protesting for their children and the belief in a 'peaceful tomorrow'. 'My children miss their
uncle greatly,' he said, coughing as his voice filled up with tears. 'Their
experiences have prepared them for life at much too young an age. It's
painful for them, very painful. It's painful for all of us – both here and
abroad. The pain has to stop.'

*

Back at the beginning of this recollection about life inside the
Republican war machine in late 2004, I told you how I'd gone to a
screening of the film George W Bush – Faith in the White House on the
third floor of the New Yorker Hotel, right opposite Madison Square
Garden where Bush was holding court.

A few days before I attended that screening, I also paid a visit to a
rather different religious meeting. It was a discussion panel organised by
the American Muslim Taskforce on Civil Rights and Elections. Its leadership had spent $1,200 hiring a conference room in a hotel to meet
with Republican Party delegates to discuss their concerns about the on-
going backlash against Muslim-Americans.

When I got there, at least an hour after the event was supposed to
have started, there was a forlorn little group of maybe five Muslims, sitting around a table. They brightened up considerably when I arrived
and told them I was a journalist interested in writing about them. It
turned out there hadn't been any other visitors but me. Why? I asked.

Well, it seems that the Republican Party has the power to control
where any meeting connected to its convention gets placed. In their wisdom the Republican Party apparatchiks chose to put the Muslim group
in a hotel where there were no delegates and few journalists staying.

With a dash of a pen, the party made sure that nobody knew about the Muslim group, and that meant that nobody heard what they had to say.

They were charming people. As soon as I arrived they brought in a banquet of food – enough samosas and kebabs to feed the hundreds they had expected to turn up. I was lucky enough to have these people to myself for an hour and it was an education to listen to them.

Agha Saeed, the chair of the Taskforce, said the ease with which his organisation's voice was silenced showed just 'how much we are under siege at the moment in this country'. He added: 'This was a chilling way to keep us quiet. The lack of inclusion for my community is more than apparent here – they tell us that we are included but really we are totally outside the structures.'

Saeed goes on to tell how the erosion of civil liberties by Attorney-General John Ashcroft is like a cancer gnawing away at his community. He had little good to say about the Democrats, either – they have long been silent in the face of Republican crackdowns on freedom and civil rights. Saeed said his organisation even considered endorsing a third party independent – that's how bad their predicament had become.

'Believe me when I say that 98 per cent of Muslims will not vote for Bush,' said Saeed. That's a pretty extraordinary figure considering that many Muslim small business owners backed Bush in 2000. 'The rhetoric of the Bush administration has become extremist, ominous and disturbing.'

When we spoke there were just about two months to go until the 2004 election. Saeed, an optimist in the face of ruin, truly believed back then that America was 'waking up to the futility of the Republican Party policies'. If the Democrats lost, however, and Bush continued in office, then Saeed thought 'the isolation of the USA in the world would triple'.

'Muslims in this country have been reduced to second-class citizens. A colleague from our offices in California was in a library recently and two police officers showed up. They walked up to him and told him to step outside. They questioned him and told him they were interviewing him because he had been seen reading a newspaper article about Osama bin Laden. What more can I say?'

The group told me that this was an example of what they call 'forced identity'. In other words, it doesn't matter if you live in New Jersey and have a US passport, or come from Islamabad and are dressed in robes – if you are Muslim in America, you are a suspect. America's 4.2 million Muslim voters are therefore consigned to the same security bracket as the 9-11 hijackers. There is no ambiguity, no complexity; just black and white, good and evil, with us or against us.

'We are becoming less and less involved in civic life,' says Saeed. One woman at the meeting, Debbie Almontaser, a New Yorker of Yemeni extraction, said she had to be escorted to her work as a school teacher by her husband or other male relatives. Debbie was no submissive door-mat or repressed victim of her culture, she was a highly educated, well-spoken, self-confident woman, but she wore the *hijab* – the Muslim headscarf – and it wasn't uncommon for people to verbally abuse her or even spit at her on the streets.

'Every major Muslim organisation in the USA is under some sort of investigation,' said Saeed. 'Organisations have been asked to hand over the complete list of their members. This is spreading a fear which is killing our community. Our community leaders have been arrested, our organisations shut down and ordinary people are scared to be Muslim – that is what is happening in George Bush's America.

'I'm not joking when I say that I believe that what is happening here will have serious consequences for the rest of the world. If weak and dangerous countries see a nation like America adopting this sort of behaviour then they will follow suit and the rights of everyone in the world will be eroded. We Muslims aren't asking for special favours in the USA, we are just asking America to be true to its own ideals – ideals of freedom and of liberty – the ideals which founded this great nation that we all want to live in equally.'

THE FALL
or
How torture and terror took our democracies into the abyss

The Germans have a word – much favoured by that sinister philosopher Friedrich Nietzsche – which describes what Britain and America are experiencing at the moment as democracies. The word is *Untergang*. It comes from the verb *untergehen*. It has a number of meanings: to go down or descend; to set, in the way the sun sets in the west; to be destroyed; or to go under, like a sinking ship.

The Germans also use the word the way we use the expression 'the fall': to describe the fall of man – the fall of Adam and Eve. A German director even used the word as the title for his film about Hitler's final days in the Berlin bunker as Nazi Germany collapsed around him.

Iraq has been our *Untergang*.

You don't need me to tell you this. Take a look at where and when you are living. We began this war based on lies, on motives which had everything to do with money and power and nothing to do with the higher values of democracy and freedom which we claim as our own. If you are a Christian like Blair and Bush, it would be hard not to see what has happened in Iraq as a sin – a very great sin. If you aren't a Christian, then it would be just as difficult not to see the men who plotted a war which has killed many thousands of innocent people as criminals – very grave criminals.

But our leaders weren't just content to sin and to commit crime. No. This was a new century, a new age and that required a new doctrine for war – a doctrine which looked at the Geneva Conventions as petty inconveniences to be outmanoeuvred; a doctrine which removed concepts such as 'innocent until proven guilty' and 'trial by jury'; a doctrine which raped and abused the historic principles of liberty, equality and democracy upon which both the US and the UK were founded.

We compounded our sins with acts of torture, with human rights abuses, with the murder of civilians, with the disappearances of innocent people. We became the very thing we were supposed to be fighting. To coin another expression from Nietzsche, we went beyond good and evil. Who is morally superior in this war? The tyrant Saddam? The invaders and liars Bush and Blair? The troops who kill and torture? The resistance who kill and torture? You? Me? The answer's nobody. This war – so famously described as a battle between good and evil, as a matter of being 'with me or against me' morally – has left us with no moral balance.

The last redoubt of Bush and Blair in their attempt to defend the Iraq war as a noble cause was the claim that it was a moral war – that Saddam was a monster who raped, tortured and killed his own people and had to be taken out.

We all know Saddam was a monster who raped, murdered and tortured – but then when we deposed him as the tyrant of Iraq we replaced him with our own rapists, murderers and torturers. It wasn't just the Americans who raped and killed and tortured in places like Abu Ghraib, the Brits were doing their fair share of killing and torturing. They used Iraqis as human punch-bags; they killed kids.

Britain has been betrayed by Blair. The UK has done some terrible things over the years but the nation still carried some residual respect in the eyes of the world because of what it stood for after the Second World War. The spirit of that brave, great and good generation has been defiled by Blair. Britain's standing as a country that was seen simplistically as being at heart 'good' has been squandered – British people are now the bad guys. They are the guys in black hats. People hate Britons around the world. Think on that – people who don't even know you hate you enough to kill you simply because you come from a certain country.

Not only did the Muslim world have to watch while its men, women and children were taken to medieval prisons like Abu Ghraib to be raped or murdered or tortured, they had to take that abuse while they were being told that they were being liberated, that they were being made free, that democracy was being spread. The word 'democracy' shouldn't be allowed to come from the mouths of men like Bush and Blair. They are the killers of democracy. No democratic country starts illegal wars which its people don't support, bombs innocent people or allows rape and murder and torture to be committed by its own troops. Bush and Blair are in command of the American and British armed forces, and every rape and murder and act of torture is their responsibility – morally they may as well have committed the atrocities themselves.

While such perverted hypocrisy was being poured into the ears of the Arab people, Iraq was also allowed to drift into total chaos, anarchy and sectarian civil war. The US and Britain were steeped in sin and permitted their playground by the Euphrates to become a vision of hell on earth. Iraq was looted like a helpless drunk lying in the gutter; its infrastructure – the hospitals, schools, the apparatus of state – rotted while American companies got rich; cities became vast rubbish tips; there was no effective police force; intellectuals were assassinated for the hell of it; children vanished off the streets; women were walking targets. Then the looters and insurgents started to make off with vast amounts of conventional weapons ... then the al-Qaeda guys moved in. It was the Vietnam-style quagmire that many seasoned military veterans had warned of before the war, only it was worse. Life in Iraq became nasty, brutish and short. Where there were no terrorists, terrorists were created; where there were no weapons of mass destruction, the US and Britain allowed looted universities and factory sites to gift technology that could be used to make dirty bombs to Islamic fundamentalists; where the Iraqis had one enemy before the invasion and occupation – Saddam and his secret police and his psychopathic sons – they were given enemies on all fronts and in all guises. Now, if you are an Iraqi you can be killed by Ba'athist resistance fighters, al-Qaeda affiliated crazies, British troops, trigger-happy GIs, criminals who want your money or your daughters; you can die from drinking dirty water, from malnutrition, because you've been contaminated with the dust of the depleted uranium used in British and American shells ... the permutations of death in Iraq are now endless.

If the US and the UK showed the world that they could be mean, sinful, criminal bastards in Iraq, then the arrival of the Jihadist fighters presented the world with a brave new definition of meanness, sin and criminality. The lunatics dropped by to take over the asylum.

Until his death, Abu Musab al-Zarqawi was the first among these killers. He began taking anyone from any country connected with the occupation hostage, and anyone who was seen as a war profiteer was fair game too. If you were from South Korea, Bulgaria, Britain, Italy, America or a worker with a foreign oil company, or one of the reconstructors, then you were a target. If al-Zarqawi's men got you, you were dead. No question. And it wouldn't be an easy or quick death. You would have your head cut off, live on camera, after being made to beg someone like Blair for your life. You'd be forced to denounce the crimes at Abu Ghraib and then you'd get to briefly star in your own snuff movie. Eventually, your body would be dumped at the side of the road and if your mother or father or wife or husband or children were very lucky they'd get your mutilated corpse back for burial.

Make no mistake. People like Ken Bigley, the British hostage who was beheaded by al-Zarqawi in the autumn of 2004, were killed in revenge for acts such as the atrocities committed in Abu Ghraib. I've sat through most of the propaganda films produced by the communications unit of al-Zarqawi's militia group and they make abundantly clear the connection between US and UK crimes and the fate of hostages like Bigley. Extremist films, like those from al-Zarqawi's al-Qaeda connected outfit, follow a predictable but effective propaganda pattern. They begin with pictures of dead Iraqi kids, wailing women and devastated homes played over chilling Koranic chanting, then a man masked in a black balaclava appears – when al-Zarqawi was alive it was presumably him or one of his lieutenants – and delivers a speech to camera in praise of Jihad and in denunciation of the west and any Muslim who will not take up arms against the occupation. A bound hostage cowers at his feet. The hostage is suddenly grabbed by the lead figure and his henchmen as they shout 'God is great!'. The hostage is then pinned down and their head is sawn off – the head isn't cut off with one blow; it is sawn off; and as that happens, you, the viewer, have to watch a fellow human being die slowly, humiliatingly and painfully for a war that you don't believe in and they probably didn't believe in either. When it's over, the victim's head is held aloft. There is usually one final shot of the hostage, with their head placed on their chest, lying crumpled on a blood-soaked floor in their orange Guantanamo Bay-style jumpsuit. The message is clear: what you do to us, we will pay you back ten-fold, twenty-fold; whatever it takes, you will pay, and we won't stop. Not for nothing did one British intelligence officer describe al-Zarqawi to me as a 'Prince of Terror'; for terror was his *métier*.

Al-Zarqawi became our worst nightmare made flesh. The war on terror created men for whom terror was an art form, and gave al-Zarqawi the excuse he needed to exercise his horrible gift. How did we arrive at such a place? How could even a wrong, illegal war, descend into such a hell on earth? How could a country like Britain be reviled around the world as a force for evil?

We entered a gothic world. A world of nightmares, violence, sexual abuse, torture and murder; a nihilistic empty world of no values, no morality, no escape. A world where good, selfless, peaceful people die horribly and become martyrs for innocence; a world where people like Margaret Hassan – an Irish aid worker who lived in Iraq most of her life, married an Iraqi, took Iraqi nationality, opposed sanctions, opposed the war and opposed the occupation – can be taken away in broad daylight on a Baghdad street and shot in the head for no other apparent reason than the fact that she was a westerner.

If al-Zarqawi was a gothic monster to the west – a demon-like creature, hovering on the edge of consciousness waiting to spirit innocent people away and kill them – what do you think the Muslim world made of creatures like the American GI Lynndie England, that pixie-faced little pervert who sexually abused Iraqi prisoners in Abu Ghraib? If you think she lives in the minds of ordinary Muslims the way Myra Hindley, the Moors murderer and multiple child killer, lives in the minds of British people then you wouldn't be far off the mark.

It's such a long, long way from the day after September 11 when *Le Monde* wrote the most powerful, honest and humanitarian headline that the world of journalism has ever produced: WE ARE ALL AMERICANS NOW. Back then the world meant it; America's suffering was all our suffering; the events of 9-11 were wrong and horrible and we wanted to help our American friends; but today the headline should read: WE ARE ALL MONSTERS NOW. And that waste of shared humanity – an opportunity that our leaders should have grabbed with both hands in the hope of spreading real peace across the world – is all thanks to Messrs Bush and Blair.

How did we get so very far down the road to ruin in such a short space of time? How did a few planes flying into a few buildings and killing a few thousand people debase an entire generation? Disgrace the concept of democracy? Degrade humanity?

If creatures like al-Zarqawi paid us back for what they saw as our crimes against their people, then let's start our unravelling of this 'fall' of ours with an examination of our gravest sin: the decision by governments in the west to roll back democratic freedoms and to create an environment in which torture, atrocity and human rights abuses could flourish. From this sin, all other sins flow.

Torture

Like so much to do with this war in Iraq, the first steps on the road to Abu Ghraib were taken as a result of the events of 9-11. A few months after that terrible event, on February 7, 2002, President Bush issued a memorandum to Dick Cheney, Colin Powell, Donald Rumsfeld, John Ashcroft, his Chief of Staff, the head of the CIA, the Assistant to the President for National Security Affairs and the Chairman of the Military Joint Chiefs of Staff headed *Humane treatment of al-Qaeda and Taliban detainees.*

In this memo, Bush says that he has taken a decision based on 'the opinion of the department of justice dated January 22, 2002, and on the legal opinion rendered by the Attorney-General (John Ashcroft)' that 'none of the provisions of Geneva apply to our conflict with al-Qaeda in Afghanistan or elsewhere throughout the world'. He also ruled that the Geneva Conventions did not apply to Taliban detainees. The memo spells out that al-Qaeda and Taliban prisoners are not 'legally entitled' to humane treatment. It also says, without any apparent consciousness of moral contradiction, that any state, group or person who captures Americans should treat them in accordance with international law.

Now, watch the ripple effect of this decision to alter fundamentally the legal framework surrounding the US military and its detention of prisoners by the commander-in-chief. Bush makes a sweeping statement about the need for a new 'paradigm' and soon Iraqis are being raped, attacked with dogs, stripped naked, left in their own shit, beaten, made to masturbate in front of female GIs and killed.

In August 2002, the Justice Department told the White House that – if you can believe this – international laws against torture 'may be unconstitutional if applied to interrogations' of al-Qaeda operatives. In a memo, the Justice Department added that a CIA officer who tortured an al-Qaeda terrorist 'would be doing so in order to prevent further attacks on the United States by the al-Qaeda network' and that such 'necessity and self-defence could provide justifications that would eliminate criminal liability'.

This memo was written in response to a CIA request for information and sent to the White House Counsel, Alberto R Gonzales. It was signed by Assistant Attorney-General Jay S Bybee. In it, the concept of torture is watered down. We are told that torture 'must be equivalent in intensity to the pain accompanying serious physical injury, such as organ failure, impairment of bodily functions, or even death'. Here is the Justice Department saying that as long as no kidneys are ruptured or no-one is crippled or killed, then it is fine for the CIA's thugs to put on the brass-knuckles and go for it.

The memo listed seven acts which were considered to be torture, namely severe beatings with truncheons, threats of death, burning with cigarettes, electric shocks to the genitals, rape and sexual assault and forcing one prisoner to watch the torture of another prisoner. The memo then said: 'While we cannot say with certainty that acts falling short of these seven would not constitute torture ... we believe that interrogation techniques would have to be similar to these in their extreme nature and in the type of harm caused to violate law.'

The memo continued: 'For purely mental pain or suffering to amount to torture it must result in significant psychological harm of significant duration e.g. lasting for months or even years.' As long as the experience does not cause 'post-traumatic stress disorder', or other serious mental illness, then torture is OK by the Justice Department's standards.

How does a torturer know, when he is urinating in the mouth of a detainee, or beating him on the soles of his feet, whether the victim will recover in a day or in a lifetime? The Justice Department is ready with an answer. Interrogators should show that they have taken 'such steps as surveying professional literature, consulting with experts or reviewing evidence gained in past experience'. This would prove that they had intended the torture they inflicted on their victim to 'not amount to the acts prohibited'.

Gonzales, the White House Counsel, had told Bush in January 2002, that the 'new paradigm' for fighting the war on terror 'renders obsolete Geneva's strict limitations'. He also said that the President should dump Geneva as 'prosecutors and independent counsels ... may in the future decide to pursue unwarranted charges' of war crimes. Gonzales would later go on to be appointed by Bush to replace John Ashcroft as the US Attorney-General.

In March 2003, just before the invasion of Iraq, the Pentagon conducted a review of the torture laws. Those making up the review panel included members of all the armed forces, the Joint Chiefs of Staff and representatives of intelligence agencies. The review group believed that international laws forbidding torture could be circumvented by presidential directives. The report was prepared by the Pentagon's Chief Lawyer William J Haynes. He found that 'in order to respect the President's inherent constitutional authority to manage a military campaign ... [laws forbidding torture] must be construed as inapplicable to interrogations undertaken pursuant to his Commander-in-Chief authority'. Laws banning torture were found to 'not apply to the conduct of US personnel' in Guantanamo Bay.

'If a government defendant were to harm an enemy combatant during an interrogation in a manner that might arguably violate criminal prohibition, he would be doing so in order to prevent further attacks on the United States by the al-Qaeda terrorist network. In that case, [Department of Justice] believes that he could argue that the executive branch's constitutional authority to protect the nation from attack justified his actions.'

The Department of Justice and the Pentagon were all singing from the same hymn sheet. They all wanted to get away with torture and they were looking for a legal means by which to do so. As Tom Malinowski of Human Rights Watch said: 'It appears what they were contemplating was the commission of war crimes and looking for ways to avoid legal accountability.'

The slippage in morality is brought home by a comment in the memo which shows how quickly America has forgotten the lessons learned in 1945. It states that a soldier could defend himself against criminal allegations by saying that he was merely following 'superior orders'. It was a resurrection of the Nazi concentration camp guards' defence. How strange that a man once seen as America's leading liberal, Jewish lawyer – Alan Dershowitz – should have been one of the first public figures to speak out in favour of using torture on Muslim suspects. He advocated law courts issuing 'torture warrants' to ensure that there was some degree of oversight when an American interrogator slid a sterilised stainless steel needle underneath a detainee's fingernails to extract information.

Until December 2002, the US army was only allowed to use 17 approved interrogation techniques with prisoners. These were all verbal. Interrogators could scare the daylights out of prisoners and verbally insult them but they couldn't lay a finger on them; they couldn't even really yell at them, and they weren't allowed to lie.

In December 2002, however, Donald Rumsfeld, the US Defense

Secretary, approved some 16 new interrogation techniques. These included yelling and lying – big deal – but there were some much more dangerous, abusive techniques to which he gave the green light, such as: putting prisoners in 'stress positions' – that might be squatting on the ground with your arms in front of you for hours on end – isolation in a totally dark, sound-proofed cell; hooding; stripping prisoners naked; using dogs on them during interrogations; removing religious items and blankets; 'mild non-injurious physical contact' such as grabbing, poking and pushing; and forcing prisoners to have their beards and heads shaved. Rumsfeld later authorised 'sleep adjustment' – in other words keeping someone awake for days on end.

This was 'torture-lite' or 'stress and duress' as the Pentagon liked to call it. All these erosions of protections for enemy prisoners in US detention were, in fact, part and parcel of an *ad hoc* torturers' charter that was being rolled out by the Bush administration. What was happening was the start of a slippery slope to disappearances, extrajudicial executions and rape. According to the independent review of the Pentagon's detention operations in Abu Ghraib, Rumsfeld's policies ended in 'acts of brutality and purposeless sadism'. Let me jog your memory, in the unlikely event that you have forgotten those pictures of what took place inside Abu Ghraib – Saddam's old torture HQ – when it was taken over by the Americans.

In May 2004, CBS TV in America flashed a series of pictures leaked by horrified US soldiers around the world. The paper I work for, the *Sunday Herald*, called them 'The Pictures That Lost the War'. They were all images that would have made Saddam proud. Among the most grimly iconic, was a photograph of a prisoner, hooded and dressed in rags, his hands outstretched, electrodes attached to his fingers and genitals. He'd been forced to stand on a box about one-foot square. His captors had told him that, if he fell off the box, he'd be electrocuted. That picture captured the moment when members of the coalition forces, who styled themselves liberators, were exposed as torturers.

But that iconic image also gave us a clue as to how deep the roots of torture went within the US administration and military. The hood, the electrodes, the box, the outstretched arms, are all part of a specific type of torture technique known in US military circles as 'the Vietnam'. As Darius Rejali, an expert on torture, said: 'Was that something that an MP [military police] dreamed up by herself? Think again. That's a standard torture. But it's not common knowledge. Ordinary American soldiers did this, but someone taught them.'

The pictures of US soldiers torturing their captives have the added horror of sexual abuse. In many, Lynndie England, a 21-year-old from a West Virginia trailer park is playing up to the camera while her captives are tortured. In one picture, her hand rests on the buttocks of a naked and hooded Iraqi who is being forced to sit on the shoulders of another Iraqi prisoner.

Later, she's got a cigarette clenched between grinning lips and is pointing at the genitals of a line of naked, hooded Iraqis who are being forced to masturbate. A hill-billy serial killer couldn't look more disturbed and frightening, if they tried. A third snap shows her embracing a colleague as a naked Iraqi lies before them. Her most infamous picture shows her numbly dragging a naked Iraqi prisoner across the floor by a dog collar and leash. It's S&M porn. Even her blank, dumb expression is straight from the empty faces of the women who degrade themselves and others in the most extreme forms of American and European pornography. England was having sex with another one of the Abu Ghraib torturers during her time in Baghdad. His name was Corporal Charles Graner and she became pregnant by him. God help the child.

Little Lynndie turned sexual torture into home entertainment and al-Zarqawi trumped her in return with real life snuff movies.

Another disgraceful image from Abu Ghraib shows an Iraqi known to have a severe mental condition lying on the floor with a banana in his anus. In other pictures, the same man is covered in human faeces and tied up.

In still more holiday snaps from hell, two naked Iraqis are forced to simulate oral sex and a group of naked Iraqi men are made to clamber on to each other's backs. Others were 'ridden like animals', according to military investigators, and beaten while being forced to masturbate. One dreadful picture features nothing but the bloated face of an Iraqi who has been beaten to death. His body is wrapped in plastic.

Other pictures showed snarling dogs lunging at naked, cowering prisoners. Some dog handlers used to place bets with each other to see how many prisoners they could make lose control of their bladder and bowels through the use of dogs.

A male rape also took place in Abu Ghraib. One Iraqi PoW claims that a civilian translator, hired to work in the prison, raped a male juvenile prisoner. He said: 'They covered all the doors with sheets. I heard the screaming ... and the female soldier was taking pictures.'

The US torture pictures were taken by members of the US army's Military Police Brigade. Brigadier General Mark Kimmitt, Deputy Director of Coalition Operations in Iraq, said he was 'appalled'. He added: 'These are our fellow soldiers. They wear the same uniform as us, and they let their fellow soldiers down. Our soldiers could be taken prisoner as well – and we expect our soldiers to be treated well by the adversary, by the enemy – and if we can't hold ourselves up as an example of how to treat people with dignity and respect ... we can't ask that other nations do that to our soldiers as well. This is wrong. This is reprehensible.'

These soldiers weren't mavericks. Some of the accused claim they acted on the orders of military intelligence and the CIA, and that some of the torture sessions were under the control of mercenaries hired by the US to conduct interrogations. Two 'civilian contract' organisations which took part in interrogations at Abu Ghraib are linked to the Bush administration. The California-based Titan Corporation – linked to former CIA Director James Woolsey – says it is 'a leading provider of solutions and services for national security'. In 2003–04, it gave nearly $40,000 to George W Bush's Republican Party. Titan supplied translators to the military. CACI International Inc. describes its aim as helping 'America's intelligence community in the war on terrorism'. Richard Armitage, the Deputy US Secretary of State, sat on CACI's board.

No civilians, however, are facing charges as military law does not apply to them. Colonel Jill Morgenthaler, from CentCom, said that at least one civilian contractor was accused along with six soldiers of mistreating prisoners. However, it was left to the contractor to 'deal with him'. The contract companies vigorously deny any wrongdoing. One civilian interrogator did admit to army investigators, however, that he had 'unintentionally' broken several tables during interrogations as he was trying to 'fear-up' detainees.

Lawyers for some accused say their GI clients are scapegoats for a rogue prison system, which allowed mercenaries to give orders to serving soldiers. A military report said private contractors were at times supervising the interrogations.

CACI Vice-president Jody Brown said: 'The company supports the Army's investigation and acknowledges that CACI personnel in Iraq volunteered to be interviewed by army officials in connection with the investigation. The company has received no indication that any CACI employee was involved in any alleged improper conduct with Iraqi prisoners. Nonetheless, CACI has initiated an independent investigation.'

However, military investigators said: 'A CACI investigator's contract was terminated because he allowed and/or instructed military police officers who were not trained in interrogation techniques to facilitate interrogations which were neither authorized nor in accordance with regulations.'

One of the US soldiers involved in the abuse was reservist Staff Sergeant Chip Frederick – the equivalent of a part-time British Territorial Army squaddie. In civvy street, he was a prison warder in Virginia. Frederick said he would plead not guilty and blame the army for the torture at Abu Ghraib. 'We had no support, no training whatsoever,' he said, claiming he had never even been shown the Geneva Convention. 'I kept asking my chain of command for certain things like rules and regulations and it just wasn't happening.'

Frederick also blamed the intelligence services for encouraging the brutality. Among the agencies coming to the prison were 'military intelligence', says Frederick, adding: 'We had all kinds of other government agencies, FBI, CIA.'

In letters and emails home, he wrote: 'Military intelligence has encouraged and told us "Great job".' He added: 'They usually don't allow others to watch them interrogate. But since they like the way I run the prison, they have made an exception ... We help getting [the PoWs] to talk with the way we handle them ... We've had a very high rate with our style of getting them to break. They usually end up breaking within hours.'

Frederick said prisoners were made to live in cramped, windowless cells with no clothes, running water or toilet facilities for up to three days. Others were held for 60 days before interrogation. He said one prisoner with a mental health condition was 'shot with non-lethal rounds'. An interrogator told soldiers to 'stress one prisoner out as much as possible [as] he wanted to talk to him the next day'. Frederick also said one prisoner was 'stressed so bad that the man passed away'. Prisoners were covered in lice and some had tuberculosis. None was allowed to pray. Frederick said all this was sanctioned by superiors. Frederick, unlike the contractor mercenaries, was looking at jail and being thrown out of the army. His lawyer, Gary Myers, said: 'The elixir of power, the elixir of believing that you're helping the CIA, for God's sake, when you're from a small town in Virginia, that's intoxicating. And so, good guys sometimes do things believing that they are being of assistance and helping a just cause ... and helping people they view as important.' Where have we heard that before? At the Nuremburg trials, perhaps?

Kimmitt admitted: 'I'd like to sit here and say that these are the only prisoner abuse cases that we're aware of, but we know that there have been others.'

Describing the images of abuse as an 'atrocity', Abdel Bari Atwan, editor of the newspaper *Al-Quds Al-Arabi*, said: 'The liberators are worse than the dictators.' His sentiments have been echoed around the world. It is hard to find a country or agency that hasn't condemned the torture of Iraqi prisoners. From the Red Cross to the UN and from Amnesty to the coalition's loyal 'deputy in the Pacific', the Australian Premier John Howard, the world is united in horror against the actions of the coalition forces.

The awful cost of these acts of barbarism by Britain and America is summed up by ex-US Marine Lieutenant Colonel Bill Cowan: 'We went to Iraq to stop things like this from happening, and, indeed, here they are happening under our tutelage ... If we don't tell this story, these kind of things will continue, and we'll end up getting paid back 100 or 1,000 times over.'

Chip Frederick was the highest-ranking soldier from Abu Ghraib to be charged with 'abusing and humiliating' detainees. He received eight years' imprisonment in October 2004. Another accused soldier, Jeremy Sivits, is serving a one-year sentence after pleading guilty to three charges. Armin Cruz, 24, a military intelligence soldier, was also sentenced in September 2004 to eight months.

Frederick blamed his chain of command, telling the court that prisoners were forced to submit to public nudity and degrading treatment 'for military intelligence purposes'. He testified he was given no training or support in supervising detainees and only learned of regulations against mistreatment after the abuses occurred. He said that when he discussed matters about detainees with his commanders, 'they told me to do what MI told me to do', referring to military intelligence.

Lynndie England got three years for her part in the torture of Iraqi prisoners. She's now taking bible classes at her prison – the Naval Consolidated Brig Miramar in San Diego – and blames everything on her former Abu Ghraib lover and baby-daddy Charles Graner, who got ten years.

There have been hundreds of allegations of abuse made against US troops in Afghanistan, Iraq and Guantanamo Bay. Those appointed by Donald Rumsfeld as part of an 'independent' review of US detention procedures said that there was both 'institutional and personal responsibility at higher levels' for the torture. In other words, the soldiers who carried out these acts in Abu Ghraib were right at the bottom of the food chain. Those really culpable were much, much higher up.

The Department of Justice's Office of Legal Counsel said in August 2002, with its mind focused on al-Qaeda fighters and Taliban soldiers in Afghanistan, that for an act to constitute torture, it must be 'specifically intended to inflict severe physical or mental pain and suffering that is difficult to endure'. That very loose definition of what it means to degrade a fellow human being was another key moment in the journey towards accepted and institutionalised torture.

The military intelligence battalion which arrived in Abu Ghraib in July and August 2003 cut its teeth in Afghanistan where America had ruled that the Geneva Conventions weren't worth the paper they were written on. In Afghanistan, the military intelligence troops worked hard using brutal interrogation techniques, unhindered by international law, in support of Special Forces. When they came to Abu Ghraib, they simply took their torture practices with them – an import from Geneva-free Afghanistan – even though America accepted that Iraqis were protected by international law. Two soldiers with military intelligence in Abu Ghraib were known by commanders to have been suspects in the 'questionable death' of a detainee in Afghanistan. Those same soldiers went on to lead interrogations in Iraq and to be part of the abuse of Iraqi detainees.

By mid-September 2003 military intelligence 'started directing nakedness at Abu Ghraib ... to humiliate and break down detainees', the US military report into the abuse says. Sleep deprivation also came with the military intelligence squad from Afghanistan. The military police were told to keep the prisoners awake so they decided the best way to keep the Iraqis on their feet was to strip them and throw cold water on them.

At least five detainees died in US custody – and that's according to the people Rumsfeld appointed to investigate the atrocities committed under his watch. A further 23 detainee deaths are still under investigation – 20 in Iraq, and three in Afghanistan. But I think we all know that we are looking at the tip of a very large iceberg.

Rumsfeld's independent panel to review Pentagon detention operations said that the Defense Secretary's own 'augmented' interrogation techniques created a situation which made the tricks of 'Guantanamo migrate to Afghanistan and Iraq where they were neither limited or safe-guarded ... Policies approved for use on al-Qaeda and Taliban detainees, who were not afforded the protection of the Geneva Conventions, now applied to detainees who did fall under the Geneva Convention protections.'

Although, the Guantanamo – Gitmo in US army-jargon – techniques should never have been used in Iraq, the US government knew what was happening and ignored the on-going atrocities. They knew because by at least the autumn of 2003, the International Committee for the Red Cross (ICRC) had told the US government what was going on in Abu Ghraib after visiting the jail. One ICRC report said that MPs were con-ducting 'acts of humiliation such as [detainees] being made to stand naked ... with women's underwear over their head, while being laughed at by guards, including female guards, and sometimes photographed in this position'. But no action was taken until the media rumbled the scandal. The ICRC visited Abu Ghraib three times between September 16, 2003 and January 31, 2004. Military commanders were told twice about 'serious violations of international humanitarian law and of the Geneva Conventions'.

The US army's own investigations into what was happening at Abu Ghraib make for disturbing but monotonous reading. The army found that some 27 military intelligence personnel 'requested, encouraged, condoned or solicited military police to abuse detainees and/or partici-pated in detainee abuse'. Four civilian contractors also took part in abuse. The US army added that 'most, though not all, of the violent and sexual abuses occurred separately from scheduled interrogations and did not focus on persons held for intelligence purposes'. In other words, it was sadistic and pointless. However, many interrogators who abused detainees during questioning did so as they believed their crimes – such as stripping a prisoner naked and threatening him with savage dogs – were condoned by the government and the military.

There was, according to US military investigations, 'confusion about what interrogation techniques were authorised'. This was compounded by a 'failure to effectively screen, certify, and then integrate contractor interrogators/analysts/linguists'. These contractors, and agencies such as the CIA, were working in Abu Ghraib to 'different rules regarding inter-rogation and detention operations' and 'encouraged soldiers to deviate from prescribed techniques'. The use of contractors exacerbated the problems caused by the lack of trained military personnel within Abu Ghraib – a fact which itself contributed to the level of abuse and torture. The command structure was also weak, with little or no discipline for uncouth grunts like Frederick and England.

Abu Ghraib was a legal black hole just like Guantanamo. A report by official US military investigators says: 'At Abu Ghraib, detainees were accepted from other agencies and services [for that read the CIA and Special Forces] without proper in-processing, accountability or documentation. These detainees were referred to as "ghost detainees" ... The number of ghost detainees temporarily held at Abu Ghraib and the audit trail of personnel responsible for capturing, medically screening, safeguarding and properly interrogating the "ghost detainees" cannot be determined.' That means people were simply 'disappeared' off the streets of occupied Iraq and stuck in Abu Ghraib – there wasn't even a bit of paper to prove they were there. It's a bit like Chile or Argentina during the bad old fascist days of the 1970s. Abu Ghraib, says the report, was 'an environment that would appear to condone depravity and degradation rather than humane treatment of detainees'. And this from investigators who were military top brass themselves.

Military investigators listed some 44 incidents of abuse at Abu Ghraib. Here's a sample of some of the acts uncovered in their secret report to the Pentagon:

> On October 7, 2003 three military intelligence officers sexually assaulted a female detainee. One stayed outside her cell, the other held her hands and the third started to kiss her. She was taken to another cell where she was shown a naked male prisoner and told that if she didn't 'co-operate' with the soldiers that she'd end up in the same state. She was then taken back to her cell, forced to kneel and ordered to raise her arms while one of the soldiers took her top off. Thankfully, when she started to cry the soldiers just swore at her and left saying they would be back for her at night. Pictures also exist of a female prisoner being made to lift up her top and expose her breasts.
>
> On October 25, three detainees were stripped, cuffed together and forced to lie on the ground and simulate sex with each other. This happened repeatedly over a number of days. They were photographed each time. The abuse was carried out by military police, but Lynndie England – the Irma Grese of Abu Ghraib – said 'MI

[military intelligence] instructed them [the military police] to rough them up'. The MPs would go on to improve on this routine, making six or more prisoners at a time clamber, naked, on top of each other, bags on heads, into human pyramids. None of these detainees were part of the resistance, they were all being held for civilian criminal offences.

Two days later, another detainee was stripped naked for nine days. He had pepper thrown in his face and was beaten for half an hour by military police. He recalls being hit with a chair until it broke and punched and kicked until he lost consciousness. Military intelligence said that military police officers like Staff Sergeant Fredrick should 'fear-up' the prisoner as they felt he was withholding information. Fredrick liked to tell prisoners 'Come with me, piggy' when he took them to 'the hole' – the dark, solitary confinement cell in Abu Ghraib which was used for days on end. Fredrick later told military intelligence soldiers after one torture session: 'I want to thank you guys, because up until a week or two ago, I was a good Christian.'

Also in October, a 'high value' prisoner was 'left naked in his cell for extended periods, cuffed in stressful positions [such as being 'high cuffed' to the top bunk of a bed frame] left with a bag over his head for extended periods, and denied bedding and blankets ... made to bark like a dog, being forced to crawl on his stomach while MPs spit and urinated on him, and being struck causing unconsciousness ... tied to a window in his cell and forced to wear women's underwear on his head ... forced to lie down while MPs jumped onto his back and legs ... beaten with a broom and a chemical light was broken and poured over his body ... during this abuse a police stick was used to sodomise the detainee and two female MPs were hitting him, throwing a ball at his penis and taking photographs'. The prisoner was also hit so severely in the ear by a contract interpreter that he needed several stitches.

On November 4, a detainee under CIA control who had been captured by a Navy SEAL team died in custody. His death occurred after he was taken to the shower room by two CIA agents. About 45 minutes later the MPs were told he was dead. Witnesses said he had a sandbag on his head. 'The body was placed in a body bag, packed in ice, and stored in the shower area ... the body was removed from Abu Ghraib the next day on a lit-ter to make it appear as if the detainee was only ill, thereby not drawing the attention of the Iraqi guards and detainees.' The prisoner died from a blood clot on the brain.

The rape of a 15-year-old boy. An adult detainee 'heard screaming and climbed to the top of his cell door to see over the sheet covering the door of the cell where the abuse was occurring. [The adult detainee] observed [a civilian contractor] who was wearing military uniform, raping the detainee. A female soldier was taking pictures.' Military investigators found that the description of the civilian contractor matched that of an interpreter working in the jail.

As I said earlier, the catalogue of abuse is numbing and revolting – it goes on and on and on. GIs trying to suffocate prisoners by holding their mouths and noses closed; prisoners thrown from the back of moving vehicles; guns pressed to their heads.

Religion was exploited in the same way as sex. One detainee was 'forced to eat pork' and had alcohol poured into his mouth. The same man was beaten on his broken leg, made to curse Islam and terrified with dogs. The Arab world has a distinctly different view of man's best friend than we in the west do. It's unusual in the Arab world to keep dogs as pets like Brits and Americans. Thus, Fido is more a fiend than a friend to them. An Egyptian journalist friend of mine once came round to my house for dinner and nearly passed out in terror when confronted with my idiotic pet spaniel trying to slobber on his hand. The US military understood this cultural quirk and were quick and happy to exploit it.

The same prisoner who was tormented with dogs was also threatened with rape. Like in all good torture camps, the doctors at Abu Ghraib were no better than the guards. One prisoner was fitted with a catheter but was not given a bag; his wounds were bleeding and the colonel who was on duty as prison doctor refused to help the man.

The abuse of detainees with dogs started as soon as the animals arrived in Abu Ghraib on November 20, 2003. The dog teams came to Abu Ghraib on the instructions of Major General Geoffrey Miller from Guantanamo Bay. He'd been ordered by the US government to improve the quality of the intelligence coming from Iraqi detainees using his experience of dealing with captives in Guantanamo. In order to fulfil his job of Gitmo-ising Abu Ghraib for the US government he brought in the dogs. As a report by official US military investigators said: 'Interrogations at Abu Ghraib were also influenced by several documents that spoke of exploiting the Arab fear of dogs ... the use of dogs in interrogations to "fear-up" detainees was generally unquestioned.' On the first night the dogs arrived a detainee was bitten on the arm while being yelled at in his cell by a CACI interrogator. Dogs were used, in the words of Abu Ghraib soldiers, to 'go nuts' in the cell of two juveniles; a mentally ill detainee was also bitten; and dogs were used to rip up the bedding of detainees. Staff Sergeant Fredrick and other soldiers referred to the use of dogs to terrify prisoners as 'doggy dance sessions'.

The army could put no gloss on what happened in Abu Ghraib. Nudity as a punishment, said an official report by US military investigators, 'contributed to an escalating "dehumanisation" of the detainees and set the stage for additional and more severe abuses to occur'. Enforced nudity and abuses such as placing women's underwear on the heads of prisoners were part of what interrogators called 'ego-down' techniques. To you and me, that's using humiliation and degradation to totally break a captive. One MP log notes that a detainee 'was stripped down per MI [military intelligence] and he is neked (sic) and standing tall in his cell'. The trailer park vernacular gives some indication of the type of creatures that were running this torture chamber. Another detainee was made to wear a MRE (meals ready to eat) bag – an army rations pouch – over his genitals. He was then ordered to raise his arms so the bag fell away while two women interrogators watched.

One soldier told of the incessant level of sadistic violence used against prisoners. 'MPs were using detainees as practice dummies. They would hit the detainees as practice shots. They would apply strikes to their necks and knock them out. One detainee was so scared; the MPs held his head and told him everything would be alright, then they would strike him. The detainees would plead for mercy and the MPs thought it was all funny.'

Another said: 'The prisoners are captured by soldiers, taken from their familiar surroundings, blindfolded and put into a truck and brought to this place (Abu Ghraib); and then they are pushed down a hall with guards barking orders and thrown into a cell, naked; and that not knowing what was going to happen or what the guards might do caused them extreme fear.'

In one ghastly way, the prisoners in Abu Ghraib were luckier than many other victims of American power. At least a couple of hundred

War on Terror suspects have been 'rendered' to foreign governments by the US. That means a captured suspect is stuck on a plane after being kidnapped by the CIA and flown to a country like Egypt where they are disappeared, tortured and probably killed. British and American intelligence agencies then receive details of the inevitably bogus information that is extracted under torture. MI6 and the CIA also often assist in the interrogations by passing information about the suspects to their friendly torturers overseas. So many suspects have been 'rendered' that the CIA had to set up a covert chartered airline to deal with the numbers, and secret 'black site' prisons in former Soviet states in eastern Europe have also been established.

There was little place for decency under the new American 'paradigm' of prisoner detention. When the first Gitmo commander – Brigadier General Rick Baccus – proved too kind to prisoners, he was relieved of his duty. Baccus had given prisoners the Koran, special meals for Ramadan and cards explaining their rights.

That wasn't what Rumsfeld wanted, so after Baccus was given his marching orders, a new type of solider was brought in to run Gitmo – Major General Geoffrey Miller. Out went the Koran and halal chicken on holy days and in came hooding, stripping, dogs and the hole. When the insurgency really started to kick off in Iraq, Rumsfeld realised that he just wasn't getting the kind of intelligence he wanted. He was desperate for interrogations to yield info on where Saddam and the other top Ba'athists were hiding out. That just wasn't happening. So, Miller, after his raging success at Gitmo, was sent on his way to Iraq to beef up the interrogations process there.

Brigadier General Janis Karpinski, who was in charge of the military police unit in Abu Ghraib, describes a discussion with Miller which shows just how far up the chain of command the decision to humiliate and debase detainees went. He told her: 'At Guantanamo Bay we learned that the prisoners have to earn every single thing that they have.' Karpinski added: 'He said they are like dogs and if you allow them to believe at any point that they are more than a dog then you've lost control of them.'

Terror

If you beat a dog, it either lies down and dies or it bites you back. It's the abused child syndrome. If someone is weak and is beaten, raped and humiliated because of their weakness, then one day, when they finally have power, they themselves will become the abuser or the rapist. Over the years, I've interviewed many brutal criminals – killers, rapists, paedophiles – and nearly all of them were the victims of abuse themselves when they were young and defenceless. When they grew up they committed the very crimes that they had been made to endure upon others who were just as weak, young and defenceless as they once were. There seems to be something terrible in the human psyche that demands that we repay the suffering that we have experienced on innocent others.

We've already seen this abused child syndrome played out on the world's stage in the shape and history of the state of Israel. The Jewish people were treated monstrously in Europe for centuries and then faced with extermination at the hands of the Nazis. They were the ultimate victims – homeless, nation-less, unorganised, totally defenceless. They were abused by Hitler and his followers the way an innocent child would be tormented by a sadistic, psychopathic, murderous adult. When Hitler finally fell, the Jewish people were owed the world's support, friendship and assistance. The world had a debt to repay the Jewish people. They found a nation; they organised; they were able to defend themselves at last. But the abused child then grew up into a young adult. And then, with terrible inevitability, the young adult began to abuse those nearby who were weakest.

So, the world found itself with a new abused child on its hands – the homeless, nation-less, unorganised and totally defenceless Palestinian people.

Today, many people in the Arab and Muslim world are no longer prepared to hang around and wait to be turned into the next geo-political equivalent of an abused kid. They want an end to the abuse of the Palestinians and they don't want a taste of the same experiences that those in Gaza and Ramallah and Jenin have experienced. They've seen what kind of suffering is doled out to those in the Muslim world who are the weakest. They've watched America prop up Israel, the nation that has heaped humiliation on the Palestinian people, and it has terrified them. Their weakness, helplessness and anger has only one outlet – violence. But it's the violence of the weak and the terrified – the pyrrhic violence of the puniest kid in the playground who makes one last, desperate flying assault on the school bully, knowing that they will be hammered into the ground for their pains, but determined not to get beaten to a pulp without drawing some of the bully's blood first. Weakness and victimhood breed illogical, disturbed, mindless actions. So, the suicide bombs are strapped on; the hostages are taken; planes are blown up; car bombs wipe out civilians. The weak can't fight Apache helicopters and unmanned drones, but they can fly planes into buildings and kill hostages. They can think up – *in extremis* – the kind of nightmares that even a bully like the west – like America, Britain or Israel – will blanch at. Abu Musab al-Zarqawi was one creature able to dream the nightmares of the west; a man who crawled inside the western mind like an invisible worm and found our darkest fears, found ways to manipulate us that we never contemplated before. He used his unmeasured sickness and cruelty to expose our own callousness and violence.

Al-Zarqawi has been behind the worst of the hostage taking in Iraq. It was he who took hostages like Ken Bigley, the Briton, and Nick Berg, the American, and turned their deaths into a perverted spectator sport on television; and he who used the suffering of these innocent hostages as a means to terrorise the entire western world.

Of course, the greatest victims of people like al-Zarqawi and his ilk were, and still are, the people of Iraq who every week die in their hundreds at the hands of al-Qaeda inspired murder squads and suicide bombers. We will come to the horror that this sectarian civil war has brought to the Iraqi people later; this section, however, is meant to appeal directly to your self-interest, not higher values such as empathy for the suffering of fellow human beings in Iraq. Your government created the circumstances which unleashed terror from the likes of al-Zarqawi that is directed straight at you. When the al-Qaeda franchise in Iraq chops off the head of a westerner like Ken Bigley, the assassins are symbolically killing you, your children, your parents, your partner, your friends and your next-door neighbours. Your government made you the target of hatred from the al-Zarqawis of this world. And, as we know from the events in London of July 7, 2005, such hatred is shared by men and women in Europe who, unlike the followers of al-Zarqawi, are close enough at hand to actually take your life.

Prior to his death, al-Zarqawi's words and deeds were disseminated by his own 'information department'. His organisation was once known as Tawhid wal Jihad (Monotheism and Holy War) until it swore allegiance to Osama bin Laden in the autumn of 2004 and took the name The al-Qaeda Organisation of Jihad in the Land of the Two Rivers – the rivers being Iraq's Tigris and Euphrates. Common shorthand for the organisation is now 'the al-Qaeda organisation in Iraq'. It's the biggest franchise leased by the McDonald's of Terror.

The west has the uncanny ability to portray its worst enemies as mindless thugs or fanatics. We seem to wish to avoid any complexity or attempt at understanding when it comes to getting a handle on the people who hate us and would kill us. If a nation has no depth of understanding of its enemies then it will never beat them. Beating an enemy does not mean merely killing a figurehead like al-Zarqawi. For every militia leader killed and left like a bloody stain on the ground, there are plenty of second-in-commands waiting in line to take their place.

Al-Zarqawi was constantly described as some semi-literate psycho who had scrambled out of Jordan's criminal underworld slums and then somehow, miraculously, found himself as the leader of one of the world's most effective terror groups. Never has such a portrayal been so wrong or so misguided.

Take one of al-Zarqawi's most detailed propaganda statements – which came in the form of an audiotape released in July 2004 under the title 'Important commandments to the Mujahidin, and in reply to the defeatists, from the amir of Tawhid wal Jihad, Sheikh Abu Musab al-Zarqawi'. This was not the work of some hoodlum; this was the work of a man who was as much a natural in the field of propaganda as he was in the field of terror. Al-Zarqawi combined Goebbels' modern mastery of mass communications with Himmler's barbarous gift for boundless sadism. He had as much an understanding of modernity and the 21st-century psyche as he did of theocracy and the medieval mindset of the prophet Mohammad's seventh century.

Al-Zarqawi began the taped speech with a quote from the Koran: 'So lose no heart, nor fall into despair, for ye must gain mastery if ye are true in faith. If a wound hath touched you, be sure similar wound hath touched the others.'

In this tape, al-Zarqawi shifted between quoting freely and at length from the Koran to recalling the words of Islam's greatest thinkers and poets, to analysing the policies of current Muslim leaders and to powerful bursts of his own rhetoric, which were at times punctuated with his own tears, his voice breaking as he called the faithful to Jihad or recounted the nobility of patriotic resistance. This was no thug; he may have been a sadistic, brutal psychopath and a religious extremist, but he was not a thick-headed boot-boy lacking in intellect. His intellect, coupled with his perverted bloodthirstiness, made him the most terrible of opponents. If a western terrorist released tapes that referenced the Bible,

Plato, Kant, Shakespeare, Darwin and Keats and critiqued the behaviour of Jacques Chirac, Tony Blair and George Bush, we wouldn't dismiss them as a creature who was no more than a snarling brute, would we? Al-Zarqawi understood the west almost as well as he understood his own culture; in fact, he probably understood the west better than most westerners do – and that is what gave him his edge.

His most effective verbal assaults were levelled against his critics within the Muslim world – the scholars and politicians who denounced him in tandem with the west. 'Being submissive slaves,' he said, 'they indeed cannot picture themselves killing the US master. Yes, they have imbibed the milk of humiliation from the breasts of their mothers and it lies deep in their veins.' His wrath was also directed at the 'infidel crusader media' for 'brainwashing the Muslims'.

Al-Zarqawi made very clear that those who fell into his hands as hostages would never see the light of day again. He quoted the response of the first Caliph of Islam, Abu Bakr – for whom, al-Zarqawi says, 'I would have given my father and mother' – when he was offered ransom money in return for the sparing of an 'infidel' prisoner. Abu Bakr said: 'Kill him because killing a man from the polytheists is preferable to me than all other things.'

Al-Zarqawi then said that 'some mediators tried to save this lout [he is referring to Nick Berg whom, it is said, he personally beheaded] and offered us whatever sums of money we could ask for. Despite our dire need for money for use for Jihad we preferred to avenge our sisters and nation'.

When al-Zarqawi mentioned 'our sisters' he was making a direct reference to women prisoners detained in Abu Ghraib. In his public statements, al-Zarqawi often justified the ghastly murders he committed as revenge for the torture of Muslims in Abu Ghraib. By our misdeeds in Abu Ghraib, we gave men like al-Zarqawi the excuse, the cause to hide behind, or perhaps, even, the moral justification – in their minds at least – which they needed in order to capture, mutilate and kill innocent westerners.

'Where is my nation?' he cried out on the tape. 'Can my nation not see what is happening to Muslims in Iraq, Palestine, Afghanistan, Indonesia, the Chechen Republic and others? Can my nation do anything apart from weeping and crying, staging peaceful demonstrations and issuing denunciations and condemnations? ... Woe to you, my nation. Your honour is in the hands of the worshippers of the cross.'

Al-Zarqawi – as well as being a psychopath's psychopath, a terrorist's terrorist and a propagandist's propagandist – was also a religious maniac of the same stripe that the Roman Catholic Church would have been proud of during the Spanish Inquisition. He hated Christians, the way a Klansman hates blacks or a Nazi hates Jews. We created a creature like this. Without our actions, he would have been a squalid little fanatic, albeit a highly intelligent and apparently quite charismatic one, spouting his hateful drivel to a few desperate, lonely followers. Instead, we set up the moral vacuum which allowed him to become a hero to radical Islamists the world over. Remember all those warnings by military and intelligence analysts in the run-up to the March 2003 invasion that the UK and US would turn Saddam-free Iraq into a chaotic haven for anti-western fundamentalists? Well, the free-style terror developed by al-Zarqawi and his militia proved that those guys deserved a hike in their pay-grade. Al-Zarqawi wasn't content in simply getting the west out of the Middle East. What he wanted – and what his legion of followers still want – is 'to conquer the White House, the Kremlin and London'. We created a creature that we simply had to kill, because if we didn't kill him, he'd just go on and on killing us. It was the Frankenstein effect. Our actions rendered any form of peaceful negotiation with our worst enemies impossible. We forced ourselves into a position in which we had to be violent rather than diplomatic – where we had to follow our most brutal instincts rather than our higher ones. As the story of al-Zarqawi's life, his killings and his own death at the hands of the west shows, morally, everyone involved in this conflict is in a lose–lose situation.

Just seconds before he decapitated Nick Berg, al-Zarqawi addressed 'the mothers and wives of American soldiers'. Slipping the murder weapon into the light of day, he said: 'You will see nothing from us except corpse after corpse and casket after casket of those slaughtered in this fashion.'

In response to his unbelievable acts, the western press threw insults at al-Zarqawi – that he was a 'medieval barbarian', a 'headhunter' and a 'demon'. That must have been music to his ears. As long as his enemies in the west kept reducing him to the status of a bogeyman, they would continue to underestimate him. And anyone who underestimated a man like al-Zarqawi did so at his own risk.

Al-Zarqawi was skilful enough to play a macabre cat-and-mouse game of international relations with the life of the British hostage, Kenneth Bigley – keeping his victim alive for weeks, dragging out the

horror for the British public and putting enormous pressure on the Blair
government through the phased release of statements and videos. I
spoke to British intelligence officers – both current and retired – and a
number of men who have been volunteers in the IRA, to try to understand the nature of the dance of death that al-Zarqawi embarked upon
with the British people during the Bigley crisis.

They were united in their opinion that al-Zarqawi was a 'Prince of
Terror'. Some thought his name might have been used as a blanket identity by a collection of leading al-Qaeda figures in Iraq to ramp up the
terror and mythology that he fomented. One intelligence officer said
that al-Zarqawi's form of terror 'operated a bit like a McDonald's franchise. In Argentina or France or the UK, McDonald's will serve up slight
variations on the original to reflect the tastes of the country. Groups like
al-Zarqawi's do the same. They share the overall ethos of al-Qaeda and
take inspiration from it, but they are subtly different and fairly
autonomous.'

Like all the al-Qaeda affiliated groups, al-Zarqawi's outfit had intelligence officers who made up for their lack of resources and funding
with an enviable vision and tenacity. The Bigley kidnapping was almost
a textbook example on how to run a psyop – intelligence jargon for a
'psychological operation'.

Al-Zarqawi's understanding of British politics, and its press and culture is very sophisticated and very nuanced. Martin Ingram, the cover
name of a former British military intelligence officer who was engaged
in 'the dirty war' against the IRA, said, in the midst of the Bigley hostage
crisis, before the Liverpudlian was killed on tape: 'Al-Zarqawi's intelligence cell is quite something. They understand the British psyche. They
quickly killed the two American hostages [who were also taken captive
with Bigley] as they knew that Bush would make no deals, but they
milked the British hostage-taking for all it was worth.

'They seem to know how our newspapers work. They couldn't have
wished for this amount of publicity. They realised Tony Blair was in a
precarious position, as many voters and many of his backbenchers
oppose the war. They chose the right side of the Atlantic on which to
cause a storm.

'They even exploited the tensions between the UK and the US. When
the Americans stepped in to say that there would be no release of prisoners [al-Zarqawi wanted female prisoners released from detention in
Iraq in return for the hostages' lives], it added to the resentment that

some people in Britain felt towards America.

'Al-Zarqawi took the British people onto a plateau of terror that we had never reached before the kidnapping of Bigley. He really is our worst nightmare come true. Quite simply, this man doesn't give a damn what happens or who dies.'

Ingram's view tallied with those of other intelligence officers, who said that we needed to see al-Zarqawi as the leader of a 'death cult', not a conventional terrorist. Al-Zarqawi's name, Musab, was taken from Musab bin Umayer – a follower of the prophet Muhammed – who is a kind of patron saint for suicide bombers. Before his own end, al-Zarqawi referred to his organisation as the 'battalion of death', and often talked of loving death as much as the west loved life. It is as if he took the western blueprint of a monster and modelled himself on it to the letter.

The west was also faced with the almost impossible task of properly penetrating organisations like al-Zarqawi's – not just because of the loose cell structure used, but also because British and American intelligence didn't have the men on the ground in Iraq who were capable of either joining the organisation as infiltrated agents or of 'turning' current members into spies. It's a bleak truth, but al-Zarqawi's intelligence on the west was often far better than the west's intelligence on him.

The horrific nature of his crimes meant few were willing to turn informer, despite the $25 million bounty the US offered for him. 'If that kind of money had been put on the head of one of the IRA's top commanders,' says Ingram, 'we'd have had him in a week. But we are dealing with an alien psyche, and that means we have to prepare to be in this for the long haul.'

Outfits like the one al-Zarqawi headed up before his death have a wide reach, so the long haul might be very long indeed.

The bitterest irony for families like the Bigleys is that al-Zarqawi was in fact a creature of the western powers' action. If the US–UK coalition hadn't gone into Iraq, it wouldn't have become a vortex for killers like him. His terror – of assassination, suicide bombing, kidnap and beheading – would never have existed without our terror – of civilian bombings, invasion, occupation, detention and torture. We are all terrorists – that's the truth of this war. A pre-war assessment by Britain's Joint Intelligence Committee found that al-Qaeda and associated groups continue to represent by far the greatest threat to western interests, and that threat would be heightened by military action against Iraq'.

During the worst days of the Bigley hostage crisis, when some of Bigley's relatives were saying that Blair had 'blood on his hands', al-Zarqawi was able to keep the Prime Minister literally and politically boxed in. The Prime Minister was hardly visible for days on end, fearing that a wrong statement could either cause Bigley's death or be seen as an attempt at negotiation with a terrorist. Not talking to terrorists is something of a matter of phoney dogma within the British political Establishment. The Tories in government pretended that they didn't talk to the IRA, when in actual fact they had been negotiating with Republican leaders for years.

The intelligence services say that al-Zarqawi's grasp of the differences between the UK and US press was also probably more sophisticated than that of many Britons and Americans. The UK press has a rapacious reputation for picking events to pieces. British newspaper journalists are renowned for going into 'feeding frenzy' mode when big stories crop up. American newspaper journalists, on the other hand, are much more sedate – even plodding. It is a difference that al-Zarqawi exploited with cruel zeal. The British press is also unlikely to follow the demands of the government when it comes to self-censorship. There is no way that UK newspapers or broadcasters would agree not to air images of the coffins of British servicemen draped in Union Jacks as they arrived home from Iraq, in the same way that the US media complied with requests not to show images of the Stars and Stripes-clad caskets of dead GIs. Likewise, the desire of the UK government to have kidnappings played down in Britain is never reflected in press coverage in the same way that similar government wishes would be respected, or at least listened to and taken into consideration, in America. Al-Zarqawi knew these subtle differences well and manipulated them with sadistic panache.

By keeping Bigley alive for weeks on end before brutally finishing him off, al-Zarqawi pushed the UK media into near-hysteria and kept the pressure cranked up to the max on Blair. Every day that the hostage drama continued made Blair look cruel, remote, not in control, at the beck and call of America and cowardly. Ahmad al-Rikaby, founder of Baghdad's first talk radio station, described the UK coverage as 'blood shows', adding: '[The publicity] is helping them to recruit more members to terrorist groups such as al-Qaeda.' You can also be sure that the publicity achieved another al-Zarqawi aim: to make sure that Brits who wanted to hold onto their heads either got out of Iraq quick or decided not to go in the first place.

Peter Preston, former editor of *The Guardian*, said British papers needed to be 'more muted'. Comparing US and UK coverage of the hostage crisis, he said: '[The US press] have not actually not reported it, but I think the *Washington Post* put it on page 27. That's the kind of mid-way I think we ought to be thinking about.'

Former members of the IRA whom I also spoke to during Bigley's capture said that while al-Zarqawi's actions were disgusting and beyond the pale, they were also 'tactically brilliant'. One said: 'If you want to terrorise the UK, that is the best way to do it.'

Kevin Fulton, the pseudonym of a British soldier who served undercover inside the IRA as a double agent, said: 'A good terrorist knows what makes his enemy tick and will do whatever he can to exploit it. Al-Zarqawi knew that killing one innocent person was worth the lives of many soldiers in terms of the effect it would have on the UK. The idea was to scare the shit out of people. It was shock-and-awe on his terms and it worked.

'When a soldier dies, we hear little of it in the UK. But for many weeks the Bigley hostage-taking was front-page news. Al-Zarqawi put Blair's balls in a vice. Whatever happened, he was going to win. The IRA just played at being terrorists compared to guys like him. He was the real thing.'

Ian Stephen, one of the UK's most esteemed forensic psychologists on whom the TV series *Cracker* was based, said al-Zarqawi's personality showed strong 'classic psychopathic' traits, not least of which was the fact that he was said to have personally decapitated some of his victims.

'He wanted to be in total control,' Stephen said. 'He looked to the world and saw that he could be more powerful than other leaders. Stringing a tragedy out simply added to his power.

'He knew that he was splitting the UK and pitting people against the Prime Minister. Bringing down a government is the ultimate power. Within a small group like this [al-Zarqawi had just a few hundred active militiamen] the leader can often become God-like to his followers.'

Dr Magnus Ranstrop, a terrorism expert at St Andrews University, said al-Zarqawi had shown that he could take out high-profile targets – such as Laurence Foley, the US diplomat assassinated in Jordan, and Izzadine Saleem, head of Iraq's governing council – and could also use low-profile targets such as hostages for huge propaganda coups.

'He wanted to create massive debate on the British contribution to the coalition,' said Ranstrop, 'and influence public opinion. He knew that psychological warfare was one of the strongest weapons in his arsenal.'

At its very end, the Bigley hostage-taking turned into the final reel of a video nasty horror film – compounding the revulsion and terror that the British people felt. Bigley managed to escape for around half an hour on the day he died. Like the last minutes of a slasher movie, Bigley ran for his life, dressed in an orange jumpsuit, fleeing to God knows where in a place he neither knew nor understood, pursued by men who would behead him live on TV if they got hold of him. As we know, they caught Bigley and recorded his murder on videotape after making him beg Blair once more for his life.

British military intelligence were actively hunting al-Zarqawi. In fact, there is some suspicion that intelligence could have played a role in aiding Bigley's temporary escape – perhaps even recruiting someone connected loosely to al-Zarqawi's outfit to assist in the getaway plan. Unlike the Americans, the British have decades – centuries even – of expertise in infiltrating 'domestic terror groups' like the IRA. Organisations like the Force Research Unit (FRU), a wing of British military intelligence, took part in the hunt for al-Zarqawi. The members of such units played a significant role in the 'Dirty War' in Ulster which saw the British army using members of loyalist terror gangs like the Ulster Defence Association as proxies to murder members of the IRA and other leading Catholic and Republican figures. The FRU also recruited senior members of the IRA and allowed them to continue carrying out terrorist operations so that they could keep their cover and remain in the Republican movement as key sources without being identified as informers. As Ireland has taught the UK: to defeat those you consider terrorists, you need to behave like a terrorist – and that means any military victory is accompanied by a moral defeat.

A channel of negotiation was opened between al-Zarqawi's organisation and the British in Baghdad during the last days of Ken Bigley's life. That was a bad idea on al-Zarqawi's behalf. One intelligence source told me that as a result of al-Zarqawi exposing himself – through the use of an intermediary to talk to the British in Baghdad, as well as in his public pronouncements on the internet and in audio and videotapes – he allowed the coalition to start to build up a 'first base' intelligence profile on him.

Any contact from an emissary of al-Zarqawi would be a vital intelligence foothold for organisations like British military intelligence or MI6. From surveillance on this 'first point of contact' – an al-Zarqawi go-between, say – the intelligence services could then build up a picture of the go-between's friends and associates, and of their friends and associates. The thinking was that this 'intelligence ripple' would eventually lead to al-Zarqawi himself. As we know, al-Zarqawi was eventually located and killed – or rather martyred, as he and his followers and sympathisers would say – but his death just created even more zealots and potential al-Zarqawis, and did little or no damage to the al-Qaeda in Iraq movement. In fact, al-Qaeda in Iraq has a new leader, Abu Ayyub al-Masri, and he, like his predecessor, is happily passing the time executing captives on tape and proselytising for Jihad.

The 'good guy' thinking within British intelligence was jolted massively by the actions of al-Zarqawi. Prior to al-Zarqawi being killed, one intelligence source – who has always described himself to me as 'one of the guys in the white hats' – suggested that the UK and US should take al-Zarqawi's own family hostage. Their whereabouts in Jordan has long been known to the British. 'We should parade them on TV and if he doesn't comply with our demands then we should start killing them – or throwing them alive out of helicopters over Baghdad.'

When I asked him why the west would do this when such actions would cut all moral ground from beneath Britain and America, he said: 'What moral ground? Have you forgotten about Abu Ghraib and Guantanamo Bay?'

In early June 2006, al-Zarqawi's story reached its inevitable conclusion. Although al-Qaeda in Iraq was still pretty much unpenetrated by western intelligence, al-Zarqawi was living on borrowed time. He'd been the poster boy for al-Qaeda in Iraq for three years and his organisation had claimed thousands of innocent Iraqi lives. In turn, these killings had created tens of thousands of ordinary Iraqis who would have given their own lives to see al-Zarqawi rubbed out in revenge for the deaths of their loved ones. Also, over the years, more and more members of his militia had been captured or killed, yielding the coalition forces valuable snippets of intelligence on his activities. Just a month before al-Zarqawi was killed, one of his lieutenants, Ziad Khalaf Raja al-Karbouly, was captured by Jordanian intelligence officers. It's thought that he may have given up information that helped in the pinpointing of al-Zarqawi shortly afterwards.

It appears that on June 7, 2006, Iraqi civilians spotted al-Zarqawi's right-hand man and spiritual advisor, Sheikh Abd al-Rahman, entering a safe house north-east of Baghdad in an orchard near the town of

Baquba and tipped off the authorities. American F-16s dropped two 500lb bombs on the building. The five other people in the property – including a child – were killed instantly, but al-Zarqawi survived briefly, although he was terribly wounded. He died not long after the attack on his base, and the Americans released pictures of his bloated corpse to the world.

Western newspapers and TV stations reacted to al-Zarqawi's death as if it presaged the end of hostilities in Iraq, but even President Bush was muted when it came to hyping the significance of the assassination. 'A war is not won with the death of one person,' he said. Bush and Blair knew well that the human meat grinder in Iraq would continue to mince up lives and bodies for years to come, and so were loath to look too cheery about the prospects of less bloodless times in Iraq now that their bogeyman-in-chief was dead. They also knew that there were plenty of seasoned, ruthless men in the al-Qaeda franchise in Iraq who were more than capable of filling al-Zarqawi's shoes almost immediately.

Bush and Blair were right to be relatively meek. Since the death of al-Zarqawi, attacks across Iraq have actually increased. The country is now in the grip of the sectarian conflict that al-Zarqawi helped create even more than it was when he was alive. Regardless of his death, al-Zarqawi 'won'. He achieved martyrdom at the hands of Americans, lasting fame within the pantheon of Islamic extremism, and he was able to use the sins of the US and the UK as an excuse to launch his own – now unending – version of a holy war which has left Iraq, and the democratic claims of Britain and America, nothing but a blood-soaked mess.

BRITAIN'S WAR CRIMINALS

or

Winning hearts and minds in Basra with the boys from Blighty

It wasn't just the Americans who steeped themselves in pain and perversion, carrying out acts of torture, murder and sexual abuse against Iraqi captives – British forces also committed wanton acts of cruelty.

By early May 2004, in the week that those terrible pictures from Abu Ghraib hit the headlines, my newspaper, the *Sunday Herald*, set out to try and establish just what the UK forces had been up to in occupied Iraq as well.

Here's what I found out. As of May 1, British soldiers were accused of killing at least seven prisoners as a result of mistreatment. The Ministry of Defence also admitted that a further three cases of torture and abuse, which did not result in death, were being investigated. Nine of the accused men were in the army and one was in the RAF.

An Amnesty International report into the abuse found that 'coalition forces appear in many cases to be using the climate of violence to justify violating the very human rights standards they are supposed to be upholding. Thousands of Iraqis have been detained, often in extremely harsh conditions, in unacknowledged centres. Many have been tortured or ill-treated; some have died as a result.'

I spoke to Susan Karim, an Iraqi exile who lives in Edinburgh, Scotland, and asked her what she thought about the crimes committed by UK forces. She said there wasn't much difference between the punishment she suffered at the hands of Saddam's torturers and the treatment of Iraqis today by the British and the Americans.

Karim was urinated on by Saddam's henchmen, and, like that poor Iraqi detainee in Abu Ghraib captured in those infamous photographs, she was forced into the Vietnam torture position and made to stand on a chair for hours on end after being warned that if she fell off she would be electrocuted. 'I can't believe it is happening all over again,' she said. 'Nothing has changed, only now there are different faces doing the torturing.'

By May 2004, at the time the Abu Ghraib scandal broke, Amnesty was already aware that at least four people had died in British custody in Basra – one, it was claimed, under torture. The toll of war crimes accusations against British soldiers, however, was to mount – considerably. And I was to learn that the UK government had known about the torture allegations all along, but done nothing.

Since the early days of the occupation, British soldiers have been accused of perpetrating acts of wanton cruelty against innocent Iraqis; of covering up torture sessions carried out against civilians, and of colluding together to avoid investigation.

Amnesty International's UK Media Director Lesley Warner has said that the human rights organisation's researchers have taken detailed 'witness testimony' stating that appalling beatings were inflicted on Iraqi prisoners and 'were conducted as part of the interrogation process by UK Armed Forces. The beatings were reportedly conducted in the presence of officers and in some cases officers actually took part in beating the detainees. These reports are particularly serious and underline the need for a full, independent inquiry into ... allegations of abuse in UK custody. Those responsible must be brought to justice.'

There are also horrific tales of prisoners being doused with urine and subjected to kick-boxing rituals while in UK custody. Laughing squaddies have apparently competed to see how far they could kick an Iraqi across a room. The beatings were allegedly carried out by 'shifts' of soldiers. Hooding, sleep deprivation and placing captives in 'stress positions' were reportedly also used as detention techniques by British forces. One detainee was allegedly threatened with burning petrol and a 14-year-old boy claimed to have been urinated on and had his head held over a stinking toilet.

Soldiers were even accused of turning captive, beaten prisoners into a grotesque 'choir'. Groups of Iraqis would be, by these accounts, placed together and then kicked one by one in the kidneys so that each man would let out a howl of pain. That was the choir.

A war crimes court martial is also underway relating to events which allegedly took place at 6am on September 14 2003, when UK forces in Basra began Operation Salerno, designed to uncover weapons caches.

Ten Iraqis were arrested that day by British soldiers from Camp Steven in Basra and allegedly tortured. The men had worked in the Hotel Ibn al-Haitham where weapons were found. The hotel receptionist and desk manager, Baha Musa, died in custody three days later. Musa's body was covered in blood and bruises. Another detainee was admitted to hospital in a critical condition suffering from renal failure. The raid was conducted by men from the Queen's Lancashire Regiment, now renamed the Duke of Lancaster's Regiment. Musa was 26 when he died. He was a single parent following his young wife's death from cancer and was raising his two sons aged three and five. The owner of the hotel had stored guns there; Musa, it is said, knew nothing about the arsenal.

Already, one soldier has pleaded guilty to treating Iraqi civilians inhumanely. This admission gives 35-year-old Corporal Donald Payne the proud distinction of being the first member of the British armed forces to be official classified as a war criminal, and puts him in the same category as a Nazi death camp guard. The charge he admitted to came under the International Criminal Court Act regarding the treatment of civilians protected by the Geneva Conventions.

Payne has denied the manslaughter of Baha Musa and a charge of obstructing justice. Six other soldiers are also charged. A lance-corporal and a private are accused of the war crime of treating civilians inhumanely. A sergeant is charged with assault causing actual bodily harm. A colonel is charged with negligently performing his duty - namely, failing to take proper steps to make sure that soldiers under his command did not abuse their captives. A major and a warrant officer from the Intelligence Corps are also charged with negligence of duty. The hearing will not be held before the International Criminal Court in the Hague but will be an ordinary court martial at an army barracks in the English countryside. A video of Corporal Payne and Iraqi detainees has been banned from being aired on British TV for fear that its contents will inflame anger against the UK in the muslim world.

By September 2004 – a year after Baha Musa's death – the British military had launched 131 investigations into deaths and injuries to Iraqis, in fatal incidents ranging from combat killings to deaths in detentions and in road accidents. Some 19 British soldiers were being investigated for murder and brutality. One was a 21-year-old British soldier called Trooper Kevin Williams, of the 2nd Royal Tank Regiment. He was charged by police with the murder of an Iraqi civilian – this was the first civilian murder charge in connection with the war in Iraq. The charges of shooting Hassan Abbad Said were later dropped against Williams and he walked free from court. The trooper said he believed the Iraqi was going to grab a comrade's weapon.

By late October 2004, the MoD had investigated and closed some 51 cases. But some 84 investigations were still on-going. It seemed that the tide of allegations and crimes just kept rising, although few made it as far as prosecution. Four investigations had been completed and were being considered for further action; eight were with the prosecuting authorities pending a decision by them on what action should be taken; and four had been directed for trial. The MoD said all these cases ranged from the murder of Iraqis in detention to the deaths of Iraqis who had died in road traffic accidents involving British forces.

By the summer of 2005, one lawyer acting for the alleged victims of UK war criminals had taken more than 50 cases against the Ministry of Defence. Phil Shiner, of the firm Public Interest Lawyers, said 22 of those cases involved the torture and death of civilians in custody.

Despite the welter of charges against soldiers alleged to have violated, abused and killed Iraqi civilians, many investigations have fallen by the wayside. Criminal cases are dependent on witnesses coming forward to give evidence – if the only witnesses to a soldier beating a detainee are the soldier's comrades, then the chance of getting corroborative witnesses' testimony is pretty slim.

By July 2005, at least half of the 14 murder investigations that were still being looked into by military prosecutors had either collapsed or were about to collapse.

Among the cases that fell apart was the shooting of a taxi-driver who was gunned down when he hit a soldier with his car door. Another case, hamstrung due to a lack of witnesses, involved a group of soldiers who were accused of throwing a looter down a well and drowning him. The case was in tatters even though the government admitted that there was 'substantive evidence of deliberate abuse in custody'.

Another case was dropped against three members of the RAF who were alleged to have beaten an Iraqi prisoner to death on a helicopter.

While many cases collapsed, others quietly wound their way through the labyrinthine military investigations procedures – so, by the summer of 2005, some 30 members of the UK armed forces were either facing charges or had been prosecuted for offences related to the alleged abuse, killing or torturing of Iraqi civilians. There had been a total of 176 investigations, with 156 closed and 20 still active. Of the 20, four related to abuse of civilians. Most of the 170-plus investigations related to shootings following the British army returning fire, according to the MoD.

One of the most disgusting crimes investigated by the Royal Military Police came replete with shades of the sadism of Abu Ghraib. It began when 'trophy' photographs of soldiers from the Royal Regiment of Fusiliers torturing Iraqi prisoners came to light. Some showed Iraqis suspended in netting from a forklift truck; others were pictures of Iraqi prisoners being forced to take part in a 'sex show' for the pleasure of squaddies at Camp Breadbasket in southern Iraq in which the 'victims [were made to] engage in sexual activity between themselves'. The offences took place 'while the civilians were temporarily detained but not in a prison or detention facility'. The investigation was spurred forward following the May 2003 arrest of Fusilier Gary Bartlam, aged 18, after he took a camera film containing some of the images to be developed in Tamworth.

At court martial, Lance Corporal Mark Cooley was jailed for two years for 'disgraceful conduct of a cruel kind'; Lance Corporal Darren Larkin, who was photographed standing on an Iraqi prisoner, got 140 days for assault; Corporal Daniel Kenyon was jailed for 18 months; and Fusilier Gary Bartlam was also jailed for 18 months for aiding and abetting the taking of photographs.

Some investigations, for offences which allegedly took place in the immediate wake of the invasion, only got to trial three years later.

Charges of murder levelled against seven members of the 3rd Battalion of the Paratroop Regiment were dropped after the judge said there was insufficient evidence as the case was not properly investigated. They had been accused of killing an 18-year-old.

Allegations of violence mounted. There was even a claim from an Australian citizen of Iraqi origin, who was working in Iraq for an Australian marine and oil company, that he had been beaten and tortured by British soldiers from the Royal Regiment of Wales. Nouri Alwan, a marine surveyor, had a high-ranking job with the company; his main task was to inspect oil cargoes leaving Iraq. He was mistakenly rounded up by the British in a crackdown on suspected Ba'athists. Alwan, who had been persecuted under Saddam's regime before fleeing to Australia and getting citizenship, claims he was racially abused, stripped and beaten, and suffered a broken rib while being held by the British.

The MoD denies any liability, despite medical reports conducted when he was in British detention in Basra, confirming his injuries. Alwan was held for three days until his company and the Australian High Commission in Baghdad secured his release from British custody.

Allegations were also made in August 2005 on the BBC's *Newsnight* programme by two Iraqi brothers, Marhab and As'ad Zaaj-al-Saghir, who say they were beaten with sticks, urinated on, refused water and deprived of sleep while under British detention after their home was raided in Basra.

According to Marhab, British soldiers tied up his brother and stole money and the family car before taking them away to a prison camp. 'While I was tied up,' said Marhab, 'they threw me on the floor and hit me with a stick. You couldn't draw breath afterwards and I lost consciousness. I thought they would throw water over us, but he got his penis out and urinated on my head. If I'd had a weapon I'd have killed myself.'

Another prisoner, Hani Jahoush, was held for two months without charge. Soldiers made him holler like a monkey, bark like a dog and punched him. A third prisoner, Talib Abu Daoud, claimed to have been detained for a full month without being allowed proper sleep. Allegations have also been made that British female soldiers sexually humiliated prisoners under questioning.

Two other investigations centred on the deaths of Hazam Jumah Kati, aged 60, and Abd Al Karim Hassan, 25, who were killed by British troops near Basra. The men were unarmed and were shot as they walked in the dark. One soldier, when asked by investigators why the men were shot, replied: 'It was dark.'

Another alleged killing being investigated is that of headmaster Abd Al Jabbar Mossa, who died while being taken prisoner by British soldiers. He was hit on the head with empty rifle magazines and a helmet as he was bundled into a vehicle.

In another incident, Abbas Abid Ali, a policeman, says that prisoners were badly beaten and abused by British soldiers after a major gun battle on May 14, 2004 near the town of Majar al-Kabir. Abbas Abid Ali, who claimed he had nothing to do with any fighting, said: 'We saw people by the side of the road with hands tied behind their backs and who were hooded and lying on their chests in the dirt. They did the same with us and made us lie on the hot and dirty earth for maybe two hours.'

The captives were put on top of each other in a military vehicle 'with soldiers' feet on top of us', he said, adding: 'We remained hooded until the next morning, when I could hear the birds sing. Then they started interrogating us one by one. They were using abusive language, shouting at us and kicking and beating us around the face and head and body. I saw one prisoner with his jaw so swollen I couldn't recognise him. They wanted to know who had told us to fight. I said I was a policeman and a farmer, not an insurgent.'

Former Scots Guard and current Tory MP Ben Wallace says he blames Blair just as much for the atrocities as the men who perpetrated them. 'If we are charging some of these men with neglect of their duties,' he said, 'then we must recognise that the chain of command does not stop with commanding officers but goes right to the door of Number 10.' Many senior figures in the armed services agree wholeheartedly with Wallace.

The idea that Iraqis are somehow safer with British troops is nonsensical. The misconception that British soldiers go around wearing soft hats and winning Iraqi hearts and minds, while gun-nut American GIs do all the abusing is ludicrous. Just look at the case of Abdallah Khudhran al-Shamran. He was arrested in April 2003 by US forces. He was beaten, given electric shocks, suspended by his legs, had his penis tied and was deprived of sleep. After four days, he was transferred to a camp hospital at Umm Qasr. When he was released, he approached a British patrol, was re-arrested and once again interrogated and tortured. This time he was exposed in the sun for prolonged periods, locked in a container and threatened with execution.

Did Tony Blair know that this kind of abuse was going on? Yes. Did he do anything about it? No.

From May 2003 onwards – when Bush declared the Iraq War 'Mission Accomplished' – both the US and the British governments started receiving International Committee of the Red Cross (ICRC) reports 'month after month' detailing the abuse and torture of Iraqi prisoners.

Yet both Bush and Blair chose to say nothing in public to condemn the horrors which they knew in private were being committed by soldiers under their command. The acknowledgement of the torture and mistreatment of Iraqis was only made by Bush and Blair when the horrific pictures of torture from inside Abu Ghraib were publicised.

A senior source at the ICRC told me in May 2004: 'We had been telling the US and UK authorities in Baghdad for over a year about the scale of this [abuse and torture] problem. They had been given 10 or more reports. All detailed the same findings. They knew this had been going on for a year.'

Paul Bremer, the former US ambassador who headed the coalition's provisional authority in Iraq prior to the 'handover' of power to the Iraqi interim government, was also handed a report by Amnesty International which described prisoner abuse and Geneva Convention violations throughout US-run camps in Iraq in July 2003.

Rumsfeld admitted to Congress that the Pentagon and a US general had tried to block CBS, the US TV network, from broadcasting abuse pictures taken inside Abu Ghraib. He also said 'more photographs and videos exist', adding: 'It's going to make matters worse if these are released to the public.'

The US and the UK knew all along that these shaming, horrific, illegal war crimes were taking place but they deliberately adopted a policy of hiding them from us.

The US and the UK also had plenty of opportunities to fix the endemic level of criminality within the military ranks. Human rights activists had been telling them since the invasion of Afghanistan in October 2001 that crimes were being committed – but still they did nothing.

Teresa Richardson, of Amnesty, said: 'We have been delivering reports on these violations to the US authorities since the period between 9/11 and the beginning of the Iraq war. The abuse and torture, in Afghanistan, goes back years.'

She said Amnesty reports on abuse by British soldiers in Iraq had also been handed to the Ministry of Defence in London in the months immediately after the official end of hostilities in May 2003.

'But we've received no response from the MoD,' Richardson added. That meant that for a full year – from May 2003 to May 2004 when the Abu Ghraib scandal went public – Blair was aware that abuses were occuring but he did nothing. 'Our experience with the MoD, going back to Northern Ireland, is that investigations should not be carried out by the MoD, but by a civilian-led organisation.'

Blair knew that such reports from Amnesty and the ICRC existed, so he could have moved to re-establish human decency in the army's ranks and gone public with an apology, instead he remained silent.

Although the British government expressed regret and sympathy for the deaths of Iraqi civilians, it still decided to fight a lawsuit by the families of six Iraqis allegedly killed by British troops, who went to the high court in London seeking to force an independent investigation.

By late 2004, the government said it had paid a paltry £142,000 in compensation to settle 106 cases of death, injury and property damage in Iraq. With Iraq an impoverished dustbowl, even a pittance, in western terms, in compensation for a dead relative is a small fortune. Another 537 claims were denied, while 149 remained under investigation.

Crimes by British troops were constantly played down and suppressed by the Blair government. At one point, when military police were investigating some 75 cases of crimes against Iraqis, it came to light that this figure was twice the number of offences that government ministers had admitted to publicly. Similarly, at a time when British troops were actually accused of killing 36 Iraqi civilians, the government was only acknowledging a third of that figure.

A shooting by a King's Own Scottish Borderers' squaddie shows the level of contempt in which the British army and government hold the lives of Iraqi children. Alexander Johnston of Shotts, Lanarkshire, was on his first tour of duty in southern Iraq when he shot a 13-year-old boy in September 2003. He admitted negligently discharging his gun and was fined £750 and ordered to pay the boy, who was left paralysed from the waist down, £2,000.

An Amnesty International report in May 2004, found that an eight-year-old girl and a guest at a wedding party were among the Iraqi civilians shot and killed by UK armed forces. The victims were no threat to themselves or others, the report said.

Many cases of civilian killings by UK armed forces have not even been investigated, says the report. Investigations by the Royal Military Police (RMP) have been secretive, with Iraqi families given little or no information about their progress. Amnesty International want the findings of all investigations made public.

Amnesty International UK Director Kate Allen said: 'We are told in the UK that southern Iraq is comparatively safe and secure. Yet Iraqis on the ground have painted a very different picture ... Killings by UK forces, in situations where they should not be using lethal force, are examined in secrecy and behind closed doors. Instead of the army deciding whether to investigate itself when civilians are killed, there must be a full, impartial and civilian-led investigation into all allegations of killings by UK troops.'

The Amnesty report, *Killings of Civilians in Basra and al-Amara*, is based on research carried out by Amnesty International delegates in February and March of 2004. The organisation interviewed families and eyewitnesses, Iraqi police officers and Coalition Provisional Authority officials responsible for law and order. It details numerous case studies of killings by UK armed forces. One such case is that of eight-year-old Hanan Saleh Matrud, reportedly shot by a soldier from B Company of the First Battalion of the King's Regiment in August 2003. An eyewitness disputes the UK army's account of her death, according to which she may have been hit accidentally by a warning shot. The eyewitness told Amnesty International that Hanan was killed when a soldier aimed and fired a shot at her from around 60 metres away. The British army later paid her family a pitiful £390.

You have to ask yourself why such a degradingly small sum was paid to the dead Iraqi child's family, when in the UK the killing of a child by the British armed forces – even if the killing was accidental – would trigger millions of pounds in damages pay-outs. The answer, I can only guess, is that the army and the government know they can get away with it – and simply don't care.

In January 2004, Ghanem Kadhem Kati, a 22-year-old unarmed man was reportedly shot in the back outside his front door while celebrating a family wedding. UK soldiers, responding to the sound of bullets fired into the air in celebration, reportedly fired five shots at him from 50 yards away despite being told by a neighbour not to fire and that the earlier shots were part of the wedding festivities. The victim's relatives were not told how to go about claiming compensation.

Families are frequently given no information by the British military on how to lodge a compensation claim for the killing of family members. In some cases they are given wrong information, including being told that responsibility for compensation will rest with a new Iraqi government. The British army's Area Claims Officer, to whom claims must be submitted, is usually situated in an area difficult to access for ordinary civilians – like Basra airport – and there is little explanatory information provided on the process in English or in Arabic. As a result, few ordinary Iraqis have any confidence in the compensation system.

Kate Allen, Director of Amnesty International UK, said: 'The rule of law must prevail ... If there is to be true security in Iraq, it is essential that justice is done and is seen to be done.'

WALKING WITH DANTE

or

Miscellaneous ways of descending into Hell

Torture and terror aren't the only forces pulling the world into the kind of mass collective horror that we haven't seen in 60 years. There are more roads to perdition that are being paved at the moment. Here are just a few ...

Driving out the good guys

Al-Zarqawi's serial-killer followers were behind the August 2003 bombing of the United Nations headquarters in Baghdad. Crimes like this, and the kidnapping of aid workers such as Margaret Hassan from Care International, have left ordinary Iraqis to the mercies of the insurgents, the criminals, the terror groups and the coalition.

According to one of the UN's most internationally respected former leaders, the reason the HQ was bombed in Baghdad was because the United Nations had been taken over by the US and turned into a 'dark joke' and a 'malignant force'.

Denis Halliday, the former UN Assistant Secretary-General and Humanitarian Coordinator in Iraq, condemned the United Nations as an aggressive arm of US foreign policy in the immediate aftermath of the truck bomb attack on the mission station in Baghdad which killed at least 23 people – many of whom were Halliday's former friends and colleagues.

'The west sees the UN as a benign organisation, but the sad reality in much of the world is that the UN is not seen as benign,' I was told by Halliday, who was nominated for the 2001 Nobel Peace Prize. 'The UN Security Council has been taken over and corrupted by the US and UK, particularly with regard to Iraq, Palestine and Israel.

'In Iraq, the UN imposed sustained sanctions that probably killed up to one million people. Children were dying of malnutrition and water-borne diseases. The US and UK bombed the infrastructure in 1991, destroying power, water and sewage systems against the Geneva Convention. It was a great crime against Iraq.

'Thirteen years of sanctions made it impossible for Iraq to repair the damage. That is why we have such tremendous resentment and anger against the UN in Iraq. There is a sense that the UN humiliated the Iraqi people and society. I would use the term genocide to define the use of sanctions against Iraq. Several million Iraqis are suffering cancers because of the use of depleted uranium shells. That's an atrocity. Can you imagine the bitterness from all of this?'

He warned that 'further collaboration' between the UN and the US and Britain 'would be a disaster for the United Nations as it would be sucked into supporting the illegal occupation of Iraq'.

'The UN has been drawn into being an arm of the US – a division of the State Department. Kofi Annan was appointed and supported by the US and that has corrupted the independence of the UN. The UN must move quickly to reform itself and improve the Security Council – it must make clear that the UN and the US are not one and the same.'

Halliday said the US should get out of Iraq. The UN could then start the work of helping the Iraqis rebuild their nation. 'Bush has blown $75 billion on this war, so he should spend $75 billion on reconstruction – and the money shouldn't just go to Halliburton and the boys either. Once the US goes from Iraq, the terrorist will go as well.

'Bush and Blair have misled their countries into war. By invading Iraq and placing the US inside the Islamic world, America is inviting terror-ists to come on the attack.'

Halliday, who resigned from the UN in 1998, knew the conversation he had with me would upset London, Washington and Kofi Annan, but he claimed it had to be said as many senior UN figures feel the same anger.

Installing lunatics as democratic leaders of 'free' Iraq

Iyad Allawi, briefly Iraq's interim Prime Minister, allegedly shot dead as many as six suspected insurgents just days before Washington handed political control over to his new government in June 2004. This revela-tion was quite a scoop for my good friends and newspaper colleagues

David Pratt and Torcuil Crichton.

Two separate witnesses said that the prisoners, blindfolded and hand-cuffed, were lined up against a wall in a courtyard next to a maximum security cell at al-Amariyah prison in Baghdad. Allawi then pulled out a pistol and shot them in the head, telling policemen that he was setting an example of how to deal with resistance fighters. Allawi is said to have told onlookers that the men 'deserved worse than death'.

Some 30 witnesses are said to have been present in the compound when Allawi paid a surprise visit to the security facility to reassure police officers that they would be protected from reprisals if they killed insurgents in the course of their duty.

The claims have raised fears that the leaders of the newly 'free Iraq' are returning to the cold-blooded tactics of their predecessor, Saddam Hussein. The allegations led to urgent calls for the Red Cross to launch an investigation.

'These are dreadful allegations. It is vital that they are cleared up one way or another and that needs an independent inquiry,' said former Foreign Secretary Robin Cook. 'An international body such as the Red Cross would be best able to give authority to the investigation that the situation now demands.'

Senior US officials did not make an outright dismissal of the allega-tions but Allawi's office denied the claims concerning the conduct of one of the key figures meant to be leading Iraq towards democracy. It said Allawi had never visited the prison, did not carry a gun, and that the allegations were rumours instigated by enemies of Allawi.

Reports of the killings were also dismissed by some sections of the UK government. A spokesman for the Foreign Office said its staff in Baghdad had no knowledge of the allegations. 'There are thousands of rumours sweeping the city and this is just one of them,' he said.

In contrast, Downing Street said it was aware of the report but added that the matter was an issue for the Iraqi government. Allawi had denied the allegations, the official said, adding: 'As far as we are concerned the matter is dealt with.'

The reports, in a country where rumour is as powerful as fact, were a devastating blow to the interim Iraqi government's claim that it wanted to create a climate conducive to free democratic elections.

As well as his own security staff, Allawi is accompanied at all times by a close protection unit of soldiers drawn from US special forces. Allawi, a former hit man for the Saddam regime, has shown signs of flexing his power to its limits and breaking out of US control.

'If we attempted to refute each rumour, we would have no time for other business, as far as this press office is concerned, this case is closed,' said a spokesman at the US Embassy in Baghdad.

News of the allegations of the mass murder carried out by Allawi was followed by a suicide bombing by a group led by Osama bin Laden's ally al-Zarqawi. In the attack, Iraq's Justice Minister Malik al-Hassan escaped but five bodyguards were killed when the bomber drove his car into the government convoy.

If the allegations about government top brass popping caps in the heads of insurgents is reminiscent of the bad old Saddam days, then revelations about state-run torture chambers in the newly liberated Iraq are a first-class trip down Ba'athist memory lane.

US troops stumbled onto the set of a horror movie in November 2005 when they uncovered a secret detention bunker and torture chamber in the middle of Baghdad which was run by the Interior Ministry of the new 'democratic' Iraq.

The dungeon was located near the Interior Ministry's Baghdad compound. Inside were 173 starving and abused men and teenagers. Mohammed Duham, who runs an organisation which fights for the rights of prisoners in Iraq said, after interviewing some of the survivors: 'This is even worse than what was happening before [under the Saddam regime]. A lot of torture implements were found in the bunker, like saws to cut people's limbs and also razors to peel the skin off people's bodies.'

Corpses are regularly found dumped in the streets of Baghdad – sometimes by the busload. Some have been mutilated with knives and electric drills. While the insurgents are responsible for many of these disappearances and murders, government paramilitary death squads are also carrying out abductions, torture and extrajudicial executions. The Iraqi government has admitted that some members of the state security forces were 'resorting to the same sort of torture and abuses as were seen under Saddam'.

One of the guards at the torture chamber, an 18-year-old called Seif Saad, unapologetically told the Reuters news agency, how suspects were snatched off the streets. 'We placed sacks on their heads and tied their hands behind their backs,' he said.

Human Rights Watch has testimony from some of the captives. One man, Ali Bargouth Alwan, who was arrested after being found with a grenade, said he was told he would be freed if he could come up with a 50,000-dinar bribe. He couldn't, so he was tortured with prolonged beatings and had cables and pipes taken to his back and head. Another man, Tahsin Dar'am Balasem said: 'They started beating me with cables. They also used electric shocks by tying wires to my ears and to my penis. After that I confessed [to carrying out robberies and abductions].'

But to make matters even more terrifying, ordinary Iraqis don't just have to worry about government sponsored death squads snatching people off the streets and killing them, they've also got to keep an eye out for al-Qaeda infiltrators inside the police force as well.

Iraq's National Security Advisor, Muwafaq al-Rubaie, admitted that insurgents had infiltrated the country's security forces. He told the BBC's *Newsnight* programme: 'Our Iraqi security forces in general, and these in particular in many parts of Iraq, I have to admit that they have been penetrated by some of the insurgents, some of the terrorists as well, so I can't deny this.'

It is also suspected that the Shi'ite Badr Organisation has infiltrated the security services. The Badr organisation is a militia group allied to the Supreme Council for the Islamic Revolution in Iraq. The SCIRI is a hardline political party in the Iraqi government, and the Badr organisation was formed in exile in Iran in the 1980s as the SCIRI's military wing.

The level of torture in Iraq is now worse than it was under the tyrant Saddam, the UN says. According to Manfred Nowak, the United Nations Special Rapporteur on Torture, abuses by state security forces, insurgents and militias is 'out of control'. The UN has listed the types of cruelty inflicted on Iraqi victims, including: the removal of eyes, skinning, acid burns and the extraction of teeth.

Had a tough day in the Green Zone?
Unwind by 'smoking' an Iraqi ...

Three American soldiers – a captain and two sergeants – from the 82nd Airborne Division stationed at Forward Operating Base (FOB) Mercury near Fallujah in Iraq have told Human Rights Watch how prisoners were tortured as a form of 'stress relief'.

The 82nd Airborne soldiers at FOB Mercury earned the nickname 'The Murderous Maniacs' from local Iraqis and took the moniker as a badge of honour.

The soldiers referred to their Iraqi captives as PUCs – persons under control – and used the expressions 'fucking a PUC' and 'smoking a PUC' to refer respectively to torture and forced physical exertion.

One sergeant provided graphic descriptions to Human Rights Watch investigators about acts of abuse carried out both by himself and others. He now says he regrets his actions. His regiment arrived at FOB Mercury in August 2003. He said: 'The first interrogation that I observed was the first time I saw a PUC pushed to the brink of a stroke or a heart attack. At first I was surprised, like, "This is what we are allowed to do?"'

The troops would put sandbags on prisoners' heads and cuff them with plastic zip-ties. The sergeant, who spoke on condition of anonymity, said, if he was told that prisoners had been found with home-made bombs, 'we would fuck them up, put them in stress positions and put them in a tent and withhold water ... It was like a game. You know, how far could you make this guy go before he passes out or just collapses on you?'

He explained: 'To "fuck a PUC" means to beat him up. We would give them blows to the head, chest, legs and stomach, pull them down, kick dirt on them. This happened every day. To "smoke" someone is to put them in stress positions until they get muscle fatigue and pass out. That happened every day. 'Some days we would just get bored so we would have everyone sit in a corner and then make them get in a pyramid. We did that for amusement.'

Iraqis were 'smoked' for up to 12 hours. That would entail being made to hold five-gallon water cans in both hands with outstretched arms, made to do press-ups and star jumps. At no time, during these sessions, would they get water or food apart from dry biscuits. Sleep deprivation was also 'a really big thing', the sergeant added.

To prepare a prisoner for interrogation, military intelligence officers ordered that the Iraqis be deprived of sleep. The sergeant said he and other soldiers did this by 'banging on their cages, crashing them into the cages, kicking them, kicking dirt, yelling'.

They'd also pour cold water over prisoners and then cover them in sand and mud. On some occasions, prisoners were tortured for revenge. 'If we were on patrol and caught a guy that killed our captain or my buddy last week ... man, it is human nature,' said the sergeant – but on other occasions, he confessed, it was for 'sport'.

Many prisoners were completely innocent and had no part in the insurgency, he said – but intelligence officers had told soldiers to exhaust the captives to make them cooperate. He said he now knew his behaviour was 'wrong', but added 'this was the norm'. 'Trends were accepted. Leadership failed to provide clear guidance so we just developed it. They wanted intel [intelligence]. As long as no PUC came up dead, it happened. '

According to Captain Ian Fishback of the 82nd Airborne Division, army doctrine had been broken by allowing Iraqis who were captured by them to remain in their custody, instead of being sent 'behind the lines' to trained military police.

Pictures of abuse at FOB Mercury were destroyed by soldiers after the scandal of Abu Ghraib broke. However, Fishback told his company commander about the abuse. The reply was 'Remember the honour of the unit is at stake' and 'Don't expect me to go to bat for you on this issue if you take this up'. Fishback then told his battalion commander who advised him to speak to the Judge Advocate General's (JAG) office, which deals with issues of military law.

The JAG told Fishback that the Geneva Conventions 'are a grey area'. When Fishback described some of the abuses he had witnessed the JAG said it was 'within' Geneva Conventions.

Fishback added: ' If I go to JAG and JAG cannot give me clear guidance about what I should stop and what I should allow to happen, how is an NCO or a private expected to act appropriately?'

Fishback, a West Point graduate who has served in both Afghanistan and Iraq, spent 17 months trying to raise the matter with his superiors. When he attempted to approach representatives of US Senators John McCain and John Warner about the abuse, he was told that he would not be granted a pass to meet them on his day off.

Fishback says that army investigators were more interested in finding out the identity of the other soldiers who spoke to Human Rights Watch than dealing with the systemic abuse of Iraqi prisoners.

Colonel Joseph Curtin, a senior army spokesman at the Pentagon, said: 'We do take the captain seriously and are following up on this.' Fishback was removed from special forces training because of the army investigation.

Massacres and how they are justified by God

Amnesty International has said that 'Iraqis have been collectively punished for attacks on coalition forces by having their crops and houses deliberately destroyed. Amnesty International has on numerous occasions reminded the occupying powers of their obligations and in many areas they have failed to respect them.' Reprisals against civilians included bombing homes using planes, tanks and helicopters.

Here's an example of one of these terrible reprisals – a reprisal in this case for the mere discharge of a firearm at, yet again, a wedding party – which turned into a massacre; a wedding day massacre.

The bombing started at 3 a.m. on Wednesday, May 19, 2004. The villagers from the tiny desert community of Makr al-Deeb were fast asleep, exhausted after a day spent celebrating. By the time the bombing had stopped and the advancing GIs had finished marauding and shooting their way through the remains of the village, the Americans had killed at least 42 innocent people.

Among the dead were 27 members of the Rakat family who had just a few hours earlier been dancing and laughing at a double family wedding. Many of their guests died, as did the band of musicians who played throughout the wedding and one of Iraq's most popular singers, Hussein al-Ali from Ramadi.

One of the few people to live through the night was Haleema Shihab, the sister-in-law of the groom. She described to reporters from her hospital cot how she was sleeping in bed with her husband and children in the Rakat family villa when the bombs started to fall.

'We went out of the house and American soldiers started to shoot at us,' she said. 'They were shooting low on the ground and targeting us one by one.'

Picking up her youngest child in her arms, with two of her sons running at her side, she was hit by shrapnel from a shell that landed nearby fracturing her legs. Her two boys were dead on the ground beside her and as she lay next to them she was wounded again when another round hit her in the arm. One of her children had been decapitated.

'I fell into the mud and an American soldier came and kicked me,' she said. 'I pretended to be dead so he wouldn't kill me. My youngest child was alive next to me.'

Not long before daybreak, Shihab saw GIs reduce the home of the Rakat family and the house next door to a pile of rubble. When a relative carried her and her surviving child to hospital, she learned that her husband Mohammed had also died. Mohammed was the eldest son of the Rakat family.

One witness, Dahham Harraj, said: 'This was a wedding and the planes came and attacked the people at a house. Is this the democracy and freedom that Bush has brought us?'

An unnamed witness said that bombs fell on the village one after another and three houses with the guests inside were hit. 'They fired as if there were an armoured brigade inside not a wedding party.'

A third witness said: 'The US military planes came and started killing everyone in the house.' One of the causes for the mass killings is likely to have been the failure by US forces to understand Iraqi culture.

At weddings, many Iraqis fire guns into the air as a sign of celebration. The Americans may have misinterpreted what was happening and sent in their bombers and infantry without pausing for thought. If they had stopped to think they might have remembered an incident in 2002 when 48 innocent Afghanis celebrating a wedding were blown to bits by US jets. Another 100 were injured. That time, too, the guests had fired guns into the air to celebrate the bride and groom.

Ma'athi Nawaaf, a neighbour of the Rakats whose daughter and grandchildren died in the attack, said: 'We were happy because of the wedding. People were dancing and making speeches.' Then after the ceremony, the jets and a military convoy approached.

'The first thing they bombed was the tent for the ceremony,' Nawaf said. 'We saw the family running out of the house. The bombs were falling destroying the whole area.'

Armoured personnel carriers then drove into Makr al-Deeb, firing machine-guns and backed up by helicopters. 'They started to shoot at the house and the people outside the house,' Nawaf added.

Chinooks later landed and dozens of troops charged out. Explosives were set in the Rakat house and minutes later it and a neighbouring home were just smouldering rubble.

'I saw something that nobody ever saw in this world,' Nawaf went on. 'There were children's bodies cut into pieces, women cut into pieces, men cut into pieces.'

Nawaf found his grandson dead in his daughter's arms. 'The other boy was lying beside her,' he said. 'I found only his head. The Americans call these people foreign fighters. It is a lie. I just want one piece of evidence of what they are saying.'

In the al-Qaim general hospital, Dr Hamdi Noor al-Alusi said 11 of the dead were women and 14 were children. 'I want to know why the Americans targeted this small village. These people are my patients. I know each one of them. What has caused this disaster?'

In the face of such overwhelming evidence that they had killed innocent revellers, the US stubbornly insisted that the raid was against a 'suspected foreign fighter safe house'. A statement even claimed that 'during the operation, coalition forces came under hostile fire and close air
support was provided'.

Brigadier Mark Kimmitt, Deputy Director of Operations for the US
military in Iraq, said: 'We took ground fire and we returned fire. We
estimate that around 40 were killed. But we operated within our rules
of engagement.'

Television footage showed a truck filled with bodies killed in the
attack. Men were seen lifting the bodies from the truck, wrapped in
blankets, and taking them to the desert for burial in deep pits. The
corpse of a little girl of six was seen wrapped in a white shawl. Other
bodies were shown with horrific injuries.

Showing an astonishing arrogance and lack of understanding for the
culture or geography of the country his men are occupying, Major-
General James Mattis, commander of the 1st Marine Division, mocked
anyone who claimed his troops had massacred innocent Iraqis.

'How many people go into the middle of the desert to hold a wedding
80 miles from the nearest civilisation?' he said, claiming there 'were
more than two dozen military-aged males' in the area.

Makr al-Deeb has been a village for a long time. Before the attack it
had around two dozen homes. When Mattis was asked about TV
images of a dead child, he said he had not seen the pictures and did not
have to justify the actions of his men.

Deputy Police Chief Lieutenant Colonel Ziyad al-Jbouri said American helicopters attacked the village at around 2.45 a.m. in the morning.

The wedding party was the biggest celebration in the village for years.
It marked the moment when two local families – the Rakats and Sabahs
– came together with the long negotiated marriage of Ashad Rakat and
his cousin Rutba Sabah. There was also a second ceremony between a
Rakat girl and a Sabah man. Much of the party took place under can-
vas in the gardens of the Rakat villa.

Incredibly, the survivors included the two married couples and the
patriarch of the extended family who owns the Rakat villa. Some of the
graves of those who died were marked with this sole epitaph: THE
AMERICAN BOMBING.

Inevitably, the massacre at Makr al-Deeb – taken together with the US
onslaughts against Fallujah which claimed hundreds of Iraqi lives –

erodes any moral foundations of the US invasion down to zero. The Arab media completely discounted the US version of events, describing it as a 'savage massacre'.

And the suffering of the people of Makr al-Deeb will only fuel the resistance against the occupying forces. Not far from where the victims lay buried, Ahmed Saleh said: 'For each one of those graves, we will get 10 Americans.'

The kind of boiling, blinding hatred which grew inside Ahmed Saleh's heart after the wedding party massacre is the same kind of hatred that inspired an Iraqi mob to lynch and burn four civilian American contractors who were caught in the streets of Fallujah in the spring of 2004. The images of the men's blackened and hacked-up limbs hanging from a bridge shocked the world.

But such inhuman savagery has to be seen for what it actually is: a terrible and cruel revenge exacted against innocent westerners for suffering that had been inflicted on innocent Iraqis by the west. In Iraq, an eye for an eye really is making everyone blind. Fallujah, the killers hoped, would be 'the Americans' graveyard'. Instead, by the autumn of 2004, the US Marines – against the wishes of the United Nations – had bombed the city into submission.

Before the Americans went into the rebel stronghold, many GIs were baptised. They bowed their heads before open-air gospel services on the outskirts of Fallujah and prayed on their knees in full combat gear, still clutching their machine-guns, in the sand.

One photograph showed US soldiers in prayer with their guns held before them. They looked like those romantic 19th-century pre-Raphaelite drawings of crusader knights in shining armour praying on their knees during the night before battle. Like the praying knights in those vigil paintings, the GIs held their guns like the knights held their swords – in front of them, with the handle and blade, as the barrel and magazine, standing in as makeshift crucifixes to worship.

That simmering, creepy image of 'Christianity versus Islam' is a potentially apocalyptic one. It hints that we are really engaged in some struggle which has, at its heart, the medievalism and madness of organised religion.

Sadly, thanks to President Bush, it appears that this is truly the case. We are, indeed, embarked on a fresh Crusade. The loon on Pennsylvania Avenue actually said this to Palestinian Foreign Minister Nabil Sha'ath: 'I'm driven with a mission from God. He told me, "George, go and fight those terrorists in Afghanistan". And I did ... and then, "George, go and end the tyranny in Iraq". And I did. And now again, I feel God's words coming to me, "Go get the Palestinians their state, and the Israelis their security". And by God, I'm gonna do it.'

Oh Lord ...

Intercontinental Ballistic Missionaries

Speaking of God, I thought you'd like to know this little titbit that I found out: Blair and Bush pray together. They actually prayed to their God in the run-up to the Iraq war at 'crucial moments'. They share a 'spiritual affinity', I was told.

It was a chap called David Aikman who filled me in on all this holy fellowship mullarky between the Prez and the PM. Aikman is British, a former senior writer on *Time* magazine and the author of *A Man Of Faith: The Spiritual Journey of George W Bush*. According to Aikman, the Prime Minister and the President shared moving moments of private prayer.

The revelations will embarrass Blair. For a supposedly religious man, he has a strangely deep-seated fear of being portrayed as the same sort of evangelical Christian as Bush. The Prime Minister had an infamously bruising encounter with BBC *Newsnight* presenter Jeremy Paxman just before the war started in which he reacted angrily when asked repeatedly if he and Bush prayed together. In another interview in 2003, for *Vanity Fair* magazine, Blair was also asked about his faith but his spin doctor, Alastair Campbell, interrupted to say: 'I'm sorry, we don't do God.' I'm sure Campbell managed to make God understand in no uncertain terms that his divine presence wasn't needed that day by our devout PM.

Aikman based his book on extensive interviews with some of Bush's closest aides and confidants – such as the key Bush advisors Karen Hughes and Karl Rove, aka Bush's Brain. He also spoke to old friends Don Evans from Texas and the Christian pop star Michael W Smith and interviewed two of Bush's pastors in Texas as well as the President's mother, Barbara, who, incidentally, is an apparently very mean and scary woman.

'I spoke to a lot of the inner circle,' Aikman said. 'It is very obvious that they [Bush and Blair] understood each other on a faith level and that they prayed together at least once. They are both conviction politicians. They are convinced of the same things and their shared faith gives them a commonality. It seals the package of their special relationship.'

The White House was delighted with Aikman's book. Aikman's daughter was married in the summer of 2004 and Bush sent a personal letter to her on account of her father's work. Downing Street, however, was not so cock-a-hoop when I called to ask if the PM liked to get down on his knobbly knees and pray to God with Bush.

Can you imagine them together? Blair, watching Dubya nervously out of the corner of one half-shut eye, as he prays desperately not to be thrown into the fiery pit of hell and toasted on the forks of Satan's imps for taking the UK to war in Iraq; and the President, lips moving silently and frantically as he recites the 'Lawd's Praya', shivering with rapturous pleasure as he senses the hand of God guiding him in new ways to deliver high-explosive ordnance onto the homes of Arabs.

When I made that call to Downing Street, the senior press officer on the other end of the phone actually sighed – a long, low, sad exhalation of breath. 'You know we don't talk about these things, Neil,' he said. But you must have some comment, I asked. He thought for a moment, and then said: 'Yes. Yes, I do. Here it is: Downing Street does not comment on what is said in people's books.'

My Lai in Iraq

Civilians who spent time at the Haditha Dam base of the Third Battalion of the First Marines describe the place as something out of *Apocalypse Now* or *Lord of the Flies*. It was 'feral', one said. Soldiers didn't wash; they'd abandoned their regulation billets and built makeshift, primitive huts bearing skull and crossbones signs; the place stank. One American civilian engineer attached to the camp and tasked to keep the huge, nearby hydro-electric dam operating, said he was terrified of the soldiers he had to live alongside.

Kilo Company was part of the Third Battalion. At 7.15 a.m. on November 19, 2005, as a column of Kilo Company Humvees drove down the Hay al-Sinnai Road in Haditha, a bomb exploded under the last vehicle – 'the tail-end charlie' – killing the driver, 20-year-old Lance Corporal Miguel Terrazas.

What happened next will go down in US military history as the worst deliberate atrocity carried out against unarmed civilians by American forces since the notorious massacre at My Lai in Vietnam when GIs killed around 500 people – mainly women, children and the elderly.

Minutes after Terrazas died, the remaining 13-strong unit of marines went on a bloody rampage; wiping out whole families, killing women, children and an elderly man in a wheelchair, and hurling grenades into homes. In all some 24 Iraqi civilians were murdered by American troops. The killings are already having a corrosive effect on US society – war-weary from scandals like the torture of detainees at Abu Ghraib and the ever-mounting death toll of American troops. US government sources say that some of the marines involved will be put on trial, and could face the death penalty for their crimes.

The men of Kilo Company have been involved in some of the worst horrors of the Iraq War, including the assault on Fallujah which involved close-up killing and hand-to-hand fighting. Many of the marines in Kilo Company were on their second tour of duty in Iraq at the time of the massacre in Haditha.

As soon as the shooting stopped, the marines started to lie and cover up the truth about the Haditha killings. The faked-up version of events went something like this: as a taxi drove up Hay al-Sinnai Road, towards the Humvee column, the marines waved to it to stop. When the Humvees and the taxi came to a halt, a bomb detonated, indicating, the marines claimed, that the taxi was either meant to lure the Humvees over the bomb or that someone in the taxi detonated the bomb. The marines claimed they immediately came under fire from nearby houses once the bomb exploded. The four passengers in the taxi and the driver fled, the marines claimed, and were all shot dead. Soldiers then returned fire on the positions shooting at them, killing eight insurgents in total. Fifteen civilians, they said, also died in the explosion which killed the Humvee driver Terrazas.

Investigations by the military, accounts by survivors and reports by human rights organisations and medics have proved this version of events to contain barely a grain of truth.

Eman Waleed, a nine-year-old girl, was a few minutes' walk from the site of the bomb which caught the Humvee, at the home of her grandfather Abdul Hamid Hassan Ali, an 89-year-old amputee in a wheelchair. Eman recalls the moment the killings started. 'We heard a big noise that woke us all up. Then we did what we always do when there's an explosion – my father goes into his room with the Koran and prays that the family be spared any harm.'

While her father prayed, Eman and her mother, her wheelchair-bound grandfather, grandmother, two brothers, two aunts and two uncles stayed together in the main room. Eman recalls sitting in her pyjamas and hearing shooting as the marines moved towards her home. They stormed into the house, went to the room where Eman's father was praying and shot him dead.

Next, they entered the room where the rest of the family were huddled together. 'I couldn't see their faces very well,' said Eman, 'only their guns sticking into the doorway. I watched them shoot my grandfather, first in the chest and then in the head. Then they killed my granny.'

The marines started to spray the corner of the room with automatic fire where Eman and her eight-year-old brother Abdul where being shielded by the other adults. Both Eman and Abdul were wounded but survived. Eman's aunt fled the house as the shooting started, taking her five-month-old niece with her. She escaped. Her husband, who also tried to escape, was shot in the head. In total seven family members died. Eman's grandfather was shot nine times. His death certificate notes that his intestines had spilled through the exit wounds in his back. His wife, Eman's grandmother; three sons – including Eman's father; Eman's mother; and a four-year-old child were also murdered. Only one of the adults in the house that day survived. Eman and her brother hid under a bed, with their family lying dead around them, and waited two hours before Iraqi soldiers arrived to help them.

The marines then moved to the house of Younis Salim Khafif, which he shared with his wife, Aida, and their six children. Aida was in bed recovering from an operation so her sister was in the house to help out with family chores. A neighbour says he heard Younis beg for his life, telling the marines in English: 'I am a friend, I am good.' They shot him anyway. Everybody in the house that day – apart from a 12-year-old girl – were murdered as the marines opened fire and then lobbed hand-grenades at the civilians. The children who died were aged 14, 10, five, three and one. In total, eight died. The surviving child, Safa, said she lay on the ground, pretending to be dead and covered in her sister's blood. She recalls the blood spurting out of her sister like water from a tap, and the soldiers kicking the bodies of the dead on the ground. 'I was wishing to be alive,' she said. 'Now I wish I had died with them.'

Further up the street, four brothers aged 20 to 38, were at home. The women inside were forced outside at gunpoint by marines and the men shot dead. A relative said the Americans put the brothers in a wardrobe and machine-gunned them.

Finally, back at the bomb site, a taxi entered the street and was stopped by marines. The four students inside and the driver were ordered out of the car and shot dead. Of the 24 people killed, only one had a weapon.

After the killings were over, the marines cordoned off the area and then later took the dead to Haditha hospital, left them in body bags in the garden and drove off. An Iraqi journalism student, called Taher Thabet, later videotaped the bodies in the morgue and the scenes of the killings. It was passed to the Iraqi organisation, the Hammurabi Human Rights Group, and it confirms that the dead were killed not by the booby-trap which took the life of Terrazas in the Humvee, but by Terrazas's enraged comrades. The rooms where the civilians were killed were riddled with bullets and splattered with blood. A doctor at the hospital said there were no signs of shrapnel wounds from explosives on the bodies, instead 'the bullet wounds were very apparent. Most of the victims were shot in the chest and head from close range'. Death certificates for all the murdered Iraqi civilians showed they were all shot – many in the head and chest.

One marine who had to help clear up the bloody aftermath of the murders and remove the bodies, Lance-Corporal Roel Ryan Briones, said he was traumatised by what he'd seen. 'They ranged from little babies to adult males and females. I'll never be able to get that out of my head. I can still smell the blood. This left something in my head and heart,' he said. His mother added: 'He had to carry a little girl's body. Her head was blown off and her brain splattered on his boots.'

After the killings, a group of elders from Haditha, led by the mayor, protested to local marine commanders and were dismissed with the claim that the killings were an accident. Even when the student's tape was handed to marine commanders, they claimed that it was 'AQI [al-Qaeda in Iraq] propaganda'. When it became clear that the civilians had been shot by US soldiers, the marines switched to saying that the deaths were the fault of insurgents who 'placed non-combatants in the line of fire as the marines responded to defend themselves'. However, that claim also fell apart when other senior US commanders in Baghdad saw the tape and a criminal investigation was opened. Military police travelled to Haditha, examined the murder scenes, spoke to survivors and interviewed marines. The marine story quickly collapsed and members of Kilo Company started to implicate each other.

Military investigators have now briefed a group of US congressmen, telling them a number of men in Kilo Company may soon be charged with murder. There are also likely to be other charges of dereliction of duty and making false statements. Representative John Kline, a Republican and a former marine said: 'This was a small number of marines who fired directly on civilians and killed them. This is going to be an ugly story ... There is no doubt that the marines allegedly involved in doing this lied about it. They certainly tried to cover it up.' John Murtha, an anti-war Democratic Congressman and decorated marine war veteran, added: 'They killed innocent civilians in cold blood and that's what the report [by the military into the killings and the cover-up] is going to tell. It is as bad as Abu Ghraib, if not worse.'

So far, three marine officers, including the commander of Kilo Company and the commander of the third battalion, have been relieved of duty. The investigation is centred on the NCO who was leading Kilo Company on the day of the murders, and allegedly at the scene of nearly every killing, and a number of other soldiers who are said to have taken part directly in the killings. Up to nine other men witnessed the killings but did nothing. Sources close to the investigation have named the ranking marine in the group, who entered the homes and is a focus of the inquiry, as 25-year-old Sgt Frank Wuterich.

President Bush has said of the marine massacre that 'those who violated the law will be punished'. Bush also apparently roasted his Secretary of Defense, Donald Rumsfeld, for not informing him of the killings promptly when Rumsfeld learned of the events in March.

Following the killings, Iraq's current Prime Minister, Nouri Maliki, heavily criticised what he described as habitual attacks on civilians by coalition forces. Maliki said many troops had 'no respect for civilians ... and killed on a suspicion or a hunch'. In response, senior US army commanders ordered that troops would undergo a two-hour course on 'moral and ethical values'. The US army denied it was a limp and late face-saving exercise.

Suspicions have been raised that senior commanders were aware of what was happening in Haditha on the day of the killings. Although some Iraqis claim that US marines burned houses in the area, others have said that warplanes dropped bombs on a number of houses. Senior commanders would have had to green-light such an action.

So far, the marines have paid out $2,500 (just over £1,300) to the families of 15 of the victims. The senior officer who ordered the payments ruled that those killed had not taken part in any attacks on US forces.

Shortly after the massacre, the marines from Kilo Company held a memorial service for their dead comrade Terrazas. Messages like 'TJ you were a great friend' were written on stones and piled up in a funeral mound. The bodies of the 24 men, women and children killed in Haditha in the hours after Terrazas's death are in a cemetery known as 'the Martyrs' Graveyard'. On a nearby wall some graffiti reads: DEMOCRACY ASSASSINATED THE FAMILY THAT WAS HERE.

Waleed Mohammed, a lawyer representing some of the families, said the survivors were waiting desperately for news of criminal charges being pressed against the marines of Kilo Company. 'They are convinced that the sentence will be like one for someone who has killed a dog in the United States,' he said, 'because Iraqis have become like dogs in the eyes of Americans.'

*

Haditha is not the only town where US forces have been accused of carrying out atrocities and murdering innocent Iraqi civilians in reprisal operations.

Iraqi police have directly accused American soldiers of killing 11 people – ranging from a baby of six months to a 75-year-old woman – during a raid on March 15, 2006, in the Abu Sifa village of the Ishaqi district some 60 miles to the north of Baghdad.

Along with the baby, four other children all aged five or under, were also shot dead. The villagers were killed together when GIs rounded them up, put them in a room and opened fire, the Iraqi police said. The US troops then burned the villagers' cars, killed their animals and blew up the house in which the bodies had been left.

After a brief investigation, the US military came to the conclusion that there was no misconduct by the soldiers and claimed reports that GIs executed civilians were 'absolutely false'. The army says it was trying to capture insurgents and explained away most of the civilian deaths as 'collateral damage'. According to army commanders the troops 'operated in accordance with the rules of engagement'.

However, what gives the claims so much credence is the fact that an official report has been compiled by senior Iraqi security force officers at the Joint Coordination Centre (JCC) in Tikrit. The JCC is a regional security centre set up by Iraqi police in partnership with the US military.

The report on the killings reads: 'American forces used helicopters to drop troops on the house of Faiz Harat Khalaf [a 30-year-old man who also died in the raid]. The American forces gathered the family members in one room and executed 11 people, including five children, four women and two men, then they bombed the house.'

The report lists the dead and is signed by Fadhil Muhammed Khalaf, the Assistant Chief of the JCC. Brigadier General Issa al-Juboori, the head of the JCC, said the report was accurate and the officer who wrote it was thoroughly trusted. 'He's a dedicated policeman and a good cop,' al-Juboori added.

Officially, the US claims the raid was the result of a tip-off that an al-Qaeda operative was at the house. Neighbours confirmed that an al-Qaeda member had been at the house, which was owned by a relative, but said the owner was a school-teacher and he and the rest of the family had nothing to do with terrorism or the insurgency.

Local Police Commander Lt Col Farooq Hussain said autopsies 'revealed that all the victims had bullet shots in the head and all bodies were handcuffed'. Hussain added that the killings were 'a clear and perfect crime'.

Ibraheem Hirat Khalaf, the brother of Faiz Harat Khalaf whose house was attacked, said he saw US helicopters firing six missiles at the house as they left. Another local man, Rasheed Thair, said: 'Everyone attended the funeral. We want the Americans to give an explanation for this horrible crime which took the smile and the dream of a spring night from 11 people and destroyed even the toys of children.'

Apart from the attack on Abu Sifa, other allegations of war crimes and atrocities carried out against Iraqi civilians by US forces in 2006 alone include:

> March 18, troops from the 101st Airborne Division shoot dead a 13-year-old boy and his parents at their home in Dhuluiya claiming they were among eight people killed after a patrol was ambushed;
>
> April 26, a man from Hamandiya is reportedly taken from his home and shot by marines;
>
> May 4, two unarmed women and a mentally handicapped man are killed in Samarra by the 101st Airborne Division;
>
> May 30, another shooting in Samarra in which US soldiers killed two Iraqi women – one about to give birth. The car they were in was racing to a maternity hospital when soldiers shot at it for failing to stop.

The cost of these killings is a growing hatred of America and increased recruits for the insurgency. As an example, look at the case of Jalal Abdul Rahman. The car that he and his son, 12-year-old Abdul, were travelling in came under fire from US soldiers in January this year on their way home from buying a PlayStation game in Baghdad.

The soldiers say they gave the order to stop; Rahman says he heard no such command. As his child lay dead, the soldiers threw a body-bag on the ground saying 'This is for your son' and left. Rahman, who had nothing to do with the insurgency before this incident, said: 'This is America, the so-called guardian of humanity, and killing people for them is like drinking water. I shall go after them until I avenge the blood of my son.'

Some 600 cases of abuse by GIs against civilians in Iraq and Afghanistan have so far been investigated by the Pentagon. Although around 230 soldiers have been disciplined, most military personnel found guilty of abusing civilians received 'administrative' punishment such as being reduced in rank, loss of pay, confinement to base or extra duty.

Out of 76 courts martial only a few resulted in jail terms of more than a year. Most resulted in sentences of between two and four months. John Sifton of Human Rights Watch said: 'That's not punishment, and that's the problem. Our concern is that abuses in the field are not being robustly investigated and prosecuted, and that they are not setting an example with people who cross the line ... That sends the message that you can commit abuse and get away with it.'

Child prisoners

It was early in October 2003 that Kasim Mehaddi Hilas says he witnessed the rape of a boy prisoner aged about 15 in the notorious Abu Ghraib prison in Iraq. 'The kid was hurting very bad and they covered all the doors with sheets,' he said in a statement given to investigators probing prisoner abuse. 'Then, when I heard the screaming I climbed the door ... and I saw [the rapist's name is deleted] who was wearing a military uniform.' Hilas, who was himself threatened with being sexually assaulted in Abu Ghraib, then describes in horrific detail how the soldier raped 'the little kid'.

In another witness statement, which I have seen, former prisoner Thaar Salman Dawod said: '[I saw] two boys naked and they were cuffed together face to face and [a US soldier] was beating them and a group of guards were watching and taking pictures and there was three female soldiers laughing at the prisoners. The prisoners, two of them, were young.'

It's not certain exactly how many children are being held by coalition forces in Iraq, but my investigations have led to a conservative estimate that suggests there were up to 107 children in coalition custody by the end of the summer in 2004. Their names are not known, nor is the location of where they are being kept, how long they will be held or what has happened to them during their detention.

Proof of the widespread arrest and detention of children in Iraq by US and UK forces is contained in an internal Unicef report written in June 2004. The report has – surprisingly – not been made public. A key section on child protection, headed 'Children in Conflict with the Law or with Coalition Forces', reads: 'In July and August 2003, several meetings were conducted with CPA [Coalition Provisional Authority] ... and Ministry of Justice to address issues related to juvenile justice and the situation of children detained by the coalition forces ... Unicef is working through a variety of channels to try and learn more about conditions for children who are imprisoned or detained, and to ensure that their rights are respected.'

Another section reads: 'Information on the number, age, gender and conditions of incarceration is limited. In Basra and Karbala children arrested for alleged activities targeting the occupying forces are reported to be routinely transferred to an internee facility in Um Qasr. The categorisation of these children as "internees" is worrying since it implies indefinite holding without contact with family, expectation of trial or due process.'

The report also states: 'A detention centre for children was established in Baghdad, where according to ICRC a significant number of children were detained. Unicef was informed that the coalition forces were planning to transfer all children in adult facilities to this "specialised" child detention centre. In July 2003, Unicef requested a visit to the centre but access was denied. Poor security in the area of the detention centre has prevented visits by independent observers like the ICRC since last December [2003].

'The perceived unjust detention of Iraqi males, including youths, for suspected activities against the occupying forces has become one of the leading causes for the mounting frustration among Iraqi youths and the potential for radicalisation of this population group,' the report added.

Journalists in Germany have also been investigating the detention and abuse of children in Iraq. One reporter, Thomas Reutter of the TV programme *Report Mainz*, interviewed a US army sergeant called Samuel

Provance, who is banned from speaking about his six months stationed in Abu Ghraib but still told Reutter of how one 16-year-old Iraqi boy was arrested.

'He was terribly afraid,' Provance said. 'He had the skinniest arms I've ever seen. He was trembling all over. His wrists were so thin we couldn't even put handcuffs on him. Right when I saw him for the first time, and took him for interrogation, I felt sorry for him.

'The interrogation specialists poured water over him and put him into a car. Then they drove with him through the night, and at that time it was very, very cold. Then they smeared him with mud and showed him to his father, who was also in custody. They had tried out other interrogation methods on him, but he wasn't to be brought to talk. The interrogation specialists told me, after the father had seen his son in this state, his heart broke. He wept and promised to tell them everything they wanted to know.'

An Iraqi TV reporter Suhaib Badr-Addin al-Baz saw the Abu Ghraib children's wing when he was arrested by Americans while making a documentary. He spent 74 days in Abu Ghraib.

'I saw a camp for children there,' he said. 'Boys, under the age of puberty. There were certainly hundreds of children in this camp.' Al-Baz said he heard a 12-year-old girl crying. Her brother was also held in the jail. One night guards came into her cell. 'She was beaten,' said al-Baz. 'I heard her call out, "They have undressed me. They have poured water over me."' He says he heard her cries and whimpering daily – this, in turn, caused other prisoners to cry as they listened to her. Al-Baz also told of an ill 15-year-old boy who was soaked repeatedly with hoses until he collapsed. Guards then brought in the child's father with a hood over his head. The boy collapsed again.

Although most of the children are held in US custody, I established that some are held by the British army. British soldiers tend to arrest children in towns like Basra, which are under UK control, then hand the youngsters over to the Americans who interrogate them and detain them.

Between January and May 2004 the Red Cross registered a total of 107 juveniles in detention during 19 visits to six coalition prisons. The aid organisation's Rana Sidani said they had no complete information about the ages of those detained, or how they had been treated. The deteriorating security situation has prevented the Red Cross visiting all detention centres.

Amnesty International is outraged by the detention of children. It is aware of 'numerous human rights violations against Iraqi juveniles, including detentions, torture and ill-treatment, and killings'. Amnesty has interviewed former detainees who say they've seen boys as young as 10 in Abu Ghraib.

The organisation's leaders have called on the coalition governments to give concrete information on how old the children are, how many are detained, why and where they are being held, and in what circumstances they are being detained. They also want to know if the children have been tortured.

Alistair Hodgett, Media Director of Amnesty International USA, said the coalition forces needed to be 'transparent' about their policy of child detentions, adding: 'Secrecy is one thing that rings alarm bells.' Amnesty was given brief access to one jail in Mosul, he said, but has been repeatedly turned away from all others. He pointed out that even countries 'which don't have good records', such as Libya, gave Amnesty access to prisons. 'Denying access just fuels the rumour mill,' he said.

Hodgett added that British and US troops should not be detaining any Iraqis – let alone children – following the so-called handover of power from the coalition to the Iraqi interim government. 'They should all be held by Iraqi authorities,' he said. 'When the coalition handed over Saddam they should have handed over the other 3,000 detainees.'

The British Ministry of Defence confirmed UK forces had handed over prisoners to US troops, but a spokesman said he did not know the ages of any detainees given to the Americans.

When I spoke to officials, the MoD also admitted it was holding at least one prisoner aged under 18 at Shaibah prison near Um Qasr. Since the invasion, Britain has detained, and later released, more than 65 under-18s. The MoD claimed the ICRC had access to British-run jails and detainee lists.

High-placed officials in the Pentagon and Centcom told me that children as young as 14 were being held by US forces. 'We do have juveniles detained,' a source said. 'They have been detained as they are deemed to be a threat or because they have acted against the coalition or Iraqis.'

Officially, the Pentagon said it was holding 'around 60 juvenile detainees primarily aged 16 and 17', although when it was pointed out that the Red Cross estimate was substantially higher, a source admitted 'numbers may have gone up, we might have detained more kids'.

Officials would not comment about children under the age of 16 being held prisoner. Sources said: 'It's a real challenge ascertaining their ages. Unlike the UK or the US, they don't have IDs or birth certificates.' I was told, however, that at least five children aged under 16 are being kept at Abu Ghraib and Camp Bucca.

A highly placed source in the Pentagon said: 'We have done investigations into accusations of juveniles being abused and raped and can't find anything that resembles that.'

The Pentagon's official policy is to segregate juvenile prisoners from the rest of the prison population, and allow young inmates to join family members also being detained. 'Our main concern is that they are not abused or harassed by older detainees. We know they need special treatment,' an official said.

Pentagon sources said they were unaware how long child prisoners were kept in jail but said their cases were reviewed every 90 days. The sources confirmed the children had been questioned and interrogated when initially detained, but could not say whether this was 'an adult-style interrogation'.

The Norwegian government, which is part of the 'Coalition of the Willing', has told the US that the alleged torture of children is intolerable. Odd Jostein Sæter, Parliamentary Secretary at the Norwegian Prime Minister's office, said: 'Such assaults are unacceptable. It is against international laws and it is also unacceptable from a moral point of view. This is why we react strongly ... We are addressing this in a very severe and direct way and present concrete demands. This is damaging the struggle for democracy and human rights in Iraq.'

In Denmark, which is also in the coalition, Save the Children called on its government to tell the occupying forces to order the immediate release of child detainees. Neals Hurdal, head of the Danish Save the Children, said they had heard rumours of children in Basra being maltreated in custody since May 2004.

Human Rights Watch (HRW) said it was 'extremely disturbed' that the coalition was holding children for long periods in jails notorious for torture. HRW also criticised the policy of categorising children as 'security detainees', saying this did not give carte blanche for them to be held indefinitely. HRW said if there was evidence the children had committed crimes then they should be tried in Iraqi courts, otherwise they should be returned to their families.

Unicef is 'profoundly disturbed' by reports of children being abused in coalition jails. Alexandra Yuster, Unicef's senior advisor on child detention, said that under international law children should be detained only as a last resort and only then for the shortest possible time.

They should have access to lawyers and their families, be kept safe, healthy, educated, well-fed and not be subjected to any form of mental or physical punishment, she added. Unicef is now 'desperately' trying to get more information on the fate of the children currently detained in coalition jails.

Giving al-Qaeda WMD

During the autumn of 2004, in the corridors of the United Nations, diplomats embarked on an angry whispering campaign against the Americans and the British, blaming the Coalition of the Willing for the disappearance across Iraq, since the occupation began, of countless items of machine equipment which could be used to build nuclear bombs.

These machines and tools do not in anyway constitute weapons of mass destruction – quite the opposite, in fact. The United Nations allowed Iraq to have these pieces of equipment because they did not breach laws about the control of nuclear, biological or chemical weapons.

These machines were 'dual-use' – they could be used safely and legally in industry, science and academia; or used illegally to create nuclear bombs. The view within the UN was expressed by one diplomatic source this way: 'There weren't any weapons of mass destruction when we went into Iraq, but now any piece of equipment that Iraq had that could be used to make nuclear bombs has gone missing. We don't know who has this stuff or where it is. It's frightening. It's deadly serious. And it's unforgivable.'

Mark Gwozdecky, the Director of Public Information with the International Atomic Energy Agency – the UN's nuclear weapons inspection body – said: 'We know that dozens of sites which we once carefully monitored have been either completely or partially dismantled.'

These sites – some of which were sprawling factory complexes with dozens of buildings within the grounds – were fiercely monitored by the IAEA in the wake of the First Gulf War as they were home to an assortment of dual-use items like electron beam welders, milling machines and precision measurement equipment. Other materials which have vanished include high-strength aluminium, which could be turned into aluminium tubing for the centrifuges needed in the construction of a nuclear bomb. Satellite images show widespread dismantling at the sites, says Gwozdecky.

To put it more brutally, the sites themselves have literally vanished. It isn't just the dual-use technology that the factories contained that's disappeared off the face of the earth on the coalition's watch, the actual buildings in their entirety – walls, floors, windows, roofs, the lot – have gone. The problem is that no-one – not the IAEA, the CIA, MI6 – knows where in the world this stuff is.

Diplomats say the equipment could still be in Iraq in the hands of terrorists or it could be floating around on the global black market. The looting was organised, well-equipped and had plenty of manpower. The dismantling of the buildings couldn't have been undertaken without the use of heavy equipment to break up the factories and take large parts, like roofs and metal walls, away.

The looting lasted almost a year, taking place throughout 2003 in the wake of the invasion and into the early months of 2004. The dismantling of just one of the sites affected would have taken weeks to complete. UN diplomats want to know why the coalition didn't post guards around these sites given that they were known – due to weapons inspections – to have contained dual-use equipment.

'This was a big screw-up,' one said. UN resolutions made the coalition powers responsible for the security of all dual-use technology in Iraq. Britain and America were obliged to tell the IAEA if any of the material which had been previously checked by its staff was moved or interfered with. The IAEA pointed out that Iraq reported any changes to this equipment twice a year for more than a dozen years. The coalition made no reports to the IAEA; it was the IAEA which discovered that dangerous equipment was missing from studying satellite photos.

'If Iraq moved a milling machine from location X to location Y, they'd inform us and we'd verify it and make sure that there was no nuclear purpose,' said Gwozdecky. 'This happened for scientists as well as machines.'

Gwozdecky added that investigators who are trying to find the missing equipment have discovered that large amounts of scrap material from the looted sites have been shipped to the Netherlands and Jordan. A dozen missile engines have also been located in Rotterdam, and UNMOVIC – the other UN weapons inspections team – is pursuing this lead.

Some of this traced equipment was radioactively contaminated.

However, none of the high quality dual-use equipment has been discovered. Mohammed ElBaradei, who heads the IAEA, has told the UN Security Council that the missing material is of 'proliferation significance' – which means the bomb could fall into the wrong hands because this material is missing.

Although some UN sources believe that the discovery of bits of the missing equipment in countries like Holland is a good thing, as it shows that the looters are selling it on the black market rather than directly to terrorists, other diplomatic figures aren't so optimistic.

'The fact that they are selling it on the black market worries me as well,' one diplomat said. 'If someone is prepared to sell dual-use technology on the black market then they are prepared to sell it to anyone and that poses a serious risk that this stuff will get into the wrong hands.'

The IAEA says that none of the 'scary stuff' – radioactive material like enriched uranium – is missing, as Iraq didn't have any in the first place to go missing; it was safely taken care of by weapons inspectors after the First Gulf War. Even if someone managed to get their hands on all the dual-use material that is missing they still would be unable to build a home-made nuclear bomb – as they wouldn't have the requisite fissionable material.

UN diplomats are also furious with the Americans and British for preventing the IAEA getting back into Iraq to deal with the looting of sites with dual-use equipment. Diplomats feel this should be treated as a priority – not something to be repeatedly delayed and delayed.

However, the UN Security Council, which is dominated by America and the UK, has not yet taken a decision on what the IAEA's role in Iraq should be. 'The US and the UK don't want the IAEA to go back in because the weapons inspectors – the IAEA and UNMOVIC – embarrassed them because of what they didn't find in Iraq prior to the war,' a UN diplomatic source said.

'The US and the UK, therefore, don't want to hand the ball to these guys. What matters, however, is that the IAEA has the history, the record and the legitimacy needed to go back in there and clear up what exactly is happening to all this stuff.'

The draft

It looks like America is effectively laying the groundwork to bring back conscription. Two bills have been lodged in the United States – one in the Senate and one in the House of Representatives – for the introduc-tion of the military draft due to pressure on the overstretched US army in dealing with the occupation of Iraq and the war on terror.

Senior military commanders say the army is at breaking point. Senator Ernest F Hollings introduced the 'Universal National Service Act', which has already had two readings and has now been referred to the Armed Service Committee. An identical bill was lodged by Charles Rangel in the House of Representatives.

The bill says that every citizen of the US, aged between 18 and 26 will have to perform a two-year period of National Service. There will be some deferment chances for those still in high school, those who are in 'extreme hardship' or those who suffer from physical or mental illness. The bill rules that conscientious objectors will be forced to undertake military service but they will be exempt from combat. Any claim to con-scientious objector status can only be made on religious grounds – so atheists and agnostics can't be pacifists in America, it seems.

How the US public will greet this bill when both Bush and Dick Cheney infamously dodged the draft is anyone's guess, but there has barely been a mention of these moves in the American media. Hollings and Randel jointly said: 'With major military operations in Iraq and Afghanistan, 14 current peacekeeping missions and prior troop com-mitments around the globe, our forces are spread thin.

'President Bush's dependence on endless deployments of the National Guard and Reserves – who are supposed to serve in the event of emer-gencies – is an unsustainable military policy. Our legislation to reinstate the draft is designed to help create a force size appropriate to meet the nation's expanding military obligations.'

The US army has instituted a 'Stop-Loss' programme which means that thousands of soldiers have had to stay in Iraq longer than they were promised. America is struggling to find fresh recruits to serve in the Middle East. Andrew Exum, a former army captain, described 'Stop-Loss' as 'shameful', saying: 'Many, if not most of the soldiers in this lat-est Iraq-bound wave are already veterans of several tours in Iraq and Afghanistan. They have honourably completed their active duty obliga-tions. But like draftees, they have been conscripted to meet the addi-tional needs in Iraq.'

High-level British military sources said they would be concerned about the 'standard of the American conscripted soldier that profes-sional British soldiers would have to fight alongside' if the draft was reimposed. They added: 'We don't like the idea at all.'

Nearly two-thirds of the US army's 500,000 troops are serving overseas, with the largest deployment – some 115,000 in the middle of 2004 – in Iraq. There are American military units in some 130 countries. All ten of the army's active service divisions are either in Iraq or Afghanistan, preparing to deploy there or resting from a tour of duty.

Morale is at an all-time low. More and more soldiers are resigning at the earliest possible moment and troops are starting to refuse orders from military commanders. Low-level mutinies are even underway. Professor Antony Cordesman of the Centre for Strategic and International Studies says that the Iraq war 'has shown that the US faces serious strains in fighting even one prolonged low-intensity conflict'.

The Select Service Board in America – which would be responsible for administering the draft in the US – has been advertising for volunteers to become members of local draft boards. This has fuelled speculation that conscription is just around the corner.

Professor Leonard Wong, a retired colonel who is now teaching at the US Army War College, says the draft would simply add to the American military woes. 'We have a high-quality army because we have people who want to be in it,' he said. 'Our volunteer force is really a professional force. You can't draft people into a profession.'

The British blood price

By autumn 2004, the British army was being asked by Blair to pay a greater price for this US overstretch. Hundreds of soldiers from Scotland's Black Watch regiment were ordered to leave the British zone in and around Basra in the south of Iraq and to move up north into the Sunni triangle, aka the Triangle of Death, near Baghdad to be placed under US control.

The intention was to free up US troops in that area so they would be able to concentrate on brutally suppressing the rebellious city of Fallujah. The casualty rate for the Scottish regiment quickly mounted up with five dead in the month of November 2004 alone. Was this part of the 'blood price' needed to secure the special transatlantic relationship with the US that Tony Blair spoke of back in September 2002?

Many anti-war politicians and sceptical military commanders believe that Britain is being asked to 'bleed' as badly as America in order for Bush to prove to US public opinion that other nations are bearing an equal brunt of the violence in occupied Iraq.

One of Britain's top military experts, Lord Timothy Garden, former Assistant Chief of the defence staff and a leading analyst with the Royal Institute of International Affairs, has described the sending of Scotland's Black Watch regiment to back up American troops in Iraq's most dangerous areas as a 'critical, serious and ultimately unnecessary decision that makes no logistical sense'.

Garden believes the plan will eventually lead to the UK sending even more troops to Baghdad or Fallujah. He said that decision would blur the present boundaries, which see Britain in a peace-keeping role in the south of Iraq while America takes on insurgents in the main trouble spots.

Garden branded the strategy 'bizarre': 'There are 130,000 US troops in Iraq and the 600 British troops will find it difficult to be integrated with them. What is being attempted here is to blur the boundaries that divide US and UK control.'

The blurring of the boundaries between the US and UK forces led inevitably to the escalation of violence in the British-controlled southern sector of Iraq. British troops were more and more seen in the same light as the oppressive US forces and in turn the level of attacks against UK soldiers mounted in an area that had once been relatively peaceful compared with the mayhem to the north.

Garden said that if the security situation worsened, and UK forces had to continue to be redeployed to support the Americans, then Britain would have no reserve soldiers in southern Iraq, and an increase in British troops being sent to the Gulf would have to follow. Other military sources asked what possible purpose a few hundred British troops could have in terms of relieving the US military. Such a small number of troops would not lighten the American burden and this thinking ramped up the belief that the underlying principle of the redeployment was to demonstrate that Britain was prepared to suffer the same type of casualties as the US. The UK has lost just over 100 soldiers during the occupation, while the US has lost more than 2,450 in some of the worst fighting since the invasion.

The leader of the Scottish National Party, Alex Salmond, who is bitterly opposed to the war, said the decision to redeploy the Black Watch had 'politics stamped all over it and it looks repugnant that Blair is still asking this "blood price" to be paid'.

Robin Cook, the former Foreign Secretary who resigned over the invasion of Iraq, warned that if British soldiers were deployed in the

American sector they could find themselves tagged with the more aggressive tactics associated with US troops. Cook, before his death, also said there was a danger that 'if Britain frees up US forces for the next assault, we may be held equally responsible by Iraqis for what happens to the residents of Fallujah'.

Of course, this being Britain, the Black Watch couldn't be dispatched to pay the British 'blood price' for Bush without getting a slap in the face from Blair as well. Their posting to the Sunni Triangle came just as they were told that not only were they going to have to do two back-to-back tours of duty in Iraq and miss Christmas leave, but also – much more importantly for a tradition-rich regiment like the Black Watch – that the centuries old outfit was to be disbanded and amalgamated with the rest of Scotland's locally raised regiments – in which sons had followed fathers into uniform down the generations – into one very Blairite Scottish 'super regiment'.

Sitting in the bar of the Black Watch Club in Perth in Scotland, John Nichol, a former Colour Sergeant in the Black Watch, Vice-Chairman of the Black Watch Club and Treasurer of the Black Watch Association, bristled with patriotic indignation as he contemplated this state of affairs – something which his former comrades-in-arms consider a 'stab in the back' from the government.

This is what he told me over a drink, with his regimental beret on his head, its red hackle as vibrant as his anger: 'We have fought the enemies of the UK down the centuries. Now it seems we're fighting our own government as well as fighting our countries' enemies. Every Black Watch soldier out there is putting their life on the line – for what? A Labour government that doesn't want to have anything to do with them? There isn't a soldier I know who would say otherwise.'

Not far from the Black Watch Club in Perth is the home of Jessie Lamond. Her grandson, Chris Cargill, celebrated his 25th birthday in Basra, the day before I spoke to her. She is 84 and as mad as hell that her 'wee laddie', a Lance-Corporal in the Black Watch, faces another tour of duty in Iraq when the regiment in which generations of her family have served faces disbandment.

She reeled off the names of her menfolk who have fought with the Black Watch and said: 'It will be terrible if they aren't home by Christmas after they have been promised this. I want to see him. Like all the family – I miss him. The threat to disband the regiment was a kick in the teeth, and now we're told about this second tour. I only hope they all come through it and get home soon.'

As we know, not every Black Watch soldier did 'come through it'.

Mutiny and Desertion

The overstretch of US troops is also highlighting the lack of support among ordinary American GIs for the war. In October 2004, 18 US soldiers staged a mutiny and refused to go on a convoy in Iraq as they felt that commanders had ignored their fears when they complained about the safety and condition of their vehicles.

The soldiers refused to accompany fuel tankers on a supply run from south-eastern Iraq to Baghdad, arguing that the fuel was contaminated and their un-armoured vehicles were in bad shape.

The tankers had previously been carrying jet fuel and had not been cleaned before the new cargo of diesel fuel was loaded, said Teresa Hill, who received a frantic telephone message from her daughter, Specialist Amber McClenny.

'Hi mom, this is Amber. This is a real, real big emergency. I need you to contact someone, I mean, raise pure hell. We yesterday refused to go on a convoy ... We had broken-down trucks, non-armoured vehicles and we were carrying contaminated fuel,' said McClenny in the message aired on US television networks.

Hill said her daughter referred to the convoy as a suicide mission. 'She felt like the army was just leaving them out there to drown,' said Hill, who added that her daughter feared the contaminated fuel might be put in a helicopter that could ultimately crash and add to the US death toll in Iraq.

Johnny Coates said his son complained on one occasion that his truck broke down four times on the way to deliver fuel. Like other relatives, Coates called his son a good soldier who felt he had to take a stand. 'I think he did the right thing. He lived to talk about it for one more day.'

Such righteous rebelliousness is quickly seeping into British ranks, as well, as our professional soldiers become increasingly sickened by what is happening in the Gulf.

More than 1,000 British squaddies have deserted and vanished since the invasion of Iraq. Figures for the numbers of soldiers going absent without leave have also skyrocketed. In 2003, when the war broke out, 2,825 soldiers went AWOL, but in 2004, the number had jumped to 3,050. John McDonnell, a Labour MP, said in parliament that troops were 'questioning the morality and legality of the occupation'.

In spring 2006, RAF doctor Flight Lieutenant Malcolm Kendall-Smith was sentenced to eight months in prison for refusing to serve in Iraq. He claimed that the British occupation was illegal. Kendall-Smith had previously served two tours of duty in Iraq.

A former SAS soldier, Ben Griffin, was allowed to leave the army after telling his commanding officer that he wouldn't serve in Iraq as he believed illegal acts were being carried out by coalition forces. Griffin says his views are shared by many British soldiers. Major General Patrick Cordingley, who commanded the 7th Armoured Brigade – the famed 'Desert Rats' – in the First Gulf War admitted that soldiers were indeed leaving the army because of Iraq.

The British Parliament is currently – in late 2006 – debating a law that will forbid all military personnel from refusing to participate in the occupation of a foreign country.

A rising tide of blood

Before the *de facto* civil war between Sunni and Shia militias really started to hot up from late autumn 2004, sending death tolls into the stratosphere, the world's most prestigious medical magazine, *The Lancet*, reported that around 100,000 civilians, mainly women and children, had been killed as a result of the invasion of Iraq, mostly due to military activity. Jack Straw, the UK's Foreign Secretary, said the British government would 'examine with very great care' the findings. After *The Lancet* published its research, the mounting sectarian violence turned Iraq into an even more rapacious human meat-grinder with deaths of up to 100 people a day not out of the ordinary.

The study by US and Iraqi researchers was led by Johns Hopkins Bloomberg School of Public Health in Baltimore. It said that poor planning, air strikes by coalition forces and a 'climate of violence' had led to the spiralling death toll in Iraq.

The risk of death from violence for civilians in Iraq was now 58 times higher than before the war, it said. Violence was now the 'primary cause of death'; the study attributed most of these deaths to coalition forces. The major causes of death before the war were heart attack, stroke and chronic illness.

Straw said: 'Because it is in *The Lancet*, it is obviously something we have to look at in a very serious way.'

The researchers compared civilian mortality for periods spanning more than a year, before and after the invasion. They interviewed 988

Iraqi households from 33 randomly selected neighbourhoods. *The Lancet* said the findings were 'convincing'.

Lancet Editor Richard Horton said: 'Democratic imperialism has led to more deaths, not fewer. This political and military failure continues to cause scores of casualties among non-combatants.'

He urged the coalition forces to rethink their strategy to 'prevent further unnecessary human casualties'. There is no official estimate from the coalition of the number of Iraqi civilians who have died since the outbreak of the war in Iraq. To not even count the people that we have killed shows, perhaps, more than any other action, the wanton disregard that Britain and America have for the lives of the ordinary Iraqis that our leaders say they wish to liberate. Bush and Blair seem to be using the Vietnam theory of liberation, which runs along the lines of that old US military saying that 'in order to liberate the village, we had to destroy it'. That kind of perverted logic is now churning around in the brains of Bush and Blair, and liberty in Iraq now seems to be found only inside a coffin after a violent death.

Human rights groups say the occupying powers have failed in their duty to catalogue the deaths, giving the impression that ordinary Iraqis' lives are worth less than those of their soldiers for whom detailed statistics are available. Prior to the *Lancet* findings in late 2004, unofficial estimates of the civilian toll had varied from around 10,000 fatalities to more than 37,000.

Torture, terror, murder, reprisals, executions, child prisoners, rape, weapons proliferation, mutiny, desertion, the draft, the levelling of cities, mountains of dead – this is the war our governments chose for us; this is the war that makes you and me culpable for the crimes that our nations are committing collectively in our name; this is the war that has fostered unspeakable hatred against westerners; against you, against me, and against our children and our children's children.

THANK YOU FOR A LOVELY WAR, MR. MURDOCH!
or
The corruption of the press and the silencing of dissent in a time of war—as proved by maths

You know by now that you've been lied to and dragged into one of the most horrific wars in the history of mankind. That's what this entire book has been about, after all. So, what are you going to do about it? You can't just blame Blair and Bush and their hangers-on for the lies that have seeped into our brains and souls, our culture and our way of life; they're politicians, they're programmed to lie to us. You also have to blame folk like me – the journalists who wittingly or unwittingly spread the politicians' lies for them; and you also have to blame yourself. A lot of us knew that we were being lied to, but what did we do about it? We sat at home and fumed in front of the TV, threw the remote control at the screen, screamed at our wives or husbands or boyfriends or girlfriends about the iniquities of the world and then did – what exactly?

Nothing.

We bought another game for the PlayStation. Went to a new club. Bought some new clothes. An iPod. Maybe you went to Prague for the weekend on a cheap flight, or you took a jaunt to the Big Apple for some shopping in Macys. It's easy, in the world we live in, to get drugged by consumerism; to forget just how shitty the world is with a little retail therapy or a hedonistic holiday that makes it all go away for a wee while. And then what with the mortgage and the kids and the weekly shopping and the bills, it's hard to keep in the forefront of your mind that there are people worse off than you: the British and American soldiers dying in the first flush of their youth in some godforsaken strip of desert or a back-street slum in Baghdad; the people of Iraq; the families of all those thousands of dead people who loved them and don't have their loved ones in their lives anymore.

Blame the press. We aren't supposed to let you down like this. We're supposed to be the one thing that stands between you and the government. We are the ones who are meant to tell you when they are lying; not collude with their lies; and not let their power blind us. People forget how important the press is meant to be in a democracy. Our job isn't really to entertain you, or show you some pretty girl from Essex on page three with her tits out. We are meant to be the fourth estate. Here's a reminder of what the fourth estate is supposed to be about. Historically, the fourth estate, the press, watches over the other 'three estates of the realm' – the clergy, the nobility and the people. The philosopher Edmund Burke said there were three estates in the British Parliament – the commoners, the aristocracy and the clergy, but then he turned his attention to the Reporter's Gallery and added: 'Yonder, there sat a fourth estate more important far than they all.' A journalist is an ordinary citizen whose job is to pass on the truth to fellow citizens, and to challenge those in power on behalf of fellow citizens. Screw with the press and you may as well elect Hitler as your leader. No free press means no freedom.

We are meant to be one of the guardians of democracy, not a lapdog for the Establishment. But that failed somewhere along the way in the last few years. Instead of questioning what our elected leaders were up to, we became their cheerleader. And it is disgusting. Any journalist who acts as a rah-rah boy for the government should be taken out and shot. The Establishment journalist is more of a threat to your safety and well-being than any power-hungry politician because if it wasn't for the Establishment journalist then the abusive government would not be allowed to exploit you, to pull the wool over your eyes, to make a fool of you. The Establishment journalist is the lynchpin in the corruption of democracy by our political leaders.

If you want to see just how insidious the press can be, and how deadly to democracy, then watch Rupert Murdoch's Fox News. I began watching this channel - which has been called the 'Pravda of America' - in-depth in the days following September 11. The Stars and Stripes flutters in the corner of the screen; the President is fawningly referred to as the Commander-in-Chief; liberals are treated like witches; men like Oliver North – he of Irangate infamy – are all-American heroes.

Rupert Murdoch owns nine satellite TV networks, 100 cable channels, 175 newspapers, 40 book imprints, 40 TV stations and one – only one, mind you – movie studio. His global audience is 4.7 billion – that is three-quarters of the people on the entire planet. What does the dirty digger from down under give his global audience? Right-wing pap and lies.

Investigative film-maker Robert Greenwald has led the way in exposing just what Mr Murdoch has been up to. His documentary, *Outfoxed: Rupert Murdoch's War on Journalism*, is essential viewing for anyone who wants to understand the power of the media and the danger of misusing it. I have drawn heavily on his sterling work in this chapter, and also on the equally probing research of US broadcaster Amy Goodman who has explored the influence that Fox and similar networks wield, and the role the media plays in propping up the establishment.

Frank O'Donnell, an ex-Fox News producer from Washington DC, says he remembers back in the early days, when Murdoch had just taken over the channel, that he was told by 'Murdoch apparatchiks' to pay 'fawning tributes' to Ronnie Reagan, who Murdoch was clearly head-over-heels in love with. 'Suddenly,' says O'Donnell, 'we were ordered from the top to carry Republican right-wing propaganda.'

Of course, Murdoch was ably assisted by the man he appointed CEO of Fox News – none other than Roger Ailes, a former media strategist for Messrs Nixon, Reagan and Bush Senior. You can see why Fox uses logos like 'Fair and Balanced', 'We report, you decide' and 'The network America trusts', can't you? It's nothing less than consumer fraud and attempts have been made to sue Fox in order to prevent it using its disgraceful, perverted logo 'Fair and balanced'.

Ailes is responsible for screwing with the minds of millions of Americans. As a consequence of those screwed American minds, Bush was able to take the US to war. When Bush decided he was going to war, our Prime Minister, in turn, made up his mind to follow America come what may, and did everything in order to hang on to Bush's coat-tails and drag the UK into an illegal conflict. The result is that British soldiers are now dying and killing in Iraq, and the UK is seen as an evil occupier. That is the point of this chapter. America's bankrupt media helped bring about the current busted flush that is democracy in the UK.

Larry Johnson is an ex-CIA officer, the former Deputy Director of the US State Department's Office of Counter-Terrorism and a one-time Fox News contributor. He says staff at Fox were 'monitored by a Stalinist system' and lived in an 'environment of fear'. If they stepped out of line ideologically they were finished. Johnson was dropped from Fox because he had the temerity to say that the invasion of Iraq would over-stretch the US army.

'The media is supposed to be the fourth estate,' he says, 'but they decided to completely climb into bed with the administration.'

John Du Pre, a one-time Fox anchor, adds: 'We weren't so much a news-gathering organisation, more a proponent of a point of view.' That would be Murdoch's point of view handed down by his minions like Ailes. As David Brock, the CEO of Media Matters for America, says of Murdoch: 'He doesn't believe in objectivity ... He wants all news to be a matter of opinion, as opinion can't be proved false.'

One of Fox's chief opinion formers is John Moody, the Vice-president in charge of news – in other words, he's the go-to guy for propaganda decisions. He was famous for the 'Moody memos' – little edicts that came down from on high inside Fox telling the drudge and drone reporters what to say and how to say it.

Take this memo dated April 28, 2004, from Moody to news staff: 'Let's refer to the US marines we see as "sharpshooters" not snipers, which carries a negative connotation.'

Or this one from May 6, 2004, headed 're: Abu Ghraib': 'Today, we have a picture – carried on Al-Arabiya [a Middle-Eastern TV station] – of an American hostage being held with a scarf over his eyes, clearly against his will. Who's outraged on his behalf?'

This right-wing bent mutates quickly into astonishing vitriol. John Kerry – the Democratic nominee against Bush in 2004 – was called 'Jane Fonda with a Burberry scarf' on Fox News. The station also allowed this to be said on air: 'John Kerry has Kim Jong-il [the dictator of North Korea] on his side and Barbra Streisand.'

Viewers were told that 'North Korea loves John Kerry'; he was even described as 'French-looking', for Christ's sake! I actually heard one reporter greet viewers with this cheery little line: 'Hello! Or as John Kerry would say "Bon jour"!'

I now have to watch Fox on the sneak in my house. My wife says that if I even watch it for research purposes I'm still putting money in the Fox coffers and so she hides the remote control. I have to wait until she's fast asleep and then creep downstairs in the dead of night, like some per-vert or junkie, to get my far-right fix of Fox's fibs.

On Fox, liberals are treated like shit on the shoe of the nation. The best the channel has to offer when it comes to a so-called liberal member of staff is a weasly little fella called Alan Combes. He appears alongside a megalomaniac über-jock and Republican attack dog called Sean Hannity, and Hannity regularly subjects Combes and any liberal guests to a verbal raping. Hannity has even been known to refer to Combes as a 'good liberal' as if he was some sort of trained dog. Apart from the puny Combes, the freaks that Fox uses to front its shows are modelled on the big-balled alpha male stereotype. I guess the theory is that they are supposed to be so manly that the viewing public couldn't conceive of their chiselled faces spouting lies. Watch them closely though and you can see the sheen of hairspray and just a smudge of make-up. Alpha males? More like beta girls with delusions of grandeur.

Hannity had a nice little routine in the run-up to the 2004 presidential election which saw him tell viewers that it was only 250 days or 120 days until George W Bush was re-elected. He was there day in and day out doing the Republican Party's propaganda legwork. The conservative, Republican guests are always clever, well-turned out, well-known public figures; the liberals and Democrats are all losers with crap hair and no brains, or else they are closet Republicans who turn traitor on air and start sticking up for right-wing values. It is so loaded that you wonder, while watching it, how anyone could buy it. It's not that it is wrong to have right-wing views; but, bloody hell, can't they let the odd leftie at least make a point without howitzering them?

Liberals are hunted down and killed for sport. Richard Clarke, the former counter-terrorism czar for both Clinton and Dubya, became public enemy number one in the eyes of the White House and Fox when he said that he and the rest of the administration had failed America over 9-11 and asked for the people's forgiveness. First, the White House attacked him, and then Fox moved to do a nasty up-close-and-personal assassination job. Clarke was accused of sucking up to Kerry, of trying to get a job in a Kerry administration, of being an opportunist, of profiteering and trying to sell a book. It was a text-book smear campaign.

Staff also say that they were told that people like Jesse Jackson, the black liberal politician and churchman, were 'our targets'. Suffice to say any story about the plight of immigrants, single mums, drug addicts or anyone else who doesn't really matter to this lot is canned immediately, and reporters who value their jobs have learned not to bring such wishy-washy bullshit to the news meetings. This kind of journalism has the brutality of the Coliseum and the political integrity of a Leni Reifensthal movie.

One Fox reporter was seen as too confrontational with James Baker during the Florida debacle at the 2000 presidential elections and was pulled off the story. John Du Pre was told to treat Ronnie Reagan's birthday like a holy day and was dispatched to film smiling children celebrating the great man. The only problem was there weren't any crowds to film cheering the ex-President. Du Pre got suspended.

FAIR – the pressure group Fairness and Accuracy in Reporting – studied 25 weeks of a Fox news show called *Special Report with Brit Hume*. It is meant to be one of the week's main flagship programmes. The folk at FAIR found that 83 per cent of the guests on the show were Republicans and most of the remaining 17 per cent of guests were centrist Democrats.

The biggest beast in the Fox News zoo is Bill O'Reilly, quite simply the *capo di capo tuti* as he does Master Murdoch's bidding to the letter and beyond – either instinctually or because he realises it is the best way to climb the particular greasy pole he has chosen to scale.

O'Reilly has committed many disgusting sins in his life, but the one that will send this dissembling, lying fool rocketing into the outer reaches of hell when he finally expires was his shameless attack on the son of one of the victims of September 11. Jeremy Glick signed a petition against the invasion of Afghanistan and was a guest on O'Reilly's show – it's called *The O'Reilly Factor* and has the tagline 'the no spin zone'.

Glick's logic was sound: the US had armed the lunatics who killed his father by sending weapons and cash to the Mujahedin in the 1980s in order for them to fight the Soviet invasion of Afghanistan, so it was hardly fair to start killing innocent Afghani civilians. Many would disagree with Glick on principal, but not on his right to say what he felt. And surely no human being would stoop to insulting a young man who was still grieving for the loss of his father. But, then, we have to ask ourselves, 'Are people like O'Reilly really human?' Can a journalist maintain any humanity when they have to lie in the pursuit of their pay cheque? When their lies are furthering wars? And if someone can really go out to hurt a man whose father died in 9-11 simply because of a political disagreement, then the rest of us have to ask serious questions about their mental state. Empathy for other people is one of the distinguishing characteristics of being human. People devoid of empathy are just a couple of clicks on the old loony scale away from being full-blown sociopaths, in my opinion.

O'Reilly started by calling Glick 'far-left' and claiming Glick's own father wouldn't approve of his position. How he knew this, nobody knows, but Bill is so sure of his right to say whatever he feels that he obviously thinks he can channel the political opinions of the dead Mr Glick from Ground Zero.

Glick Junior then pointed out that his dad actually thought Bush's presidency was illegitimate because of the fiasco surrounding the 2000 election. O'Reilly flipped. His god was being called into question. Glick added that O'Reilly was trying to use 9-11 to 'rationalise a narrow right-wing agenda'.

O'Reilly – on air – said: 'That's a bunch of crap. I've done more for the 9-11 families than you'll ever hope to do so keep your mouth shut.' The Fox freak then told Glick that he was 'warped' and screamed at him: 'I hope your mom isn't watching this.' When Glick protested, O'Reilly ordered him to shut up again and then called on the backroom boys to 'cut his mic'. O'Reilly said: 'Out of respect for your father I'm not gonna dress you down anymore.'

Once the show was off the air, O'Reilly said to Glick: 'Get out of my studio before I fucking tear you apart.' Glick left and went to the green room to chill out after this horrendous encounter only to be told by a producer that he had to get out of the building as the crew believed O'Reilly would physically attack him. The next day, O'Reilly accused Glick of 'vile propaganda' against America. Six months later, O'Reilly was still hounding Glick – in the sickest and most frightening example of predatory bullyboy journalism that I have ever come across in my career. Talk about a lack of empathy? The guy should have been put in a straitjacket.

Finally, Glick asked the comedian, pundit, writer and broadcaster Al Franken – who had attacked Fox and O'Reilly in his book, *Lies and the Lying Liars who Tell Them* – how he could go about suing O'Reilly. Franken spoke to his own lawyer and was told the most astonishing thing: to sue O'Reilly, Glick would have to prove that O'Reilly knew he was lying and 'as O'Reilly is so crazy, [and] he lies so pathologically, it's harder to prove that O'Reilly knew he was lying'. In other words, O'Reilly is a professional foaming-at-the-mouth propagandist maniac and as lying is his stock-in-trade it's almost impossible to legally call him to account.

O'Reilly vowed when the invasion of Iraq took place that the war would be reported without ideology on his 'no spin zone' show. No sooner had he said that than he was telling viewers that Martin Sheen, the Hollywood actor who opposes the war, was 'against what we stand for'. People like Sheen are 'enemies of the state', O'Reilly went on. He also sent a personal 'warning to Barbra Streisand'. Sean Hannity chipped in as well to suppress dissent by calling protesters 'traitors'.

When liberals aren't being verbally mutilated, stories designed to ramp up fear are played for high stakes – like reports on terror plots that never happen, or what to do if your plane is hijacked, or endless stories on the latest 'orange alert' terror threat level. For as long as they could sustain the lie, Fox tried to portray Iraq as a happy country awash with freedom and smiling faces post-liberation.

The channel's reporters are always chirpy and full of *bonhomie* when they meet a Republican. Just take Carl Cameron, for example. During the 2000 election, he got to interview Bush. Before the interview started the cameras were running and Carl and George were chatting – getting warmed up for the first take. In that little unaired scene we learn that Cameron's wife is campaigning for Bush; the pair laugh and joke and Bush tells Cameron that his wife is a 'good soul'.

Cameron later wrote a story filled with fake quotes attributed to Kerry that made out that the Democrat nominee was a big gay girl. The story even went up on the Fox News website in the middle of the presidential race in 2004. Here's a sample of what this top political reporter wrote:

> Rallying supporters in Tampa, Friday, Kerry played up his performance in Thursday night's debate in which many observers agreed the Massachusetts senator outperformed the president.
>
> 'Didn't my nails and cuticles look great? What a good debate!' Kerry said Friday.
>
> With the foreign-policy debate in the history books, Kerry hopes to keep the pressure on and the sense of traction going.
>
> Aides say he will step up attacks on the president in the next few days, and pivot somewhat to the domestic agenda, with a focus on women and abortion rights.
>
> 'It's about the Supreme Court. Women should like me! I do manicures,' Kerry said.

The story also quoted Kerry saying of himself and President Bush: 'I'm a metrosexual – he's a cowboy.' Of course, Fox had to apologise for Cameron's 'little joke' – for that, inevitably, was the excuse – but you've got to ask yourself what kind of loose-cannon idiots this channel attracts as senior members of staff? Cameron is supposed to be one of

Fox's chief political correspondents, for God's sake.

I suppose I should remind you here that when Fox News became the first TV network to call the 2000 election for Bush – an act which was patently and mathematically flawed – the decision was taken by none other a than a certain staff member, Mr John Ellis, first cousin to one Mr George W Bush.

Once that election was won, Fox switched from crucifying liberals to singing collective hymns in praise of the new, super-dooper, ideologically sound President Bush. John Cohen, an ex-Fox News contributor, said: 'In the old Soviet Union you used to hear about the party line shifting 180 degrees.' He compared this Soviet-style *volte-face* to 'watching Fox News at the end of Clinton, where it was all attack mode, where they were just vicious watchdogs, and then Bush takes power and they were just little lapdogs. It was like night and day. It was a party line shift.'

Then in the run-up to the next election in 2004, Bush was called 'extraordinary' by Fox News, praised for his 'strong leadership' and described as a 'gentleman', while Kerry was dissed constantly over his war record. When Kerry said Bush would cut entitlement cheques for the elderly, Fox News reported that John Kerry was 'scaring old people as usual' and described Kerry's claims as 'lies'. Other Fox shows said that a Kerry win was 'unthinkable'. All the while, the TV network would constantly cut live to Bush, no matter what old tosh he was delivering on the hustings, and air his rally speeches almost in their entirety.

Fox did the White House's job for it. This is where the 'echo chamber' effect comes into play. A comment is made by senior Republicans and then repeated again and again by commentators on Fox until the collective mind of the nation is saturated with the message. Remember Kerry being described as a 'flip-flopper' – as a guy who couldn't make his mind up? Well, that phrase was first coined by the Republican Party and then leapt upon by Fox. After the Republicans used the expression, Head of News John Moody wrote a March 16, 2004 memo saying: 'Kerry, starting to feel the heat for his flip-flop record, is in West Virginia.' And then the dogs were released to kill the flip-flopper which they did with most deadly efficiency. The phrase 'flip-flop' was repeated, and repeated, and repeated, and repeated, and repeated until soon no-one – not even Kerry's wife – could think of him without imagining beach footwear.

Kerry was actually blamed by Fox for making the markets fall. When the economy did well, it was thanks to Bush, but when it did badly it was because traders had got panicked over some poll showing Kerry in the lead for the presidency.

Fox couldn't be more up Bush's ass if the news anchors got themselves hiking boots and crampons and actually climbed inside the President's orifice. One Fox News big-name presenter, Tony Snow, even became the White House Press Secretary in 2006. He'd previously been a speech writer for Dubya's daddy during the Bush Senior presidency.

One of Fox's favoured targets is what its anchors and newscasters like to call 'the liberal elite media'. O'Reilly sometimes refers to it as the 'pinhead media'. Fox likes to make it clear that it speaks for the hard-working common man and woman from the American heartlands, while those leftie-feminists in the 'liberal elite media' are just yammering to the type of stuck-up know-it-alls with a liberal arts degree that you find on the east and west coasts. The liberal elite media – papers like the *New York Times* and the *San Francisco Chronicle* – are demonised by Fox for messing with family values, being unpatriotic, getting all antsy about a woman's right to choose whether or not to have an abortion, having the temerity to bang on about the separation of church and state – those kind of things.

Maybe Murdoch has a point here, though. Don't you think? I mean, shouldn't a billionaire media tycoon from Australia be congratulated for taking on all those 'elitists' out there in the US press and broadcasting and calling them to heel?

I watch this twisted little network filled with right-wing ideologues and toadies to get a handle on what my enemies are up to. You should watch it for the same reason. It's so deranged and over the top that it is actually quite funny, and can be almost entertaining at times – if only because it makes you want to get a gun and hunt Bill O'Reilly naked through the canyons of Manhattan. But before you watch it, get yourself a copy of a fascinating little academic study called *Misperceptions, The Media and The Iraq War*. It was carried out by The Programme on International Policy Attitudes (PIPA) – a joint endeavour by the Center on Policy Attitudes and the Center for International and Security Studies based out of the University of Maryland. PIPA worked on the study with Knowledge Networks, a polling, social science and market research firm from California. PIPA's board of advisors includes the likes of Bill Frenzel, from the Brookings Institute; Anthony Lake from Georgetown University; Catherine Kelleher from the US Naval War

College and Alexander George from Stanford University. As you can see, these are some big academic hitters.

Let me sum up, in my rather coarse fashion, what the *Misperceptions* study shows: if you watch Fox News you are more likely than any other zipper-head on the face of the planet to be a stupid, ill-informed nyerk who's been brainwashed by your government and gullible enough to believe the lies that your leaders pour in your big, dumb ears. You will also be a paranoid, war-like fool with no more understanding about what is really going on in the world than my dog. In other words, Fox News does the job of the Republican government, instead of doing the job it is meant to do, which is to protect and inform you.

Between January and September 2003 – the time-frame covering the run-up to war, the war itself and the aftermath of the war – PIPA/Knowledge carried out seven different polls on Iraq. In their very restrained words: 'It was discovered that a substantial portion of the public had a number of misperceptions that were demonstrably false.'

The kind of stuff that 'a substantial portion' of the American people believed to be true included:

> Iraq played an important role in September 11 and supported al-Qaeda;
>
> Evidence was found by British and American troops in Iraq which proved a relationship between secular Iraq and God-crazy al-Qaeda;
>
> That the British and Americans found weapons of mass destruction in Iraq;
>
> Saddam had used WMD against British and American forces;
>
> World opinion – including the opinion of the Islamic nations – was behind the attack on Iraq.

'A large majority' of those polled by PIPA/Knowledge held at least one of these misperceptions.

'In polls conducted throughout the world before and during the war,' say the folk from PIPA/Knowledge, 'a very clear majority of world opinion opposed the US going to war with Iraq without UN approval. However, PIPA/Knowledge found in polls conducted during and after the war that only a minority of Americans were aware of this. A significant minority even believed that a majority of people in the world favoured the US going to war with Iraq.'

Now, this is clearly freaky. It's easier to accept that the Americans and British who supported this war did so regardless of the overwhelming evidence which proved that government claims about Iraq – primarily over WMD – were totally wrong. But to find out that the people who supported the war were just stupid and ignorant is pretty scary.

But were they just stupid and ignorant? It would actually appear not. It seems, in fact, that these people were callously misled and – I know this is a pretty far-out expression to use – even brainwashed to some extent. After reading the PIPA/Knowledge report, I was left with a nasty feeling that the people were being exploited for terrifying reasons and by terrifying people.

What had happened here? Hadn't these people seen all the protests across the world against the war? Well, of course they hadn't. These protests – as we'll see later in this chapter – were being ignored or downplayed by the media. In fact, some demonstrations were even hidden from members of the public walking the streets. Protesters were placed in 'Free Speech Zones'. That's another lovely neocon Orwellianism.

Let's say you and 5,000 of your friends wanted to demonstrate against me because you hate this book and think I'm a big stinky liar. I say, fair enough. You can stand outside my house and hurl abuse at me until the cows come home if you want – that's democracy for you. But if I were the President and I was coming to your town and you wanted to stand on the main drag in your town, where I'd be driving by, then I'm afraid you would be told that this just wasn't possible. You'd be told that you had to assemble in a 'Free Speech Zone'. That zone would probably be down by the docks a few miles from where the Prez was scuttling through. It works perfectly as an illusion of democracy. Sure, people get to rant and rave and wave their little banners saying NOT IN MY NAME and feel that they are participating in a real democracy, but who cares? Nobody cares because nobody knows they are there. The President doesn't care because he can't see them; the public don't care because the protesters are stuck in the middle of nowhere and the media sure as hell don't care because they've come to report verbatim and unquestioningly what the Commander-in-Chief is going to say and if there ain't no hippies around waggling their placards then they aren't going to get a mention in the story. And if the press *do* catch sight of some outraged citizens calling the President a murderer, well then they can't really rely on one of those peacenik pinko demonstration organisers to give accurate numbers of protesters, now can they? So they call the local cops – and guess what? Those cop figures are always way lower than the numbers the demonstrators give. Now, if I was reporting that demonstration – and I've reported on plenty – I'd either try to count the protesters myself, or if that was impossible then I'd give the figure from the police and the figure from the organisers for a bit of balance – but that sure doesn't happen either.

Real reporters are pretty much dead in the west. They've been replaced by two types of journalist: the one who's obsessed with sex scandals, footballers, soap stars, reality shows and celebrity; and the Establishment hack, the one who regurgitates the shit fed to him or her by corporations, political parties and anyone else with the faintest whiff of power emanating from them. A few reporters still exist who like to dig up real filth – the kind of filth that hurts people in power and protects people with no power – but they are seen as oddities, mavericks, part of the awkward squad.

Thus we get a news environment which is tilted away from facts and towards titillation and subservience to those in power. From this incestuous, brain-dead realm spring the findings of PIPA/Knowledge. The researchers say that the 'misperceptions' that they uncovered in their study 'played a key role in generating and maintaining approval for the decision to go to war'.

In January 2003, before the war started, some 68 per cent of those polled believed that Iraq 'played an important role in September 11'. Some 13 per cent believed that 'conclusive evidence' had been found to prove this. I don't need to spell that out for the average American, anyone who was linked to September 11 needed to be dealt with hard and removed from power. After the invasion, some 57 per cent still believed that Iraq was either directly involved in September 11 or had given substantial support to al-Qaeda. Only 7 per cent – an incredibly low figure – believed correctly that there was no link between Saddam and Osama.

Now you can see that all those comments by Bush and Cheney conflating Iraq and al-Qaeda, and Saddam and 9-11, sure worked. If a lie is thrown out into the public domain by politicians, reported unchallenged as fact and allowed to trickle down with no filter into the culture, permeating and corrupting civil discourse, then inevitably people will believe that lies are the truth and that the truth is a lie.

In June 2003, after the invasion, the researchers asked the public: 'Is it your impression that the US has or has not found clear evidence in Iraq that Saddam Hussein was working closely with the al-Qaeda organisation?' An amazing 52 per cent said the US had found evidence.

Where did they get this information from? Were they referencing their dreams? Their hopes? Their nightmares? Because they sure as shit weren't quoting from the real world.

Then we come to weapons of mass destruction. In May, when a cod-piece-clad Bush declared 'Mission Accomplished' on the deck of an aircraft carrier, PIPA/Knowledge asked whether or not the US had found Iraqi weapons of mass destruction. Thirty-four per cent said America had found WMD. PIPA/Knowledge then asked whether 'Iraq did or did not use chemical or biological weapons in the war that had just ended?' Twenty-two per cent believed Saddam had used weapons of mass destruction.

Believing in a war crime and an atrocity that never happened is a bit like forgetting about Horoshima or the Holocaust in my opinion. How could nearly a quarter of the people surveyed have imagined that Saddam had blasted our troops with sarin or anthrax when it had never taken place? How could people be so dangerously deluded?

Before the war started, PIPA/Knowledge asked: 'How do all the people of the world feel about the US going to war with Iraq?' Here's what PIPA/Knowledge found: 'Only 35 per cent perceived correctly that the majority of people opposed the decision. Thirty-one per cent expressed the mistaken assumption that views were evenly balanced on the issue, and another 31 per cent expressed the egregious misperception that the majority favoured it.' Maybe PIPA/Knowledge shouldn't have used the word 'egregious' as it's pretty much a racing cert that the 31 per cent who felt that the world favoured war with Iraq won't have a clue what it means.

Some 48 per cent of Americans polled believed – incorrectly – that 'a majority of people in the Islamic world favour US-led efforts to fight terrorism', and 35 per cent thought people in the Muslim world believed that US policies were making the Middle East more safe.

When PIPA/Knowledge asked Americans if they believed that Iraq was linked to al-Qaeda, that WMD were found in Iraq and if world opinion backed the US going to war, the pollsters discovered that 32 per cent believed one of those 'misperceptions', 20 per cent believed two 'misperceptions' and eight per cent believed all three. Only 30 per cent didn't believe any. That's a lot of American people believing a lie and not enough in touch with the truth.

In case you need reminding, here's what the world really thought of the decision to go to war without UN approval. Of 38 countries, including 20 European nations, polled by Gallup in the run-up to war, not a single one showed a majority support for America and the UK acting alone without UN backing. In 34 of the countries – including 17 out of 20 European states – a majority said that their nation should not support the US and UK going it alone in Iraq.

Turkey, Indonesia, Pakistan, Lebanon, Jordan, Kuwait, Morocco and the Palestinian Authority were all polled by the Pew Global Attitudes Survey in May 2003. Apart from Kuwait, opposition to the war in the six other states ranged from between 67 to 97 per cent of those polled.

Unsurprisingly, those Americans who believed in one or more of the Big Three misconceptions – links to al-Qaeda, WMD found in Iraq and that world opinion was behind Dubya – were more likely to support the war. It kind of reminds me of that terrible/hilarious event in the UK at the height of one of our annual panics over paedophiles when the home of a paediatrician was attacked by a pervert-hating mob who believed that a child doctor was actually a child molester. If people are frightened, ill-informed, confused and not given the means to put their terrors into context then they rush for the security-blanket of force to protect them and comfort them. If they don't understand the world around them, then they can be encouraged to commit untold acts of wanton cruelty and stupidity.

After repeated polling by PIPA/Knowledge in 2003 it was found that 69 per cent of punters who believed that 'Saddam Hussein was directly involved in September 11' said they supported the war. Fifty-four per cent of those who felt Iraq 'had given al-Qaeda substantial support but was not involved in the September 11 attacks' backed the war. Thirty-nine per cent who felt 'a few al-Qaeda individuals had contact with Iraqi officials' backed Bush, but only 11 per cent who said 'there was no connection at all' between Saddam and al-Qaeda supported Bush going it alone. Of those who believed there was no connection at all, 73 per cent opposed the war. So, the more you believe the lie, the more you'll support the war; and vice-versa, the more you know the truth, the more you oppose the war.

An April 2006 poll for *Investors Business Daily* and the *Christian Science Monitor* asked the 72 per cent who they found supported the war to give the top reason for attacking Iraq. The primary motive was: 'Iraq's connection with groups like al-Qaeda.'

The same pattern is played out for the other Big Three misperceptions. Seventy-three per cent of people who believed WMD were found in Iraq supported the war; only 41 per cent of those who didn't believe that weapons of mass destruction had been found backed the invasion.

Support for the war ran at 64 per cent among those who thought Iraq had used WMD during the war. Only 48 per cent of those who knew that Saddam hadn't used banned weapons supported the war.

Just before the start of the war in March 2003, PIPA/Knowledge found that 81 per cent of people who believed that the world was behind America going to war, with or without the backing of the UN, supported the invasion. Of those who knew that the world was against America, only 28 per cent said they backed Bush's push for war. The percentages remained relatively unchanged after the invasion.

Eighty-six per cent of those who held all three 'misperceptions' – that WMD had been found, that Iraq backed al-Qaeda and that the world supported America – were in favour of the invasion. Of those who held two of the big 'misperceptions', 78 per cent backed the war. Among those who held one of the 'misperceptions' 53 per cent backed the war and only 23 per cent of those who didn't hold any of the misperceptions supported the invasion.

You see the pattern, by now? Here is where the statistics and the figures get really strange. PIPA/Knowledge decided to have a wee look at where these people, who were labouring under such woeful ignorance, were getting their information from. 'The extent of Americans' misperceptions vary significantly depending on their source of news,' the PIPA/Knowledge researchers said. And now for the killer proof that propaganda is alive and well and screwing us all up. The PIPA/Knowledge study proved that: 'Those who receive most of their news from Fox News are more likely than average to have misperceptions. Those who receive most of their news from NPR or PBS [the equivalent of the BBC] are less likely to have misperceptions.'

It has been proved by maths! Fox makes you thick! Add to this the fact that only 19 per cent of Americans get their news from papers and 80 per cent stare goggle-eyed at the boob-tube spewing out infotainment and you have a society ripe for being exploited by misinformation. If people don't really care about the truth and about facts, then you can just spoon-feed them any old garbage and they will happily digest it and regurgitate it unquestioningly. Why would they bother trying to work out whether what they were being told was true or not, anyway, what with a pizza and *The Simpsons* to get through?

When punters were asked by PIPA/Knowledge which channels they watch, the stats broke down like this:

Two or more channels 30%
Fox 18%
CNN 16%
NBC 14%
ABC 11%
CBS 9%
PBS/NPR 3%

'Standing out in the analysis are Fox and NPR/PBS,' the PIPA/ Knowledge study says, 'but for opposite reasons. Fox was the news source whose viewers had the most misperceptions. NPR/PBS are notable because their viewers and listeners consistently held fewer mis- perceptions than respondents who obtained their information from other news sources ... Fox News watchers were most likely to hold mis- perceptions – and were more than twice as likely than the next nearest network to hold all three misperceptions. In the audience for NPR/PBS, however, there was an overwhelming majority who did not have any of the three misperceptions and hardly any had all three.'

Frequency of Misperceptions (belief in evidence of al-Qaeda links, WMD found, world public opinion favourable)
Respondents with one or more misperceptions by channel of choice:
Fox 80%
CBS 71%
ABC 61%
NBC 55%
CNN 55%
Print 47%
PBS/NPR 23%

When it came to believing that the US had found 'clear evidence in Iraq that Saddam Hussein was working closely with the al-Qaeda terrorist organisation', 67 per cent of Fox viewers believed that crock of ca-ca. Only 40 per cent of newspaper readers and 16 per cent of NPR-PBS fans bought the same lie.

Thirty-three per cent of Fox watchers fell for the lie that 'since the war has ended the US has found Iraqi weapons of mass destruction'. Twenty per cent of CNN viewers believed the same lie, with 17 per cent of news- paper readers and only 11 per cent of people who got their information from PBS-NPR getting suckered. There was a similar picture regarding the belief that the world supported the US attack on Iraq. Thirty-five per cent of Fox viewers, 24 per cent of CNN viewers, 17 per cent of newspaper readers and five per cent of PBS-NPR viewers and listeners believed the global community was giving a big old thumbs-up for shock-and-awe.

Some other tasty tit-bits dug up by those diligent data-miners over at PIPA/Knowledge make for pleasant reading too. 'Republicans with lower education are more likely to have misperceptions,' the report claims. Big surprise, there.

If you split the Republicans up into itty-bitty groups based on where they get their information you also discover that it is the Republicans who watch Fox who believe the most lies, rather than the Republicans who get their news from more 'normal' channels.

Some 43 per cent of all Republicans believed each one of the Big Three lies. But 54 per cent of Republicans who watch Fox believed all three lies. Only 32 per cent of Republicans who get their news from PBS-NPR believed all three.

Do you realise just how horrible these facts are? It means that down there at the bottom of the gene-pool, and leading us into world war, are a bunch of thick-as-shit couch potatoes who are sucking up the lies and disinformation peddled by Rupert Murdoch's big fat fib machine along with their nachos and cheesy puffs. The suckers, the gullible, the lazy, the uninterested and the simple-minded have brought us to a place where torture and terror and war are the fabric of our lives.

Sure, people can say 'That's democracy, boy, the people have spoken and just 'cos you don't like it, don't mean we're gonna change it'. That kind of glib answer is fine if people are making democratic decisions based on the truth, but when they make decisions based on flagrant lies told to them by their leaders which are routinely amplified by the corporate media then I have to say that I, at least, don't believe that that is democracy in action. It seems more like a cosy little sham to me.

Now, wait for some truly frightening statistics; frightening because they seem to show the ruthless and inescapable nature of modern propaganda. What PIPA/Knowledge also found out was that if you listen attentively to Fox News you are more likely to believe lies than if you just have Fox on in the background like a form of TV wallpaper. So by trying to be a good citizen – by trying to get yourself informed – you are actually exposing yourself to the virus of propaganda and lies if you tune into a right-wing thought-machine like Fox and watch it closely.

'While it would seem that misperceptions are derived from a failure to pay attention to the news, overall, those who pay greater attention to the news are no less likely to have misperceptions,' the boffins over at PIPA/Knowledge found out from their marathon number-crunching endeavours. 'Among those who primarily watch Fox, those who pay more attention are more likely to have misperceptions. Only those who mostly get their news from print media, and to some extent those who primarily watch CNN, have fewer misperceptions as they pay more attention.'

Just the act of watching Fox is likely to frig around with your brain. How scary is that? Forty-two per cent of Fox viewers who said they didn't really pay attention to the news believed al-Qaeda and Saddam were linked. But wait for this ... 80 per cent of Fox viewers who said they paid 'very close' attention to the news believed the same particular lie.

The stats are reversed when you look at newspaper readers. Forty-nine per cent of folk who primarily use newspapers to get facts, but don't really pay attention, believed the Saddam and al-Qaeda lie. But only 32 per cent of newspaper readers who really did pay close attention believed the same lie.

That makes sense. If I skip through a newspaper and only read the headlines, look at the pictures and read the sports section then I might well come away from my daily news feast a little fuzzy on the facts. But Fox turns logic on its head. The more you watch, the dumber you get; the less you watch, the smarter and safer you are.

As you would expect, the same figures are replicated among Fox viewers when their positions on the other two big lies are examined. Forty-four per cent of people who said they watched Fox 'very closely' believed WMD had been found in Iraq – but only 24 per cent of people who said they didn't pay very much attention to Fox when they watched it believed the same thing.

The more that CNN viewers watched the news, however, the more understanding they had. Twenty-four per cent of viewers who hardly bothered watching believed WMD had been found, but only 11 per cent who watched 'very closely' believed banned weapons had been discovered.

Of Fox viewers who 'did not follow the news at all closely', 22 per cent believed world opinion was behind America, but 48 per cent of Fox viewers who 'followed the news very closely' believed the same lie.

Among newspaper readers, 25 per cent who didn't follow the news closely believed the world backed America, falling to just 16 per cent for those who did follow the news closely. 'For CNN, only 11 per cent of those who followed the news very closely had this misperception, while for those who followed the news not closely at all the percentage was 27 per cent.'

The PIPA/Knowledge study just keeps getting better. The researchers found that 'the level of misperceptions varies according to Americans' political positions'. Can you guess which particular political position will find its followers to be a little more gullible, out-there, daft and mad than anyone else's? Why, that's right! It's Bush supporters.

Here's what PIPA/Knowledge have to say: 'Supporters of the President are more likely to have misperceptions. Republicans are also more likely, but this appears to be a function of support for the President.' Liking Bush, therefore, makes you dumb and gullible – even more dumb and gullible than fellow Republicans who don't dig the President. Well, I suppose all good sheep like a good shepherd, so it's not really that surprising, is it?

Prior to the November 2004 presidential election, PIPA/Knowledge said: 'When Bush supporters and supporters of the Democratic nominee [that was John 'Lurch' Kerry in case you've forgotten] are compared, it is clear that supporters of the President are more likely to have misperceptions than those who oppose him.

'Republicans are also more likely to have misperceptions. However, further analysis reveals that support for the President is the critical factor, not Republican identity.'

Thankfully, just because you are a Republican it doesn't mean that you swallow the garbage from Bush hook, line and sinker – it is the devotees of Bush who have the funny brains. That means Republicans can be allowed to continue breeding, but Bush supporters, I'm afraid, must be controlled by eugenics. I'm joking of course.

'On average,' says the PIPA/Knowledge study, 'those who would vote for the President held misperceptions 45 per cent of the time, while those who say they will vote for a Democrat misperceived, on average, 17 per cent of the time.'

Support for the President/Kerry and belief in the Big Three Key Misperceptions
Evidence of links to al-Qaeda
   Bush supporters 68%
   Democrats 31%

WMD found
Bush supporters 31%
Democrats 10%
World opinion favourable
Bush supporters 36%
Democrat 11%

Nearly 30 per cent of Bush supporters said 'Iraq was directly involved in the 9-11 attacks,' compared to 15 per cent of Democrats.

'While Bush supporters are more likely than supporters of a Democratic nominee to have misperceptions,' the PIPA/Knowledge researchers said, 'for both groups, respondents' choices of a news source make a significant difference in how prevalent misperceptions are'. For example, 78 per cent of Bush supporters who watch Fox News thought the US has found evidence of a direct link to al-Qaeda, but only 50 per cent of Bush supporters in the PBS and NPR audience thought this.

'On the other side, 48 per cent of Democrat supporters who watch Fox News thought the US has found evidence of a direct link to al-Qaeda, but not one single respondent who is a Democrat supporter and relies on PBS and NPR for network news thought the US had found such evidence.'

PIPA/Knowledge went on: 'Among those who say they will vote for the President, those with higher exposure to news are more likely to misperceive and to support the war. The opposite is true for those who say they will vote for a Democratic nominee: those with higher exposure to news are less likely to misperceive and to support the war ... Among Bush supporters who say they follow the news 'not at all' on average 40 per cent misperceive. This rises to an average of 54 per cent misperceiving among those who follow the news very closely. The opposite dynamic occurs for those who say that they will support a Democratic nominee. Among Democratic supporters who do not pay attention at all, an average of 22 per cent misperceive. At higher levels of attention, misperceptions drop so that among those who follow the news very closely only an average of 11 per cent misperceive.'

Misperception rate by Bush supporters and Democrat supporters related to attention paid to news sources
Belief in Iraqi links to al-Qaeda
Bush supporters:
Not following the news closely 57%
Following the news closely 74%

Democrats:
Not following the news closely 35%
Following the news closely 22%
Belief in WMD being found in Iraq
Bush supporters:
Not following the news closely 29%
Following the news closely 44%
Democrats:
Not following the news closely 18%
Following the news closely 4%
Belief that world opinion backs America
Bush supporters:
Not following the news closely 34%
Following the news closely 43%
Democrats:
Not following the news closely 14%
Following the news closely 8%

'Among those who say they will vote for the President, support for the war rises as they pay more attention to the news (and, apparently, have more misperceptions), going from 53 per cent among those who do not follow the news closely at all to 86 per cent among those who follow the news very closely,' PIPA/Knowledge explained.

That's a whole lot of numbers and stats, but you know exactly what it means: we're screwed. Idiots who watch lies on TV obediently vote for the governments spewing the lies on TV, and we have to live with the consequences.

But then, if you're an optimist like me, you might think that some decent souls tried to explain to these scramble-brained war-dogs that they were totally wrong in their beliefs.

This is where we come up against the most wicked and insidious tool of a press which is embedded, and in bed, with the government: the suppression of information.

You can't persuade people that they are wrong if the media will not air your message – if the TV won't show your demonstrations or if the newspapers won't report them. And if your voice is being suppressed at a time when dissent is being defined as unpatriotic, treacherous and even criminal, then sometimes, understandably, people get scared and they start to shut up.

Below, I have directly reproduced an article which I wrote for the

Sunday Herald back in June 29, 2003 – right in the middle of the time when PIPA/Knowledge researchers were carrying out their study. It was headlined RAGE. FEAR. MISTRUST. UNCLE SAM'S ENEMIES WITHIN, and the sub-deck said 'While the US fights a war on terror, it is also systematically crushing its citizens' rights. Neil Mackay on the alarming rise of a new tyranny.' It also had a real cute picture of me on the page.

Now, let me tell you, this little piece elicited quite a flurry of email correspondence. I got emails – well, hatemails – from all across the US of A, and, boy, were they pissed off. I was called ... oh, let me count the insults: 'limey bastard', 'gay-loving, nigger-loving English fruit' (I'm Irish)', 'a-hole', 'asshole', 'fuckin' asshole', 'haggis' (the reader had obviously worked out the paper I write for is Scottish), 'Jew-hating', 'Nazi', 'commie', 'pinko', 'Sovietist-Liberalist' (my personal favourite), 'the Queen's ass licker', 'Tony Blair's fag', 'a hack', 'a yellow journalist', 'a turd', 'a knave' (I thought that was cool) and 'a stupid fucker'.

If there are any mums and dads out there who are now cross with me as their children – switched-on little liberals that they are, I'm sure – have read a whole string of bad swear words, then I am sorry. But that is what angry right-wing people write to journalists these days – and I have to say I think it's both hilarious and scary. If I were at a party and you overheard me saying that I disagreed passionately with Tony Blair, would you walk up to me, tap me on the shoulder and call me a fag or a turd?

But it's also good that I got these horrible hatemails, as it shows that people are seeking out different forms of information from across the world. And for every hatemail that I got for the piece that you are going to read I got four nice ones. The article really isn't the most incendiary of stories at all, in fact I got far more hatemail for running pieces like the investigation into the PNAC or reports about the use of depleted uranium shells as coalition munitions.

The nicemails were from the States as well, and they were saying different things. They were thanking the *Sunday Herald* for running articles that they'd never read before or heard before in the US media. They were delighted to see someone challenge the Establishment. They were saying 'keep on writing, man' and some were even signed with things like 'peace' and 'love'. Now I know that the nicemails sound like they came from hideous old hemp-sucking hippies but they were from teachers, factory workers, academics, nurses, soldiers, students, ex-intelligence community folk, single moms (I use 'mom', not 'mum', as they were American) and musicians and all sorts of everyday people.

The piece has got a really poor intro (first paragraph in journalist-talk), and I wish I'd written it better, but I need to reproduce it in full (without rewriting the dodgy intro, much as I would like to) to explain why all those bewildered Fox News viewers who thought that up was down, and left was right, and black was white never got to hear the truth. Didn't they see the protests? Didn't they listen to the anti-war campaigners? Or were they somehow swept away by a media trammelling up the passions of patriotism, fear, glory and anger? And were the voices of dissent and opposition being gently silenced and quietly frightened into acquiescence?

Like I said, this piece might explain that conundrum – just a wee bit. RAGE. FEAR. MISTRUST. UNCLE SAM'S ENEMIES WITHIN.

June 29, 2003

When the Hollywood actor Tim Robbins took to his feet before the National Press Club in Washington DC in April this year, he delivered a speech laced with deliberate echoes of Bob Dylan's protest song 'Blowin' in the Wind'. While Dylan, however, sang of freedom and liberty one day triumphing over repression and control, Robbins was saying that the greatest democracy on earth, the United States of America, was heading in the opposite direction under President Bush: to a future where freedom had lost out to repression and liberty to control.

'A chill wind is blowing in this nation,' said Robbins – who, along with his partner, the actress Susan Sarandon, has been routinely denounced by the American right. 'A message is being sent through the White House and its allies in talk radio: if you oppose this administration, there can and will be ramifications. Every day the airwaves are filled with warnings, veiled and unveiled threats, spewed invective and hatred directed at any voice of dissent. And the public sits in mute opposition and fear.'

Just days before this speech, Saddam's statue in Baghdad was wrapped in the Stars and Stripes and dragged to earth by US tanks. To millions of Americans like Robbins, the image must have been replete with irony. Here was democratic America destroying one of the most tyrannical regimes on earth in the name of freedom – yet in the process of fighting for democracy abroad, America's own freedoms were being systematically eaten away at home.

A few things have happened recently that show just how powerful – and, perhaps, unstoppable – is the march of the right-wing machine in the US. This month the American Enterprise Institute (AEI), a right-wing think-tank umbilically tied to the Bush administration, declared open warfare on non-governmental organisations (NGOs) deemed too left-wing and set up an organisation called NGOWatch to monitor these liberal pressure groups. NGOs that have fallen foul of its wrath include groups promoting human rights, women, the environment and freedom of speech; among its targets are the American Civil Liberties Union (ACLU), Amnesty International, Greenpeace and the World Organisation Against Torture. Only this February, George Bush boasted that 20 AEI members were working for his administration. AEI fellows include Lynne Cheney, the Vice-president's wife, and Richard Perle, the most influential of all neoconservative hawks.

NGOWatch has issued scathing reports on the following groups:

> Human Rights Watch, which investigates government abuses around the world. According to NGOWatch, it is an organisation that 'recommends groups that promote same-sex marriage', 'promotes sexual orientation rights', 'denounces abstinence [from sex] programmes', 'advocates gays in the military' and 'demands release of some detainees at Camp X-Ray in Guantanamo Bay'. Nearly 700 men are held at the camp without charge, trial or access to legal help.
>
> CARE International, which works in the Third World. It is attacked because its president, Peter Bell, criticises Bush's Mexico City Policy, which prohibits international groups that perform or promote abortion from receiving tax dollars to teach family planning.
>
> The NOW (National Organisation For Women) Foundation, which promotes abortion rights and equality in the workplace. NGOWatch says: 'With lesbianism and left-wing politics, NOW conferees cling to the fringe.'

Naomi Klein, author of the anti-corporate bestseller *No Logo*, points out that Andrew Natsios, head of the government-run United States Agency for International Development (USAid), attacked NGOs this May 'for failing to play a role many of them didn't realise they had been assigned: doing public relations for the US government'. Klein says NGOWatch is a 'McCarthyite blacklist, telling tales on any NGO that dares speak against the Bush administration's policies or in support of international treaties opposed by the White House'.

But the Bush administration might not find the term 'McCarthyite' all that insulting if the poster-girl of the American right, Ann Coulter, gets her way. Coulter is set to knock Hillary Clinton, the former First Lady, off the top of the US bestseller lists with her book *Treason: Liberal Treachery from The Cold War to The War On Terrorism*. Its central thesis is that Senator Joe McCarthy, the man behind the communist witch-hunts of the 1950s, was a good guy and an all-American patriot. Coulter is the woman who said after September 11: 'We should invade their countries, kill their leaders and convert them to Christianity.' She also said US citizens should carry passports on domestic flights to make it easier to identify any 'suspicious-looking swarthy males'.

McCarthy was censured by his Senate colleagues: despite levelling charges of communism at all and sundry, he was unable to produce the name of a single card-carrying communist in the US government. The *Encyclopaedia Britannica* says he was seen by his detractors as a 'self-seeking witch-hunter who was undermining the nation's traditions of civil liberties', yet his accusations led to the persecution of many of those he condemned.

Coulter says: 'The myth of McCarthyism is the greatest Orwellian fraud of our times. Liberals are fanatical liars, then as now. Everything you think you know about McCarthy is a hegemonic lie. Liberals denounced McCarthy because they were afraid of getting caught. McCarthy was not tilting at windmills. Soviet spies in the government were not a figment of right-wing imaginations. He was tilting at an authentic communist conspiracy.'

Coulter's article of faith is that liberals have managed to shout harder than the right and twist society with propaganda. It is a remarkable claim given the approach to journalism by one of the US's most popular TV stations, Fox News. Vilification of liberals is almost a sport on Fox, which is owned by Rupert Murdoch. One of its main anchors, Bill O'Reilly, told viewers the US should 'splatter' Iraqis; another anchor referred to the veil worn by a Muslim-American woman as a 'thing'.

While Europeans might recoil at a subservient press and a government with such blatantly right-wing policies, others will say: 'So what? The administration is simply pushing its agenda and the media is reflecting the support of the public.' But that is not the case. Scratch the surface and many more disturbing cases of government control and attacks on dissent in the name of patriotism spring to light – and it is obvious that a vast swathe of the US public is horrified by what is happening.

Take the case of John Clarke, an organiser with the Ontario Coalition Against Poverty (OCAP). In February 2002 he was crossing into the US from Canada to speak at Michigan State University. He was taken into the immigration offices and asked what anti-globalisation protests he had attended and whether he 'opposed the ideology of the United States'. His car was searched and he was frisked. He was denied entry to the US, then interrogated by a special agent with the State Department's Diplomatic Security Service. He was asked if the OCAP was a cover for anarchism and if he was a 'socialist'. The agent had a file on the OCAP, leaflets from public-speaking engagements Clarke had taken part in and the name of a man Clarke had stayed with in Chicago. Clarke was accused of being an 'advocate for violence' and threatened with jail. Astonishingly, the interrogator asked him questions about Osama bin Laden.

Sounds like a rogue agent? Not if you take into account the six French journalists who arrived at Los Angeles Airport this May to cover a video games conference. They were detained – three of them in cells for 26 hours – interrogated, subjected to body searches and then forcibly repatriated.

It is not just foreigners that are deemed dangerous and un-American. There was Tom Treece, a teacher who gave a class in 'public issues' at a high school in Vermont. A uniformed police officer entered his classroom in the middle of the night because a student art project on the wall showed a picture of Bush with duct tape over his mouth and the words: 'Put your duct tape to good use. Shut your mouth.' Local residents said they would refuse to pass the school budget unless Treece was sacked. He was eventually removed from that class.

Or how about Jason Halperin? This March he was in an Indian restaurant in New York when it was raided by five police officers with guns drawn. Halperin says they kicked open the doors, then pointed guns in the faces of staff and made them crawl out of the kitchen. Ten other officers from the Department of Homeland Security then entered. One patron said the police had no right to hold him; he was told the Patriot Act allowed his detention without warrant. Halperin asked if he could see a lawyer; he was told only if he came to the station, and then in 'maybe a month'. When he told police he was leaving, an officer walked over, his hand on his gun, saying: 'Go ahead and leave, just go ahead.' Another officer said: 'We are at war and this is for your safety.'

The American Civil Liberties Union had to take court action to help

15-year-old Bretton Barber, who faced suspension from school when he refused to take off a T-shirt showing Bush with the words 'International Terrorist' beneath. A J Brown, a college student from North Carolina, was visited at home by secret service agents who told her: 'Ma'am, we've gotten a report that you have anti-American material.' She refused to let them in, but eventually showed them what she thought they were after – an anti-death-penalty poster showing Bush and a group of lynched bodies over the epithet 'We hang on your every word'. The agents then asked her if she had 'any pro-Taliban stuff'.

Art dealer Doug Stuber, who ran the presidential campaign in North Carolina for the Green Party's Ralph Nader, was told he could not board a plane to Prague because no Greens were allowed to fly that day. He was questioned by police, photographed by two secret service agents and asked about his family and what the Greens were up to. Stuber says he was shown a Justice Department document that suggested Greens were likely terrorists.

Michael Franti, front man of the progressive hip-hop band Spearhead, says the mother of one of his co-musicians, who has a sibling in the Gulf, was visited by 'two plain-clothes men from the military' in March this year. Franti says: '[The military] came in and said, "You have a child who's in the Gulf and you have a child who's in this band Spearhead who's part of the resistance."' The military had pictures of the band at peace rallies, their flight records for several months, the names of backstage staff and their banking records.

Chris Hedges, a Pulitzer Prize-winning *New York Times* reporter, was booed off stage after making what was perceived to be an anti-war speech at a graduation ceremony at Rockford College in Illinois. College officials unplugged his mic twice while he was making the speech, which he had to cut sharply in order to keep the situation under control; some students blared foghorns and turned their backs, while others rushed up the aisles screaming and throwing caps and gowns.

A report by the American Civil Liberties Union called *Freedom under Fire: Dissent in Post-9/11 America* says: 'There is a pall over our country. The responses to dissent by many government officials so clearly violate the letter and the spirit of the supreme law of the land that they threaten the underpinnings of democracy itself.'

The words of Justice Antonin Scalia, an avid Bush supporter and member of the Supreme Court, seem to support these fears. In March, during a lecture at John Carroll University in Ohio, Scalia told his audience: 'Most of the rights you enjoy go way beyond what the Constitution requires.' He added that in wartime 'the protections will be ratcheted down to the constitutional minimum'.

Under current laws, anyone even suspected of terrorism can be held indefinitely without charge or access to a lawyer. A new proposed law would lead to anyone deemed a sympathiser of an organisation classed as terrorist having their US citizenship revoked; they would also be deported. The Pentagon's Total Information Awareness plans will allow the state to analyse every piece of data held on each US citizen.

Many are frightened to fight back. In September 2002, around 400 peaceful demonstrators near the White House were attacked and arrested; in Oakland California, police used rubber and wooden bullets at a peace rally. Yet there is resistance. The Bill of Rights Defense Committee has been supported by more than 114 legislatures in cities, towns and counties, as well as the states of Alaska and Hawaii. They have all passed resolutions opposing draconian legislation: that accounts for 11.1 million people.

[Update. At the last time of checking, the Bill of Rights Defense Committee had made sure and steady progress. Seven states and 387 cities and counties around America had passed resolutions against the Patriot Act. The population of the areas opposing the Patriot Act stood at nearly 62 million people. Hundreds more resolutions were in the process of being prepared across the country. You heard much about that on Fox? No, I didn't think so.]

Still, with massive donations rolling in from corporate backers, many fear it is unlikely Bush will be dethroned in 2004. With a supine Democratic Party, save a few maverick voices, and a craven media, it is left to a handful of fringe voices to speak out for Americans who are angered and disgusted at the state of their nation.

These voices belong to people such as Bruce Jones, an author and Vietnam veteran. He recently wrote about what he saw as 'the ugly side of patriotism – those who insist that "you are either with us or against us"'. He added: 'There is no more important patriot in this nation than the citizen who has the guts to stand up and tell the official establishment that it is wrong.

'I know who my enemies are – the idiots who burned down the dry-cleaning establishment I use here in Modesto because it had the word French in its name, or because it had Assyrian owners who immigrated from the Middle East. I know who I must fear the most – those

Americans who do not understand what freedom of speech means;
those who equate patriotism with blind obedience.'

*

So, you can see that it was pretty hard for the average Joe or Josephine
to get out there and convincingly change the minds of the Fox News
herd. They couldn't get their voices heard and they were often under
nasty, subtle pressure to shut up. The security state that people now live
under in Britain and America has taken to saying: 'Sssh, citizen. Stop
making so much noise. There is nothing to worry about. Go home and
go back to sleep. You are scaring people with all your talk and we don't
want to have to get cross with you, do we? Go and buy yourself some
nice stuff and forget about it.'

Remember, that we are only in this war because of America. And
America is only in this war because that's what the neocons wanted.
And the neocons couldn't have taken America to war unless the press
had picked up the megaphone and blasted the government's lies into the
ears of decent Americans. And all of this was beautifully finessed by the
machine of state quietly – and in the most insidiously gentle of ways –
terrifying people, shutting them up, silencing them. What happens in
America affects us all. The lies of the Bush presidency and Rupert
Murdoch's relentless war on journalism and bastardisation of reporting
have poisoned the British just as much as they have the Americans.

Things haven't really changed since the summer of 2003. They've just
got worse. In October 2004, not long before the US election, three
schoolteachers from the town of Medford in Oregon found out just how
cross the state can get when its citizens speak up.

They were all threatened with arrest when they turned up at a venue
where Bush was speaking wearing T-shirts saying PROTECT OUR CIVIL
LIBERTIES. Intimidated by the state for wearing a T-shirt that champions
democracy? Wouldn't most politicians in a western democracy have
wanted to see people at their rally calling out for the protection of civil
liberties? Does Bush see civil liberties as something else he has to declare
war on? Maybe we should ready ourselves for the declaration of a new
'Axis of Evil': civil liberties, human rights and the rule of law.

The three teachers all had valid tickets for the event but were told to
leave the meeting when Republican organisers pulled them to one side.
'I wanted to see if I would be able to make a statement that I feel is
important but not offensive, in a rally for my President,' said 48-year-
old teacher Janet Voorhies.

Her friend, Tania Tong, a 34-year-old special needs teacher, added: 'We chose this phrase specifically because we didn't think it would be offensive or degrading or obscene.'

The Bush/Cheney presidential campaign was ruthless in keeping dissenting voices away from their rallies. Access to events was limited to people mad enough to volunteer for their campaign, and those who did protest at their events faced being arrested and charged with criminal conduct. But to threaten to arrest three teachers who weren't disrupting anything and were only wearing clothes with a completely party-neutral message that any American should be proud to support takes the suppression of opinion to a new and extremely dangerous place.

In September 2004, a 54-year-old woman called Perry Patterson was charged with criminal trespass when she said one word – 'No' – in response to a comment by Cheney that Bush had made the world safer. The day before Patterson's arrest, Sue Niederer, the 55-year-old mother of a soldier who was killed in Iraq, was also arrested for criminal trespass when she interrupted a speech by Laura Bush in New Jersey. Both had legit tickets for both events.

I asked some of my American friends to send me similar stories. They sent out emails to their pals, spoke to local activists where they lived and soon hundreds of emails were flooding into my office from across the States. They were telling me how local rallies against the war weren't being reported, how dissenting voices were being silenced in their local press and on local TV, how they were being made to feel enemies of the state in their own home towns.

These were people like Linda Ford from Tacoma in Washington State. 'I attended demonstrations in the Seattle area,' she wrote to me, 'where upwards of 10–15,000 people marched, yet the news reported "several hundred".

'In Tacoma, where I live, I stood in one spot and personally hand-counted 2,000 people march past. That evening the news reported "a few dozen protesters". This is the situation across the country. Our protests are minimised or ignored entirely by the media who wish to reduce the impact such protests have. .

'Most Americans were opposed to going to war with Iraq. The media insisted that the majority favoured the war even though it was necessary to lie to the public and to continually question the loyalty of anyone who dared to raise his or her voice against it.

'They bamboozled us. And it was shamelessly simple for them to do so. Now that it has become clear they conned us, do they express any remorse? No. Instead, they endlessly repeat their mantra: "Aren't we better off without Saddam?" I want to shout back: "Wouldn't the poor of the world be better off without you?" We are none of us innocent.'

Linda later emailed one of her friends to comment on my asking Americans to relate what they thought of their press and how protesters had been treated. Here's what she said to her friend: 'We get so little media attention that a Scottish guy [I'm Irish, but I forgive her] expresses interest in our stories and everyone is flabbergasted. Someone would care to hear our views? Hasn't he got the memo from Karl Rove?'

Martin Totusek from Seattle sent me a tape of an anti-war demo that took place in that supposedly great liberal west coast city on March 22, 2003 which was shot by Ken Slusher. The demo – from what I could see on screen – was maybe 5,000 strong. Which isn't that big. But there were thousands of police there to control a crowd which was perfectly peaceful.

The cops were dressed like Judge Dredd – all sci-fi body armour, knee boots, riot helmets, the lot. They were black-clad heavies armed with guns, tear gas and six-foot billy clubs, and backed up with more cops on horseback. I've seen it plenty of times before: armour-clad tools of the state, paid for by the tax-payer, being used to frighten tax-paying peasants who dare to legally protest against the state. The police job, it appeared from the film, was simply to stop the demonstration from taking place. The people waggled their No IRAQ WAR signs and shouted 'Our streets' and 'Let us walk!', but the sheriffs weren't for listening. 'This is what a police state looks like!' shouted one guy.

Kids with banners started getting pushed about, guns were drawn, the crowd got pissed off and so did the police, so they started to clear the road. One protester fell down and the cops were on him like wasps, dragging him around and off the street to shouts of 'Shame on you!' from other demonstrators.

Then a young woman protester was knocked to the ground and cuffed. Her bloodied face – splattered red around the nose and mouth – looked scared and stunned. An onlooker said that the girl just stepped off the curb and was 'viciously attacked' by police who threw her to the ground. The onlooker added that she was scared to move in case she was beaten by police clubs. She'd just had a gun pointed in her face, she said.

The police, clearly sick of messing about and playing soft, lined the road and just drew a halt to the demonstration. 'Hitler would have been proud of you,' one guy said as a police officer, clad in a balaclava and looking more like a military sniper, paced around in the road while a helicopter buzzed overhead. The tape ends with a message: 'This is our history ... will it be our future?'

Another American correspondent was Sarah Morris from Covington, Georgia. She wrote to me and told me how she went to protest against Bush when he popped down to her home town for a fundraiser. After a little email activity to coordinate the protest she and her pals left work early – Sarah works in an architect's office – and headed to the 'posh neighbourhood' where Bush's financial *soireé* was to be held. There was 'tons of security in the area' she said and no-one was allowed in. 'We instead had to go to a "Free Speech Zone" about a half-mile away,' Sarah explained. She and other protesters gathered there and got heck-led by rich folk driving past.

'The police wouldn't even let us go to the street where his motorcade would leave on. He won't see any protests. Shutting himself off from people who oppose him in anyway is starting to have quite the opposite effect than the President's handlers wanted.

'On a side note on how free speech is no longer free in this country: I live 35 miles outside the metro Atlanta area, in a heavily Republican town, but my neighbourhood is actually very Democratic (I've seen the voter rolls). I have three Kerry-Edwards signs in my yard, two on either side of my driveway and one up close to my house. My neighbour, two houses down, has one sign as well.

'We both put ours out on Tuesday morning, September 28, 2004. Just last night, October 1, someone (or a group of people) spray-painted BUSH on both my signs and my neighbour's. They kicked my neighbour's in the middle and ripped it and bent its stakes. I see that differing opinions are no longer allowed in Bush's Amerika [Sarah's spelling].'

We all know that funny spelling – Amerika – is meant to denote a kind of proto-fascist state. But it's not just leftie activists who are starting to imply that there is something a little of 'Berlin 1933' about America of late – and Britain, I should add, isn't that far behind the US in the authoritarian stakes either. Gore Vidal, one of America's most respected men of letters, said of the Bush administration: 'Many commentators of a certain age have noted how Hitlerian our *junta* sounds as it threatens first one country for harbouring terrorists and then another. It is true that Hitler liked to pretend to be the injured – or threatened – party before he struck.' Vidal went on to play with similarities between his country and Imperial Rome.

Hairy-chested he-man and Hemingway for today, Norman Mailer, said he felt the patriotism swimming in the blood-stream of America could quickly turn to fascism. Here's a bit of the great man's riff: 'This century is going to be the most awesome of all centuries to contemplate – there is a real question whether humankind will get to the end of it ... America's so big, so powerful, so vain ... I get angry when I see it being less than it can be.

'The British have a love of their country that is profound. They can revile it, tell dirty stories about it. But deep down their patriotism is deep. In America, we're playing musical chairs – don't get caught without a flag or you're out of the game.

'Why do we need all this reaffirmation? It's as if we're a three hundred-pound man who's seven feet tall, superbly shaped, absolutely powerful, and every three minutes he's got to reaffirm the fact that his armpits have a wonderful odour. We don't need compulsive, self-serving patriotism. It's odious.'

Mailer says 'when you have a great country, it's your duty to be critical of it so it can become even greater ... Culturally, emotionally, America is growing more loutish, arrogant and vain. I detest this totally promiscuous patriotism. Wave a little flag and become a good person? Ugly ... There's too much anger here, too much ruptured vanity, too much shock, too much identity crisis. And worst of all, too much patriotism. Patriotism in a country that's failing has a logical tendency to turn fascistic.'

Thanks, Norm.

We live in a world where journalists happily get 'embedded' with the military. Has there ever been a more accurate word for the state which journalism has got itself into in the early 21st century? Our media is quite literally in bed with the Establishment. The journalists have opened their legs for the men in power like tarts in a Nevada chicken ranch.

On the day that the statue of Saddam was torn down in Baghdad, CNN and CNN International showed two different sets of images. CNN – for domestic US consumption – just showed pictures of the US army tearing down the monument to Saddam, but CNN International – which is shown across the world – intercut the images with pictures of the Iraqi casualties of war. To America, the pain of other people doesn't exist. Their protests and suffering are hidden and therefore unknown and unimportant. Aaron Brown of CNN said the pictures of suffering civilians weren't shown stateside as they were 'tasteless'.

What we are left with, says Amy Goodman of the progressive and independent media outlet Democracy Now, is war as a video game with souped-up graphics and rolling news filled with comment by ex-generals and night-sight pictures of bombs falling on buildings in which we are told lurk the evil enemies of democracy. While movie-war beams from our TVs nightly, channels like ABC allow their staff, with a straight face, to tell viewers that anti-war protesters don't even know what they are protesting about. MSNBC, another major US channel, is owned by General Electric, which just happens to be a massive weapons manufacturer.

US TV stations called their war coverage things like 'Target Iraq' or flashed up graphics of the Pentagon's own code-name for the war – 'Operation Iraqi Freedom'. Images of Saddam with a rifle target over his head were used as logos for stories about Iraq. As Amy Goodman says: 'If this were state media how would it be any better?' FAIR – Fairness and Accuracy in Reporting – noted that in the run-up to the war the main news casts of CBC, NBC, ABC and PBS aired 393 interviews on the war – only three of the voices were anti-war. And those guys – CBC, NBC *et al* – are all way more 'fair and balanced' than the likes of Fox.

Journalists need to fight this – if only so we can sleep in our beds at night and look our children in the eye. We journalists live in this media world, so we have to make it clean and honest to inhabit. Right now, it's a slum filled with whores, thieves, liars and creeps. MTV dropped songs with 'war' in the title from play lists; Clear Channel – which owns 1,400 radio stations in America because Michael Powell (son of Bush's former Secretary of State Colin Powell, and head of the Federal Communications Commission) allowed the industry to deregulate – sponsors pro-war rallies and bans anti-war songs. We are in trouble. Our profession is dying. We have lied to the public. We have to apologise to the people we serve and never do what we did again. We have to change now, before it's too late and we lose the people's trust just as much as the politicians have done. Pretty soon no-one will be able to believe anything at all, and all of us will be living in a real-life version of *Alice in Wonderland*, or something even more creepy and Kafkaesque.

We all know that politicians will never apologise for the lies they told us, but have any journalists bothered to apologise either for totally failing you? Well, a few have – an exceptional few – but even they said sorry in the way I used to say sorry to my headmaster when I was caught smoking behind the cricket hut. It was a case of swallow your pride or have your arse beaten with a big stick. I said sorry because I had to, not because I wanted to, or really was sorry. I wouldn't have smoked cigarettes in school if I really wanted to say sorry. And a journalist who writes a story which they know isn't accurate only says sorry because they were rumbled. They wouldn't have written the disinformation and lies in the first place if they had really cared about not misleading the people.

That's why I got totally sick of hearing British journalists bang on about what a huge *mea culpa* the *Washington Post* gave in the summer of 2004 when it squeaked out an apology for being blind cheerleaders for a criminal war and rehashing White House propaganda.

'There was an attitude among editors: Look, we're going to war, why do we even worry about all this contrary stuff?' said the paper's Pentagon correspondent Thomas Ricks.

Executive Editor Leonard Downie Jr, added: 'We were so focused on trying to figure out what the administration was doing that we were not giving the same play to people who said it wouldn't be a good idea to go to war and were questioning the administration's rationale. Not enough of those stories were put on the front page. That was a mistake on my part.'

And Assistant Managing Editor Bob Woodward – he of Watergate fame – added: 'We did our job, but we didn't do enough, and I blame myself mightily for not pushing harder. We should have warned readers we had information that the basis for [the war] was shakier than widely believed.' He went on: 'Those are exactly the kind of statements that should be published on the front page.'

In May 2004, the *New York Times* performed a similar, limp, hand-wringing exercise. 'Some of the *Times*' coverage in the months leading up to the invasion of Iraq was credulous; much of it was inappropriately italicised by lavish front-page display and heavy-breathing headlines,' Public Editor Daniel Okrent said at the time. *The Times*' own *mea culpa* admitted that the newspaper was taken in by spurious information from a few Iraqi exiles – especially over the issue of weapons of mass destruction – with their own agenda to oust Saddam Hussein.

Okrent cited instances in which reporters who raised substantive questions about certain stories were not heeded, while others with substantial knowledge of the subject at hand seemed not to have been given the chance to express reservations.

'*Times* reporters broke many stories before and after the war – but when the stories themselves later broke apart, in many instances *Times* readers never found out,' he said. 'Some remain scoops to this day. This is not a compliment.'

Not a compliment? Journalists have injected lies into the minds of the people and they should have their notebooks torn up and their pencils broken before their eyes. We can all make mistakes as journalists; it's a rapid, quick-turn-around, cut-throat business and I don't believe that any article in any paper is truly 100 per cent accurate. But if the journalist and their editor has hand-on-heart tried to make a story as accurate as they possibly can, then they have done their job. But to knowingly withhold information, spin information or just make stuff up ... that's an act of journalistic abortion. Phoneys like that should go and write speeches for politicians or lobby for pharmaceutical companies – the people have no time for them and so newspapers and television should have no place for them as disseminators of facts. Sack 'em.

Incidentally, not only do you have to deal with a craven western press, you should also be worrying about what Britain and America are up to with overseas newspapers and TV stations, in order to further the aims of Bush and Blair. A memo from Number 10, marked TOP SECRET and dated April 2004, referred to Bush mentioning the use of 'military action' against the Arab television network al-Jazeera. The American government has consistently accused al-Jazeera of aiding and abetting terrorism. You should note that in 2001, the station's Kabul office was blown up by US bombs, and in 2003 a member of staff was killed when another American bomb hit al-Jazeera's Baghdad bureau. *The Los Angeles Times* has also reported that the American military paid Iraqi newspapers to run positive stories about the invasion and occupation written by army propaganda specialists.

So, what do you do? The press lies to you and suppresses your voice, the government uses the media like a propaganda arm and chills dissent with its softly-softly fear tactics; when journalists are caught out punting the government's lies they dribble out a feeble apology and carry on regardless; when the politicians are caught out, they give you the finger and keep straight on with the lies. What do you do, citizen?

Do you remember me talking earlier in this chapter about all those angry and happy Americans who read articles on the internet like the ones I've written for my paper, and then flamed me with hatemails or ego-stroked me with nicemails? Well, therein lies your answer.

The internet gives you access to everything that is written for public consumption on the face of the planet. Be your own journalist. I don't think we really understand the internet yet. This invention is as precious as the printing press but we still haven't really worked that out. The Net will one day make people like me redundant. More and more of you are beginning to work out that only a few media outlets are trustworthy – and I sincerely hope that you think that my own paper, the *Sunday Herald*, is one of them. Eventually, you will tire of the corporate spin and the lies that are sprinkled on the information you suck up in the papers or on the telly. Why tolerate lies in your newspaper and spin on your TV screens any more than you'd tolerate asbestos in your home or someone spitting in your coffee? If you don't like it stop reading it and watching it.

The dawn of the age of the 'fifth estate' is not that far away. We have come to such an *impasse* in the world of information that the members of the fourth estate – guys like me – need a rugged and independent watchdog to keep an eye on us; to make sure we don't get too cosy with government. That's you – you're the watchdog. Ordinary punters can control the press. Write to editors if you think they are spinning stories. Write to journalists if you know they got something wrong. Set up your own website and start filling it up with articles that you think are important. Read overseas papers. Vote out the politicians that lie. Vote for truth and honesty. If America and Britain say Iran is a deadly nuked-up nation don't just take it from Fox or *The Sun*, watch al-Jazeera too or see what the French and the Canadians and the Aussies and the Germans are rabbiting on about. You don't need someone to tell you how to think, you just need to go and find the truth for yourselves – and then tell someone else what you found. Believe me, the truth really is out there.

DEMOCRACY INACTION

or

**A tale of two elections, some news on civil war
and a short aside on why boiling people alive allows
freedom to flourish**

In May 2005, the British people voted for their sons and daughters to be allowed to die in bad, illegal wars; we also voted for our sons and daughters to be allowed to kill in bad, illegal wars.

Or rather 35.2 per cent of the British people who bothered to vote voted for bad, illegal wars by sticking an X in a box beside the name of a Labour Party candidate. The rest of us – the majority of the British people – didn't vote for bad, illegal wars. We voted for other parties, or we stayed at home – either out of apathy or disgust.

With just 35.2 per cent of the total vote, the Labour party secured a majority in the House of Commons of 66 seats – that gave them more than 55 per cent of the seats in the House. Fifty-five per cent of the seats with just 35.2 per cent of the vote? That just doesn't compute.

It took just 26,877 votes to elect one Labour MP; 44,521 votes to elect a Conservative MP and 96,378 votes to elect a Lib-Dem MP. The Lib-Dems were the only mainstream party to take a consistent, intelligent anti-war stance. Maths was never Britain's strongest subject.

In terms of the whole electorate, however, even less people supported Blair. Turn-out was woeful. Of all those entitled to vote, only 61.3 per cent bothered to do so. If you do the arithmetic (working out 35.2 per cent of 61.3), you discover that only 21.6 per cent of the entire eligible electorate voted for Labour. That means just one in four Britons, therefore, really support Blair.

Sure, Blair got a bit of a bloody nose and saw his majority cut severely from the previous election in 2001, but the brutish, blunt, British electoral system gave him a healthy enough majority to get cracking on some really nasty pieces of legislation as soon as he was re-elected – such doozies as his Big Brother-style ID cards and the wholesale trashing of civil liberties in the UK.

Here's what the British Electoral Reform Society had to say about the depressing democratic shambles that was the May 2005 British General Election: 'No majority government in British history has ever rested on a flimsier base of public support – or, more accurately, none has since the extension of the franchise in 1918. In terms of active public consent for government, Britain is almost back in the pre-reform era of rotten boroughs.'

The war in Iraq has claimed one very big casualty that none of us have really noticed: British democracy. In a democracy, if a government lies to the people about the reasons for going to war, then the government should fall. In real, vibrant democracies, do parties come to power with just over 21 per cent of the electorate behind them? And how many of those 21 per cent didn't feel their stomachs do a disgusted back-flip when they put their X in the box by Labour?

What was the alternative? The tired, discredited Tories – a party which was still hauling out the same old faces from the Thatcher era of the 1980s; a party which supported the war but hypocritically still liked to hurl insults at Blair for lying over the way he took the country into the conflict? The Tories confused and revolted the electorate just as much as Labour. The party's politics were consummately craven and their leaders were ready to switch opinions and sell out their grannies at the drop of a hat.

The Lib-Dems were untried and untested and still too small to have any real hope of success. The one good thing from the election was the Lib-Dems gradually increasing their share of the vote and coming closer to appearing as a legitimate alternative opposition party – although they were still horribly hamstrung by the anti-democratic 'first past the post' system. The Lib-Dems got 5.98 million votes which translated into just 62 seats. Labour got 9.57 million votes and secured 356 seats.

Then there was the rest of the fringe parties out there. The Green Party polled 0.28 million votes and got precisely zero seats. The DUP in Northern Ireland polled 0.24 million votes and got nine seats; Respect – the anti-war rabble led by George Galloway, an MP who turned the collective skin of Britain into goose-flesh when he acted like a pussy (that's a cat, by the way) on the reality show *Celebrity Big Brother* – polled 0.11 million votes and got one seat.

The mathematics behind the British electoral process is ridiculous. It can only make voters think that something is badly amiss with the system designed to govern them. Put against the back-drop of our leader – Mr Blair – being caught lying his pants off about the reasons for war, and suffering nary a consequence save for a bit of a cut to his Commons majority, and you have a major problem: British democracy looks to be on its last legs. It can no longer express the true will of the people; it can be distorted and twisted and paid no account by politicians; it can be forgotten and shunned by British voters who can't even be bothered to get up off their sofas and go to their local polling station to draw a couple of lines in a box.

There's no wiser adage than the expression 'If it ain't broke, don't fix it'. Our parliamentary system is broke, and it needs fixed – sharpish. Something radical needs to be done to patch it up pretty quickly. Ask any historian who understands how extremism flourished in Europe between the two world wars, and they will tell you that when liberal democracies start to malfunction the extremists move into the spaces where democracy has failed, and start to build up their strengths. Just look at the small but steady advances being made by the far-right British National Party in recent years. Even a public debate on electoral reform would be a start; at least that would show the British people that those who purport to have the best interests of the country at heart – the politicians – realise that something is badly amiss and want to seek out a remedy. We need to throw everything out on the table: compulsory voting, internet voting, proportional representation; everything should be up for grabs and up for discussion in a moment seized to secure the revival of British democracy in the 21st century.

The election was played out against an unfolding story that proved – again – that Blair had lied and lied and lied to take us to war. But even that wasn't enough to off-set the imbalances of our electoral system.

The story that unfolded during the electioneering was that Britain's own Attorney-General, Lord Goldsmith, had told Blair that the war was illegal before the invasion. To anyone who'd closely followed the path to war, this revelation was nothing surprising – but to the vast majority of the British public this was the first time they were finding out just how duplicitous Blair had been.

This is what the British people learned in the run-up to the general election of May 2005: we discovered that on March 7, 2003, just before the war began, the Attorney-General had passed a memo to Blair saying it was up to the UN Security Council to decide whether Iraq was in breach of disarmament obligations – it was not for a cabal of countries lead by America and Britain to make the call. The Attorney-General added: 'The safest legal course would be to secure the adoption of a further resolution to authorise the use of force.' If that wasn't forthcoming then the next best alternative would be 'to demonstrate hard evidence of non-compliance and non-cooperation' with disarmament requirements and weapons inspections. But Goldsmith added that given the reports by weapons inspectors Blair would 'need to consider very carefully whether the evidence of non-cooperation and non-compliance by Iraq is sufficiently compelling to justify the conclusion that Iraq has failed to take its final opportunity'.

Professor Philippe Sands, QC, said the memo would be seen by lawyers – and he could have added historians, as well – to be 'written by a man who, in his heart, recognises that, without a second resolution, the war would be unlawful'.

The British cabinet wasn't shown the Attorney-General's memo because Blair felt some of the members of his cabinet – his own hand-picked top team – couldn't be trusted with its contents. So much for the protocol of 'collective responsibility' in British government. Blair's treatment of the cabinet shows that the directors of the board of Britain plc are just whipped dogs who'll do their master's bidding no matter what.

One man whose opinion was courted a little more actively than that of the members of the cabinet was the Chief of the Defence Staff, Admiral Sir Michael Boyce. When he got the gist of what was in the memo he reacted the way any sane person would when confronted with such findings on the eve of war. He said it simply wasn't good enough. British troops could face war crimes charges if they engaged in an illegal action, and soldiers and their families in turn could also sue the government if they were injured or killed in an illegal war. The Head of the Army, General Sir Michael Jackson, reportedly said behind closed doors: 'I have spent a good deal of time in the Balkans to make sure Milosevič [former Serbian ruler Slobodan Milosevič] was put behind bars. I have no intention of ending up in the cell next to him in The Hague.'

Lord Goldsmith's memo to Blair – warning him about the illegality of the war – was more than 6,000 words long. In contrast, the next memo the Attorney-General wrote Blair just over a week later was a mere few hundred words long. It was handed to Blair on March 17, 2003. This time it backed up the case for war, claiming the invasion was legal. It was a complete reversal of opinion – an intellectual and legal *volte-face* – in a mere ten days. Miraculous.

The March 17 memo said the 'authority to use force against Iraq exists from the combined effect of Resolution 678, 687 and 1441' and that Iraq has failed to comply with UN disarmament orders. Thus, Britain had the right to use force against Iraq – even without an additional UN resolution specifically saying Iraq was in breach and therefore risked invasion.

Goldsmith only wrote the March 17 memo after carrying out a clear act of CYA – cover your ass. On March 14, he'd written to Blair asking for confirmation that 'it is unequivocally the Prime Minister's view that Iraq has committed further material breaches' of UN disarmament resolutions.

Blair's Private Secretary replied: 'It is indeed the Prime Minister's unequivocal view that Iraq is in further material breach of its obligations.'

It should be pointed out that Goldsmith decided to seek these assurances from Blair the day after he met with Baroness Morgan, Blair's Director of Political and Government Relations, to discuss Iraq and the desires of the Prime Minister.

After this meeting Goldsmith – very pragmatically – put the responsibility for the war directly on the shoulders of Blair. If the PM said Iraq was in breach of its disarmament requirements, then, without evidence from the weapons inspectors, Blair's word was all the Attorney-General had left to legally prop up the invasion. It was quite fitting that the Prime Minister should be left to carry the can alone given that Blair had castrated his cabinet, made any debate on the matter irrelevant and turned the invasion of Iraq into his own personal crusade.

On March 17, the cabinet was read Lord Goldsmith's second, brief memo backing the invasion. (If you remember, just ten days previously Blair had decided not to allow them sight of Lord Goldsmith's initial, lengthy memo saying the war was effectively illegal.) The result: within days, Iraq was invaded.

On March 18 – in one of those rare but wonderful examples of an insider having the courage of their convictions in the Britain of today – Elizabeth Wilmshurst, the Deputy Legal Advisor to the Foreign Office, resigned in protest over the legality of the war.

Her simple, short, eloquent letter of resignation should be read in full.

Here it is:

> A minute dated 18 March, 2003 from Elizabeth Wilmshurst (Deputy Legal Advisor) to Michael Wood (The Legal Advisor), copied to the Private Secretary, the Private Secretary to the Permanent Under-Secretary, Alan Charlton (Director Personnel) and Andrew Patrick (Press Office):
>
> 1. I regret that I cannot agree that it is lawful to use force against Iraq without a second Security Council resolution to revive the authorisation given in SCR [Security Council Resolution] 678. I do not need to set out my reasoning; you are aware of it.
>
> My views accord with the advice that has been given consistently in this office before and after the adoption of UN Security Council Resolution 1441 and with what the Attorney-General gave us to understand was his view prior to his letter of 7 March. (The view expressed in that letter has of course changed again into what is now the official line.)
>
> I cannot in conscience go along with advice – within the Office or to the public or Parliament – which asserts the legitimacy of military action without such a resolution, particularly since an unlawful use of force on such a scale amounts to the crime of aggression; nor can I agree with such action in circumstances which are so detrimental to the international order and the rule of law.
>
> 2. I therefore need to leave the Office: my views on the legitimacy of the action in Iraq would not make it possible for me to continue my role as a Deputy Legal Advisor or my work more generally. For example, in the context of the International Criminal Court, negotiations on the crime of aggression begin again this year. I am therefore discussing with Alan Charlton whether I may take approved early retirement. In case that is not possible this letter should be taken as constituting notice of my resignation.
>
> 3. I joined the Office in 1974. It has been a privilege to work here. I leave with very great sadness.

You should note carefully Wilmshurst's concern that the invasion would amount to a 'crime of aggression'. One of the central charges levelled against the Nazi defendants in the Nuremberg Trials after the Second World War was the offence of 'planning, initiating and waging wars of aggression and other crimes against peace'.

Of course, the Wilmshurst letter and the Attorney-General's initial memo warning Blair that war was basically illegal weren't made available to the public. All that was made available to the public was the crappy snippet – which weakly asserted that the war was illegal – that Lord Goldsmith gave Blair on March 17. This was later read out to Parliament in order to bolster the faked-up legal case for an invasion. The government insisted that the full legal advice from the Attorney-General should remain strictly confidential.

Blair's chicanery was sickening. A handful of decent souls in the Labour Party packed up their bags and left, including Brian Sedgemore who defected to the Lib-Dems after 27 years as a Labour MP. 'I voted against the war on Iraq,' he said, 'and it becomes clearer every day that Blair decided to go to war after meeting Bush on his Texas ranch in 2002. After that he lied to persuade the country to support him.

'The stomach-turning lies on Iraq were followed by the attempt to use the politics of fear to drive through Parliament a deeply authoritarian set of law and order measures that reminded me of the Star Chamber [a tyrannical court used by Britain's most despotic kings and queens]. The Star Chamber used torture but at least they allowed a proper trial before throwing someone into prison. That is when I decided enough was enough.'

Sedgemore denounced Labour's 'descent into hell'. The 68-year-old Sedgemore knew well the cost of war. Here was a man whose own father, as he pointed out, 'died in the war to protect liberty'. His conscience wouldn't let him sleep at night and he had to make a stand. He told the British public: 'In this election above all, people should vote for liberty and freedom and against the increasingly repressive and authoritarian measures of this government.'

Sedgemore had hit on something horribly true: the Labour Party, like the Republican Party in America, is not a party of freedom or liberty, it is a party that has stolen and perverted the words 'freedom' and 'liberty'; twisted them, turned them on their heads and made them expressions of control and repression both for the citizens of the US and the UK, and for the citizens of far-off lands with funny names.

Yet Britons looked to other electoral issues rather than Iraq to decide the fate of the country in the five years following the election of May 2005. Even with black-and-white proof of Blair's lies in front of them, thanks to the leaking of the Attorney-General's legal opinion and the Wilmshurst letter, Britons made their minds up over economics, the

THE WAR ON TRUTH

414   THE WAR ON TRUTH

health service, crime, immigration and education. Iraq barely registered on the list of voter priorities.

The attitude of most British voters is understandable.

health service, crime, immigration and education. Iraq barely registered on the list of voter priorities.

The attitude of most British voters is understandable. Foreign wars in far-away lands are hard to get passionate about when you are worrying about your bank balance, mortgage repayments, the kids' education and the fact that there are no police officers pounding the local beat.

But what we missed as a nation was an opportunity to say that it is not OK to lie in order to invade another country and kill its people. Think of Reg Keys. Reg's son, Tom, was one of the six British military policemen shamefully kitted out with hardly any ammunition thanks to a tight-fisted MoD and killed in Iraq by a mob.

Keys stood against Tony Blair in the Prime Minister's north-east Sedgefield constituency – and of course lost – but the reason he stood is a powerful reminder to the British people of what politics is really about. He said that if the war in Iraq had been a legal one, he would have grieved for his dead son, but not campaigned. Instead, when faced with the truth that this war was indeed illegal he had no option but to both grieve and campaign. All politics are personal, and for Keys he was forced into politics by the impact of the war on his life – through the loss of his son. But all of us Britons – in a little way – have lost something through this war: the faith in ourselves to do the right thing. The war wasn't right – it was wrong; and we should have and could have addressed that at the ballot box. But maybe collective loss – the disappearance of a tiny bit of self-esteem as a nation – and the knowledge that we as the citizens of this country allowed something to happen in our name that was quite wrong isn't as effective a change on a person's worldview as the loss of a son or daughter.

The Iraqis also had their own taste of democracy in 2005 with the country's first 'open' elections in January. Sunni Arabs – from where Saddam drew his support – either boycotted the elections or didn't vote as violence in their areas prevented them getting to polling stations; this left the way wide open for Shia Muslims to soak up votes and power. In some Sunni areas turnout was as low as 2 per cent. The result is that the Sunnis who make up about 20 per cent of the Iraqi population have just six per cent of the seats in the new National Assembly.

In terms of truly representing the views of the people, the electoral process in Iraq is as wrecked as democracy in the UK – a democracy which forced an illegal war to create 'free democratic Iraq'. To illustrate: the Sunnis offered up 22 candidates for posts in the new Defence

Ministry and all were vetoed.

That electoral dysfunction was just another ingredient to add to the recipe for yet more bloodshed in a country already stained with too much for any one nation to bear. One month after the Iraqi elections, came the bloodiest single attack since the fall of Saddam. Some 115 people were killed and more than 130 injured when a suicide car-bomber blew himself to smithereens in the city of Hillah. The street looked like the bloody effluent of a sewer had backed-up and spilled onto the road. The victims had been queuing for jobs – in a country where now more than half the population is unemployed.

One British commentator referred to the birth of democracy in Iraq as 'politics in a bloody mist'. On May 12, 2005 – one week after the British general election – 71 people died in and around Kirkuk, Baghdad and Tikrit in multiple suicide bombings. Not long before, there had been a big song and dance made in Washington and London about the insurgency in Iraq waning. Ansar al-Sunna, the Sunni group which carried out the attack in Tikrit – Saddam's old home turf – said the 33 Shias it murdered were 'apostates' working for the 'crusaders'.

The next day, thousands fled their homes in the town of Qaim because of fighting between American troops and insurgents. The US killed at least 100 'rebels' that day. In the west, our eyes are now beginning to glaze over when we hear about the number of Iraqi casualties – but 100 dead people is the equivalent to everyone in your street dying. That would have a pretty profound effect on you – if you survived it, that is – especially if you had to leave your home amidst the bodies. The name for the US operation? Operation Matador. The same day, the first Prime Minister of 'free' Iraq, Ibrahim al-Jaafari (whose premiership just about lasted for one year), extended a six-month-old state of emergency. The birth of democracy in Iraq came with terror and repression as midwives.

Also that day, a few other nasty things happened: three Iraqis, two of them soldiers, died in a car bomb in Baquba; a policeman was shot dead in Baghdad; mortars killed three Iraqi soldiers at a check-point in Hilla; gunmen ambushed an interior ministry official and killed a guard, and a bomb hit a US convoy near Baghdad airport. The insurgency was waning, right?

Democracy comes from within. You don't punch your child in the face on Christmas morning because they don't happen to like the Barbie doll or Action Man you bought them; you don't inflict violence on your little boy or girl because you want to make them happy. After all, one day they might end up punching you back.

And you can't bomb and shoot a nation into representative government. You can't kill people in order to make them free.

What Iraq is left with is a recipe for lengthy, horrific civil war and possible partition of the country. Iraq is in pretty much the same place that Ireland found itself in, in 1919, at the outbreak of the War of Independence against Britain – except this time the repression, sectarianism and violence come with all the lovely horrors that modern-day technology has to offer. The country is in anarchy, the violence is unbearable, civil society has broken down, the rule of the gun is all and sectarian divisions – be they Catholic and Protestant back in 1919 or Sunni and Shia today – are verging on the genocidal. The only solution seems to be exhaustion – eventually the insurgents and state forces will bleed themselves white with suffering and death until just the thought of more prolonged violence drags everyone to the negotiating table.

Don't be fooled by the garbage that British and American propagandists and war apologists spew out – claiming that opposition to the British and American occupation is centred solely on Sunnis. It implies the Sunnis are a bunch of recalcitrant Saddam-worshippers and al-Qaeda acolytes, and the Shias are delighted to be under the heel of Bush and Blair. If that's the case then why did a crowd of 300,000, comprised mainly of Shias, but also including Sunnis, march through Baghdad in April 2005 protesting against Bush and Blair as well as absolutely rejecting Saddam? Moqtada al-Sadr, the Shia cleric who organised the demonstration is part of the National Foundation Congress. Comprised of both Sunni and Shia, it rejects 'terrorism aimed at innocent Iraqis, institutions, public buildings and places of worships' but also promotes 'the legitimate right of the Iraqi resistance to defend their country and its destiny'. And, of course, resistance to British control in the Shia-dominated south is becoming more violent by the day.

The portrait of Iraq is this: the most nightmarish form of violence comes from the extremist Sunni ranks – the suicide bombers who will happily blow themselves all the way to Paradise, and their promised 72 virgins, while standing in the middle of a crowded mosque or a high street just to kill Shias in order to whip up a full-scale civil war. The fascist Salafi or Wahhabi militant strain of Sunni Islam, from which al-Qaeda springs, sees the Shias as infidels who must be exterminated. These lunatics – many of whom are Sunnis from outside Iraq – have no desire ever to be brought into the fold of peace. Poverty, fundamentalism, ignorance and malice mean they will go on killing until they are killed – and in a country now over-run by the evils of poverty, fundamentalism, ignorance and malice, they will win more and more recruits to their cause. These people have moved from the fringes to centre stage thanks to Britain and America. The invasion was a beacon for these cultists; and the west's war fomented their hatred. But the vast majority of Sunnis and Shias want to live in peace – and without British or American boots trampling all over their country. How long will that attitude last?

Already, the sectarian hatred is making cooperation between the two communities almost impossible. Iraq is an unstoppable, broiling, bloody mess. The Shia community is only just keeping the desire for mindless revenge in check – as are ordinary Sunnis. In May 2005 alone, some 14 Sunni clerics were murdered. More than 150 Sunni mosques had also been attacked by that date and 62 worshippers killed.

When one of Shia Islam's most holy sites in Iraq – the Golden Mosque of Samarra – was blown up in February 2006 by al-Qaeda-inspired Sunni extremists, all pretence that Iraq was not now in the throes of a very real civil war was abandoned by everyone but the most idiotic. It was as if European Protestant terrorists blew the Vatican to bits. Within 24 hours, more than 130 people had lost their lives as sectarian violence between the Sunni and Shia communities swept the country in the wake of the bombing.

In June 2006, Abu Musab al-Zarqawi, the frontman of al-Qaeda in Iraq, called on Sunnis to 'confront the Shia snakes' accusing the Shia militias of killing and raping Sunnis. 'Forget about those advocating the end of sectarianism,' he said in a taped *communiqué*.

The ethnic tensions are cranked up even further by the Iraqi security forces finding most recruits from within the Shia community – pitting Sunnis and Shias against each other in yet another way.

Again, you can see the shades of Ireland in the unfolding history – only Iraq will make Ireland and its Troubles seem like a punch-up between Millwall and Chelsea fans on a Saturday afternoon.

And what about Ibrahim al-Jaafari, who briefly ruled in 2005–06 as the first Iraqi Prime Minister? Callers to a Kurdish radio station, Radio Nawa, early in 2006 said that there was no difference between al-Jaafari and Saddam Hussein. One caller said: 'America managed to get rid of one Saddam, but thousands of Saddams have emerged.'

Iraq's first PM hailed from the Shia Dawa Party. It carried out suicide bombings in Baghdad, and tried to blow up US and French embassies in Kuwait in the 1980s. Dawa is connected umbilically to the Iranian theocracy just over the Iraqi border – another ingredient to stoke up Iraq's bubbling pot of horror. Although the first PM was at pains to portray himself as a moderate, Dawa wants to see Sharia law implemented across Iraq. When pushed, this is what al-Jaafari had to say about that nasty little matter: 'Islam should be ... one of the main sourccs for legislation.' Great news. In future, all thieves in Baghdad can rest assured that their rehabilitation from a life of crime is a dead cert – they will, after all, be unable to rob shops or pick-pockets if they have no hands.

Ibrahim al-Jaafari was succeeded by a fellow member of the Dawa Party, Nouri al-Maliki, as PM in mid-2006.

So, the Dawa Party wanted to bring in Sharia law when it got elected in 2005. Big deal. Look what Blair wanted to force onto poor old democratic Britain when we were daft enough to re-elect him in the same year: draconian anti-terror laws and ID cards. Could anyone be fool enough to trust New Labour with these powers that they are so desperate to have? Effectively interning suspects without trial is another weapon that Blair would love to have in his authoritarian arsenal. On alleged terrorists, Blair's manifesto said that 'wherever possible suspects should be prosecuted through the courts in the normal way'. Wherever possible? So much for due process of the law in New Labour Britain.

The Blair-backed proposed laws also targeted those who 'glorify or condone' terrorism. Does that mean that Dr Jenny Tonge, the former Lib-Dem children's spokeswoman, would face jail for saying that she might have become a suicide bomber if she'd lived in the Palestinian occupied territories? Tonge said she wasn't condoning suicide bombing – and she wasn't, she appeared to be empathising with the hopelessness of Palestinian women who are driven to extremes because of the heartbreak of losing their loved ones – but she was depicted as a supporter of terrorism by the pro-war lobby. Jenny seems ripe for a stint in Belmarsh, aka Britain's Guantanamo, in New Labour eyes.

The New Labour manifesto also made a big hoo-ha about how there were more than 700 terror arrests in the UK between September 11, 2001 and December 2004. What it didn't point out is that only 17 of those arrests resulted in a conviction. During the Labour Party Conference in the late autumn of 2005 some 600 totally innocent people were detained under the Terrorism Act. These people weren't terrorists; they were protestors who wanted Blair to hear them denounce his policies and his wars. Infamously, these people included Walter Wolfgang, an 82-year-old Jewish refugee from Nazi Germany, who shouted 'Nonsense!' during a speech on the Iraq war by Jack Straw, then Foreign Secretary, and was manhandled out of the conference and later detained under terror laws. Another campaigner, this time aged 80, was stopped for wearing an anti-Blair T-shirt.

The new anti-terror powers include 'control orders' which put British citizens under house arrest without trial on the say-so of a judge. We should count ourselves lucky. New Labour initially wanted these 'control orders' to be handed out on the whim of the Home Secretary – former Communist Party of Great Britain member, John Reid, our very own political commissar. Now we only have to worry about tame Establishment judges confining us to our homes indefinitely because we might commit some thought-crime that Tony thinks is tantamount to flying planes into buildings.

New Iraq has its leaders clamouring for nasty laws; and New Labour is clamouring for its own nasty laws. The Iraqi election was a representative disaster and so was Britain's election. There are grim, if distant, echoes between the two nations in these sickening times. Perhaps it is a case of 'if you lie down with dogs you get fleas' but quite who the dog is, I can't decide.

In Britain, just one month before the election, UK courts confirmed that the Labour Party in Birmingham had been up to a bit of extracurricular vote-rigging. There had been 'massive, systematic and organised fraud'. The judge also said the postal voting system was 'hopelessly insecure', and damned New Labour's defence of postal voting with these words: 'Anybody who has sat through the case I have just tried and listened to evidence of electoral fraud that would disgrace a banana republic would find this statement surprising.'

Three New Labour activists had been running a 'vote-rigging factory' in an abandoned warehouse where police had found them handling unsealed postal ballots relating to local council elections.

There were jokes during the British election in 2005 that election monitors from Robert Mugabe's Zimbabwe should come and make sure that New Labour wasn't rigging the count. Well, over in Iraq, there was some time-honoured banana-republicing going on during their elections, too. Dr Odisho Malko, President of the Assyrian National Assembly in Iraq, said that no ballot boxes ever arrived in areas where the Assyrian people live. He estimated that between 200,000 and 400,000 Assyrians were unable to vote. No Assyrian has a place in the New Iraqi democracy. Britain and America, in the eyes of the Assyrian people, have made a mockery out of democracy and welched on their vows to bring freedom to the many peoples of Iraq. Dr Malko added: 'To Tony Blair, we say: honour your promises.'

Blair and Bush – and other similar creatures, like the Australian Premier John Howard, who have become omnipresent spectres on the world's stage – called the elections in Iraq 'a blow to global terrorism' or some such glib guff. Some voters in Iraq only voted because they were afraid that if they didn't then they would have no ink-stain on their finger (all people who voted had their finger inked at polling stations) and the religious parties who wanted power would attack them on the streets. The lack of an ink-blot on your index finger acted like some reverse mark of Cain in Iraq – without it you were a marked man. Other Iraqis, like so many of us back in Britain, held their noses and voted for one of the many appalling people on the voting list simply in the hope that anything was better than the bloody mess of terror and occupation.

In many polling stations, there were no election monitors at all. One party representative said he'd been given credentials for 134 election monitors when he really needed 386 to do the job properly.

The Iraqi election did not prove the invaders right. It justified nothing. After the elections, we were told by Washington and London – erroneously as we have seen from the daily carnage in Iraq – that the insurgency was slowing down. As if that was going to do the Iraqis any damn good, anyway. The Iraqi Ministry of Health showed that in the last six months of 2004 the occupational forces – and primarily the Americans – were killing three times as many people as the insurgents.

Sami Ramadani, an Iraqi exile under Saddam and Senior Lecturer at London Metropolitan University, wisely pointed out that after the 1967 elections in Vietnam, US papers were declaring a defeat for 'Vietcong terror'. History has a way of making any contemporary statement look ridiculous – but to trumpet the defeat of global terror because of a vote in Iraq is not only pin-headery of the highest order but an insult to every man, woman and child who has died in that country.

Salim Lone, former Director of Communications for the United Nations in Iraq, said this of the Iraqi election: 'It was illegitimate, and cannot resolve the rampant insecurity resulting from occupation. The only way to stop the destruction of Iraq is to end the occupation and enfranchise the Sunnis, who are leading the resistance because they see the US as systematically excluding them from the role they deserve to play in Iraq.' This was an 'illegal occupiers' election', Lone added.

There was another election around the same time that the Iraqis were going to the polls which it might be worth paying a little attention to as well. It took place in Uzbekistan in December 2004 – and can roughly be characterised as the historic moment when the Uzbek people voted on whether to elect Islam Karimov as their President or whether to elect Islam Karimov as their President. Islam Karimov, aka the Tyrant of Tashkent, has been the Uzbek President since 1991.

In December 2004, all opposition parties had been banned, so the lucky old Uzbeks were saved all that unnecessary thinking time that is involved in making democratic choices. They didn't have to worry at all about democracy in fact. All they had to do was vote for a man who has literally boiled his enemies alive in cauldrons in his torture chambers.

· Surely, America and Britain want to take this despotic bastard out as part of the onward march of freedom? Umm, not really. You see, old Islam Karimov is a big ally of the west in the War on Terror, so it's best not to upset him. As long as a despot boils people alive in a way favourable to Britain and America then the cooking of other human beings is perfectly acceptable; it's when dictators cook people in ways that aren't favourable to Britain and America that such acts become really intolerable.

There are about 6,000 political prisoners in Uzbekistan; there's no free press; religious freedom is a joke; and the state controls the market – put bluntly. It is a totalitarian hell-hole and its head of state should be in The Hague awaiting trial for crimes against humanity.

But Mr Islam Karimov has made sure he's kissed the correct butts to allow him to continue boiling dissidents alive without the irritation of interference from Washington or London. He gave the US an airbase on his turf; he protected oil and gas supplies from central Asia; and he allowed Uzbekistan to be used for 'renditions'. We've talked about renditions before: renditions occur when the Coalition of the Willing wants to torture someone they believe is a terrorist, but can't because the public at home in Dallas or Newcastle would start squealing about the abuse of human rights. So, the allies find some nice, tamed tyrant like Islam Karimov and send the unfortunate terror suspect to Tashkent for a spin in the tongue-loosening cauldrons of his gulags. Of course, all the nonsense that the poor soul blabs under torture is passed by Uzbek secret police to the CIA and MI6. So, when torture victim X has his arm dipped in boiling water and says that his mother is the al-Qaeda go-to girl in Stoke-on-Trent, then that ludicrous pile of crap ends up in the data-stream of British and American intelligence and is subsequently used by people like Bush and Blair to make public statements on the war on terror. The lies come straight from the torture chamber to your ears via a few spooks and a speech writer in the White House or Number 10.

So, as you can guess not much was said by Britain or America about the rigged elections in Uzbekistan of December 2004. One British diplomat, Craig Murray, former UK Ambassador to Tashkent, did point out that the UK was 'selling its soul' by dealing with a monster like Karimov, but, obviously, he was removed from his position for making such silly statements. Murray was particularly worried that information extracted from terror suspects under torture in Tashkent could end up being used as evidence in UK courts. Silly old Murray made a bit of a fool of himself by actually caring about the British justice system – no wonder New Labour thought him a little odd and got rid of him.

Then, in May 2005, not long after the British general election, Karimov decided to shoot dead about 750 pro-democracy demonstrators. Britain and America, as you may remember, had hailed similar democratic protests by ordinary people in countries like Ukraine and Lebanon – countries with leaders towards whom Messrs Blair and Bush were nowhere nearly as well disposed as Islam Karimov – as wonderful moments; as occasions when the thirst for democracy bubbled to the surface; as events to be grasped, nourished and cherished; as a blooming of freedom. It wasn't quite the same in Uzbekistan.

Washington muttered something about all sides in Uzbekistan showing restraint. This must have gone down like a cup of cold sick with the families of the 750 or so dead in Uzbekistan. Have you ever been so unrestrained that you deliberately ran into the bullet of a secret policeman's gun?

Jack Straw, the British Foreign Secretary until Blair demoted him to leader of the House of Commons in mid-2006 for not being militaristic enough, was equally Janus-faced. Although he said the killings were 'appalling', he didn't call for new elections or attack Karimov. All in all, you can see how the British and American attitude towards 'a great flowering of democracy' in Uzbekistan really does prove that they care wholeheartedly about liberty and freedom. No matter where it may struggle to bloom, democracy has no truer friend than the British and

American governments – and if you believe that, you'll believe that I have six toes on each foot.

Straw, perhaps, is the one man who sums up the failure of politics in the west. A young radical in his youth, he has sold himself body and soul to the politics of power. Take the following story as a meditation on the nature of politicians today – the people into whose hands we give ourselves.

During the November 2004 memorial service in Liverpool Anglican Cathedral for Ken Bigley, the Briton beheaded on video tape by al-Qaeda in Iraq, Tony Blair was approached by one of his most fearsome critics, Ken Bigley's brother, Paul.

Paul had savaged Blair for taking Britain into a war built on lies. In the spirit of the moment and still trembling with emotion after reading a public eulogy to his brother, Paul walked up to Blair and said he had no personal grudge against the PM. He said he considered the Prime Minister to be a gentleman but that he had serious moral concerns about the invasion of Iraq.

Blair replied: 'I understand. It's quite alright, Paul.' I know this, as Felicity Arbuthnot, a good friend and colleague of mine, was in regular contact with Paul Bigley throughout the abduction and murder of his brother. He later wrote her a letter outlining the events of the day of the memorial for his brother. Felicity forwarded it to me. It's from this letter that I quote.

Not long after his brief exchange with Blair, Jack Straw approached Paul Bigley. Paul wrote: 'I also thanked him for attending and said I wanted to apologise if I had offended him in any way personally as a human being. If in the heat of the moment in my frantic campaign to save my brother's life I had said something out of line on a personal level then I was sorry.' Straw said that no offence had been taken. Paul was about to make his good-byes and leave, when Straw pulled him to one side and whispered: 'Oh, by the way, Paul, you have a rapport and good connections with the media. Do you think the next time you are on air you could mention this fact, reiterate it, you know, apologise, because Mr Blair is rather concerned about his re-election chances?'

This was Paul's take on the conversation: 'He wanted me to say in public that I was sorry. I couldn't believe it. I was being humble, approaching him and apologising as a gentleman to a gentleman, having taken the message of forgiveness to heart and he takes immediate advantage.

'I was flabbergasted, I had offered him the hand of friendship and he bit it, and in a cathedral of all places. Then he takes me to one side and asks if I could possibly go public with this – well, I am going public with it now.'

And public he has gone – to you. Listen to what Paul Bigley has to tell you.

He is telling you that this is the quintessence of a politician. Blair was treated with humanity and decency by Paul Bigley. Then the Prime Minister and his little side-kick Straw thought about what Bigley had said and the pair of them smelt blood and plot and spin and votes. They saw Paul Bigley's honour and courage and humility as weaknesses to exploit, not to respect. They are the mirror image of what you hope and pray you are. They are humanity reversed. That's what we voted for: whether we live in Baghdad, Bristol or Buffalo – we voted for people who are not like us, who do not think or feel like us, who do not represent us, who do not care about us, who live off us, laugh at us, use us, discard us. They have to go. We are only now at the beginning of the 21st century. The project of the future should be the eradication of people like this from politics. If that is the only good thing that the war on Iraq can achieve, then maybe all those deaths will not have been in vain – because, with politicians like Straw and Blair banished from the realm of government, such wasted, useless deaths as Ken Bigley's just might become a thing of the past as well. Next time you vote, think of Paul Bigley and ask yourself if the person standing in your ward or constituency would act the way Straw and Blair did to Paul. If the answer is 'yes', consign them to hell and the history books; if the answer is 'no', elect them and change your country.

CRIME AND PUNISHMENT

or

How both chickens and suicide-bombers tend to come home to roost

Let's talk about karma and pay-back.

We began this book by uncovering the secret plans of Team Bush to whack Iraq. If you recall, we found the scheme lurking in a frightening blueprint paper for world domination: the Project for the New American Century's version of *Mein Kampf* called *Rebuilding America's Defenses*.

Now, we are going to unlock more nasty militaristic secrets hidden away in another secret memo. This time, however, it's a British document – the so-called 'Downing Street Memo'.

Rebuilding America's Defenses, to remind you, was written prior to Bush taking power. Unless you are blind, deaf, mad and a Republican, it proves conclusively that the neocons wanted to remove Saddam long before they took over the White House so they could expand America militarily in the Gulf and get their mitts on all that lovely Iraqi oil.

The PNAC document was the set-up for the whole horrific enterprise that was and is the invasion and occupation of Iraq. It gives you the political context to understand why what happened happened, and why the world is so screwed at the moment. Reading it provides you with an understanding of the motives behind the war; it allows you to cut through the crap that the politicians spewed out and see their lies for what they are. It gives you a scary glimpse of the thought processes of the men and women who embarked on this criminal enterprise and lets you know why they started the war.

Now, if you want to know how they pulled off this caper and carried out their crime, then you have to turn to another document – the

Downing Street Memo. It lifts the veil on the way crimes of historic proportions are committed, reveals the scheming behind the invasion and shows you how the Bush and Blair governments manipulated us all.

Read it for yourself:

SECRET AND STRICTLY PERSONAL – UK EYES ONLY
David Manning
From: Matthew Rycroft
Date: 23 July 2002
S 195 /02
cc: Defence Secretary, Foreign Secretary, Attorney-General, Sir Richard Wilson, John Scarlett, Francis Richards, CDS, C, Jonathan Powell, Sally Morgan, Alastair Campbell
Iraq: Prime Minister's Meeting, 23 July
Copy addressees and you met the Prime Minister on 23 July to discuss Iraq.
This record is extremely sensitive. No further copies should be made. It should be shown only to those with a genuine need to know its contents.

John Scarlett summarised the intelligence and latest JIC assessment. Saddam's regime was tough and based on extreme fear. The only way to overthrow it was likely to be by massive military action. Saddam was worried and expected an attack, probably by air and land, but he was not convinced that it would be immediate or overwhelming. His regime expected their neighbours to line up with the US. Saddam knew that regular army morale was poor. Real support for Saddam among the public was probably narrowly based.

C [the Head of MI6] reported on his recent talks in Washington. There was a perceptible shift in attitude. Military action was now seen as inevitable. Bush wanted to remove Saddam, through military action, justified by the conjunction of terrorism and WMD. But the intelligence and facts were being fixed around the policy. The NSC had no patience with the UN route, and no enthusiasm for publishing material on the Iraqi regime's record. There was little discussion in Washington of the aftermath after military action.

CDS [Chief of Defence Staff] said that military planners would brief CENTCOM on 1–2 August, Rumsfeld on 3 August and Bush on 4 August.

The two broad US options were:

(a) *Generated Start*. A slow build-up of 250,000 US troops, a short (72-hour) air campaign, then a move up to Baghdad from the south. Lead time of 90 days (30 days preparation plus 60 days deployment to Kuwait).

(b) *Running Start*. Use forces already in theatre (3 x 6,000), continuous air campaign, initiated by an Iraqi *casus belli*. Total lead time of 60 days with the air campaign beginning even earlier. A hazardous option.

The US saw the UK (and Kuwait) as essential, with basing in Diego Garcia and Cyprus critical for either option. Turkey and other Gulf states were also important, but less vital. The three main options for UK involvement were:

(i) Basing in Diego Garcia and Cyprus, plus three SF squadrons.

(ii) As above, with maritime and air assets in addition.

(iii) As above, plus a land contribution of up to 40,000, perhaps with a discrete role in Northern Iraq entering from Turkey, tying down two Iraqi divisions.

The Defense Secretary said that the US had already begun 'spikes of activity' to put pressure on the regime. No decisions had been taken, but he thought the most likely timing in US minds for military action to begin was January, with the timeline beginning 30 days before the US Congressional elections.

The Foreign Secretary said he would discuss this with Colin Powell this week. It seemed clear that Bush had made up his mind to take military action, even if the timing was not yet decided. But the case was thin. Saddam was not threatening his neighbours, and his WMD capability was less than that of Libya, North Korea or Iran. We should work up a plan for an ultimatum to Saddam to allow back in the UN weapons inspectors. This would also help with the legal justification for the use of force.

The Attorney-General said that the desire for regime change was not a legal base for military action. There were three possible legal bases: self-defence, humanitarian intervention, or UNSC authorisation. The first and second could not be the base in this case. Relying on UNSCR 1205 of three years ago would be difficult. The situation might of course change.

The Prime Minister said that it would make a big difference politically and legally if Saddam refused to allow in the UN inspectors. Regime change and WMD were linked in the sense that it was the regime that was producing the WMD. There were different strategies for dealing with Libya and Iran. If the political context were right, people would support regime change. The two key issues were whether the military plan worked and whether we had the political strategy to give the military plan the space to work.

On the first, CDS said that we did not know yet if the US battle plan was workable. The military were continuing to ask lots of questions. .

For instance, what were the consequences, if Saddam used WMD on day one, or if Baghdad did not collapse and urban war fighting began? You said that Saddam could also use his WMD on Kuwait. Or on Israel, added the Defence Secretary.

The Foreign Secretary thought the US would not go ahead with a military plan unless convinced that it was a winning strategy. On this, US and UK interests converged. But on the political strategy, there could be US/UK differences. Despite US resistance, we should explore discreetly the ultimatum. Saddam would continue to play hard-ball with the UN.

John Scarlett assessed that Saddam would allow the inspectors back in only when he thought the threat of military action was real.

The Defence Secretary said that if the Prime Minister wanted UK military involvement, he would need to decide this early. He cautioned that many in the US did not think it worth going down the ultimatum route. It would be important for the Prime Minister to set out the political context to Bush.

Conclusions:

(a) We should work on the assumption that the UK would take part in any military action. But we needed a fuller picture of US planning before we could take any firm decisions. CDS should tell the US military that we were considering a range of options.

(b) The Prime Minister would revert on the question of whether funds could be spent in preparation for this operation.

(c) CDS would send the Prime Minister full details of the proposed military campaign and possible UK contributions by the end of the week.

(d) The Foreign Secretary would send the Prime Minister the background on the UN inspectors, and discreetly work up the ultimatum to Saddam.

He would also send the Prime Minister advice on the positions of countries in the region, especially Turkey, and of the key EU member states.

(e) John Scarlett would send the Prime Minister a full intelligence update.

(f) We must not ignore the legal issues: the Attorney-General would consider legal advice with FCO/MOD legal advisors.

(I have written separately to commission this follow-up work.)

Mathew Rycroft

That's it.

OK. Let's run through this document now that you've read it and get some understanding of what it is really revealing to us.

The author is Matthew Rycroft, a Downing Street aide on foreign policy and national security, and he is sending the memo to the following people: the PM's former Foreign Policy Advisor and now UK Ambassador to Washington, David Manning; Defence Secretary, Geoff Hoon; Foreign Secretary, Jack Straw; Attorney-General, Lord Goldsmith; Cabinet Secretary, Richard Wilson; Joint Intelligence Committee Chairman, John Scarlett; GCHQ Chief, Francis Richards; Chief of the Defence Staff, Sir Michael Boyce; Head of MI6, Richard Dearlove; Blair's Chief of Staff, Jonathan Powell; Director of Government Relations, Sally Morgan; and, of course, Director of Communications and Strategy, Alastair Campbell.

To summarise: MI6 Chief Richard Dearlove has been told in Washington that George Bush is definitely going to invade Iraq and remove Saddam, and Blair in return has secretly committed Britain to war on America's behalf. The date of the memo is July 25, 2002 – nearly a year before the actual invasion. In that same month, Blair was telling the British people that no decision had been made about the war. On July 17, Blair specifically told the House of Commons: 'As I say constantly, no decisions have yet been taken.'

The memo makes clear that in order to invade Iraq more lies have to be spun. It says that 'intelligence and the facts were being fixed around policy' in the United States. In other words, Team Bush came up with a set of objectives, misused intelligence and the truth to fit the plan and Britain tagged along behind like a creepy little side-kick to its psychopathic, lumbering mate.

The memo makes it quite clear that there is no desire by America to use the legal route of going through the UN, and no mind was paid to the consequences of military action – it was just a case of jumping on their horses and riding into the sunset to kill some bad guys.

A possible date had already been fixed by the US for an invasion – and its timing seemed designed to help the Republican Party during congressional elections. Britain happily acquiesces despite admitting that the case for the invasion 'was thin' and that Saddam wasn't as great a danger as Libya, Iran or North Korea.

Britain also knows abundantly well, as the memo shows, that the case for war is effectively illegal without UN approval. Blair is shown to be plotting a way of getting Saddam to irritate the UN by refusing to admit weapons inspectors – an act which would give the US and UK a chance to whack him, and provide the necessary trigger for war. Finally, the memo shows that regardless of all these concerns about illegality the UK is intent on fighting this war alongside the US. The first conclusion is: 'we should work on the assumption that the UK would take part in any military action'. By the summer of 2002, therefore, the UK was committed to taking the nation to war irrespective of what the UN, the world, the British people or justice might have to say about it.

That is the long and the short of the Downing Street Memo. It is a chain-smoking gun of a memo. There was another memo written around the same time and this memo, marked SECRET and written by the Cabinet Office, was headed 'Iraq: conditions for military action (a note by officials)'. It stated baldly that the British government had to 'create the conditions necessary to justify military action' – that is, make things up, scare people and generally behave in a disgraceful manner. It referred to Blair's recent discussions with Bush at the President's ranch in Crawford, Texas, where the Prime Minister 'said that the UK would support military action to bring about regime change, provided that certain conditions were met: [these include] efforts had been made to construct a coalition/shape public opinion'. And it added: 'It is necessary to create the conditions in which we could legally support military action ... Time will be required to prepare public opinion in the UK that it is necessary to take military action against Saddam Hussein.'

The whole policy by Blair from the get-go was to manipulate us into war – or as the Cabinet Office would put it: 'shape public opinion'.

Bush and Blair have, through their public statements and rhetoric, repeatedly told us that we live in a Manichaean world – a world where there are no shades of grey, no ambiguity, no complexity. Theirs is a world of 'good versus evil', of being 'either with us or against us'.

In that black-and-white world, the Downing Street memo is proof of an act of evil. No question about it. The document shows that Bush and Blair lied to us and were planning to invade Iraq and topple Saddam no matter what; it also reveals that they were happy to manipulate intelligence and mislead the public.

In this simplistic Manichaean world of theirs, sin is always punished. Good conquers evil.

Yet Blair hasn't been punished. The British people, however, have. We've been punished for his crimes. When suicide bombers strapped explosives to their bodies and blew themselves up on three London Tube trains and a bus on July 7, 2005, what do you think that was? It was punishment. It was pay-back for Blair's crimes in Iraq.

While the guts and brains of British citizens were being swept off the streets and rail-tracks of London, Mr Blair had the audacity to tell us that the war in Iraq was nothing to do with the London bombings. Not only does he utterly insult the intelligence of the British people, he's also shameless enough to lie straight to our faces, while hiding his blood-stained hands behind his back. His claims were tantamount to spitting on the graves of the July 7 dead.

For proof of Blair's lies just read the transcript of the tape that Mohammed Siddique Khan – the pathetic, deluded, hate-filled, religious maniac who was also the apparent ring-leader of the London bombing cell – made before going off on his barbaric mission that cost the lives of 52 innocent people.

Think about Mr Blair insisting that Khan and his cohorts were not motivated by Iraq when you read the transcript.

Here's what Khan said:

> I am going to keep this short and to the point, because it's all been said before by far more eloquent people than me.
>
> But our words have no impact upon you, therefore I'm going to talk to you in a language that you understand. Our words are dead until we give them life with our blood.
>
> I'm sure by now the media has painted a suitable picture of me, this predictable propaganda machine will naturally try to put a spin on it to suit the government and to scare the masses into conforming to their power and wealth-obsessed agendas.
>
> I and thousands like me are forsaking everything for what we believe. Our driving motivation doesn't come from tangible com-

modities that this world has to offer. Our religion is Islam, obedience to the one true God, Allah, and following in the footsteps of the final prophet and messenger Muhammad.

This is how our ethical stances are dictated. Your democratically elected governments perpetuate atrocities against my people and your support of them makes you responsible, just as I am directly responsible for protecting and avenging my Muslim brothers and sisters.

Until we feel security, you'll be our target. Until you stop the bombing, gassing, imprisonment and torture of my people, we'll not stop this fight. We are at war and I am a soldier. Now you too will taste the reality of this situation.

Khan's words are simple to understand – even though he's insane enough to believe that splattering himself and any man, woman or child around him over a train carriage will get him a free pass into Paradise. This man, who was born and bred in Leeds, says that he is going to kill his fellow countrymen and women because of what Blair has done in the Middle East, and because Muslims are being bombed and killed and imprisoned in Iraq. It is no more complicated that that. Blair's actions and policies have ripped the heart out of Britain. They have set Asian against white and white against Asian. Khan – who worked as a teaching mentor, visited the home of his local MP and even met Blair's International Development Secretary, Hilary Benn – turned from an apparently upstanding member of the community to a murdering fanatic. This man, who should have felt himself as British as Buckingham Palace, was driven to hate his own country so much that he chose to see his fellow citizens as the enemy. Blair's greatest crime is that he triggered such hatred and created such an 'enemy within'.

Khan and his fellow bombers weren't a bunch of daft kids who got caught up in a revenge fantasy and then carried it out – they were *bona fide* well-connected international terrorists. Khan is said to have trained in a variety of Islamic terror camps around the world, and to have had connections with the Indonesian terror group Jemaah Islamiah which carried out the Bali bombing in 2002. He was also known to British intelligence as a potential terrorist, and linked to other terrorists who had planned attacks against the UK.

There are many Khans in the UK today. The British intelligence and security services say they have uncovered some 20 'major conspiracies', and MI5 has said that there could be up to 1,200 terrorists in the UK today. Men like Khan – inspired by their god and British actions in Iraq – will be hunting humans in Britain for many years to come.

Remember how, before the war, Blair attempted to bring to life a pretend phantom – the nexus between Iraq and terror – that was used to try to scare us into supporting the invasion. We were told that Saddam was up to his armpits in international terror prior to the war. That was a crock. Now, however, Iraq – or rather the coalition's actions in Iraq – is inspiring international terrorists to kill Brits in their own cities.

It's easy to dismiss Khan and his three co-conspirators as primitive-thinking Jihadi nutcases – medieval idiots who slavishly kill for their god. Certainly, they are medieval in their thinking and their ideas are intellectually bereft, but the UK government knew full well that our policies in the Middle East, and in Iraq in particular, would inflame hatred and bring terror to our doorstep.

For proof that the UK government knew that it was fomenting Islamic terrorism at home just look at this report from the UK's Joint Terrorism Analysis Centre, which said, a mere three weeks before the bombings: 'Events in Iraq are continuing to act as motivation and a focus of a range of terrorist-related activity in the UK.'

Then there was the warning letter from Foreign Office Permanent Secretary Michael Jay which was written on May 18, 2004 – more than a year before the bombings – to Sir Andrew Turnbull, the Cabinet Secretary.

In it, Jay says: 'Colleagues have flagged up some of the potential underlying causes of extremism that can affect the Muslim community, such as discrimination, disadvantage and exclusion. But another recurring theme is the issue of British foreign policy, especially in the context of the Middle East Peace Process and Iraq.

'Experience of both ministers and officials working in this area suggests that the issue of British foreign policy and the perception of its negative effect on Muslims globally plays a significant role in creating a feeling of anger and impotence amongst especially the younger generation of British Muslims. The concept of the 'Ummah', ie, that the Believers are one 'nation', has led to HMG's [Her Majesty's Government] policies towards the Muslim world having a very personal resonance for British Muslims, many of whom are taking on the burden of both the perceived injustices and of the responsibility of putting them right, but without the legitimate tools to do so.

'This seems to be a key driver behind recruitment by extremist organisations (eg, recruitment drives by groups such as Hizb-ut-Tahrir and al-Mahajiroon).'

The Foreign Office knew full well that Iraq bred hatred at home within the Muslim community. And they weren't the only ones. Two internationally acclaimed think-tanks, The Royal Institute of International Affairs and the Economic and Social Research Council, let the government know in no uncertain terms that Iraq was fuelling terrorism. In a 2005 report, *Security, Terrorism and the UK*, written in the run-up to the July 7 bombings, they said: 'The UK is at particular risk [of terrorism] because it is the closest ally of the United States, has deployed armed forces in the military campaigns to topple the Taliban regime in Afghanistan and in Iraq ... The UK government has been conducting counter-terrorism policy "shoulder to shoulder" with the US, not in the sense of being an equal decision-maker, but rather as pillion passenger compelled to leave the steering to the ally in the driving seat. There is no doubt that the situation over Iraq has imposed particular difficulties for the UK, and for the wider coalition against terrorism. It gave a boost to the al-Qaeda network's propaganda, recruitment and fund-raising, caused a major split in the coalition, provided an ideal targeting and training area for al-Qaeda-linked terrorists, and deflected resources and assistance that could have been deployed to assist the Karzai government [in Afghanistan] and to bring bin Laden to justice. Riding pillion with a powerful ally has proved costly in terms of British and US military lives, Iraqi lives, military expenditure, and the damage caused to the counter-terrorism campaign.'

In other words, the government couldn't have made a bigger balls-up if they had tried. Iraq made British Muslims hate their country, fuelled terrorism, recruited insane Jihadis to be torturers, murderers and martyrs, diverted attention away from the real bad guys – people like bin Laden – and turned Iraq into a magnet for every head-lopping lunatic this side of the Euphrates.

And I should mention one other little fact that proves once and for all that Blair is lying when he says that Iraq did not inflame the thought-processes of the London bombers. On MI5's own website, under the heading 'Threat to the UK from international terrorism', it states: 'Iraq is a dominant issue for a range of extremist groups and individuals in the UK and Europe.' It also says: 'Some individuals who support the insurgency are known to have travelled to Iraq in order to fight against coalition forces. It is possible that they may return to the UK and consider mounting attacks here.' This was on MI5's own website while Blair was saying that Iraq had nothing to do with the July 7 atrocities.

Even former Tory Prime Minister John Major admitted that Iraq made the threat of terrorism in the UK 'more potent and more immediate'. Blair has to be the only human being on earth who refuses to accept that Iraq made innocent people die in London on his watch.

What is Blair's solution to the problem of Islamic extremism in Britain? Well, he does the worst possible thing – he panders to religious leaders and then goes on to virtually rip up the human rights legislation in the UK. The third strand of Blair's thinking on how he should tackle terrorism was to allow his policemen to shoot dead an innocent civilian on the London Underground. When Jean Charles de Menezes was shot dead shortly after the bombings, the police told the public that the Brazilian was 'directly linked' to anti-terrorist operations. There were also leaks to the press that the victim wore clothing that could have concealed explosives; that he vaulted over ticket barriers; ran from police onto the train; and that a warning was shouted by officers.

It turned out, however, that not one of these claims was true. De Menezes literally had his head blown off for no reason, and the police denied it was their fault. But what do you expect? When the Prime Minister can lie countless times with impunity, why shouldn't Scotland Yard be allowed the odd ass-saving fib too?

Incidentally, and just to make matters all the more scary, British army special forces took part in the operation which led to the killing of de Menezes. They'd previously had experience of the so-called 'Dirty War' in Ulster which led to military intelligence officers helping loyalist terrorists target Republicans and Catholics, and to the use, by the British army, of terrorist proxy assassins. These men are now helping fight the War on Terror on the home front – I can't say I find that particularly reassuring.

Here are some rather angry musings of mine about the New Labour reaction to the London bombings in a newspaper column published a few weeks after the attacks.

*

Why don't we just get on with it and ban love in this country? Now that New Labour has all but legislated hate out of existence, we may as well go the whole hog and outlaw every uncontrollable human emotion that the government doesn't like.

Anyone engaged in acts of condoning, supporting or glorifying love could be subjected to house arrest, face exile and charges of treason. Let's deport the 'preachers of love', and begin consultations on whether fear, joy, hope and despair should also be proscribed. Anything which tilts a person's emotional Richter scale beyond zero should be criminalised immediately.

We're being told that it's our patriotic duty to support the government's 'war on hate'. After all, banning people from feeling an emotion that's always been part of the human condition, is clearly the only way to protect our democracy and our liberties. It's the only way to preserve our Britishness. If you can't help feeling bad emotions, like hate, you will have to go to jail – for the new crime of 'justifying or glorifying terrorism' – or pack your bags, get out of Britain and head for somewhere in the Middle East.

But hate, it seems, will soon be gone forever, thanks to Tony Blair. There's a whole flotilla of hate-busting legislation looming on the horizon. The Religious Hatred Bill will soon make it illegal to mock or insult any religion. That'll deal with those damned atheists and sectarian-haters. Thanks to the July 7 suicidal religious nutters (can I still say that?), Blair's going to deport people from the UK for uttering hateful words and close mosques, bookshops or anywhere suspected of fomenting hate. So that's those pesky Jihadist haters dealt with, too. There's even talk in Westminster that since we're banning extremist Muslim groups like al-Muhajiroun, now might be the time to make a clean sweep and ban the BNP into the bargain – which will deal with race hatred as well.

The desire to clamp down hard on what goes on inside the minds of individual citizens is written in the DNA of New Labour. With former Communist Party members like John Reid helping run the show, it was only a matter of time before the thought-crime allegations started flying. Tony always prefers to pass headline-snatching new legislation when faced with a problem – whether it's yobs or suicide bombers. Why bother checking whether existing powers and laws can deal adequately with the situation?

So now, as part of the PM's attempt to eradicate unpleasant emotions, we are to send 'the preachers of hate' back to tin-pot regimes where they can be tortured, rather than imprisoning them in the UK if they have broken laws by conspiring to carry out acts of terrorism and murder, or putting them under 24-hour surveillance if we suspect they will break the law. Why be civilised when you can be authoritarian?

You will no longer be able to think or say that you support suicide bombers. That sounds sensible; who would support blowing up innocent people? But shouldn't you be able to think whatever you want – even if it is disgusting? And there's a world of difference between a guy from Dewsbury, who's had the same lifestyle as you or me, strapping a bomb to his back and killing passengers on the Tube, and a Chechen woman who's seen her daughters raped and murdered by Russian soldiers, sticking on a bomb belt and taking out a patrol because she's crazed by grief. Both are criminal, dreadful acts, but, morally, a gulf separates them. One is mass murder; the other desperate, pyrrhic resistance. Am I still allowed to say that I empathise with the Chechen mother?

Instead of banning people from saying hateful things, shouldn't we allow them to speak openly so we know who the dangerous people are and can penetrate their organisations through intelligence?

Recently, while filming a documentary on the far right, I spent six months with some of the most extreme Nazis on the planet. These people want an all-white Europe and many contemplate using violence to achieve that end. Most think the Holocaust was a jolly good idea worth repeating. Should we ban them? Of course not. Do we jail them? What for – thought-crime? Because they fantasise about gas chambers? They might need a long lie-down in a mental institution but I can't remember violent fantasies ever being illegal. People are free to think monstrous thoughts. That's democracy and liberty for you. We don't ban paedophiles from having their sick little fantasies spin around in their heads; what we do is arrest them the moment the thought starts to transform into a criminal deed which will hurt another person: when the paedophile accesses child pornography or conspires to harm a child, the law acts. We can't legislate to outlaw thoughts.

Stalin murdered millions in his gulags, but did we ban people like John Reid from supporting a political party which embraced that totalitarian hero? Should every trendy leftie with a bust of Lenin on their desk be deported for idolising a man who unleashed the Red Terror on Russia? Do we lock up every religious believer because, down the ages, people have carried out acts of mass murder in the name of their faith?

Just because people think nasty, ugly thoughts it doesn't mean we have to send them to the Tower. Hate all you want. Hate may not be nice, but it is as human to hate as to love. Anyone who says different has had their brain washed by Tony Blair.

Our latest haters – the sad Jihadi suicide-supporters – are primitive-thinking losers who believe in childish nonsense dreamed up by some bloke who had a way with words and lived in the desert more than 1,000 years ago. The same can be said for any Jew or Christian or Hindu or Pagan.

But should their hate be banned? Or should the rule of law in a liberal democracy be respected? Something tells me that I once lived in a country where people who did bad things – not thought bad things or made stupid, evil comments – were put on trial and sent to prison.

You don't have to respect the haters, nor do you need you risk your safety by allowing them to wander around. If they've broken the law, jail them. Don't ride roughshod over civil liberties, dusting off the treason charges and telling judges to toe the party political line and get behind Team Britain for a spate of thought-crime prosecutions. New Labour, it seems, is no longer content with sabre-rattling at recalcitrant judges; the Lord Chancellor plans to push through new laws that will tell judges exactly how they should and should not interpret laws such as the Human Rights Act in order to allow 'hate-peddlers' to be booted out of the UK.

Home truth number one: Tony Blair fanned the flames of hate, now he wants to ban it. Is it just me, or is there a pattern here? We arm Osama bin Laden so he can kill Russians on the Afghan plains, then he comes looking for us, so we have to take him out; we sell weapons of mass destruction to Saddam so he can chemicalise the Ayatollah's armies during the Iran–Iraq war, then we decide we'd better go after him just in case he still has a few vials of anthrax kicking about; we give a home in Britain to a bunch of Jihadists who hate the west, then ask them to sit back and watch while we invade the Muslim world – surprise, surprise, they get mad and blow us up.

So now, in order to squash the hatred he helped spawn, Blair wants to ban their thoughts and words, to ban the emotion of hate and rip up the law books. And we're told not to worry; that this 'change of the rules of the game', as the Prime Minister styles his bonfire of freedom, will have no effect on decent folk like you and I. Really? If a despicable character like Abu Qatada, Osama's go-to guy in the UK, is sent back to Jordan and has jump-leads attached to his nipples, mightn't I be perceived as having a share in that crime simply because I'm a British citizen? When the rules of the game – the game being the administration of justice in a liberal democracy – are changed, big, bad mistakes are made. Remember internment without trial in Northern Ireland? Very bad idea. Thanks to that little rule-change, the IRA got a windfall of new recruits and the UK looked like a banana republic.

Let the haters hate. Don't let them hand an opportunity to this government to take away your right to think and feel and say what you believe in, even if your opinions are repellent. Our current crop of haters want a caliphate in this country where freedom of thought and expression would be punished by death. Pay these nasty little men the ultimate insult by allowing them to be free to hate in a way that, given half the chance, they would forbid you from doing, and show them that the kind of country they want will never come to Britain – no matter how much Tony Blair tries.

*

So we got a bloody pay-back for our crimes as a nation, right? As one famous Islamist, Malcolm X, once said, of the death of President John F Kennedy, 'The chickens have come home to roost.' For us the chickens were home-grown suicide bombers and the roost was the London Underground. You have to be outraged at Blair for leading us by the nose into this horror-show and creating a set of circumstances which caused more than 50 people to die in London on July 7, 2005. You have to be outraged because it could have been you. Blair could have caused your death, too.

But if we are honest with ourselves, we realise that our pain as a nation and as a people over these murders isn't really that great in the scheme of things. Fifty people dying in Iraq barely merits a mention in the news these days. It's the norm. The death toll of the London bombings is nothing compared to the daily butchery in Iraq. If we as a country have been punished by lunatics like Mohammed Siddique Khan for our collective crime against Iraq then the Iraqis, each and every one of them, are paying for our crime many times over simply by existing in a country which is such a dreadful, grinding parade of misery that we couldn't begin to envisage it in our worst nightmares.

Any hopes for the nation finding a form of peace were dashed by the outright rejection of the Iraqi constitution at the ballot box by the country's Sunni minority in mid-2005. The vote on the constitution, however, passed thanks to the overwhelming support of most of the Shia majority and the Kurds who voted for it in their millions. Saddam's Ba'ath Party, you will recall, drew its support primarily from the Sunnis.

Adnan Dulaimi, spokesman for the General Conference for Sunnis, had earlier promised that his people would reject the constitution when it came time for the population to vote on it. 'We will do our best to make sure this draft fails at the referendum,' he said – with the US Ambassador to Iraq, Zalmay Khalilzad, sitting at his elbow. Many Sunnis believe the vote to accept the constitution was rigged.

Make no mistake – this is a recipe for the kind of sectarian hatred which will make Northern Ireland's 30-year 'Troubles' look like a playground squabble. If the Sunnis can't be brought on board – and believe me they don't want to be brought on board – then the insurgency will become a conveyor belt of death that will go on churning out corpses for decades. Any hope of the US and UK starting to pull out by Christmas 2006 – and Bush and Blair are desperate to start troop reductions by then – can be forgotten.

One Sunni negotiator, Soha Allawi, said: 'We will not be silent … The constitution has elements that will lead to the break-up of Iraq and civil war.' Inevitably, Sunni gunmen and murder gangs – the main bulk of the insurgents – issued threats to unleash hell (if it is possible to make Iraq more hellish) in the wake of the constitution's acceptance. They were good to their word.

In July 2006, senior Iraqi government officials were quoted as saying that 'Iraq as a political project is finished' and that planning was now underway for the partition of Iraq between Shias, Sunnis and Kurds. Baghdad might even become the new Berlin, with the city bisected into territory under the control of Sunnis in West Baghdad and Shias in East Baghdad. If anyone thinks that it isn't a recipe for continuing violence to divide a country into three under the control of ethnic and religious groups which can't stand the sight of each other, then they need their head examined.

Amid their daily horror, then, the Iraqis know that the violence will only get worse. They have only tasted the starter that the terrorists have to offer; the main course is on its way. If you listen, you can hear the Four Horsemen of the Apocalypse sharpening their spurs already.

When the constitution was formally signed on the last Sunday of August 2005, all 15 Sunni representatives stayed away from the ceremony. The Sunnis believe that the constitution is paving the way for them to be excluded from the highest offices in the land; that its shift towards federalism will lead to the break-up and partition of the country with the Shias taking the south and the Kurds the north; and that it will put Islam at the centre of the new republic, jettisoning the secularism of Saddam's old regime.

Isn't it fantastic that our war to spread freedom and democracy across the world has led to newly liberated Iraq seeking to embrace Sharia law and the most primitive elements of Islam. One leak from the draft constitution said: 'It is not permitted to legislate anything which conflicts with the principles and rules of Islam'. In a nation where secular women are now going out veiled in order to prevent them being assaulted by religious maniacs, women might soon be legally compelled to dress in a bag thanks to the pro-Allah lobby. It'll be back to stoning adulteresses (have you noticed that not many adulterers ever get a rock on the head), lopping off the hands of thieves and burying gays alive. Truly, Iraq will be a beacon of liberty in a desert of oppression.

In fact, we might even end up creating a whole new theocratic nation called Shiastan. The Supreme Council for the Islamic Revolution in Iraq (SCIRI) is one of the boss men when it comes to the Shia bloc in Iraq. Needless to say, the clerics which run the organisation are umbilically linked to the old mullahs of Tehran – they are puppets of Iranian theocrats. The head of SCIRI, Abdul Aziz al-Hakim, says he wants the southern part of Iraq – the Shia homeland – turned into a federal state. When he made a speech to this effect in front of tens of thousands of supporters in the holy city of Najaf he received enormous support.

In many parts of the south, the people already effectively live under Sharia law, with fundamentalist Shias banning alcohol and music, and forcing women to wear the *burka*. The Iraqi Women's Association (IWA) says the development of an autonomous religious state in the south would be the end of liberty for the women under its control. Sharia, says Ghareba Ghareb of the IWA, 'is our fear'.

Regardless of all the fear and loathing that foreign al-Qaeda affiliated fighters generate, some 90 per cent of insurgency attacks are blamed by CENTCOM, the US command post for the region, on home-grown Sunnis. Attacks in Iraq over the summer months of 2005 were averaging 70 a day, the worst since the war was officially declared 'over' by Bush. If the Sunni insurgents wanted to they could make the first few years of the occupation look like a dummy-run for a real terror campaign.

The head of the Arab League, Secretary-General Amr Moussa, described the constitution as 'a recipe for chaos', adding that it was 'perhaps a catastrophe for Iraq' and its neighbours. His fears for a further

Iraqi descent into hell are shared by Iraq's most powerful Shia scholar and cleric, Grand Ayatollah Ali al-Sistani. He says he believes that Iraq is drifting into a 'genocidal war'.

For a reminder of the kind of nightmare that we are putting Iraq through, cast your mind back to the Baghdad stampede which happened just a few days after the drafting of the constitution in August 2005.

More than 900 Shia pilgrims died during the day of remembrance for the martyrdom of Imam Moussa al-Khadhem. Most of the deaths happened when rumours about a suicide bomber swept through the crowd causing people to hurl themselves from a bridge as they desperately tried to escape the phantom Jihadi. Earlier, the crowd had been mortared, killing at least seven and injuring dozens more. The deaths and killings happened on the very last day that Iraqis could register to vote on the constitution.

Incidentally, isn't it exceptionally thoughtful of the UK to start deporting Iraqi refugees in Britain back to their hellish nation? There are 7,000 failed asylum-seekers in Britain waiting to be deported. Many are already in refugee detention centres awaiting removal. Refugee detention centres are little more than glorified jails for men, women and children. When they come here we put them in these awful cages, where they can drift into mental illness and commit suicide while awaiting forced deportation to a homeland that may well execute them and their children on arrival. Britain's Chief Inspector of Prisons has condemned these places. The Refugee Council says the move to send refugees back to Iraq 'goes against the advice of the UN'.

Our crimes – our sins – in Iraq did, then, bring pay-back to our doorstep in the shape of murderous home-grown British-Muslim terrorists. But such woes are as nothing when set alongside the suffering of the Iraqi people. To compare the pay-back that the British people received for the invasion of Iraq, to the price that ordinary Iraqis are paying every day for our adventures in their country would be like comparing a pinprick to a crucifixion. And so, one is left with the feeling, that in terms of karma, the people of Britain have a long, long way to go before we have fully paid for the sins of our leader Tony Blair.

THERE WERE WEAPONS OF MASS DESTRUCTION IN IRAQ...BUT IT WAS US WHO USED THEM

or

How to help yourself against a bunch of lying bastards

The ultimate, most wicked, form of lying, is to blame your own sins on another person or to attack others for having committed the very crimes or misdeeds that you yourself are guilty of.

People like that crop up in our daily news every other day, and they have become figures of hate for us: people like the police officers, teachers and social workers who are tasked to protect children, but whom, we later discover, have stashes of child pornography on their computers at home. These are the people who are meant to arrest abusers and comfort child victims, but all the while they've been getting their kicks from images of child abuse, from pictures of innocent children being raped and degraded. Their hypocrisy is equal to their crime.

We have politicians who stand in moral judgement of us, the people; politicians who espouse family values publicly, while taking mistresses, visiting bondage dungeons, paying for sex with rentboys and hookers, and snorting coke.

Personally, I don't have that much of a problem with people who want to take lovers, visit bondage dungeons, or snort coke. If you want to do it then you should be free to indulge your consensual, adult vice in privacy – as long, however, as you don't claim in public to be a high moral guardian of the public good; as long as you don't tell the world publicly that mistresses, dungeons and coke are all wrong, are all things or acts for which people should be judged. If you don't say one thing in public, but do another in private, then your life should be your own and no-one should pass judgement on your personal affairs.

If a man or a woman has the regular moral weaknesses that we all have – if they have had an adulterous affair, or used drugs or hurt their loved ones for stupid selfish reasons – then that doesn't take away their right to state what they think are moral truths about the world. As long as the moral statements they make are not in conflict with the realities of their lives.

New Labour doesn't seem to understand that. New Labour in the shape of Tony Blair told us that Saddam had weapons of mass destruction which threatened the UK and the rest of the world, and, for that reason alone, we, the people, were told that we should back a war against Iraq.

We know that Blair lied to us about Saddam having weapons of mass destruction. That was bad enough, but he compounded his lies. For Tony Blair, and Bush, went on to use weapons of mass destruction themselves – in the shape of shells tipped with depleted uranium against the Iraqi people in this war. The men who claimed to stand against weapons of mass destruction ended up killing men, women and children with weapons of mass destruction. Who are the war criminals? Who are the hypocrites? Who are the dangers to world peace?

Let me tell you about these weapons of mass destruction that the UK and the US used against the Iraqi people.

The United Nations defines depleted uranium shells as weapons of mass destruction. To use these weapons in warfare – as the UK and US have done time and time again – is to defy the will of the world. Britain and America obviously believe that some very special sort of morality and some exclusive code of law is set aside for rich, English-speaking western democracies. Well, Britain and America are wrong. Saddam gassed the Kurds. Britain and America used DU shells against Iraqis. What's the difference? People still end up dead at the hands of a government using banned weapons.

Depleted uranium – DU – contaminates land and causes horrific birth defects and cancers among the soldiers using the weapons, the armies they target and the civilians unlucky enough to be around when these illegal bombs are dropped.

Professor Doug Rokke is the ex-Director of the Pentagon's depleted uranium project, a former Professor of Environmental Science at Jacksonville University and a one-time US army colonel who was tasked by the US Department of Defense with the desert clean-up of depleted uranium after the First Gulf War. I've had many conversations with this remarkable man over the years.

Rokke, a true blue American patriot, is unequivocal in his view that the use of DU is a 'war crime'. His rage is evident as he talks about the disgusting truth: that two nations which levelled one country for having mythical weapons of mass destruction actually ended up using real weapons of mass destruction themselves. 'There is a moral point to be made here,' he told me. 'This war was about Iraq possessing illegal weapons of mass destruction – yet we are using weapons of mass destruction ourselves. Such double-standards are repellent.'

DU is used constantly in Iraq by the UK and the US – its application is not something that occurs rarely or only *in extremis*; rather, it is used regularly and in a casual everyday fashion. Firing a shell tipped with DU is no big deal for a grunt in the British or American armed forces.

According to an August 2002 report by the UN sub-commission which studied DU, laws which are breached by the use of depleted uranium shells include; the Universal Declaration of Human Rights; the Charter of the United Nations; the Genocide Convention; the Convention Against Torture; the four Geneva Conventions of 1949; the Conventional Weapons Convention of 1980; and The Hague Conventions of 1899 and 1907. Even as far back as the 19th century the world expressly forbade employing 'poison or poisoned weapons' and 'arms, projectiles or materials calculated to cause unnecessary suffering'. All of the above laws are designed to spare civilians from the unwarranted horror that an army which is prepared to commit atrocities with illegal weapons can rain down on a beleaguered population.

Depleted uranium has been blamed widely for the effects of Gulf War Syndrome – typified by chronic muscle and joint pain, fatigue and memory loss – suffered by thousands of US and UK soldiers after the 1991 conflict with Iraq.

DU is also cited as the most likely cause of the 'increased number of birth deformities and cancer in Iraq' after the First Gulf War. The UN Sub-Commission which looked into DU adds: 'Cancer appears to have increased between seven and ten times, and deformities between four and six times.'

The Pentagon admits that 320 tonnes of DU were left on the battlefield after the First Gulf War. Russian military experts, however, say 1,000 tonnes is a more accurate figure. In 1991, the allies fired 944,000 DU rounds or some 2,700 tonnes of DU-tipped bombs. A UK Atomic Energy Authority report said that some 500,000 people would die due to radioactive debris left in the desert. The use of DU has also led to

birth defects in the children of allied veterans and is believed to be the
cause of the 'worrying number of *anophthalmos* cases – babies 'born
without eyes' in Iraq. Only one in 50 million births should be anoph-
thalmic, yet one Baghdad hospital had eight cases in just two years.
Seven of the fathers had been exposed to American DU anti-tank rounds
in 1991.

There have also been cases of Iraqi babies born without the crowns of
their skulls, a deformity also linked to DU shelling. A study of First Gulf
War Iraqi veterans showed that 67 per cent had children with severe illnesses, missing eyes, blood infections, respiratory problems and fused
fingers. DU also causes neuro-psychotic disorders and damage to the
immune system.

Not only does DU kill and deform innocent Iraqis and their children,
it also kills and deforms British and American servicemen and their children. Blair and Bush will have their crime echo down the generations –
their guilt evidenced in the bodies of mutated infants.

'A nation's military personnel cannot wilfully contaminate any other
nation, cause harm to persons and the environment and then ignore the
consequences of their actions,' said Rokke. 'To do so is a crime against
humanity. We must do what is right for the citizens of the world – ban
DU.'

Rokke also called on the US and UK to 'recognise the immoral consequences of their actions and assume responsibility for medical care
and thorough environmental remediation'. In other words, we should
pay the hospital bills for all those deformed kids and their dads who are
dying of cancer, and we should clean up the radioactive junk that we've
left scattered around Iraq – junk which can go on killing human beings
for thousands and thousands of years unless we remove it and deconta-
minate the area where it landed. 'We can't just use munitions which
leave a toxic wasteland behind them and kill indiscriminately,' Rokke
growls. 'It is equivalent to a war crime.'

The Ministry of Defence has lied to the people of the UK about DU
in every respect. From the start, the MoD said that DU didn't pose any
health risk. As Doug Rokke says, that statement resulted in our troops
going into action without adequate respiratory protection against DU
contamination from the rounds they were using. But not only that; the
MoD needed to test-fire DU shells, so between 1989 and 1999 some
6,350 DU rounds were shot into the Solway Firth in Scotland.

But come the Second Gulf War, the MoD's lies about DU were rumbled – by yours truly. Through a circuitous route, military sources passed a card to me that was being handed out to British soldiers on the frontline in Iraq in 2003 and 2004.

The card read:

> 'You have been deployed to a theatre where depleted uranium (DU) munitions have been used. DU is a weakly radioactive heavy metal which has the potential to cause ill-health. You may have been exposed to dust containing DU during your deployment. You are eligible for a urine test to measure uranium. If you wish to know more about having this test, you should consult your unit medical officer on return to your home base. Your medical officer can provide information about the health effects of DU.'

The card proved that the MoD knew that DU was a threat to human health – even though they were still, unforgivably, playing down the risks to British soldiers. Until that card was discovered, the MoD had one very simple public line on depleted uranium and it was this: 'DU does not pose a risk to health or the environment.' It was a gross, dirty lie which led to the needless and painful deaths of countless people from Baghdad to Birmingham.

So much for the claim from the MoD that depleted uranium is not a risk to life. When I was sent this card, back in February 2004, it outraged scientists, the military and, even, some politicians.

The MoD, then, was, by its own admission, responsible for not only killing innocent Iraqi civilians with DU, but was also culpable for the illnesses affecting British soldiers contaminated by DU. And what about all those Scottish folk living near the Solway Firth where thousands of DU rounds had been fired? Locals there have complained about illnesses they think are connected to DU contamination and understandably, were incandescent when the card was revealed. Doug Rokke, predictably, was horrified. 'The MoD card acknowledges the risks,' he said to me. 'It contradicts the position the MoD has taken publicly – that there was no risk – in order to sustain the use of DU rounds and avoid liability.'

You have to ask yourself why the US and the UK want to continue using DU shells. DU is supposed to make for a super-tough shell, but is that really the reason for its continual use in the face of such overwhelming evidence that it is a cruel and barbaric weapon? The problem is that when government leaders lie on such a scale – and then are caught out – it's impossible to believe them ever again. It becomes second nature to believe the worst of a government that could lie about a country having weapons of mass destruction and then go on to use weapons of mass destruction itself against that very same nation. Could the US and the UK have known the risks of DU, but just not cared? Or might they secretly be glad of the catastrophe that DU is bringing to Iraq? Is a population crippled by disease, cancer and birth defects part of their plan? Are the deaths of our own DU-contaminated soldiers just collateral damage?

I honestly don't know. How can I divine the motives of liars, fantasists and self-deceivers; of men who would use radioactive weapons against civilians and children? But this I do know, if someone never tells you the truth, then you have to believe the worst of them for your own self-preservation. So, when it comes to working out the government's motive for continuing with the use of DU, I can only fall back on my worst suspicions: that Blair knows these shells will create cancer and foetal mutations and cause the countless deaths of innocent Iraqis and our own troops, but he just doesn't fucking care.

One other point. I've known since I was about five that radioactivity kills and deforms people. I'd worked that out by watching black-and-white B-movies on a Saturday afternoon like *Them!* or *Tarantula*. If radioactivity could turn an ant into something the size of a house, or a spider into a mountain, then I realised that it might not be very beneficial for human health. Now, I'm not saying that 1950s creature features are a good teaching tool for advanced physics, but I'm sure that if I was able to grasp the danger of the atom when I was straight out of kindergarten then our military planners and politicians must have known that radioactive stuff is not a good substance to throw in the faces of civilians, soldiers or anyone, for that matter.

Rokke says that Britain and America have been 'contaminating the world' with DU munitions. The issuing of the MoD warning card to UK soldiers meant that the British government, at least, had 'a moral obligation to provide care for all those affected', including Iraqis, and to clean up the environment in Iraq.

'DU is in residential areas in Iraq,' Rokke said. 'Troops are going by sites contaminated with it, with no protective clothing or respiratory protection, and kids are playing in the same areas. What right does anyone have to throw radioactive poison around and then not clean it up or offer people medical care? This war was about weapons of mass destruction, but the US and the UK were the only people using WMD in the form of DU shells.'

Need I remind you that America also used white phosphorous shells during the battle for Fallujah in late 2004? White phosphorous – nicknamed 'shake and bake' by the US military – is an incendiary that's like napalm and its use against civilians in also banned under international weapons treaties. So far, the allies have also used cluster bombs in civilian areas, and the Mark 77 firebomb which is basically napalm under another name.

Ray Bristow is the trustee of the UK's National Gulf Veterans and Families Association. To him, the MoD card 'confirms what independent scientists have said for years', and what the government has denied for years. It was with very mixed feelings that Bristow received the news. Sure, he was vindicated after years of fighting for the government to admit that DU kills, but Bristow, a man of only 45, suffers from chromosomal abnormalities and conditions which doctors say are similar to the state of those who survived the nuclear bombing of Hiroshima. Being proved right must feel like something of a pyrrhic victory. A former Warrant Officer in the medical corps during the First Gulf War, Bristow is now only able to walk short distances with the use of a walking frame. Often, he has to use a wheelchair.

'While the card may have been issued to British troops we have to ask, "What about the Iraqi people?" They are living among DU contamination. And what about the people in Scotland? The MoD line has always been that DU is safe – it has been caught in a lie,' said Bristow, showing more generosity of spirit and humanity in just a few, short seconds of his ruined life than someone like Blair could show in an entire lifetime.

According to Bristow, some 29,000 British troops could be contaminated. He was found to have uranium in his system more than 100 times the safety limit. 'I put on a uniform because I believe in democracy and freedom,' he told me. 'Now, I can't believe a word my government says.'

Alasdair Morgan, a Nationalist member of the Scottish Parliament for the Dundrennan area, near where DU shells were test-fired, has said he wants DU banned: 'This find vindicates those who have said DU should never have been used or tested. Testing should stop in this area completely.' Chris Ballance, a Green party member for the area, said: 'DU is a weapon of mass destruction that must be banned.' Ballance wants the government to remove all DU shells from the Solway Firth and to explain to the people of Dundrennan what exactly has been going on.

Malcolm Hooper, Emeritus Professor of Medicinal Chemistry at Sunderland University and a government advisor on DU, said the MoD had committed 'administrative deception' by claiming DU was not a health risk while simultaneously issuing health warnings to UK troops. He went further, however, describing the government's behaviour as 'a dreadful experiment, an obscenity and a war crime against our own troops'. The issuing of the card was, Hooper added, 'a confession of failure' by Blair's administration. Peter Kilfoyle, a former Labour Defence Minister, said: 'I can remember similar denials about the chemical Agent Orange [which caused horrific deaths and deformities after it was used to strip away forest cover in Vietnam by America], but invariably we discover these substances do have long-term consequences.'

Armed with all this information, and the little laminated card which told British troops that DU was a health risk, I went to the Ministry of Defence and told them what I'd learned. I reminded them that on its own website, the MoD stated categorically that DU wasn't a risk to health.

I feel sorry, in a way, for these poor press officers in government ministries. They don't make up the lies that they have to defend daily, but they still have to find some way to wriggle out of the truth and to save the government's skin. When they go home at night they must feel soiled. If I did what they did just to earn a living then I couldn't look at my own reflection in the bathroom mirror, or kiss my kids good-night. My soul would be ashes.

In desperation, the poor press officer to whom I spoke told another whopper straight back at me, when I asked if the MoD card proved the government was up to its neck in lies – lies which could kill. He responded: 'We never said it was a safe substance.'

'OK,' I said, 'so you are agreeing that DU is dangerous to our troops and to Iraqi civilians?'

Lies inevitably lead to confusion. 'It is radioactive,' he replied, 'but there is no evidence to link it to ill-health.' I wondered if he allowed his kids to play with plutonium rods when they got bored.

The DU cards, he told me, were issued to 'reassure' troops, adding that the take-up of the urine test had been very low as 'most soldiers understand the risks are minimal'. Perhaps, I wondered, maybe most soldiers are too busy trying to avoid getting their arms and legs blown off by suicide bombers, to have time to worry about the risk DU poses to their health and the health of their unborn children. But, the press officer assured me rather weakly, there was no way the MoD had changed its policy on DU. He sounded like a whipped dog now. He was lying for a living and he knew I knew.

The kind of lies this government tells are like a virus – like HIV. They weave themselves into the fabric and DNA of society, corrupting it, distorting it. Black is white, up is down, and left is right. These lies are an abuse – an abuse of you and me and the society we live in. If you play with someone's mind enough eventually they will see the world in a different way – in a back-to-front, crazy way. The lies that our leaders tell us each day have made us see the world the wrong way around.

If we see the world upside down, then our whole lives are lived on a false premise; our very existence becomes a sick joke. Our leaders, by lying to us, are robbing us of the reality of the world around us and stealing the truth from us – the one thing that each person should have an inalienable right to. The thoughts that we think after our minds are poisoned by the nonsense that our leaders spin for us bear no relation to reality. We see the world through a glass darkly – and the glass has been darkened by our prime ministers and presidents lying to us and telling us that 2+2=5.

British soldiers are being drawn ever deeper into this terrible conflict; in Fallujah, a city was emptied by the Americans, and Iraqi bodies were left to be eaten by cats and dogs in the streets; the insurgents kill daily; suicide bombers blow up lines of men waiting to join the police; US forces shoot dead injured combatants instead of taking them prisoner; our civil liberties are ripped up at home in the name of security; racism, hatred and fear become the common currency of day-to-day civil discourse.

How can we make any sense of any of these events – and events yet to come – if we have no context in which to understand them? If our framework for interpreting these events is based on lies then we cannot find the right answers to the right questions. To live in a world constructed out of someone else's lies leaves each one of us unable to even identify what the right questions which we should be asking in the first place are. Our leaders have exploited us ruthlessly, and worse, they have corrupted our minds and our souls, making us culpable in their mass murders. Their ultimate sin is that they twisted our minds, took reality and the truth from us, fed us a diet of lies which infantilised us and made us dependent on them. Their lies were designed to frighten us, stifle us, keep us quiet, meek and bewildered; our fear helped further their ends and keep them in power and us powerless. Trapped inside their lies, we are unable to challenge them. The truth, as the old saying goes, really will set you free.

George W Bush won four more years as the ruler of the United States, and Tony Blair was re-elected as the Prime Minister of my country. America and Britain are drugged with lies and fear and confusion. That's why both countries made such terrible electoral mistakes. It's time now to wake up and throw the whole lying, filthy crew out. Forget Labour and forget the Tories, and forget the Democrats and the Republicans – they all backed this war. Let's look elsewhere for leadership. Let's look for vision, independence of thought, humanity, honesty and integrity. If we don't, then we may as well shred the true concept of democracy. Democracies don't exist through the rule of lies and fear and stagnant party politics.

Democracies thrive and become great through openness and freedom of thought. Our democracies need governments which treat their citizens as equally as those who have been voted into power and given the temporary honour and job of enabling us, the people, to live good and decent lives. They are not meant to be our leaders, they are meant to be our enablers.

Tony Blair has long told us that Britain has a 'blood price' to pay in this war; that the British people have to bleed collectively for a war he created out of a fog of his own lies. He asked us to send our sons and daughters and mothers and fathers and brothers and sisters to Iraq to kill and be killed for his deception.

Well, there is a blood price that can be paid for his lies. And here's how this particular debt can be honoured: if Tony Blair won't send his own children who have reached military age to kill and die in Iraq, then he should do the decent British thing. He should call in to the Ministry of Defence one day soon and ask if he can borrow a revolver from one of his generals. When he gets his hands on it, he should make sure that there is one bullet left in the chamber and then he should go back to Number 10 Downing Street. On his return he should write an apology to the British, American and Iraqi people on his hands and knees, with tears of contrition running down his face. He should then lock the door of his office and, like the good Christian he says he is, send himself to his maker for his final judgement. I sincerely hope his God forgives him. Because I can't.

CODA:
IT'S GREAT TO BE RIGHT
or
Smoking really does give you cancer and
invading Iraq really will ruin your country

Damn, timing is everything. The presses were just about to start running on this book you are reading when all of a sudden news emerged that proved we were right all along. This wasn't a matter of argument anymore – the very people who were wrong, were admitting they were wrong.

I genuinely had just hours to write this chapter. I'm writing this on Sunday, October 1, 2006 at 3.30 a.m. – and I have to give the finished version of this book to my publisher at 9 a.m. on Monday, October 2.

So, let's not waste anymore time.

This article ran in the *Sunday Herald* today – October 1, 2006. Read it.

> TWO LEAKED REPORTS, JUST ONE CONCLUSION: THE WAR ON
> TERROR IS FUELLING TERRORISM
> Neil Mackay investigates
> So, Britain and America's intelligence services believe that the Iraq war has fuelled international terrorism aimed against the West, and made the world a much more dangerous place to live if you happen to come from Belfast or Boston, Glasgow or Galveston, Manchester or Miami, Swansea or Seattle.
> Leaks, throughout the week, on the Iraq war's 'terror dividend' were deeply embarrassing to both Whitehall and Washington. Evidence that both the invasion and occupation of Iraq have, in the eyes of US and UK intelligence, provided succour and support for the international al-Qaeda franchise may have come as something of a mild shock to ordinary British and American citizens,

but to intelligence operatives, military leaders and political insiders the revelation was a no-brainer.

Here is the bitterly sarcastic response from one British security source to news that leaked secret reports, from within both the Ministry of Defence and the American intelligence establishment, found that the invasion of Iraq was the number one recruiting sergeant for jihadi extremists: 'No shit, really? What are you going to tell me next – that smoking gives you cancer?'

Not only have the leaked intelligence reports from Britain and America red-flagged just how counter-productive the war in Iraq has been, but they have also highlighted the fragmenting state of the alliances forged as part of the war on terror. As leaks dribbled out about what the spooks really thought about the fall-out from the decision to hit Saddam, relations between the US and the UK, on one side, and Pakistan, on the other, turned increasingly sour.

The head of Pakistan's Directorate for Inter-Services Intelligence (ISI) claimed, said President Pervez Musharraf, that former US Deputy Secretary of State Richard Armitage threatened to bomb the country into the 'Stone Age' unless it supported the war on terror. This was followed by leaks from British intelligence that the UK's spying agencies felt the ISI had supported terrorism in Britain and Afghanistan. Amidst this East–West split, Pakistan and Afghanistan also fell out over who had or hadn't done the most to deal with Osama bin Laden's terrorist network and the Taliban.

The British leak came from the Defence Academy, a think-tank for the UK's Ministry of Defence. Written by a naval commander, it was a distillation of thinking from within the military and intelligence services. Its key finding reads: 'The war in Iraq ... has acted as a recruiting sergeant for extremists across the Muslim world ... The al-Qaeda ideology has taken root within the Muslim world and Muslim populations within Western countries. Iraq has served to radicalise an already disillusioned youth and al-Qaeda has given them the will, intent, purpose and ideology to act.'

It goes on to say that 'the wars in Afghanistan and particularly Iraq have not gone well and are progressing slowly towards an as yet unspecified and uncertain result'. So bad is the situation, that military brass want to pull out of Iraq so they can attempt to win the fight against the Taliban in Afghanistan.

The paper says: 'British armed forces are effectively held hostage in Iraq following the failure of the deal being attempted by the chief of staff to extricate UK armed forces from Iraq on the basis of doing Afghanistan, and are now fighting and are arguably losing, or potentially losing, on two fronts.'

The West is 'in a fix', the report says, adding that the British government sent its troops into Afghanistan 'with its eyes closed'. Senior British military commanders are now at loggerheads with their political masters over their desire to get British troops out of Iraq and into Afghanistan. For the time being, their efforts have been knocked down by the government. Troop levels will remain unchanged in Iraq for at least six months, although there have been hints that there might be a reduction in the British deployment to Iraq around the same time that Tony Blair leaves office.

Next, the leaked British intelligence paper went on to attack Pakistan, saying: 'The army's dual role in combating terrorism and at the same time promoting the MMA [the hardline Mutahida Majlis-e-Amal, a coalition of religious parties], and so indirectly supporting the Taliban through the ISI, is coming under closer and closer international scrutiny … Indirectly, Pakistan, through the ISI, has been supporting terrorism and extremism.'

Some of the British suicide bombers who attacked the London transport system in July of last year had visited Pakistan. Other British-born Muslims have travelled to training camps in Pakistan. There have been allegations that members of the Pakistani intelligence services provided military lessons at such camps.

Musharraf has hit back at such claims, saying that the London bombers were radicalised in Britain. 'Let us not absolve the United Kingdom from their responsibilities,' he said. 'Youngsters who are 25, 30 years old, and who happen to come to Pakistan for a month or two, and you put the entire blame on these two months of visit to Pakistan and don't talk about the 27 years or whatever they are suffering in your country.'

Musharraf tackled Tony Blair about the leaked report and its interpretation during a meeting on Thursday. The document also describes the British policy of supporting President Musharraf as flawed because Pakistan is 'on the edge of chaos'. It goes on to say that links between the British and Pakistan armies at a senior level should be exploited to persuade Musharraf to stand down, accept free elections and disband the ISI.

MoD attempts to play down the leaked intelligence report were limp. The Ministry said that the paper was just reporting the views of a variety of key personnel. However, as one senior military source said: 'It is indeed the view of those in the military and in the intelligence and security services that Iraq was a mistake and that we need to concentrate on Afghanistan.' The officer also said that it was 'common knowledge – and had been for years' that the Pakistani intelligence service had aided the Taliban long before 9-11.

The MoD [in a bid to counter the accusations in the leaked intelligence document] said that Pakistan was considered 'a key ally in our efforts to combat international terrorism'. Officials added that Pakistan's security forces had made 'considerable sacrifices in tackling al-Qaeda and the Taliban'. Britain was also 'working closely with Pakistan to tackle the root causes of terrorism'.

Musharraf angrily attacked claims made about the ISI in the British intelligence paper. 'I totally, 200 per cent, reject it ... ISI is a disciplined force, breaking the back of al-Qaeda. Getting 680 [al-Qaeda suspects in custody] would not have been possible if our ISI was not doing an excellent job.'

Over on the other side of the Atlantic, the US administration experienced much the same kind of week as the British government when America's 16 intelligence agencies were revealed to have concluded that the invasion of Iraq had also made the world a much more dangerous place to live.

President Bush was eventually forced to declassify parts of his April 2006 National Intelligence Estimate (NIE) entitled *Trends in Global Terrorism: Implications For The United States*, following leaks in the US press.

One US intelligence analyst said of the document: 'The leaks in the UK were embarrassing for the government, but they couldn't have been that much of a shock for many Brits. The leaks in the US, however, were really damaging. They came out just ahead of the mid-term elections [for Congress in November 2006] ... Our voters are still much more supportive of the war than those in the UK – so for them to hear from the intelligence services that the war increases the risk of terrorism is a major blow.'

The most damaging revelation in the NIE report was that 'the Iraq conflict has become the *cause célèbre* for jihadists, breeding a deep resentment of US involvement in the Muslim world and cultivating supporters for the global jihad movement'.

Al-Qaeda, according to US intelligence, is 'exploiting the situation in Iraq to attract new recruits and donors and to maintain its leadership role'. The NIE also stated that the 'global jihadist movement – which includes al-Qaeda, affiliated and independent terrorist groups, and emerging networks and cells – is spreading and adapting to counter-terrorism efforts', and that 'activists identifying themselves as jihadists, although a small percentage of Muslims, are increasing in both number and geographic dispersion ... if this trend continues, threats to US interests at home and abroad will become more diverse, leading to increasing attacks worldwide ... The confluence of shared purpose and dispersed actors will make it harder to find and undermine jihadist groups.'

The threat from 'self-radicalised cells' will grow both 'in the Homeland' and overseas. US intelligence notes that 'jihadists regard Europe as an important venue for attacking Western interests. Extremist networks inside the extensive Muslim diasporas in Europe facilitate recruitment and staging for urban attacks, as illustrated by the 2004 Madrid and 2005 London bombings.'

Jihadist groups will continue to hit 'soft targets', with fighters who have experience of Iraq 'a potential source of leadership'. Disturbingly, the report adds that 'CBRN [chemical, biological, radiological and nuclear] capabilities will continue to be sought by jihadist groups'.

The NIE report also predicts that terror attacks against American and Western targets could spread out from Islamic groups to non-religious, non-Muslim organisations. 'Anti-US and anti-globalisation sentiment is on the rise and fuelling other radical ideologies. This could prompt some leftist, nationalist or separatist groups to adopt terrorist methods to attack US interests. The radicalisation process is occurring more quickly, more widely and more anonymously in the internet age, raising the likelihood of surprise attacks by unknown groups whose members and supporters may be difficult to pinpoint. We judge that groups of all stripes will increasingly use the internet to communicate, propagandise, recruit, train, and obtain logistical and financial support.'

It's clear that the NIE assessment was leaked in the run-up to the Congressional elections in order to destabilise a Republican Party that bases its electoral appeal on tough security policies.

Senator Jay Rockefeller, the lead Democrat on the intelligence committee, said: 'There is no question that many of our policies have inflamed our enemies' hatred toward the United States and allowed violence to flourish. But it is the mistakes we made in Iraq – the lack of planning, the mismanagement and the complete incompetence of our leadership – that has done the most damage to our security.'

It wasn't just Democrats who turned on the administration. Republican senator Arlen Specter said he was 'very concerned' about what the NIE assessment contained, adding: 'My feeling is that the war in Iraq has intensified Islamic fundamentalism and radicalism.'

Major General John Batiste, former commander of the 1st Infantry Division in Iraq in 2004-5 and also one-time military assistant to ex-Deputy Defence Secretary Paul Wolfowitz, called for the resignation of Defence Secretary Donald Rumsfeld and said that the government 'did not tell the American people the truth for fear of losing support for the war in Iraq'.

The White House tried to spin the findings of the NIE paper, with Bush saying that it was only 'because of our success against the leadership of al-Qaeda [that] the enemy is becoming more diffuse and independent'. Intelligence sources on both sides of the Atlantic mocked the attempt to put a gloss on the facts as 'pathetic'.

Tony Snow, the White House press spokesman, also tried to accentuate the positive, saying: 'Let's start with the obvious: since September 11, 2001, we have not been attacked ... We have kept America safe and we will continue to do so.' His words came amid a military announcement that the number of suicide attacks in Iraq was at its highest ever level since the invasion.

Homeland Security advisor Frances Fargos Townsend attacked the press for leaking the report, saying that journalists were endangering national security.

Bush also had to contend with trying to patch up the relationship between Pakistan and Afghanistan when the nations' two leaders – Pervez Musharraf and Hamid Karzai – were dinner guests of the President in Washington. The pair, who didn't even shake hands, have bitterly disagreed on how to fight the Taliban in the border areas between Pakistan and Afghanistan. Karzai says Pakistan is not doing enough to fight militants and deal with Taliban supporters operating in Pakistan and preparing attacks on Afghanistan. In reply, Musharraf has accused Karzai of doing little to deal with the Taliban and ignoring huge swathes of the country.

Bush also faces a revivified Bill Clinton wading into the November battle and playing the national security card. Clinton put the wind up the Republicans recently when he took an angry swipe at the Bush administration for its failures in tackling terrorism.

As one British intelligence analyst, who has worked closely with Washington, said: 'There was only so long that the administrations in both London and Washington could go on pretending that everything was OK ... It's probably lucky for both Bush and Blair that the pair of them are coming to the end of their leaderships. I don't know how much more disastrous news the public can take about what they did in Iraq.'

This article was written as a newspaper article always is – in a hurry. To compile it I used interviews carried out with my own sources, TV and radio broadcasts and other newspaper articles. While working on this report the media sources I relied on included most of the recognised news outlets in British and American press and broadcasting.

*

Do you know what the story behind this story is? Or rather, what is the lesson that we should learn from this story? It is that Tony Blair has taken the biggest gamble on Britain's future since King Harold bollocked up the Battle of Hastings. If Britain loses this stupid war in Iraq – a fight which we should never have picked in the first place – then this country will be ruined. Britain has been steadily eroded down to a rich, belligerent, mouthy nub of a world power. From an early 20th-century global empire – not something I'm a cheerleader for, please believe me – to a wounded, but still nonetheless respected, global player in 1945, Britain has dribbled away. Blair's policies won't just dribble away a bit more of Britain's dying power and prestige – this man is pissing our country up against the wall.

The Suez Crisis of 1956 burst Britain's bubble. The UK's political and military objectives – albeit colonialist and not all that pleasant – were cowed by the United States and its newly acquired superpower muscle.

Now, we fight wars on the orders of US Presidents.

This country can not take one more knock to its standing. Be selfish for a moment, and forget about all those decent values of yours – fair play, honesty, fellow-feeling – and think about what might happen to *you* if Britain doesn't fix the shambles of this war. If you are a decent human being then you know this war is wrong because of the lies it is based on and the suffering it has caused to Iraq and the rest of the world. But even if you are not a decent human being – even if you are a selfish bastard, who just happens to be British, then you must be able to see that this can not go on. And the same goes for the American people as well.

You can not shoot 'terrorists' into submission, you have to destroy their ideological base. And if they commit crimes then you treat them like the criminals they are – you arrest them and put them on trial, just as we did with the Lockerbie bombing; you do not treat a killer with a political agenda as if they are a nation state.

To destroy the ideological base of the insurgents who have – thanks to the actions of the UK and the USA – turned Iraq into a blood-circus, Britain and America have to be seen to disengage from Iraq. The attempt to bring security to the Iraqi people has to be internationalised. People with muslim names and far eastern faces and people from African countries and Latin American homes have to offer their services to the people of Iraq in the name of common humanity and democracy.

If Britain and America remain as the leaders of what is happening in Iraq, the killing will go on for generations. If the United Nations steps in – using a peace-keeping force which is truly comprised of international soldiers – and determinedly works to bring democracy, peace and stability to the Iraqi people then there is a chance that we'll see Baghdad become a city where ordinary people can live and love and play again.

The inevitable sum of Britain's Iraq adventure is that our country will be diminished. We start a war, balls up a war and then we either lose the war or walk away from the war. This isn't a war that is either worth fighting or winning. Right now, the best path for the UK – and the USA – to take is one that sees us relegated to just one of many international peace-keeping forces installed by the UN in Iraq to clean up the mess that Britain and America made in the first place.

If we take that path, then this country – although a little more hobbled by foolish foreign policy – at least will not collapse into the gutter. If we 'stay the course' – as the great neocons and the Blairite zombies say – then we'll one day drag ourselves limping out of a bloodstained hell-hole, as the US once did in Vietnam, and find ourselves an insignificant fool of a nation.

I don't want to live in a world where Britain is seen as a wasted, pathetic joke; as a country which sinned and then suffered by tumbling down the international scale of consequence. The price of losing a war is economic, social and geo-political meltdown. We can't afford that. America might be able to afford the price of failure; Britain can not. We are not a superpower. And if the USA ends up losing this war too, it's highly unlikely that it will remain a superpower very much longer either.

So, the Tony Blair who wanted to go down in history as the man who led Britain to victory after victory could very well go down in history as the man who lost Britain its place in the world and consigned us to international basket-case status.

As you can see from reading the newspaper article I wrote above, in October 2006, it isn't just me who thinks this was all a pointless, idiotic, waste-of-life mistake – the British military think it, the British intelligence services think it, the US military think it, the US intelligence services think it ... even the goddamn Republicans think it, for Christ's sake.

The answer to our problems with Iraq – and all those other countries like Iraq, that aren't very nice and we don't like – has always been diplomacy. If we use a little diplomacy now and get the US and Britain out of Iraq and the United Nations in, then Iraq may very well survive as a country – and so might Great Britain and the United States of America.

NOTES AND ACKNOWLEDGMENTS

The greatest acknowledgement I can make is to my family: my wife Nicolla and my daughters Niamh and Caitie. Without them this book would have no purpose and neither would I. Writing this took me away from them for far too long, and, inevitably, they had to put up with my tantrums, moaning and self-pity. I want to thank them from the very bottom of my heart for all their patience, love and support. They are, quite simply, the world to me, and I will love them forever.

For more information about *The War on Truth* go to *www.thewarontruth.com*. There'll you'll get the best of my journalism – including some of the published investigations on which a number of chapters of *The War on Truth* were based – as well as my current writing and reporting. The website also has the latest information on what I'm up to and a blog where readers can debate, insult, praise or just chat with me about news, current affairs, politics, defence, terrorism, intelligence and security – or whatever else happens to take their fancy. See you soon at *www.thewarontruth.com*.

The truth was actually out there

For all information on the PNAC, it's best to check out its website – *www.newamericancentury.org*. There you can find the founding statement of principles, the Clinton letter and *Rebuilding America's Defenses.*

Go to Google and you can also pull up my exclusive articles which make up much of the background research to this chapter, and were published in the *Sunday Herald*. Key in the following headlines along with my name:
'Bush planned Iraq "regime change" before becoming President', *Sunday Herald*, September 15, 2002
'Rumsfeld urged Clinton to attack Iraq', *Sunday Herald*, March 16, 2003
'The Rise of the Neocons', *Sunday Herald*, December 28, 2003
Or just go to the *Sunday Herald*'s website at *www.sundayherald.com*.

Getting away with murder

This chapter would have been impossible without the work of the George Washington University's National Security Archive and GWU's Joyce Battle. To read the entire archive relating to Rumsfeld, Regan and Saddam go to *www. gwu.edu/~nsarchive/NSAEBB/NSAEBB82/.*

Read Irene Grendzier's excellent work at *www.zmag.org/content/print_article. cfm?itemID=4832&sectionID=15*

Arming Saddam

The Riegle Report is at *www.gulfweb.org/bigdoc/report/riegle1.html*

To find out about the Early Day Motion in the British Parliament, go to *www.paulflynnmp.co.uk/mustreaddetail.jsp?id=892* and to *http://edm.ais.co.uk/ weblink/html/printable.html/ref=300*

'How did Iraq gets its weapons? We sold them', Neil Mackay and Felicity
   Arbuthnot, *Sunday Herald*, September 8, 2002

Why Britain was Saddam's dirty little whore

As well as the Scott Report itself, this chapter called on the work of the late, great Paul Foot, particularly one report in *Socialist Review*, March 1996, headlined 'Armed and Dangerous'.

The journalism of Richard Norton-Taylor in *The Guardian* throughout February 1996 was also indispensable, as was the work of his colleagues Michael White and Patrick Wintour.

John Pilger's reporting on the Scott Report was also essential reading, particu- larly 'Getting off Scott Free' in the *New Statesman*, February 23, 1996.

We must invade Iraq ... we have the receipts

Much as it depresses me, Andreas Zumach at *Die Tageszeitung* in Germany beat me to the scoop on the list of firms that supplied Saddam. You can read a trans- lation of some of his reporting at *www.scoop.co.nz/mason/stories/HL0212/ S00126.htm*

On Britain's sale of chemical weapons to the world, read my original article 'Britain's chemical bazaar', *Sunday Herald*, June 9, 2002, and the side-bar that went with it: 'Why the taxpayer ends up paying to sell arms to the most danger- ous countries on earth'.

Other helpful sources were:
'How £1bn was lost when Thatcher propped up Saddam', David Leigh and Rob
   Evans, *The Guardian*, February 28, 2003
'Who Calls the Shots' by the Campaign Against the Arms Trade

How the UN defanged Saddam
and killed half a million Iraqi kids

This chapter owes a great debt to William Rivers Pitt and his book, co-authored with Scott Ritter, *War on Iraq: What Team Bush Doesn't Want You to Know.*

Many facts, figures and quotations in this chapter were taken from Pitt's infor- mative Q&A interview with Ritter. The interview makes up the bulk of this truly excellent book.

My article, co-written with Felicity Arbuthnot, 'How did Iraq get its weapons? We sold them', *Sunday Herald*, Sept. 8, 2002, was also used to build this chapter.

For more on Denis Halliday see my article 'Former UN chief: bomb was payback for collusion with US', *Sunday Herald*, August 24, 2003

A nasty, black, three-letter word

The main source for this chapter was the report *Strategic Energy Policy Challenges for the 21st Century*. Download and read it at your leisure from the Council on Foreign Relations website at: *www.rice.edu/projects/baker*

You can check out my original investigation in the *Sunday Herald* on October 6, 2002 'Official: US oil at the heart of Iraq crisis'

Other vital sources included the work of *CBS News* correspondent Vince Gonzales. His original Enron reports are at *www.cbsnews.com*.

How the lies were told: Part I

The main source for this chapter was an interview conducted between myself and Scott Ritter in June 2003 on the workings of Operation Rockingham. To read the original articles published on June 8, 2003 go to the *Sunday Herald* website and search for 'Revealed: the secret cabal which spun for Blair' and 'Blair's secret weapon'.

For more on Operation Rockingham see Scott Ritter writing on the Hutton Report in *The Guardian* on January 30, 2004. It's headed 'The public must look at what is missing from the report'. Also see Michael Meacher MP, also in *The Guardian* on November 21, 2003, 'The very secret service'.

The best material on Operation Mass Appeal came from Nicholas Rufford of the *Sunday Times* who wrote the article 'Revealed: how MI6 sold the Iraq War', December 28, 2003.

How the lies were told: Part II

You can read my own original investigation into the OSP entitled 'Blair fell for US spin on Iraq WMD and ignored UK advice', by Neil Mackay and David Pratt, *Sunday Herald*, June 1, 2003.

Also, check the *Sunday Herald* website or Google my article, 'No weapons in Iraq? We'll find them in Iran', June 1, 2003.

Articles and journalism of high repute to be credited with helping me piece together the murky machinations of the OSP include, among many:

'The Lie Factory', *Mother Jones* magazine, Robert Dreyfuss and Jason Vest, January/February 2004 edition, *www.motherjones.com*

Rumsfeld's personal spy ring, *www.salon.com*, by Eric Boehlert

Of particular note is the fascinating essay 'Drinking the Kool-Aid' by Colonel W Patrick Lang, Middle-East Policy Vol XI, no 2, summer 2004.

Apart from my own discussions with Lt Colonel Karen Kwiatkowski, this chapter owes a debt to Marc Cooper's excellent interview with her, entitled 'Soldier for the Truth' which ran in the *LA Weekly*, February 2004.

Don't £*©$ with us!

My own original investigations into the Niger Connection were headlined 'Niger and Iraq: the war's biggest lie?', *Sunday Herald*, July 13, 2003.

There was a plethora of excellent articles that were essential in compiling this chapter and getting my brain sparking on such a convoluted and long-running story. I hope I credit them all. Among the highlights are:

'The Stovepipe', Seymour M Hersh, *The New Yorker*, October 27, 2003; and 'Who lied to whom?', Seymour M Hersh, *The New Yorker*, March 31, 2003.

Mr Hersh is, in my opinion, one of the world's greatest living journalists – a GLJ. His legendary work is a blueprint and guide on how to be a reporter. Facts, figures and quotations which I have drawn from his work throughout this book were essential to my study of the roots, causes and consequences of the Iraq war. Seymour Hersh also led the way in unravelling the truth about the abuse in Abu Ghraib prison. Many thanks.

'The Rove Problem', Nancy Gibbs; and 'What I told the grand jury', Matt Cooper, *Time*, July 25, 2005

'Ashcroft steps aside from probe of CIA leak; he hands over case to special counsel', David Stout, *International Herald Tribune*, December 31, 2003

'Bush rejects independent inquiry into security leak', James Harding, *Financial Times*, September 29, 2003

'Uranium that never was', David Pallister, *The Guardian*, July 31, 2003

'Tracked down, the man who fooled the world and was duped himself', Nicholas Rufford and Nick Fielding, *Sunday Times*, August 1, 2004

'The interrogation of George W Bush', Justin Raimondo, *www.antiwar.com*

'What I didn't find in Africa', Joseph C Wilson IV, *New York Times*, July 6, 2003

'The Niger Connection', Peter Beaumont and Edward Herlmore, *The Observer*, July 13, 2003

'Inside the lies', David Corn, *The Nation*, May 3, 2004

'Bashing Joe Wilson', David Corn, *The Nation*, July 16 2004

'Former envoy talks in book about source of CIA leak', David Johnston and Richard W Stevenson, *New York Times*, April 30 2004

'A right-wing smear is gathering steam', Joseph C Wilson IV, *LA Times*, July 21, 2004

'Plame's input is cited on Niger mission', Susan Schmidt, *Washington Post*, July 10, 2004

Interview with Joseph C Wilson IV by Buzzflash.com, March 5, 2004, see *www.workingforchange.com/article.cfm?ItemID=16880*

'White House reveals report to bolster uranium claim' Dana Bash, *CNN*, December 25, 2003

'French probe led to "fake Niger uranium papers" and evidence of Niger uranium trade "years before war"', Mark Huband, *Financial Times*, August 2, 2004 and June 27, 2004

'Scandal: who outed CIA agent Plame?', *Minneapolis Star Tribune*, October 1, 2003
'A diplomat's un-diplomatic truth', Robert Scheer, Alternet, July 8, 2003 see *www.alternet.org/story/16345/*
'If his words are his bond, we're in a bind', Arianna Huffington, Alternet, July 18, 2003, see *www.alternet.org/story/16433/*
'Does a felon Rove the White House?', Jeremy Scahill and Amy Goodman, *Democracy Now!*, September 30, 2003, see *www:alternet.org/ story/16867/*
'The importance of being Joe Wilson', Lakshmi Chaudhry, Alternet, November 3, 2003, see *www.alternet.org/story/17091*
'Columnist blows CIA agent's cover', Timothy M Phelps and Knut Royce, *Newsday*, July 22, 2003
'Cheney's notes add new CIA leak twist', *CBS*, May 15, 2006
'Bush knew about leak of CIA operative's name', June 3, 2004, see *www.capitol-hillblue.com/artman/publish/article_4629.shtml*
'What did he know and when did he know it?' Robert Scheer, Alternet, June 18, 2003, see *www.alternet.org/story/16199*
Patrick Fitzgerald's press conference on the status of the CIA leak investigation taken from Political Transcript Wires, October 28, 2005
'Bush under pressure in leak row', *BBC*, April 7, 2006

Whitewash in Whitehall

My original investigations are on *www.sundayherald.com* or Google. Check out:
'BBC warn Alastair Campbell: repeat allegations and we'll sue. Intelligence hit back: No 10 did sex up dossier and claims that they didn't are rubbish', Neil Mackay and Torcuil Crichton, June 29, 2003
'Blair on brink as Kelly family vows: we'll not rest until we know the truth', Neil Mackay, James Cusick and Torcuil Crichton, July 20, 2003
'The death of Dr David Kelly', Neil Mackay, July 20, 2003
'David Kelly must have felt terribly isolated and scared. He was crucified', Neil Mackay, July 27, 2003
'The heart of the matter ... did Iraq have WMD?', by Neil Mackay, Feb. 1, 2004
The most important research tool for this chapter was, of course, the Hutton Report itself. You can read this intimidating tome by going to *www.the-hutton-inquiry.org.uk.*
A great resource is also the *Panorama* investigation, 'A Fight to the Death', which was screened on BBC1 at 8.30 p.m. on January 21, 2004. The script should still be available from *http://news.bbc.co.uk/1/hi/programmes/panorama/3357 005.stm.* This excellent documentary helped me piece together the other side of the Hutton story. Top journalism from the BBC.

Spies and lies

As most of this chapter is based on intelligence briefings there are few notes and sources to acknowledge. Some of my original articles, which were used to help

build this chapter, are at *www.sundayherald.com* or on Google.
'Revealed: the truth behind the 45-minute warning', Neil Mackay, June 29, 2003
'Spy chiefs warn PM don't blame us for war', Neil Mackay, January 25, 2004
'Iraq's WMD: the big lie?', Neil Mackay, January 25, 2004
One interesting article that proved helpful in backing up what my spook sources
    were saying was: 'MI6 chief briefed BBC over Iraq arms fears by Kamal
    Ahmed', *The Observer*, July 6, 2003.

Tony in the Tower

This chapter would have been completely impossible without the tireless work of
Glen Rangwala and Dan Plesch on behalf of Adam Price MP. Hats off to all three
of them for 'A Case to Answer'. Read the entire report at *www.impeachblair.org*.

Congratulations as well to Michael Smith of *The Daily Telegraph* for his
scoops on September 18, 2004. These cracking stories appeared under the headlines: 'Secret papers show Blair was warned of Iraq chaos' and 'Failure is not an
option, but it doesn't mean they will avoid it'. Google *The Telegraph* scoops or
search for them at *www.telegraph.co.uk*.

Also, 'New MI6 chief walks into storm over ties to Downing Street', Daniel
McGrory, *The Times*, August 2, 2004

War on the United Nations

This chapter could never have been written if it wasn't for the revelatory work of
Martin Bright, Ed Vulliamy and Peter Beaumont of *The Observer*. Check out
their scoops:
'Revealed: US dirty tricks to win vote on Iraq war', March 2, 2003, *http://observ-
    er.guardian.co.uk/international/story/0,6903,905899,00.html*
'Britain spied on UN allies over war vote', February 8, 2004, *http://observer.
    guardian.co.uk/politics/story/0,6903,1143550,00.html*
Other important sources included:
'Woman's lawyers fight to lift GCHQ gag', Richard Norton-Taylor, *The
    Guardian*, January 20, 2004
'A single conscience v. the State', Bob Herbert, *New York Times*, January 19,
    2004
'Britain drops charges in leak of US memo', Patrick E Tyler, *New York Times*,
    February 26, 2004
'The spy who wouldn't keep a secret', Oliver Burkman and Richard Norton-
    Taylor, *The Guardian*, February 26, 2004
'Leak against the war', Daniel Ellsbert, *The Guardian*, January 27, 2004
'Official secrets', JFO McAllister, *Time*, January 25, 2004
'GCHQ translator cleared over leak', BBC online, February 26, 2004

Carving up the New Iraq

Much of the first half of this chapter was based on my own original research into the reconstruction project in the spring of 2003, just as the so-called 'combat' phase came to an end.

You can read those articles at *www.sundayherald.com* or Google them. Check out:

'Carving Up The New Iraq', Neil Mackay, April 13, 2003

'Firms that bankrolled Bush get contracts', Neil Mackay, April 13, 2003.

This was a difficult piece of research and thanks must go to the three researchers who assisted me in the project: Craig McQueen, Elizabeth McMeekin and Lucy Bannerman.

The bulk of the second half of the chapter, concerning the reconstruction project in the summer of 2004, after the US 'handover' to the interim Iraqi government, would have been impossible without the work of the Centre for Public Integrity in the USA. Its work is invaluable, and an incredible resource for journalists across the world who want to understand the nexus between government and business in the US.

Of particular value to this chapter was the centre's *Windfalls of War* study. Check it out thoroughly at *www.publicintegrity.org/wow*. Wow, indeed. This is journalism at its very, very best.

Also, 'Bush pulls the plug on Iraq reconstruction' by Suzanne Goldenberg, *The Guardian*, January 3, 2006

'The Spoils of War', Philip Thornton, *The Independent*, November 22, 2005

God, guns and government

This chapter is entirely based on my reporting of the US presidential elections in the autumn of 2004 for the *Sunday Herald*. You can read my contemporaneous reporting on the election at *www.sundayherald.com* or Google the following articles:

'Bush: a man's man in the land of the free', *Sunday Herald*, September 5, 2004

'All the President's People', *Sunday Herald*, September 8, 2004

'Kerry hits back', *Sunday Herald*, September 8, 2004

'Poll boost for Bush, but Kerry starts his fight back', *Sunday Herald*, Sept. 8, 2004

The fall

Among the key reports that were essential to compiling this chapter, there were:

'The Road to Abu Ghraib', Human Rights Watch, *www.hrw.org/reports/2004/usa0604/*

'Beyond Torture, US Violations of Occupation Law in Iraq', The Centre for Economic and Social Rights, *http://cesr.org/node/view/227*

Various Pentagon reports into the abuse at Abu Ghraib can be downloaded from the Department of Defence at *www.defenselink.mil/news/Aug2004/d20040825fay.pdf*, and the 'Final Report of the Independent Panel to Review DoD Detention Operations', can be downloaded at *www.defenselink.mil/news/Aug2004/d20040824finalreport.pdf*

Among the works of journalism that must be credited for helping unpick the paths of torture and terror, there are:

'Memo offered justification for use of torture', Dana Priest and R Jeffrey Smith, *Washington Post*, June 8, 2004

'Memo: Rumfeld OK'd dogs for interrogators', *Associated Press*, June 22, 2004

'The Roots of Torture', John Barry, Michael Hirsch and Michael Isikoff, *Newsweek*, May 24, 2004

To read one of Abu Mus'ab al-Zarqawi's most chilling statements go to *www.why-war.com/news/2004/07/05/importan.html*.

To read some of my own work which was used to build this chapter, go to *www.sundayherald.com* or Google:

'One year after mission accomplished: British troops accused of killing and torturing Iraqi prisoners by Amnesty; US army admits "sadistic criminal abuses" as Bush hails a better Iraq; Saddam's Republican Guard return to patrol Fallujah streets at US request', May 2, 2004

'The picture that lost the war', May 2, 2004

'Private contractors were implicated in abuse scandal', May 9, 2004

'Bogus end to a bogus war', June 27, 2004

'A Prince of Terror's deadly game', September 26, 2004

Britain's war criminals

The coverage in British newspapers in late September 2006 of the Baha Musa court martial also assisted in the compilation of this chapter, of particular merit was the reporting by *The Times*.

Much thanks must go to Amnesty International for a plethora of information. To check out the report 'Killings of civilians in Basra and al-'Amar' go to *http://web.amnesty.org/library/index/engmde140072004*. Amnesty's web address for other information is *www.amnestyinternational.org*.

While many, many journalists in many, many newspapers provided essential bits of information, the following were excellent sources:

'Army under fire: war crimes charges are tip of iceberg', Joshua Rozenberg, *The Daily Telegraph*, July 27, 2005

'Three Iraqi abuse soldiers are jailed and kicked out of the army', Michael Smith, *The Daily Telegraph*, February 26, 2005

'Army abuse cases dropped due to "lack of witnesses"', Severin Carrell, *The Independent on Sunday*, July 24, 2005

The coverage in *The Times* in late September 2006 of the Baha Musa court martial also assisted in the compilation of this chapter.

'Iraq: the aftermath: accused officer is just a "scapegoat" say colleagues', Kim Sengupta and Colin Brown, *The Independent*, July 21, 2005

'New allegations against British soldiers in Iraq', George Jones, *The Daily Telegraph*, August 16, 2005

'Australian "tortured and beaten" by British soldiers', Robert Verkaik, *The Independent*, April 28, 2006

'Uproar over "war crimes" trials', Neil Tweedie, *The Daily Telegraph*, July 21, 2005

'Undignified end leaves officers and men in angry mood', Neil Tweedie and Thomas Harding, *The Daily Telegraph*, July 21, 2005

Also check my own coverage of British abuses: 'One year after mission accomplished: British troops accused of killing and torturing Iraqi prisoners by Amnesty'; 'US army admits "sadistic criminal abuses" as Bush hails a better Iraq'; 'Saddam's Republican Guard return to patrol Fallujah streets at US request', May 2, 2004

Walking with Dante

Key sources, including my own original investigations which went into making up this eclectic chapter of horrors, are as follows:

Driving out the good guys:

'Former UN chief: bomb was pay-back for collusion with US', Neil Mackay, *Sunday Herald*, August 24, 2003

Installing lunatics:

'Iraq's PM Allawi shot six blindfolded prisoners "as example", say witnesses', David Pratt and Torcuil Crichton, *Sunday Herald*, July 18, 2004

'Sunnis demand international torture probe', Mariam Karouny and Michael Georgy, Reuters, November 16, 2005

'Insurgents "inside Iraqi police"', *BBC*, September 21, 2005

Had a tough day in the Green zone? Why not unwind by 'smoking' an Iraq?

'Torture of Iraqis was for "stress relief" say US soliders', Neil Mackay, *Sunday Herald*, October 6, 2005

Massacres and how they are justified by God:

'Iraq: the wedding party', Neil Mackay, *Sunday Herald*, May 23, 2004

'Wedding Party massacre: Iraqis claims more than 40 killed in US helicopter attack', Rory McCarthy, *The Guardian*, May 20, 2004

'"US soldiers started to shoot us, one by one": survivors describe wedding massacre as generals refuse to apologise', Rory McCarthy, *The Guardian*, May 21, 2004

'As villagers bury their dead, US general insists that group was not wedding party', Antony Loyd, *The Times*, May 21, 2004

'One incident. Forty dead. Two stories. What really happened?', Justin Huggler, *The Independent*, May 21, 2004

'Disputed strike by US leaves 40 dead', Dexter Filkins and Edward Wong, *New York Times*, May 20, 2004

'Dispute rages over attack that killed 40 in Iraq village', Ian Fisher and Khalid W Hassan, *New York Times*, May 21, 2004

'Dozens killed in US attack near Syria; Target disputed', Scott Wilson and Sewell Chan, *Washington Post*, May 20, 2004

Also, thanks to the BBC for getting out the scary George Bush and God information in the documentary *Israel and the Arabs: Elusive Peace* which was broadcast on BBC2 on October 24, 2005.

Intercontinental Ballistic Missionaries:

This section is based on an interview I conducted in the autumn of 2004 with David Aikman, author of the book *A Man of Faith: The Spiritual Journey of George W Bush*.

My Lai in Iraq:

Time magazine first broke the story of the Haditha massacre on March 27, 2006, in a piece called 'One morning in Haditha' by Tim McGirk and Aparisim Ghosh. *Time* followed up its investigation with 'The Shame of Kilo Company' by Michael Duffy.

My own reports on the massacre were published in the *Sunday Herald* on June 4, 2006, entitled 'Haditha: the worst US atrocity since Vietnam ... Iraqi women and children massacred by American marines. How did it happen?', and '2006: A catalogue of alleged US atrocities'.

Other important pieces of journalism include:

'Marines are good at killing. Nothing else. They like it', Oliver Poole, *The Daily Telegraph*, June 1, 2006

'The Conflict in Iraq', Megan K Stack and Raheem Salman, *Los Angeles Times*, June 1, 2006

'Iraqis killed by US troops "on rampage"', Hala Jaber and Tony Allen-Mills, *Sunday Times*, March 26, 2006

'In Haditha, Memories of a Massacre', Ellen Knickmeyer, *Washington Post*, May 27, 2006.

'The Reach of War', Eric Schmitt, *New York Times*, May 31, 2006

'US marines to face trial over killings at Haditha', Oliver Duff and Jerome Taylor, *The Independent*, May 31, 2006

'General vows complete probe of Iraqi killings', Douglass K Daniel, *Associated Press*, May 30, 2006

Allegations of the killings in the Abu Sifa area of Ishaqi were first revealed by the Knight Ridder news service in a piece entitled 'Iraqi police report details civilians' deaths at hands of US troops' by Matthew Schofield on March 19, 2006. This piece was followed up by Knight Ridder staff on March 21, 2006 with 'Multiple wounds mark bodies of Iraqis killed in disputed US raid'.

Child Prisoners:

'Revealed: coalition forces imprison Iraqi children', Neil Mackay, *Sunday Herald*, August 1, 2004

'Iraq's child prisoners', Neil Mackay, *Sunday Herald*, August 1, 2004

Hats off to Thomas Reutter of the TV programme *Report Mainz* in Germany for first sniffing out the story.

The British Blood Price

'Top military analyst: "Putting Black Watch on frontlines makes no sense"', Jim Cusick, *Sunday Herald*, October 17, 2004

'Keeping the home fires burning ... with anger', Neil Mackay, *Sunday Herald*, October 17, 2004

Mutiny:
Many thanks to the US news networks, ABC and CBS, for their coverage of the US 'fuel' mutiny.
'At least 1,000 UK soldiers desert', BBC, May 28, 2006
'Jail for Iraq refusal RAF doctor', BBC, April 13' 2006
A rising tide of blood:
Check out *The Lancet* at *www.thelancet.com*.
   The BBC's report 'Iraq deaths claim to be "studied"', October 29, 2004

Thank you for a lovely war, Mr Murdoch!

First up, I've got to give a huge round of applause and a full five stars to the documentary *Outfoxed: Rupert Murdoch's War on Journalism*, produced and directed by Robert Greenwald. Quite simply, it made this chapter. For more information go to *www.disinfo.com*.
   Here's a little hidden Easter egg for you too. If you are interested in the rambling, rabid rantings of Mr Bill O'Reilly, why not take a saunter over to the salacious internet website, The Smoking Gun, and check this web address for more on Mr O'Reilly's life-style: *www.thesmokinggun.com/archive/1013043mackris1.html*.
   Another excellent film that really contributed to this chapter is *Independent Media in a Time of War* with Amy Goodman of Democracy Now!, produced by Hudson Mohawk Independent Media Centre. Thanks to Martin Totusek for alerting me to this film and for forwarding me another important source – the film *March 22, 2003 Seattle* by Ken Slusher.
   Many important quotes, facts and figures are taken from both Greenwald's and Goodman's work. Both films are powerful pieces in the best journalistic tradition. I can not recommend them to you enough.
   Many thanks also to Meta Thorndyke for networking me in with a number of the ordinary American folk whose stories are recounted in this chapter.
   For more on the Bill of Rights Defense Committee go to *www.bordc.org*.
   Read the entire PIPA/Knowledge report, 'Misperceptions, the Media and the Iraq War' at *www.pipa.org/OnlineReports/Iraq/Media_10_02_03_Report.pdf*.
   'Closedown', Kevin Maguire and Andy Lines, *Daily Mirror,* November 22, 2005
   For more information on the chilling of dissent in the US that I touched on in my *Sunday Herald* article of June 29, 2003 – 'Rage. Fear. Mistrust. Uncle Sam's Enemies Within' – check out Alternet's website *www.alternet.org*. Particularly worth checking is Alternet's 'Rights and Liberties' online archive.

Democracy inaction

Do your democratic duty – go and check out the website of the British Electoral Reform Society at *www.electoral-reform.org.uk*.
   Among the many excellent articles that helped with the compilation of this chapter, the following are the most noteworthy:

'Don't be fooled by the spin on Iraq', Jonathan Steele, *The Guardian*, April 13, 2005

'No votes in Nineveh', Odisho Malko, *The Guardian*, February 23, 2005

'Suicide bombers, rocket blasts, curfews, boycotts and election candidates too scared to be identified ... is there any hope for democracy in Iraq's most dangerous war zone?', David Pratt, *Sunday Herald*, January 30, 2005

'Bloodbath in Iraq', Patrick Cockburn and David Enders, *The Independent*, March 1, 2005

'The Smoking Gun', Colin Brown, *The Independent*, March 24, 2005

'Links with Iran cast shadow over Iraq's new prime minister', Antonio Castaneda, *The Herald*, April 8, 2005

'An election to anoint an occupation', Salim Lone, *The Guardian*, January 31, 2005

'Dying for Democracy', David Pratt and Trevor Royle, *Sunday Herald*, January 23, 2005

'The Vietnam turnout was good as well', Sami Ramadani, *The Guardian*, February 1, 2005

'The cheers were all ours', Jonathan Steele, *The Guardian*, February 11, 2005

'Tony Blair, you are charged with leading Britain into an illegal war ... how do you plead?', Dan Plesch, *Sunday Herald*, March 27, 2005

'600 innocent people detained under terror law – and not one of them had committed an offence', Christopher Leake, *The Mail on Sunday*, October 2, 2005

'He's our sonofabitch', Jonathan Freedland, *The Guardian*, May 18, 2005

'Four words that will haunt Blair', Iain Macwhirter, *Sunday Herald*, March 27, 2005.

Many thanks to my friend and colleague of many years, Felicity Arbuthnot, for passing on to me Paul Bigley's account of his brush with Blair and Straw.

To read Elizabeth Wilmshurst's resignation letter online, go to: *http://news.bbc.co.uk/1/hi/uk_politics/4377605.stm*.

Crime and punishment

Michael Smith of the *Sunday Times* scored a real scoop on May 1, 2005 when he published his findings on the Downing Street memo under the headline 'Blair planned Iraq war from start'. Hunt for it online at *http://www.timeson line.co.uk/article/0,,2087-1593607,00.html*.

The *Sunday Times* also got hold of the memo headed 'Iraq: conditions for military action'. Download it at *www.timesonline.co.uk/article/0,,2089-1648758,00.html*.

You can read my coverage of the London bombings on the *Sunday Herald* website or by Googling the following headlines:

'Who did it?' July 10, 2005

'Man shot on Tube had no link with bombers', July 24, 2005

'After the bombs ... the fear', July 24, 2005

To read the security report by the Royal Institute of International Affairs and the Economic and Social Research Council go to: *www.chathamhouse.org.uk/pdf/research/niis/BPsecurity.pdf*.

The Observer's Martin Bright got hold of the Jay-Turnbull letter and published an article on it on August 28, 2005 under the headline 'Leak shows Blair told of Iraq War terror link'. To read the letter go to: *http://politics.guardian.co.uk/foi/images/0,9069,1558170,00.html*.

Thanks to Elaine Sciolino, Don Van Natta Jnr and Helene Fouquet of the *New York Times* for getting hold of the JTAC document and their article of July 19, 2005 headed 'June report led Britain to lower its terror alert'.

Other important articles and sources were:

'A "beacon of democracy" for Iraq? It's a recipe for civil war', Iain Macwhirter, *The Herald*, August 24, 2005

'Clerics push for Shiastan in southern Iraq', Rory Carroll, *The Guardian*, August 12, 2005

'Birth of a new Iraq, or blueprint for civil war', Kim Sengupta, *The Independent*, August 23, 2005

'Iraqi failed asylum seekers detained', Alan Travis, *The Guardian*, August 16, 2005

Also many thanks to the BBC for its excellent coverage of the draft Iraqi constitution.

There were weapons of mass destruction in Iraq ... but it was us who used them

This chapter is mostly based on my own investigations into depleted uranium. I'd like to thank Felicity Arbuthnot for all her advice and guidance into the use of DU by British and American troops.

I'd also like to thank my friends Charlie Jenks and Sunny Miller in the US. Their tireless work at the Traprock Peace Centre in Deerfield, Massachusetts, assisted with the compilation of this book in so many ways, particularly the research into DU. Go to their website and support their work at *www.traprockpeace.org*.

Check out my original stories on DU by either going to *www.sundayherald.com* or Googling them. The ones of most interest are:

'US forces use of depleted uranium weapons is "illegal"', Neil Mackay, *Sunday Herald*, March 30, 2000; and 'Ministry of Defence "lied" over depleted uranium', Neil Mackay and Amy Wilson, *Sunday Herald*, February 29, 2004

'The Big White Lie', Andrew Buncombe, Kim Sengupta and Colin Brown, *The Independent*, November 17, 2005

Coda

Based around my October 1, 2006 article in the *Sunday Herald* entitled 'Two leaked reports, just one conclusion: the war on terror is fuelling terrorism'. This article was also compiled using sources from all the main news sources in US and UK press and broadcasting.

And finally ...

Many thanks to all the wonderful staff at the *Sunday Herald* (quite simply the best newspaper on this planet or any other planet), particularly my editor Richard Walker and my old friend and colleague David Milne, the deputy editor. Sincere thanks also to Andrew Jaspan, the editor-in-chief of *The Age* newspaper in Australia, and to all the wonderful staff of the Newsquest research library – particularly Angela Laurins, Natalie Bushe, Catherine Watson and Ian Watson. A special mention also to my friend Iain S Bruce for taking the time to read this book and assist me with his valuable comments and advice. A tip of the hat also, of course, to Mr Bob Smith (a publisher with big, brave balls. I salute you, sir), designer John Henderson whose nightmarish imagination created the monster machine you can see on the cover of this book, the editor of *The War on Truth* Alison Rae – a ray of sunshine, indeed – and my co-prisoner and fellow partner-in-crime David 'Curly' Pratt.

Sincere thanks also to Craig Brown, *The War on Truth*'s publishing manager of Park Productions in sunny Falkirk. And cheers as well to the book's proofreader Cara Ellison – a fellow punk aficionado. They, along with Alison and Bob, endured my World War One-style email barrage as the publication date for *The War on Truth* loomed – something that must surely leave any human being suffering from the literary equivalent of shell-shock.

Thanks to all you readers for buying the book. Let me know what you think about it by getting in touch with me through *thewarontruth.com*.

And lastly, thanks to my dear mum, Moira, for being, as always, my much loved friend and supporter.